S0-AAZ-015

TAKING SIDES

Clashing Views on

Social Issues

SIXTEENTH EDITION, EXPANDED

TAKING SIDES

Clashing Views on

Social Issues

SIXTEENTH EDITION, EXPANDED

Selected, Edited, and with Introductions by

Kurt Finsterbusch
University of Maryland

The McGraw-Hill Companies

TAKING SIDES: CLASHING VIEWS ON SOCIAL ISSUES, SIXTEENTH EDITION, EXPANDED

Published by McGraw-Hill, a business unit of The McGraw-Hill Companies, Inc., 1221 Avenue of the Americas, New York, NY 10020. Copyright © 2012 by The McGraw-Hill Companies, Inc. All rights reserved. Previous edition(s) 2011, 2009, 2007, and 2005. No part of this publication may be reproduced or distributed in any form or by any means, or stored in a database or retrieval system, without the prior written consent of The McGraw-Hill Companies, Inc., including, but not limited to, in any network or other electronic storage or transmission, or broadcast for distance learning.

Some ancillaries, including electronic and print components, may not be available to customers outside the United States.

Taking Sides® is a registered trademark of the McGraw-Hill Companies, Inc.
Taking Sides is published by the **Contemporary Learning Series** group within the McGraw-Hill Higher Education division.

1 2 3 4 5 6 7 8 9 0 DOC/DOC 1 0 9 8 7 6 5 4 3 2 1

MHID: 0-07-805018-9
ISBN: 978-0-07-805018-3
ISSN: 95-83865

Managing Editor: *Larry Loeppke*
Senior Developmental Editor: *Jade Benedict*
Senior Permissions Coordinator: *Lenny J. Behnke*
Senior Marketing Communications Specialist: *Mary Klein*
Marketing Specialist: *Alice Link*
Project Manager: *Erin Melloy*
Design Coordinator: *Brenda Rolwes*
Cover Graphics: *Rick Noel*
Buyer: *Nicole Baumgartner*
Media Project Manager: *Sridevi Palani*

Compositor: MPS Limited, a Macmillan Company
Cover Image: © Brand X Pictures/Jupiter Images

Editors/Academic Advisory Board

Members of the Academic Advisory Board are instrumental in the final selection of articles for each edition of TAKING SIDES. Their review of articles for content, level, and appropriateness provides critical direction to the editors and staff. We think that you will find their careful consideration well reflected in this volume.

TAKING SIDES: Clashing Views on SOCIAL ISSUES

Sixteenth Edition, Expanded

EDITOR

Kurt Finsterbusch
University of Maryland

ACADEMIC ADVISORY BOARD MEMBERS

Pamela Altman
Georgia Southern University

Janet Armitage
St. Mary's University

David N. Baker
University of Toledo

Carole Campbell
California State University–Long Beach

Rod Carveth
Three Rivers Community College

Tamara Cheshire
Sacramento City College

Christopher Lee Coleman
St. Joseph's College

Andrea L. Fallenstein
Gonzaga University

Even Gorelick
Strayer University

Michele Hax
Community College of Baltimore County, Dundalk

Neil Johnson
Aspen University

Elizabeth Jones
California University of Pennsylvania

Rosalind Kopfstein
Western Connecticut State University

Leslie C. Lamb
Farmingdale State College

Celia Lo
University of Alabama

Barbara Lucas
University of Indianapolis

Peter Phipps
Dutchess Community College

Rebecca Riehm
Jefferson Community College

Jesse Rogers
Texas State University–San Marcos

Paulina Ruf
Lenoir-Rhyne University

Fortunata Songora Makene
Worcester State College

Russ Ward
Maysville Community & Technical College

Preface

The English word *fanatic* is derived from the Latin *fanum*, meaning temple. It refers to the kind of madmen often seen in the precincts of temples in ancient times, the kind presumed to be possessed by deities or demons. The term first came into English usage during the seventeenth century, when it was used to describe religious zealots. Soon after, its meaning was broadened to include a political and social context. We have come to associate the term *fanatic* with a person who acts as if his or her views were inspired, a person utterly incapable of appreciating opposing points of view. The nineteenth-century English novelist George Eliot put it precisely: "I call a man fanatical when . . . he . . . becomes unjust and unsympathetic to men who are out of his own track." A fanatic may hear but is unable to listen. Confronted with those who disagree, a fanatic immediately vilifies opponents.

Most of us would avoid the company of fanatics, but who among us is not tempted to caricature opponents instead of listening to them? Who does not put certain topics off limits for discussion? Who does not grasp at euphemisms to avoid facing inconvenient facts? Who has not, in George Eliot's language, sometimes been "unjust and unsympathetic" to those on a different track? Who is not, at least in certain very sensitive areas, a *little* fanatical? The counterweight to fanaticism is open discussion. The difficult issues that trouble us as a society have at least two sides, and we lose as a society if we hear only one side. At the individual level, the answer to fanaticism is listening. And that is the underlying purpose of this book: to encourage its readers to listen to opposing points of view.

This book contains 46 selections presented in a pro and con format. A total of 23 different controversial social issues are debated. The sociologists, political scientists, economists, and social critics whose views are debated here make their cases vigorously. In order to effectively read each selection, analyze the points raised, and debate the basic assumptions and values of each position, or, in other words, in order to think critically about what you are reading, you will first have to give each side a sympathetic hearing. John Stuart Mill, the nineteenth-century British philosopher, noted that the majority is not doing the minority a favor by listening to its views; it is doing *itself* a favor. By listening to contrasting points of view, we strengthen our own. In some cases we change our viewpoints completely. But in most cases, we either incorporate some elements of the opposing view—thus making our own richer—or else learn how to answer the objections to our viewpoints. Either way, we gain from the experience.

Organization of the Book   Each issue has an issue *Introduction*, which sets the stage for the debate as it is argued in the YES and NO selections. Each issue concludes with a *Postscript* that makes some final observations and points the way to other questions related to the issue. In reading the issue and forming your own opinions, you should not feel confined to adopt one or the other of the positions presented. There are positions in between the given views or totally outside them, and the suggestions for further reading that appear in each issue Postscript should help you find resources to continue your study of the subject. At the back of the book is a listing of all the *Contributors to This Volume,* which will give you information on the social scientists whose views are debated here. Also, on the *Internet References* page that accompanies each unit opener, you will find Internet site addresses (URLs) that are relevant to the issues in that unit.

A Word to the Instructor An *Instructor's Resource Guide with Test Questions* (multiple-choice and essay) is available through the publisher for the instructor using *Taking Sides* in the classroom. A general guidebook, *Using Taking Sides in the Classroom,* which discusses methods and techniques for integrating the pro-con approach into any classroom setting, is also available. An online version of *Using Taking Sides in the Classroom* and a correspondence service for *Taking Sides* adopters can be found at http://www.mhhe.com/cls/UsingTS2.pdf.

Taking Sides: Clashing Views on Social Issues is only one title in the Taking Sides series. If you are interested in seeing the table of contents for any of the other titles, please visit the Contemporary Learning Series Web site at http://www.mhhe .com/cls/.

Acknowledgments I wish to acknowledge the encouragement and support given to this project by my editor, Susan Brusch.

I want to thank my wife, Meredith Ramsay, for her patience and support as I birthed this new edition. I also want to thank George McKenna for many years as a close colleague and co-editor through many early editions of this book.

Kurt Finsterbusch
University of Maryland

Contents In Brief

Contents

Fred Barnes, journalist, executive editor of *The Weekly Standard* and TV commentator, argues that the mainstream media has a pronounced liberal bias. They do not hire conservatives, and an analysis of specific news stories shows their bias. Robert F. Kennedy Jr., environmentalist and political activist, agrees with Barnes that the media is biased but believes that it has a conservative bias. Surveys show that most Americans have many false beliefs that are fed to them by conservative talk radio shows and other conservative media outlets. Many media owners are very conservative and stifle investigative reporting.

Mark Krikorian, the executive director of the Center for Immigration Studies, presents the case against immigration. He emphasizes the changes in America that make immigration less beneficial for America. The current immigrants are not much different than immigrants in the past century but they do not fit the new America as well as the past immigrants fit the old America. One part of the story is that the new America will not assimilate immigrants well. Jason L. Riley, an editor of the *Wall Street Journal*, applauds immigration because it will propel, not impede, economic growth. America has a flexible labor market, where both employers and employees can change the work situation as they need or desire. "In the end, employers, workers, and consumers are all better off." America has a labor shortage that immigrants help fill without taking jobs in the aggregate from Americans. Riley also argues that new immigrants assimilate much like the old immigrants did.

Elizabeth Marquardt, Director of the Center for Marriage and Families, defends the common belief that divorce has devastating impacts on children and attacks Constance Ahrons's counter-thesis. Constance Ahrons, co-chair of the Council on Contemporary Families, found in her research on the children of divorced parents that they do quite well in later life and most think that they were not harmed by the divorce.

Issue 4.   Does the "Mommy Track" (Part-Time Work) Improve Women's Lives?   57

Brigham Young University colleagues E. Jeffrey Hill and Vjollca K. Märtinson, along with Maria Ferris of IBM and Robin Zenger Baker at Boston University, suggest that women in professional careers can successfully integrate family and career by following a new-concept part-time work model. In contrast, Mary C. Noonan, an assistant professor in the department of sociology at the University of Iowa, and Mary E. Corcoran, a professor of political science at the University of Michigan, document the various costs of the mommy track for female attorneys, including lower salaries and decreased likelihood of promotion to partner.

Issue 5.   Should Same-Sex Marriages Be Legally Recognized?   75

America's largest lesbian and gay organization, the Human Rights Campaign, presents many arguments for why same-sex couples should be able to marry. The main argument is fairness. Marriage confers many benefits that same-sex couples are deprived of. Researcher Peter Sprigg presents many arguments for why same-sex couples should not be able to marry. The main argument is that the state has the right and duty to specify who a person, whether straight or gay, can marry, so no rights are violated.

UNIT 3   STRATIFICATION AND INEQUALITY   93

James Kurth, Claude Smith Professor of Political Science at Swarthmore College, warns of very negative consequences for America of the growing income inequality from a conservative perspective. He also mentions the liberal criticisms of inequality but downplays their importance, because America has institutions that mitigate them. Gary S. Becker and Kevin M. Murphy, both economists teaching at the University of Chicago and Senior Fellows at the Hoover Institute, swim upstream on this issue by pointing out the positive consequences of the growing income inequality. The main reason for the increasing inequality is the increasing returns to education, which, in turn, inspire greater efforts by young people to increase their social capital.

Issue 7.   Has Feminism Benefited American Society?   110

History Professor Barbara Epstein argues that the feminist movement has been highly successful in changing the consciousness of Americans to "an awareness of the inequality of women and a determination to resist it." She explains how feminists succeeded at the consciousness level but have declined as a movement for social change. Journalist Kate O'Beirne argues that feminism is unpopular with women and is pushing an agenda that most women do not support. She claims that most women have concluded "that the feminist movement is both socially destructive and personally disappointing."

Issue 8.   Has Affirmative Action Outlived Its Usefulness?   131

Curtis Crawford, editor of the Web site http://www.DebatingRacialPreference .org, explores all possible options for bettering the situation of disadvantaged minorities in a truly just manner. He argues that the right of everyone, including white males, to nondiscrimination is clearly superior to the right of minorities to affirmative action. Sociologist Lawrence D. Bobo demonstrates that racial prejudice still exists even though it has become a more subtle type of racism, which he calls laissez-faire racism. Though it is harder to identify, it has significant effects that Bobo illustrates. In fact, it plays a big role in current politics.

Issue 9.   Are Barriers to Women's Success as Leaders Due to Societal Obstacles?   151

Alice H. Eagly and Linda L. Carli contend that barriers exist for women at every stage of their career trajectories, resulting in not a glass ceiling, but a labyrinth. Kingsley R. Browne asserts that the division of labor by sex is rooted in biologically based differences between women and men. Evolutionarily based natural selection has led to inclinations that make women and men better suited for different types of jobs.

UNIT 4   POLITICAL ECONOMY AND INSTITUTIONS   171

Political sociologist G. William Domhoff argues that the "owners and top-level managers in large income-producing properties are far and away the dominant power figures in the United States" and that they have inordinate influence in the federal government. Political scientist Sheldon Kamieniecki's research finds that business interests do not participate at a high rate in policy issues that affect them, "and when they do, they have mixed success in influencing policy outcomes." In fact, environmental and other groups often have considerable influence vis-à-vis business interests.

Robert B. Reich, Professor of Public Policy at the University of California, Berkeley, and former U.S. Secretary of Labor, accuses capitalism of undermining democratic governments' ability to serve the public good and advance the general welfare. The political power of the corporations exceeds that of the people so many nations with democratic elections do not function as democracies. Anthony B. Kim, a policy analyst at the Heritage Foundation's Center for International Trade and Economics, contends that economic progress through advancing economic freedom has allowed more people to discuss and adopt different views more candidly, ultimately leading societies to be more open, inclusive, and democratic.

Joseph E. Stiglitz, University Professor at Columbia University, argues that the government plays an essential role in enabling the market to work properly. Capitalism runs amok if it is not regulated to protect against abuse and ensure fairness. Walter Williams, Professor of Economics at George Mason University, argues that the founders defined a small role for government in the Constitution and protected the freedom of individuals. Now the role of government is increasing and individual freedoms are declining. The free market has achieved great prosperity for America and the intervention of government has had net negative impacts.

Issue 13. Has Welfare Reform Benefited the Poor? 218

David Coates presents the argument for welfare reform, which is that most poverty is self-induced; the previous welfare program created poverty and many other problems; and the reform reduces poverty, improves the lives of the people who left welfare, and solves other problems. Stephanie Mencimer, staff reporter for *Mother Jones,* does not denigrate the current welfare law but documents the horrible way welfare is administered in many states. Many welfare workers deny many benefits to many people who qualify for welfare. Thus, many welfare benefits do not reach the poor.

Issue 14. Is Competition the Reform That Will Fix Education? 237

Clint Bolick, vice president of the Institute for Justice, presents the argument for school choice that competition leads to improvements and makes the case that minorities especially need school choice to improve their educational performance. Educator and businessman Ron Wolk argues that school choice and most other educational reforms can only be marginally effective because they do not get at the heart of the educational problem, which is the way students learn. Too much attention is directed to the way teachers teach when the attention should be placed on how to stimulate students to learn more. Wolk advocates giving students more responsibility for their education.

Issue 15. Should Biotechnology Be Used to Alter and Enhance Humans? 255

The President's Council on Bioethics was commissioned by George Bush to report to him their findings about the ethical issues involved in the uses of biotechnology. Included in this selection are the expected positive benefits from the biotechnologies that are on the horizon. Political science professor Michael J. Sandel was on the President's Council on Bioethics but presents his private view in this selection, which is very cautionary on the use of biotechnology to alter and enhance humans. Many other uses of biotechnology he praises, but he condemns using biotechnology to alter and enhance humans. In these activities, humans play God and attempt inappropriate remaking of nature.

Brian Michael Jenkins, senior advisor to the President of the Rand Corporation, in testimony before the U.S. Senate Committee on Homeland Security and Governmental Affairs, posited that a team of terrorists could be inserted into the United States and carry out a Mumbai-style attack, as terrorism has "increasingly become an effective strategic weapon." Graham Allison, Harvard professor and director of the Belfer Center for Science and International Affairs, affirms that we are not likely to experience a nuclear 9/11 because "nuclear terrorism is preventable by a feasible, affordable agenda of actions that . . . would shrink the risk of nuclear terrorism to nearly zero."

UNIT 6 THE FUTURE: POPULATION/ ENVIRONMENT/SOCIETY 345

Michael Meyer, a writer for *Newsweek International,* argues that the new global population threat is not world overpopulation but underpopulation in many countries. Declining birth rates will ultimately lead to declining population and increasing ratios of older people to younger people in many countries. This situation creates immense problems in supporting the elderly and maintaining a healthy economy. Danielle Nievenberg and Mia MacDonald counter those who fear negative consequences of stable or declining population. The worriers fail to notice the benefits of a stable population. Furthermore, the population decline thesis is over-blown. The population of developed countries with healthy economies is likely to grow through immigration. Stable or declining population countries will only have to change some policies to avoid the anticipated serious problems.

Lester R. Brown, founder of the Worldwatch Institute and now president of the Earth Policy Institute, argues that population growth and economic development are placing increasingly harmful demands on the environment for resources and to grow food for improving diets. Bjorn Lomborg, a statistician at the University of Aarhus, Denmark, presents evidence that population growth is slowing down; natural resources are not running out;

species are disappearing very slowly; the environment is improving in some ways; and assertions about environmental decline are exaggerated.

Author Johan Norberg argues that globalization is overwhelmingly good. Consumers throughout the world get better-quality goods at lower prices because the competition forces producers to be more creative, efficient, and responsive to consumers' demands. Even most poor people benefit greatly. Martin Hart-Landsberg, Professor of Economics at Lewis and Clark College, argues that globalization has "enhanced transnational capitalist power and profits at the cost of growing economic instability and deteriorating working and living conditions."

Senator Jim DeMint argues that the federal government should be as limited as possible. It must protect the nation, guarantee freedom, provide justice and equal treatment, and provide a few other services that promote welfare, but it must avoid trying to solve all problems. Large government stifles the economy, wastes money and resources, reduces freedoms, and could expand to the point that it destroys the nation. Humanities professor Jeff Madrick argues that many government interventions in the economy since the end of World War II have been successful in furthering economic growth and addressing many problems that required government intervention. America is much better off because of many of the activities of the government.

Professor of social psychology at Northwestern University Alice Eagly and senior lecturer of psychology at Wellesley College Linda Carli review the literature on leadership and report that women have characteristics that make them better leaders for today's organizations. Professor of leadership and learning at the worldwide business school INSEAD Herminia Ibarra and her doctoral student Otilia Obodaru argue that men make better leaders because they have a genetic advantage of higher visionary skills than women. Women outperform men in some other skills useful to leadership but none as important as visioning that is critical for strategizing and understanding dynamic environments.

Correlation Guide

The *Taking Sides* series presents current issues in a debate-style format designed to stimulate student interest and develop critical thinking skills. Each issue is thoughtfully framed with an issue summary, an issue introduction, and a postscript. The pro and con essays—selected for their liveliness and substance—represent the arguments of leading scholars and commentators in their fields.

Taking Sides: Clashing Views on Social Issues, 16/e, Expanded is an easy-to-use reader that presents issues on important topics such as *Globalization, Biotechnology,* and *Affirmative Action.* For more information on *Taking Sides* and other *McGraw-Hill Contemporary Learning Series* titles, visit www.mhcls.com.

This convenient guide matches the issues in **Taking Sides: Social Issues, 16/e, Expanded** with the corresponding chapters in four of our best-selling McGraw-Hill Social Science textbooks by Schaefer, Witt, and Hughes/Kroehler.

Taking Sides: Social Issues, 16/e, Expanded	Sociology: A Brief Introduction, 9/e by Schaefer	SOC 2010, by Witt	Sociology: The Core, 10/e by Hughes/ Kroehler
Issue 1: Does the News Media Have a Liberal Bias?	**Chapter 6:** The Mass Media	**Chapter 4:** Socialization **Chapter 5:** Social Structure and Interaction	**Chapter 2:** Culture and Social Structure **Chapter 3:** Socialization
Issue 2: Is Third World Immigration a Threat to America's Way of Life?	**Chapter 8:** Stratification and Social Mobility in the United States	**Chapter 10:** Social Class **Chapter 11:** Global Inequality **Chapter 13:** Race and Ethnicity	**Chapter 6:** Social Stratification **Chapter 7:** Inequalities of Race and Ethnicity
Issue 3: Does Divorce Have Long-Term Damaging Effects on Children?	**Chapter 12:** The Family and Intimate Relationships	**Chapter 7:** Families	**Chapter 10:** The Family
Issue 4: Does the "Mommy Track" (Part-Time Work) Improve Women's Lives?	**Chapter 8:** Stratification and Social Mobility in the United States **Chapter 11:** Stratification by Gender **Chapter 12:** The Family and Intimate Relationships	**Chapter 4:** Socialization **Chapter 7:** Families **Chapter 10:** Social Class	**Chapter 6:** Social Stratification **Chapter 10:** The Family
Issue 5: Should Same-Sex Marriages Be Legally Recognized?	**Chapter 12:** The Family and Intimate Relationships	**Chapter 4:** Socialization **Chapter 7:** Families	**Chapter 10:** The Family

Taking Sides: Social Issues, 16/e, Expanded	Sociology: A Brief Introduction, 9/e by Schaefer	SOC 2010, by Witt	Sociology: The Core, 10/e by Hughes/ Kroehler
Issue 6: Is Increasing Economic Inequality a Serious Problem?	**Chapter 8:** Stratification and Social Mobility in the United States **Chapter 14:** Government and the Economy	**Chapter 11:** Global Inequality	**Chapter 6:** Social Stratification
Issue 7: Has Feminism Benefited American Society?	**Chapter 11:** Stratification by Gender	**Chapter 12:** Gender and Sexuality	**Chapter 6:** Social Stratification **Chapter 8:** Gender Inequality
Issue 8: Has Affirmative Action Outlived Its Usefulness?	**Chapter 10:** Racial and Ethnic Inequality	**Chapter 13:** Race and Ethnicity	**Chapter 7:** Inequalities of Race and Ethnicity
Issue 9: Are Barriers to Women's Success as Leaders Due to Societal Obstacles?	**Chapter 11:** Stratification by Gender	**Chapter 12:** Gender and Sexuality	**Chapter 6:** Social Stratification **Chapter 8:** Gender Inequality
Issue 10: Is America Dominated by Big Business?	**Chapter 14:** Government and the Economy	**Chapter 9:** Government and Economy	**Chapter 9:** Political and Economic Power
Issue 11: Does Capitalism Undermine Democracy?	**Chapter 14:** Government and the Economy	**Chapter 9:** Government and Economy	**Chapter 9:** Political and Economic Power
Issue 12: Should Government Intervene in a Capitalist Economy?	**Chapter 14:** Government and the Economy	**Chapter 9:** Government and Economy	**Chapter 9:** Political and Economic Power
Issue 13: Has Welfare Reform Benefited the Poor?	**Chapter 8:** Stratification and Social Mobility in the United States **Chapter 10:** Racial and Ethnic Inequality	**Chapter 9:** Government and Economy **Chapter 10:** Social Class	**Chapter 9:** Political and Economic Power
Issue 14: Is Competition the Reform That Will Fix Education?	**Chapter 13:** Education and Religion	**Chapter 8:** Education and Religion	**Chapter 11:** Religion, Education, and Medicine
Issue 15: Should Biotechnology Be Used to Alter and Enhance Humans?	**Chapter 15:** Health, Medicine, and the Environment	**Chapter 14:** Health, Medicine and Environment	**Chapter 11:** Religion, Education, and Medicine
Issue 16: Is Street Crime More Harmful Than White-Collar Crime?	**Chapter 7:** Deviance and Social Control	**Chapter 6:** Deviance	**Chapter 5:** Deviance and Crime
Issue 17: Should Laws Against Drug Use Remain Restrictive?	**Chapter 7:** Deviance and Social Control	**Chapter 6:** Deviance	**Chapter 5:** Deviance and Crime

(Continued)

Taking Sides: Social Issues, 16/e, Expanded	Sociology: A Brief Introduction, 9/e by Schaefer	SOC 2010, by Witt	Sociology: The Core, 10/e by Hughes/Kroehler
Issue 18: Are We Headed Toward a Nuclear 9/11?	**Chapter 14:** Government and the Economy	**Chapter 9:** Government and Economy	**Chapter 9:** Political and Economic Power
Issue 19: Are Declining Growth Rates Rather Than Rapid Population Growth Today's Major Global Population Problem?	**Chapter 15:** Health, Medicine, and the Environment	**Chapter 11:** Global Inequality	**Chapter 12:** Population and Environment
Issue 20: Is Humankind Dangerously Harming the Environment?	**Chapter 15:** Health, Medicine, and the Environment	**Chapter 14:** Health, Medicine and Environment	**Chapter 12:** Population and Environment
Issue 21: Is Globalization Good for Humankind?	**Chapter 16:** Social Change in the Global Community	**Chapter 11:** Global Inequality	**Chapter 12:** Population and Environment **Chapter 13:** Social Change
Issue 22: Is Big Government Bad?	**Chapter 14:** Government and the Economy	**Chapter 11:** Global Inequality	**Chapter 9:** Political and Economic Power
Issue 23: Do Women Make Better Leaders?	**Chapter 11:** Stratification by Gender	**Chapter 12:** Gender and Sexuality	**Chapter 8:** Gender Inequality

Introduction

Debating Social Issues

Kurt Finsterbusch

What Is Sociology?

"I have become a problem to myself," St. Augustine said. Put into a social and secular framework, St. Augustine's concern marks the starting point of sociology. We have become a problem to ourselves, and it is sociology that seeks to understand the problem and, perhaps, to find some solutions. The subject matter of sociology, then, is ourselves—people interacting with one another in groups and organizations.

Although the subject matter of sociology is very familiar, it is often useful to look at it in an unfamiliar light, one that involves a variety of theories and perceptual frameworks. In fact, to properly understand social phenomena, it *should* be looked at from several different points of view. In practice, however, this may lead to more friction than light, especially when each view proponent says, "I am right and you are wrong," rather than, "My view adds considerably to what your view has shown."

Sociology, as a science of society, was developed in the nineteenth century. Auguste Comte (1798–1857), the French mathematician and philosopher who is considered to be the father of sociology, had a vision of a well-run society based on social science knowledge. Sociologists (Comte coined the term) would discover the laws of social life and then determine how society should be structured and run. Society would not become perfect, because some problems are intractable, but he believed that a society guided by scientists and other experts was the best possible society.

Unfortunately, Comte's vision was extremely naive. For most matters of state there is no one best way of structuring or doing things that sociologists can discover and recommend. Instead, sociologists debate more social issues than they resolve.

The purpose of sociology is to throw light on social issues and their relationship to the complex, confusing, and dynamic social world around us. It seeks to describe how society is organized and how individuals fit into it. But neither the organization of society nor the fit of individuals is perfect. Social disorganization is a fact of life—at least in modern, complex societies such as the one we live in. Here, perfect harmony continues to elude us, and "social problems" are endemic. The very institutions, laws, and policies that produce benefits also produce what sociologists call "unintended effects"—unintended and undesirable. The changes that please one sector of the society may displease another, or the changes that seem so indisputably healthy at first turn out to have a dark underside to them. The examples are endless. Modern urban life gives people privacy and freedom from snooping neighbors that the small town never afforded; yet that very privacy seems to breed an uneasy sense of anonymity and loneliness. Take another example: Hierarchy is necessary for organizations to function efficiently, but hierarchy leads to the creation of a ruling elite. Flatten out the hierarchy and you may achieve social equality—but at the price of confusion, incompetence, and low productivity.

This is not to say that all efforts to effect social change are ultimately futile and that the only sound view is the tragic one that concludes "nothing works." We can be realistic without falling into despair. In many respects, the human condition has improved over the centuries and has improved as a result of conscious social policies. But improvements are purchased at a price— not only a monetary price but one involving human discomfort and discontent. The job of policymakers is to balance the anticipated benefits against the probable costs.

It can never hurt policymakers to know more about the society in which they work or the social issues they confront. That, broadly speaking, is the purpose of sociology. It is what this book is about. This volume examines issues that are central to the study of sociology.

Culture and Values

A common value system is the major mechanism for integrating a society, but modern societies contain so many different groups with differing ideas and values that integration must be built as much on tolerance of differences as on common values. Furthermore, technology and social conditions change, so values must adjust to new situations, often weakening old values. Some people (often called *conservatives*) will defend the old values. Others (often called *liberals*) will make concessions to allow for change. For example, the protection of human life is a sacred value to most people, but some would compromise that value when the life involved is a 90-year-old comatose man on life-support machines, who had signed a document indicating that he did not want to be kept alive under those conditions. The conservative would counter that once we make the value of human life relative, we become dangerously open to greater evils—that perhaps society will come to think it acceptable to terminate all sick, elderly people undergoing expensive treatments. This is only one example of how values are hotly debated today.

Two debates on values are presented in Unit 1. Issue 1 examines a major institution that can be seen as responsible for instilling values and culture in people—the media. This issue focuses in particular on whether the news reporters and anchorpersons report and comment on the news with professional objectivity and relatively bias free. Fred Barnes argues that the major news outlets are liberal and hire liberal journalists. The selection and reporting of news, therefore, has a liberal bias. In contrast, Robert F. Kennedy Jr. counters that most people get their news from conservative sources and believe many conservative myths as a result. Issue 2 concerns the cultural and economic impact of immigration. Mark Krikorian argues that America has changed in ways that make immigration less beneficial than in the past. The main problem is that America does not assimilate as well. Jason L. Riley, on the other hand, praises immigration because it helps economic growth. America's flexible labor market enables newcomers to find jobs where they are needed. America also has a labor shortage except in recessions, so immigrants take few jobs from American citizens. He also argues that new immigrants are assimilating well.

Sex Roles, Gender, and the Family

An area that has experienced tremendous value change in the last several decades is sex roles and the family. Women in large numbers have rejected major aspects of their traditional gender roles and family roles while remaining strongly committed to much of the mother role and to many feminine characteristics. Men have changed much less, but their situation has changed considerably. Issue 3 examines the consequences of divorce on children, because it has become so common. Elizabeth Marquardt presents evidence that divorce damages children, but Constance Ahrons counters that her research with children of divorced parents shows otherwise. Issue 4 considers one of the current strains on mothers—the conflict between career and childrearing. E. Jeffrey Hill and Vjollca K. Märtinson argue that the "mommy track" is one way to successfully integrate family and career. Some aspects of the career ladder are sacrificed, but the family benefits are worth it for many women. Mary C. Noonan and Mary E. Corcoran calculate the trade-offs differently. The mommy track costs female attorneys both lower salaries and fewer promotions. Issue 5 debates whether same-sex marriages should be legal. The Human Rights Campaign presents all the arguments in its favor and Peter Sprigg presents all the arguments against it.

Stratification and Inequality

Issue 6 centers around a sociological debate about whether or not increasing economic inequality is a serious problem. James Kurth asserts that it is, while Gary S. Becker and Kevin M. Murphy argue that the increasing inequality is largely the result of the education premium, which, in turn, encourages young people to get more education and better themselves. Today one of the most controversial issues regarding inequalities is affirmative action. Is justice promoted or undermined by such policies? Curtis Crawford and Lawrence D. Bobo take opposing sides on this question in Issue 7. Issue 8 covers a major transformation in American stratification, which has been the dramatic change in women's position in society. The feminist movement was a major force in changing women's roles. Not all women, however, believe that the feminist movement has benefited society. In this vein, Kate O'Beirne blasts the feminist movement while Barbara Epstein praises feminists for the great things that they accomplished. Issue 9 deals with discrimination at the highest levels of corporate America. Alice H. Eagly and Linda L. Carli argue that women seldom reach the highest levels because they face obstacles at every stage of their career that decrease the woman/man ratio at each step upward. Thus, discrimination exists throughout the corporate world. Kingsley R. Browne disagrees. He thinks that biological differences between men and women account for many differences in their behaviors and choices which make women and men better suited for different types of jobs and differences in the way that they handle the same jobs. These differences account for male/female CEO ratios.

Political Economy and Institutions

Sociologists study not only the poor, the workers, and the victims of discrimination but also those at the top of society—those who occupy what the late sociologist C. Wright Mills used to call "the command posts." The question is whether the "pluralist" model or the "power elite" model is the one that best fits the facts in America. Does a single power elite rule the United States, or do many groups contend for power and influence so that the political process is accessible to all? In Issue 10, G. William Domhoff argues that the "owners and top-level managers in large income-producing properties are far and away the dominant power figures in the United States" and have a dominating influence in government decisions. Sheldon Kamieniecki's research tells a different story. He finds that business interests do not participate at a high rate in policy issues that affect them, have mixed results when they do, and often lose out to opposing interest groups.

Another major political economy issue is whether capitalism supports or undermines democracy. In Issue 11, Robert B. Reich argues that capitalism undermines democracy by preventing the government from serving the public good and advancing the general welfare. The political power of the corporations is greater than the influence of the people, so nominal democracies do not function as democracies. Anthony B. Kim disagrees. Economic progress advances economic freedom, public discussion, multiplication of ideas, openness, and eventually democracy. He presents data to show this.

The United States is a capitalist welfare state, and the role of the state in capitalism (more precisely, the market) and in welfare is examined in the next two issues. Issue 12 considers whether or not the government should step in and attempt to correct for the failures of the market through regulations, policies, and programs. Joseph E. Stiglitz argues that government intervention is necessary to make markets work well and to prevent various harms to society. Walter Williams argues that the Constitution sought to protect the freedom of individuals, so it strictly limited the role of government. Regrettably the role of government has increased and individual freedoms have decreased. The free market has achieved great prosperity for America but the intervention of government has had net negative effects. One way in which the government intervenes in the economy is by providing welfare to people who cannot provide for their own needs in the labor market. Issue 13 debates the wisdom of the Work Opportunity Reconciliation Act of 1996, which ended Aid to Families of Dependent Children (which was what most people equated with welfare). David Coates presents the argument that the welfare reform was a great success because it greatly reduced welfare rolls and dramatically increased the employment of welfare mothers. Stephanie Mencimer tells a different story. She documents the horrible way welfare is administered in many states. Many welfare workers deny many benefits to many people who qualify for welfare. Thus, many welfare benefits do not reach the poor.

Education is one of the biggest jobs of the government as well as the key to individual prosperity and the success of the economy. For decades the American system of education has been severely criticized. Such an important institution is destined to be closely scrutinized, and many reforms have been attempted. The main debate on how to improve public schools concerns school choice, as presented in Issue 14. Clint Bolick argues that competition improves performance in sports and business, so it should do the same in education, and the data support this theory. Also, parents should be allowed to send their children to the school of their choice. Ron Wolk presents a more radical view of school reform. Many reform proposals today, including school choice, will do little to improve schools. He proposes shifting more responsibility for education from teachers to students.

The final issue in this section deals with a set of concerns about the use of present and soon-to-emerge biotechnologies. The value of biotechnologies for healing people is accepted by all. Issue 15, however, debates their use to alter and enhance humans. The President's Council on Bioethics describes how biotechnologies could improve the genes of babies and enhance everyone. The arguments against such practices are present by Michael Sandel.

Crime and Social Control

Crime is interesting to sociologists because crimes are those activities that society makes illegal and will use force to stop. Why are some acts made illegal and others (even those that may be more harmful) not made illegal? Surveys indicate that concern about crime is extremely high in America. Is the fear of crime, however, rightly placed? Americans fear mainly street crime, but Jeffrey Reiman argues in Issue 16 that corporate crime—also known as "white-collar crime"—causes far more death, harm, and financial loss to Americans than does street crime. In contrast, David A. Anderson calculates the full costs of crime, both direct and indirect, and concludes that the costs of murder and theft far exceed the cost of white-collar crime. These contradictory findings result from differing definitions of white-collar crime. A prominent aspect of the crime picture is the illegal drug trade. It has such bad consequences that some people are seriously talking about legalizing drugs in order to kill the illegal drug business. Herbert Kleber and Joseph Califano disagree. They think that drug laws should remain restrictive because legalization would result in increased use, especially by children. They contend that drug legalization would not eliminate drug-related violence but would increase the harm caused by drugs. Peter Gorman thinks that the drug laws are harmful and should be repealed. Restrictive drug laws have been ineffective. He notes that drug use and drug addiction have increased since drug laws became more stringent. Despite the crackdown on drug use, the availability of drugs has increased while the cost of drugs has decreased. In addition, restrictive drug laws, says Gorman, are racist and endanger civil liberties.

Finally, Issue 18 deals with terrorism with weapons of mass destruction, perhaps the major problem in America today. According to Brian Michael Jenkins, a team of terrorists could easily be inserted into the United States and carry out a terrorist attack with a nuclear or radiological bomb. Graham Allison argues that we are not likely to experience a nuclear 9/11 because our counter terrorist capacities have reduced the risk of nuclear terrorism to nearly zero.

The Future: Population/Environment/Society

Many social commentators speculate on "the fate of the earth." The next two issues on population and the environment address these concerns. The environmentalists have their own vision of apocalypse. They see the possibility that the human race could degrade the environment to the point that population growth and increasing economic production could overshoot the carrying capacity of the globe. The resulting collapse could lead to the extinction of much of the human race and the end of free societies. Other analysts believe that these fears are groundless. The problems of population growth have been discussed for decades. Recently the discussion has been stood on its head. The fear before was focused on overpopulation. However, now the new fear is of problems of underpopulation. Issue 19 asks which is the real, legitimate population problem. Michael Meyer points out that declining birth rates will ultimately lead to declining population and increasing ratios of older people to younger people in many countries. This situation creates immense problems in supporting the elderly and maintaining a healthy economy. Danielle Nierenberg and Nia MacDonald claims that the real population problem is still overpopulation which still threatens the environment and its capacity to support the human family. The negative consequences of declining population can be easily solved. In Issue 20, Lester R. Brown shows how human actions are degrading the environment in ways that adversely affect humans. In contrast, Bjorn Lomborg argues that the environment is improving in many ways and that environmental problems are manageable or will have mild adverse effects.

Issue 21 assesses the benefits and costs of globalization. Johan Norberg argues that economic globalization has been a demonstration of the basic economic theory that global markets and relatively free trade economically benefit all nations that participate. Martin Hart-Landsberg counters that globalization, which increases corporate profits, hurts both workers and the environment.

The Social Construction of Reality

An important idea in sociology is that people construct social reality in the course of interaction by attaching social meanings to the reality they are experiencing and then responding to those meanings. Two people can walk down a city street and derive very different meanings from what they see around them. Both, for example, may see homeless people—but they may see them in different contexts. One fits them into a picture of once-vibrant cities dragged into decay and ruin because of permissive policies that have encouraged pathological types to harass citizens; the other observer fits them into a picture of an America that can no longer hide the wretchedness of its poor. Both feel that they are seeing something deplorable, but their views of what makes it deplorable are radically opposed. Their differing views of what they have seen will lead to very different prescriptions for what should be done about the problem.

The social construction of reality is an important idea for this book because each author is socially constructing reality and working hard to persuade you to see his or her point of view, that is, to see the definition of the situation and the set of meanings he or she has assigned to the situation. In doing this, each author presents a carefully selected set of facts, arguments, and values. The arguments contain assumptions or theories, some of which are spelled out and some of which are unspoken. The critical reader has to judge the evidence for the facts, the logic and soundness of the arguments, the importance of the values, and whether or not omitted facts, theories, and values invalidate the thesis. This book facilitates this critical thinking process by placing authors in opposition. This puts the reader in the position of critically evaluating two constructions of reality for each issue instead of one.

Conclusion

Writing in the 1950s, a period that was in some ways like our own, the sociologist C. Wright Mills said that Americans know a lot about their "troubles" but they cannot make the connections between seemingly personal concerns and the concerns of others in the world. If they could only learn to make those connections, they could turn their concerns into *issues*. An issue transcends the realm of the personal. According to Mills, "An issue is a public matter: some value cherished by publics is felt to be threatened. Often there is a debate about what the value really is and what it is that really threatens it." It is not primarily personal troubles but social issues that I have tried to present in this book. The variety of topics in it can be taken as an invitation to discover what Mills called "the sociological imagination." This imagination, said Mills, "is the capacity to shift from one perspective to another—from the political to the psychological; from examination of a single family to comparative assessment of the national budgets of the world. . . . It is the capacity to range from the most impersonal and remote transformations to the most intimate features of the human self—and to see the relations between the two." This book, with a range of issues well suited to the sociological imagination, is intended to enlarge that capacity.

Internet References . . .

Internet Philosophical Resources on Moral Relativism

This Web site for *Ethics Updates* offers discussion questions, a bibliographical guide, and a list of Internet resources concerning moral relativism.

http://ethics.sandiego.edu/

The National Institute on Media and the Family

The National Institute on Media and the Family Web site is a national resource for teachers, parents, community leaders, and others who are interested in the influence of electronic media on early childhood education, child development, academic performance, culture, and violence.

http://www.mediafamily.org

The International Center for Migration, Ethnicity, and Citizenship

The International Center for Migration, Ethnicity, and Citizenship is engaged in scholarly research and public policy analysis bearing on international migration, refugees, and the incorporation of newcomers in host countries.

http://www.newschool.edu/icmec/

National Immigrant Forum

The National Immigrant Forum is a pro-immigrant organization that examines the effects of immigration on U.S. society. Click on the links for discussion of underground economies, immigrant economies, race and ethnic relations, and other topics.

http://www.immigrationforum.org

The National Network for Immigrant and Refugee Rights (NNIRR)

The National Network for Immigrant and Refugee Rights (NNIRR) serves as a forum to share information and analysis, to educate communities and the general public, and to develop and coordinate plans of action on important immigrant and refugee issues.

http://www.nnirr.org

Culture and Values

*S*ociologists *recognize that a fairly strong consensus on the basic values of a society contributes greatly to the smooth functioning of that society. The functioning of modern, complex urban societies, however, often depends on the tolerance of cultural differences and equal rights and protections for all cultural groups. In fact, such societies can be enriched by the contributions of different cultures. But at some point the cultural differences may result in a pulling apart that exceeds the pulling together. Another cultural problem in America is whether the media has a bias that is significantly removed from the epicenter of American culture. The final problem is whether current immigrants to the United States bring appropriate values and skills.*

- Does the News Media Have a Liberal Bias?
- Is Third World Immigration a Threat to America's Way of Life?

ISSUE 1

Does the News Media Have a Liberal Bias?

YES: Fred Barnes, from "Is Mainstream Media Fair and Balanced?" *Imprimis* (August 2006)

NO: Robert F. Kennedy Jr., from *Crimes Against Nature* (HarperCollins, 2005)

ISSUE SUMMARY

YES: Fred Barnes, journalist, executive editor of *The Weekly Standard* and TV commentator, argues that the mainstream media has a pronounced liberal bias. They do not hire conservatives, and an analysis of specific news stories shows their bias.

NO: Robert F. Kennedy Jr., environmentalist and political activist, agrees with Barnes that the media is biased but believes that it has a conservative bias. Surveys show that most Americans have many false beliefs that are fed to them by conservative talk radio shows and other conservative media outlets. Many media owners are very conservative and stifle investigative reporting.

"**A** small group of men, numbering perhaps no more than a dozen 'anchormen,' commentators and executive producers . . . decide what forty to fifty million Americans will learn of the day's events in the nation and the world." The speaker was Spiro Agnew, vice president of the United States during the Nixon administration. The thesis of Agnew's speech, delivered to an audience of midwestern Republicans in 1969, was that the television news media are controlled by a small group of liberals who foist their liberal opinions on viewers under the guise of "news." The upshot of this control, said Agnew, "is that a narrow and distorted picture of America often emerges from the televised news." Many Americans, even many of those who were later shocked by revelations that Agnew took bribes while serving in public office, agreed with Agnew's critique of the "liberal media."

Politicians' complaints about unfair news coverage go back much further than Agnew and the Nixon administration. The third president of the United States, Thomas Jefferson, was an eloquent champion of the press, but after six years as president, he could hardly contain his bitterness. "The man who never looks into a newspaper," he wrote, "is better informed than he who reads them, inasmuch as he who knows nothing is nearer to truth than he whose mind is filled with falsehoods and errors."

The press today is much different than it was in Jefferson's day. Newspapers then were pressed in hand-operated frames in many little printing shops around the country; everything was local and decentralized, and each paper averaged a few hundred subscribers. Today, newspaper chains have taken over most of the once independent local newspapers. Other newspapers, like the *New York Times* and the *Washington Post,* enjoy nationwide prestige and help set the nation's news agenda. Geographical centralization is even more obvious in the case of television. About 70 percent of the national news on television comes from three networks whose programming originates in New York City.

A second important difference between the media of the eighteenth century and the media today has to do with the ideal of "objectivity." In past eras, newspapers were frankly partisan sheets, full of nasty barbs at the politicians and parties the editors did not like; they made no distinction between "news" and "editorials." The ideal of objective journalism is a relatively recent development, tracing back to the early years of the twentieth century. Disgusted with the sensationalist "yellow journalism" of the time, intellectual leaders urged newspapers to cultivate a core of professionals who would concentrate on accurate reporting and who would leave their opinions to the editorial page. Journalism schools cropped up around the country, helping to promote the ideal of objectivity. Although some journalists now openly scoff at it, the ideal still commands the respect—in theory, if not always in practice—of working reporters.

These two historical developments, news centralization and news professionalism, play off against one another in the current debate over news "bias." The question of bias was irrelevant when the press was a scatter of little independent newspapers. Bias started to become an important question when newspapers became dominated by chains, and airwaves by networks, and when a few national press leaders like the *New York Times* and the *Washington Post* began to emerge. Although these "mainstream" news outlets have been challenged in recent years by opinions expressed in a variety of alternative media—such as cable television, talk radio, newsletters, and computer mail—they still remain powerful conveyers of news.

Is media news reporting biased? The media constitutes a major socializing institution, so this is an important question. Defenders of the media usually hold that although journalists, like all human beings, have biases, their professionalism compels them to report news with considerable objectivity. Media critics insist that journalists constantly interject their biases into their news reports. The critics, however, often disagree about whether such bias is liberal or conservative, as is the case with this issue. In the following selections, Fred Barnes argues that the news media tilt to the left, whereas Robert F. Kennedy Jr. contends that the slant of the news media to which most people are exposed supports a conservative status quo.

YES

Fred Barnes

Is the Mainstream Media Fair and Balanced?

Let me begin by defining three terms that are thrown around in debates about the media today. The first is objectivity, which means reporting the news with none of your own political views or instincts slanting the story one way or another. Perfect objectivity is pretty hard for anyone to attain, but it can be approximated. Then there's fairness. Fairness concedes that there may be some slant in a news story, but requires that a reporter will be honest and not misleading with regard to those with whom he disagrees. And finally there's balance, which means that both sides on an issue or on politics in general—or more than two sides, when there are more than two—get a hearing.

My topic today is how the mainstream media—meaning nationally influential newspapers like the *Washington Post*, the *New York Times*, the *Wall Street Journal* and *USA Today*; influential regional papers like the *Miami Herald*, the *Chicago Tribune* and the *Los Angeles Times*; the broadcast networks and cable news stations like CNN; and the wire services, which now are pretty much reduced to the Associated Press—stacks up in terms of the latter two journalistic standards, fairness and balance. In my opinion, they don't stack up very well.

Twenty years ago I wrote a piece in *The New Republic* entitled "Media Realignment," and the thrust of it was that the mainstream media was shedding some of its liberal slant and moving more to the center. This was in the Reagan years, and I pointed to things like *USA Today*, which was then about five years old and was a champion of the Reagan economic recovery. CNN was younger then, too, and quite different from the way it is now; Ted Turner owned it, but he wasn't manipulating it the way he did later, which turned it into something quite different. Financial news was suddenly very big in the midst of the 401 (k) revolution, and the stock market boom was getting a lot of coverage. *The New Republic*, where I worked, had been pro-Stalin in the 1930s, but by the 1980s had become very pro-Reagan and anti-communist on foreign policy. I also cited a rise of new conservative columnists like George Will. But looking back on that piece now, I see that I couldn't have been more wrong. The idea that the mainstream media was moving to the center was a mirage. In fact, I would say that compared to what I was writing about back in the 1980s, the mainstream media today is more liberal, more elitist, more secular, more biased, more hostile to conservatives and Republicans, and more self-righteous.

Reprinted by permission from *Imprimis,* the national speech digest of Hillsdale College, www .hillsdale.edu. SUBSCRIPTION FREE UPON REQUEST. ISSN 0277-8432. Imprimis trademark registered in U.S. Patent and Trade Office # 1563325.

Liberal and Impenetrable

Liberalism is endemic in the mainstream media today. Evan Thomas—the deputy editor of *Newsweek* and one of the honest liberals in the media—noted this very thing with regard to coverage of the 2004 presidential race, which I'll discuss later. It was obvious, he said, that the large majority in the media wanted John Kerry to win and that this bias slanted their coverage. And indeed, every poll of the media—and there have been a lot of them—shows that they're liberal, secular and so on. Polls of the Washington press corps, for instance, about who they voted for in 2004 always show that nine-to-one or ten-to-one of them voted Democratic. Peter Brown, a columnist who just recently left the *Orlando Sentinel*, conducted a poll a few years ago of newspaper staffs all around the country—not just at the big papers, but midsize papers and even some small papers—and found that this disparity existed everywhere.

Nor is this likely to change. Hugh Hewitt, the California lawyer and blogger and talk radio host, spent a few days recently at the Columbia Journalism School, supposedly the premiere journalism school in America. He spoke to a couple of classes there and polled them on who they had voted for. He found only one Bush voter in all the classes he spoke to. Steve Hayes, a fine young writer and reporter at *The Weekly Standard*, went to Columbia Journalism School and says that during his time there he was one of only two or three conservative students out of hundreds.

This is not to say that there aren't many fine young conservative journalists. But they aren't likely to be hired in the mainstream media. When I was at *The New Republic* for ten years—and *The New Republic* was quite liberal, despite its hawkish foreign policy—any young person who joined the staff and wrote stories that were interesting and demonstrated that he or she could write well was grabbed immediately by the *New York Times* or other big newspapers, *Newsweek*, *Time* or the networks. But that doesn't happen at *The Weekly Standard*, where I work now. Some of our young writers are the most talented I have ever met in my 30-plus years in journalism. But they don't get those phone calls. Why? Because they're with a conservative magazine. Of course there has been one famous exception—David Brooks, who is now the conservative columnist with the *New York Times*. But he was probably the least conservative person at *The Weekly Standard*. Conservatives are tokens on most editorial pages, just as they are on the broadcast networks and on cable news stations like CNN and MSNBC. Of course, I have a vested interest, since I work for FOX News; but if you compare the number of liberal commentators on FOX—and there are a lot of them—with the number of conservatives on those other stations, you'll see what I mean.

The fact is that the mainstream media doesn't want conservatives. It doesn't matter whether they're good reporters or writers. They go out of their way not to hire them. This was true 20 years ago, and it's true today. This impenetrability is why conservatives have had to erect the alternative media—talk radio, the blogs, conservative magazines and FOX News. Together, these form a real infrastructure that's an alternative to the mainstream media. But it's still a lot smaller, it's not as influential and it's largely reactive. It's not the equal of the mainstream media, that's for sure.

Powerful and Unfair

One way to see the unequaled power of the mainstream media is in how it is able to shape and create the stories that we're stuck talking about in America. A good example is Cindy Sheehan last summer. The Sheehan story was a total creation of the mainstream media. And in creating the story, the media shamelessly mischaracterized Sheehan. It portrayed her as simply a poor woman who wanted to see President Bush because her son had been killed in Iraq. Well, in the first place, she had already seen President Bush once. Also, though you would never know it from the dominant coverage, she was in favor of the Iraqi insurgency—the beheaders, the killers of innocent women and children. She was on their side, and she said so. She was also filled with a deep hatred of Israel. Yet the media treated her in a completely sympathetic manner, failing to report the beliefs that she made little attempt to hide. In any case, the Cindy Sheehan story came to dominate the news for the latter part of the summer; only the mainstream media still has the power to *make* stories big.

To see how distorted the mainstream media's view of the world can be, one need only compare its coverage of the Valerie Plame "leak" story with its coverage of the NSA surveillance leak story. Plame is the CIA agent whose name was written about by reporter Robert Novak in a column, following which the media portrayed her as having been outed as an undercover CIA agent. The simple facts from the beginning were that she was not an undercover agent any more; she was not even overseas. The story had no national security repercussions at all—none. But that didn't stop the media, which built the story up to great heights—apparently in the groundless hope that it would lead to an indictment of Karl Rove—and kept it front page news, at least intermittently, for what seemed like forever. The NSA surveillance story, on the other hand, also created by the media—this time pursuant to a real leak, and one that was clearly in violation of the law—had tremendous national security implications. After all, it revealed a secret and crucial program that was being used to uncover plots to bomb and massacre Americans and probably rendered that program no longer effective. Not only was this important story treated on an equal basis with the non-story of Valerie Plame, but the media was not interested, for the most part, in its national security repercussions. Instead the media mischaracterized the story as a "domestic spying scandal," suggesting constitutional overreach by the Bush administration. Well, a domestic spying story is exactly what the story was *not*. Those being spied on were Al-Qaeda members overseas who were using the telephone. If some of those calls were with people in the U.S., they were monitored for that reason only. But the media's stubborn mischaracterization of the story continued to frame the debate.

This brings me to the use of unfair and unbalanced labeling by the media. How often, if ever, have you heard or read the term "ultraliberal"? I don't think I've ever heard or read it. You'll hear and see the term "ultraconservative" a lot, but not "ultraliberal"—even though there are plenty of ultraliberals. Another widely used labeling term is "activist." If people are working to block a shopping center from being built or campaigning against Wal-Mart, they are called "activists." Of course, what the term "activist" means is *liberal*. But while conservatives are called conservatives by the media, liberals are "activists." For years we've seen something similar with regard to debates over judicial nominees. The Federalist Society, with which many conservative judicial nominees tend to be associated, is always referred to as the *conservative* Federalist Society, as if that's part of its name. But the groups opposing conservative nominees are rarely if ever labeled as liberal—giving the impression that they, unlike the Federalist Society, are somehow objective.

Related to this, I would mention that conservatives are often labeled in a way to suggest they are mean and hateful. Liberals criticize, but conservatives hate. Have you noticed that the media never characterizes individuals or groups as Bush haters? There are Bush critics, but there are no Bush haters—whereas in the Clinton years, critics of the president were often referred to as Clinton haters. I'm not saying that there weren't Clinton haters on the fringes in the 1990s. But far-left groups have been treated as acceptable . . . within the mainstream of American politics today by the media, while in truth they are as clearly animated by hatred as the most rabid anti-Clinton voices ever were.

Secular and Partisan Bias

With regard to religion, Christianity in particular—but also religious faith in general—is reflexively treated as something dangerous and pernicious by the mainstream media. Back in the early 1990s when I was still at *The New Republic*, I was invited to a dinner in Washington with Mario Cuomo. He was then governor of New York, and had invited several reporters to dinner because he was thinking about running for president. At one point that night he mentioned that he sent his children to Catholic schools in New York because he wanted them to be taught about a God-centered universe. This was in the context of expressing his whole-hearted support for public schools. But from the reaction, you would have thought he had said that one day a week he would bring out the snakes in his office and make policy decisions based on where they bit him. He was subsequently pummeled with stories about how improper it was for him, one, to send his kids to religious schools, and two, to talk about it. It was amazing. The most rigid form of secularism passes as the standard in mainstream journalism these days.

President Bush is similarly treated as someone who is obsessive about his religion. And what does he do? Well, he reads a devotional every day; he tries to get through the Bible, I think, once a year; and he prays. Now, I know many, many people who do this. Tens of millions of people do it. And yet the media treats Bush as some religious nut and pursues this story inaccurately. Again, it is clear that partisan bias is involved, too, because in fact, Bush talks publicly about his faith much less than other presidents have. There is a good book about Bush's religion by Paul Kengor, who went back to every word President Clinton spoke and found out that Clinton quoted scripture and mentioned God and Jesus Christ more than President Bush has. You would never get that from the mainstream media.

The partisan bias of the mainstream media has been at no time more evident than during the last presidential election. Presidential candidates used to be savaged equally by the media. No matter who—Republican or Democrat— they both used to take their hits. But that's not true any more. Robert Lichter, at the Center for Media and Public Affairs in Washington, measures the broadcast news for all sorts of things, including how they treat candidates. He's been doing it now for nearly 20 years. And would anyone care to guess what presidential candidate in all those years has gotten the most favorable treatment from the broadcast media? The answer is John Kerry, who got 77 percent favorable coverage in the stories regarding him on the three broadcast news shows. For Bush, it was 34 percent. This was true despite the fact that Kerry made his Vietnam service the motif of the Democratic National Convention, followed weeks later by 64 Swift Boat vets who served with Kerry in Vietnam claiming that he didn't do the things he said he did. It was a huge story, but the mainstream media didn't want to cover it and didn't cover it, for week after week after week.

There was an amazingly well documented book written by a man named John O'Neill—himself a Swift Boat vet—who went into great detail about why John Kerry didn't deserve his three Purple Hearts, etc. It might have been a right-wing screed, but if you actually read it, it wasn't a screed. It backed up its claims with evidence. Normally in journalism, when somebody makes some serious charges against a well-known person, reporters look into the charges to see if they're true or not. If they aren't, reporters look into the motives behind the false charges—for instance, to find out if someone paid the person making the false charges, and so on. But that's not what the media did in this case. The *New York Times* responded immediately by investigating the financing of the Swift Boat vets, rather than by trying to determine whether what they were saying was true. Ultimately, grudgingly—after bloggers and FOX News had covered the story sufficiently long that it couldn't be ignored—the mainstream media had to pick up on the story. But its whole effort was aimed at knocking down what the Swift Boat vets were saying.

Compare this with September 8, 2004, when Dan Rather reported on documents that he said showed not only that President Bush used preferential treatment to get into the Texas National Guard, but that he hadn't even done all his service. The very next morning, the whole story—because CBS put one of the documents on its Web site—was knocked down. It was knocked down because a blogger on a Web site called Little Green Footballs made a copy on his computer of the document that was supposedly made on a typewriter 30 years earlier and demonstrated that it was a fraud made on a modern computer. Then, only a few weeks after that embarrassment, CBS came up with a story, subsequently picked up by the *New York Times*, that an arms cache of 400 tons of ammunition in Iraq had been left unguarded by the American military and that the insurgents had gotten hold of it. Well, it turned out that they didn't know whether the insurgents had gotten that ammunition or not, or whether indeed the American military had possession of it. It was about a week before the election that these major news organizations broke this unsubstantiated story, something that would have been unimaginable in past campaigns. Why would they do that? Why would Dan Rather insist on releasing fraudulent documents when even his own experts recommended against it? Why would CBS and the *New York Times* come back with an explosive but unsubstantiated arms cache story only weeks later? They did it for one reason: They wanted to defeat President Bush for re-election. There is no other motive that would explain disregarding all the precautions you're taught you should have in journalism.

⋅❀⋅

I'll wind up on a positive note, however. Forty years ago, John Kenneth Galbraith—the great liberal Harvard economist—said that he knew conservatism was dead because it was bookless. Conservatives didn't publish books. And to some extent, it was true at the time. But it's no longer true. Conservatives have become such prolific writers and consumers of books that Random House and other publishing companies have started separate conservative imprints. Nowadays it is common to see two or three or four conservative books—some of them kind of trashy, but some of them very good—on the bestseller list. Insofar as books are an indication of how well conservatives are doing—at least in the publishing part of the media world—I would say they're doing quite well. They're not winning, but they're much better off than they were before—something that can't be said about how they are faring in the unfair and unbalanced mainstream media.

 **NO**

The Disinformation Society

Many Democratic voters marveled at the election results. George W. Bush, they argued, has transformed a projected $5.6 trillion, 10-year Bill Clinton surplus into a projected $1.4 trillion deficit—a $7 trillion shift in wealth from our national treasury into the pockets of the wealthiest Americans, particularly the president's corporate paymasters. Any discerning observer, they argued, must acknowledge that the White House has repeatedly lied to the American people about critical policy issues—Medicare, education, the environment, the budget implications of its tax breaks, and the war in Iraq—with catastrophic results.

President Bush has opened our national lands and sacred places to the lowest bidder and launched a jihad against the American environment and public health to enrich his corporate sponsors. He has mired us in a costly, humiliating war that has killed more than 1,520 American soldiers and maimed 11,300. He has made America the target of Islamic hatred, caused thousands of new terrorists to be recruited to al-Qaeda, isolated us in the world, and drained our treasury of the funds necessary to rebuild Afghanistan and to finance our own vital homeland-security needs. He has shattered our traditional alliances and failed to protect vulnerable terrorist targets at home-chemical plants, nuclear facilities, air-cargo carriers, and ports. He has disgraced our nation and empowered tyrants with the unpunished excesses at Guantánamo and Abu Ghraib. These baffled Democrats were hard-pressed to believe that their fellow Americans would give a man like this a second term.

To explain the president's victory, political pundits posited a vast "values gap" between red states and blue states. They attributed the president's success in the polls, despite his tragic job failures, to the rise of religious fundamentalism. Heartland Americans, they suggested, are the soldiers in a new American Taliban, willing to vote against their own economic interests to promote "morality" issues that they see as the critical high ground in a life-or-death culture war.

I believe, however, that the Democrats lost the presidential contest not because of a philosophical chasm between red and blue states but due to an information deficit caused by a breakdown in our national media. Traditional broadcast networks have abandoned their former obligation to advance democracy and promote the public interest by informing the public about both sides of issues relevant to those goals. To attract viewers and advertising revenues, they entertain rather than inform. This threat to the flow of information, vital

From *Crimes Against Nature* by Robert Kennedy Jr. (Harper Perennial, 2005). Copyright © 2005 by Robert F. Kennedy, Jr. Reprinted by permission of HarperCollins Publishers.

to democracy's survival, has been compounded in recent years by the growing power of right-wing media that twist the news and deliberately deceive the public to advance their radical agenda.

According to an October 2004 survey by the Program on International Policy Attitudes (PIPA), a joint program of the Center on Policy Attitudes, in Washington, D.C., and the Center for International and Security Studies at the University of Maryland:

- Seventy-two percent of Bush supporters believed Iraq had weapons of mass destruction (or a major program for developing them), versus 26 percent of Kerry voters. A seven-month search by 1,500 investigators led by David Kay, working for the C.I.A., found no such weapons.
- Seventy-five percent of Bush supporters believed that Iraq was providing substantial support to al-Qaeda, a view held by 30 percent of Kerry supporters. *The 9/11 Commission Report* concluded that there was no terrorist alliance between Iraq and al-Qaeda.
- Eighty-two percent of Bush supporters erroneously believed either that the rest of the world felt better about the U.S. thanks to its invasion of Iraq or that views were evenly divided. Eighty-six percent of Kerry supporters accurately understood that a majority of the world felt worse about our country.
- Most Bush supporters believed the Iraq war had strong support in the Islamic world. Kerry's supporters accurately estimated the low level of support in Islamic countries. Even Turkey, the most Westernized Islamic country, was 87 percent against the invasion.
- Most significant, the majority of Bush voters agreed with Kerry supporters that if Iraq did not have W.M.D. and was not providing assistance to al-Qaeda the U.S. should not have gone to war. Furthermore, most Bush supporters, according to PIPA, favored the Kyoto Protocol to fight global warming, the Mine Ban Treaty to ban land mines, and strong labor and environmental standards in trade agreements, and wrongly believed that their candidate favored these things. In other words, the values and principles were the same. Bush voters made their choice based on bad information.

It's no mystery where the false beliefs are coming from. Both Bush and Kerry supporters overwhelmingly believe that the Bush administration at the time of the 2004 U.S. election was telling the American people that Iraq had W.M.D. and that Saddam Hussein had strong links to al-Qaeda. The White House's false message was carried by right-wing media in bed with the administration. Prior to the election, Fox News reporters, for example, regularly made unsubstantiated claims about Iraq's W.M.D. Fox anchor Brit Hume, on his newscast in July 2004, announced that W.M.D. had actually been found. Sean Hannity repeatedly suggested without factual support that the phantom weapons had been moved to Syria and would soon be found. An October 2003 survey by PIPA showed that people who watch Fox News are disproportionately afflicted with the same misinformation evidenced by the 2004 PIPA report. The earlier study probed for the source of public misinformation about the Iraq war that might account for the common misperceptions that Saddam Hussein had been involved in the 9/11 attacks, that he supported al-Qaeda, that W.M.D. had been found, and that world opinion favored the U.S. invasion. The study discovered that "the extent of Americans' misperceptions vary significantly depending on their source of news. Those who receive most of their news from Fox News are more likely than average to have misperceptions."

Unfortunately for John Kerry, many Americans now do get their information from Fox—according to Nielsen Media Research, in February, Fox was the cable news leader, with an average of 1.57 million prime-time viewers, nearly 2.5 times CNN's average viewership in the same time slot—and from Fox's similarly biased cable colleagues, CNBC and MSNBC. Millions more tune to the Sinclair Broadcast Group—one of the nation's largest TV franchises. After 9/11, Sinclair forced its stations to broadcast spots pledging support for President Bush, and actively censored unfavorable coverage of the Iraq war—blacking out Ted Koppel's *Nightline* when it ran the names of the U.S. war dead. It retreated from its pre-election proposal to strong-arm its 62 TV stations into pre-empting their prime-time programming to air an erroneous and blatantly biased documentary about John Kerry's war record only when its stock dropped 17 percent due to Wall Street fears of sponsor boycotts and investor worries that Sinclair was putting its right-wing ideology ahead of shareholder profits.

Americans are also getting huge amounts of misinformation from talk radio, which is thoroughly dominated by the extreme right. A Gallup Poll conducted in December 2002 discovered that 22 percent of Americans receive their daily news from talkradio programs. An estimated 15 million people listen to Rush Limbaugh alone, and on the top 45 AM radio stations in the country, listeners encounter 310 hours of conservative talk for every 5 hours of liberal talk. According to the nonprofit Democracy Radio, Inc., 90 percent of all political talk-radio programming is conservative, while only 10 percent is progressive. All the leading talk-show hosts are right-wing radicals—Rush Limbaugh, Sean Hannity, Michael Savage, Oliver North, G. Gordon Liddy, Bill O'Reilly, and Michael Reagan—and the same applies to local talk radio.

Alas, while the right-wing media are deliberately misleading the American people, the traditional corporately owned media—CBS, NBC, ABC, and CNN—are doing little to remedy those wrong impressions. They are, instead, focusing on expanding viewership by hawking irrelevant stories that appeal to our prurient interest in sex and celebrity gossip. None of the three major networks gave gavel-to-gavel coverage of the party conventions or more than an hour in prime time, opting instead to entertain the public with semi-pornographic reality shows. "We're about to elect a president of the United States at a time when we have young people dying in our name overseas, we just had a report from the 9/11 commission which says we are not safe as a nation, and one of these two groups of people is going to run our country," commented PBS newsman Jim Lehrer, in disgust at the lack of convention coverage. CBS anchor Dan Rather said that "I argued the conventions were part of the dance of democracy. I found myself increasingly like the Mohicans, forced farther and farther back into the wilderness and eventually eliminated."

The broadcast reporters participating in the presidential debates were apparently so uninterested in real issues that they neglected to ask the candidates a single question about the president's environmental record. CBS anchor Bob Schieffer, who M.C.'d the final debate, asked no questions about the environment, focusing instead on abortion, gay marriage, and the personal faith of the candidates, an agenda that could have been dictated by Karl Rove.

Where is that dreaded but impossible-to-find "liberal bias" that supposedly infects the American press? The erroneous impression that the American media have a liberal bias is itself a mark of the triumph of the right-wing propaganda machine.

⟡

The Republican Noise Machine: Right-Wing Media and How It Corrupts Democracy, by David Brock—the president and C.E.O. of Media Matters for America, a watchdog group that documents misinformation in the right-wing media— traces the history of the "liberal bias" notion back to the Barry Goldwater presidential campaign, in 1964, in which aggrieved conservatives railed against Walter Cronkite and the "Eastern Liberal Press" at the Republican National Convention. In response to Spiro Agnew's 1969 attack on the networks as insufficiently supportive of Nixon's policies in Vietnam, conservatives formed an organization called Accuracy in Media, whose purpose was to discredit the media by tagging it as "liberal," and to market that idea with clever catchphrases. Polluter-funded foundations, including the Adolph Coors Foundation and the so-called four sisters—the Lynde and Harry Bradley Foundation, the John M. Olin Foundation, Richard Mellon Scaife's foundations, and the Smith Richardson Foundation—all of which funded the anti-environmental movement, spent hundreds of millions of dollars to perpetuate the big lie of liberal bias, to convince the conservative base that it should not believe the mainstream, to create a market for right-wing media, and to intimidate and discipline the mainstream press into being more accommodating to conservatism.

According to Brock, right-wing groups such as the Heritage Foundation and Scaife's Landmark Legal Foundation helped persuade Ronald Reagan and his Federal Communications Commission, in 1987, to eliminate the Fairness Doctrine—the F.C.C.'s 1949 rule which dictated that broadcasters provide equal time to both sides of controversial public questions. It was a "godsend for conservatives," according to religious-right pioneer and Moral Majority co-founder Richard Viguerie, opening up talk radio to one-sided, right-wing broadcasters. (Rush Limbaugh nationally launched his talk show the following year.) Radical ideologues, faced with Niagara-size flows of money from the Adolph Coors Foundation, the four sisters, and others, set up magazines and newspapers and cultivated a generation of young pundits, writers, and propagandists, giving them lucrative sinecures inside right-wing think tanks, now numbering more than 500, from which they bombard the media with carefully honed messages justifying corporate profit taking.

Brock himself was one of the young stars recruited to this movement, working in turn for the Heritage Foundation, the Reverend Sun Myung Moon's

Washington Times, and Scaife's *American Spectator.* "If you look at this history," Brock told me recently, "you will find that the conservative movement has in many ways purchased the debate. You have conservative media outlets day after day that are intentionally misinforming the public." Brock, who admits to participating in the deliberate deception while he was a so-called journalist on the right-wing payroll, worries that the right-wing media are systematically feeding the public "false and wrong information. It's a really significant problem for democracy.

"We're in a situation," continues Brock, "where you have 'red facts' and 'blue facts.' And I think the conservatives intentionally have done that to try to confuse and neutralize accurate information that may not serve the conservative agenda."

The consolidation of media ownership and its conservative drift are growing ever more severe. Following the election, Clear Channel, the biggest owner of radio stations in the country, announced that Fox News will now supply its news feed to many of the company's 1,240 stations, further amplifying the distorted drumbeat of right-wing propaganda that most Americans now take for news.

Sadly enough, right-wing radio and cable are increasingly driving the discussion in mainstream broadcasting as well. At a Harvard University symposium the day before the Democratic convention, three network anchors and a CNN anchor straightforwardly discussed the effects that right-wing broadcasters, conservative money, and organized pressure have on the networks. And in February 2005, Pat Mitchell announced her resignation as president of PBS, hounded from office by right-wing critics who felt her conciliatory efforts to conservatize the network—canceling a cartoon episode with a lesbian couple and adding talk shows by such right-wingers as Tucker Carlson and Paul Gigot—did not go far enough fast enough.

Furthermore, Fox's rating success has exerted irresistible gravities that have pulled its competitors' programming to starboard. In the days leading up to the Iraq war, MSNBC fired one of television's last liberal voices, Phil Donahue, who hosted its highest-rated show; an internal memo revealed that Donahue presented "a difficult public face for NBC in a time of war." CBS's post-election decision to retire Dan Rather, a lightning rod for rightwing wrath, coincided with Tom Brokaw's retirement from NBC. He was replaced by Brian Williams, who has said, "I think Rush [Limbaugh] has actually yet to get the credit he is due." According to NBC president Jeff Zucker, "No one understands this NASCAR nation more than Brian."

Conservative noise on cable and talk radio also has an echo effect on the rest of the media. One of the conservative talking points in the last election was that terrorists supported the candidacy of John Kerry. According to Media Matters, this pearl originated on Limbaugh's radio show in March 2004 and repeatedly surfaced in mainstream news. In May, CNN's Kelli Arena reported "speculation that al-Qaeda believes it has a better chance of winning in Iraq if John Kerry is in the White House"; in June it migrated to Dick Morris's *New York Post* column. Chris Matthews mentioned it in a July edition of *Hardball.* In September, Bill Schneider, CNN's senior political analyst, declared that al-Qaeda "would very much like to defeat President Bush," signaling that Limbaugh's contrivance was now embedded firmly in the national consciousness.

That "echo effect" is not random. Brock shows in his book how the cues by which mainstream news directors decide what is important to cover are no longer being suggested by *The New York Times* and other responsible media outlets, but rather by the "shadowy" participants of a Washington, D.C., meeting convened by Grover Norquist's Americans for Tax Reform, an anti-government organization that seeks to prevent federal regulation of business.

Every Wednesday morning the leaders of 80 conservative organizations meet in Washington in Norquist's boardroom. This radical cabal formulates policy with the Republican National Committee and the White House, developing talking points that go out to the conservative media via a sophisticated fax tree. Soon, millions of Americans are hearing the same message from cable news commentators and thousands of talk jocks across America. Their precisely crafted message and language then percolate through the mainstream media to form the underlying assumptions of our national debate.

This meeting has now grown to include more than 120 participants, including industry lobbyists and representatives of conservative media outlets such as *The Washington Times* and the *National Review*. According to Brock, columnist Bob Novak sends a researcher. *The Wall Street Journal's* Peggy Noonan may attend in person. The lockstep coordination among right-wing political operatives and the press is new in American politics.

A typical meeting might focus on a new tax proposal released by President Bush. Following conference calls throughout the week, the decision will be made to call the plan "bold." Over the next 10 days, radio and cable will reiterate that it's "bold, bold, bold." The result, according to Brock, is that "people come to think that there must be something 'bold' about this plan."

This highly integrated network has given the right frightening power to disseminate its propaganda and has dramatically changed the way Americans get their information and formulate policy. In *The Republican Noise Machine*, Brock alleges routine fraud and systematically dishonest practices by his former employer the Reverend Sun Myung Moon's *Washington Times,* which is the primary propaganda organ for Moon's agenda to establish America as a Fascist theocracy. The paper doesn't reach more than a hundred thousand subscribers, but its articles are read on the air by Rush Limbaugh, reaching 15 million people, and are posted on Matt Drudge's Web site, to reach another 7 million people, and its writers regularly appear on *The O'Reilly Factor,* before another 2 million. Network TV talk-show producers and bookers use those appearances as a tip sheet for picking the subject matter and guests for their own shows. And so the capacity of the conservative movement to disseminate propaganda has increased exponentially.

This right-wing propaganda machine can quickly and indelibly brand Democratic candidates unfavorably—John Kerry as a flip-flopper, Al Gore as a liar. The machine is so powerful that it was able to orchestrate Clinton's impeachment despite the private and trivial nature of his "crime"—a lie about an extramarital tryst—when compared with President Bush's calamitous lies about Iraq, the budget, Medicare, education, and the environment. During the 2000 campaign, Al Gore was smeared as a liar—a charge that was completely false—by rightwing pundits such as gambling addict Bill Bennett and prescription-painkiller abuser Rush Limbaugh, both of whom the right wing has sold as moral paradigms. Meanwhile, George Bush's chronic problems with the truth during the three presidential debates that year were barely mentioned in the media, as Brock has noted. Americans accepted this negative characterization of Gore, and when they emerged from the voting booths in 2000, they told pollsters that Bush won their vote on "trust."

In the 2004 campaign, the so-called Swift Boat Veterans for Truth launched dishonest attacks which, amplified and repeated by the right-wing media, helped torpedo John Kerry's presidential ambitions. No matter who the Democratic nominee was, this machinery had the capacity to discredit and destroy him.

Meanwhile, there is a palpable absence of strong progressive voices on TV, unless one counts HBO's Bill Maher and Comedy Central's Jon Stewart—both comedians—or Fox's meek foil, Alan Colmes, who plays the ever losing Washington Generals to Scan Hannity's Harlem Globetrotters. There are no liberal equivalents to counterbalance Joe Scarborough, John Stossel, Bill O'Reilly, and Lawrence Kudlow. Brock points to the systematic structural imbalance in the panels that are featured across all of cable and on the networks' Sunday shows. Programs like *Meet the Press* and Chris Matthews's *Hardball* invariably pit conservative ideologues such as William Safire, Robert Novak, and Pat Buchanan against neutral, nonaligned reporters such as Andrea Mitchell, the diplomatic correspondent for NBC News, or *Los Angeles Times* reporter Ronald Brownstein in a rigged fight that leaves an empty chair for a strong progressive point of view.

There is still relevant information in the print media. But even that has been shamefully twisted by the pressures of the right. Both *The New York Times* and *The Washington Post,* which jumped on Scaife's bandwagon to lead the mainstream press in the Clinton-impeachment frenzy, have been forced to issue *mea culpas* for failing to ask the tough questions during the run-up to Bush's Iraq war.

Furthermore, America's newspapers, like most other media outlets, are owned predominantly by Republican conservatives. Newspapers endorsed Bush by two to one in the 2000 election. According to a recent survey, the op-ed columnists who appear in the most newspapers are conservatives Cal Thomas and George Will. Republican-owned newspapers often reprint misinformation from the right. And red-state journalists, whatever their personal political sympathies, are unlikely to offend their editors by spending inordinate energy exposing right-wing lies.

Print journalism is a victim of the same consolidation by a few large, profit-driven corporations that has affected the broadcasters. Today, a shrinking pool of owners—guided by big business rather than journalistic values—forces news executives to cut costs and seek the largest audience. The consolidation has led to demands on news organizations to return profits at rates never before expected of them. Last summer, just a few months after winning five Pulitzer Prizes, the *Los Angeles Times* was asked by its parent company to drop 60 newsroom positions.

The pressure for bottomline news leaves little incentive for investment in investigative reporting. Costcutting has liquidated news staffs, leaving reporters little time to research stories. According to an Ohio University study, the number of investigative reporters was cut almost in half between 1980 and 1995.

During the debate over the Radio Act of 1927, an early forerunner of the Fairness Doctrine, Texas congressman Luther Johnson warned Americans against the corporate and ideological consolidation of the national press that has now come to pass. "American thought and American politics will be largely at the mercy of those who operate these stations," he said. "For publicity is the most powerful weapon that can be wielded in a republic . . . and when a single selfish group is permitted to either tacitly or otherwise acquire ownership and dominate these broadcasting stations throughout the country, then woe be to those who dare to differ with them. It will be impossible to compete with them in reaching the ears of the American people."

The news isn't entirely bleak. Progressive voices are prevalent on the Internet, which is disproportionately utilized by the younger age groups that will exercise increasing influence in public affairs each year. The success of Air America Radio, the progressive network whose best-known host is Al Franken, offers great cause for optimism. Despite a shoestring budget and financial chaos at its inception, Air America has grown in one year to include 50 stations, from which it is accessible to half the American people. Most encouraging, a recent study shows that Air America personalities as a group rank second in popularity to Rush Limbaugh. Last fall in San Diego, a traditional Republican bastion, Air America was reported to be the No. 1 radio station among listeners 18 to 49 years old. But progressive activists need also to find a voice on television, and there the outlook is dark.

If there is a market for progressive voices, as the Air America experience suggests, why don't the big corporate owners leap in? A top industry executive recently told me that he was dead certain that there would be a large audience for a progressive TV news network to counterbalance the right-wing cable shows. "But," he said, "the corporate owners will never touch it. Multinationals, like Viacom, Disney, and General Electric, that rely on government business, contracts, and goodwill are not going to risk offending the Republicans who now control every branch of government."

This executive had recently spoken to Viacom chairman Sumner Redstone (a lifelong Democrat) about the corporation's open support of the Bush administration. "I said, 'Sumner, what about our children and what about our country?' He replied, 'Viacom is my life. I've got to do what's best for the company. I need to buy more stations, and the Republicans are going to let me do it. It's in the company's interest to support Republicans.'"

When veteran television journalist and former CBS news analyst Bill Moyers resigned as host of PBS's *Now* in December, he observed, "I think my peers in commercial television are talented and devoted journalists, but they've chosen to work in a corporate mainstream that trims their talent to fit the corporate nature of American life. And you do not get rewarded for telling the hard truths about America in a profit-seeking environment." Moyers called the decline in American journalism "the biggest story of our time." He added, "We have an ideological press that's interested in the election of Republicans, and a mainstream press that's interested in the bottom line. Therefore, we don't have a vigilant, independent press whose interest is the American people."

Moyers has elsewhere commented that "the quality of journalism and the quality of democracy are inextricably joined." By diminishing the capacity for voters to make rational choices, the breakdown of the American press is threatening not just our environment but our democracy.

POSTSCRIPT

Does the News Media Have a Liberal Bias?

As the opposing arguments in this issue indicate, we can find critics on both the Left and the Right who agree that the media are biased. What divides such critics is the question of whether the bias is left-wing or right-wing. Defenders of the news media may seize upon this disagreement to bolster their own claim that "bias is in the eye of the beholder." But the case may be that the news media are unfair to both sides. If that were true, however, it would seem to take some of the force out of the argument that the news media have a distinct ideological tilt at all.

A study by S. Robert Lichter et al., *The Media Elite* (Adler & Adler, 1986), tends to support Barnes's contention that the media slant leftward, as does Ann Coulter in *Slander: Liberal Lies about the American Right* (Crown Publishers, 2002); Bernard Goldberg in *BIAS: A CBS Insider Exposes How the Media Distort the News* (Regency Publishing, 2002); and *Arrogance: Rescuing America form the Media Elite* (Warner Books 2003). On the other hand, those who think the media are biased rightward include Ben Bagdikian, *The Media Monopoly,* 6th ed. (Beacon Press, 2000); Mark Hertsgaard, *On Bended Knee: The Press and the Reagan Presidency* (Schocken, 1989); Eric Alterman, *What Liberal Media? The Truth about Bias and the News* (Basic Books, 2003); David Edwards and David Cromwell, *Guardians of Power: The Myth of the Liberal Media* (Pluto Press, 2006); Jeffery Klaehn, ed., *Bound by Power: Intended Consequences* (Black Rose Books, 2006); and Robert Waterman McChesney, *The Problem of the Media: U.S. Communication Politics in the Twenty-First Century* (Monthly Review Press, 2004). In *South Park Conservatives: The Revolt Against Liberal Media Bias* (Regnery Publications, 2005), Brian C. Anderson observes that the media were very liberal but America revolted and now conservative voices are being heard.

S. Robert Lichter, Linda Lichter, and Stanley Rothman's *Watching America* (Prentice Hall, 1991) surveys the political and social messages contained in television "entertainment" programs. Several recent memoirs of journalists are very useful for the debate on media bias. See Tom Wicker's *On the Record* (Bedford/St. Martin's, 2002); Ted Koppel's *Off Camera* (Alfred A. Knopf, 2000); and Bill O'Reilly's *The No-Spin Zone* (Broadway Books, 2001). David Halberstam's *The Powers That Be* (Alfred A. Knopf, 1979), a historical study of CBS, the *Washington Post, Time* magazine, and the *Los Angeles Times,* describes some of the political and ideological struggles that have taken place within major media organizations.

ISSUE 2

Is Third World Immigration a Threat to America's Way of Life?

YES: Mark Krikorian, from *The New Case Against Immigration* (Sentinel, 2008)

NO: Jason L. Riley, from *Let Them In: The Case for Open Borders* (Gotham, 2008)

ISSUE SUMMARY

YES: Mark Krikorian, the executive director of the Center for Immigration Studies, presents the case against immigration. He emphasizes the changes in America that make immigration less beneficial for America. The current immigrants are not much different than immigrants in the past century but they do not fit the new America as well as the past immigrants fit the old America. One part of the story is that the new America will not assimilate immigrants well.

NO: Jason L. Riley, an editor of the *Wall Street Journal*, applauds immigration because it will propel, not impede, economic growth. America has a flexible labor market, where both employers and employees can change the work situation as they need or desire. "In the end, employers, workers, and consumers are all better off." America has a labor shortage that immigrants help fill without taking jobs in the aggregate from Americans. Riley also argues that new immigrants assimilate much like the old immigrants did.

Before September 11, 2001, many Americans favored the reduction of immigration. After the terrorist attacks on the World Trade Center and the Pentagon by immigrants, some felt even stronger about limiting immigration. But is immigration bad for America, as this sentiment assumes, or does it strengthen America?

Today the number of legal immigrants to America is close to 1 million per year, and illegal ("undocumented") immigrants probably number well over that figure. In terms of numbers, immigration is now comparable to the level it reached during the early years of the twentieth century, when millions of immigrants arrived from southern and eastern Europe. A majority of the new immigrants, however, do not come from Europe but from what has been called the "Third World"—the underdeveloped nations. The largest percentages come from Mexico, the Philippines, Korea, and the islands of the Caribbean, while European immigration has shrunk to about 10 percent. Much of the reason for this shift has to do with changes made in U.S. immigration laws during the 1960s. Decades earlier, in the 1920s, America narrowed its gate to people from certain regions of the world by imposing quotas designed to preserve the balance of races in America. But in 1965, a series of amendments to the Immigration Act put all the world's people on an equal footing in terms of immigration. The result, wrote journalist Theodore H. White, was "a stampede, almost an invasion" of Third World immigrants. Indeed, the 1965 amendments made it even easier for Third World immigrants to enter the country because the new law gave preference to those with a family member already living in the United States. Because most of the European immigrants who settled in the early part of the century had died off, and few Europeans had immigrated in more recent years, a greater percentage of family-reuniting immigration came from the Third World.

Immigrants move to the United States for various reasons: to flee tyranny and terrorism, to escape war, or to join relatives who have already settled. Above all, they immigrate because in their eyes America is an island of affluence in a global sea of poverty; here they will earn many times what they could only hope to earn in their native countries. One hotly debated question is, What will these new immigrants do to the United States—or for it?

Part of the debate has to do with bread-and-butter issues: Will new immigrants take jobs away from American workers? Or will they fill jobs that American workers do not want anyway, which will help stimulate the economy? Behind these economic issues is a more profound cultural question: Will these new immigrants add healthy new strains to America's cultural inheritance, broadening and revitalizing it? Or will they cause the country to break up into separate cultural units, destroying America's unity? Of all the questions relating to immigration, this one seems to be the most sensitive.

In 1992, conservative columnist Patrick Buchanan set off a firestorm of controversy when he raised this question: "If we had to take a million immigrants next year, say Zulus or Englishmen, and put them in Virginia, which group would be easier to assimilate and cause less problems for the people of Virginia?" Although Buchanan later explained that his intention was not to denigrate Zulus or any other racial group but simply to talk about assimilation into Anglo-American culture, his remarks were widely characterized as racist and xenophobic (related to a fear of foreigners). Whether or not that characterization is justified, Buchanan's question goes to the heart of the cultural debate over immigration—the tension between unity and diversity. In the selections that follow, Krikorian contends that immigrants are harming the United States both economically and culturally. He argues that America today does not assimilate immigrants very well, so more immigration will adversely affect American life. Riley counters that the accusations against immigrants are false and that immigrants contribute greatly to America.

YES

Mark Krikorian

The New Case Against Immigration

Introduction

It's not the immigrants—it's us.

What's different about immigration today as opposed to a century ago is not the characteristics of the newcomers but the characteristics of our society. Immigrants are what they've always been: not the poorest of the poor but one step up from the bottom, strivers looking for better lives for their children, coming from rural or small-town backgrounds in traditional—what we would call third-world—societies. But the changes that define modern America—in our society, economy, government, and technology, for example—are so fundamental that our past success in dealing with immigration is simply no longer relevant.

This is a new argument. It's not that previous critiques of immigration have been wrong—indeed, much of what follows in this book is based on the outstanding work of others over the years. Instead, the source of the problems created by immigration has usually been located in differences between *immigrants* past and present rather than in differences between *America* past and present. Immigrants in the past, it is said, were white, but now they're not; they used to want to assimilate, but now they don't; or they used to be self-sufficient, but now they seek out government assistance. We've all heard the laments: "My grandpa from Sicily learned English, and my grandma from Minsk got by without welfare—what's the problem with immigrants today?" The problem is that the America your grandparents immigrated to a century ago no longer exists. . . .

In short, mass immigration is incompatible with a modern society. As Hudson Institute scholar John Fonte has written, "It's not 1900 any more."

The subsequent chapters will spell out exactly how the changes that distinguish a modern, mature society are incompatible with continued immigration, but for now it will suffice to say that they paint a picture of a country fundamentally different from the past. Some examples:

ECONOMY. A century ago, what economists call the primary sector of the economy (farming, fishing, hunting, and herding) still employed more Americans than any other, as it had since the dawn of humankind. Today only 2 percent of our workforce occupies itself in this way. Meanwhile, the tertiary

From *The New Case Against Immigration: Both Legal and Illegal,* Sentinel, 2008, pp. 1–13, 44–45, 133–139. Copyright © 2008 by Mark Krikorian. Reprinted by permission of Penguin USA.

sector (service industries) now employs 80 percent of working Americans, and the percentage is climbing.

EDUCATION. Along with the change in the economy, education has become more widespread. Nearly a quarter of American adults had less than five years of schooling in 1910; as of 2000, that figure is less than 2 percent.

. . .

GOVERNMENT. In 1900, total government spending at all levels equaled about 5.5 percent of the economy; by 2003, it was more than 36 percent. Total government employment (federal, state, and local) went from a little more than 1 million in 1900 (about 4 percent of the workforce) to more than 22 million in 2000 (more than 16 percent of the workforce).

LIFESTYLE. America's population was still 60 percent rural in 1900; in 2000, only 21 percent of Americans lived in rural areas (and only a tiny fraction were involved in farming). The average household went from more than 4.5 people to a little more than 2.5, while the number of people per room in the average house fell from 1.1 in 1910 to 0.4 in 1997.

Other changes are harder to quantify but are just as real in marking modern society as a break with the past: a weakening sense of community and civic engagement, increased religious skepticism, a greater sense of responsibility for the less fortunate, rejection of racial and religious discrimination, and concern for our stewardship of the natural world.

. . .

These social changes marking national adulthood don't mean that mass immigration was out of place during our country's adolescence. America ended up a stronger nation because of the mass-immigration phase of our development, a phase that extended for seventy-odd years, from the late 1840s until the early 1920s. Had we not experienced that period of mass immigration, our population, derived mainly from descendants of a relatively small number of preindependence settlers, would still have grown rapidly, but it would have been smaller; in 1990, about half of America's population was attributable to post-1790 immigrants and their descendants. The first part of the immigration phase, dominated by northern Europeans, helped settle much of the land; this happened both because some immigrants went directly to the Midwest and West to establish farms and ranches and because others moved to eastern cities, filling in behind old-stock Americans who had moved west. The latter part of our nation's adolescent immigration phase was dominated by immigrants from eastern and southern Europe who settled mainly in the cities and contributed mightily to industrialization.

. . .

The closing of the frontier was irreversible—once it was gone, there was no way to get it back. But prospective immigrants continued to be available in abundance. And so, starting with the 1965 immigration law, America resumed its adolescent policy of immigration, leading to the largest wave of newcomers in its history. The total foreign-born population has ballooned, from fewer than

10 million in 1970 (less than 5 percent of the nation's population) to nearly 38 million in 2007 (12.6 percent of the population). Annual legal immigration—the number of people awarded permanent residency, potentially leading to citizenship—has gone from fewer than 400,000 in 1970 to nearly 1.3 million in 2006. And illegal immigration has become a major phenomenon, with today's illegal population totaling perhaps 12 million and growing by around half a million each year.

. . .

The objective of this book is to demonstrate how this new immigration wave clashes with modern America, how a policy that served us well in our adolescence is harmful in our maturity.

Assimilation: The Cracked Melting Pot

The most important long-term measure of success in immigration is assimilation. The American model of immigration has been based on turning immigrants and their descendants fully into Americans: Theodore Roosevelt summed up this Americanization tradition when he wrote that "if the immigrant who comes here does in good faith become an American and assimilates himself to us, he shall be treated on an exact equality with every one else, for it is an outrage to discriminate against any such man because of creed or birthplace or origin."

This is unlike the practice of other countries, such as Germany or the Persian Gulf sheikhdoms, and even our own historical lapses (African slavery, the Know-Nothing movement, and the Bracero program for Mexican guest workers), which all have one thing in common—the willingness to employ the labor of foreign workers without admitting them to membership in the society.

This process of Americanizing immigrants was tumultuous and wrenching for everyone involved but eventually very successful. The descendants of those who came in generations past—from Ireland or Poland, Mexico or Sweden, China or Germany, Britain or Armenia—have indeed become one people. This has been possible, of course, because American nationality is not based on blood relations, like a biological family, but is more like a family growing partly through adoption, where new immigrants attach themselves to their new country and embrace the cultural and civic values of their native-born brethren as their own.

. . .

But this offer of complete adoption into the American nation was always based on the requirement that the immigrant "assimilates himself to us." Such assimilation is more than the surface changes that are easily observed; future Supreme Court Justice Louis Brandeis put it well in a 1915 speech:

> But the adoption of our language, manners and customs is only a small part of the process. To become Americanized, the change wrought must be fundamental. However great his outward conformity, the immigrant is

not Americanized unless his interests and affections have become deeply rooted here. And we properly demand of the immigrant even more than this. He must be brought into complete harmony with our ideals and aspirations and cooperate with us for their attainment. Only when this has been done, will he possess the national consciousness of an American.

This adoption of "the national consciousness of an American" is what Hudson Institute scholar John Fonte calls patriotic assimilation—an identification with Americans as the immigrant's new countrymen, converting, in a secular sense, from membership in one national community to membership in another. . . .

Unfortunately, the conditions of modern society make such assimilation increasingly difficult. It is characteristic of modern societies that they have great difficulty in assimilating large numbers of newcomers into the model of a territorial nation-state, with a common language and civic culture helping to cultivate the patriotic solidarity necessary for both mutual sacrifice and respect for individual rights.

This is not because of any intrinsic differences between immigrants past and present; the simple fact that most immigrants now come from Latin America and Asia, rather than from Europe, is of less importance with regard to assimilation than some observers seem to think. Instead, it is *we* who have changed.

Our modern society is different in two major ways that relate to assimilation, one practical, the other political. The first, practical, difference is that modern technology now enables newcomers to retain ties to their homelands, even to the extent of living in both countries simultaneously; thus, becoming "deeply rooted here," in Brandeis's words, is simply less likely to happen. This leads to what scholars call transnationalism—living in such a way as not to be rooted in one nation, but rather living across two or more nations. As one student of the subject has put it, "Transnational communities are groups whose identity is not primarily based on attachment to a specific territory. They therefore present a powerful challenge to traditional ideas of nation-state belonging."

Second, and perhaps more important, is the political change. Elites in all modern societies, including ours, come to devalue their own nation and culture and thus recoil from the idea that newcomers should even be required to adopt "our language, manners and customs," let alone "be brought into complete harmony with our ideals and aspirations"—assuming we can even agree, in this contentious age, on what those ideals and aspirations are. This loss of confidence expresses itself in an ideology of multiculturalism, which rejects the idea of bonds tying together all members of a society.

The combination of these two modern traits—transnationalism and multiculturalism—means that mass immigration today is much less likely to result in the kind of deep assimilation of the vast majority of immigrants and their children that is necessary for immigration to be successful. This is true regardless of the characteristics of the immigrants—their legal status, country of origin, or even level of education—because the problem is inherent to modern society and the way that modernity limits our ability to replicate the successes of the past.

. . .

Either to maintain his own cognitive balance or preserve his professional viability in academia, [Robert Putnam a political scientist and professor at Harvard University] tries to explain away the socially corrosive effects of mass immigration by arguing that in the long run "successful immigrant societies have overcome such fragmentation by creating new, cross-cutting forms of social solidarity and more encompassing identities." That is indeed what successful immigrant societies like ours have done—*in the past.* But these "cross-cutting forms of social solidarity and more encompassing identities"— in other words, an overarching American identity held by people of different ethnic groups and classes and regions and religions—are precisely what modern societies have greater trouble developing, for the reasons, both technological and ideological, that this chapter has explored.

In short, Americanization is much more difficult under modern conditions than in the past. Rather than turning out new Americans who are "blood of the blood, and flesh of the flesh of the men who wrote that Declaration," mass immigration today is helping transform the United States into what one anthropologist approvingly calls "one node in a post-national network of diasporas." Ending mass immigration does not guarantee the restoration of a common civic culture, but continuing it does guarantee that any attempt at such restoration will fail.

Economy: Cheap Labor versus Modern America

The key to the economic facet of the conflict between mass immigration and modern society is the fact that immigration floods the job market with low-skilled workers, creating what economists call a slack, or loose, labor market. This results in a buyer's market for labor, where employers can pick and choose among workers rather than having to compete with one another to attract and keep staff.

This has two major implications for the economy: First, a loose labor market reduces the bargaining power of workers compared to employers, resulting in lower earnings and less opportunity for advancement for the poorest and most marginal of Americans. And second, by artificially keeping wages lower than they would be otherwise, mass immigration reduces the incentives for more-efficient use of labor, slowing the natural progress of mechanization and other productivity increases in the low-wage industries where immigrants are concentrated.

In other words, while immigration certainly increases the overall size of our economy, it subverts the widely shared economic goals of a modern society: a large middle class open to all, working in high-wage, knowledge-intensive, and capital-intensive jobs exhibiting growing labor productivity and avoiding too skewed a distribution of income.

. . .

Economic Change

Immigration has always added workers to the economy, of course, but today is different because our economy has changed dramatically since the end of the first great immigration wave. When millions of Irish and Germans and Scandinavians and Italians and Jews and Slavs crossed the Atlantic, America was still settling vast swathes of empty land and undergoing the titanic process of industrialization. A century ago, what economists call the primary sector of the economy (farming, fishing, and so on) still employed more Americans than any other, as it had everywhere since the dawn of humankind. Today, only 2 percent of our workforce occupies itself in this way. Meanwhile, we've passed through the industrial phase of economic development and entered the postindustrial era, with the tertiary sector (the service industry overall) employing fully 80 percent of working Americans, and the percentage is climbing.

. . .

Into this twenty-first-century economy we have resumed the importation of what amounts to nineteenth-century foreign labor. Between 1980 and 2000, immigration increased the number of workers in the United States by nearly 10 percent and the number of high school dropouts by 20 percent, causing what economists call a supply shock—a sudden infusion of a particular resource (in this case, labor, especially low-skilled labor). And this shock to the labor market is likely to continue indefinitely, barring a change in federal policy; from 2000 to 2005, 8 million more immigrants arrived, the majority of them with no education beyond high school.

The contrast with American workers is stark: Only about 8 percent of native-born workers today have less than a high-school education, but almost 30 percent of immigrant workers do. What's more, while immigrants account for about 15 percent of all workers, they make up nearly 40 percent of workers lacking a high-school degree, resulting in an artificially bloated low-skilled labor force.

This gap between native and immigrant skills has been growing as the economy and society have modernized. In 1960, immigrant men were only about 25 percent more likely to be high-school dropouts than native-born men; by 1998, after the huge wave of low-skilled immigration, immigrants were nearly *four times* more likely to be dropouts. Of course, the process of modernization has been going on everywhere, so the proportion of immigrants who lack a high-school education has also been falling over the years, but much more slowly than among Americans, causing the gap to widen.

. . .

Reducing Wages

The effect of the ongoing surge of immigration on the income of low-skilled Americans is a textbook case of supply and demand. In fact, in his famous textbook, economist Paul Samuelson wrote specifically about the pre-1965 tight-border policies: "By keeping labor supply down, immigration policy tends to keep wages high." He stated the basic principle: "Limitation of the supply of any grade of labor relative to all other productive factors can be expected to raise its wage rate; an increase in supply will, other things being equal, tend to depress wage rates."

The National Research Council, in a wide-ranging study of immigration, concluded that in economic terms, immigration "harms workers who are substitutes for immigrants while benefiting workers who are complements to immigrants." In other words, since immigrants are disproportionately low skilled, it is low-skilled American workers who see their wages drop as immigrants expand the pool of people competing for jobs appropriate to their skill level. The NRC report estimated that immigration was responsible for nearly half the decline in wages of high-school dropouts between 1980 and 1994. At the same time, higher-skilled workers may gain, as the services that low-skilled workers provide (like lawn-mowing or valet parking) become cheaper and as the high skilled can specialize more.

In fact, immigration's overall economic benefit to Americans already here (as opposed to the simple increase in the total size of the economy) comes specifically from lowering the wages of American workers who compete with the immigrants. The National Research Council found that Americans as a whole received an economic benefit of between $1 billion and $10 billion per year from immigration, a tiny amount in what was, at the time of the report, an $8 trillion economy. But this small net economic benefit arises from the redistribution of wealth away from the poor and toward the rest of society; the report found that the poorest tenth of American workers (high-school dropouts who compete with immigrants) suffer a 5 percent cut in wages because of immigration, which is then redistributed to the rest of the American workforce, making the average person with at least a high-school education a minuscule two tenths of 1 percent richer.

In other words, immigration takes a figurative pound of flesh from one low-skilled American worker, who already has little to spare, and then slices it thinly among nine other better-educated Americans, who are more prosperous to begin with, giving each of them a barely noticeable benefit. And of course, even that small benefit is swamped by the extra cost in government services generated by low-skilled immigration, as discussed in the next chapter.

More recent research has found a quite pronounced loss to native-born American workers. Harvard economist George Borjas has found that the immigration wave of the 1980s and 1990s caused a drop in the annual earnings of all categories of American workers, including a 3.6 percent drop for male college graduates and a 7.4 percent drop for male high-school dropouts. Lest these numbers seem small, Borjas calculates that immigration reduced the average American high-school dropout's income in 2000 by about $1,800, while the American college graduate saw his salary reduced by $2,600.

Since education is not distributed evenly among Americans, some groups of American workers will experience a disproportionately large effect from immigration. Borjas found that the immigrant influx from 1980 to 2000 caused the annual wages of native-born white workers overall to fall 3.5 percent, but those of black workers fell 4.5 percent, and the wages of native-born Hispanic workers fell 5 percent. As he writes: "The adverse impact of immigration, therefore, is largest for the most disadvantaged native-born minorities."

Jason L. Riley

 **NO**

Let Them In: The Case for Open Borders

. . . **T**his book expounds on two general themes. The first is that, contrary to received wisdom, today's Latino immigrants aren't "different," just newer. The second is that an open immigration policy is compatible with free-market conservatism and homeland security. I explain, from a conservative perspective, why the pessimists who say otherwise are mistaken. I argue that immigrants, including low-skill immigrants, are an asset to the United States, not a liability. Immigrants help keep our workforce younger and stronger than Asia's and Europe's. As entrepreneurs, they create jobs. As consumers, they generate economic activity that results in more overall economic growth. By taking jobs that over-qualified Americans spurn, they fill niches in the workforce that make our economy more efficient and allow for the upward mobility of the native population.

An immigration policy that acknowledges these economic realities would provide more, not fewer, legal ways for immigrants to enter the country. That, in turn, would go a long way toward reducing illegal entries. It would also alleviate pressure on the border and free up our overburdened patrols to track down terrorists, drug dealers, and other serious threats to our welfare. Unfortunately, as things stand, our border security officers spend most of their time chasing migrants who come north to mow our lawns and burp our babies. A guest-worker program for such individuals would help regulate the labor flow and isolate the criminals, thus making us much safer than any wall along the Rio Grande.

. . .

The reality is that America's foreign labor force helps to propel economic growth, not impede it, because the U.S. job market, properly understood, is not a zero-sum game. The number of jobs in the United States is not static. It's fluid, which is how we want it to be. In 2006, 55 million U.S. workers (or just less than 4.6 million per month) either quit their jobs or were fired. Yet 57 million people were hired over the same period. In a typical year, a third of our workforce is turning over. In about half of those cases the separation is voluntary; in the other half, the worker has been shown the door. But either way, this messy churn, which can disrupt lives and even make obsolete entire industries, has positive macroeconomic consequences in the long run.

From *Let Them In: The Case for Open Borders,* Gotham, 2008, pp. 12–13, 54–65, 145–147, 153–157.
Copyright © 2008 by Jason L. Riley. Reprinted by permission of Penguin Group USA.

That's because flexible labor markets, the kind that minimize the costs to a business of hiring and firing employees, enable workers and employers alike to find the employment situation that suits them best. Flexible labor markets make it easier for an employee who doesn't like a job, is let go, or simply feels underappreciated by his boss to find another position somewhere else. And flexible labor markets make it more likely that an employer will expand his workforce, or take a chance on a job seeker who isn't very skilled or perhaps has a spotty record.

A better fit between employers and employees increases productivity and prosperity and makes markets more responsive to consumer demand. In the end, employers, workers, and consumers are all better off. Immigrants, be they Salvadoran dishwashers, Indian motel operators, or Russian microbiologists, increase the fluidity of U.S. labor markets. Access to fewer of them would reduce the flexibility that makes America so productive.

A nation's ability to produce goods and services determines its wealth. Productivity, defined as the quantity of goods and services produced from each hour of a worker's time, is why some nations are wealthier than others. It's a major reason why GDP per capita in the United States was $39,676 in 2007, but only $29,300 in France, $6,394 in Ukraine, and $1,237 in Mozambique. Productivity, writes Harvard economist N. Gregory Mankiw, "is the key determinant of living standards" and "the key determinant in growth of living standards." For our purposes, the question is whether immigrant labor ultimately contributes to America's productivity and economic growth, or detracts from it.

Fundamentally, immigration to the United States is a function of a labor shortage for certain kinds of jobs here. Of course, work is not the only reason foreigners migrate to America, but judging from their overrepresentation in the labor force, and the fact that immigrants (excluding refugees) resort to welfare less often than the native-born population, we know that work is the main reason they come.

Rather than appropriating jobs from natives, however, immigrants are more likely to be simply filling them—and often facilitating more employment opportunities in the process. The job-displacement myth, which fuels so much of the national immigration debate, can be rebutted empirically. In 2006, for example, there were around 146 million workers in the United States, and 15 percent, or 21 million, were foreign born. If immigrants are stealing jobs, 21 million U.S. natives, or something approximating that number, should have been out of work. But as economics reporter Roger Lowenstein noted in a July 2006 *New York Times Magazine* article, "the country has nothing close to that many unemployed. (The actual number is only seven million.) So the majority of immigrants can't literally have 'taken' jobs; they must be doing jobs that wouldn't have existed had the immigrants not been here."

The reason that immigrant workers tend not to elbow aside natives for jobs and depress wages has to do with the education and skills that foreigners typically bring to the U.S. labor market. Most immigrants fall into one of two categories: low-skilled laborers or high-skilled professionals. One-third of all immigrants have less than a high school education, and one-quarter hold a bachelor's or advanced degree. Most native workers, by contrast, are concentrated betwixt those two extremes. Hence, immigrant workers tend to act as complements to the native U.S. workforce rather than substitutes. There is some overlap, of course, but this skill distribution is the reason immigrants and natives for the most part aren't competing for the same positions.

. . .

A 2007 study published by economist Giovanni Peri analyzed the effects of immigrant labor on California, a state that wasn't chosen arbitrarily. The Golden State, the nation's most populous, is home to nearly a third of all foreign-born U.S. workers. Los Angeles, the nation's second-largest city after New York, is nearly half Hispanic. In the past decade, California's population growth has been almost entirely due to immigration, much of it illegal. The term "Mexifornia" has entered the lexicon. If, as conventional wisdom holds, immigration does in fact have a negative impact on the job security of Americans, California is one of the more likely places that the phenomenon would be manifest.

Yet Peri, a professor of economics at the University of California at Davis, found "no evidence that the inflow of immigrants over the period 1960–2004 worsened the employment opportunities of natives with similar education and experience." With respect to wages, he found that "during 1990–2004, immigration induced a 4 percent real wage increase for the average native worker. This effect ranged from near zero (+0.2 percent) for wages of native high school dropouts and between 3 and 7 percent for native workers with at least a high school diploma." In other words, immigrants tended to expand the economic pie, not displace native workers. These foreign workers lifted all socioeconomic boats; it was just a matter of how much.

At first blush, Peri's findings might seem counterintuitive. It's assumed that because immigrants increase the supply of labor, they necessarily decrease both the wages and the employment opportunities of the native workers. If most immigrant workers were interchangeable with U.S. natives, that might indeed be the case. But the assumption is problematic because immigrants on average aren't stand-ins for natives.

. . .

Peri found that since workers with different levels of education perform different tasks, the majority of native-born workers—high school graduates with some college—experience benefits, more than competition, from the foreign-born workers who are concentrated in high and low educational groups. The result is a more efficient domestic labor market, which leads to more capital investment, higher overall economic growth, and, ultimately, more choices for consumers.

But it also leads to better jobs and higher pay for American workers, explains Peri. "In nontechnical terms," he writes, "the wages of native workers could increase because the increased supply of migrants is likely to put native workers in jobs where they perform supervisory, managerial, training, and . . . coordinating tasks, which makes them more productive." More workers also means more consumers, "so that immigration might simply increase total production and demand without depressing wages."

. . .

In 1994 economist Richard Vedder of Ohio University, working with Lowell Gallaway and Stephen Moore, conducted a historical analysis of immigration's impact on the entire U.S. labor force. They found "no statistically reliable correlation between the percentage of the population that was foreign-born and the national unemployment rate over the period 1900–1989, or for just the postwar era (1947–1989)." Moreover, Vedder found that if there is any correlation between immigration and unemployment, it would appear to be negative. Which is to say that higher immigration is associated with lower unemployment.

. . .

Like Peri, Vedder concluded that the reason immigration doesn't cause unemployment is because immigrants help enlarge America's economic pie. "Immigrants expand total output and the demand for labor, offsetting the negative effects that a greater labor supply might have," he writes. "They fill vital niches at the ends of the skill spectrum, doing low-skilled jobs that native Americans rebuff (at prevailing wages) as well as sophisticated high-skill jobs."

Among high-skilled immigrant workers, these dots are perhaps easier to connect. Think of a silicon chip manufacturer in the United States that hires a bright immigrant engineer from China to redesign its products with the goal of making them more cost-efficient and marketable. If the hire is a success, the firm winds up making more chips, which requires more employees. These additional hires—from the managers to the secretaries—are all more likely to be U.S. natives. So are the additional advertisers and marketers who will be sought as the company expands. Why? In part because the skills necessary to do those jobs generally include a familiarity with the native language and culture that a recent immigrant is less likely to possess. As for the American consumer, he's now getting a better product, more choices, and lower prices. Thus has an immigrant hire resulted in more jobs for U.S. natives, not fewer, and increased overall productivity.

. . .

Of course, high-skill immigrants from Europe, Asia, and Southeast Asia do more than create extra jobs for U.S. employers. They also seem to have a knack for creating entirely new companies that employ thousands of people. Lucky for us. Technology firms, in particular, have made possible the U.S. productivity boom of the past decade. And immigrants have had a hand in starting a disproportionate number of the most successful ones—from Google and eBay to Yahoo! and Sun Microsystems.

A National Foundation for American Policy paper by Stuart Anderson and Michaela Platzer assessed the impact of immigrant entrepreneurs and professionals on U.S. competitiveness. Between 1991 and 2006, they discovered, immigrants started 25 percent of U.S. public companies that were venture-backed. These businesses employed some 220,000 people in the United States and boasted a market capitalization that "exceeds $500 billion, adding significant value to the American economy."

. . . Linguistic assimilation is key, not least because it amounts to a job skill that can increase earnings. And while restrictionists claim otherwise, there's simply no evidence that Latinos are rejecting English. "The model that we have from the European experience," sociologist Richard Alba told me in an interview, "is that the children of immigrants born in the U.S. grow up in homes where they learn, to some extent, the mother tongue. They understand it and may speak it, but they prefer English. And when they grow up, they establish homes where English is the dominant language."

According to 2005 census data, just one-third of immigrants who are in the country for less than a decade speak English well, but that fraction climbs to nearly three-quarters for those here thirty years or more. There may be more bilingualism today among the children of immigrants, but there's no indication that Spanish is dominant in the second generation. The 2000 census found that 91 percent of the children and 97 percent of the grandchildren of Mexican immigrants spoke English well. Nor are there signs, bilingual-education advocates notwithstanding, that immigrant parents *want* their children speaking Spanish. A 2002 Pew Hispanic Center/Kaiser Foundation survey found that 89 percent of Latinos "believe immigrants need to learn to speak English to succeed in the United States."

Longitudinal analyses also reveal that homeownership is up and poverty is down among the Latino immigrants. Using as his sample California, which has the country's largest concentration of Mexican foreign nationals, Myers notes that 16 percent of Latinos arriving in the Golden State in the 1970s owned homes by 1980. But more than 33 percent owned homes by 1990, and over half by 2000. The average rate of homeownership nationally was just over 66 percent in 2000.

The 2000 census found that the foreign-born poverty rate had fallen slightly, to 19.1 percent from 19.8 percent in. 1990. Myers reports that this small decrease was not due to an influx of more prosperous immigrant groups, such as Asians. The disaggregated data show that poverty fell among Latinos and Asians alike. Nor can it be attributed to a temporary upturn in the economy, since the economic conditions measured in the 1990 and 2000 censuses were similar. Again using as his sample California, Myers found that poverty reversal was directly attributable to the maturing of California's immigrant population. Longer-residing immigrants generally experience substantial improvements in poverty, but in the past those gains were overshadowed by the increasing numbers of newcomers. He explains: "Now that the longer-settled immigrants are beginning to outweigh the newcomers in number, the force of upward mobility is no longer being offset by the relatively high poverty of newcomers, and the total poverty rate of the foreign-born has turned around."

Myers is hardly the only social scientist to notice Latino upward mobility, and California isn't the only place it's happening. In a definitive longitudinal study in the 1990s, sociologists Alejandro Portes and Ruben Rumbaut found substantial second-generation progress among Latinos in Miami and Fort Lauderdale as well. Nationwide cross-generational studies show the same results. In 2006, economist James Smith of the RAND Corporation found that successive generations of Latinos have experienced significant improvements in wages relative both to their fathers and grandfathers and to the native whites with whom they compete for jobs. And Roger Waldinger and Renee Reichl, two UCLA social scientists, found that while first-generation Mexican men earned just half as much as white natives in 2000, the second generation had upped their earnings to three-quarters of their Anglo counterparts.

. . .

Assimilation is less about immigrants adopting our culture than about immigrants adopting our values. And America has been uniquely successful in this regard. Canada has utterly failed to bridge its linguistic divide. French Canadians in Quebec aren't just pro–French language but also anti-English. The United States has as many French Canadians as does Canada, and a large percentage of them live in New England, yet there has been no such tension on this side of the border.

. . .

The key to the success of the U.S. assimilation model, says Peter Salins, a senior fellow at the Manhattan Institute, is that "we put so much more stress on shared values rather than shared cultures." In an interview, Salins explained that immigrants find America's values and ideals as attractive as its economic opportunities. Yes, they come here to get rich, but it's more than that. It's also our value framework, with its emphasis on individual initiative and individual opportunity. Foreigners like the fact that you can make more money *because* you are hard-working or diligent or clever.

Salins says the other major value component is our civic institutions. We're the land of liberty and democracy. Here, people can say what they want, be what they want, do what they want. These are attractive values. And Americans are much more concerned about people sharing their values than sharing their cultural artifacts.

. . .

Key elements of America's Anglo-Protestant culture, [Salins] says, "include: the English language; Christianity; religious commitment; English concepts of the rule of law, the responsibility of rulers, and the rights of individuals; dissenting Protestant values of individualism, the work ethic, and the belief that humans have the ability and the duty to try to create a heaven on earth, a 'city on a hill.'"

Nothing indicates that today's immigrants, like those who came before them, don't share Huntington's commitment to those ideals.

. . .

For all the loud talk of late, the American public seems not to have lost confidence in the melting pot. If it had, you'd know it. There would be "English-only" signs and militarized border zones. There would be ubiquitous police checkpoints and far-right political parties like France's National Front. Michelle Malkin would be considered a serious pundit, not Ann Coulter without the nuance.

Of course, there is some bigotry and stupidity out there, which we'll always have. But when people really believe they can't live another day with other kinds of people, they don't send e-mails to *The O'Reilly Factor.* They engage in ethnic warfare. You get the Serbs and the Croats in the Balkans, the Hindus and the Muslims in India, the Hutus and the Tutsis in Rwanda. What we have in America is periodic grumpiness, short-lived sniffing about the most recent arrivals, a vague and ambivalent disdain that doesn't settle too deeply into the psyche. Americans still believe that our assimilationist model is working, even if the elites on the left and right who claim to speak on their behalf do not.

POSTSCRIPT

Is Third World Immigration a Threat to America's Way of Life?

Former representative Silvio Conte (R-Massachusetts) said at a citizenship ceremony, "You can go to France, but you will never be a Frenchman. You can go to Germany but you will never be a German. Today you are all Americans, and that is why this is the greatest country on the face of the earth." At one time, America's open door to immigrants was one of the prides of America. For some people, like Riley, it still is. He thinks that immigration is making America stronger. Many people disagree because they fear the consequences of today's immigration. Krikorian worries that the new immigrants will not assimilate very well in America as it is today. The results could be tragic.

The following works describe or debate the immigration issue: Mary C. Waters and Reed Ueda, with Helen B. Marrow, eds., *The New Americans: A Guide to Immigration since 1965* (Harvard University Press, 2007); Jane Guskin and David L. Wilson, *The Politics of Immigration: Questions and Answers* (Monthly Review Press, 2007); Spencer Abraham and Lee H. Hamilton, *Immigration and America's Future: A New Chapter: Report of the Independent Task Force on Immigration and America's Future* (Migration Policy Institute, 2006); Nancy Foner, ed., *Not Just Black and White: Historical and Contemporary Perspectives on Immigration, Race, and Ethnicity in the United States* (Russell Sage Foundation, 2004); Carol M. Swain, ed., *Debating Immigration* (Cambridge University Press 2007); and Lina Newton, *Illegal, Alien, or Immigrant: The Politics of Immigration Reform* (New York University Press, 2008).

Stanley Lieberson and Mary C. Waters, in *From Many Strands* (Russell Sage Foundation, 1988), argue that ethnic groups with European origins are assimilating, marrying outside their groups, and losing their ethnic identities. Richard D. Alba's study "Assimilation's Quiet Tide," *The Public Interest* (Spring 1995), confirms these findings. Latinos, however, are assimilating more slowly. Dowell Myers, in *Immigrants and Boomers: Forging a New Social Contract for the Future of America* (Russell Sage Foundation, 2007), emphasizes the positive benefits of immigration for America. Several major works debate whether immigrants, on average, benefit America economically and whether they are assimilating. Sources that argue that immigrants largely benefit America include Julian L. Simon, *The Economic Consequences of Immigration*, 2nd ed. (University of Michigan Press, 1999), and *Immigration: The Demographic and Economic Facts* (Cato Institute, 1995). Aviva Chomsky, *"They Take Our Jobs!": And 20 Other Myths about Immigration* (Beacon Press 2007). Sources that argue that immigrants have more negative than positive impacts include George Borjas, *Heaven's Door: Immigration Policy and the American Economy* (Princeton

36

University Press, 1999); Roy Beck, *The Case Against Immigration* (W. W. Norton, 1996); Patrick Buchanan, *The Death of the West: How Dying Populations and Immigrant Invasions Imperil Our Country and Civilization* (Thomas Dunne Books, 2002); and Otis L. Graham, Jr., *Unguarded Gates: A History of American's Immigration Crisis* (Rowman and Littlefield, 2004).

Internet References . . .

American Men's Studies Association

The American Men's Studies Association is a not-for-profit professional organization of scholars, therapists, and others interested in the exploration of masculinity in modern society.

http://mensstudies.org

Feminist Majority Foundation

The Feminist Majority Foundation Web site provides affirmative action links, resources from women's professional organizations, information for empowering women in business, sexual harassment information, and much more.

http://www.feminist.org

GLAAD: Gay and Lesbian Alliance Against Defamation

The Gay and Lesbian Alliance Against Defamation (GLAAD), formed in New York in 1985, seeks to improve the public's attitudes toward homosexuality and to put an end to discrimination against lesbians and gay men.

http://www.glaad.org

International Lesbian and Gay Association

The resources on the International Lesbian and Gay Association Web site are provided by a worldwide network of lesbian, gay, bisexual, and transgendered groups.

http://www.ilga.org

SocioSite: Feminism and Women's Issues

The Feminism and Women's Issues SocioSite provides insights into a number of issues that affect family relationships. It covers wide-ranging issues regarding women and men, family and children, and much more.

http://www.sociosite.net/index.php

Sex Roles, Gender, and the Family

*T**he modern feminist movement has advanced the causes of women to the point where there are now more women in the workforce in the United States than ever before. Professions and trades that were traditionally regarded as the provinces of men have opened up to women, and women now have easier access to the education and training necessary to excel in these new areas. But what is happening to sex roles, and what are the effects of changing sex roles? How have men and women been affected by the stress caused by current sex roles, the demand for the right to same-sex marriages, and the deterioration of the traditional family structure? The issues in this part address these sorts of questions.*

- Does Divorce Have Long-Term Damaging Effects on Children?
- Does the "Mommy Track" (Part-Time Work) Improve Women's Lives?
- Should Same-Sex Marriages Be Legally Recognized?

ISSUE 3

Does Divorce Have Long-Term Damaging Effects on Children?

YES: Elizabeth Marquardt, from "The Bad Divorce," *First Things* (February 2005)

NO: Constance Ahrons, from *We're Still Family: What Grown Children Have to Say about Their Parents' Divorce* (Harper Collins, 2004)

ISSUE SUMMARY

YES: Elizabeth Marquardt, Director of the Center for Marriage and Families, defends the common belief that divorce has devastating impacts on children and attacks Constance Ahrons's counter-thesis.

NO: Constance Ahrons, co-chair of the Council on Contemporary Families, found in her research on the children of divorced parents that they do quite well in later life and most think that they were not harmed by the divorce.

T he state of the American family deeply concerns many Americans. About 40 percent of marriages end in divorce, and only 27 percent of children born in 1990 are expected to be living with both parents by the time they reach age 17. Most Americans, therefore, are affected personally or are close to people who are affected by structural changes in the family. Few people can avoid being exposed to the issue: violence in the family and celebrity divorces are standard fare for news programs, and magazine articles decrying the breakdown of the family appear frequently. Politicians today try to address the problems of the family. Academics have affirmed that the family crisis has numerous significant negative effects on children, spouses, and the rest of society.

But is the situation as bad as portrayed? Many of you reading this come from divorced homes and can evaluate how much you suffered and whether you have been scarred for life. All of you can look around you and judge for yourselves how your acquaintances have been affected by divorce. Obviously, divorce is much worse for children than a good marriage, but is it worse than a bad marriage? Because the answer is not obvious, the debate heats up.

One reason divorce is a very important issue is the important role that the family plays in the functioning of society. For a society to survive, its population must reproduce (or take in many immigrants), and its young must be trained to perform adult roles and to have the values and attitudes that will motivate them to contribute to society. Procreation and socialization are two vital roles that families traditionally have performed. In addition, the family provides economic and emotional support for its members, which is vital to their effective functioning in society. Stable, well-functioning families best perform these roles and divorce jeopardizes them.

Although most experts agree that the American family is in crisis, there is little agreement about what, if anything, should be done about it. After all, most of these problems result from the choices that people make to try to increase their happiness. People end unhappy marriages. When they do, most of them also carefully consider the best interests of the children. These considerations obviously prevent or delay many divorces and probably should prevent many more. Obviously, however, many situations are improved by divorce, especially if the divorce and aftermath arrangements are conducted in a compassionate manner. So, which way is best is a judgment call, both by the potentially divorcing parents and by the academics who study the issue.

In the selections that follow, Constance Ahrons draws from her extensive work on the children of divorce to show that divorce has far fewer negative consequences on children than is commonly assumed. Elizabeth Marquardt's article is totally devoted to refuting Ahrons's thesis.

YES

Elizabeth Marquardt

The Bad Divorce

It is often said that those who are concerned about the social and personal effects of divorce are nostalgic for the 1950s, yearning for a mythical time when men worked, women happily stayed home baking cookies for the kids, and marriages never dissolved. Yet often the same people who make the charge of mythology are caught in a bit of nostalgia of their own, pining for the sexual liberationism of the 1970s, when many experts began to embrace unfettered divorce, confident that children, no less than adults, would thrive once "unhappy" marriages were brought to a speedy end.

Constance Ahrons, who coined the term "the good divorce" in the title of an influential 1992 book that examined ninety-eight divorcing couples, is very much a member of the latter camp. In her new book, *We're Still Family: What Grown Children Have to Say about Their Parents' Divorce,* Ahrons returns to those ninety-eight couples to survey their now-grown children. The result is a study based on telephone interviews with 173 young adults from eighty-nine families that tries to advance the idea it is not divorce itself that burdens children but rather the way in which parents divorce. As in her earlier book, Ahrons argues that the vocabulary we use to discuss divorce and remarriage is negative; she would prefer that we regard divorced families as "changed" or "rearranged" rather than broken, damaged, or destroyed. She claims that upbeat language will, above all, help children feel less stigmatized by divorce. Both of her books offer many new terms, such as "binuclear" and "tribe," to describe divorced families. The specific novelty of the new book is Ahrons' claim that her interviewees view their parents' divorces in a positive light.

It is with delight, then, that Ahrons shares surprising new findings from her on-going study. According to Ahrons, over three-quarters of the young people from divorced families who she interviewed do not wish their parents were still together. A similar proportion feel their parents' decision to divorce was a good one, that their parents are better off today, and that they themselves are either better off or not affected by the divorce. To general readers who have been following the debates about children of divorce in recent years, such findings might sound like big news. But there are problems.

According to Ahrons, over three-quarters of the young people whom she interviewed do not wish that their parents were still together. A similar proportion feel that their parents' decision to divorce was a good one, that their parents are better off today, and that they themselves are either better off

From *First Things,* February 2005. Copyright © 2005 by Institute on Religion and Public Life. Reprinted by permission.

because of the divorce or have not been affected by it. Statistically, that sounds overwhelmingly convincing. But an answer to a survey question tells us very little unless we have a context for interpreting it and some grasp of the actual experiences that gave rise to it.

Like those whom Ahrons interviewed, I grew up in a divorced family, my parents having split when I was two years old. Like Ahrons, I am a researcher in the field, having led, with Norval Glenn, a study of young adults from both divorced and intact families that included a nationally representative telephone survey of some 1,500 people. As someone who studies children of divorce and who is herself a grown child of divorce, I have noticed that the kinds of questions that get asked in such studies and the way the answers are interpreted often depend on whether the questioner views divorce from the standpoint of the child or the parent.

Take, for example, Ahrons' finding that the majority of people raised in divorced families do not wish that their parents were together. Ahrons did not ask whether as children these young people had hoped their parents would reunite. Instead, she asked if they wish today their parents were still together. She presents their negative answers as gratifying evidence that divorce is affirmed by children. But is that really the right conclusion to draw?

Imagine the following scenario. One day when you are a child your parents come to you and tell you they are splitting up. Your life suddenly changes in lots of ways. Dad leaves, or maybe Mom does. You may move or change schools or lose friendships, or all of the above. Money is suddenly very tight and stays that way for a long time. You may not see one set of grandparents, aunts, uncles, and cousins nearly as much as you used to. Then, Mom starts dating, or maybe Dad does. A boyfriend or girlfriend moves in, perhaps bringing along his or her own kids. You may see one or both of your parents marry again; you may see one or both of them get divorced a second time. You deal with the losses. You adjust as best you can. You grow up and try to figure out this "relationship" thing for yourself. Then, some interviewer on the telephone asks if you wish your parents were still together today. A lifetime of pain and anger and adjustment flashes before your eyes. Any memory of your parents together as a couple—if you can remember them together at all—is buried deep under all those feelings. Your divorced parents have always seemed like polar opposites to you. No one could be more different from your mother than your father, and vice versa. "No," you reply to the interviewer, "I don't wish my parents were still together." Of course, one cannot automatically attribute such a train of thought to all of Ahrons' interview subjects. Still, it is plausible, and it might explain at least some of the responses. But Ahrons does not even consider it.

Ahrons tells us that the vast majority of young people in her study feel that they are either better off or not affected by their parents' divorce. For a child of divorce there could hardly be a more loaded question than this one. The generation that Ahrons is interviewing grew up in a time of massive changes in family life, with experts assuring parents that if they became happier after divorce, their children would as well. There wasn't a lot of patience for people who felt otherwise—especially when those people were children, with their aggravating preference for conventional married life over the adventures of divorce, and their tendency to look askance at their parents' new love interests.

However, a child soon learns the natural lesson that complaining about a parent's choices is a surefire way to be ignored or worse, and that what parents want above all is praise for those choices. Few things inspire as much admiration among divorced parents and their friends as the words of a child reassuring them that the divorce was no big deal—or even better, that it gave the child something beneficial, like early independence, or a new brother or sister. Parents are proud of a resilient child. They are embarrassed and frustrated by a child who claims to be a victim. And who among us wants to be a victim? Who would not rather be a hero, or at least a well-adjusted and agreeable person? When the interviewer calls on the telephone, what will the young adult be more likely to say? Something like "I'm damaged goods"? Or "Yes, it was tough at times but I survived it, and I'm stronger for it today." It is the second reply that children of divorce have all their lives been encouraged to give; and the fact that they are willing to give it yet again is hardly, as Ahrons would have it, news.

Thus, Ahrons' statistics on their own hardly constitute three cheers for divorce. Far more meaningful and revealing are the extended quotations from interview subjects with which the book is liberally studded. She writes, for instance, that Andy, now thirty-two, sees "value" in his parents' divorce. Why? Because:

> "I learned a lot. I grew up a lot more quickly than a lot of my friends. Not that that's a good thing or a bad thing. People were always thinking I was older than I was because of the way I carried myself."

Treating a sad, unfortunate experience (like being forced to grow up more quickly than one's peers) as something neutral or even positive is merely one example of what can happen when a person attempts to conform to a culture that insists that divorce is no big deal. To take such an ambivalent response as clear evidence that divorce does no damage, as Ahrons does is inexcusable.

Ahrons cheerfully reports other "good" results of divorce. Here for example is Brian, whose parents split when he was five:

> "In general, I think [the divorce] has had very positive effects. I see what happens in divorces, and I have promised myself that I would do anything to not get a divorce. I don't want my kids to go through what I went through."

Tracy, whose parents divorced when she was twelve, sees a similar upside to divorce:

> "I saw some of the things my parents did and know not to do that in my marriage and see the way they treated each other and know not to do that to my spouse and my children. I know [the divorce] has made me more committed to my husband and my children."

These are ringing endorsements of divorce as a positive life event? Like the testimony of a child who's learned a painful but useful lesson about the dangers of playing with fire, such accounts indicate that the primary benefit of divorce is to encourage young people to avoid it in their own lives if at all possible.

Then there are the significant problems with the structure of Ahrons' study itself. While the original families were recruited using a randomized method, the study lacks any control group. In other words, Ahrons interviewed plenty of young people from divorced families but spoke to no one of similar ages from intact families. So she really can't tell us anything at all about how these young people might differ from their peers.

Rather than acknowledging that her lack of a control group is a serious limitation, Ahrons sidesteps the issue. In several places she compares her subjects to generalized "social trends" or "their contemporaries" and decides, not surprisingly, that they are not all that different. Thus, Ahrons notes that many of the young people from divorced families told her they frequently struggled with issues of "commitment, trust, and dealing with conflict," but on this finding she comments, "These issues are precisely the ones that most adults in this stage of their development grapple with, whether they grow up in a nuclear family or not." Never mind that she has not interviewed any of those other young people, or cited any studies to back up her contention, or acknowledged the possibility that, while all young people do have to deal with these kinds of interpersonal issues, some have a much harder time doing it than others. Ahrons instead wholly dismisses the pain expressed by the children of divorce and assures us that they are simply passing through a normal development phase.

When it comes to her conclusions, Ahrons claims that "if you had a devitalized or high-conflict marriage, you can take heart that the decision to divorce may have been the very best thing you could have done for your children." While research does show that children, on average, do better after a high-conflict marriage ends (the same research, by Paul Amato and Alan Booth, also shows that only one-third of divorces end high-conflict marriages), no one—Ahrons included—has shown that children do better when an adult ends a marriage he or she perceives as "devitalized." Children don't much care whether their parents have a "vital" marriage. They care whether their mother and father live with them, take care of them, and don't fight a lot. . . .

Ahrons also remains preoccupied with the concept of stigma. She writes, for instance, that we are seeing "progress" because a high divorce rate has the effect of reducing the stigma experienced by children of divorce. That's all well and good, but one wonders why Ahrons gives stigma so much attention while saying nothing about a far more damaging social problem for children of divorce—namely, silence. Consider my own experience. The type of family in which I grew up was radically different from the intact family model. Yet no one around me, not even therapists, ever once acknowledged that fact. Never mind that my beloved father lived hours away, or that the mother I adored was often stressed as she tried to earn a living while also acting as a single parent. I was left to assume, like many children of divorce, that whatever problems I struggled with were no one's fault but my own. The demand that children of divorce keep quiet and get with the program puts them in the position of protecting adults from guilt and further stress—effectively reversing the natural order of family life in which the adults are the protectors of children.

Ahrons is remarkably unsympathetic to the children on whom this burden is laid. What do children of divorce long for? According to Ahrons, they nurture unrealistic hopes for "tidy," "perfect" families. She uses these words so frequently—the first term appears at least six times in the book and the second at least four times—that she sometimes appears to be portraying children of divorce as weird obsessives. Speaking directly to children of divorce, Ahrons offers the following advice: "You may not have the idyllic family you dreamed of . . . [but] often the only thing within our control is how we perceive or interpret an event." "For example, you can choose to see your family as rearranged, or you can choose to see it as broken." Indeed, the curative powers of social constructivism are nothing short of miraculous. Encouraging readers to stop using the descriptive term "adult child of divorce," she asserts that "it's a stigmatizing label that presumes you are deficient or traumatized. . . . If you have fallen prey to using it to explain something about yourself, ask yourself if it is keeping you from making changes that might bring you more satisfaction in your life." Apparently, coming to grips with one's family history and the deepest sources of one's sadness and loneliness is the worst thing a child can do. . . .

Ahrons surely knows more about the tragedies of divorce than her thesis allows her to admit. She has studied divorced families for years. She has worked with them as a clinician. She has been through divorce herself. Yet she inevitably follows up heartbreaking observations of interviewees with the confident assertion that everyone involved would be so much happier if only they talked themselves out of—and even walked away from—their anguish. As she writes in one (unintentionally haunting) passage, "Over the years I have listened to many divorcing parents in my clinical practice talk about how much they look forward to the day when their children will be grown and they won't have to have anything more to do with their exes." Is it possible to image a sadder or more desperate desire than this one—the longing for one's children to grow up faster so that relations with one's ex-spouse can be more effectively severed? In such passages it becomes obvious that all of Ahrons' efforts to explain away the tragedy of divorce and its legacy are in vain. In the end, the theory collapses before reality.

Ahrons' poorly structured study and far too tendentious thesis are of no help to us in thinking through our approach to divorce and its consequences. Children of divorce are real, complex people who are deeply shaped by a new kind of fractured family life—one whose current prevalence is unprecedented in human history. These children are not nostalgic for "tidy," "perfect," "idyllic" families. They grieve the real losses that follow from their parents' divorce. They don't need new words to describe what they've been through. Ordinary words will serve quite well—provided that people are willing to listen to them.

No Easy Answers: Why the Popular View of Divorce Is Wrong

. . . **A**lthough it may appear strange, my exhusband's untimely death brought his second and first families closer together. I had mourned at his funeral and spent time with his family and friends for several days afterward. A different level of kinship formed, as we—his first and second families—shared our loss and sadness. Since then, we have chosen to join together at several family celebrations, which has added a deeper dimension to our feelings of family.

You may be thinking, "This is all so rational. There's no way my family could pull this off." Or perhaps, like the many people who have shared their stories with me over the years, you are nodding your head knowingly, remembering similar occasions in your own family. The truth is we are like many extended families rearranged by divorce. My ties to my exhusband's family are not close but we care about one another. We seldom have contact outside of family occasions, but we know we're family. We hear stories of each other's comings and goings, transmitted to us through our mutual ties to my daughters, and now, through grandchildren. But if many families, like my own, continue to have relationships years after divorce, why don't we hear more about them?

Quite simply, it's because this is not the way it's supposed to be. My family, and the many others like mine, don't fit the ideal images we have about families. They appear strange because they're not tidy. There are "extra" people and relationships that don't exist in nuclear families and are awkward to describe because we don't have familiar and socially defined kinship terms to do so. Although families rearranged and expanded by divorce are rapidly growing and increasingly common, our resistance to accepting them as normal makes them appear deviant.

Societal change is painfully slow, which results in the situation wherein the current realities of family life come into conflict with our valued images. Sociologists call this difference "cultural lag," the difference between what is real and what we hold as ideal. This lag occurs because of our powerful resistance to acknowledging changes that challenge our basic beliefs about what's good and what's bad in our society.

From *We're Still Family: What Grown Children Have to Say about Their Parents' Divorce* by Constance Ahrons (HarperCollins, 2004). Copyright © 2004 by Constance Ahrons, Ph.D. Reprinted by permission of the author and Sandra Dijkstra Literary Agency.

Why Good Divorces Are Invisible

Good divorces are those in which the divorce does not destroy meaningful family relationships. Parents maintain a sufficiently cooperative and support-ive relationship that allows them to focus on the needs of their children. In good divorces children continue to have ties to both their mothers and their fathers, and each of their extended families, including those acquired when either parent remarries.

Good divorces have been well-kept secrets because to acknowledge them in mainstream life threatens our nostalgic images of family. If the secret got out that indeed many families that don't fit our "mom and pop" household ideal are healthy, we would have to question the basic societal premise that marriage and family are synonymous. And that reality upsets a lot of people, who then respond with familiar outcries that divorce is eroding our basic val-ues and destroying society.

Although we view ourselves as a society in which nuclear families and life-long monogamous marriages predominate, the reality is that 43 percent of first marriages will end in divorce. Over half of new marriages are actually remarriages for at least one of the partners. Not only have either the bride or groom (or both) been divorced but increasingly one of them also has parents who are divorced.

Families are the way we organize to raise children. Although we hold the ideal image that marriage is a precursor to establishing a family, mod-ern parents are increasingly challenging this traditional ideal. Families today arrange—and rearrange—themselves in many responsible ways that meet the needs of children for nurturance, guidance and economic support. Family his-torian Stephanie Coontz, in her book *The Way We Never Were,* shows how the "tremendous variety of workable childrearing patterns in history suggests that, with little effort, we should be able to forge new institutions and values."

One way we resist these needed societal changes is by denying that divorce is no longer deviant. We demean divorced families by clinging to the belief that families can't exist outside of marriage. It follows then that sto-ries of healthy families that don't fit the tidy nuclear family package are rare and stories that show how divorce destroys families and harms children are common. In this way, bad divorces appear to represent the American way of divorce and good divorces become invisible.

Messages That Hinder Good Divorces

When the evils of divorce are all that families hear about, it makes coping with the normal transitions and changes that inevitably accompany divorce all the more difficult. Negative messages make children feel different and lesser, lead-ing to feelings of shame and guilt. Parents who feel marginalized in this way are less likely to think about creative solutions to their problems. That all of this unnecessary anxiety is fueled by sensationalized reports of weak findings, half-truths and myths of devastation is deplorable. Only by sorting out the truths about divorce from the fiction can we be empowered to make better decisions, find healthy ways to maintain family relationships, and develop important family rituals after divorce. Let's take a close look at the most common misconceptions about divorce.

Misconception 1: Parents Should Stay Married for the Sake of the Kids

This is message that pervades our culture, and it rests on a false duality: Marriage is good for kids, divorce is bad. Underlying this premise is the belief that parents who divorce are immature and selfish because they put their personal needs ahead of the needs of their children, that because divorce is too easy to get, spouses give up on their marriages too easily and that if you're thinking about divorcing your spouse, you should "stick it out till the kids are grown." A popular joke takes this message to its extreme. A couple in their nineties, married for seventy years, appears before a judge in their petition for a divorce. The judge looks at them quizzically and asks, "Why now, why after all these years?" The couple responds: "We waited until the children were dead."

The research findings are now very clear that reality is nowhere near as simple and tidy. Unresolved, open interparental conflict between married spouses that pervades day-to-day family life has been shown again and again to have negative effects on children. Most experts agree that when this is the case it is better for the children if parents divorce rather than stay married. Ironically, prior to the initiation of no-fault legislation over twenty years ago, in most states this kind of open conflict in the home was considered "cruel and inhumane" treatment and it was one of the few grounds on which a divorce would be granted—if it could be proved.

But the majority of unsatisfying marriages are not such clearcut cases. When most parents ask themselves if they should stay married for the sake of their children, they have clearly reached the point where they are miserable in their marriages but wouldn't necessarily categorize them as "high-conflict." And here is where, in spite of the societal message, there is no agreement in the research findings or among clinical experts. That's because it's extremely complex and each individual situation is too different to allow for a "one-size-fits-all" answer.

A huge list of factors comes into play when assessing whether staying married would be better for your kids. For example,

- Is the unhappiness in your marriage making you so depressed or angry that your children's needs go unmet because you can't parent effectively?
- Do you and your spouse have a cold and distant relationship that makes the atmosphere at home unhealthy for your children?
- Do you and your spouse lack mutual respect, caring or interests, setting a poor model for your children?
- Would the financial hardships be so dire that your children will experience a severely reduced standard of living?

Add to this your child's temperament, resources and degree of resilience, and then the personal and family changes that take place in the years after the divorce, and you can see how the complexities mount.

It is a rare parent who divorces *too easily*. Most parents are responsible adults who spend years struggling with the extremely difficult and complex decision of whether to divorce or stay married "for the sake of the children." The bottom line is that divorce is an adult decision, usually made by one spouse, entered into in the face of many unknowns. Without a crystal ball, no one knows whether their decision will be better for their children. As you read further in this book, however, you may gain some perspective on what will be most helpful in your situation, with your children, by listening carefully to the reactions and feelings of various children of divorce *as they have changed over twenty years*.

Misconception 2: "Adult Children of Divorce" Are Doomed to Have Lifelong Problems

. . . The truth is that, for the great majority of children who experience a parental divorce, the divorce becomes part of their history but it is not a defining factor. Like the rest of us, most of them reach adulthood to lead reasonably happy, successful lives. Although children who grew up with divorced parents certainly share an important common experience, their ability to form healthy relationships, be good parents, build careers, and so on, are far more determined by their individual temperaments, their sibling relationships, the dynamics within their parents' *marriages* and the climate of their *postdivorce* family lives.

Misconception 3: Divorce Means You Are No Longer a Family

There's this myth that as long as you stay married your family is good but as soon as you announce you're separating, your family is thrown into the bad zone. Your family goes from being "intact" to being "dissolved," from two-parent to single parent, from functional to dysfunctional. Even though we all know that people don't jump from happy marriages right into divorce, there is an assumption that the decision to separate is the critical marker. It doesn't seem to matter whether your marital relationship was terrible, whether you were miserable and your children troubled. Just as long as you are married and living together in one household, the sign over the front door clearly states to the world, "We're a normal family."

The inaccurate and misleading message that divorce destroys families is harmful to both parents and children because it hides and denies all the positive ways that families can be rearranged after divorce. It sends the destructive message to children that divorce means they only get to keep one parent and they will no longer be part of a family. Although two-parent first-married households now represent less than 25 percent of all households, and an increasing number of children each year are raised by unmarried adults, many people cling to the belief that healthy families can only be two-parent married families and social change is always bad and threatening to our very foundations. . . .

The truth is that although some divorces result in family breakdown, the vast majority do not. While divorce changes the form of the family from one household to two, from a nuclear family to a binuclear one, it does not need to change the way children think and feel about the significant relationships within their families. This does not mean that divorce is not painful or diffi-cult, but over the years, as postdivorce families change and even expand, most remain capable of meeting children's needs for family.

Misconception 4: Divorce Leaves Children without Fathers

This message is linked closely with the preceding one because when we say that divorce destroys families we really mean that fathers disappear from the family. The myths that accompany this message are that fathers are "deadbeat dads" who abandon their kids and leave their families impoverished. The mes-sage strongly implies that fathers don't care and are unwilling or unable to make continuing commitments to their children. While this reflects the real-ity for a minority of divorced fathers, the majority of fathers continue to have loving relationships with their children and contribute financially to their upbringing. . . .

Misconception 5: Exspouses Are Incapable of Getting Along

. . . Although we have come to realize that parents who divorce still need to have some relationship with one another, the belief that it's not really pos-sible still lingers. In fact, when exspouses remain friends they are viewed as a little strange and their relationship is suspect. Yet, the truth is that many divorced parents *are* cooperative and effective coparents. Like good divorces and involved fathers, they are mostly invisible in the media. . . .

Misconception 6: Divorce Turns Everyone into Exfamily; In-Laws Become Outlaws

When it comes to the semantics of divorce-speak, all of the kinship ties that got established by marriage dissolve abruptly. On the day of the legal divorce, my husband and all of his relatives suddenly became exes. But even though the kinship is *legally* terminated, meaningful relationships often continue. My friend Jan, during her fifteen-year marriage, formed a very close relationship with her mother-in-law. Now, twenty years later, she still calls her eighty-two-year-old exmother-in-law "Mom," talks with her several times a week and has dinner with her weekly. Exmother-in-law is certainly not an adequate descrip-tion of this ongoing relationship.

As a culture we continue to resist accepting divorce as a normal end-point to marriage even though it is an option chosen by almost half of those who marry. It is this cultural lag, this denial of current realities that causes the inaccurate language, not only for the family ties that continue but also for the family we inherit when we, our former spouses, our parents or our children remarry. Kinship language is important because it provides a short-hand way for us to identify relationships without wading through tedious explanations. . . .

Misconception 7: Stepparents Aren't Real Parents

. . . Children and their new stepparents start off their relationships with two strikes against them. They have to fight an uphill battle to overcome negative expectations, and they have to do so without much help from society. Since almost 85 percent of the children with divorced parents will have a stepparent at some time in their lives, it is shocking that we know so little about how these relationships work. Clearly, societal resistance to recognizing the broad spectrum of postdivorce families has hindered the development of good role models for stepchildren and their stepparents.

Painting a False Picture

Taken together, these negative messages paint a false picture of divorce, one that assumes family ties are irretrievably broken so that postdivorce family relationships appear to be nonexistent. Despite these destructive messages, many divorced parents meet the needs of their children by creating strong families after divorce. Without a doubt, divorce is painful and creates stress for families, but it is important to remember that most recover, maintaining some of their kinship relationships and adding new ones over time.

By making good divorces invisible we have accepted bad divorces as the norm. In so doing, children and their divorced parents are being given inaccurate messages that conflict with the realities they live and make them feel deviant and stigmatized. It is time we challenge these outdated, ill-founded messages and replace them with new ones that acknowledge and accurately reflect current realities.

The Distortions of Oversimplifying

Just a little over a decade ago, in January 1989, the *New York Times Magazine* ran a cover story called "Children after Divorce," which created a wave of panic in divorced parents and their children. Judith Wallerstein and her coauthor, Sandra Blakeslee, a staff writer for the *New York Times*, noted their newest unexpected finding. Calling it the "sleeper effect," they concluded that only ten years after divorce did it become apparent that girls experience "serious effects of divorce at the time they are entering young adulthood."

When one of the most prestigious newspapers in the world highlights the findings of a study, most readers take it seriously. "That 66 percent of young women in our study between the ages of nineteen and twenty-three will suffer debilitating effects of their parents' divorce years later" immediately became generalized to the millions of female children with divorced parents. The message—just when you think everything may be okay, the doom of divorce will rear its ugly head—is based on a *mere eighteen out of the grand total of twenty-seven women* interviewed in this age group. This detail wasn't mentioned in the fine print of the article but is buried in the appendix of the book that was scheduled for publication a month after the *New York Times* story appeared. And it is on this slim data that the seeds of a myth are planted. We are still living with the fallout.

In sharp contrast to Wallerstein's view that parental divorce has a powerful devastating impact on children well into adulthood, another psychologist made headlines with a completely opposite thesis. In her book, *The Nurture Assumption: Why Children Turn Out the Way They Do*, Judith Rich Harris proposes that what parents do makes little difference in how their children's lives turn out. Half of the variation in children's behavior and personality is due to genes, claims Harris, and the other half to environmental factors, mainly their peer relationships. For this reason, Harris asserts parental divorce is not responsible for all the ills it is blamed for.

These extreme positions—of divorce as disaster and divorce as inconsequential—oversimplify the realities of our complex lives. Genes and contemporary relationships notwithstanding, we have strong evidence that parents still make a significant difference in their children's development. Genetic inheritance and peer relationships are part of the story but certainly not the whole story.

Sorting Out the Research Findings

Drawing conclusions across the large body of research on divorce is difficult. Studies with different paradigms ask different questions that lead to different answers. A classic wisdom story shows the problem. Three blind men bumped into an elephant as they walked through the woods. They didn't know what it was, but each prided himself on his skill at "seeing." So one blind man reached out and carefully explored the elephant's leg. He described in great detail the rough, scratchy surface that was huge and round. "Aha, this is an ancient mighty tree. We're in a new forest." "No, no," said the blind man who had taken hold of the elephant's trunk. "We're in great danger—this is a writhing snake, bigger than any in our hometown. Run!" The third man laughed at them both. He'd been touching the elephant's tusk, noticing the smooth hard surface, the gentle curve, the rounded end. "Nonsense! We have discovered an exquisitely carved horn for announcing the emperor's arrival."

The blind men described what they "saw" accurately. Their mistake was to claim that what they saw was the whole. Much like the three blind men, researchers see different parts of the divorce elephant, which then frames their investigations.

It should come, then, as no surprise that reports of the findings about divorce are often contradictory and confusing. It is impossible for any study to take account of all the complexities of real life, or of the individual differences that allow one family to thrive in a situation that would create enormous stress, and frayed relationships, in another. But it is in these variations that we can begin to make sense of how divorce impacts the lives of individuals and families.

Facing Reality

Hallmark Cards recently launched a line of greeting cards called "Ties That Bind" aimed at various nontraditional unions—from stepfamilies to adopted child households to unmarried partnerships. "Our cards reflect the times," says Marita Wesely-Clough, trend group manager at Hallmark. "Relationships today are so nebulous that they are hard to pin down, but in creating products, we have to be aware that they are there. Companies need to respect and be sensitive to how people are truly living their lives now, and not how they might wish or hope for them to live."

Advertising agencies and marketing services make it their business to assess social realities. To sell their products, they have to evaluate the needs and desires of their potential consumers. They do not share the popular cultural anxiety about the changes in families. Instead they study them and alter their products to suit. Policy makers would do well to take some lessons from them and alter their preconceived notions about families to reflect current realities.

While the political focus today is on saving marriages and preserving traditional family values, Americans in large numbers are dancing to their own drummers. They're cohabiting in increasingly large numbers, having more children "out of wedlock" and engaging in serial marriages. While the rates of divorce have come down from their 1981 highs, they have leveled off at a high rate that is predicted to remain stable. To meet the needs of children and parents, we need to burst the balloon about idealized families and support families as they really live their lives. And that means we have to face the true complexities of *our* families and not search for simple answers.

As you read this book, keep in mind that we can all look back on our childhoods and note something about our mothers or fathers or sisters or brothers that has had lasting effects on our personalities. If you are looking to answer the question of whether a parental divorce results in children having more or less problems than children who grew up in other living situations, you will be disappointed. Nor will you find answers to whether the stresses of divorce are worse for children than other stresses in life. However, you will find answers here to questions about how and why individual children respond in different ways to the variations in their divorced families.

Divorce is a stressful life event that requires increased focus on parenting. The effort and care that parents put into establishing their postdivorce families are crucial and will pay off over the years in their many benefits to the children. But remember, families are complex, and if you find easy answers, they are likely to be wrong.

POSTSCRIPT

Does Divorce Have Long-Term Damaging Effects on Children?

Because about 45 percent of first marriages and about 60 percent of second marriages end in divorce, it is a major problem for the individuals involved and, potentially, for the society as a whole. Most writings emphasize the negative effects of divorce, especially for the children. These include Maggie Gallagher, *The Abolition of Marriage: How We Destroy Lasting Love* (Regnery, 1996); Barbara Dafoe Whitehead, *The Divorce Culture: How Divorce Became an Entitlement and How It Is Blighting the Lives of Our Children* (Alfred A. Knopf, 1997); Richard T. Gill, *Posterity Lost: Progress, Ideology, and the Decline of the American Family* (Rowman & Littlefield, 1997); James Q. Wilson, *The Marriage Problem: How Our Culture Has Weakened Families* (HarperCollins, 2002); Judith Wallerstein, *The Unexpected Legacy of Divorce* (Hyperion, 2000); Elizabeth Marquardt, *Between Two Worlds: The Inner Lives of Children of Divorce* (Crown, 2006); and Linda Waite and Maggie Gallagher, *The Case for Staying Married* (Oxford University Press, 2005).

The writings that minimize the harmful effects of divorce include Constance Ahrons, *We're Still Family: What Grown Children Have to Say about Their Parents' Divorce*, (Harper Collins, 2004); E. L. Kain, *The Myth of Family Decline* (D. C. Heath, 1990); and Mavis Hetherington and John Kelly, *For Better or for Worse: Divorce Reconsidered* (W. W. Norton, 2002). David Popenoe and Jean Bethke Elshtain's book *Promises to Keep: Decline and Renewal of Marriage in America* (Rowman & Littlefield, 1996) discusses the negative impacts of divorce but also discusses signs of the renewal of marriage.

Works that analyze changes in marriage and the family along with divorce include Betty Farrell's *Family: The Making of an Idea, an Institution, and a Controversy in American Culture* (Westview Press, 1999); Karla B. Hackstaff's *Marriage in a Culture of Divorce* (Temple University Press, 1999); Jessica Weiss's *To Have and to Hold: Marriage, the Baby Boom, and Social Change* (University of Chicago Press, 2000); Barbara J. Risman's *Gender Vertigo: American Families in Transition* (Yale University Press, 1998); Ronald D. Taylor and Margaret C. Wang, eds., *Resilience Across Contexts: Family, Work, Culture, and Community* (Lawrence Erlbaum, 2000); Linda J. Waite and Maggie Gallagher, *The Case for Marriage: Why Married People Are Happier, Healthier, and Better Off Financially* (Doubleday, 2000); Daniel P. Moynihan et al., eds., *Future of the Family* (Russell Sage Foundation, 2004); and Lynne M. Casper and Suzanne M. Bianchi, *Continuity and Change in the American Family* (Sage, 2002). For counsel on how to strengthen marriages, see David P. Gushee, *Getting Marriage Right: Realistic Counsel for Saving and Strengthening Relationships* (Baker Books, 2004). For information on divorce among seniors, see Deirdre Bair, *Calling It Quits: Late-life Divorce and Starting Over*, 1st ed. (Random House, 2007). For advice on handling divorce issues, see Mark A. Fine and John H. Harvey (eds.), *Handbook of Divorce and Relationship Dissolution* (Lawrence Erlbaum, 2006). Finally, for information on the adjustment of children, see Robert E. Emery, *Marriage, Divorce, and Children's Adjustment,* 2nd ed. (Sage Publications, 1999).

ISSUE 4

Does the "Mommy Track" (Part-Time Work) Improve Women's Lives?

YES: E. Jeffrey Hill, Vjollca K. Märtinson, Maria Ferris, and Robin Zenger Baker, from "Beyond the Mommy Track: The Influence of New-Concept Part-Time Work for Professional Women on Work and Family," *Journal of Family and Economic Issues* (2004)

NO: Mary C. Noonan and Mary E. Corcoran, from "The Mommy Track and Partnership: Temporary Delay or Dead End?" *The Annals of the American Academy of Political and Social Science* (2004)

ISSUE SUMMARY

YES: Brigham Young University colleagues E. Jeffrey Hill and Vjollca K. Märtinson, along with Maria Ferris of IBM and Robin Zenger Baker at Boston University, suggest that women in professional careers can successfully integrate family and career by following a new-concept part-time work model.

NO: In contrast, Mary C. Noonan, an assistant professor in the department of sociology at the University of Iowa, and Mary E. Corcoran, a professor of political science at the University of Michigan, document the various costs of the mommy track for female attorneys, including lower salaries and decreased likelihood of promotion to partner.

Women account for about 47 percent of the workforce in the United States and work approximately the same number of hours as men (35–50 hours/week); 60 percent of all women over age 16 are in the workforce. However, women earn less than men on average; this is true across full-time and part-time work, as well as across race, class, and educational levels. One explanation for the earning discrepancy is that women experience more job discontinuity due to family obligations, such as taking time off for childbirth, as well as dual-career conflicts, such as following a spouse who relocates to improve his job status. That is, women are expected to choose family over career in any work-family conflicts. Job interruptions and lower wages can result in women experiencing lower self-esteem and a reduced sense of accomplishment. Often these patterns are attributed to women's own choices and that they "deserve" less. However, others have suggested that society would benefit from recognizing that the childbearing years are also the years during which one is most likely to make the greatest career advancements. Thus, if women get off the career track to have children, they begin to lag and struggle to ever get back on the track. As a solution to this problem, the "mommy track" was proposed in 1989, a phrase coined in the *New York Times* to describe a "career and family" path that would serve as a viable alternative to the traditional "career primary" path typically followed by men. The "career and family" path was intended to offer women—only temporarily—flexible schedules, with reduced salaries and less responsibilities, while they tended to family matters, with the opportunity to return later to the fast track. The debate is whether the mommy track adequately allows for a temporary delay in women's career trajectory or if it really is a dead end. Skeptics question whether it is ever possible to truly get back on the fast track following a timeout for family. Although the concept of the mommy track was to prevent women from being unfairly treated, many argue that all it has done is perpetuate the stereotype that women, who chose, even temporarily, family over career, are not really committed to the workplace. As recently as July 2007, a *U.S. News & World Report* article was focused on how the mommy track can derail a career. In the selections that follow, Hill and colleagues use data from a study of IBM workers to argue that women in professional careers can successfully integrate family and career by following a new-concept part-time work model. The selection by Noonan and Corcoran counters with data from University of Michigan law school graduates to show the costs of the mommy track for female attorneys, including lower salaries and decreased likelihood of promotion to partner.

YES ← E. Jeffrey Hill, Vjollca K. Märtinson, Maria Ferris, and Robin Zenger Baker

Beyond the Mommy Track: The Influence of New-Concept Part-Time Work for Professional Women on Work and Family

The demographic composition of the United States workforce now includes more dual-earner couples who have responsibility to care for children, as well as more dual-professional couples who both have careers, not just jobs. In addition, the trend is toward longer work hours for many segments of American workers, especially for highly educated managers and professionals. The United States is one of the countries with the highest percentage of employees working 50 hours per week or more. This creates what has been termed a time famine for today's families. The time deficit is especially severe for women who choose to have children while pursuing a full-time career in a professional occupation.

Becoming a mother can make having a balanced life very difficult for a professional woman. Some new mothers try to do it all, continuing to work long hours in their professional careers while at the same time investing heavily in their family career. This option often takes a toll in stress and health. Others opt for, or are channeled into the so-called mommy track, moderating their ultimate career aspirations in order to raise their children. Some of these women choose to drop out of the workforce completely or for some period of time. Others take less demanding jobs in order to have more time and energy for their children. Still others choose part-time work.

Voluntary part-time employment after childbirth or adoption is consistently cited as a desirable option to facilitate work and family balance, especially for women. Studies show that part-time work options, especially for women, are increasing, and that this work is associated with lower work-to-family interference, better time-management ability, and improved life satisfaction. However, most professional women do not opt for reduced-hours options because, like other work-life programs, the economic costs in the form of forgone wages and career advancement are perceived to be too great. Generally these part-time jobs are of lower status with less pay and fewer career opportunities.

From *Journal of Family and Economic Issues*, March, 2004, 121–126, 129–133. Copyright © 2004 by Springer Journals (Kluwer Academic). Reprinted by permission.

Because job prestige, income, and career opportunity are important to many professional women, some companies have begun to offer new-concept part-time employment options, call[ing] it customized work; it [is] a growing trend. In contrast to most part-time jobs, these are high-status, career-oriented reduced-hours options that conserve pro-rated professional salaries and benefits. The hope is that this option might ameliorate the tendency toward mommy track career outcomes and convince women to continue to make professional career contributions as they embark on their family career. [O]ffering reduced work schedules that fit well with employee needs is an important weapon in "winning the war for talent" by retaining "professional employees and managers with critical skills."

Work and Family Balance

Research offers support for the notion that flexible work arrangements allowing individuals to integrate and overlap work and family responsibilities in time and space are instrumental in achieving a healthy work and family balance. Examples of outcomes associated with negative work-to-family spillover include withdrawal from family interaction, increased conflict in marriage, less knowledge of children's experiences, less involvement in housework, shorter period of breast-feeding for mothers with full-time employment, depression, greater likelihood to misuse alcohol, and overall decrease in the quality of life.

Less research has focused on family-to-work spillover, the "neglected side of the work-family interface." Examples of outcomes associated with negative family-to-work spillover include more pronounced psychological distress at work due to poor marital and parental role quality, decreased job satisfaction, greater likelihood of leaving the company, and increased absenteeism. $6.8 billion worth of annual work loss in the United States as a result of the absenteeism that is associated with marital distress [has been documented].

Part-Time Employment

The most persistent work characteristic that predicts work-family imbalance is long work hours, especially for women. For those financially able to do so, part-time work seems an obvious option for dealing with the problems associated with long work hours. In fact, many professionals desire to work fewer hours. More than half of the companies in America have a part-time option for parents to transition back to the workforce after childbirth or adoption. A recent study shows that 8% of men and 21% of women employees in the United States work part time. However, due to work responsibilities, perceived diminished career opportunities, and reduction in salary and benefits, relatively few professionals choose to work less than full time. The emergence of new-concept, part-time work, attempts to address these concerns. "These jobs are viewed as permanent, have career potential, include fringe benefits, and their rate of pay is prorated relative to that of comparable full-time jobs." Though many studies examine part-time work in general, relatively few have specifically examined professional women who work reduced hours while their children are young in these new-concept, part-time professional positions. This study attempts to fill that gap.

Research Questions

This study will expand the extensive literature on part-time employment by exploring the influence of new-concept part-time options, used by professional women who are mothers of preschoolers, on work-family balance and perceived career opportunity. In essence, we speculate that these new-concept part-time jobs will enable female professionals to go beyond the mommy track and successfully start their family careers while they simultaneously move forward in their occupational careers. We will attempt to answer the following specific research questions for a sample of new mothers in professional positions:

1. What is the relationship between new-concept part-time work and work-family balance?
2. What is the relationship between new-concept part-time work and perceived career opportunity?
3. How do part-time professional women and full-time professional women differ in how they allocate time to work, child care, and household chores?
4. How do part-time professional women and full-time professional women differ in total income and pay rates?
5. What do those participating in new-concept part-time positions perceive they would have done, had that option not been available?

Method

The data for this paper came from a work and life issues survey administered on-line by IBM in the United States in 1996. The focus of this study was female professionals with preschool children (birth to age 4) who utilized the new-concept part-time option. Originally the study was to look at part-time work for men as well, but there were insufficient male responses for reliable statistical analyses.

Internal surveys revealed that IBM employees perceived the flexibility to choose when, where, and how many hours are worked to be the most beneficial IBM offering to enhance work-family balance. In 1991, as part of an overall flexibility initiative, IBM implemented the Flexible Work Leave of Absence Program, which enabled employees to reduce their scheduled work hours from 40 to 20–32 hours per week. This qualified as a new-concept, part-time program because those participating continued in their same professional position, received pro-rated pay and benefits equivalent to what they had received when working full time, and were eligible for promotion and recognition. This research was conducted when the maximum length of part-time employment allowed by IBM was five years.

Data Collection and Sample

A 9% representative sample of all IBM employees in the United States was invited to take this online survey; 58% ($N = 6,451$) responded. Sample respondents were similar to the broader U.S. population of workers, except that this IBM sample was more highly educated and more highly paid than national norms. The option of part-time employment was probably more feasible in this population than in the overall population.

The survey was administered electronically. IBM has conducted on-line surveys since 1986, and survey data indicate a high degree of confidence in confidentiality and anonymity. For confidentiality reasons, the electronic mail addresses were deleted from the data before data were sent to the survey administrator. . . .

Results

Results related to the research questions are summarized below.

Relationship Between New-Concept Part-Time Work and Work-Family Balance

Being in a new-concept part-time position vis-à-vis a full-time position was strongly and positively correlated to work-family balance. This relationship was maintained in multivariate analyses after controlling for occupational level, family income, age, and job flexibility.

Relationship Between New-Concept Part-Time Work and Perceived Career Opportunity

Being in a new-concept part-time professional position vis-à-vis a full-time position was not significantly correlated to perceived career opportunity. No significant relationship was found in multivariate analyses after controlling for occupational level, family income, age, and job flexibility.

Allocation of Time to Work, Child Care and Household Chores

Those in new-concept part-time professional positions reported that they worked an average of 23 fewer hours per week than those in full-time professional positions (26.3 hours per week vs. 49.3 hours per week). They reported slightly more hours per week in child care (27.3 vs. 25.5) and in household chores (16.1 vs. 13.5).

Differences in Total Income and Pay Rates

Those in the new-concept part-time professional positions reported $20,022 less annual family income than those in full-time professional positions ($100,568 per year vs. $120,590 per year). They also reported $26,624 less annual individual income ($37,954 per year vs. $64,578 per year). When converted to an hourly pay equivalent, those in new-concept part-time professional positions earned slightly more per hour than those in full-time professional positions ($27.94 per hour worked vs. $25.36 per hour worked).

What Professional Women Report They Would Have Done Had the Program Not Been Offered

Most of those participating in new-concept part-time professional positions (74%) reported they would have left IBM if this program had not been available. Almost three-fifths (59%) reported they would have left IBM to find a job with more flexibility. Almost one-fourth (23%) reported they would have left the workforce altogether. Only about one-fifth (19%) reported they would have stayed with IBM and continued to work full time.

Discussion

In this study we consider the possibility that new-concept part-time professional positions might be an alternative to the mommy track. We consider whether this option may better enable professional women to embark on their family career with less stress and fewer negative consequences to long-term career prospects.

Personal/Family Implications

It was not surprising that mothers in new-concept part-time professional positions reported much better work-family balance than those working full time. Considering they work 23 fewer hours per week, it would have been surprising if the part-time group did not report better balance. However, it was surprising that they did not report less perceived career opportunity. This is counter to what would be expected had they been working in traditional part-time jobs based on previous research. Why is this so? It may be the higher status, greater responsibility, and pro-rated pay of new-concept part-time professional positions creates an environment where the employee feels in the loop of future career opportunities.

The personal decision for a professional woman to work a part-time schedule is a matter of trade-offs. This study quantifies some of the advantages and disadvantages for this population. The most obvious advantage of new-concept part-time work for professional women is that more than four and one-half hours per work day are freed up for personal and family needs. This extra time was certainly a major factor in why work-family balance was less problematic for the professional women working part time.

An interesting finding is that women in the full-time group reported an average of almost as many hours in child care as the part-time group (26 vs. 27 hours per week) and almost as much time doing household chores (14 vs. 16 hours per week). Apparently both full- and part-time professional women take the time needed to care for home and family responsibilities. The real benefit for the part-time women, therefore, appears to be the extra 19 more hours per week available to use in individual activities that might reduce stress, such as additional sleep, recreation, and other renewal activities. The literature cited earlier indicates that possible benefits for these new mothers include less marital conflict, increased period of breast-feeding after the birth of an infant, less depression, and better monitoring of children.

The most obvious disadvantage for a new mother considering a new-concept part-time professional position is reduced income. This study documents that the salaries of the part-time professionals averaged about 41% less (about $27,000 less per year) than the full-time professionals. However, because they reported working 47% fewer hours (26 vs. 49 hours per week), their pay equivalent was actually higher than the full-time group ($27.94 vs. $25.50 per hour). The family income of the part-time group was only about 17% less than the full-time group (about $20,000 less per year).

Organizational Implications

Companies today are engaged in what is known as a talent war to "recruit and retain professional employees and managers with critical skills." Data from this study support the notion that offering new-concept part-time professional positions may be a useful weapon in that war. Difficulty managing the demands of work and personal/family life is very problematic, especially for professional women who have chosen to have children. It is considered to be the most important reason why professional women with preschool children would choose to leave their job. Of the reduced-hours group in this study, 23% reported they would have left their job to stay home full time had the part-time work option not been available. Another 58% said they would have left their job to work for another company that offered greater flexibility. Only 19% indicated they would have continued working full time for the company. It appears that new-concept part-time employment is a strategy that may have enabled 81% of these women to stay employed with IBM, rather than going to work for someone else or leaving the workforce altogether.

In summary, the results of this study indicate that new-concept part-time employment offers the promise of enabling professional women opportunities to better balance work and family life while maintaining career opportunity. This option appears to be a true win-win solution to help mitigate the personal toll of increased work demands, with relatively few costs. If visionary business leaders and empowered individuals adopt greater flexibility, we may see the end to the zero-sum game and set up a virtuous cycle in which work-family balance programs leverage on each other to promote individual well-being, family solidarity, and organizational success.

Limitations

One limitation of this study is that respondents all worked for IBM in the United States. IBM employees, in general, are highly educated, have higher salaries, and have more experience with computer technology than the general population. For these reasons, the degree to which these results may be generalized to other companies and in other parts of the world is uncertain.

Even if the IBM sample is representative of employees working for large corporations, it may not be representative of the majority of professional women who work for smaller firms or are self-employed. In addition, most IBMers work in or near urban centers, so the applicability of this research to those who work in rural settings is uncertain.

Conclusion

Just as flexibility in family processes diminishes potential family stress, so flexibility in work processes may be key in helping employees effectively manage contemporary stress associated with work and family demands. In fact, this study documents that new-concept, part-time positions may provide the time professional women need at the beginning of their family career when children require the greatest parental investment. Given that these women represent key talent required for meeting business objectives, data like these can reinforce management's efforts to provide greater flexibility in the workforce, especially when the results are so clear and the costs of such efforts are relatively small. Just as important, these data may help encourage professional women to take advantage of the flexibility offered so they can more effectively care for their young children. As more companies offer viable new-concept part-time options and more employees use these options, perhaps we can move beyond the mommy track to enable women to contribute their best to both work and home, at the same time.

Mary C. Noonan and
Mary E. Corcoran

 **NO**

The Mommy Track and Partnership: Temporary Delay or Dead End?

More than 40 percent of recent law school graduates are women, and almost 40 percent of associates in large firms are women. In 2003, women made up 63 percent of Berkeley Law School's graduating class, 51 percent of Columbia Law School's graduating class, and 47 percent of Harvard Law School's graduating class. Despite the rapid feminization of law since the 1970s, women associates are far less likely than male associates to become partners. According to a recent American Bar Association Commission report, the most pervasive underrepresentation of women lawyers is among partners in law firms. Only 16 percent of partners in law firms are women. . . .

Women now graduate from top law schools and enter prestigious law firms at roughly the same rates as do men. [W]omen "start strong out of the gate." But after leaving law school and entering firms, women increasingly fall behind men. Why is this? [It has been] asserted that women associates make partner at lower rates than do male associates because women face "multiple glass ceilings" that men do not at many stages of the career hierarchy. One such stage is the decision to remain in a firm long enough to be considered for partnership. Partnership typically occurs after six to eight years at a firm, but many women associates drop out of large law practices by their fourth year. Donovan claimed that "the single most important element of women's inability to make partner is the high attrition rate of women from firms . . . women cannot make partner if they have left the firm." Foster (1995, 1658) stated that "attrition perpetuates the glass ceiling as fewer women are available for promotion and more men remain in decision-making positions as a result."

High attrition in the first years after joining firms is not the only reason offered for women's underrepresentation in partnership ranks. [G]lass ceilings operate at other career stages as well—resulting in lower promotion chances for women associates who remain in firms and in lower earnings and equity shares for women who become partners.

[T]he following institutional factors may marginalize women associates: "rainmaking" demands (i.e., generating new clients for the firm), lack of mentors, sexual harassment and discrimination, high work hours, and part-time work tracks that permanently derail lawyers from partnership tracks. [F]emale

From *The Annals of the American Academy of Political and Social Science,* vol. 596, no. 1, 2004, pp. 130–135, 137, 139–142, 146–149. Copyright © 2004 by Sage Publications. Reprinted by permission.

associates have fewer opportunities than male associates to develop "social capital" within law firms. Researchers who interview women lawyers find that many report experiencing sex discrimination within the firm. [B]oth men and women lawyers identify sex discrimination as one of the main reasons for women's early attrition from private firms and lower rates of promotion to partnership. [W]omen lawyers report lower levels of discrimination at the "front door" (hiring) than on the job (salary, promotion, and assignments).

The primary personal factor identified as constraining women's partnership chances is that some cut back labor supply (e.g., work part-time for a period, take a family leave, work fewer hours per year) to balance the demands of motherhood with the demands of practicing law. As Donovan put it, "The most notorious reason for women to leave [a firm] is motherhood." [C]hild care responsibilities and family leave policies play a significant role in career decisions—jobs, specialties, cases, and work hours—for women but not for men. Common reasons women report for leaving the field of law are the lack of flexibility offered by law firms, long hours, child care commitments, and the stressful nature of the work. Men are less likely to cite "work-family conflict" as a reason for leaving law and are more likely to state the desire to use different skills.

As these authors noted, the distinction between institutional and personal constraints is fuzzy. For instance, a woman associate may "choose" to work part-time for several years, and this choice may reduce her chances of making partner. But this choice may be a response to discrimination within a firm, or this choice may be all that is available in a firm. Furthermore, the "choice" itself may be strongly conditioned by the expectations of others—family, colleagues, the larger culture—expectations that do not constrain men's labor supply choices. . . .

[Many] authors hypothesized that work-family conflicts lead women to reduce their labor supply in ways that increase their chances of exiting law firms and reduce their chances of becoming partners. Two studies of attrition from law firms and several studies of partnership have used relatively recent data on lawyers' outcomes to test this hypothesis.

What do these researchers find? First, sex strongly predicted exits from law firms and promotion to partnership even when controlling for law school quality, academic distinction in law school, *potential* work experience (i.e., years since called to the bar, years since law school graduation), legal specialization, having taken a leave for child care, marital status, children, current work hours, and measures of social capital. Second, labor supply matters. Having taken a family leave was more common among women and reduced chances of partnership in [a] sample of Toronto lawyers. A work-family constraint lowered women's but not men's chances of partnership in [a] sample of Chicago lawyers. Current work hours positively predicted partnership.

The usefulness of this research in assessing for the extent to which women's labor supply choices reduce their chances of becoming partners is limited given the relatively weak measures of labor supply used. No study had a measure of years worked part-time to care for children. Yet [it has been] argued that choosing to work-part time on a "mommy track" can stigmatize women as "not serious" and permanently damage chances of becoming partners. . . .

No study had a measure of years practicing law. Instead, all of these prior studies included a measure of potential experience (years since called to the bar or years since law school graduation), but actual years practiced is likely lower for women than for men. . . . Those who do not make partner might well cut back work hours.

Given the limitations of the labor supply measures used in past research, it may be surprising to learn that even with these weak controls for labor supply, mothers are no less likely than childless women to become partners. This does not mean that *sex* does not matter for partnership; mothers and childless women are equally *less* likely than men to become partners.

We use detailed information on the fifteen-year careers of graduates of the University of Michigan Law School to investigate sex differences in promotion to partnership. Because women may be disadvantaged relative to men at multiple career stages, we examine three steps in the partnership process: (1) the decision to attrite early from private practice, (2) the attainment of partnership among those who do not attrite, and (3) determinants of partners' earnings. Because we have direct measures of the labor supply choices made to handle child care responsibilities (e.g., months time out for kids, months worked part-time for kids, and years worked in law), we can more precisely estimate the extent to which cutbacks in labor supply are associated with reduced chances of becoming partner for women who start out in private practice than have past researchers. If, after controlling for sex differences in these precise measures of labor supply, women still have higher early attrition rates from private practice than men, women who stay in private practice are still less likely to be promoted than men, and women who become partners still have lower earnings than men, then this is strong indirect evidence that glass ceilings constrain women's opportunities at multiple points in their legal careers. In addition, if after controlling for labor supply, motherhood has no further effects on early attrition, partnership among stayers, and wages of partners, then it seems unlikely that parenting concerns account for the remaining sex differences in early attrition, partnership, and earnings.

Examining women's experiences at multiple stages of their careers after they first enter firms is important because the experiences of women long-termers in a firm likely inform the career decisions made by new women entrants. If cutting back on labor supply has derailed the partnership of older women, then new entrants who are concerned about balancing work and family may quit private practice for another legal setting. If older women who have not cut back labor supply are less likely than men with similar work histories to become partners, and if women partners earn less than men partners with similar work histories, then even new women entrants who are not concerned about balancing family demands may decide their opportunities are restricted and leave. . . .

We use a sample of University of Michigan Law School graduates to examine these questions. The law school surveys all graduates fifteen years after graduation about their earnings, work hours, work histories (including interruptions and years worked part-time), work settings, and families. These survey data are matched with law school records, giving additional information on graduates' performance while in law school.

The sample includes the graduating classes of 1972 to 1985. Outcomes are observed from 1987 to 2000. The average response rate across all years was 60 percent for women and 64 percent for men. We exclude women and men with missing data on the variables used in the analyses (about 18 percent of the total sample). We use three samples in our analyses: those who spent at least one year in private practice (433 women and 1,876 men), those who spent at least four years in private practice (354 women and 1,694 men), and those who were partners in their fifteenth year (144 women and 1,116 men). . . .

Women were less likely than men to have tried out private practice for at least one year (82 vs. 87 percent), to have stayed in practice for four or more years (67 vs. 79 percent), and to have made partner (27 vs. 52 percent). Among graduates who did not attrite early (those with four or more years' of private practice), 40 percent of women and 65 percent of men were partners.

. . . At three years of experience, the gap between the percentage of men and women still in private practice is minor—94 versus 89 percent, respectively. The gap widens to approximately 10 percentage points after four and five years of work experience. We suspect that this is the period when women become discouraged about their chances of making partner. Between five and eight years, the years in which partnership decisions are typically made, the gap widens another 10 percentage points, reaching nearly 20 percent at year eight. It seems likely that women leave private practice at higher rates after five to eight years of practice either because they expect not to make partner or they do not make partner. The gender gap in attrition is constant over the period from eight to fifteen years.

. . . Sex differences in family characteristics were large: women were more likely to be childless, less likely to be married, and more likely to be married to a lawyer. Women, on average, also worked significantly fewer hours than men—1,966 hours versus 2,493 hours. Women and men were equally likely to have had a mentor and were equally satisfied with the balance of family and work in their lives.

Sex differences in the labor supply of parents are striking. Only 19 of the 1,574 fathers in our sample had worked part-time, and only 17 had taken a leave from work to care for children. In contrast, 47 percent of mothers had worked part-time and 42 percent had taken a leave from work. Mothers who had worked part-time averaged forty-two months of part-time work over the fifteen years since law school graduation, and those who took a leave from work averaged twenty-four months not working. Fathers worked more hours in year fifteen than did mothers—2,519 versus 2,005 hours. . . .

Although women lawyers were more likely than men lawyers to cut back labor supply, 56 percent of women lawyers *never* worked part-time or took a leave. This 56 percent consists of childless women (29 percent of the sample) and mothers who never worked part-time or took time out to care for children (27 percent of the sample). Women who had not worked part-time or dropped out worked high hours—roughly twenty-four hundred at year fifteen. . . .

Women are more likely than men to exit, even after controlling for GPA, marriage, children, labor supply, mentoring, and satisfaction. GPA and years practiced law are significantly associated with lower rates of leaving for both men and women. Marriage, children, time out, and part-time work are not significantly associated with rates of leaving for women or men. . . . Men who left are more likely than men who stayed to be satisfied with their work-family balance at the fifteenth year; this is not true for women. Further analyses show that, for women, having children, taking time out of work, and working part-time are all positively associated with work-family satisfaction. Women who leave private practice are more likely to take time out of work, women who stay in private practice are more likely to work part-time, and both groups are equally likely to have children. Therefore, it appears that both women "leavers" and "stayers" have balanced their work and family lives in different ways, but both approaches are equally satisfying. Since very few men who remain in private practice actually work part-time, it may be that—for men—work-family satisfaction only comes through leaving the stressful world of private practice for other less demanding lines of work.

Sex also affects promotion rates for lawyers who remain in firms for at least four years. Women are less likely than men to be promoted to partner, even when GPA, race, years practiced law, months part-time, months nonwork, marital status, number of kids, mentorship, and satisfaction are controlled. . . . [M]arriage and children are *positively* associated with the probability of becoming partner when experience measures are included. . . . GPA, years practiced law, and having a mentor are positively associated with partnership, and months not worked is negatively associated with partnership. The effects of time out on partnership are significantly larger for men, and the effects of GPA on partnership are significantly larger for women. Part-time work significantly decreases the likelihood of becoming a partner for women but not for men; however, the difference in the effect is not large enough to be statistically different by sex. Having a lawyer as a spouse increases women's but not men's chances of becoming a partner. . . .

The "base" lawyer is a white man who is married with children, has an average GPA, 13.5 years of private practice experience, no leave, no part-time experience, a mentor, is satisfied with his work-family balance, and has a spouse who is not a lawyer. This "base" lawyer has a 9 percent chance of leaving private practice before his fourth year and a 57 percent chance of making partner if he remains in private practice for at least four years. A woman with these same characteristics has a 15 percent chance of leaving practice within four years and a 40 percent chance of making partner if she remains in private practice for at least four years. Thus, "being female" increased the predicted chances of attrition by 6 percentage points and reduced the chances of becoming partner by 17 percentage points.

Conclusion and Discussion

In this article, we use data on graduates of the University of Michigan Law School, a highly ranked law school that provides specialized training and access to well-paid jobs, to examine sex differences in the path to partnership. These men and women started off on an equal footing in the legal marketplace. Despite this, men were almost twice as likely as women to become partners.

How did this happen? The pattern is one of cumulating disadvantages. Women fell behind men in each stage in the progression to partnership. . . .

Some argue that women are more likely than men to select themselves out at each stage of the partnership process because men and women handle family responsibilities differently. Certainly, a large minority of women in our sample cut back labor supply to deal with family responsibilities, and virtually no men did so. These cutbacks in labor supply were negatively associated with partnership chances and with partners' earnings. But we found large gaps between the early attrition rates, chances of partnership, and annual earnings of men and women partners with the *same* work histories. . . . At most, one-quarter to one-third of the male/female differences in early attrition and promotion and one-half of the earnings gap between men and women partners are due to labor supply differences. These estimates of reductions may be on the high side since women's labor supply choices are likely influenced by the options firms offer and by women's perceptions of sex differences in promotion opportunities.

A family leave of one year reduced women's chances of making partner by one-third and reduced women partners' earnings by 28 percent. But law school performance and connections had equally strong effects on women lawyers' careers. A woman with a B+ average GPA in law school was 1.5 times as likely to attrite early as was one with an A average (14 vs. 9 percent) and was less likely to make partner (35 vs. 49 percent). Women with mentors were almost 1.5 times as likely to become partners as were those without mentors (35 vs. 24 percent), and women married to lawyers were 1.8 times as likely to make partner as women who were not married to lawyers (54 vs. 35 percent).

The few male lawyers who reduced their labor supply to care for children fared badly economically. A year of leave reduced men's predicted chances of making partner from 58 to 0 percent, and a year of part-time work reduced male partners' predicted earnings by 41 percent. The meaning of these drops is unclear. These could be very unusual men, or it could be that male lawyers who behave in nontraditional ways face high penalties. If the latter were true, it is not surprising that so few male lawyers reduce labor supply. . . .

One could argue that parenting responsibilities reduce women's productivity at work in ways not captured by these analyses. But controlling for labor supply, mothers had the same early attrition rates, promotion rates, and earnings as did childless women; and ever-married women were more likely to be promoted than never-married women. It seems implausible that women's commitment to home and hearth accounts for the remaining sex-based gaps in early attrition, partnership, and partners' earnings.

This brings us to sex-based differences in the ways women are treated in law firms. Posited that direct discrimination and sexual harassment, as well as a wide array of embedded institutional practices, marginalize women within law firms. We could not directly test this proposition, . . . [b]ut our finding of large sex differences at each stage of the progression to partnership, controlling for labor supply differences, suggests that women are disproportionately selected out and discouraged at each of these stages. This is strong indirect evidence that women face multiple glass ceilings.

Researchers who have conducted in-depth, in-person interviews with associates and partners in law firms describe two sets of mechanisms that could systematically disadvantage women. One set constrains associates' labor supply choices and determines the effects these choices have on partnership. For instance, although firms offer part-time tracks, official policies differ on whether part-time work counts for partnership and on whether part-timers can return to partnership tracks. Even when the official policy is that family leaves and part-time work do not disqualify women from partnership, several studies find that some women reported being assigned less important cases and being labeled as less motivated after having worked part-time (Epstein et al. 1995; Gannon 2003). This social stigma and fear of not being taken seriously likely keeps many lawyers from pursuing part-time options. . . . A second set of mechanisms can systematically disadvantage women in ways that are unrelated to their actual labor supply choices. [H]igh rainmaking demands, a lack of mentoring, sex discrimination, disproportionate shares of pro bono work, and mixed messages about personal style all may reduce women's chances of making partner.

It is easy to describe institutional arrangements that might make law firms more family-friendly. A report in the *Harvard Law Review* (1996) suggested reducing "billable hours" requirements, billing approaches that move away from reliance on billable hours to other indicators of performance, officially counting part-time work toward partnership, developing a work climate in which individuals who work part-time and take family leaves are not stigmatized, part-time partnership, employer-assisted emergency day care, and mixed compensation (compensation consisting partly of time and partly of money).

It is equally easy to list approaches that can change institutional barriers to women's mobility. To the extent that sex discrimination and sexual harassment limit women's chances, there may be legal avenues to pursue. Of course, the individual costs of pursuing such strategies may be high. Other strategies include programs that improve the mentoring women associates receive, broaden the criteria for partnership, and reduce the extent to which women's personal styles are viewed as less effective in a legal setting. We find mentoring has a big impact on women's partnership chances.

Implementing family-friendly policies and changing embedded institutional policies that disadvantage women may require shifts in law firm culture. This is the rub. The *Harvard Law Review* study (1996, 1381) warned that such changes can "conflict with (firms') institutional norms" and that "law firms and their clients are understandably reluctant to challenge deeply ingrained business practices." [T]hree social processes—traditionalism, stereotyping, and ambivalence—contribute to this institutional inertia.

The *Harvard Law Review* study (1996, 1376) succinctly summed up the dilemma facing women associates: "Women cannot reach true equality within firms as large numbers of women are considered atypical because they fail to conform to the male-based definition of the ideal worker." Despite this gloomy assessment, the *Harvard Law Review* study contended that the benefits to changing firm culture may be powerful enough to overcome inertia. The *Harvard Law Review* report argues that high hour demands have led to a "time famine" among lawyers and that this "lack of time" can adversely affect health by increasing stress and can inhibit professional development by reducing available time for community service, pro bono work, scholarship, and education.

POSTSCRIPT

Does the "Mommy Track" (Part-Time Work) Improve Women's Lives?

The irony of the mommy track–fast track debate is that it is based on the assumption that women have a choice regarding work. In fact, most women have no choice. Either they are single parents or part of a family that needs two paychecks to meet the family's financial needs. Thus, for large numbers of working women this is a meaningless debate. Choice is reserved for the educational elite, according to Mary Blair-Loy in *Competing Devotions*. Rather, the debate serves to perpetuate stereotypes regarding women's commitment to family over work. The reality is that most working women have little control over the hours they work. Indeed, for the lowest income jobs working hours are not family-friendly hours. Consider the schedules of waitresses and housekeeping staff, for example.

It is worth noting that the family–career conflict that is receiving so much attention currently is in fact a rather current phenomenon. Claudia Goldin (2004) has suggested that this "conflict" has changed over time. For women graduating from college in the early 1900s the choice was clear: family or career. From 1920 to 1945 many women opted for a "job then family" model. From about 1946 to the 1960s, the pattern was reversed to "family then job." In the late 1960s the language shifted from "job" to "career," with a pattern of "career then family" dominating through the 1980s. Since then the trend has been toward "career and family." Goldin contends that these shifts have been possible due largely to increased career opportunities for women, especially white collar jobs, with improved contraceptive methods also making it easier for women to control their fertility.

Some scholars have suggested that it is the issue of care-giving that needs to be rethought in our society. If society as a whole were committed to the well-being of children, then conceptualizations of child care might well rest on a foundation of shared community support, freeing up all parents to provide quality care to their children. No longer would the parent who wants/needs to stay home with a sick child or attend preschool graduation be looked upon as less than the ideal worker. Only when there is a shift in perceptions of who is responsible for child care will even the subtle, but nevertheless powerful, effects of the assumption of women holding the primary responsibility for children subside.

There is a rich literature on the current career/family choices of women. See Sharon Hays, *The Cultural Contradictions of Motherhood* (Yale University Press, 1996); Ann Crittenden, *The Price of Motherhood* (Metropolitan Books, 2001);

Diane Eyer, *Motherguilt* (Times Book, 1997); Susan Chira, *A Mother's Place: Choosing Work and Family Without Guilt or Shame* (Perennial, 1999); Kjell Erik Lommerud and S. Vagstad, *Mommy Tracks and Public Policy: On Self-Fulfilling Prophecies and Gender Gaps in Promotion* (Center for Economic Policy Research, 2000); Mary Blair-Loy, *Competing Devotions: Career and Family among Women Executives* (Harvard University Press, 2003); Jeanne Marecek, "Mad Housewives, Double Shifts, Mommy Tracks and Other Invented Realities," *Feminism and Psychology* (vol. 13, 2003); Phyllis Moen (ed.), *It's about Time: Couples and Careers* (Cornell University Press, 2003).

For some recent discussions of the demands of work and family on women, see Arlie Russell Hochschild, *The Second Shift* (Penguin Books, 2003); Daphne Spain and Suzanne M. Bianchi, *Balancing Act: Motherhood, Marriage, and Employment among American Women* (Russell Sage Foundation, 1996); Nancy Kaltreider, ed., *Dilemmas of a Double Life: Women Balancing Careers and Relationships* (Jason, Aronson, 1997); and Anna Fels, *Necessary Dreams: Ambition in Women's Changing Lives* (Pantheon Book, 2004). For the facts on the changes in women's participation in the labor force, see The National Bureau of Economic Research, *From the Valley to the Summit: The Quiet Revolution That Transformed Women's Work* (NBER Working Paper No. 10335). Mary Eberstadt is the major critic of the working mothers who leave much of the childrearing to others. See her *Home-Alone America: The Hidden Toll of Daycare, Behavioral Drugs, and Other Parent Substitutes* (Penguin, 2004).

On the issue of time scarcity and time use, which factors into the debate on the tension between work and family, see *Fighting for Time: Shifting Boundaries of Work and Social Life,* edited by Cynthia Fuchs-Epstein and Arne L. Kalleberg (Russell Sage Foundation, 2004); Phyllis Moen, *It's about Time: Couples and Careers* (Cornell University Press, 2003); Harriet B. Presser *Working in a 24/7 Economy: Challenges for American Families* (Russell Sage Foundation, 2003); John Robinson and Geoffrey Godbey, *Time for Life: The Surprising Ways Americans Use Their Time*, 2nd ed. (State University Press, 1999); Juliet Schor, *The Overworked American: The Unexpected Decline of Leisure* (Basic Books, 1991); Jerry A. Jacobs and Kathleen Gerson, *The Time Divide: Work, Family, and Gender Inequality* (Harvard University Press, 2004); and Cynthia Fuchs Epstein et al., *Paradox: Time Norms, Professional Life, Family, and Gender* (Routledge, 1999).

The issue of the tension between family and work is recently receiving much attention. See Jerry A. Jacobs, *The Time Divide: Work, Family, and Gender Inequality* (Harvard University Press, 2004); and Janet C. Gornick and Marcia K. Meyers, *Families That Work Policies for Reconciling Parenthood and Employment* (Russell Sage Foundation, 2003). Brid Featherstone points out that government policies can reduce this stress in *Family Life and Family Support: A Feminist Analysis* (Palgrave Macmillan, 2004).

ISSUE 5

Should Same-Sex Marriages Be Legally Recognized?

YES: Human Rights Campaign, from "Answers to Questions about Marriage Equality" (Human Rights Campaign, 2009)

NO: Peter Sprigg, from "Questions and Answers: What's Wrong with Letting Same-Sex Couples 'Marry'?" (Family Research Council, 2004)

ISSUE SUMMARY

YES: America's largest lesbian and gay organization, the Human Rights Campaign, presents many arguments for why same-sex couples should be able to marry. The main argument is fairness. Marriage confers many benefits that same-sex couples are deprived of.

NO: Researcher Peter Sprigg presents many arguments for why same-sex couples should not be able to marry. The main argument is that the state has the right and duty to specify who a person, whether straight or gay, can marry, so no rights are violated.

In 1979, in Sioux Falls, South Dakota, Randy Rohl and Grady Quinn became the first acknowledged homosexual couple in America to receive permission from their high school principal to attend the senior prom together. The National Gay Task Force hailed the event as a milestone in the progress of human rights. It is unclear what the voters of Sioux Falls thought about it, because it was not put up to a vote. However, if their views were similar to those of voters in Dade County, Florida; Houston, Texas; Wichita, Kansas; and various localities in the state of Oregon, they probably were not pleased. In referenda held in these and other areas, voters have reversed decisions by legislators and local boards that banned discrimination by sexual preference.

Yet the attitude of Americans toward the rights of homosexuals is not easy to pin down. Voters have also defeated resolutions such as the one in California in 1978 that would have banned the hiring of homosexual schoolteachers, or the one on the Oregon ballot in 1992 identifying homosexuality as "abnormal, wrong, unnatural and perverse." In some states, notably Colorado, voters have approved initiatives widely perceived as antihomosexual. But, almost invariably, these resolutions have been carefully worded so as to appear to oppose "special" rights for homosexuals. In general, polls show that a large majority of Americans believe that homosexuals should have equal rights with heterosexuals with regard to job opportunities. On the other hand, many view homosexuality as morally wrong.

Currently, same-sex marriages are not legally recognized by Congress. In the Defense of Marriage Act of 1996, Congress defined marriage as heterosexual. A state does not have to recognize another state's nonheterosexual marriage. The legal situation is constantly changing. Several states have legalized same-sex civil unions, and San Francisco and Massachusetts have legalized same-sex marriages, though the new law in California nullifies the San Francisco law. These developments have prompted President Bush to propose a constitutional amendment limiting marriage to the union of a man and a women, but this law did not pass Congress.

The issue of same-sex marriage fascinates sociologists because it represents a basic change in a major social institution and is being played out on several fields: legal, cultural/moral, and behavioral. The legal debate will be decided by courts and legislatures; the cultural/moral debate is open to all of us; and the behavioral debate will be conducted by the activists on both sides. In the readings that follow, the Human Rights Campaign presents the major arguments for same-sex marriages, and Peter Sprigg argues that marriage must remain heterosexual.

YES

Answers to Questions about Marriage Equality

Why Same-Sex Couples Want to Marry

Many same-sex couples want the right to legally marry because they are in love—many, in fact, have spent the last 10, 20 or 50 years with that person—and they want to honor their relationship in the greatest way our society has to offer, by making a public commitment to stand together in good times and bad, through all the joys and challenges family life brings.

Many parents want the right to marry because they know it offers children a vital safety net and guarantees protections that unmarried parents cannot provide. And still other people—both gay and straight—are fighting for the right of same-sex couples to marry because they recognize that it is simply not fair to deny some families the protections all other families are eligible to enjoy. Currently in the United States, same-sex couples in long-term, committed relationships pay higher taxes and are denied basic protections and rights granted to married straight couples. Among them:

- **Hospital visitation.** Married couples have the automatic right to visit each other in the hospital and make medical decisions. Same-sex couples can be denied the right to visit a sick or injured loved one in the hospital.
- **Social Security benefits.** Married people receive Social Security payments upon the death of a spouse. Despite paying payroll taxes, gay and lesbian partners receive no Social Security survivor benefits—resulting in an average annual income loss of $5,528 upon the death of a partner.
- **Immigration.** Americans in bi-national relationships are not permitted to petition for their same-sex partners to immigrate. As a result, they are often forced to separate or move to another country.
- **Health insurance.** Many public and private employers provide medical coverage to the spouses of their employees, but most employers do not provide coverage to the life partners of gay and lesbian employees. Gay and lesbian employees who do receive health coverage for their partners must pay federal income taxes on the value of the insurance.
- **Estate taxes.** A married person automatically inherits all the property of his or her deceased spouse without paying estate taxes. A gay or

From *Human Rights Campaign Report*, 2009, pp. i, 1–17. Copyright © 2009 by Human Rights Campaign Foundation. Reprinted by permission.

lesbian taxpayer is forced to pay estate taxes on property inherited from a deceased partner.

- **Family leave.** Married workers are legally entitled to unpaid leave from their jobs to care for an ill spouse. Gay and lesbian workers are not entitled to family leave to care for their partners.
- **Nursing homes.** Married couples have a legal right to live together in nursing homes. The rights of elderly gay or lesbian couples are an uneven patchwork of state laws.
- **Home protection.** Laws protect married seniors from being forced to sell their homes to pay high nursing home bills; gay and lesbian seniors have no such protection.
- **Pensions.** After the death of a worker, most pension plans pay survivor benefits only to a legal spouse of the participant. Gay and lesbian partners are excluded from such pension benefits.

Why Civil Unions Aren't Enough

Comparing marriage to civil unions is a bit like comparing diamonds to rhinestones. One is, quite simply, the real deal; the other is not. Consider:

- Opposite-sex are couples who are eligible to marry may have their marriage performed in any state and have it recognized in every other state in the nation and every country in the world.
- Couples who are joined in a civil union, for example in Vermont, New Jersey or New Hampshire, have no guarantee that its protections will travel with them to other states. Moreover, even couples who have a civil union and remain in Vermont, New Jersey or New Hampshire receive only second-class protections in comparison to their married friends and neighbors. While they receive state-level protections, they do not receive any of the more than 1,100 federal benefits and protections of marriage.

In short, civil unions are not separate but equal—they are separate and unequal. And our society has tried separate before. It just doesn't work.

Marriage:
- State grants marriage licenses to couples.
- Religious institutions are not required to perform marriage ceremonies.

Civil unions:
- State would grant civil union licenses to couples.
- Couples receive legal protections and rights under state law only.
- Civil unions are not necessarily recognized by other states or the federal government.
- Religious institutions are not required to perform civil union ceremonies.

"I Believe God Meant Marriage for Men and Women. How Can I Support Marriage for Same-Sex Couples?"

Many people who believe in God—as well as fairness and justice for all—ask this question. They feel a tension between religious beliefs and democratic values that has been experienced in many different ways throughout our nation's history. That is why the framers of our Constitution established the principle of separation of church and state.

That principle applies no less to the marriage issue than it does to any other. Indeed, the answer to the apparent dilemma between religious beliefs and support for equal protections for all families lies in recognizing that marriage has a significant religious meaning for many people, but that it is also a legal contract. And it is strictly the legal—not the religious—dimension of marriage that is being debated now.

Granting marriage rights to same-sex couples would not require leaders of Christian, Jewish, Islamic or any other religious leaders to perform these marriages. It would not require religious institutions to permit these ceremonies to be held on their grounds. It would not even require that religious communities discuss the issue. People of faith would remain free to make their own judgments about what makes a marriage in the eyes of God—just as they are today.

Consider, for example, the difference in how the Roman Catholic Church and the U.S. government view couples who have divorced and remarried. Because church tenets do not sanction divorce, the second marriage is not valid in the church's view. The government, however, recognizes the marriage by extending to the remarried couple the same rights and protections as those granted to every other married couple in America. In this situation—as would be the case in marriage for same-sex couples—the church remains free to establish its own teachings on the religious dimension of marriage while the government upholds equality under law.

A growing number of religious communities bless same-sex unions, including Reform Judaism, the Unitarian Universalist Association and the Metropolitan Community Church. The Presbyterian Church (USA) allows ceremonies to be performed but they're not considered the same as marriage. The Episcopal Church, United Church of Christ and the United Synagogue of Conservative Judaism allow individual congregations to set their own policies on same-sex unions.

"This Is Different from Interracial Marriage. Sexual Orientation Is a Choice."

> "We cannot keep turning our backs on gay and lesbian Americans. I have fought too hard and too long against discrimination based on race and color not to stand up against discrimination based on sexual orientation. I've heard the reasons for opposing civil marriage for same-sex couples. Cut through the distractions, and they stink of the same fear, hatred, and intolerance I have known in racism and in bigotry."
>
> —Rep. John Lewis, D-Ga., a leader of the black civil rights movement, writing in the Boston Globe, Nov. 25, 2003

Decades of research all point to the fact that sexual orientation is not a choice, and that a person's sexual orientation cannot be changed. To whom one is drawn is a fundamental aspect of who we are. In this way, the struggle for marriage equality for same-sex couples is just as basic as the successful fight for interracial marriage. It recognizes that Americans should not be coerced into false and unhappy marriages but should be free to marry the person they love—thereby building marriage on a true and stable foundation.

"Won't This Create a Free-for-All and Make the Whole Idea of Marriage Meaningless?"

Many people share this concern because opponents of LGBT equality have used this argument as a scare tactic—but it is not true. Granting same-sex couples the right to marry would in no way change the number of people who could enter into a marriage (or eliminate restrictions on the age or familial relationships of those who may marry). Marriage would continue to recognize the highest possible commitment that can be made between two adults, plain and simple.

"I Strongly Believe Children Need a Mother and a Father."

Many of us grew up believing that everyone needs a mother and father, regardless of whether we ourselves happened to have two parents, or two good parents.

But as families have grown more diverse in recent decades, and researchers have studied how these different family relationships affect children, it has become clear that the quality of a family's relationship is more important than the particular structure of families that exist today. In other words, the qualities that help children grow into good and responsible adults—learning how to learn, to have compassion for others, to contribute to society and be respectful of others and their differences—do not depend on the sexual orientation of their parents but on their parents' ability to provide a loving, stable and happy home, something no class of Americans has an exclusive hold on. That is why research studies have consistently shown that children raised by gay and lesbian parents do just as well as children raised by straight parents in all conventional measures of child development, such as academic achievement, psychological well-being and social abilities.

That is also why the nation's leading child welfare organizations, including the American Academy of Pediatrics, the American Academy of Family Physicians and others, have issued statements that dismiss assertions that only straight couples can be good parents—and declare that the focus should now be on providing greater protections for the 1 million to 9 million children being raised by gay and lesbian parents in the United States today.

"How Could Marriage for Same-Sex Couples Possibly Be Good for the American Family—or Our Country?"

"We shouldn't just allow gay marriage. We should insist on gay marriage. We should regard it as scandalous that two people could claim to love each other and not want to sanctify their love with marriage and fidelity."

—Conservative columnist David Brooks,
writing in the New York Times, *Nov. 22, 2003*

The prospect of a significant change in our laws and customs has often caused people to worry more about dire consequences that could result than about the potential positive outcomes. In fact, precisely the same anxiety arose when some people fought to overturn the laws prohibiting marriage between people of different races in the 1950s and 1960s. (One Virginia judge even declared, "God intended to separate the races.")

But in reality, opening marriage to couples who are so willing to fight for it could only strengthen the institution for all. It would open the doors to more supporters, not opponents. And it would help keep the age-old institution alive.

As history has repeatedly proven, institutions that fail to take account of the changing needs of the population are those that grow weak; those that recognize and accommodate changing needs grow strong. For example, the U.S. military, like American colleges and universities, grew stronger after permitting African Americans and women to join its ranks.

Similarly, granting same-sex couples the right to marry would strengthen the institution of marriage by allowing it to better meet the needs of the true diversity of family structures in America today.

"Can't Same-Sex Couples Go to a Lawyer to Secure All the Rights They Need?"

Not by a long shot. When a gay or lesbian person gets seriously ill, there is no legal document that can make their partner eligible to take leave from work under the federal Family and Medical Leave Act to provide care—because that law applies only to married couples.

When gay or lesbian people grow old and in need of nursing home care, there is no legal document that can give them the right to Medicaid coverage without potentially causing their partner to be forced from their home—because the federal Medicaid law only permits married spouses to keep their home without becoming ineligible for benefits.

And when a gay or lesbian person dies, there is no legal document that can extend Social Security survivor benefits or the right to inherit a retirement plan without severe tax burdens that stem from being "unmarried" in the eyes of the law.

These are only a few examples of the critical protections that are granted through more than 1,100 federal laws that protect only married couples.

In the absence of the right to marry, same-sex couples can only put in place a handful of the most basic arrangements, such as naming each other in a will or a power of attorney. And even these documents remain vulnerable to challenges in court by disgruntled family members.

"Won't This Cost Taxpayers Too Much Money?"

No, it wouldn't necessarily cost much at all. In fact, treating same-sex couples as families under law could even save taxpayers money because marriage would require them to assume legal responsibility for their joint living expenses and reduce their dependence on public assistance programs such as Medicaid, Temporary Assistance to Needy Families, Supplemental Security Income disability payments and food stamps.

Put another way, the money it would cost to extend benefits to same-sex couples could be outweighed by the money that would be saved as these families rely more fully on each other instead of state or federal government assistance.

For example, two studies conducted in 2003 by professors at the University of Massachusetts, Amherst, and the University of California, Los Angeles, found that extending domestic partner benefits to same-sex couples in California and New Jersey would save taxpayers millions of dollars a year.

Specifically, the studies projected that the California state budget would save an estimated $8.1 million to $10.6 million each year by enacting the most comprehensive domestic partner law in the nation. In New Jersey, which passed a new domestic partner law in 2004, the savings were projected to be even higher—more than $61 million each year.

(Sources: "Equal Rights, Fiscal Responsibility: The Impact of A.B. 205 on California's Budget," by M. V. Lee Badgett, Ph.D., IGLSS, Department of Economics, University of Massachusetts, Amherst, and R. Bradley Sears, J.D., Williams Project, UCLA School of Law, University of California, Los Angeles, May 2003, and "Supporting Families, Saving Funds: A Fiscal Analysis of New Jersey's Domestic Partnership Act," by Badgett and Sears with Suzanne Goldberg, J.D., Rutgers School of Law-Newark, December 2003.)

"Where Can Same-Sex Couples Marry Today?"

In 2001, the Netherlands became the first country to extend marriage rights to same-sex couples. Belgium passed a similar law two years later. Spain followed suit in July 2005, and in December 2005, the South African Supreme Court ruled that the country had to extend the rights of marriage to same-sex couples by the end of 2006. Some of these countries, however, have strict citizenship or residency requirements that do not permit American couples to take advantage of the protections provided. In 2003, Ontario became the first Canadian province to grant marriage to same-sex couples, and in July 2005, Canada's federal government passed a law extending marriage equality nationwide.

In November 2003, the Massachusetts Supreme Judicial Court recognized the right of same-sex couples to marry, giving the state six months to begin issuing marriage licenses to same-sex couples. It began issuing licenses May 17, 2004.

In October 2008, the Connecticut Supreme Court recognized the right of same-sex couples to marry. Connecticut began issuing licenses to same-sex couples Nov. 12, 2008.

On Nov. 4, 2008, California voters approved Proposition 8, which amends the state constitution to prohibit marriage by same-sex couples. The amendment overrules a May 2008 decision by the California Supreme Court recognizing marriage equality. California continues to provide rights and responsibilities to registered domestic partners.

Follow the latest developments in California, New Jersey, New Mexico, New York, Oregon, Washington and other communities across the country at the HRC Marriage Center. Other nations have also taken steps toward extending equal protections to all couples, though the protections they provide are more limited than marriage. Croatia, Denmark, Finland, France, Germany, Iceland, Israel, New Zealand, Norway, Portugal, Slovenia, Switzerland, Sweden and the United Kingdom all have nationwide laws that grant same-sex partners a range of important rights, protections and obligations.

Beginning in December 2005, same-sex couples in the United Kingdom have been able to apply for civil partnership licenses to certify their relationships before the government. These licenses provide same-sex couples hospital visitation rights, pension benefits, the ability to gain parental responsibility for a partner's children and other rights granted to opposite-sex couples.

"What Protections Other Than Marriage Are Available to Same-Sex Couples?"

At the federal level, there are no protections at all available to same-sex couples. In fact, a federal law called the "Defense of Marriage Act" says that the federal government will discriminate against same-sex couples who marry by refusing to recognize their marriages or providing them with the federal protections of marriage.

Some members of the U.S. Congress have tried to go even further by attempting to pass a federal marriage amendment that would write discrimination against same-sex couples into the U.S. Constitution. This was defeated twice, in 2004 and 2006.

At the state level, Vermont, New Jersey and New Hampshire offer civil unions (as of 2008), which provide important state benefits but no federal protections, such as Social Security survivor benefits. There is also no guarantee that civil unions will be recognized outside these states. Forty-four states also have laws or state constitutional amendments explicitly prohibiting the recognition of marriages between same-sex partners.

Domestic partner laws have been enacted in California, Maine, Hawaii, Oregon, Washington and the District of Columbia. The benefits conferred by these laws vary; some offer access to family health insurance, others confer co-parenting rights. Some offer a broad range of rights similar to civil unions.

10 FACTS

1. Same-sex couples live in 99.3 percent of all counties nationwide.

2. There are an estimated 3.1 million people living together in same-sex relationships in the United States.

3. Fifteen percent of these same-sex couples live in rural settings.

4. One out of three lesbian couples is raising children. One out of five gay male couples is raising children.

5. Between 1 million and 9 million children are being raised by lesbian, gay and bisexual parents in the United States today.

6. At least one same-sex couple is raising children in 96 percent of all counties nationwide.

7. The highest percentages of same-sex couples raising children live in the South.

8. Nearly one in four same-sex couples includes a partner 55 years old or older, and nearly one in five same-sex couples is composed of two people 55 or older.

9. More than one in 10 same-sex couples include a partner 65 years old or older, and nearly one in 10 same-sex couples is composed of two people 65 or older.

10. The states with the highest numbers of same-sex senior couples are also the most popular for straight senior couples: California, New York and Florida.

These facts are based on analyses of the 2000 Census conducted by the Urban Institute and the Human Rights Campaign. The estimated number of people in same-sex relationships has been adjusted by 62 percent to compensate for the widely reported undercount in the Census. (See "Gay and Lesbian Families in the United States: Same-Sex Unmarried Partner Households.")

Questions and Answers: What's Wrong with Letting Same-Sex Couples "Marry"?

What's Wrong with Letting Same-Sex Couples Legally "Marry"?
There are two key reasons why the legal rights, benefits, and responsibilities of civil marriage should not be extended to same-sex couples.

The first is that homosexual relationships are not marriage. That is, they simply do not fit the minimum necessary condition for a marriage to exist—namely, the union of a man and a woman.

The second is that homosexual relationships are harmful. Not only do they not provide the same benefits to society as heterosexual marriages, but their consequences are far more negative than positive.

Either argument, standing alone, is sufficient to reject the claim that same-sex unions should be granted the legal status of marriage.

Let's Look at the First Argument. Isn't Marriage Whatever the Law Says It Is?
No. Marriage is not a creation of the law. Marriage is a fundamental human institution that predates the law and the Constitution. At its heart, it is an anthropological and sociological reality, not a legal one. Laws relating to marriage merely recognize and regulate an institution that already exists.

But Isn't Marriage Just a Way of Recognizing People Who Love Each Other and Want to Spend Their Lives Together?
If love and companionship were sufficient to define marriage, then there would be no reason to deny "marriage" to unions of a child and an adult, or an adult child and his or her aging parent, or to roommates who have no sexual relationship, or to groups rather than couples. Love and companionship are usually considered integral to marriage in our culture, but they are not sufficient to define it as an institution. . . .

Why Should Homosexuals Be Denied the Right to Marry Like Anyone Else?
The fundamental "right to marry" is a right that rests with *individuals,* not with *couples.* Homosexual *individuals* already have exactly the same "right"

From *The National Review,* July 2004. Copyright © 2004 by Senator John Cornyn. Reprinted by permission of the author.

to marry as anyone else. Marriage license applications do not inquire as to a person's "sexual orientation.". . .

However, while every individual person is free to get married, *no* person, whether heterosexual or homosexual, has ever had a legal right to marry simply any willing partner. Every person, whether heterosexual or homosexual, is subject to legal restrictions as to whom they may marry. To be specific, every person, regardless of sexual preference, is legally barred from marrying a child, a close blood relative, a person who is already married, or a person of the same sex. There is no discrimination here, nor does such a policy deny anyone the "equal protection of the laws" (as guaranteed by the Constitution), since these restrictions apply equally to every individual.

Some people may wish to do away with one or more of these longstanding restrictions upon one's choice of marital partner. However, the fact that a tiny but vocal minority of Americans desire to have someone of the same sex as a partner does not mean that they have a "right" to do so, any more than the desires of other tiny (but less vocal) minorities of Americans give them a "right" to choose a child, their own brother or sister, or a group of two or more as their marital partners.

Isn't Prohibiting Homosexual "Marriage" Just as Discriminatory as Prohibiting Interracial Marriage, Like Some States Used to Do?

This analogy is not valid at all. Bridging the divide of the sexes by uniting men and women is both a worthy goal and a part of the fundamental purpose of marriage, common to all human civilizations.

Laws against interracial marriage, on the other hand, served only the purpose of preserving a social system of racial segregation. This was both an unworthy goal and one utterly irrelevant to the fundamental nature of marriage.

Allowing a black woman to marry a white man does not change the definition of marriage, which requires one man and one woman. Allowing two men or two women to marry would change that fundamental definition. Banning the "marriage" of same-sex couples is therefore essential to preserve the nature and purpose of marriage itself. . . .

How Would Allowing Same-Sex Couples to Marry Change Society's Concept of Marriage?

As an example, marriage will open wide the door to homosexual adoption, which will simply lead to more children suffering the negative consequences of growing up without both a mother and a father.

Among homosexual men in particular, casual sex, rather than committed relationships, is the rule and not the exception. And even when they do enter into a more committed relationship, it is usually of relatively short duration. For example, a study of homosexual men in the Netherlands (the first country in the world to legalize "marriage" for same-sex couples), published in the journal *AIDS* in 2003, found that the average length of "steady partnerships" was not more than 2 < years (Maria Xiridou et al., in *AIDS* 2003, 17:1029–1038).

In addition, studies have shown that even homosexual men who are in "committed" relationships are not sexually faithful to each other. While infidelity among heterosexuals is much too common, it does not begin to compare to the rates among homosexual men. The 1994 National Health and Social Life Survey, which remains the most comprehensive study of Americans' sexual practices ever undertaken, found that 75 percent of married men and 90 percent of married women had been sexually faithful to their spouse. On the other hand, a major study of homosexual men in "committed" relationships found that only seven out of 156 had been sexually faithful, or 4.5 percent. The Dutch study cited above found that even homosexual men in "steady partnerships" had an average of eight "casual" sex partners per year.

So if same-sex relationships are legally recognized as "marriage," the idea of marriage as a sexually exclusive and faithful relationship will be dealt a serious blow. Adding monogamy and faithfulness to the other pillars of marriage that have already fallen will have overwhelmingly negative consequences for Americans' physical and mental health. . . .

Don't Homosexuals Need Marriage Rights so That They Will Be Able to Visit Their Partners in the Hospital?

The idea that homosexuals are routinely denied the right to visit their partners in the hospital is nonsense. When this issue was raised during debate over the Defense of Marriage Act in 1996, the Family Research Council did an informal survey of nine hospitals in four states and the District of Columbia. None of the administrators surveyed could recall a single case in which a visitor was barred because of their homosexuality, and they were incredulous that this would even be considered an issue.

Except when a doctor limits visitation for medical reasons, final authority over who may visit an adult patient rests with that patient. This is and should be the case regardless of the sexual orientation or marital status of the patient or the visitor.

The only situation in which there would be a possibility that the blood relatives of a patient might attempt to exclude the patient's homosexual partner is if the patient is unable to express his or her wishes due to unconsciousness or mental incapacity. Homosexual partners concerned about this (remote) possibility can effectively preclude it by granting to one another a health care proxy (the legal right to make medical decisions for the patient) and a power of attorney (the right to make all legal decisions for another person). Marriage is not necessary for this. It is inconceivable that a hospital would exclude someone who holds the health care proxy and power of attorney for a patient from visiting that patient, except for medical reasons.

The hypothetical "hospital visitation hardship" is nothing but an emotional smokescreen to distract people from the more serious implications of radically redefining marriage.

Don't Homosexuals Need the Right to Marry Each Other in Order to Ensure That They Will Be Able to Leave Their Estates to Their Partner when They Die?

As with the hospital visitation issue, the concern over inheritance rights is something that simply does not require marriage to resolve it. Nothing in current law prevents homosexual partners from being joint owners of property such as a home or a car, in which case the survivor would automatically become the owner if the partner dies.

An individual may leave the remainder of his estate to whomever he wishes—again, without regard to sexual orientation or marital status—simply by writing a will. As with the hospital visitation issue, blood relatives would only be able to overrule the surviving homosexual partner in the event that the deceased had failed to record his wishes in a common, inexpensive legal document. Changing the definition of a fundamental social institution like marriage is a rather extreme way of addressing this issue. Preparing a will is a much simpler solution.

Don't Homosexuals Need Marriage Rights so That They Can Get Social Security Survivor Benefits when a Partner Dies?

. . . Social Security survivor benefits were designed to recognize the non-monetary contribution made to a family by the homemaking and child-rearing activities of a wife and mother, and to ensure that a woman and her children would not become destitute if the husband and father were to die.

The Supreme Court ruled in the 1970s that such benefits must be gender-neutral. However, they still are largely based on the premise of a division of roles within a couple between a breadwinner who works to raise money and a homemaker who stays home to raise children.

Very few homosexual couples organize their lives along the lines of such a "traditional" division of labor and roles. They are far more likely to consist of two earners, each of whom can be supported in old age by their own personal Social Security pension.

Furthermore, far fewer homosexual couples than heterosexual ones are raising children at all, for the obvious reason that they are incapable of natural reproduction with each other. This, too, reduces the likelihood of a traditional division of labor among them.

Survivor benefits for the legal (biological or adopted) *children* of homosexual parents (as opposed to their partners) are already available under current law, so "marriage" rights for homosexual couples are unnecessary to protect the interests of these children themselves. . . .

Even if "Marriage" Itself Is Uniquely Heterosexual, Doesn't Fairness Require That the Legal and Financial Benefits of Marriage Be Granted to Same-Sex Couples—Perhaps Through "Civil Unions" or "Domestic Partnerships?"

No. The legal and financial benefits of marriage are not an entitlement to be distributed equally to all (if they were, single people would have as much reason to consider them "discriminatory" as same-sex couples). Society grants benefits to marriage because marriage has benefits for society—including, but not limited to, the reproduction of the species in households with the optimal household structure (i.e., the presence of both a mother and a father).

Homosexual relationships, on the other hand, have no comparable benefit for society, and in fact impose substantial costs on society. The fact that

AIDS is at least ten times more common among men who have sex with men than among the general population is but one example. . . .

What about the Argument That Homosexual Relations Are Harmful? What Do You Mean by That?

Homosexual men experience higher rates of many diseases, including:

- Human Papillomavirus (HPV), which causes most cases of cervical cancer in women and anal cancer in men
- Hepatitis A, B, and C
- Gonorrhea
- Syphilis
- "Gay Bowel Syndrome," a set of sexually transmitted gastrointestinal problems such as proctitis, proctocolitis, and enteritis
- HIV/AIDS (One Canadian study found that as a result of HIV alone, "life expectancy for gay and bisexual men is eight to twenty years less than for all men.")

Lesbian women, meanwhile, have a higher prevalence of:

- Bacterial vaginosis
- Hepatitis C
- HIV risk behaviors
- Cancer risk factors such as smoking, alcohol use, poor diet, and being overweight . . .

Do Homosexuals Have More Mental Health Problems as Well?

Yes. Various research studies have found that homosexuals have higher rates of:

- Alcohol abuse
- Drug abuse
- Nicotine dependence
- Depression
- Suicide

Isn't It Possible That These Problems Result from Society's "Discrimination" Against Homosexuals?

This is the argument usually put forward by pro-homosexual activists. However, there is a simple way to test this hypothesis. If "discrimination" were the cause of homosexuals' mental health problems, then one would expect those problems to be much less common in cities or countries, like San Francisco or the Netherlands, where homosexuality has achieved the highest levels of acceptance.

In fact, the opposite is the case. In places where homosexuality is widely accepted, the physical and mental health problems of homosexuals are greater, not less. This suggests that the real problem lies in the homosexual lifestyle itself, not in society's response to it. In fact, it suggests that increasing the level of social support *for* homosexual behavior (by, for instance, allowing same-sex couples to "marry") would only increase these problems, not reduce them. . . .

Haven't Studies Shown That Children Raised by Homosexual Parents Are No Different from Other Children?

No. This claim is often put forward, even by professional organizations. The truth is that most research on "homosexual parents" thus far has been marred by serious methodological problems. However, even pro-homosexual sociologists Judith Stacey and Timothy Biblarz report that the actual data from key studies show the "no differences" claim to be false.

Surveying the research (primarily regarding lesbians) in an *American Sociological Review* article in 2001, they found that:

- Children of lesbians are less likely to conform to traditional gender norms.
- Children of lesbians are more likely to engage in homosexual behavior.
- Daughters of lesbians are "more sexually adventurous and less chaste."
- Lesbian "co-parent relationships" are more likely to end than heterosexual ones.

A 1996 study by an Australian sociologist compared children raised by heterosexual married couples, heterosexual cohabiting couples, and homosexual cohabiting couples. It found that the children of heterosexual married couples did the best, and children of homosexual couples the worst, in nine of the thirteen academic and social categories measured. . . .

Do the American People Want to See "Marriages" Between Same-Sex Couples Recognized by Law?

No—and in the wake of the June 2003 court decisions to legalize such "marriages" in the Canadian province of Ontario and to legalize homosexual sodomy in the United States, the nation's opposition to such a radical social experiment has actually grown.

Five separate national opinion polls taken between June 24 and July 27, 2003 showed opponents of civil "marriage" for same-sex couples outnumbering supporters by not less than fifteen percentage points in every poll. The wording of poll questions can make a significant difference, and in this case, the poll with the most straightforward language (a Harris/CNN/Time poll asking "Do you think marriages between homosexual men or homosexual women should be recognized as legal by the law?") resulted in the strongest opposition, with 60 percent saying "No" and only 33 percent saying "Yes."

POSTSCRIPT

Should Same-Sex Marriages Be Legally Recognized?

The issue of the rights of homosexuals creates a social dilemma. Most people would agree that all members of society should have equal rights. However, the majority may disapprove of the lifestyles of a minority group and pass laws against some of their behaviors. The question is, When do these laws violate civil rights? Are laws against same-sex marriage such a violation?

There is a considerable literature on homosexuality and the social and legal status of homosexuals. Recent works on gay marriage include Craig A. Rimmerman and Clyde Wilcox, eds., *The Politics of Same-Sex Marriage* (University of Chicago Press, 2007); Daniel R. Pinello, *America's Struggle for Same-Sex Marriage* (Cambridge University Press, 2006); Donald J. Cantor et al., *Same-Sex Marriage: The Legal and Psychological Evolution in America* (Wesleyan University Press, 2006); R. Claire Snyder, *Gay Marriage and Democracy Equality for All* (Rowman & Littlefield Publishers, 2006); David Moats, *Civil Wars: A Battle for Gay Marriage* (Harcourt, 2004); Evan Gerstmann, *Same-Sex Marriage and the Constitution* (Cambridge University Press, 2004); Lynn D. Wordle et al., eds., *Marriage and Same-Sex Unions: A Debate* (Praeger, 2003); Martin Dupuis, *Same-Sex Marriage, Legal Mobilization, and the Politics of Rights* (Peter Lang, 2002); and Kevin Bourassa, *Just Married: Gay Marriage and the Expansion of Human Rights* (University of Wisconsin Press, 2002). Recent works on the history of the gay rights movement include Dudley Clendinen and Adam Nagourney, *Out for Good: The Struggle to Build a Gay Rights Movement in America* (Simon & Schuster, 1999); Ronald J. Hunt, *Historical Dictionary of the Gay Liberation Movement* (Scarecrow Press, 1999); JoAnne Myers, *Historical Dictionary of the Lesbian Liberation Movement: Still the Rage* (Scarecrow Press, 2003); and John Loughery, *The Other Side of Silence: Men's Lives and Gay Identities: A Twentieth-Century History* (Henry Holt, 1998). For broad academic works on homosexuality, see Kath Weston, *Long Slow Burn: Sexuality and Social Science* (Routledge, 1998), and Michael Ruse, *Homosexuality: A Philosophical Inquiry* (Blackwell, 1998). Recent works that focus on homosexual rights include David A. J. Richards, *Identity and the Case for Gay Rights* (University of Chicago Press, 1999); Daniel R. Pinello, *Gay Rights and American Law* (Cambridge University Press, 2003); Carlos A. Ball, *The Morality of Gay Rights: An Exploration in Political Philosophy* (Routledge, 2003); Brette McWhorter Sember, *Gay and Lesbian Rights: A Guide for GLBT Singles, Couples, and Families* (Sphinx Publishing, 2003); and Nan D. Hunter, *The Rights of Lesbians, Gay Men, Bisexuals, and Transgender People: The Authoritative ACLU Guide to a Lesbian, Gay, Bisexual, or Transgender Person's Rights*, 4th ed. (Southern Illinois University Press, 2004).

Internet References . . .

Statistical Resources on the Web: Sociology

This Statistical Resources on the Web site provides links to data on poverty in the United States. Included is a link that contains both current and historical poverty data.

http://www.lib.umich.edu/government-documents-center/explore

Institute for Research on Poverty (IRP)

The Institute for Research on Poverty researches the causes and consequences of social inequality and poverty in the United States. This Web site includes frequently asked questions about poverty and links to other Internet resources on the subject.

http://www.ssc.wisc.edu/irp/

About.com: Affirmative Action

About com's Web site on affirmative action contains information about resources and organizations that focus on affirmative action policies and current events. This site also enables you to search other topics related to race relations.

http://www.racerelations.about.com/
cs/affirmativeaction

Stratification and Inequality

***W**hy is there so much poverty in a society as rich as ours? Why has there been such a noticeable increase in inequality over the past quarter century? Although the ideal of equal opportunity for all is strong in the United States, many charge that the American political and economic system is unfair. Does extensive poverty demonstrate that policymakers have failed to live up to United States egalitarian principles? Are American institutions deeply flawed in that they provide fabulous opportunities for the educated and rich and meager opportunities for the uneducated and poor? Is the American stratification system at fault or are the poor themselves at fault? And what about the racial gap? The civil rights movement and the Civil Rights Act have made America more fair than it was, so why does a sizeable racial gap remain? Various affirmative action programs have been implemented to remedy unequal opportunities, but some argue that this is discrimination in reverse. In fact, California passed a referendum banning affirmative action. Where should America go from here? Social scientists debate these questions in this part.*

- Is Increasing Economic Inequality a Serious Problem?
- Has Feminism Benefited American Society?
- Has Affirmative Action Outlived Its Usefulness?
- Are Barriers to Women's Success as Leaders Due to Societal Obstacles?

ISSUE 6

Is Increasing Economic Inequality a Serious Problem?

YES: James Kurth, from "The Rich Get Richer," *The American Conservative* (September 25, 2006)

NO: Gary S. Becker and Kevin M. Murphy, from "The Upside of Income Inequality," *The American* (May–June 2007)

ISSUE SUMMARY

YES: James Kurth, Claude Smith Professor of Political Science at Swarthmore College, warns of very negative consequences for America of the growing income inequality from a conservative perspective. He also mentions the liberal criticisms of inequality but downplays their importance, because America has institutions that mitigate them.

NO: Gary S. Becker and Kevin M. Murphy, both economists teaching at the University of Chicago and Senior Fellows at the Hoover Institute, swim upstream on this issue by pointing out the positive consequences of the growing income inequality. The main reason for the increasing inequality is the increasing returns to education, which, in turn, inspire greater efforts by young people to increase their social capital.

T he cover of the January 29, 1996, issue of *Time* magazine bears a picture of 1996 Republican presidential candidate Steve Forbes and large letters reading: "DOES A FLAT TAX MAKE SENSE?" During his campaign, Forbes expressed his willingness to spend $25 million of his own wealth in pursuit of the presidency, with the major focus of his presidential campaign being a flat tax that would reduce taxes substantially for the rich. It seems reasonable to say that if the rich pay less in taxes, others would have to pay more. Is it acceptable for the tax burden to be shifted away from the rich in America? Forbes believed that the flat tax would benefit the poor as well as the rich. He theorized that the economy would surge ahead because investors would shift their money from relatively nonproductive, but tax-exempt, investments to productive investments. Although Forbes has disappeared from the political scene, his basic argument still thrives today. It is an example of the trickle-down theory, which states that helping the rich stimulates the economy, which in turn helps the poor. In fact, the trickle-down theory is the major rationalization for the view that great economic inequality benefits all of society.

Inequality is not a simple subject. For example, America is commonly viewed as having more social equality than do the more hierarchical societies of Europe and Japan, but America has more income inequality than almost all other industrial societies. This apparent contradiction is explained when one recognizes that American equality is not in income, but in the opportunity to obtain higher incomes. The issue of economic inequality is further complicated by other categories of equality/inequality, which include political power, social status, and legal rights.

Americans believe that everyone should have an equal opportunity to compete for jobs and rewards. This belief is backed up by free public school education, which provides poor children with a ladder to success, and by laws that forbid discrimination. Americans, however, do not agree on many specific issues regarding opportunities or rights. For example, should society compensate for handicaps such as disadvantaged family backgrounds or the legacy of past discrimination?

This issue has divided the country. Americans do not agree on programs such as income-based scholarships, quotas, affirmative action, or the Head Start compensatory education program for poor preschoolers.

America's commitment to political equality is strong in principle, though less strong in practice. Everyone over 18 years old gets one vote, and all votes are counted equally. However, the political system tilts in the direction of special interest groups; those who do not belong to such groups are seldom heard. Furthermore, as in the case of Forbes, money plays an increasingly important role in political campaigns.

The final dimension of equality/inequality is status. Inequality of status involves differences in prestige, and it cannot be eliminated by legislation. Ideally, the people who contribute the most to society are the most highly esteemed. To what extent does this principle hold true in the United States? The Declaration of Independence proclaims that "all men are created equal," and the Founding Fathers who wrote the Declaration of Independence went on to base the laws of the land on the principle of equality. The equality they were referring to was equality of opportunity and legal and political rights for white, property-owning males. In the two centuries following the signing of the Declaration, nonwhites and women struggled for and won considerable equality of opportunity and rights. Meanwhile, income gaps in the United States have been widening.

In the readings that follow, James Kurth mentions the danger of ever greater concentration of market power but thinks that antitrust laws and global competition will keep this problem in check. Other economic problems are also manageable. He is most concerned about the numerous political consequences of inequality, which include increased terrorist threats. Gary S. Becker and Kevin M. Murphy focus on the increased value of higher education that is at the root of the increasing inequality. The main consequence is the substantial increase in college attendance of all groups in society.

YES

James Kurth

The Rich Get Richer

In 1914, Henry Ford paid his factory workers $5 a day, twice the going rate, with the aim of creating a broad middle class able to buy the cars they were building. Today, that project isn't faring so well: *The Economist* reports that in the U.S. "the gap between rich and poor is bigger than in any other advanced country." And it's growing. According to the Congressional Budget Office, from 1979 to 2001, the after-tax income of the top 1 percent of U.S. households soared 139 percent, while the income of the middle fifth rose only 17 percent and the income of the poorest fifth climbed just 9 percent. Last year American CEOs earned 262 times the average wage of their workers—up tenfold from 1970.

This widening gap can be seen virtually everywhere we look—in America; within other countries, even those hitherto distinguished by a high degree of equality (in particular, Japan, South Korea, and China); and between rich and poor countries in the world at large. This pervasive reality has been explored ably and comprehensively in recent books by the popular and learned conservative writer Kevin Phillips. But it has also been recognized by professional analysts at the very heart of the capitalist system: a recent study by Citigroup Global Markets entitled "Plutonomy: Buying Luxury, Explaining Global Imbalances" suggested investment strategy on the basis of these trends.

Since most of the writing on inequality is done by economists, it is natural that they focus on the fiscal consequences. But in this essay, our focus will be on the ramifications for politics and culture, both within America and within the world more generally.

As Phillips documents, there have been several previous eras in American history that were characterized by growing economic inequality. They include not only the famous (and infamous) Gilded Age of the 1880s but also the 1830s and the 1920s. These previous eras and their eventual end may provide some prototypes for our own. But as we shall see, there are certain unique features of our era of growing inequality that make it something new under the sun.

It would be one thing, and bad enough, if great personal wealth were simply expended on more goods, in order to engage in conspicuous consumption. The consequences for society would include ever greater public displays of materialistic values. But this phenomenon seems to be as old as recorded history, and it is hard for a conservative to get really angry about something that has so much tradition behind it.

From *The American Conservative*, September 25, 2006, pp. 6–11. Copyright © 2006 by The American Conservative. Reprinted by permission.

It would be another thing, and even worse, if great personal wealth were simply translated into more great wealth—if capital were invested in capital in order to get even more capital. The consequences for society would include ever greater concentration of market power. But in the United States, this phenomenon has been around for more than a century, and we have dealt with it by permitting more competition, not only by antitrust legislation but also by opening the American economy to similar goods imported from abroad and, even more effectively, to entirely new goods and services that have resulted from technological innovation. It is difficult to get anxious about a problem that has been so readily and so often solved in the past.

A more serious problem results because the rich also like to buy people—personal servants who work in their homes and grounds as maids, cooks, nannies, painters, and gardeners. Nowadays, this largely means Mexican and Central American immigrants—and illegal ones at that. Of course, U.S. agricultural and manufacturing businesses want to hire illegal immigrants, too. However, the really animated core of the political lobby that supports illegal immigration—its mass base, so to speak—is composed of rich homeowners, who desperately want someone to do their dirty work and to do it cheaply. Although they are the largest beneficiaries of the American way of life, including the rule of law, when it comes to the issue of illegal immigration, the rich do everything they can to undermine the American way for the vast majority of other Americans. There is nothing conservative about these actions by the rich; rather, the true conservatives are the less well-off who oppose illegal immigration and who are trying to preserve (and conserve) what was once an established and respected order.

But immigration policy is only one example of the most serious problem with increasing economic inequality: the holders of great wealth—especially if they are organized into a political lobby of similar holders of great wealth—can buy not only more goods, more capital, and more people. They can also buy (through the vehicle of campaign contributions) more important people: politicians and other public officials and therefore public policies.

Some of these bought policies may be for the purpose of making the rich even richer, most obviously the current regressive tax policies of the Bush administration. The wealth of the very rich is never the product of free enterprise and the free market alone but comes by operating within and exploiting a network of government supports, such as licenses, regulations, subsidies, and contracts. It is the product of a sort of giveaway. Consequently, to reduce the taxes on wealth (estate taxes) or on the income from wealth (capital-gains taxes), when that wealth has been acquired with one or another kind of government support, is in effect to give the wealth holder an additional giveaway. Again, there is nothing authentically conservative about this process.

Having even more wealth than they had before, the very rich can thus buy even more government supports and giveaways and acquire even more wealth, enabling them to buy even more government supports and giveaways. And so on. The result of great wealth buying public policies is a positive feedback loop, or perhaps a vicious cycle, which transfers ever greater wealth and power to the very rich and away from everyone else.

What is to prevent this cycle from going on forever? Historically, there have been two major constraining (or reversing) processes: one derives from macroeconomics, and the other derives from mass politics. Both constraints were once very powerful but neither are really operating today.

If the rich are getting richer, and the poor, if they are not getting poorer in real terms are not seeing their fortunes rise at comparable rates, this would seem to mean that the increasingly opulent consumption by the rich will have as its counterpart the increasingly austere consumption by the poor, and even by the now shrinking middle class. Eventually, the newly poor will not be able to earn enough to maintain their previous levels of consumption. Consequently, some goods produced will not be consumed, thus there will be fewer goods produced, there will be fewer producers or workers, there will be fewer goods consumed, and so on. We have yet another kind of cycle. It is exactly this process that has long been identified (by John Maynard Keynes, among others) as one of the classical explanations of how the growing inequality of the 1920s led to a crisis of underconsumption and overproduction and then to the Great Depression of the 1930s. A similar cycle had occurred earlier, when the growing inequality of the 1880s had issued in the depression of the 1890s (which, at that time, had also been called the Great Depression).

Given this simple model and given the recent pattern of growing economic inequality, one would have expected that the American economy would already be in a new Great Depression. What element has been added that has suspended, perhaps only temporarily, the execution of this macroeconomic iron law? The answer, of course, is consumer credit and record levels of consumer debt. Over one billion credit cards are in circulation in the U.S.—four for every man, woman, and child—and with 40 percent of families spending more than they earn, this keeps consumption rising, even as income may be declining.

In addition, some of the American consumption is also financed, albeit in an indirect and complex way, through the credit extended to the U.S. government and to U.S. lending institutions by the producers (or more precisely, by their governments) of many of the very goods that Americans are consuming—those of China, Japan, and South Korea. On the one hand, these foreign creditors have enabled the United States to avoid another Great Depression. On the other, this has come at the cost of a growing Great Dependence: the proportion of foreign-held debt is half what we owe as a nation and interest alone totals nearly $100 billion per year. That dependence is more immediate and obvious with respect to the U.S. government than it is for the American consumer. It does mean, however, that our government will have to tax American citizens more in order to finance its debt. With the tax policies of the Bush administration, this will in turn add to the growing inequality. It also meansx that the U.S. government may come to be more constrained in confronting the creditor governments on a variety of foreign-policy issues.

It strains credulity to believe that this cycle of increasing credit—be its sources domestic or foreign—can go on forever. When it ends, the old macroeconomic iron law will impose its penalties.

When we turn from economic responses to growing inequality to political ones, we quickly recall a dramatic parade of social—and socialist—movements marching across the historical landscape, from the beginning of the Industrial Revolution to the end of the Cold War. In America, these included the Jacksonian movement of the 1830s; the Populist movement of the 1880s–1890s; and the New Deal, along with a variety of Marxist movements, in the 1930s. Each of these represented a popular, even mass, reaction to growing economic inequality.

In Europe, of course, these social movements were more massive and more radical. They included the Labour Party in Britain in its early decades; Marxist parties in most nations on the Continent; anarchist movements in Southern Europe; and of course a successful Communist revolution in Russia. Each of these also represented a mass reaction to growing inequality. Communist movements and parties also spread to Asia, where they represented not only the class conflict between rich and poor within countries but also the international conflict between rich and poor countries within the world at large, with these Communist movements becoming anti-colonialist and nationalist ones as well (as in China and Indochina). Marxist movements also spread to Latin America, but there the reaction against growing inequality more often took the form of populist ones (the most familiar case being Peronism in Argentina).

Wherever their locale, most of these mass social movement were eventually able to impose some kind of constraint upon, or even reversal of, the growing inequality within their countries (but not, however, upon the inequality between countries). Sometimes the constraint was imposed by democratic elections and egalitarian legislation as with the American New Deal, the British Labour Party, and the Scandinavian social democratic parties. Sometimes an electoral triumph by socialist parties was followed by a repressive reaction imposed by parties of the Right as in much of Continental Europe during the 1920s–1930s. And on a few occasions, a Communist party succeeded in making a revolution and imposing a reversal of inequality that was ruthless and terrible indeed as in Russia, China, and Indochina.

But of course, this long historical parade of mass social movements effectively came to an end with the end of the Cold War and with the discrediting and collapse of Communism and of much of Marxism more generally. With the end of the Marxist version of mass social movements, it is not surprising that the past 15 years have been a period of growing economic inequality that is now almost completely unconstrained.

Given the extensive historical record of equalitarian social movements and the recent pattern of growing economic inequality, however, one might have expected that some such movement would have already arisen. If we look around the world, perhaps we will be able to see it before our very eyes. Indeed, when we eventually turn our attention to particular poor countries or regions, this will be the case.

In regard to contemporary America, however, there is no evidence of any social movement at all. Has a new element been added to American politics that has suspended, perhaps only temporarily, operation of the social-movement constraint in our own time? Actually, we can identify three such new elements.

First, there has been a change in the nature of the working population, which always constitutes a good part of the poor or increasingly poor within a society. The conditions of the working class, including the conditions conducive to political organization, are one thing in an industrial economy and a very different thing in a post-industrial, or information, economy such as our own. Sociologists have long observed and specified the many reasons it is much more difficult to politically organize workers who perform clerical, technical, or professional tasks in offices than workers who perform industrial or manufacturing tasks in factories. In any event, there are very few labor unions that are composed of clerical, technical, or professional employees. When we remember that unions of industrial workers were a fundamental and major pillar of the Democratic Party in America, the Labour Party in Britain, and the socialist and Marxist parties in continental Europe, we can see how, by itself, the shift to an information economy has removed the most powerful political constraint on growing economic inequality.

Second, there has also been a change in the economic self-identification of the general population. The way people define themselves is different in a consumer society, with a total focus upon individual self-gratification, than it is in a producer society, with an emphasis on the social consequences and connections of one's work. It is obviously much more difficult to politically organize masses of people if they all think of themselves as individual consumers or as expressive individualists, each freely choosing his own unique (even if vapid and banal) lifestyle, than to organize masses of people who think of themselves as members of working classes or local communities, who share in common most of the important conditions of their lives.

Third, and a variation on the consumer mentality, there has been a change in the non-working or leisure activities—the preoccupations and not just the occupations—of much of the population. For many Americans today, especially those in what was once the working class, there is indeed a kind of mass activity, but it is not mass political or social activism. Rather, it involves spectator entertainment, especially sports. For them, there is no participation in anything involving real interaction with other human beings, be it political parties, labor unions, community associations, fraternal societies, or, if they have become adults, even in participatory team sports themselves. It is the poorer classes, in contrast to the richer ones, that spend most of their free time with spectator entertainment. As more and more people become poor or poorer and lose any reasonable hope of improving their economic status, either by their own economic efforts or by anything like political activism, it is not surprising that they would seek to fill their bleak hours and vent their sullen frustrations with escapist (and violent) entertainment. What would have been seen as juvenile and abnormal preoccupations in the society of half a century or more ago have become normal ones in the society of our own time.

The same three shifts that have essentially demolished the social-movement constraint on growing inequality in America have also gone far toward doing so in other Western countries as well and even in Japan. All of these have now followed America far along the path of becoming information economies, consumer societies, and spectator cultures. . . .

What happens when we turn our attention from America and the West to the world at large? Of course, due to the promotion of globalization by successive U.S. governments and by American elites, the United States is now very much in that world—and in its face.

As it happens, globalization adds to the processes producing a widening gap between rich and poor. First, as is well known, in any country that is immersed and enmeshed in globalization, it has resulted in both winners (those who already have international connections, English-language proficiency, or information-age skills) and losers (those engaged in traditional agricultural, industrial, and cultural occupations). Those who are already rich tend to benefit from globalization, and many of those who are already poor tend to be hurt by it. It is no accident that the era of globalization—which has largely been the era since the end of the Cold War—has also been an era of a widening gap between rich and poor. Anyone who claims that globalization is a conservative process is either a liar or a fool.

What has been true within countries has been true between countries as well. Over the past 15 years or so, globalization has generally increased the GNP per capita of the countries that were already rich—the United States, Europe, and Japan—although of course even in these countries there are some sectors and groups that have been hurt by it. More momentously, globalization has also increased the GNP per capita of some countries that were once poor or near-poor, particularly many countries in Asia and including such immense ones as China and India. This is a very impressive result indeed, although again, even in these countries there are very large sectors and groups in the traditional economy that have been hurt by globalization.

However, there are three big regions where a very large majority of the people have lost out from globalization, or are at least convinced that they have: Africa, Latin America, and most consequentially, the Middle East and more generally the Muslim world. The increasing economic inequality within the countries of these regions combined with the increasing economic inequality between these regions and the rest of the world has generated vast reservoirs of resentment toward the globalization process, toward the West, and especially toward that arch-promoter of globalization, the United States. And starting in the early 2000s, that popular resentment has developed into actual resistance movements, which bear some resemblance to the egalitarian movements of earlier eras.

The resistance to globalization has developed least in Africa, which in any case is the least developed—the poorest and the most anarchic—region of the world. In Latin America, however, populist—and anti-globalization and anti-American—movements have surged in the past few years. Radical versions have been voted into power in Venezuela and Bolivia; more moderate versions have been successful in Argentina, Chile, and Uruguay; and populist candidates have come close to electoral victory in Mexico and Peru. In many ways, these contemporary populist movements and leaders are reminiscent of earlier ones in Latin America history. If the United States were not now bogged down in the quagmire of Iraq, the attention of the U.S. government and the American media would be fixated upon what they would perceive as a dangerous populist threat sweeping Latin America.

But the really serious resistance movement to globalization, the West, and the United States has arisen within the Muslim world. This is Islamism, which is also often called political Islam. When we in America consider Islamism, we do not think of it as an egalitarian social movement. However, the theology (more accurately, ideology) of political Islam is permeated with egalitarian norms and sentiments, and Islamists are often animated by egalitarian resentments and anger as well. Islamists speak frequently about the injustices and exploitation inflicted by the rich upon the poor, and by the rich West upon the poor Muslim world. "Social justice" is a central concept in most Islamist programs. They have their own way of claiming, as the Communists claimed in an earlier era, to speak for "the wretched of the earth." . . .

Perhaps the most interesting place where the Islamist ideology of social justice will resonate is that part of the Muslim world within the West itself: Western Europe's communities of Muslim Immigrants and their European-born children and descendents. By now several major European countries—Spain, Britain, France, and the Netherlands—have suffered either Islamist terrorist attacks or Muslim youth riots and violence, and there will doubtless be more of this in the future.

Indeed, many Western European countries are becoming two nations. The first is the original, ethnic-European nation; it is now largely secular or even pagan, rich, and aging. And because of its extraordinarily low birth rates, it is shrinking in numbers. The second is the immigrant, non-European nation, the Muslim nation or *umma;* it is substantially religious or even Islamist, poor, and young. And because of its high birth rate, it will continue to grow in numbers.

The two nations are coming to view each other with mutual contempt, but in the new Muslim nation there is a growing rage, and in the old, ethnic-European nation there is a growing fear. This will provide the perfect conditions for a widespread Islamist sense of social injustice, a deep Islamist hatred of what are perceived as rich Europeans, and as a natural consequence, an endemic threat of Islamist violence. . . .

And finally, of course, Islamist terrorists may soon acquire weapons of mass destruction, something that only states have possessed up to now. States, being established, hierarchical institutions, have not really wanted to put their WMD at the service of egalitarian projects. With Islamist transnational networks, however, there is no obvious reason why they would not be willing, even eager, to use WMD to bring the rich and the powerful, and rich and powerful states, crashing down. Although Islamist terrorist networks are not really very good examples of mass social movements, they will be very good at achieving mass social destruction. And, brimming over with egalitarian envy and self-righteous wrath, they will delight in doing so.

And so, what will be the eventual fate of the current drive toward greater economic inequality, in America and around the world? Within America and the other rich countries (or rather, the countries with a lot of rich), there do not now seem to be any internal forces that will arrest this drive. As for external forces, only Islamism is now beginning to mount a serious threat to the security of the rich, and that threat is also directed at all the other groups and peoples that the Islamists despise as well. Still, whoever might be the specific target of a particular Islamist attack with a weapon of truly mass destruction, it will take a lot of the rich along with it. Furthermore, by exploding established expectations about the future of economic and financial assets, and therefore by reducing the value of those assets, it will take a lot of their wealth too.

In the course of the 20th century, there were several years of growing economic inequality. On a few occasions, they came to an end in a relatively gentle way, with democratic elections and more egalitarian legislation. More often, however, they were ended by a catastrophe, such as the Great Depression, a violent social revolution, or a world war. When the rich went out, it seems, they normally did so with a bang, and not with a whimper. The way things are now going, it is likely to be so in the future.

**Gary S. Becker and
Kevin M. Murphy**

 **NO**

The Upside of Income Inequality

Income inequality in China substantially widened, particularly between households in the city and the countryside, after China began its rapid rate of economic development around 1980. The average urban resident now makes 3.2 times as much as the average rural resident, and among city dwellers alone, the top 10 percent makes 9.2 times as much as the bottom 10 percent. But at the same time that inequality rose, the number of Chinese who live in poverty fell—from 260 million in 1978 to 42 million in 1998. Despite the widening gap in incomes, rapid economic development dramatically improved the lives of China's poor.

Politicians and many others in the United States have recently grown concerned that earnings inequality has increased among Americans. But as the example of China—or India, for that matter—illustrates, the rise in inequality does not occur in a vacuum. In the case of China and India, the rise in inequality came along with an acceleration of economic growth that raised the standard of living for both the rich and the poor. In the United States, the rise in inequality accompanied a rise in the payoff to education and other skills. We believe that the rise in returns on investments in human capital is beneficial and desirable, and policies designed to deal with inequality must take account of its cause.

To show the importance to inequality of the increased return to human capital, consider Figure 1 . . . , which shows the link between earnings and education by displaying the wage premium received by college-educated workers compared with high school graduates. In 1980, an American with a college degree earned about 30 percent more than an American who stopped education at high school. But, in recent years, a person with a college education earned roughly 70 percent more. Meanwhile, the premium for having a graduate degree increased from roughly 50 percent in 1980 to well over 100 percent today. The labor market is placing a greater emphasis on education, dispensing rapidly rising rewards to those who stay in school the longest.

This trend has contributed significantly to the growth in overall earnings inequality in the United States. And just as in China and India, this growing inequality gap is associated with growing opportunity—in this case, the opportunity to advance through education. The upward trend in the returns to education is not limited to one segment of the population. Education premiums for women and African Americans have increased as much as, or more than, the premiums for all workers.

From *The American*, May–June 2007, pp. 20–23. Copyright © 2007 by American Enterprise Institute. Reprinted by permission via Copyright Clearance Center.

Figure 1

Percentage by which the wage of workers with college and graduate school educations exceeds that of workers with high school only.

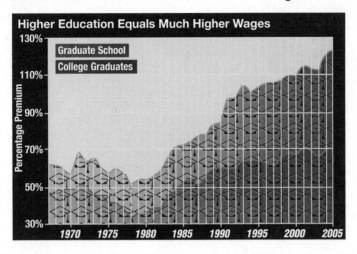

Source: Current Population Survey, U.S. Bureau of Labor Statistics.

Figure 2 shows that the growth in returns to education for women has paralleled that for men over the past 25 years, but has remained at a somewhat higher level. Figure 3 shows that returns for blacks have increased as much

Figure 2

Percentage by which the wages of college-educated men and women exceed those of men and women with high school only.

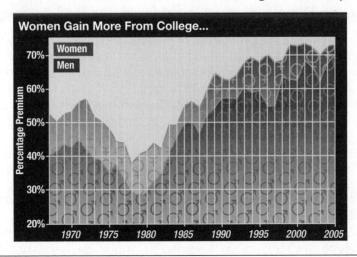

Source: Current Population Survey, U.S. Bureau of Labor Statistics.

Figure 3

Percentage by which the wages of blacks and whites with college educations exceed those of both races with high school only.

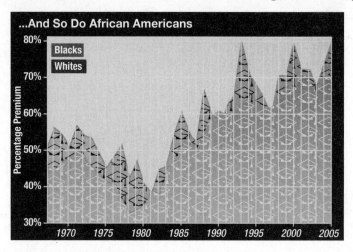

Source: Current Population Survey, U.S. Bureau of Labor Statistics.

as those for whites. As these two figures show, the potential to improve one's labor-market prospects through higher education is greater now than at any time in the recent past, and this potential extends across gender and racial lines.

The growth in returns to college has generated a predictable response: as the education earnings gap increased, a larger fraction of high school graduates went on to college. As Figure 4 shows, the proportion of men and women ages 20 to 25 who attended college jumped by about half over the past 40 years, tracking the rise in the wage premium. When returns fell in the 1970s, the fraction going on to college declined. The rise in returns since 1980 has been accompanied by a significant rise in the fraction going on to college.

This increase in the proportion of persons going on to higher education is found among all racial and ethnic groups, but it is particularly important for women, who, in 2004, outnumbered men as students in degree-granting institutions of higher education by 33 percent.

Women have also shifted toward higher-earnings fields, such as business, law, and medicine: the number of women in graduate schools rose 66 percent between 1994 and 2004, while the number of men rose just 25 percent. And the greater education achievement of women compared to men is particularly prominent among blacks and Latinos: the proportion of black women who attend colleges and universities jumped from 24 percent to 43 percent between 1974 and 2003, while the proportion of white men rose only from 41 percent to 49 percent.

The potential generated by higher returns to education extends from individuals to the economy as a whole. Growth in the education level of the population has been a significant source of rising wages, productivity,

Figure 4

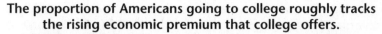

The proportion of Americans going to college roughly tracks
the rising economic premium that college offers.

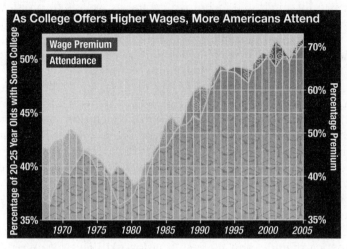

Source: Current Population Survey, U.S. Bureau of Labor Statistics.

and living standards over the past century. Higher returns to education will
accelerate growth in living standards as existing investments have a higher
return, and additional investments in education will be made in response to
the higher returns. Gains from the higher returns will not be limited to GDP
and other measures of economic activity; education provides a wide range of
benefits not captured in GDP, and these will grow more rapidly as well due to
the additional investments in schooling.

Why is the earnings gap widening? Because the demand for educated
and other skilled persons is growing. That is hardly surprising, given developments in computers and the Internet, advances in biotechnology, and a
general shift in economic activity to more education-intensive sectors, such
as finance and professional services. Also, globalization has encouraged the
importing of products using relatively low-skilled labor from abroad. At the
same time, world demand has risen for the kinds of products and services that
are provided by high-skilled employees.

When calculating the returns to education, we look at the *costs* of education as well. And even accounting for the rise in university tuition (it more than
doubled, on average, in constant dollars between 1980 and 2005), overall returns
to college and graduate study have increased substantially. Indeed, it appears
that the increases in tuition were partly induced by the greater return to college
education. Pablo Peña, in a Ph.D. dissertation in progress at the University of
Chicago, argues convincingly that tuition rose in part because students want to
invest more in the quality of their education, and increased spending per student
by colleges is partly financed by higher tuition levels. More investment in the
quality and quantity of schooling will benefit both individuals and society.

This brings us to our punch line. Should an increase in earnings inequality due primarily to higher rates of return on education and other skills be considered a favorable rather than an unfavorable development? We think so. Higher rates of return on capital are a sign of greater productivity in the economy, and that inference is fully applicable to human capital as well as to physical capital. The initial impact of higher returns to human capital is wider inequality in earnings (the same as the initial effect of higher returns on physical capital), but that impact becomes more muted and may be reversed over time as young men and women invest more in their human capital.

We conclude that the forces raising earnings inequality in the United States are beneficial to the extent that they reflect higher returns to investments in education and other human capital. Yet this conclusion should not produce complacency, for the response so far to these higher returns has been disturbingly limited. For example, why haven't more high school graduates gone on to a college education when the benefits are so apparent? Why don't more of those who go to college finish a four-year degree? (Only about half do so.) And why has the proportion of American youth who drop out of high school, especially African-American and Hispanic males, remained fairly constant?

The answers to these and related questions lie partly in the breakdown of the American family, and the resulting low skill levels acquired by many children in elementary and secondary school—particularly individuals from broken households. Cognitive skills tend to get developed at very early ages while, as our colleague James Heckman has shown, noncognitive skills—such as study habits, getting to appointments on time, and attitudes toward work—get fixed at later, although still relatively young, ages. Most high school dropouts certainly appear to be seriously deficient in the noncognitive skills that would enable them to take advantage of the higher rates of return to education and other human capital.

So instead of lamenting the increased earnings gap caused by education, policy makers and the public should focus attention on how to raise the fraction of American youth who complete high school and then go on for a college education. Solutions are not cheap or easy. But it will be a disaster if the focus remains so much on the earnings inequality itself that Congress tries to interfere directly with this inequality rather than trying to raise the education levels of those who are now being left behind.

For many, the solution to an increase in inequality is to make the tax structure more progressive—raise taxes on high-income households and reduce taxes on low-income households. While this may sound sensible, it is not. Would these same individuals advocate a tax on going to college and a subsidy for dropping out of high school in response to the increased importance of education? We think not. Yet shifting the tax structure has exactly this effect.

A more sensible policy is to try to take greater advantage of the opportunities afforded by the higher returns to human capital and encourage more human capital investment. Attempts to raise taxes and impose other penalties on the higher earnings that come from greater skills could greatly reduce the productivity of the world's leading economy by discouraging investments in its most productive and precious form of capital—human capital.

POSTSCRIPT

Is Increasing Economic Inequality a Serious Problem?

The list of negative consequences mentioned by James Kurth is quite long and varied. It includes conspicuous consumption, corporate concentration, biased immigration policies, regressive tax policies, many subsidies for the welloff, limitations on many policies benefitting lower groups, the coming of a crisis of overproduction and under consumption and thus a bad recession, excessive debt, trade imbalances, and even greater danger from terrorism. Can anything good be said about the growing inequality?

According to Gary S. Becker and Kevin M. Murphy, it is making America much stronger. Inequality puts a high premium on higher education, which has driven up college enrollments and caused many Americans to better themselves.

Inequality, stratification, and social mobility are central concerns of sociology, and they are addressed by a large body of literature. Important discussions of income inequality include Robert H. Frank, *Falling Behind: How Rising Inequality Harms the Middle Class* (University of California Press, 2007); Allan C. Ornstein, *Class Counts: Education, Inequality, and the Shrinking Middle Class* (Rowman & Littlefield, 2007); Barry Bluestone and Bennett Harrison, *Growing Prosperity: The Battle for Growth with Equity in the Twenty-First Century* (Houghton Mifflin, 2000); D. G. Champernowne and F. A. Cowell, *Economic Inequality and Income Distribution* (Cambridge University Press, 1998); Sheldon Danziger and Peter Gottschalk, *America Unequal* (Harvard University Press, 1995); Richard B. Freeman, *When Earnings Diverge: Causes, Consequences, and Cures for the New Inequality in the U.S.* (National Policy Association, 1997); Andrew Hacker, *Money: Who Has How Much and Why* (Scribner's Reference, 1997); Chuck Collins and Felice Yeskel, *Economic Apartheid in America* (New Press, 2005); Paul Ryscavage, *Income Inequality in America: An Analysis of Trends* (M. E. Sharpe, 1999); Edward N. Wolff, *Top Heavy: The Increasing Inequality of Wealth in America and What Can Be Done about It* (New Press, 2002); *The Causes and Consequences of Increasing Inequality*, edited by Finis Welch (University of Chicago Press, 2001); James Tardner David Smith (eds.), *Inequality Matters: The Growing Ecomomic Divide in America and Its Poisonous Consequences* (New Press, 2005); and Samuel Bowles, et al. (eds.) *Unequal Chances* (Princeton University Press, 2005). A big part of the inequality picture is the conditions of the working poor, which are analyzed by Lawrence Mishel et al., *The State of Working America, 2002–2003* (Cornell University Press, 2003); *Low-Wage America: How Employers Are Reshaping Opportunity in the Workplace*, edited by Eileen Appelbaum et al. (Russell Sage Foundation, 2003); and David K. Shipler, *The Working Poor: Invisible in America* (Knopf, 2004). For a poignant ethnographic study of the poor and their disadvantages, see Elliot Liebow, *Tell Them Who I Am: The Lives of Homeless Women* (Free Press, 1993).

ISSUE 7

Has Feminism Benefited American Society?

YES: Barbara Epstein, from "The Successes and Failures of Feminism," *Journal of Women's History* (Summer 2002)

NO: Kate O'Beirne, from *Women Who Make the World Worse* (Sentinel, 2006)

ISSUE SUMMARY

YES: History Professor Barbara Epstein argues that the feminist movement has been highly successful in changing the consciousness of Americans to "an awareness of the inequality of women and a determination to resist it." She explains how feminists succeeded at the consciousness level but have declined as a movement for social change.

NO: Journalist Kate O'Beirne argues that feminism is unpopular with women and is pushing an agenda that most women do not support. She claims that most women have concluded "that the feminist movement is both socially destructive and personally disappointing."

$\mathbf{T}$he publication of Betty Friedan's *The Feminine Mystique* (W. W. Norton, 1963) is generally thought of as the beginning of the modern women's movement, and since that time significant changes have occurred in American society. Data on advanced degrees and on income mark the profound changes. In 1960, only 35 percent of B.A.s were awarded to women but in 2003 that percentage had increased to 57 percent. The comparable figures for M.A.s were 32 percent in 1960 and 59 percent in 2003, for Ph.D.s were 11 percent in 1960 and 48 percent in 2003, and for law degrees were 2.5 percent in 1960 and 48 percent in 2003. The number of women in Congress in 1960 was 20 and in 2002 was 73. In 1963, the average full-time adult women worker earned 58 percent of what the average adult male worker earned, while in 2003 they earned 75 percent.

Many other changes marking women's progress are readily available. Occupations and professions, schools, clubs, associations, and governmental positions that were by tradition or law previously reserved for men only are now open to women. Women are found in increasing numbers among lawyers, judges, physicians, and elected officials. In 1981, President Ronald Reagan appointed the first woman, Sandra Day O'Connor, to the Supreme Court. In 1983, the first American woman astronaut, Sally Ride, was included in the crew of a space shuttle, and now women are on many of the space shuttle missions. The service academies have accepted women since 1976, and women in the military participated in the U.S. invasion of Panama in December 1989, the Persian Gulf War in 1990–1991, and the war to liberate Iraq in 2003. Elizabeth Watson became the first woman to head a big-city police department when the mayor of Houston appointed her chief of police in January 1990. New breakthroughs for women are now common and a woman president may not be far off.

These sorts of changes—quantifiable and highly publicized—signal a change in women's roles in the direction that feminists have championed. But more than three decades after Friedan's book, there are still many inequalities that favor men including income and poverty indicators. Much change toward greater equality has also occurred in the cultural area, but full parity has not yet been achieved. Femininity and femaleness are not valued as highly as maleness and masculinity. Housework and child rearing are not shared equally in two career families, though substantial progress has been made. Women are still adapting to a man's world.

Feminism—an ideology that, in its most basic form, directly opposes sexism by supporting gender equality and portraying women and men as essentially equals—has been a driving force in shaping the modern women's movement. The final legal victory of the women's movement was supposed to be the passage of the Equal Rights Amendment (ERA) to the Constitution, which would have made a person's sex an irrelevant distinction under the law. The ERA passed both houses of Congress by overwhelming margins in 1972, but it failed to win ratification from the required three-fourths of the state legislatures. The amendment was not ratified in part due to the efforts of a coalition of groups, composed overwhelmingly of women, who went to battle against it. Obviously, the women's movement did not represent the views of all women; many continued to believe in traditional gender roles. This pattern continues to today. Some of the prominent opponents against today's feminism are women.

In the readings that follow, a favorable view of feminism is presented by Barbara Epstein. The strongest arguments for feminism are the intolerable inequities that existed before the women's movement and the accomplishments of feminists since then, as Epstein demonstrates. In contrast, Kate O'Beirne argues that feminists falsely reconstruct gender realities to portray men as exploiters and women as victims and to blame women's unhappiness on being chained to child raising and homemaking. Her main criticism is that feminism attacks the family and seeks policies that run counter to natural differences between the sexes. She concludes that the feminist program of action will have largely adverse impacts such as undermining the family, encouraging divorce, and harming children.

YES

Barbara Epstein

The Successes and Failures of Feminism

I have been trying to figure out for several years how feminism should go forward. This seems to me to be the perfect audience to present these ideas to, and get reactions from, so I am going to try out some of my thoughts on you. I want to talk about what the achievements of the women's movement have been and what remains undone—what the strengths were and what some of the weaknesses are.

Leaving aside the antiwar movement of the 1960s, which I think played an important role in bringing the war to an end, the women's movement was the most successful movement of the 1960s and 1970s. The idea that women should enjoy full equality with men was a startlingly radical idea then. That idea has been widely accepted. It seems clear that women in the United States think differently about themselves now than they did 30 years ago because of the women's movement. There have been advances in opportunities for women, especially in the professions, also to, I think, a lesser degree in working-class jobs. Such issues as child care, violence against women, and reproductive rights have been placed on the public agenda as legitimate issues—dramatically different from the political agenda of the 1950s and through the 1960s. There have also been some actual advances in other areas, around such issues as women's health and violence against women, though, given the rightward drift of politics in the United States generally over the last several decades, the record on these concerns has been somewhat mixed. But on a rhetorical level at least, women's equality has been accepted as a goal by mainstream society. The gap between rhetoric and reality remains, but the fact that women's equality has been accepted as a legitimate goal creates an opportunity for changing the reality. It seems to me that probably the most important contribution of the women's movement of the 1960s and 1970s was that it gave women a sense of their collective power. And I think it is useful to look at the difference between second-wave feminism and first-wave feminism in relation to this sort of issue. Women who participated in the women's movement of the late nineteenth and early twentieth centuries also learned this lesson, but the lesson had a narrower impact. First of all, that movement, particularly in the latter part of the nineteenth and early twentieth centuries, was largely confined to middle-class and upper-middle-class, overwhelmingly white women. Working-class women also participated, but they constituted quite a small element of the

From *Journal of Women's History*, 14:2 (2002), pp. 118–125. Copyright © Journal of Women's History. Reprinted by permission.

movement and the memory of that movement was quite effectively obliterated during the 1940s and 1950s, such that feminism in a sense had to be reinvented in the 1960s. The impact of the second wave of feminism has been broader and deeper and the obliteration of that lesson is not going to happen. So that's a very major accomplishment.

The second wave of feminism was successful not only because it led to changes in the lives of huge numbers of women, but also because the movement evolved over time. And I think in many ways, the movement evolved in positive directions. When the women's movement first emerged in the mid 1960s, it was largely confined to university students, other young people of more or less the same class and a slightly older group of women professionals. There were women of color and working-class women in these movements, but they tended to enter the movements through the same routes that everybody else did, namely the fact that they were in college or in the professions despite unusual origins. Their presence in the movement in the late 1960s did not mean that feminism was being adopted within working-class communities or within communities of color. In those years, there was a wide gap between the feminist claim to speak for all women and the reality, which had to do with the specific class and social origins of the women making up the movement. Most of them were from the middle class or the upper middle class, and I suspect actually that most of them were from the suburbs. In the 1970s and into the 1980s, women of color began to articulate their own versions of feminism, and working women, who had not been part of feminism's earlier university student cohort, began to organize around demands of equal treatment in the workplace and other issues working-class women faced. If one were to contrast the women's movement of the 1960s and beyond with the women's movement of the nineteenth and early twentieth centuries, I think one might say that while the first movement narrowed over time, in terms of its constituency and its class perspective, the latter movement—our movement—widened over time. Another way of putting this is to remember that the nineteenth-century women's movement emerged out of an alliance between white women and African Americans in the struggle for abolitionism. But after the Civil War, in the context of a white middle class shifting toward the political right in the late nineteenth century, the women's movement shifted away from earlier alliances. By the early twentieth century, the activists were arguing for women's suffrage on racist and anti-immigrant grounds. So there was a shift away from the alliance with black people specifically, and with a broader, progressive agenda, more generally. I do not think the women's movement of our era has ever been racist in that sense, but I also think it has improved over time. In the mid-1960s, the movement was largely composed of white women who were often blind to the fact that they could not actually speak for all women, but by the 1970s and certainly by the 1980s, there was a much greater awareness of the need to recognize difference within the women's movement, and a much greater awareness of the need to build alliances with other progressive constituencies, particularly groups of color.

Over the 1980s and 1990s, feminism as a perspective or as an identity spread widely and a kind of diffuse feminist consciousness has become a mass phenomenon. There are enormous numbers of women who identify as feminists or who think about women's issues in a different way as a result of feminism. There are also now countless projects, groups, and organizations that are, in one way or another, infused by a feminist perspective. But it is also the case that the main organizations of the women's movement, the most visible organizations such as the National Organization for Women and others, have narrowed in their perspective and are no longer mass-based. They are no longer connected to mass movements, and they have become organizations that are run by staffs rather than on the basis of membership engagement. These organizations have become more cautious in their approach than was the case with even the liberal wing of the women's movement in the late 1960s and 1970s, and they have become more identified with professional, middle-class women and their perspectives. This is not true of the whole women's movement, and actually this conference represents other strands within the movement. There are many organizations that rest on grassroots organizing among women, such as the National Congress of Neighborhood Women. There are many local groups focused on women of color and working women's concerns. There are many such groups in California, including the Mothers of East Los Angeles and the Women's Action for New Directions. While there are many grassroots-based women's organizations with broad social concerns, these do not make up the most visible wing of the women's movement. Despite a great deal of grassroots organizing, there is a way in which the women's movement has lost a sense of coherent direction and urgency. The wind has gone out of the sails. And I would like to address why.

The wind has gone out of the sails, not only of the women's movement but also of the progressive movement as a whole in the United States generally. There are hopeful signs. Among these is the struggle against globalization and corporate control that emerged in Seattle, and in which feminism has been a major component. Though it has not yet congealed into a movement, it holds out the possibility of something new and exciting. There are probably more people involved in grassroots organizing around progressive issues in the United States now than there were in the 1960s and 1970s. But despite these positive signs, the progressive movement as a whole has become institutionalized. It has become an arena in which many of us live and find consensus on many issues. But this progressive sector is not having much effect on the political direction of the country as a whole. Why is that? What has happened?

Part of the answer is that feminism has become more an idea than a movement. And even as a movement, it lacks some of the impetus that it once had. I think that in the case of the women's movement, the gap between the breadth of the original vision and the current state of activism comes from the gap between the feminism's broad and radical vision and the much narrower character of its actual tangible accomplishments—something Linda Gordon alluded to in her contribution to this conference when she said that the inspiration within the feminist movement came very largely from women's liberation in the 1960s and 1970s, but the liberal wing of feminism accomplished the concrete victories. I would go a little bit further and say that not only was it liberal feminists that were able to accomplish those victories, but that their victories were narrower than the intentions of the larger movement. There are many historical cases of popular movements that made broad and radical demands which then became winnowed down such that the final achievement was the least threatening element of the original set of demands. So it is not a big surprise that this should happen to the women's movement as it has happened to other movements, but it is worth looking at the fact that it did happen, and what the consequences have been.

Linda Gordon also mentioned that there were the two wings of the women's movement. People have categorized these differently. On the one hand, there was liberal feminism; on the other hand, there was women's liberation. People also sometimes talked about that wing as comprised of radical feminism and socialist feminism, with radical feminists regarding women's oppression as the root of all oppression, and socialist feminists placing women's oppression within the context of other forms of oppression, particularly race and class. But if one contrasts radical feminism with the liberal wing, you could say that the main goal of the liberal wing of the movement was to win equal access for women to the public sphere on equal terms with men, particularly to the sphere of work. While women's liberation or radical feminism supported that goal, it also aimed for two broader visions. One was that women's liberation insisted that the subordination of women in the public realm could not be separated from the subordination of women in the private realm—both had to be addressed simultaneously. Radical feminists also insisted that it was not possible to win equality for women without winning equality in society across the board. In other words, women could not be equals in a society deeply stratified by race and class.

In the 1960s and 1970s, there was actually a lot of overlap between women's liberation or radical feminism, and liberal feminism. I think the influence tended to go from the radical sphere towards the liberal sphere; that liberal feminists were pushed by radical activists. Many liberals adopted radical ideas. Another element, particularly in the 1970s, was that people from women's liberation participated in an enormous amount of organizing around feminist issues among working-class women. Working-class women's caucuses demanded affirmative action to help themselves and others like them. So in a certain sense, it's not accurate to divide the women's movement up into different spheres because they overlapped, and because the goal of affirmative action—which is usually, and I think appropriately, associated with liberal feminism—also contained a very important working-class element.[1] However, despite the sort of ferment and intersection of liberal and radical demands that took place in the 1960s and 1970s, the fact of the matter is that demands and results are not always the same thing. Affirmative action campaigns in the end were more effective in the professions than elsewhere, and educated and overwhelmingly white women took the greatest advantage of these opportunities. I think that these gains in affirmative action, combined with the growing gap between the lower and higher rungs of the economy (which continued to increase divisions among women despite the gains of affirmative action), pushed the women's movement as a whole away from the radical demands of the 1960s and 1970s.

Meanwhile, radical feminism itself became stalled in the 1970s. It was torn apart by two things. The first was the kind of factionalism, ideological conflicts, and internal struggles that Linda Gordon addressed, which led to the decline of radical feminism and the emergence of a much less political version of feminism that we called cultural feminism by the end of the decade.[2] Such sectarianism is ordinarily associated with movements that are in decline, but feminism at the time was strong and growing. My analysis of why this happened is that the radical wing of the women's movement became a bit crazed in the late 1960s and early 1970s, for the same reason that radicalism in the United States as a whole was becoming a bit crazed (and I speak as someone who was part of this movement). Radicals not only adopted revolution as their aim, but also thought that revolution was within reach. Now there were many versions of revolution—feminist, Marxist/Leninist, Black, and so on. But everybody thought revolution was a good idea, and virtually everybody thought it was around the corner. In my view at least, there was nothing wrong with the commitment to revolution; I wish we had more of it now. But there was something unrealistic about the view that if we did just the right thing, it would happen.

At bottom, the war in Vietnam produced a major crisis in U.S. society. Protest against the war combined with protests against racism and sexism made it seem possible to create a new society. But the fact of the matter was that once the war was over, the major basis for protest evaporated. And those of us who thought that protest would go on to become a revolutionary movement in the United States turned out to be wrong. In fact, what happened was that when the war came to an end, the largest sector of the movement evaporated, and the radical core of the various movements began to find itself isolated. I think it took longer for this to happen in the case of radical feminism than it did in the case of other sectors of the radical movement simply because the mainstream feminist movement was strong and growing, and within the feminist movement, there were many people who were quite open to radical ideas. But nevertheless, the trajectory of American society as a whole was toward the right, and the idea that revolution would happen tomorrow if you did just the right thing was clearly not accurate. By the 1980s, radical feminism too had been pushed to the margins and it was no longer a central current within American politics.

So I am arguing that two things happened more or less simultaneously. First, affirmative action was more or less accomplished, but in a form that was relatively conservative. At the same time, the radical sector of the movement more or less evaporated—or more accurately, it moved into academia. While most radicals did not become academics, enough people did that there was a sort of a critical mass of radicals in academia. Because it was a safe space for radicals and because of access to publishing and whatnot, the university became one of the spaces where feminism was defined. At the same time, academic feminism was gradually losing its ties to activism outside the academy.

This did not happen to all academics, of course, and this conference is in a certain sense about the people who took a different path. I am very pleased that this conference and the collections have highlighted the work of Frances Fox Piven, for example, who is a model in continuing to construct that bridge between activism and academia. Academic feminism, by and large, took a different path.

I suggested earlier that the politics and constituency of first-wave feminism narrowed and that was not the case with our feminist movement. But I think I was careful to say that there were also some problems. Even though I think our movement has not narrowed, particularly in relation to race, I think there is another respect in which the current women's movement has rather unconsciously narrowed its politics, which mirrors what happened in the nineteenth century. As the women's movement aged, so to speak, it became vulnerable to absorbing trends within its own class. And I think that is what has happened to the most visible and prominent aspects of our women's movement.

The women's movement of the 1960s and 1970s, especially the radical core of that movement, demanded not only equality for women, but also equality across the board. Feminists sought an egalitarian society governed by humane values. But since the early 1970s, economic inequalities have steadily widened in the United States. Most people now work longer hours at less secure jobs. Often these jobs are associated with increasing stress. Many people have spoken of work having become a religion in the United States. I think it might be more accurate to say that for many people, work has become the only meaningful source of identity. In a broader sense, the United States is becoming an increasingly individualistic, cold, and selfish society. It seems to me that we now live in a society in which people's concern for other people is becoming a kind of quaint, archaic value. People seem to assume that you should really be mostly concerned with yourself and maybe for other members of your nuclear family, if you happen to have one, but beyond that, it is a sort of silliness to be concerned with anybody else. Many progressives seem to have absorbed these ideas too. And I think the ways we have absorbed them has been by throwing ourselves into work and adopting or absorbing the view into the way we value ourselves. I know that this is true of me. I have the sense that it is also true of other people in our general community. I cannot really speak for the United States as a whole, but I am struck, even in visiting other countries, with the reigning individualism in the United States, which seems to be much further advanced than it is elsewhere in the world—even though I also think that individualism is a kind of global tendency.

Feminism is not marking a noticeable challenge to this cultural shift. In fact, I think that the version of feminism that was formed through the demand for women's equality in the workplace, and then, in practice, became focused around the success of the demand for affirmative action for professional women, has blindly absorbed many of the dominant cultural values of the middle class. In the 1970s, many feminists thought that if only we could get enough women into academic jobs, academia would change. It would become a less elitist, more humane place, concerned with social good. Well, a fair number of women are in the academy and I do not think that the academy has changed in those directions. Instead, I think the academy has gone in the opposite direction. This is not women's fault; it is because we are caught up in a wildly accelerating global version of capitalism that is drawing everything, including the universities, into its vortex and bringing market values to every area of life. Simply having more women in the academy does nothing to oppose this. As more people are in institutions that are adopting greater market values, the greater the pressures are for those people to adopt those values. We need a movement that explicitly and overtly criticizes this shift and the values associated with it.

I am suggesting here—and this is all completely impressionistic—that although the values of individualism, market values, and so forth, have taken on increased importance throughout the United States as a whole, there is a way in which the professional middle class has been the carrier of these values. We live in a society that is rapidly dividing between those who make it to the top and those who fall to the bottom, and generally speaking, people in the professional middle class would much rather rise than fall. There is a kind of scramble going on, and we are in the sector of society that is engaged in that scramble rather than critical of it. The media image of feminists as career-ists was not entirely invented by a hostile press but feminists are no more careerists than other members of the same class. If this is true, then we are admitting that we have lost a grip on the social vision that feminism originally embraced. So I am calling for a return to a sort of revised version of radical feminism. It seems to me that we have to place feminism within the demand for an egalitarian society and a demand for a society that respects human con-nection and respects communities and promotes them rather than destroying them. And I do think we can look back to the legacy of women's liberation for at least some very good hints about how to do this.

Notes

1. I learned about this from Nancy Maclean, whose very important article on the use of affirmative action by working-class women appeared in a recent issue of *Feminist Studies*.

2. These developments are wonderfully described by Alice Echols in her book *Daring to Be Bad: Radical Feminism in America, 1967–1975*, and also by Ruth Rosen in her recent book *The World Split Open: How the Modern Women's Movement Changed America*. What is striking about both these books is that they are written from a perspective which is deeply feminist and deeply respectful of the women's movement, but also very clear-eyed about its problems.

Women Who Make the World Worse

How Radical Feminists Have Weakened the Family

The traditional family boosts the health, happiness, and wealth of husbands, wives, and children and raises the blood pressure of a certain kind of woman. Betty Friedan's 1963 *The Feminine Mystique* is typically included on lists of the one hundred most influential books of the last century. In a chapter entitled "The Comfortable Concentration Camp," she likened the passivity and hopelessness of American POWs in Korea to American women trapped at home with children in the suburbs. She later wrote, "For fear of being alone, I almost lost my own self-respect trying to hold on to a marriage that was based no longer on love but on dependent hate. It was easier for me to start the women's movement which was needed to change society than to change my own personal life."

Friedan got a divorce in 1969, but unfortunately not before she expounded on the merits of Marxist economics, persuaded far too many women that a selfless devotion to their families was a recipe for misery, helped to create the National Organization for Women (NOW), and destructively politicized relations between the sexes. Over the next decades, Friedan's fans moved beyond her criticisms of mothers at home and launched a hostile assault on marriage and family life.

The radical demand for androgyny and personal autonomy is irreconcilable with the need for different sex roles and mutual self-sacrifice between parents raising their offspring. Influential feminists see two major problems with the family that inhibit women's equality—husbands and fathers. Their advocacy and propaganda have eroded support for the family as an indispensable institution for both individuals and society.

Marriage Under Assault

In 1969, Marlene Dixon, a sociology professor at the University of Chicago, wrote, "The institution of marriage is the chief vehicle for the perpetuation of the oppression of women; it is through the role of wife that the subjugation of

From *Women Who Make the World Worse* by Kate O'Beirne (Sentinel, 2006). Copyright © 2006 by Kate O'Beirne. Reprinted by permission of Penguin Group USA.

women is maintained. In a very real way the role of wife has been the genesis of women's rebellion throughout history."

That same year, Kate Millett's *Sexual Politics* was published. What began as a thesis for the Columbia University doctoral candidate became a celebrated call for the end of a patriarchal Institution that treated women like chattel. In 1970, Robin Morgan, a founder of *Ms.* magazine, was calling marriage "a slavery-like practice," and arguing, "We can't destroy the inequities between men and women until we destroy marriage." The following year, Australian feminist Germaine Greer's *The Female Eunuch* argued that married women had to save themselves by fleeing from their marriages in favor of "rambling organic structures."

By 1972, the angry screeds against marriage were being dressed up with academic adornments. In her influential book *The Future of Marriage*, Pennsylvania State University sociologist Jessie Bernard claimed that the "destructive nature" of marriage harmed women's mental and emotional health. In short, according to Bernard, "Being a housewife makes women sick." The fact that married women regularly reported that they were happier than unmarried women was dismissed as a symptom of this marital illness. "To be happy in a relationship which imposes so many impediments on her, as traditional marriage does, women must be slightly mentally ill." It was their oppression speaking when wives reported satisfaction with their lives. "Women accustomed to expressing themselves freely could not be happy in such a relationship."

Although the late Professor Bernard's pronouncements were those of a left-wing ideologue with a radical agenda, she was considered one of the top women sociologists in the world, and according to *The Boston Globe*, her twenty-three books established her as "the preeminent scholar of the women's movement." She held visiting professorships at Princeton and at the University of California. In *The Future of Motherhood* she argued that being a mother was also hazardous to women's health. She saw the desire for children as a sexist social construction and believed that many women preferred celibacy to "the degradation of most male-female sexual relationships." Professor Bernard sounded a warning about what truly liberated women could expect: "Men will resist and punish them; unliberated women, brainwashed not only to accept their slavery in marriage but also to love it, will resist them." The Center for Women's Policy Studies established a Jessie Bernard Wise Women award to recognize similar worthy insights.

Many establishment figures share Bernard's views. Laura Singer, who was president of the American Association for Marriage and Family Therapy in the 1970s, has explained, "I wouldn't say that marriage and self-actualization are *necessarily* mutually exclusive, but they are difficult to achieve together."

If these attacks on marriage strike you as extreme, you have some surprising company. Twenty years after she helped launch the modern women's movement, even Betty Friedan was criticizing her feminist sisters for their hostility to family life. In her 1981 book *The Second Stage*, she wrote: "The women's movement is being blamed, above all, for the destruction of the family." She cited the increase in divorces, in single-parent households, and in the number of women living alone and asked, "Can we keep on shrugging all this off as enemy propaganda—'their problem, not ours'? I think we must at least admit and begin openly to discuss feminist denial of the importance of family, of women's own needs to give and get love and nurture, tender loving care."

This time Betty Friedan's appeals fell on deaf feminist ears. The scholarship and sentiment that sounded dire warnings about marriage's harmful effects on women's well-being and ambitions had found an enthusiastic audience in women's studies programs and was popularized by journalists like Barbara Ehrenreich, a former columnist for *Time* magazine.

Writing from that powerful perch, Ehrenreich repeatedly denigrated marriage and family life. She advocated that the government concentrate on promoting "good divorces" rather than attempt to strengthen marriages and argued that the only problem with single-parent households was the lack of sufficient government support. She used the Menendez brothers and O.J. Simpson cases as an opportunity to share her opinion about the malevolent forces afoot in American families. The murders should prompt us to think "that the family may not be the ideal and perfect living arrangement after all—that it can be a nest of pathology and a cradle of gruesome violence." She asserted that "millions flock to therapy groups" and "we are all, it is often said, 'in recovery.' And from what? Our families, in most cases." She cited the "long and honorable tradition of 'anti-family' thought" and quoted Edmund Leach, the renowned British anthropologist, stating that "far from being the basis of a good society, the family, with its narrow privacy and tawdry secrets, is the source of all discontents."

Marlo Thomas and her pals, including Lily Tomlin, Bea Arthur, and Whoopi Goldberg, literally sang the praises of never-formed or broken families. Thomas's earlier *Free to Be . . . You and Me* attempted to overcome nasty sex stereotypes and create a more welcoming world for boys who played with dolls. In her *Free to Be . . . a Family,* any arrangement at all was promoted as just fine for raising children. The book and album wanted to teach children that "if the people whom you live with are happy to see your face, that's a family." The stories, songs and poems were "really about the family as it exists today, not the family as a storybook idea."

During the 2004 campaign, Teresa Heinz Kerry reflected a casual contempt for the role of wife and mother when she proclaimed that Laura Bush hadn't worked at a "real job . . . since she's been grown up." Laura Bush worked as a teacher and librarian for ten years, before giving up her career in education to raise her twin daughters. Most people, who haven't inherited a condiments empire and the resources to allow them to keep busy handing out fat foundation grants, think being a wife and mother is a "real job" for a "grown-up."

Before long, the antipathy to marriage infected the academy and was reflected in social science textbooks. When a nonpartisan group studied twenty textbooks used in eight thousand college courses in the mid-nineties, they found, "These books repeatedly suggest that marriage is more a problem than a solution. The potential costs of marriage to adults, particularly women, often receive exaggerated treatment, while the benefits of marriage, both to individuals and society, are frequently downplayed or ignored."

In *Changing Families*, Judy Root Aulette, a sociology professor at the University of North Carolina at Charlotte, didn't mention a single beneficial effect of marriage in the three chapters she devoted to the subject (one of which was titled "Battering and Marital Rape"). She did find room to approvingly cite Friedrich Engels stating that marriage was "created for a particular purpose: to control women and children."

While Professor Aulette had a lot to learn about the institution of marriage, she was well schooled in the politics of phony grievances. She accused the report's author of trying "to get rid of my voice, and my right to be in a classroom and present a feminist point of view."

In her textbook, Marine Baca Zinn proved herself worthy of a Jessie Bernard Wise Women award when she wrote, "If marriage is so difficult for wives, why do the majority surveyed judge themselves as happy? . . . [The reason] is that happiness is interpreted by wives in terms of conformity. Since they are conforming to society's expectations, this must be happiness."

The study's author, Professor Norval Glenn of the University of Texas, explained that the textbooks studied represented "the distilled essence of the current conventional wisdom" and were used to train the next generation of counselors, social workers, therapists, and teachers. He illustrated the conventional wisdom by contrasting the number of pages in each book focusing on the benefits of marriage for adults—less than one—with the pages per book devoted to domestic violence—twelve."

Marriage Benefits Men and Women

Professor Linda Waite of the University of Chicago filled a well-researched book with the good news about marriage. In *The Case for Marriage: Why Married People Are Happier, Healthier, and Better Off Financially*, Waite, a self-described liberal Democrat, and her conservative co-author, Maggie Gallagher, detailed the research findings that thoroughly refute Jessie Bernard and her acolytes' case against marriage. Linda Waite saw the notion that marriage was a much better deal for men than women as "the most powerful and persuasive" of the modern myths about marriage. She thought it was important for young women to be well-informed before they make their choices. "If we pretend that women are not advantaged by being married, we are doing them a great disservice."

Among Waite and Gallagher's findings: Because wives influence husbands to take better care of themselves, men do get more health benefits from marriage than women, but both married men and women express "very high and very similar levels of satisfaction with their marriages" and are similarly committed to their spouses. Women gain more financially from marriage than men do, and while both sexes are winners in sexual satisfaction, women gain even more owing to the sense of commitment that improves their sex life. And, when a wide range of disorders is considered, both sexes enjoy a boost in mental health. In fact, married women are generally less depressed than *Sex and the City*'s Carrie Bradshaw and her single sisters.

A well-respected study found that similar percentages of married women and men (41 percent and 38 percent) report they are "very happy," rates that are far higher than for those who have never married or are divorced. Social psychologist David G. Myers, author of *The Pursuit of Happiness*, strongly endorses Waite and Gallagher's conclusions. "The idea that women are happier if they are unmarried and men happier if they are married is blatantly untrue. The evidence is mountainous in the other direction."

Unlike other liberal women engaged in research on family issues, Dr. Waite had no preconceived notions or ideological axes to grind when she began to look at the data on marital status and mortality ten years ago. She was aware of other researchers looking at earnings data and health issues, but no one had put together the big picture. Waite recognized, "There's a general pattern here that nobody's noticed. All of the big things in life—good outcomes for children, health, long life—depend on marriage." This insight became the subject of a speech she delivered to the Population Association of America as its president in 1995.

Divorce Hurts

Professor Waite and her colleagues have more recently published a study on divorce that showed that unhappily married people were no happier after their marriages ended. They analyzed data from a national survey on families and households and found, "When the adults who said they were unhappily married in the late 1980s were interviewed again five years later, those who had divorced were on average still unhappy or even less happy, while those who stayed in their marriages on average had moved past the bad times and were at a happier stage."

Waite, who has been married for over thirty years, has a married daughter and a daughter with cerebral palsy who lives at home. She was married as an undergraduate and divorced from her first husband after four years with no children. She explains that her case against divorce is less applicable to the kind of short, early union she had. "It's very different. You're not leaving somebody who's financially dependent, you haven't built years of friendships, you don't have kids, you're not as much a working single unit as people who are married for a long time."

Waite explains that once children are present, the case against divorce becomes stronger. Professor Waite and Maggie Gallagher looked at the effect of divorce on children in their book and concluded that children were usually not better off when their parents split up. They pointed out that divorce might end marital conflict for parents, but it doesn't end "what really bothers kids: parental conflict." Their research indicates, "Children of divorce also have less money, live in poorer neighborhoods, go to poorer schools, and do worse in school than children of married parents—even if those marriages have a high degree of conflict."

In their book *Generation at Risk*, two liberal social scientists estimated that only about a third of divorces with children involved are so troubled that children are likely to benefit from the break-up. The remaining 70 percent of divorces involve low-conflict marriages where children are less harmed than they would be if their parents separated.

Fractured Families and Disposable Dads

In the past, the majority of Americans believed that unhappily married couples should stay together for the sake of their children. Now, only 15 percent agree that "when there are children in the family, parents should stay together even if they don't get along." When the traditional virtues of self-sacrifice and duty lose in a conflict with the feminist doctrine of self-fulfillment and personal autonomy, children pay a very steep price.

In an ominous sign that the well-being of children is unlikely to take precedence over the desires of adults any time soon, among young people there is little appreciation for the benefits of marriage and widespread support for "alternative lifestyles" as perfectly suitable for raising children. A national survey of high school seniors found that although a large majority of these teenagers expect to marry, less than a third of girls and only slightly more than a third of boys believe "that most people will have fuller and happier lives if they choose legal marriage rather than staying single or just living with someone." More than half of both boys and girls think out-of-wedlock childbearing is a "worthwhile lifestyle."

In 1988, among never-married people between the ages of eighteen and thirty-four, 64 percent of males and 56 percent of females thought "those who want children should get married." In 2002, only 51 percent of males and 42 percent of females in this age group thought having children and being married shouldn't be separate pursuits.

While the pathetic plight of wives and mothers was being peddled by women like Bernard, Aulette, and Zinn, others were making the case that dads are dispensable.

Male lions roar to protect their young from threatening predators, penguin pops balance fragile eggs on their feet in frigid temperatures, while adult male elephants temper the delinquent behavior of the young bulls. When the National Fatherhood Initiative used these arresting thirty-second images from the animal kingdom to depict the importance of fathers in their "Nature of Fatherhood" ad campaign, they drove some feminists wild. NOW raised an alarm about the "dangerous policy" of paternal responsibility being promoted by the initiative, which hoped to encourage fathers to commit to marriage and parenting.

An article that argued "neither mothers nor fathers are unique or essential" was promoted to bolster the case that "NOW Knows Best." In "Deconstructing the Essential Father," published in the influential *American Psychologist* in 1999, the authors maintained that children are perfectly fine as long as they have "parenting figures" of either sex, who need not be biologically related. Predictably, the authors favored policies that support the legitimacy of "diverse family structures" rather than "privileging the two-parent, heterosexual, married family." Fatherhood is a retrograde gender role and therefore verboten.

The academics did not just dismiss the unique contributions of fathers as unimportant. It was argued that a father's presence in the home extracts an overlooked cost because "some fathers' consumption of family resources in terms of gambling, purchasing alcohol, cigarettes, or other nonessential commodities, actually increases women's workload and stress level." So, message to moms: Throw the bums out.

Professor Louise B. Silverstein, a Yeshiva University psychology professor and family therapist, co-authored the study that sought "to create an ideology that defines the father-child bond as independent of the father-mother relationship." Professor Silverstein is a past president of the American Psychological Association's Division of Family Psychology and chairman (a title that could put her in therapy) of the Feminist Family Therapy Task Force within the APA Division of the Psychology of Women. Her 1999 article making the case for throwaway dads won the Association for Women in Psychology's Distinguished Publication Award.

From the indispensable Maggie Gallagher it won condemnation. Gallagher graduated from Yale University in 1982. Married with two sons, this Portland, Oregon, native lives in New York and is a syndicated columnist and president of the Institute for Marriage and Public Policy. The author of three books, she has been an editor of *National Review* and a senior editor of the Manhattan Institute's *City Journal*. George Gilder called her first book, *Enemies of Eros: How the Sexual Revolution Is Killing Family, Marriage, and Sex, and What We Can Do About It*, published in 1989, "the best book ever written on men, women and marriage."

Maggie Gallagher has mastered the social science research on marriage, the family, and child well-being to become a leading authority on the most personal public-policy questions we face. She devotes her formidable skills to debunking clichés and conventional wisdom about love, marriage, and children and has the fortitude to challenge a culture more interested in self-gratification to confront the consequences of our failure to keep our commitments.

After having some fun with Dr. Silverstein's conclusion that "both men and women have the same biological potential for nurturing" based on her examination of the behavior of marmoset fathers, Gallagher deconstructs Silverstein's deconstruction handiwork. "Our new desire to strengthen marriage is in their view just a scary attempt to reassert 'the cultural hegemony of traditional values, such as heterocentrism, Judeo-Christian marriage, and male power and privilege.' It leads to horrible, unrealistic policies—like giving job help to low-income married fathers (and not just welfare mothers), or a more marriage-friendly tax code. Instead, these hard-headed professors urge more practical solutions, like reconstructing traditional masculine ideology so men care for infants as much as women."

Maggie Gallagher incisively confronts the fundamental questions that Silverstein ignores. "Under what conditions are children likely to fare best? And, are adults obligated to provide, if they can, the best situation for their kids?" Answers: Living with their married biological parents, and Yes.

Louise Silverstein is the glorified guru of gender warriors, but Cornell University professor Urie Bronfenbrenner, who was widely regarded as one of the world's leading scholars in developmental psychology, child-rearing, and human ecology—the interdisciplinary field he created—strongly disagreed with her Dispensable Dad thesis. "Controlling for factors such as low income, children growing up in father-absent households are at a greater risk for experiencing a variety of behavioral and educational problems, including extremes of hyperactivity and withdrawal; lack of attentiveness in the classroom; difficulty in deferring gratification; impaired academic achievement; school misbehavior; absenteeism; dropping out; involvement in socially alienated peer groups; and the so-called 'teen-age syndrome' of behaviors that tend to hang together—smoking, drinking, early and frequent sexual experience, and in the more extreme cases, drugs, suicide, vandalism, violence and criminal acts."

In his defense of responsible fatherhood, Karl Zinsmeister counters Marlo Thomas's dismissal of the traditional family as a "storybook idea" by reminding us of its indispensability for men, women, and children. "It's when a culture stops upholding the paternal rituals, rules, and rewards that fathering withers. . . . Some people have actually convinced themselves families can do fine without fathers. They're wrong. Wherever men are not lured or corralled into concerning themselves with their children and mates, decent human society fades . . . the magic ingredients needed to tie men to their children are the ancient ones: Sexual restraint and enduring marriage." When men are committed to protecting and providing for their families, wives and children benefit and so too do husbands.

Studies show that men become more economically productive after they marry, with married men earning between 10 and 40 percent more than single men with similar education and job experience. Marriage also increases median family income, which more than doubled between 1947 and 1977. Over the past twenty years, the growth in median family income has slowed, increasing by just 9.6 percent, in large part because married couples, who do better economically, make up a decreasing proportion of all families.

In Britain, 49 percent of all births are illegitimate. In a sign that the British public has had its fill with the social and financial costs of unwed child-bearing, three unmarried sisters and their babies recently made front-page news. MUM AT 12, MUM AT 16, MUM AT 14, the headlines blared. The father of the sixteen-year-old's baby is a thirty-eight-year-old man in a "long-term relationship" with her; he lives with his parents. Their divorced mother had been married twice, but never to the fathers of her daughters. She became a grandmother three times in a year.

While most of the commentary criticized the intergenerational illegitimacy and complained that taxpayers had to pick up the considerable tab, Germaine Greer surfaced to celebrate the self-actualization of young girls doing their own thing. "Social historians will tell you that illegitimacy is highly hereditary. There have always been women like Yeats' Crazy Jane whose gardens grow 'nothing but babies and washing.' They live in an alternative society that is matrilineal, matrifocal, and matrilocal, a society that the patriarchy has always feared and hated." The "alternative society" Greer celebrates is on the brink of representing a majority of British births.

In 1960, only 9 percent of all children lived in single-parent households. Presently in the United States, almost one-third of children are born to single mothers. A large number of children will see their parents divorced before their eighteenth birthday. Two-thirds of black children are born out of wedlock. Over half of American children will spend all or part of their childhood without their father in the home.

According to my former colleague, the Heritage Foundation's poverty guru Robert Rector, "The collapse of marriage is the principal cause of child poverty and a host of other social ills. A child raised by a never-married mother is seven times more likely to live in poverty than a child raised by his biological parents in an intact marriage." Nearly two-thirds of poor children live in single-parent homes, and an additional 1.3 million children are born out of wedlock every year. We have never experienced so many children growing up without knowing what it means to live with the daily support and attention of their fathers.

Half of children living without their fathers have never been in their father's home, and one study found that only 27 percent of children over age four saw their father at least once a week, while 31 percent had no contact at all in the previous year.

In *The Abolition of Marriage*, Maggie Gallagher reminds us, "When we tell our girls that becoming a single mother—through divorce or failure to marry—is a perfectly acceptable lifestyle choice, we forget that our boys are listening too. And this is what they hear: Men aren't necessary. Women can do it alone. Women and children are usually better off without men. Breadwinning oppresses women and children. Marriage and breadwinning can be hard. Why do it, if you are only oppressing the ones you love?"

Barbara Dafoe Whitehead is co-director of the National Marriage Project at Rutgers University. She famously concluded in *Atlantic Monthly* article that "Dan Quayle Was Right" following the feminist fits over the vice president's *Murphy Brown* comments. Dr. Whitehead recently reported, "According to some researchers, growing up with both married parents in a low-conflict marriage is so important to child well-being that it is replacing race, class, and neighborhood as the greatest source of difference in child outcomes."

According to the National Marriage Project, men today are increasingly staying single longer, fathering more illegitimate children, cohabiting rather than marrying, and divorcing in large numbers. In 1970, only 7 percent of men between the ages thirty-five and forty-four had never married, compared with 18 percent today.

The National Fatherhood Initiative that NOW's feminists rail against as a patriarchal plot offers some inescapable "Father Facts." The rate of child abuse in single-parent households is nearly twice the rate of child abuse in two-parent families. Even after controlling for factors like family background and neighborhood variables, boys who grew up outside of intact marriages were, on average, more than twice as likely to end up in jail as other boys, and twice as likely to use illegal drugs.

Intact families are a far more effective "program" than are most government schemes to reduce poverty, child abuse, crime, and drug abuse, or to boost educational outcomes.

Although costly to men, women, children, and taxpayers, opposition to the traditional family is growing. The influential American Law Institute (ALI) recently released a report arguing that family law should be reformed so that marriage and cohabitation are treated equally and that marriage should be redefined as a gender-neutral arrangement in order to accommodate same-sex couples. These lawyers want to wipe out biology as a basis for parenthood in order to ensure "family diversity."

Professor Katharine Bartlett, a feminist scholar and dean of Duke University's law school, is one of the principal authors of the ALI report. She explains that her passion is "the value I place on family diversity and on the freedom of individuals to choose from a variety of family forms. This same value leads me to be generally opposed to efforts to standardize families into a certain type of nuclear family because a majority may believe this is the best kind of family or because it is the most deeply rooted ideologically in our traditions." Ignoring the overwhelming evidence about the benefits to family members and society from traditional marriage, Professor Bartlett attributes its support to either ignorant belief or blind ideology, befitting her status as a celebrated feminist scholar.

POSTSCRIPT

Has Feminism Benefited American Society?

The most convincing arguments of the antifeminists are made against extremist positions, which "reasonable feminists" might not hold. For example, one can be a feminist and still love a husband, desire to mother children, and even leave the labor force in order to raise them. Nonetheless, there are legitimate issues in the debate about feminism. Does their demand for truly equal opportunity and affirmative action require the premise that men and women are essentially the same? Does feminist activism cultivate an antipathy to men as their oppressors? Has the feminist program adversely affected the family and gender relations? Do feminists deny that nondiscriminatory bases exist for many inequalities between men and women?

Over the past 40 years, there has been a deluge of books, articles, and periodicals devoted to expounding feminist positions. Among the earliest feminist publications was Betty Friedan's book *The Feminine Mystique* (W. W. Norton, 1963). Friedan later wrote *The Second Stage* (Summit Books, 1981), which was less antagonistic to men and more accepting of motherhood and traditional women's roles. In her latest book, *Life So Far* (Simon & Schuster, 2000), she presents her memoirs, which largely cover the women's movement that she helped start. Important statements by other past feminist leaders are Gloria Steinem, *Outrageous Acts and Everyday Rebellions*, 2nd ed. (Henry Holt, 1995) and "Revving Up for the Next 25 Years," *Ms* (September/October, 1997); Patricia Ireland, *What Women Want* (Penguin, 1996); and Susan Brownmiller, *In Our Time: Memoir of a Revolution* (Dial Press, 1999). For an attack on the attackers and misrepresenters of the women's movement, see Susan Faludi's *Backlash: The Undeclared War on American Women* (Crown Publishers, 1991). For histories of the women's movement see Kathleen C. Berkeley, *The Women's Movement in America* (Greenwood Press, 1999); Dorothy Sue Cobble, *The Other Women's Movement: Workplace Justice and Social Rights in Modern America* (Princeton University Press, 2004); Barbara J. Love (ed.), *Feminists Who Changed America, 1963–1975* (University of Illinois Press, 2006); and Judith M. Bennett, *History Matters: Patriarchy and the Challenge of Feminism* (University of Pennsylvania Press, 2006). For discussions of the current state of feminism see Kristin Rowe-Finkbeiner, *The F-Word: Feminism in Jeopardy: Women, Politics, and the Future* (Seal Press, 2004); Judith Lorber, *Breaking the Bowls: Degendering and Feminist Change* (W. W. Norton, 2005); Maureen Dowd, *Are Men Necessary?* (G. P. Putnam's Sons, 2005); Phyllis Chesler, *The Death of Feminism: What's Next in the Struggle for Women's Freedom* (Palgrave Macmillan, 2005); Naomi Zack, *Inclusive Feminism: A Third Wave Theory of Women's Commonality* (Rowman & Littlefield, 2005); Stacy Gillis, Gillian Howie, and Rebbeca Munford (eds.), *Third Wave Feminism*

(Palgrave Macmillan, 2004). A superb analysis of the full range of gender issues is found in *Paradoxes of Gender* by Judith Lorber (Yale University Press, 1994). For radical feminist views, see Catharine A. MacKinnon's *Feminism Unmodified* (Harvard University Press, 1987); Marilyn French's *Beyond Power* (Summit Books, 1985); and Margaret Randall's *Gathering Rage: The Failure of Twentieth-Century Revolutions to Develop a Feminist Agenda* (Monthly Review Press, 1992). For a radical feminist analysis of the oppression of women, see Marilyn French, *The War Against Women* (Summit Books, 1992). For an insightful analysis of how ideology has been used by men to mute the rebellion of women against exploitative and subordinate relations, see Mary R. Jackman, *The Velvet Glove: Paternalism and Conflict in Gender, Class, and Race Relations* (University of California Press, 1994). A rich analysis of gender inequality and its social and psychological roots is provided by Sandra Lipsitz Bem in *The Lenses of Gender: Transforming the Debate on Sexual Inequality* (Yale University Press, 1994). For discussions of feminism around the world, see Myra Marx Ferree and Aili Marl Tripp, eds., *Global Feminism: Transnational Women's Activism, Organizing, and Human Rights* (New York University Press, 2006); Mary E. Hawkesworth, *Globalization and Feminist Activism* (Rowan & Littlefield, 2006); Valentine M. Moghadam, *Globalizing Women: Transnational Feminist Network* (Johns Hopkins University Press, 2005); Shamillah Wilson, Anasuya Sengupta, and Kristy Evans, eds., *Defending Our Dreams: Global Feminist Voices for a New Generation* (Zed Books, 2005); Peggy Antrobus, *The Global Women's Movement* (Zed, 2004); Trudie M. Eklund, *Sisters around the World: The Global Struggle for Female Equality* (Hamilton Books, 2004). For a discussion of women's rights see Catharine A. MacKinnon, *Are Women Human?* (Belknap Press, 2006) and *Women's Lives, Men's Laws* (Belknap Press); and Linda M. G. Zerilli, *Feminism and the Abyss of Freedom* (University of Chicago Press, 2005).

Antifeminist works are rarer. One antifeminist, Nicholas Davidson, charges that it is "extremely difficult to find a publisher for a work critical of feminism." See Davidson's *The Failure of Feminism* (Prometheus Books, 1988). Other antifeminist arguments may be found in Elizabeth Powers' "A Farewell to Feminism," *Commentary* (January 1997); Ellen R. Klein, *Feminism under Fire* (Prometheus, 1996), and *Undressing Feminism: A Philosophical Exposé* (Paragon House, 2002); Ariel Levy, *Female Chauvinist Pigs: Women and the Rise of Raunch Culture* (Free Press, 2005); and Neil Boyd, *Big Sister: How Extreme Feminism Has Betrayed the Fight for Sexual Equality* (Greystone Press, 2004). Some, like Christine Hoff Sommers, in *Who Stole Feminism: How Women Have Betrayed Women* (Simon & Schuster, 1994), advocate equity (liberal) feminism while criticizing feminist extremists and sloppy research.

For a defense of men against the accusations of feminists, see Warren Farrell, *The Myth of Male Power* (Simon & Schuster, 1993), and David Thomas, *Not Guilty: The Case in Defense of Men* (William Morrow, 1993). For a pro-feminist male viewpoint, see Steven P. Schact and Doris W. Ewing, *Feminism with Men: Bridging the Gender Gap* (Rowan & Littlefield, 2004).

ISSUE 8

Has Affirmative Action Outlived Its Usefulness?

YES: Curtis Crawford, from "Racial Preference versus Nondiscrimination," *Society* (March/April 2004)

NO: Lawrence D. Bobo, from "Inequalities that Endure?" in Maria Krysan and Amanda E. Lewis, eds., *The Changing Terrain of Race and Ethnicity* (Russell Sage Foundation, 2004)

ISSUE SUMMARY

YES: Curtis Crawford, editor of the Web site http://www.Debating RacialPreference.org, explores all possible options for bettering the situation of disadvantaged minorities in a truly just manner. He argues that the right of everyone, including white males, to nondiscrimination is clearly superior to the right of minorities to affirmative action.

NO: Sociologist Lawrence D. Bobo demonstrates that racial prejudice still exists even though it has become a more subtle type of racism, which he calls laissez-faire racism. Though it is harder to identify, it has significant effects that Bobo illustrates. In fact, it plays a big role in current politics.

In America, equality is a principle as basic as liberty. "All men are created equal" is perhaps the most-well known phrase in the Declaration of Independence. More than half a century after the signing of the Declaration, the French social philosopher Alexis de Tocqueville examined democracy in America and concluded that its most essential ingredient was the equality of condition. Today we know that the "equality of condition" that Tocqueville perceived did not exist for women, blacks, Native Americans, and other racial minorities, nor for other disadvantaged social classes. Nevertheless, the ideal persisted.

When slavery was abolished after the Civil War, the Constitution's newly ratified Fourteenth Amendment proclaimed, "No State shall . . . deny to any person within its jurisdiction the equal protection of the laws." Equality has been a long time coming. For nearly a century after the abolition of slavery, American blacks were denied equal protection by law in some states and by social practice nearly everywhere. One-third of the states either permitted or forced schools to become racially segregated, and segregation was achieved elsewhere through housing policy and social behavior. In 1954, the Supreme Court reversed a 58-year-old standard that had found "separate but equal" schools compatible with equal protection of the law. A unanimous decision in *Brown v. Board of Education* held that separate is *not* equal for the members of the discriminated-against group when the segregation "generates a feeling of inferiority as to their status in the community that may affect their hearts and minds in a way unlikely ever to be undone." The 1954 ruling on public elementary education has been extended to other areas of both governmental and private conduct, including housing and employment.

Even if judicial decisions and congressional statutes could end all segregation and racial discrimination, would this achieve equality—or simply perpetuate the status quo? Consider that the unemployment rate for blacks today is much higher than that of whites. Disproportionately higher numbers of blacks experience poverty, brutality, broken homes, physical and mental illness, and early deaths, while disproportionately lower numbers of them reach positions of affluence and prestige. It seems possible that much of this inequality has resulted from 300 years of slavery and segregation. Is termination of this ill treatment enough to end the injustices? No, say the proponents of affirmative action.

Affirmative action—the effort to improve the educational and employment opportunities for minorities—has had an uneven history in U.S. federal courts. In *Regents of the University of California v. Allan Bakke* (1978), which marked the first time the Supreme Court dealt directly with the merits of affirmative action, a 5-4 majority ruled that a white applicant to a medical school had been wrongly excluded in favor of a less qualified black applicant due to the school's affirmative action policy. Yet the majority also agreed that "race-conscious" policies may be used in admitting candidates—as long as they do not amount to fixed quotas. The ambivalence of *Bakke* has run through the Court's treatment of the issue since 1978. In 2003, the Supreme Court found the University of Michigan's admissions policy discriminatory but the University of Michigan Law School's admissions policy nondiscriminatory. As a result, race can still be used as one factor among many to create a diverse student body, but the weight of that factor must be far less than some universities had been using.

In the following selections, Curtis Crawford and Lawrence D. Bobo debate the merits of affirmative action. Crawford carefully lays out the options and arguments and balances the various rights and values involved. In the end, he argues, we must hold fast to the principle that the right to not be discriminated against supercedes all other values in this case and will produce the best results. Bobo counters that discrimination against minorities still exists, and affirmative actions—if not egregious—are still needed to bring about greater justice in society.

YES

Curtis Crawford

Racial Preference versus Nondiscrimination

After a 25-year silence on the subject, the Supreme Court has pronounced on the constitutionality of race-based affirmative action in university admissions. Those who had hoped that the issues would be wisely clarified and weighed must have been greatly disappointed. The two cases accepted for review, *Grutter v. Bollinger* and *Gratz v. Bollinger,* provided valuable information on how universities actually implement preferential admissions. . . .

The litigation of these two cases revealed large racial inequalities in the treatment of applicants with similar academic credentials. For example, at the trial in federal district court, the Michigan Law School admission grid for 1995 (the year Ms. Grutter was rejected) was offered in evidence. For all applicants, identified by race but not by name, the grid included data on their Undergraduate Grade Point Average (UGPA), Law School Aptitude Test score (LSAT), and admission or rejection. Each cell of the grid combined a small range of grades and scores. . . .

The size of the preference is indicated by the gap between the rates of admission for Favored Minorities and for Other Applicants. In the cell containing the median grade and score for all applicants (UGPA 3.25–3.49, LSAT 161–163), all Favored Minorities were admitted but only 5% of Other Applicants. . . . Down at the 30th percentile (applicants with grades and scores below 70% of their rivals), 83% of Favored Minorities but just 1% of Other Applicants gained admission. . . . In sum, Favored Minorities in the 10th percentile cell had a slightly better chance of admission than Other Applicants in the median cell, while Favored Minorities in the median cell had a slightly better chance than Other Applicants in the top cell. . . .

Racial affirmative action began almost forty years ago with efforts to make sure that people were not being treated unequally because of their race. It soon developed into programs conferring special treatment based on race, especially in higher education and employment. Decisions typically affected have been admission to college and graduate school; and hiring, promotion and training for private and government jobs. The groups now regularly designated for favorable treatment based on race or ethnicity are blacks, Latinos and Native Americans. Asians sometimes receive it; whites, almost never. The advantage is usually conferred by applying a double standard, whereby the requirements for selection are less exacting for members of the favored group.

From *Society,* March/April 2004, pp. 51–58. Copyright © 2004 by Springer Science and Business Media. Reprinted by permission.

These programs have been upheld as a remedy for past injustice, yet condemned as an instrument of present injustice. They have been praised for increasing minority access to business and professional careers, and blamed for debasing standards in the process. They are supposed by some to have raised and by others to have undermined the self-esteem of their recipients and the value placed on them by others. The controversy is fierce, partly because people on both sides believe that their position is what justice requires. But contrary views cannot both be right. We must dig deeper than usually occurs in public discussion to uncover and disentangle the relevant standards for moral judgment.

Unequal Treatment in General

At the outset, we need to distinguish between unequal treatment in general, and unequal treatment based on race. The latter may or may not be a special case, with special rules. Unequal treatment is simply treatment that favors one person over another. People are treated unequally for so many reasons, in so many contexts, that the existence of a general moral rule may seem impossible. But I suggest that we have such a rule. Ask yourself if and when you think that treating people unequally is the right thing to do. Is it all right when there is no reason for it? That would be arbitrary. Is it morally permissible if there is a good reason? For example, is it permissible to favor one applicant over another if they differ in ability, character, training, experience, and the like? Of course. Concerning something as important as the opportunity for education or employment, should people ever be treated unequally without good reason? No. But if there is a good reason, is it morally permissible to treat them unequally? It is not only permissible, it may be required.

What if the individual difference on which special treatment is based has nothing to do with an applicant's ability or need? Suppose that a public university gives an admissions preference to in-state residents, or a scholarship preference for veterans. Does the rule still hold, that unequal treatment is morally permissible when it is reasonable? The reasons commonly offered are, in the first case, that a state university is financed by, and owes a primary educational responsibility to, the residents of the state; in the second case, that such scholarships are both reward and incentive for service in the armed forces. The reasons seem good to me, and my sense of right and wrong does not bar the unequal treatment in either example. Others may think the reasons poor and the treatment wrong. In either view, whether unequal treatment is permissible depends on whether there is a good reason for it.

Preferential admission to a private university for the children of alumni is supposed to strengthen the school's relationship with its former students, thereby solidifying their continued interest and financial support, without which the quality and even the survival of the school might be jeopardized. Whether these are good reasons is disputed, but again the point is that, if one thinks the reasons good, one does not consider the preference immoral.

Supporters of racial preference think that the reasons for it are good: better, indeed, than for many kinds of preference that are generally accepted.

Hence they conclude that there is nothing morally wrong with the unequal treatment they advocate. This conclusion is valid, if the rule for unequal treatment based on race is the same as the rule for unequal treatment in general. But are the rules the same?

Does the rule, that unequal treatment is morally permissible when there is good reason, still hold when it is based on race? During the campaign to overthrow American discrimination against blacks and others, it was never suggested that if the discriminators had good reason, their actions would be morally acceptable. The legislatures, schools, professions, businesses and unions that practiced racial discrimination were not asked about their reasons; they were simply told to quit. Any claims that their policies were "reasonable means to legitimate ends" were rejected as rationalizations for racial injustice. The overriding conviction was that racial discrimination was morally out of bounds, no matter what reasons the discriminators might offer.

Based on this moral principle, laws were enacted between 1940 and 1970 at the local, state and national levels, barring unequal treatment in voting, housing, health care, public accommodations, public facilities, education and employment. These statutes established the right not to be discriminated against, and the corresponding duty not to discriminate, on account of "race, color or national origin." Rights are not absolute: they may be overridden by superior rights or by public necessity. But when unequal treatment on a particular basis is barred *as a matter of right*, people are not free to discriminate on that basis simply because they have good reasons. The right not to be racially discriminated against was not reserved for members of particular groups, but ascribed equally to every person in the United States.

Was the moral principle behind this legislation mistaken? For blacks it can be seen as a two-edged sword, banning adverse discrimination to be sure, but also prohibiting any discrimination in their favor. The antidiscrimination statutes left blacks with two important disadvantages. They were still held back by deficiencies in ability, training and motivation attributable at least in part to past discrimination; and they faced the prospect that discrimination against them in the future, though illegal, would often occur. No one doubts that the social and economic condition of American blacks would be better, absent their history of racial oppression. A plausible remedy would be racial preference, until both the effects of past, and the practice of current, anti-black discrimination had dissipated. But such a remedy would require important exceptions to the general ban on racial discrimination.

Any society that decides to end an era of discrimination faces the same moral dilemma. If everyone is granted the right not to be discriminated against on account of race, the possibility of helping the victims of past discrimination through racial preference is lost. If members of the previously excluded groups are favored on the basis of race, the right of others not to suffer racial discrimination is denied.

There is a way to slice through the dilemma, which would assist many disadvantaged individuals. Instead of racial preference, a program could assist those who had suffered specific, oppressive treatment, such as chronic and substantial racial discrimination. Any person, regardless of race, who could demonstrate such treatment in his own case would be eligible for the assistance. Such a program would satisfy the racial nondiscrimination rule, since the basis for assistance would be individual injury, not racial identity. But it would help only a fraction of those who currently benefit from race-based affirmative action.

Are there superior rights or public necessities that might override the right to racial nondiscrimination? The right to racial nondiscrimination, though momentous, is not the only care of the republic. Other (sometimes conflicting) rights and interests must also be protected. The moral dilemma of racial preference for some *versus* racial nondiscrimination for all might be avoided if, in certain circumstances, the right to racial nondiscrimination were superseded by a higher right or by public necessity.

Equity and Compensation

Some argue that there is a right to equal participation for racial groups, which overrides the individual right to nondiscrimination. According to this view, 'equal participation' means equal success in wealth, status, and achievement, not for every individual, but for the average person in each group, as compared with the average American. A belief in this right is often the moral basis for affirmative-action goals, adopted for the purpose of increasing the percentage of "underrepresented" minorities in the higher echelons of education and employment, to match their share of the general population. If such a right exists, it would conflict with the right to nondiscrimination, and might overrule it. . . .

If individuals who have been subjected to racial discrimination can be given compensatory help without running afoul of the nondiscrimination rule, why not an entire racial group? Could we thus escape from our moral dilemma? Is it possible that all we need is a finding by the national legislature that discrimination against certain racial groups has been and continues to be so pervasive that every member of the group is entitled to compensatory preference? Many proponents of affirmative action proceed as if such a finding had occurred, in their own minds if not in the legislative process. This helps them to think of racial preference as compensation, rather than discrimination.

A legislative finding of this sort, though based on evidence of injury to some, would be mere supposition concerning others. But the right of just compensation requires proof of specific injury to the person who invokes it. A legislative decision to compensate an entire racial group could not meet this criterion; it would be discrimination masquerading as compensation. Moreover, a legislature permitted to stereotype racial groups sympathetically would be free to do the contrary. Based on data that discrimination against Blacks is much more frequent than against whites, it would declare every black a victim. Based on statistics that crime by Blacks is much more frequent than by Whites, it could declare every Black a criminal. . . .

A Public Necessity to Achieve Diversity?

Some, giving a broader definition to public necessity, uphold two propositions, (a) that racial diversity in education and employment is a public necessity, and (b) that racial preference is essential to achieve such diversity. If by "diversity" they simply mean difference or variety, proposition (a) may be true, but proposition (b) is manifestly untrue. In a society composed of many different groups, all one needs in order to ensure racial and ethnic variety in colleges and workplaces is not to discriminate. But among supporters of race-based affirmative action, "diversity" often means having a larger number from "underrepresented groups" than would occur without racial preference. Using this definition, proposition (b) is true, but proposition (a) is false. There is no public necessity that racial groups be represented in education or employment in proportions higher than warranted by the fitness of their members, individually and impartially assessed.

A Need to Reduce Bias against Minorities?

Some argue that racial preference helps to prevent racial discrimination. They believe that unlawful discrimination against nonwhites in education and employment is common, since those in power are mostly white; they argue that when decision-makers have to meet goals for increasing minority participation, antiminority discrimination is effectively prevented. Racial goals and quotas are therefore imposed, by institutions over their officials or by courts over institutions, to ensure that people who might discriminate will not do so.

Paradoxically, this policy prevents violations of the right to racial nondiscrimination by making certain that they occur. . . .

The Right to Racial Nondiscrimination

We have found that, if we recognize a general moral right to racial nondiscrimination, racial preference cannot be justified as serving a superior right or a public necessity. The supposed rights and necessities either do not exist, or do not conflict with the right to nondiscrimination. Is there another approach that might clear the way for racial preference?

The moral right to racial nondiscrimination could be expunged or limited. One could (1) scrap the right altogether, (2) define the right more narrowly, (3) exempt education and employment from the nondiscrimination rule, (4) permit discrimination favorable to blacks, or (5) permit discrimination favorable to all "underrepresented" minorities. Should the United States have chosen (or now choose) one of these options?

1. Scrap the Right Entirely?
This option would require us to repeal our antidiscrimination laws and to reject the moral principle on which they are based. No one advocates this. . . .

Wherever practiced, racial discrimination generates racial oppression, hostility and violence. Nondiscrimination is not easy, but it is the only standard to which members of every racial and ethnic group might agree, since it is the only standard that places no one at a disadvantage because of his group membership. . . .

2. Redefine Wrongful Discrimination?

Instead of forbidding all unequal treatment based on race, we might bar such treatment only when it is motivated by racial prejudice or hostility. This would clear the way for "benign" discrimination in behalf of a previously excluded group, without sacrificing anyone's right to be free from "malign" discrimination.

A principal disadvantage to this approach is the extensive harm that it would legalize. A major reason for antidiscrimination laws is to protect people from being deprived of products, services, and opportunities by discriminatory acts. But this deprivation is just as great, whether the discrimination is motivated by prejudice or not. Discrimination is not benign to the person it injures. . . .

3. Exempt Education and Employment?

No one contends that racial discrimination should be outlawed in every kind of decision; to bar it in choosing a friend, a spouse, or a legislative representative would be invasive or unenforceable. Why not, then, withdraw the prohibition from the two areas in which preferential treatment might be most helpful for members of a previously excluded group, by bringing them more quickly into prestigious occupations and encouraging their fellows to aim higher and work harder?

A decision to exempt education and employment from the ban on discrimination would place both society and government in moral contradiction with themselves. The society, having decided that racial discrimination in general is wrong, would nevertheless be treating it in crucial areas as beneficial. The government, in its roles as educator and employer, would freely practice here that which elsewhere it must prosecute and punish. Such broad contradictions are fatal to the public consensus that racial discrimination is ordinarily unjust, a consensus that is necessary for general adherence to antidiscrimination laws. . . .

4. Favor Blacks Only?

This would respond forthrightly to the moral dilemma posed early in this essay, by making Blacks an exception to the nondiscrimination rule. The exception could apply to all areas of life that are covered by the rule, including housing, business, finance, voter registration, shopping, entertainment, criminal and civil justice, *etc.*, as well as education, employment, and government contracting. But an exception this large, which could easily sink the rule, has no champions. What is proposed instead is to limit the exception primarily to employment and higher education.

The exception faces two ways: Blacks would gain the privilege of favorable discrimination, by themselves or in their behalf; while all others would lose the right not to racially discriminated against when blacks are the beneficiaries.

A major argument against this option is the absence of a principled basis for making blacks the only beneficiaries of racial discrimination. If, when the nation decided to ban racial discrimination, blacks were the only group to have suffered it in the past, a basis for this exception would be clear. But Blacks were not alone. American Indians; Mexicans, Puerto Ricans, and other Latinos; Japanese, Chinese, and other Asians; Poles, Italians, Slavs, Arabs, Jews, and other whites could all point to group wounds from past discrimination. . . .

5. Favor "Underrepresented" Minorities?

It may be argued that this, in effect, is the option we have chosen, not by amending the nondiscrimination statutes, but by creating affirmative-action programs. Under them, Blacks, Latinos, and Native Americans receive racial preference and are supposedly not discriminated against; whites do not receive preference and are often discriminated against; Asians are sometimes the beneficiaries, sometimes the victims. That many whites and Asians have lost their right to racial nondiscrimination in these areas is not made explicit. But it is surely implied, by the view that racial preference at their expense is morally permissible when serving a good purpose, and by the argument that they have no more reason to complain when disadvantaged by racial preference, than if the preference had been based on place of residence or family connections. . . .

Supporters of racial preference for black, Hispanic and Native Americans in education and employment typically invoke principles of racial justice, such as the right to compensation for past injury and/or a right to equal racial success. We have argued above that the latter right does not exist and the former right, properly applied, does not require special treatment based on race. We have argued also that the plea of public necessity is unfounded. . . .

Our inquiry began with a moral dilemma. If all have the right not to be subject to racial discrimination, no one may be assisted via racial preference; if racial preference is authorized for some, the right not to suffer racial discrimination is thereby denied to others. Two ways out of the dilemma were examined.

May the right to racial nondiscrimination, especially in education and employment, though belonging to everyone, be overridden by certain higher rights or public necessities? By a right to equal success for racial groups, or to just compensation for past discrimination? Or by a public necessity for racial preference as a means to racial peace, to racial diversity, or to the prevention of discrimination? These supposed rights and necessities were found to be either non-existent, or not in conflict with the right to racial nondiscrimination, and therefore incapable of overriding it.

Should we rescind or limit the right to racial nondiscrimination, in order to make racial preference available? Five options were considered. The nondiscrimination rule could be scrapped altogether, redefined to cover only prejudiced or hostile acts, dropped from education and employment, or modified in these areas to allow preference for blacks only or for all "underrepresented" minorities. The arguments against these limits were in every case preponderant.

We cannot have the individual and social benefits of the nondiscrimination rule if we decline to obey it. We cannot teach our children that racial discrimination is wrong if we persistently discriminate. We cannot preserve the right to nondiscrimination by systematically violating it. But, without breaking or bending the rule, we can respond to many people who need and deserve help. The racial nondiscrimination rule does not preclude compensation for specific injury. It does not bar special assistance, by the public or private sector, to persons who labor under social, cultural, or economic disadvantages, provided that the purpose of the help and the criteria for eligibility are colorblind.

Besides excluding racial preference, there are other important respects in which a desirable assistance program would not imitate current affirmative action. It would help people increase their ability to meet regular standards, instead of lowering standards to accommodate inferior ability. The role of government would be primarily determined by the legislative branch, not the bureaucracy or the judiciary. The participation of the private sector would be voluntary or contractual, not compulsory. The rules and operation of the program would be honestly described and freely accessible to public scrutiny. These guidelines are not mandates of the nondiscrimination rule, just counsels of good sense. They will be easier to meet in a racial policy that we really believe is right.

Lawrence D. Bobo

Inequities That Endure? Racial Ideology, American Politics, and the Peculiar Role of the Social Sciences

As part of research on the intersection of poverty, crime, and race, I conducted two focus groups in a major eastern city in early September 2001, just prior to the tragic events of September 11. The dynamics of the two groups, one with nine white participants and another with nine black participants, drove home for me very powerfully just how deep but also just how sophisticated, elusive, and enduring a race problem the United States still confronts. An example from each group begins to make the point that the very nature of this problem and our vocabularies for discussing it have grown very slippery, very difficult to grasp, and therefore extremely difficult to name and to fight.

First let's consider the white focus group. In response to the moderator's early question, "What's the biggest problem facing your community?" a young working-class white male eagerly and immediately chimed in, "Section 8 housing." "It's a terrible system," he said. The racial implications hung heavy in the room until a middle-aged white bartender tried to leaven things a bit by saying:

> All right. If you have people of a very low economic group who have a low standard of living who cannot properly feed and clothe their children, whose speech patterns are not as good as ours [and] are [therefore] looked down upon as a low class. Where I live most of those people happen to be black. So it's generally perceived that blacks are inferior to whites for that reason.

The bartender went on to explain: "It's not that way at all. It's a class issue, which in many ways is economically driven. From my perspective, it's not a racial issue at all. I'm a bartender. I'll serve anybody if they're a class [act]." At this, the group erupted in laughter, but the young working-class male was not finished. He asserted, a bit more vigorously:

> Why should somebody get to live in my neighborhood that hasn't earned that right? I'd like to live [in a more affluent area], but I can't

Bobo, Lawrence D., "Inequalities That Endure? Racial Ideology, American Politics, and the Peculiar Role of the Social Sciences." In *The Changing Terrain of Race and Ethnicity,* edited by Maria Krysan and Amanda E. Lewis. ©2004 Russell Sage Foundation, 112 East 64th Street, New York, NY 10021. Reprinted with permission.

afford to live there so I don't. . . . So why should somebody get put in there by the government that didn't earn that right?

And then the underlying hostility and stereotyping came out more directly when he said: "And most of the people on that program are trashy, and they don't know how to behave in a working neighborhood. It's not fair. I call it unfair housing laws."

Toward the end of the session, when discussing why the jails are so disproportionately filled with blacks and Hispanics, this same young man said: "Blacks and Hispanics are more violent than white people. I think they are more likely to shoot somebody over a fender bender than a couple of white guys are. They have shorter fuses, and they are more emotional than white people."

In fairness, some members of the white group criticized antiblack prejudice. Some members of the group tried to point out misdeeds done by whites as well. But even the most liberal of the white participants never pushed the point, rarely moved beyond abstract observations or declarations against prejudice, and sometimes validated the racial stereotypes more overtly embraced by others. In an era when everyone supposedly knows what to say and what not to say and is artful about avoiding overt bigotry, this group discussion still quickly turned to racial topics and quickly elicited unabashed negative stereotyping and antiblack hostility.

When asked the same question about the "biggest problem facing your community," the black group almost in unison said, "Crime and drugs," and a few voices chimed in, "Racism." One middle-aged black woman reported: "I was thinking more so on the lines of myself because my house was burglarized three times. Twice while I was at work and one time when I returned from church, I caught the person in there."

The racial thread to her story became clearer when she later explained exactly what happened in terms of general police behavior in her community:

> The first two robberies that I had, the elderly couple that lived next door to me, they called the police. I was at work when the first two robberies occurred. They called the police two or three times. The police never even showed up. When I came in from work, I had to go . . . file a police report. My neighbors went with me, and they had called the police several times and they never came. Now, on that Sunday when I returned from church and caught him in my house, and the guy that I caught in my house lives around the corner, he has a case history, he has been in trouble since doomsday. When I told [the police] I had knocked him unconscious, oh yeah, they were there in a hurry. Guns drawn. And I didn't have a weapon except for the baseball bat, [and] I wound up face down on my living room floor, and they placed handcuffs on me.

The moderator, incredulous, asked: "Well, excuse me, but they locked you and him up?" "They locked me up and took him to the hospital."

Indeed, the situation was so dire, the woman explained, that had a black police officer who lived in the neighborhood not shown up to help after the patrol car arrived with sirens blaring, she felt certain the two white police officers who arrived, guns drawn, would probably have shot her. As it was, she was arrested for assault, spent two days in jail, and now has a lawsuit pending against the city. Somehow I doubt that a single, middle-aged, churchgoing white woman in an all-white neighborhood who had called the police to report that she apprehended a burglar in her home would end up handcuffed, arrested, and in jail alongside the burglar. At least, I am not uncomfortable assuming that the police would not have entered a home in a white community with the same degree of apprehension, fear, preparedness for violence, and ultimate disregard for a law-abiding citizen as they did in this case. But it can happen in black communities in America today.

To say that the problem of race endures, however, is not to say that it remains fundamentally the same and essentially unchanged. I share the view articulated by historians such as Barbara Fields and Thomas Holt that race is both socially constructed and historically contingent. As such, it is not enough to declare that race matters or that racism endures. *The much more demanding challenge is to account for how and why such a social construction comes to be reconstituted, refreshed, and enacted anew in very different times and places.* How is it that in 2001 we can find a working-class white man who is convinced that many blacks are "trashy people" controlled by emotions and clearly more susceptible to violence? How is it that a black woman defending herself and her home against a burglar ends up apprehended as if she were one of the "usual suspects"? Or cast more broadly, how do we have a milestone like the *Brown* decision and pass a Civil Rights Act, a Voting Rights Act, a Fair Housing Act, and numerous acts of enforcement and amendments to all of these, including the pursuit of affirmative action policies, and yet still continue to face a significant racial divide in America?

The answer I sketch here is but a partial one, focusing on three key observations. First, as I have argued elsewhere and elaborate in important ways here, I believe that we are witnessing the crystallization of a new racial ideology here in the United States. This ideology I refer to as laissez-faire racism. We once confronted a slave labor economy with its inchoate ideology of racism and then watched it evolve in response to war and other social, economic, and cultural trends into an explicit Jim Crow racism of the de jure segregation era. We have more recently seen the biological and openly segregationist thrust of twentieth-century Jim Crow racism change into the more cultural, free-market, and ostensibly color-blind thrust of laissez-faire racism in the new millennium. But make no mistake—the current social structure and attendant ideology reproduce, sustain, and rationalize enormous black-white inequality.

Second, race and racism remain powerful levers in American national politics. These levers can animate the electorate, constrain and shape political discourse and campaigns, and help direct the fate of major social policies. From the persistently contested efforts at affirmative action through a historic expansion of the penal system and the recent dismanding of "welfare as we know it," the racial divide has often decisively prefigured and channeled core features of our domestic politics.

Third, social science has played a peculiar role in the problem of race. And here I wish to identify an intellectual and scholarly failure to come to grips with the interrelated phenomena of white privilege and black agency. This failure may present itself differently depending on the ideological leanings of scholars. I critique one line of analysis on the left and one on the right. On the left, the problem typically presents as a failure of sociological imagination. It manifests itself in arguments that seek to reduce racialized social dynamics to some ontologically more fundamental nonracialized factor. On the right, the problem is typically the failure of explicit victim-blaming. It manifests itself in a rejection of social structural roots or causation of racialized social conditions. I want to suggest that both tactics—the left's search for some structural force more basic than race (such as class or skill levels or child-rearing practices) and the right's search for completely volitional factors (cultural or individual dispositions) as final causes of "race" differences—reflect a deep misunderstanding of the dynamics of race and racism. Race is not just a set of categories, and racism is not just a collection of individual-level anti-minority group attitudes. Race and racism are more fundamentally about sets of intertwined power relations, group interests and identities, and the ideas that justify and make sense out of (or challenge and delegitimate) the organized racial ordering of society. The latter analytic posture and theory of race in society is embodied in the theory of laissez-faire racism.

On Laissez-Faire Racism

There are those who doubt that we should be talking about racism at all. The journalist Jim Sleeper denounces continued talk of racism and racial bias as mainly so much polarizing "liberal racism." The political scientists Paul Sniderman and Edward Carmines write of the small and diminishing effects of racism in white public opinion and call for us to "reach beyond race." And the linguist John McWhorter writes of a terrible "culture of victimology" that afflicts the nation and ultimately works as a form of self-sabotage among black Americans. Even less overtly ideological writers talk of the growing victory of our Myrdalian "American Creed" over the legacy of racism. Some prominent black intellectuals, such as the legal scholar Randall Kennedy, while not as insensitive to the evidence of real and persistent inequality and discrimination, raise profound questions about race-based claims on the polity.

These analysts, I believe, are wrong. They advance a mistaken and counterproductive analysis of where we are today, how we got here, and the paths that we as a nation might best follow in the future. In many respects, these analysts are so patently wrong that it is easy to dismiss them.

Let's be clear first on what I mean by "racism." Attempts at definition abound in the scholarly literature. William Julius Wilson offers a particularly cogent specification when he argues that racism is an "an ideology of racial domination or exploitation that (1) incorporates belief in a particular race's cultural and/or inherent biological inferiority and (2) uses such beliefs to justify and prescribe inferior or unequal treatment for that group." I show here that there remains a profound tendency in the United States to blame racial inequality on the group culture and active choices of African Americans. This is abundantly clear in public opinion data, and it is exemplified by more than a few intellectual tracts, including McWhorter's *Losing the Race*. Closely attendant to this pattern is the profound tendency to downplay, ignore, or minimize the contemporary potency of racial discrimination. Again, this tendency is clear in public opinion and finds expression in the scholarly realm in the Thernstroms' book *America in Black and White*. These building blocks become part of the foundation for rejecting social policy that is race-targeted and aims to reduce or eliminate racial inequality. In effect, these attitudes facilitate and rationalize continued African American disadvantage and subordinated status. Our current circumstances, then, both as social structure and ideology, warrant description and analysis as a racist regime. Yet it is a different, less rigid, more delimited, and more permeable regime as well.

Laissez-faire racism involves persistent negative stereotyping of African Americans, a tendency to blame blacks themselves for the black-white gap in socioeconomic status, and resistance to meaningful policy efforts to ameliorate U.S. racist social conditions and institutions. It represents a critical new stage in American racism. As structures of racial oppression became less formal, as the power resources available to black communities grew and were effectively deployed, as other cultural trends paved the way for an assault on notions of biologically ranked "races," the stage was set for displacing Jim Crow racism and erecting something different in its place.

I have taken up a more complete development of the historical argument and the contemporary structural argument elsewhere. What is worth emphasizing here is, first, the explicit social groundedness and historical foundation of our theoretical logic—something that sets this theory of racial attitudes apart from notions like symbolic racism. Although not directly inspired by his work, our theoretical logic is a direct reflection of ideas articulated by the historian Thomas Holt. As he explains: "Racial phenomena and their meaning do change with time, with history, and with the conceptual and institutional spaces that history unfolds. More specifically they are responsive to major shifts in a political economy and to the cultural systems allied with that political economy."

The second point to emphasize here is that this is an argument about general patterns of group relations and ideology—not merely about variation in views among individuals from a single racial or ethnic category. As such, our primary concern is with the central tendency of attitudes and beliefs within and between racial groups and the social system as such, not within and between individuals. It is the collective dimensions of social experience that I most intend to convey with the notion of laissez-faire racism—not a singular attitude held to a greater or lesser degree by particular individuals. The intellectual case for such a perspective has been most forcefully articulated by the sociologist Mary R. Jackman. We should focus an analysis of attitudes and ideology on group-level comparisons, she writes, because doing so

> draws attention to the structural conditions that encase an intergroup relationship and it underscores the point that individual actors are not free agents but caught in an aggregate relationship. Unless we assume

that the individual is socially atomized, her personal experiences constitute only one source of information that is evaluated against the
backdrop of her manifold observations of the aggregated experiences
(both historical and contemporaneous) of the group as a whole.

The focus is thus more on the larger and enduring patterns and tendencies
that distinguish groups than on the individual sources of variation.

With this in mind, I want to focus on three pieces of data, the first of
which concerns the persistence of negative stereotypes of African Americans
[in a survey he conducted]. . . . Several patterns stand out. It is easier for
both blacks and whites to endorse the positive traits when expressing views
about the characteristics of blacks than the negative traits. However, African
Americans are always more favorable and less negative in their views than
whites. Some of the differences are quite large. For instance, there is a thirty-
percentage-point difference between white and black perceptions on the trait
of intelligence and a thirty-three-percentage-point difference on the "hard-
working" trait. . . .

Negative stereotypes of African Americans are common, though not uniform, and to a distressing degree they exist among both blacks and whites
and presumably influence perceptions and behaviors for both groups. However, there is a sharp difference in central tendency within each group, in predictable directions. One cannot escape the conclusion that most whites have
different and decidedly lesser views of the basic behavioral characteristics of
blacks than do blacks themselves. And that generally these patterns indicate
that African Americans remain a culturally dishonored and debased group in
the American psyche. . . .

On American Politics

As a historic fact and experience as well as a contemporary political condition,
racial prejudice has profoundly affected American politics. A wide body of
evidence is accumulating to show that racial prejudice still affects politics.
Black candidates for office typically encounter severe degree of difficulties
securing white votes, partly owing to racial prejudice. There is some evidence,
to be sure, that the potency of racial prejudice varies with the racial composition of electoral districts and the salience of race issues in the immediate
political context.

Moreover, political candidates can use covert racial appeals to mobilize
a segment of the white voting public under some circumstances. For example, the deployment of the infamous Willie Horton political ad during the
1988 presidential campaign heightened the voting public's concern over race
issues. It also accentuated the impact of racial prejudice on electoral choices
and did so in a way that did not increase concern with crime per se. That is,
what appears to give a figure like Willie Horton such efficacy as a political symbol is not his violent criminal behavior per se, but rather his being a violent
black man whose actions upset a racial order that should privilege and protect
whites.

Major social policy decisions may also be driven by substantially racial considerations. The political psychologists David Sears and Jack Citrin make a strong case that antiblack prejudice proved to be a powerful source of voting in favor of California's historic property tax reduction initiative (Proposition 13), a change in law that fundamentally altered the resources available to government agencies.

On an even larger stage, the very design and early implementation of core features of the American welfare state were heavily shaped by racial considerations. Robert Lieberman has shown that the programs that became Social Security, Aid to Families with Dependent Children (AFDC), and unemployment insurance were initially designed to either exclude the great bulk of the black population or leave the judgment of qualification and delivery of benefits to local officials. The latter design feature of AFDC (originally ADC) had the effect in most southern states of drastically curtailing the share of social provision that went to African Americans. . . .

There are good reasons to believe that the push to "end welfare as we know it"—which began as a liberal reform effort but was hijacked by the political right and became, literally, the end of welfare as we had known it—was just as surely impelled by heavily racial considerations. The political sociologist Martin Gilens (1999) has carefully analyzed white opinion on the welfare state in the United States. Some features of the welfare state, he finds, lack an overtone of black dependency (such as Social Security) and enjoy high consensus support. Other programs (AFDC, food stamps, general relief) are heavily racialized, with much of the white voting public regarding these programs as helping lazy and undeserving blacks.

Indeed, the fundamental alignment of the U.S. national political panics has been centrally driven by a racial dynamic. Over the past thirty-five years we have witnessed a fundamental transformation in the Democratic and Republican party system, a transformation that political scientists call realignment. The more the Democratic Party was seen as advancing a civil rights agenda and black interests—in a manner that clearly set them apart from the Republican Party—the more race issues and race itself became central to party affiliations, political thinking, and voting in the mass white public. What was once a solid white Democrat-controlled South has thus shifted to a substantially white Republican-controlled South.

The end result of all of these patterns, simply put, is that African Americans do not enjoy a full range of voice, representation, and participation in politics. Black candidates, particularly if they are identified with the black community, are unlikely to be viable in majority white electoral districts. Even white candidates who come to be strongly associated with black interests run the risk of losing many white voters. As a consequence, party leaders on both sides have worked to organize the agenda and claims of African Americans out of national politics. In particular, the national Democratic Party, which should arguably reward its most loyal constituents in the black community, instead has often led the way in pushing black issues off the stage. As the political scientist Paul Frymer has explained, party leaders do so because they are at risk of losing coveted white "swing voters" in national elections if they come to be perceived as catering to black interests. Thus is the elite discourse around many domestic social policies, and their ultimate fate, bound up in racial considerations.

Against this backdrop it becomes difficult, if not counterproductive, to accept the widely shared view that American democracy is on an inexorable path toward ever-greater inclusivity and fuller realization of its democratic potential. In the context of such enduring and powerful racialization of American politics, such an assumption is naive at best.

There is an even more incisive point to be made. The presumption of ever-expanding American liberalism is mistaken. For example, the Pulitzer Prize winning–historian Joseph Ellis writes of the terrible "silence" on the subject of slavery and race that the "founding fathers" *deliberately* adopted. They waged a Revolutionary War for freedom, declared themselves the founders of a new nation, and in very nearly the same moment *knowingly* wedded democracy to slave-based racism. The philosopher Charles Mills extends the reach of this observation by showing the deep bias of Enlightenment thinkers toward a view of those on the European continent—whites—as the only real signatories to the "social contract." Others, particularly blacks, were never genuinely envisioned or embraced as fully human and thus were never intended to be covered by the reach of the social contract.

Considerations of this kind led the political theorist Rogers Smith to suggest that the United States has not one but rather multiple political traditions. One tradition is indeed more democratic, universalistic, egalitarian, and expansive. But this tradition competes with and sometimes decisively loses out to a sharply hierarchical, patriarchal, and racist civic tradition. The ultimate collapse of Reconstruction following the Civil War and the subsequent gradual development of de jure segregation and the Jim Crow racist regime provide one powerful case in point.

POSTSCRIPT

Has Affirmative Action Outlived Its Usefulness?

Crawford and Bobo approach the issue of affirmative action from different directions. Bobo starts with the end or goal of fairness to disadvantaged minorities and argues that affirmative action is a necessary means to that end. Crawford starts with the means and argues that affirmative action is morally unjustifiable. On the other hand, compensation for individuals who have been discriminated against is morally justifiable, but most of the people who benefit from affirmative action programs are not in this category. This argument would not persuade anyone who is passionate about justice for disadvantaged minorities, because our laws already allow discrimination victims to seek redress in the courts and that has not stopped or compensated for discrimination. Many believe that something more is needed, and affirmative action properly conducted is the best means.

The writings on this subject are diverse and numerous. For an in-depth discussion of the legal standing of affirmative action, see Girardeau A. Spann, *The Law of Affirmative Action: Twenty-Five Years of Supreme Court Decisions on Race and Remedies* (New York University Press, 2000). For a review of affirmative action programs, see M. Ali Raza et al., *The Ups and Downs of Affirmative Action Preferences* (Greenwood, 1999). William G. Bowen and Derek Bok review affirmative action in college admissions in *The Shape of the River: Long-Term Consequences of Considering Race in College and University Admissions* (Princeton University Press, 1998). Robert K. Fullinwider and Judith Lichtenberg provide a more recent assessment in *Leveling the Playing Field: Justice, Politics, and College Admissions* (Rowman & Littlefield, 2004), and Patricia Gurin et al. defend affirmative action at the University of Michigan in *Defending Diversity: Affirmative Action at the University of Michigan* (University of Michigan Press, 2004). For a history of affirmative action, see Philip F. Rubio, *A History of Affirmative Action* (University Press of Mississippi, 2001). The need for affirmative action or another effective means to address racial and gender inequality is provided in *Problem of the Century: Racial Stratification in the United States,* edited by Elijah Anderson and Douglas S. Massey (Russell Sage Foundation); Andrew Hacker, *Mismatch: The Growing Gulf between Women and Men* (Scribner, 2003); and David Neumark, *Sex Differences in Labor Markets* (Routledge, 2004). The debate on affirmative action is covered by Carl Cohen and James P. Sterba in *Affirmative Action and Racial Preference: A Debate* (Oxford University Press, 2003). Recently an anti-affirmative action movement has mobilized. Three works that try to counter this movement are Fred L. Pincus, *Reverse Discrimination: Dismantling the Myth* (Lynne Rienner, 2003); Faye J. Crosby, *Affirmative Action Is Dead: Long*

Live Affirmative Action (Yale University Press, 2004); and Lee Cokorinos, *The Assault on Diversity: An Organized Challenge to Racial and Gender Justice* (Rowman & Littlefield, 2003). Andrew Hacker argues that affirmative action has relatively minor adverse consequences for whites in *Two Nations: Black and White, Separate, Hostile, Unequal* (Charles Scribner's Sons, 1992). Dinesh D'Souza, in *The End of Racism* (Free Press, 1995), argues that white racism has pretty much disappeared in the United States. The opposite is argued by Joe R. Feagin and Hernan Vera in *White Racism: The Basics* (Routledge, 1995) and by Stephen Steinberg in *Turning Back* (Beacon Press, 1995). For international comparisons, see Thomas Sowell, *Affirmative Action around the World: An Empirical Study* (Yale University Press, 2004).

ISSUE 9

Are Barriers to Women's Success as Leaders Due to Societal Obstacles?

YES: Alice H. Eagly and Linda L. Carli, from "Women and the Labyrinth of Leadership," *Harvard Business Review* (September 2007)

NO: Kingsley R. Browne, from *Biology at Work: Rethinking Sexual Equality* (Rutgers University Press, 2002)

ISSUE SUMMARY

YES: Alice H. Eagly and Linda L. Carli contend that barriers exist for women at every stage of their career trajectories, resulting in not a glass ceiling, but a labyrinth.

NO: Kingsley R. Browne asserts that the division of labor by sex is rooted in biologically based differences between women and men. Evolutionarily based natural selection has led to inclinations that make women and men better suited for different types of jobs.

Women continue to face career barriers. Although women hold 40 percent of managerial positions in the United States today, only 2 percent of *Fortune* 500 CEOs are women. The question remains as to why. Explanations tend to fall into one of two camps: human capital theory and discrimination theory. Human capital theories focus on obstacles from within the person. These theories focus on explanations such as differences in women's and men's abilities, interests, education, qualifications, personal investment in their careers, and leadership style, as well as choices related to family-work conflicts that are more likely to result in job discontinuity and turnover for women than for men. On the other hand, discrimination theorists focus on sociocultural factors that result in differential treatment of women and men. Three forms of employment discrimination have been identified: within-job wage discrimination (i.e., disparities within the same job, or unequal pay for equal work), valuative discrimination (i.e., lower wages in female- than male-dominated fields), and allocative discrimination (i.e., biases in hiring, promotion, and dismissal). This latter form of discrimination has invoked various descriptors of discrimination, including the "glass ceiling," "concrete wall," and "glass escalator." The image of the glass ceiling suggests that women ascend the career ladder with the top in sight, but at some rung on that ladder they hit the "glass ceiling." This image was transformed to that of a "concrete wall" to describe the even greater challenges faced by ethnic minority women. The "glass elevator" was a term coined to express the rapid career advancement of men who enter nontraditional, historically female-dominated fields, such as nursing. In the selections that follow the excerpt from Browne is an example of an explanation from the human capital perspective in which he argues that by nature women and men have different interests and talents that better suits them for different jobs. In contrast, Eagly and Carli's selection represents a discrimination theory perspective. In addition to describing all the various ways in which women can be targets of discrimination in the workplace, they coin a new term for allocative discrimination, the "labyrinth."

YES    Alice H. Eagly and Linda L. Carli

Women and the Labyrinth of Leadership

If one has misdiagnosed a problem, then one is unlikely to prescribe an effective cure. This is the situation regarding the scarcity of women in top leadership. Because people with the best of intentions have misread the symptoms, the solutions that managers are investing in are not making enough of a difference.

That there is a problem is not in doubt. Despite years of progress by women in the workforce (they now occupy more than 40% of all managerial positions in the United States), within the C-suite they remain as rare as hens' teeth. Consider the most highly paid executives of *Fortune 500* companies—those with titles such as chairman, president, chief executive officer, and chief operating officer. Of this group, only 6% are women. Most notably, only 2% of the CEOs are women, and only 15% of the seats on the boards of directors are held by women. The situation is not much different in other industrialized countries. In the 50 largest publicly traded corporations in each nation of the European Union, women make up, on average, 11% of the top executives and 4% of the CEOs and heads of boards. Just seven companies, or 1%, of *Fortune* magazine's Global 500 have female CEOs. What is to blame for the pronounced lack of women in positions of power and authority?

In 1986 the *Wall Street Journal's* Carol Hymowitz and Timothy Schellhardt gave the world an answer: "Even those few women who rose steadily through the ranks eventually crashed into an invisible barrier. The executive suite seemed within their grasp, but they just couldn't break through the glass ceiling." The metaphor, driven home by the article's accompanying illustration, resonated; it captured the frustration of a goal within sight but somehow unattainable. To be sure, there was a time when the barriers were absolute. Even within the career spans of 1980s-era executives, access to top posts had been explicitly denied. . . .

Times have changed, however, and the glass ceiling metaphor is now more wrong than right. For one thing, it describes an absolute barrier at a specific high level in organizations. The fact that there have been female chief executives, university presidents, state governors, and presidents of nations gives the lie to that charge. At the same time, the metaphor implies that women and men have equal access to entry- and mid-level positions. They do not. The image of a transparent obstruction also suggests that women are being misled

From *Harvard Business Review*, September 2007, pp. 63–71. Copyright © 2007 by Harvard Business School Publishing. Reprinted by permission.

about their opportunities, because the impediment is not easy for them to see from a distance. But some impediments are not subtle. Worst of all, by depicting a single, unvarying obstacle, the glass ceiling fails to incorporate the complexity and variety of challenges that women can face in their leadership journeys. In truth, women are not turned away only as they reach the penultimate stage of a distinguished career. They disappear in various numbers at many points leading up to that stage.

Metaphors matter because they are part of the storytelling that can compel change. Believing in the existence of a glass ceiling, people emphasize certain kinds of interventions: top-to-top networking, mentoring to increase board memberships, requirements for diverse candidates in high-profile succession horse races, litigation aimed at punishing discrimination in the C-suite. None of these is counterproductive; all have a role to play. The danger arises when they draw attention and resources away from other kinds of interventions that might attack the problem more potently. If we want to make better progress, it's time to rename the challenge.

Walls All Around

A better metaphor for what confronts women in their professional endeavors is the labyrinth. It's an image with a long and varied history in ancient Greece, India, Nepal, native North and South America, medieval Europe, and elsewhere. As a contemporary symbol, it conveys the idea of a complex journey toward a goal worth striving for. Passage through a labyrinth is not simple or direct, but requires persistence, awareness of one's progress, and a careful analysis of the puzzles that lie ahead. It is this meaning that we intend to convey. For women who aspire to top leadership, routes exist but are full of twists and turns, both unexpected and expected. Because all labyrinths have a viable route to the center, it is understood that goals are attainable. The metaphor acknowledges obstacles but is not ultimately discouraging.

If we can understand the various barriers that make up this labyrinth, and how some women find their way around them, we can work more effectively to improve the situation. What are the obstructions that women run up against? Let's explore them in turn.

Vestiges of prejudice.   It is a well-established fact that men as a group still have the benefit of higher wages and faster promotions. In the United States in 2005, for example, women employed full-time earned 81 cents for every dollar that men earned. . . .

One of the most comprehensive of these studies was conducted by the U.S. Government Accountability Office. The study was based on survey data from 1983 through 2000 from a representative sample of Americans. Because the same people responded to the survey repeatedly over the years, the study provided accurate estimates of past work experience, which is important for explaining later wages.

The GAO researchers tested whether individuals' total wages could be predicted by sex and other characteristics. They included part-time and full-time employees in the surveys and took into account all the factors that they could estimate and that might affect earnings, such as education and work experience. Without controls for these variables, the data showed that women earned about 44% less than men, averaged over the entire period from 1983 to 2000. With these controls in place, the gap was only about half as large, but still substantial. The control factors that reduced the wage gap most were the different employment patterns of men and women: Men undertook more hours of paid labor per year than women and had more years of job experience.

Although most variables affected the wages of men and women similarly, there were exceptions. Marriage and parenthood, for instance, were associated with higher wages for men but not for women. In contrast, other characteristics, especially years of education, had a more positive effect on women's wages than on men's. Even after adjusting wages for all of the ways men and women differ, the GAO study, like similar studies, showed that women's wages remained lower than men's. The unexplained gender gap is consistent with the presence of wage discrimination.

Similar methods have been applied to the question of whether discrimination affects promotions. Evidently it does. Promotions come more slowly for women than for men with equivalent qualifications. . . . Even in culturally feminine settings such as nursing, librarianship, elementary education, and social work, men ascend to supervisory and administrative positions more quickly than women.

The findings of correlational studies are supported by experimental research, in which subjects are asked to evaluate hypothetical individuals as managers or job candidates, and all characteristics of these individuals are held constant except for their sex. Such efforts continue the tradition of the Goldberg paradigm, named for a 1968 experiment by Philip Goldberg. His simple, elegant study had student participants evaluate written essays that were identical except for the attached male or female name. The students were unaware that other students had received identical material ascribed to a writer of the other sex. This initial experiment demonstrated an overall gender bias: Women received lower evaluations unless the essay was on a feminine topic. Some 40 years later, unfortunately, experiments continue to reveal the same kind of bias in work settings. Men are advantaged over equivalent women as candidates for jobs traditionally held by men as well as for more gender-integrated jobs. Similarly, male leaders receive somewhat more favorable evaluations than equivalent female leaders, especially in roles usually occupied by men.

. . . [A] general bias against women appears to operate with approximately equal strength at all levels. The scarcity of female corporate officers is the sum of discrimination that has operated at all ranks, not evidence of a particular obstacle to advancement as women approach the top. The problem, in other words, is not a glass ceiling.

Resistance to women's leadership. What's behind the discrimination we've been describing? Essentially, a set of widely shared conscious and unconscious mental associations about women, men, and leaders. Study after study has affirmed that people associate women and men with different traits and link men with more of the traits that connote leadership. . . .

In the language of psychologists, the clash is between two sets of associations: communal and agentic. Women are associated with communal qualities, which convey a concern for the compassionate treatment of others. They include being especially affectionate, helpful, friendly, kind, and sympathetic, as well as interpersonally sensitive, gentle, and soft-spoken. In contrast, men are associated with agentic qualities, which convey assertion and control. They include being especially aggressive, ambitious, dominant, self-confident, and forceful, as well as self-reliant and individualistic. The agentic traits are also associated in most people's minds with effective leadership—perhaps because a long history of male domination of leadership roles has made it difficult to separate the leader associations from the male associations.

As a result, women leaders find themselves in a double bind. If they are highly communal, they may be criticized for not being agentic enough. But if they are highly agentic, they may be criticized for lacking communion. Either way, they may leave the impression that they don't have "the right stuff" for powerful jobs.

Given this double bind, it is hardly surprising that people are more resistant to women's influence than to men's. . . .

Studies have gauged reactions to men and women engaging in various types of dominant behavior. The findings are quite consistent. Nonverbal dominance, such as staring at others while speaking to them or pointing at people, is a more damaging behavior for women than for men. Verbally intimidating others can undermine a woman's influence, and assertive behavior can reduce her chances of getting a job or advancing in her career. Simply disagreeing can sometimes get women into trouble. Men who disagree or otherwise act dominant get away with it more often than women do.

Self-promotion is similarly risky for women. Although it can convey status and competence, it is not at all communal. So while men can use bluster to get themselves noticed, modesty is expected even of highly accomplished women. . . .

Another way the double bind penalizes women is by denying them the full benefits of being warm and considerate. Because people expect it of women, nice behavior that seems noteworthy in men seems unimpressive in women. For example, in one study, helpful men reaped a lot of approval, but helpful women did not. Likewise, men got away with being unhelpful, but women did not. . . .

While one might suppose that men would have a double bind of their own, they in fact have more freedom. Several experiments and organizational studies have assessed reactions to behavior that is warm and friendly versus dominant and assertive. The findings show that men can communicate in a warm or a dominant manner, with no penalty either way. People like men equally well and are equally influenced by them regardless of their warmth.

It all amounts to a clash of assumptions when the average person confronts a woman in management. . . . In the absence of any evidence to the contrary, people suspect that such highly effective women must not be very likable or nice.

Issues of leadership style. In response to the challenges presented by the double bind, female leaders often struggle to cultivate an appropriate and effective leadership style—one that reconciles the communal qualities people prefer in women with the agentic qualities people think leaders need to succeed. . . .

It's difficult to pull off such a transformation while maintaining a sense of authenticity as a leader. Sometimes the whole effort can backfire. In the words of another female leader, "I think that there is a real penalty for a woman who behaves like a man. The men don't like her and the women don't either." Women leaders worry a lot about these things, complicating the labyrinth that they negotiate. For example, Catalyst's study of *Fortune* 1000 female executives found that 96% of them rated as critical or fairly important that they develop "a style with which male managers are comfortable."

Does a distinct "female" leadership style exist? There seems to be a popular consensus that it does. . . .

More scientifically, a recent meta-analysis integrated the results of 45 studies addressing the question [comparing three leadership styles]. . . . Transformational leaders establish themselves as role models by gaining followers' trust and confidence. They state future goals, develop plans to achieve those goals, and innovate, even when their organizations are generally successful. Such leaders mentor and empower followers, encouraging them to develop their full potential and thus to contribute more effectively to their organizations. By contrast, transactional leaders establish give-and-take relationships that appeal to subordinates' self-interest. Such leaders manage in the conventional manner of clarifying subordinates' responsibilities, rewarding them for meeting objectives, and correcting them for failing to meet objectives. Although transformational and transactional leadership styles are different, most leaders adopt at least some behaviors of both types. The researchers also allowed for a third category, called the laissez-faire style—a sort of non-leadership that concerns itself with none of the above, despite rank authority.

The meta-analysis found that, in general, female leaders were somewhat more transformational than male leaders, especially when it came to giving support and encouragement to subordinates. They also engaged in more of the rewarding behaviors that are one aspect of transactional leadership. Meanwhile, men exceeded women on the aspects of transactional leadership involving corrective and disciplinary actions that are either active (timely) or passive (belated). Men were also more likely than women to be laissez-faire leaders, who take little responsibility for managing. These findings add up to a startling conclusion, given that most leadership research has found the transformational style (along with the rewards and positive incentives associated with the transactional style) to be more suited to leading the modern organization. The research tells us not only that men and women do have somewhat different leadership styles, but also that women's approaches are the more generally effective—while men's often are only somewhat effective or actually hinder effectiveness.

Another part of this picture, based on a separate meta-analysis, is that women adopt a more participative and collaborative style than men typically favor. The reason for this difference is unlikely to be genetic. Rather, it may be that collaboration can get results without seeming particularly masculine.

As women navigate their way through the double bind, they seek ways to project authority without relying on the autocratic behaviors that people find so jarring in women. A viable path is to bring others into decision making and to lead as an encouraging teacher and positive role model. . . .

Demands of family life.   For many women, the most fateful turns in the labyrinth are the ones taken under pressure of family responsibilities. Women continue to be the ones who interrupt their careers, take more days off, and work part-time. As a result, they have fewer years of job experience and fewer hours of employment per year, which slows their career progress and reduces their earnings. . . .

There is no question that, while men increasingly share housework and child rearing, the bulk of domestic work still falls on women's shoulders. We know this from time-diary studies, in which people record what they are doing during each hour of a 24-hour day. So, for example, in the United States married women devoted 19 hours per week on average to housework in 2005, while married men contributed 11 hours. That's a huge improvement over 1965 numbers, when women spent a whopping 34 hours per week to men's five, but it is still a major inequity. And the situation looks worse when child care hours are added.

Although it is common knowledge that mothers provide more child care than fathers, few people realize that mothers provide more than they did in earlier generations—despite the fact that fathers are putting in a lot more time than in the past. . . . Thus, though husbands have taken on more domestic work, the work/family conflict has not eased for women; the gain has been offset by escalating pressures for intensive parenting and the increasing time demands of most high-level careers.

Even women who have found a way to relieve pressures from the home front by sharing child care with husbands, other family members, or paid workers may not enjoy the full workplace benefit of having done so. Decision makers often assume that mothers have domestic responsibilities that make it inappropriate to promote them to demanding positions. . . .

Underinvestment in social capital.   Perhaps the most destructive result of the work/family balancing act so many women must perform is that it leaves very little time for socializing with colleagues and building professional networks. The social capital that accrues from such "nonessential" parts of work turns out to be quite essential indeed. One study yielded the following description of managers who advanced rapidly in hierarchies: Fast-track managers "spent relatively more time and effort socializing, politicking, and interacting with outsiders than did their less successful counterparts . . . [and] did not give much time or attention to the traditional management activities of planning, decision making, and controlling or to the human resource management activities of motivating/reinforcing, staffing, training/developing, and managing conflict." . . .

Even given sufficient time, women can find it difficult to engage in and benefit from informal networking if they are a small minority. In such settings, the influential networks are composed entirely or almost entirely of men.

Breaking into those male networks can be hard, especially when men center their networks on masculine activities. The recent gender discrimination lawsuit against Wal-Mart provides examples of this. For instance, an executive retreat took the form of a quail-hunting expedition at Sam Walton's ranch in Texas. Middle managers' meetings included visits to strip clubs and Hooters restaurants, and a sales conference attended by thousands of store managers featured a football theme. One executive received feedback that she probably would not advance in the company because she didn't hunt or fish.

Management Interventions That Work

Taking the measure of the labyrinth that confronts women leaders, we see that it begins with prejudices that benefit men and penalize women, continues with particular resistance to women's leadership, includes questions of leadership style and authenticity, and—most dramatically for many women—features the challenge of balancing work and family responsibilities. It becomes clear that a woman's situation as she reaches her peak career years is the result of many turns at many challenging junctures. Only a few individual women have made the right combination of moves to land at the center of power—but as for the rest, there is usually no single turning point where their progress was diverted and the prize was lost.

What's to be done in the face of such a multifaceted problem? A solution that is often proposed is for governments to implement and enforce antidiscrimination legislation and thereby require organizations to eliminate inequitable practices. However, analysis of discrimination cases that have gone to court has shown that legal remedies can be elusive when gender inequality results from norms embedded in organizational structure and culture. The more effective approach is for organizations to appreciate the subtlety and complexity of the problem and to attack its many roots simultaneously. More specifically, if a company wants to see more women arrive in its executive suite, it should do the following:

> **Increase people's awareness of the psychological drivers of prejudice toward female leaders, and work to dispel those perceptions.** . . .
>
> **Change the long-hours norm.** . . . To the extent an organization can shift the focus to objective measures of productivity, women with family demands on their time but highly productive work habits will receive the rewards and encouragement they deserve.
>
> **Reduce the subjectivity of performance evaluation.** . . . To ensure fairness, criteria should be explicit and evaluation processes designed to limit the influence of decision makers' conscious and unconscious biases.
>
> **Use open-recruitment tools, such as advertising and employment agencies, rather than relying on informal social networks and referrals to fill positions.** . . . Research has shown that such personnel practices increase the numbers of women in managerial roles.

Ensure a critical mass of women in executive positions—not just one or two women—to head off the problems that come with tokenism. Token women tend to be pegged into narrow stereotypical roles such as "seductress," "mother," "pet," or "iron maiden." . . . When women are not a small minority, their identities as women become less salient, and colleagues are more likely to react to them in terms of their individual competencies.

Avoid having a sole female member of any team. Top management tends to divide its small population of women managers among many projects in the interests of introducing diversity to them all. But several studies have found that, so outnumbered, the women tend to be ignored by the men. . . . This is part of the reason that the glass ceiling metaphor resonates with so many. But in fact, the problem can be present at any level.

Help shore up social capital. As we've discussed, the call of family responsibilities is mainly to blame for women's underinvestment in networking. When time is scarce, this social activity is the first thing to go by the wayside. . . . When a well-placed individual who possesses greater legitimacy (often a man) takes an interest in a woman's career, her efforts to build social capital can proceed far more efficiently.

Prepare women for line management with appropriately demanding assignments. Women, like men, must have the benefit of developmental job experiences if they are to qualify for promotions. . . .

Establish family-friendly human resources practices. These may include flextime, job sharing, telecommuting, elder care provisions, adoption benefits, dependent child care options, and employee-sponsored on-site child care. Such support can allow women to stay in their jobs during the most demanding years of child rearing, build social capital, keep up to date in their fields, and eventually compete for higher positions. . . .

Allow employees who have significant parental responsibility more time to prove themselves worthy of promotion. This recommendation is particularly directed to organizations, many of them professional services firms, that have established "up or out" career progressions. People not ready for promotion at the same time as the top performers in their cohort aren't simply left in place—they're asked to leave. But many parents (most often mothers), while fully capable of reaching that level of achievement, need extra time—perhaps a year or two—to get there. . . .

Welcome women back. It makes sense to give high-performing women who step away from the workforce an opportunity to return to responsible positions when their circumstances change. . . .

Encourage male participation in family-friendly benefits. Dangers lurk in family-friendly benefits that are used only by women. Exercising options such as generous parental leave and part-time work slows down women's careers. More profoundly, having many more women than men take such benefits can harm the careers of women in general because of the expectation that they may well exercise those options. Any effort toward greater family friendliness should actively recruit male participation to avoid inadvertently making it harder for women to gain access to essential managerial roles.

Managers can be forgiven if they find the foregoing list a tall order. It's a wide-ranging set of interventions and still far from exhaustive. The point, however, is just that: Organizations will succeed in filling half their top management slots with women—and women who are the true performance equals of their male counterparts—only by attacking all the reasons they are absent today. Glass ceiling-inspired programs and projects can do just so much if the leakage of talented women is happening on every lower floor of the building. Individually, each of these interventions has been shown to make a difference. Collectively, we believe, they can make all the difference.

The View from Above

Imagine visiting a formal garden and finding within it a high hedgerow. At a point along its vertical face, you spot a rectangle—a neatly pruned and inviting doorway. Are you aware as you step through that you are entering a labyrinth? And, three doorways later, as the reality of the puzzle settles in, do you have any idea how to proceed? This is the situation in which many women find themselves in their career endeavors. Ground-level perplexity and frustration make every move uncertain.

Labyrinths become infinitely more tractable when seen from above. When the eye can take in the whole of the puzzle—the starting position, the goal, and the maze of walls—solutions begin to suggest themselves. This has been the goal of our research. Our hope is that women, equipped with a map of the barriers they will confront on their path to professional achievement, will make more informed choices. We hope that managers, too, will understand where their efforts can facilitate the progress of women. If women are to achieve equality, women and men will have to share leadership equally. With a greater understanding of what stands in the way of gender-balanced leadership, we draw nearer to attaining it in our time.

Biology at Work: Rethinking Sexual Equality

Modern evolutionary biology and psychology pose an even more direct challenge to the [Standard Social Sciences Model] (SSSM) with their insight that human behavioral predispositions are ultimately attributable to the same cause as the behavioral predispositions of other animals—evolution through natural selection. The centrality of mating and reproduction to evolutionary success, coupled with the differential investment of mammalian males and females in offspring, makes behavioral and temperamental identity of the sexes highly improbable. Just as no farmer expects to see identical patterns of behavior from the mare as from the stallion, from the cow as from the bull, or from the hen as from the rooster, no social scientist should expect to see identical patterns of behavior from men and women.

Claims for the existence of a recognizable "human nature" or for predictable behavioral differences between the sexes should be inherently suspect only to those who believe that the forces that created humans were importantly different from those that created the rest of the animal kingdom. If males and females are at their core psychologically identical, they are unique among mammals. This is not to deny the importance of social influences or the fact that societies have certain emergent characteristics that no amount of atomistic study of individuals could ever predict. But it is critical to understand that some social practices are more likely to arise than others precisely because human *minds* are more likely to settle on some social practices than others and that males and females tend to have different psychologies independent of the influence of cultures that expect them to be different.

The Division of Labor by Sex

A proper understanding of psychological sex differences would go far toward an understanding of the modern workplace, the study of which has heretofore been heavily biased toward the SSSM orientation. One human universal that is apparently a product of human nature is the division of labor by sex. All societies label some work "men's work" and other work "women's work." Although the content of the categories is by no means fixed—what some cultures label "men's work" is "women's work" in others—there are, nonetheless, some consistent patterns. Big-game hunting and metalworking are almost always "men's

From *Biology at Work: Rethinking Sexual Equality,* Rutgers University Press, 2002. Copyright © 2002 by Rutgers University Press. Reprinted by permission.

work" and cooking and grinding grain are almost always "women's work." While some divisions are obviously related to physical capacity, this is not always the case. For example, carrying water is almost always "women's work," and manufacture of musical instruments is almost always "men's work."

Modern Western societies are breaking down these age-old divisions, so that workers increasingly find themselves in what anthropologists call an "evolutionarily novel environment"—an environment that differs from that in which our hominid ancestors evolved—in this case a workplace environment in which men and women work side by side and compete for position in the same status hierarchies. Today, almost all positions in the labor market are formally open to women, the primary exception being certain combat positions in the military. Nonetheless, a high degree of de facto occupational segregation continues to exist, so that in practice there are many occupations that remain "men's work" and "women's work." Thus, most men work mostly with other men, and most women work mostly with other women. Moreover, even in largely integrated occupations, men are more likely than women to achieve the highest organizational positions.

The architects of sexual equality appear to have assumed that lifting formal barriers to women in the workplace would result in parity with men because men and women inherently have identical desires and capacities. When prohibitions on formal discrimination have not resulted in sexual parity, hidden discrimination is often assumed responsible. If hidden discrimination can be disproved, then informal barriers, such as sexist attitudes of parents or teachers are identified as the culprit. If direct external forces must finally (and reluctantly) be abandoned because the paths that women's lives have taken must be attributed to their own choices, then their choice becomes a "choice" that is attributed to their internalization of "patriarchal" notions about the proper role of the sexes and to their life constraints. While the causal attribution may shift over time, what does not change is the persistent invocation of causes other than women's inherent predispositions. Given the human propensity for self-deception, it may not be possible to answer the question whether these shifting arguments reflect actual beliefs or are merely opportunistic arguments to advance a political agenda.

The social-role view of sex differences is that "men and women have inherited essentially the same evolved psychological dispositions" and that behavioral sex differences are simply results of "two organizing principles of human societies: the division of labor according to sex and gender hierarchy." How is it that a sexually monomorphic mind came up with the division of labor by sex and gender hierarchy? Certainly the social explanation is not the most parsimonious explanation for sex differences in behavior. Humans evolved from other creatures surely having sexually dimorphic minds. The notion that humans evolved away from the primate pattern of behavioral sex differences—presumably because it was advantageous to do so—but simultaneously replaced the preexisting biological pattern with cultural patterns having the same effect is difficult to credit. Moreover, the direction of causation in this explanation is implausibly unidirectional. Even if behavioral sex differences originated from a sexually monomorphic mind, one would expect that they would be reinforced through selection over the hundreds of thousands or millions of years that these social phenomena existed.

Stasis and Change

Trends in women's work-force participation are not easily explained in terms of broad themes such as "patriarchy," "subjugation of women," or even the waning power of a monolithic male hierarchy. The progress of women has not been uniformly slow or uniformly fast, as might be expected if it were solely a consequence of such wide-ranging forces; instead, the pattern has been much more complex, and it is that pattern that any theory of workplace sex differences must attempt to explain.

In some respects, the role of women in the work force has been massively transformed in just a few decades. In 1960, women constituted just one-third of the American work force compared to over 46 percent today. During that same period, the percentage of married women who work doubled to 61 percent. Only 4 percent of lawyers in 1970 were women, while today the figure for law school graduates exceeds 42 percent. The percentage of female physicians increased from 10 to 24 percent between 1970 and 1995, and the percentage of female medical students now exceeds 40 percent. In business, the change has been no less impressive. In 1972, women held only 18 percent of managerial and administrative positions, compared to 43 percent of such positions in 1995. These changes represent a genuine revolution in the American workplace.

Despite these striking advances, however, women are far from achieving parity in a number of areas. They constitute only 5 to 7 percent of senior executives in the largest corporations, and the average full-time female employee makes less than 75 cents for every dollar earned by the average full-time male, if factors that influence wages such as hours worked and nature of the occupation are not considered. Many occupations remain highly sex segregated. Among the occupations in the United States that remain 90 percent or more female are bank teller, receptionist, registered nurse, and preschool and kindergarten teacher. Among the occupations that are less than 10 percent female are engineer, firefighter, mechanic, and pest exterminator. Large numbers of women pursue education in some scientific fields—such as biology and medicine—yet far fewer are found in other scientific fields—such as mathematics, physics, and engineering. Despite frequent assertions that women are victims of widespread discrimination, for the past two decades unemployment rates of the two sexes have not diverged by as much as a percentage point.[14] Thus, women's progress has not been uniformly stifled nor has it uniformly advanced; instead it has been quite patchy.

The question is why. Part of the answer lies in the sexually dimorphic human mind. . . . The means by which any animal "makes a living" is intimately related to the animal's physical and psychological makeup. If the physical and psychological makeup of a species varies substantially by sex, we would expect that males and females may make their livings in a somewhat different manner. The culturally universal division of labor by sex appears to be a manifestation of that principle.

Even in today's relatively egalitarian Western societies, men and women tend to seek different jobs, favor different occupational attributes, and sometimes even perform the same jobs in a somewhat different manner. Because workplace choices often influence both tangible and intangible rewards, systematically different preferences tend to result in systematically different rewards. A social environment in which individuals of both sexes are free to pursue their own priorities cannot therefore be expected, a priori, to produce identical rewards to members of the two sexes.

Sex differences in temperament and cognitive abilities, as well as occupational preferences, are at least partially responsible for a number of workplace phenomena that are sometimes labeled "problems"—the "glass ceiling," the "gender gap" in compensation, and occupational segregation. Although sex discrimination can also play a role, complete understanding of workplace patterns requires us to look honestly at other factors. Some individuals, for example, are more likely to seek, and make the requisite sacrifices and investments to achieve, the highest positions in business, government, and academia. Those who achieve positions of high status tend to be those for whom status is a high priority. Those who have high earnings tend to be those for whom high earnings are a sufficiently high priority that the sacrifices and tradeoffs necessary to achieve them are worthwhile. Because men and women vary systematically along these and other dimensions, occupational outcomes for men and women are not identical. Whether this is a problem or merely a fact is to some extent a value judgment. However, one's beliefs about the causes of the outcomes—for example, discrimination by employers or personal choice of the affected individuals—may influence the extent to which the outcomes are deemed acceptable. . . .

Conclusion

The evidence and arguments put forward in this book will be troubling to many. Some may believe that invocation of biology is implicitly (or perhaps even explicitly) a defense of the status quo—a paean to the virtue of existing arrangements or at least a testament to their inevitability. The defense, however, is more limited. It is that many of the workplace patterns that are laid at the foot of nefarious causes such as discrimination by employers or sexist socialization have causes that are less invidious and less attributable to an antifemale ideology than is commonly recognized.

A consensus about the causes of workplace patterns does not foreordain consensus about policy responses. One's values are important, and values are not directly derivable from scientific fact. Proponents of laissez-faire policies will likely draw free-market implications, while those more inclined toward governmental intervention may settle on more activist approaches. Everyone interested in workplace policy, however, whatever his political or social outlook, should desire an accurate understanding of the underlying causes of current patterns.

It would be a mistake to interpret average temperamental or cognitive sex differences as limitations on the potential of individual girls and women. Nothing contained in this book implies that women cannot or should not

be corporate presidents or theoretical physicists, only that equal representation of women in these positions is unlikely to occur unless selection processes are modified with the specific purpose of guaranteeing proportional
representation.

Sufficient overlap exists on most traits that there are few occupations that
should be expected to remain the exclusive domain of one sex, but many occupations will remain overwhelmingly male or overwhelmingly female if people
continue to select occupations on the basis of their preferences and abilities.
Expansion of the choices available to women (and to men) increases the influence of individual preferences on workplace outcomes. To the extent that individuals' preferences differ, we should expect them to seek different workplace
rewards. Because the average endowment of men and women differs—in temperament, cognitive ability, values, and interests—it would be astonishing if
their occupational preferences and behaviors were identical.

Modern attitudes about preferences are somewhat conflicted. The value
that Western liberals place upon individual liberty rests heavily on the assumption that the preferences of individuals differ. Each individual should be free,
within broad limits, to pursue his own ends. There is, therefore, something
vaguely illiberal about both the assumption that all individuals *should* have
the same preferences and attempts to ensure the outcomes that would result
if they did.

Some people believe that even if sex differences exist, there is harm in
publicizing them because they can become self-fulfilling prophecies. Even if
the "correct" ratio of professional mathematicians is, say, 5 males to 1 female,
it is harmful to make that fact widely known, because then mathematics
will be labeled a "male field," and girls will assume that it is *only* for males.
Although that is a rational concern, it is not well supported empirically. Clark
McCauley found, for example, that when asked to estimate the proportion of
males or females in a number of sex-stereotyped occupations, subjects showed
no evidence of stereotypic exaggeration. The correlation between estimates
and actual percentages was high, indicating that people rank-ordered them
accurately, but where the subjects erred, it was almost always in the direction of underestimating the difference between men and women in the occupation. Similarly, Mary Ann Cejka and Alice Eagly found that participants
systematically underestimated the extent to which male-dominated and
female-dominated occupations were segregated.

It may seem odd that this book implies the near-inevitability of disproportionate male representation at the highest levels in corporate and other
hierarchies, at least under current incentives, at the same time that other
writers are predicting seemingly contrary trends. In 1999, two books appeared
on the market, coincidentally both by Rutgers University anthropologists: *The
First Sex* by Helen Fisher and *The Decline of Males* by Lionel Tiger. Both chronicled changes in the workplace, in education, and in broader social forces such
as increasing female control over reproduction. Fisher's book emphasized the
positive—the ascendancy of females—but gave little attention to the social
effects of the "displaced males" that ascendancy of females implies. Tiger analyzed many of the same trends, but his view was more pessimistic, as the specter

of large numbers of marginalized males does not bode well for any society. Neither Fisher's nor Tiger's analysis is inconsistent with that provided here, however. [T]he gender gap in compensation shrinks with changes in work that favor women. Nonetheless, men will continue to dominate the scarce positions at the top of hierarchies as long as it is necessary to devote decades of intense labor-market activity to obtain them, even if women come to predominate in middle-management positions and even if men also disproportionately occupy the bottom of hierarchies. Men will similarly continue to dominate math-intensive fields, as well as fields that expose workers to substantial physical risks.

The extent of one's willingness to live with the sex differences in outcomes described here depends to some extent on one's definitions of equality. If current workplace outcomes are a cumulative consequence of millions of individual choices made by men and women guided by their sexually dimorphic psyches, are the outcomes of those choices rendered suspect because those sexually dimorphic minds incline men and women to make their choices in systematically different ways? This question resembles, if not entails, the familiar question of whether the equality that ought to be of importance to policy makers is "equality of opportunity" or "equality of result." Those who place primary importance on equality of opportunity may say that as long as both men and women are given the opportunity to pursue the opportunities that the workplace provides, the outcomes are unimportant. Those who look to group outcomes, on the other hand, may say that the critical question is what the different groups end up with. However, we cannot say that the "outcome" for women is deficient without specifying with precision what that outcome is. We cannot, that is, simply look at women's income and occupational attainment without also considering what they get in return for the occupational tradeoffs that they make.

The question of agency is at the core. Are women, like men, active agents in their own lives, making rational decisions based upon their own preferences? Or are they pawns of both men and society—making suboptimal "choices" that are forced on them by others? All indications are that the former is closer to the mark. Women, though somewhat constrained by life circumstances, as are men, make rational and responsible choices that are most compatible with their temperaments, abilities, and desires.

POSTSCRIPT

Are Barriers to Women's Success as Leaders Due to Societal Obstacles?

Women's leadership style has been cited frequently as a barrier to success at the top of the corporate ladder. Leadership can be viewed from either the human capital perspective or the discrimination perspective. The human capital view would suggest that women, due to their natures, simply do not have the dominance-related and assertive dispositions that are presumed to be correlates of leadership. From a discrimination perspective, one can argue that women have not been given opportunities to learn and practice leadership skills. Furthermore, research shows that many people prefer a male to a female boss. The irony is that much of the research suggests that women's leadership styles, when they differ from those of men, can be more effective, although the job description rather than the sex of the person usually better predicts what type of leadership style one will use.

How can the contradictions between women being effective leaders and still have difficulty exercising leadership be resolved? Alice Eagly has suggested that the view of female leadership is complex and is a mixture of advantage and disadvantage. On the one hand, women's styles have been described as transformative, in that they promote innovation, trust, and empowerment in followers. On the other hand, expectations regarding competitiveness and toughness, coupled with old-fashioned prejudice against women, can interfere with effective leadership, especially in male-dominated domains.

Suggested Readings

Jean Lau Chin, B. Lott, J. Rice, and J. Sanchez-Hucles, *Women and Leadership: Transforming Visions and Diverse Voices* (Teachers College Press, 2007).

E. E. Duehr and J. E. Bono, "Men, Women and Managers: Are Stereotypes Finally Changing?" *Personnel Psychology* (Winter 2006).

Robin. J. Ely, D. E. Meyerson, and M. N. Davidson, "Rethinking Political Correctness," *Harvard Business Review* (September 2006).

Anna Fels, "Do Women Lack Ambition?" *Harvard Business Review* (March 2005).

B. R. Ragins, J. M. Cornwell, and J. S. Miller, "Heterosexism in the Workplace: Do Race and Gender Matter?" *Group & Organizational Management* (vol. 28, 2003).

Internet References . . .

Economic Report of the President

The Economic Report of the President Web site includes current and antici-pated trends in the United States and annual numerical goals concerning topics such as employment, production, real income, and federal budget outlays. The database notes employment objectives for significant groups of the labor force, annual numeric goals, and a plan for carrying out program objectives.

http://www.gpoaccess.gov/eop/index.html

National Center for Policy Analysis

Through the National Center for Policy Analysis site you can read discussions that are of major interest in the study of American politics and government from a sociological perspective.

http://www.ncpa.org/

Speakout.com

The Speakout.com Web site contains a library of online information and links related to public policy issues, primarily those in the United States. The issues are organized into topics and subtopics for easy searching.

http://www.speakout.com/activism/issues/

Policy.com

Visit Policy.com, the site of the "policy community," to examine major issues related to social welfare, welfare reform, social work, and many other topics. The site includes substantial resources for researching issues online.

http://www.policy.com

Political Economy
and Institutions

*W*hat is the proper role of government in the economy? Some believe that the government must correct for the many failures of the market, while others think that the government usually complicates the workings of the free market and reduces its effectiveness. The next debate concerns public policy: What is the impact of the end of the Federal AFDC program? The fourth issue examines alternative educational policies for significantly improving public education. Finally, the last issue in this part looks at the use of biotechnology to alter and enhance humans.

- Is America Dominated by Big Business?

- Does Capitalism Undermine Democracy?

- Should Government Intervene in a Capitalist Economy?

- Has Welfare Reform Benefited the Poor?

- Is Competition the Reform That Will Fix Education?

- Should Biotechnology Be Used to Alter and Enhance Humans?

ISSUE 10

Is America Dominated by Big Business?

YES: G. William Domhoff, from *Who Rules America? Power, Politics, and Social Change,* 5th ed. (McGraw-Hill, 2006)

NO: Sheldon Kamieniecki, from *Corporate America and Environmental Policy* (Stanford University Press, 2006)

ISSUE SUMMARY

YES: Political sociologist G. William Domhoff argues that the "owners and top-level managers in large income-producing properties are far and away the dominant power figures in the United States" and that they have inordinate influence in the federal government.

NO: Political scientist Sheldon Kamieniecki's research finds that business interests do not participate at a high rate in policy issues that affect them, "and when they do, they have mixed success in influencing policy outcomes." In fact, environmental and other groups often have considerable influence vis-à-vis business interests.

$\mathbf{S}$ince the framing of the U.S. Constitution in 1787, there have been periodic charges that America is unduly influenced by wealthy financial interests. Richard Henry Lee, a signer of the Declaration of Independence, spoke for many Anti-Federalists (those who opposed ratification of the Constitution) when he warned that the proposed charter shifted power away from the people and into the hands of the "aristocrats" and "moneyites."

Before the Civil War, Jacksonian Democrats denounced the eastern merchants and bankers who, they charged, were usurping the power of the people. After the Civil War, a number of radical parties and movements revived this theme of anti-elitism. The ferment—which was brought about by the rise of industrial monopolies, government corruption, and economic hardship for western farmers—culminated in the founding of the People's Party at the beginning of the 1890s. The Populists, as they were more commonly called, wanted economic and political reforms aimed at transferring power away from the rich and back to "the plain people."

By the early 1900s, the People's Party had disintegrated, but many writers and activists have continued to echo the Populists' central thesis: that the U.S. democratic political system is in fact dominated by business elites. Yet the thesis has not gone unchallenged. During the 1950s and the early 1960s, many social scientists subscribed to the *pluralist* view of America.

Pluralists argue that because there are many influential elites in America, each group is limited to some extent by the others. There are some groups, like the business elites, that are more powerful than their opponents, but even the more powerful groups are denied their objectives at times. Labor groups are often opposed to business groups; conservative interests challenge liberal interests, and vice versa; and organized civil libertarians sometimes fight with groups that seek government-imposed bans on pornography or groups that demand tougher criminal laws. No single group, the pluralists argue, can dominate the political system.

Pluralists readily acknowledge that American government is not democratic in the full sense of the word; it is not driven by the majority. But neither, they insist, is it run by a conspiratorial "power elite." In the pluralist view, the closest description of the American form of government would be neither majority rule nor minority rule but *minorities* rule. (Note that in this context, "minorities" does not necessarily refer to race or ethnicity but to any organized group of people with something in common—including race, religion, or economic interests—not constituting a majority of the population.) Each organized minority enjoys some degree of power in the making of public policy.

In extreme cases, when a minority feels threatened, its power may take a negative form: the power to derail policy. When the majority—or, more accurately, a coalition of other minorities—attempts to pass a measure that threatens the vital interests of an organized minority, that group may use its power to obstruct their efforts. (Often cited in this connection is the use of the Senate filibuster, which is the practice of using tactics during the legislative process that cause extreme delays or prevent action, thus enabling a group to "talk to death" a bill that threatens its vital interests.) But in the pluralist view, negative power is not the only driving force: When minorities work together and reach consensus on certain issues, they can institute new laws and policy initiatives that enjoy broad public support. Pluralism, though capable of producing temporary gridlock, ultimately leads to compromise, consensus, and moderation.

Critics of pluralism argue that pluralism is an idealized depiction of a political system that is in the grip of powerful elite groups. Critics fault pluralist theory for failing to recognize the extent to which big business dominates the policy-making process. In the selections that follow, G. William Domhoff supports this view, identifies the groups that compose the power elite, and details the way they control or support social, political, and knowledge-producing associations and organizations that advance their interests. Sheldon Kamieniecki, in opposition, argues that, thanks to new consumer, environmental, and other citizen groups, big business has a much more limited influence on Washington policymakers than Domhoff claims.

YES

G. William Domhoff

Who Rules America?
Power, Politics, and Social Change

Introduction

Using a wide range of systematic empirical findings, this book shows how the owners and top-level managers in large companies work together to maintain themselves as the core of the dominant power group. Their corporations, banks, and agribusinesses form a *corporate community* that shapes the federal government on the policy issues of interest to it, issues that have a major impact on the income, job security, and well-being of most other Americans. At the same time, there is competition within the corporate community for profit opportunities, which can lead to highly visible policy conflicts among rival corporate leaders that are sometimes fought out in Congress. Yet the corporate community is cohesive on the policy issues that affect its general welfare, which is often at stake when political challenges are made by organized workers, liberals, or strong environmentalists. The book therefore deals with another seeming paradox: How can a highly competitive group of corporate leaders cooperate enough to work their common will in the political and policy arenas?

Partly because the owners and high-level managers within the corporate community share great wealth and common economic interests, but also due to political opposition to their interests, they band together to develop their own social institutions—gated neighborhoods, private schools, exclusive social clubs, debutante balls, and secluded summer resorts. These social institutions create social cohesion and a sense of group belonging, a "we" feeling, and thereby mold wealthy people into a *social upper class*. In addition, the owners and managers supplement their small numbers by financing and directing a wide variety of nonprofit organizations—e.g., tax-free foundations, think tanks, and policy-discussion groups—to aid them in developing policy alternatives that serve their interests. The highest-ranking employees in these nonprofit organizations become part of a general leadership group for the corporate community and the upper class, called the *power elite*.

Corporate owners and their top executives enter into the electoral arena as the leaders of a *corporate-conservative coalition*, which they shape through large campaign contributions, the advocacy of policy options developed by their hired experts, and easy access to the mass media. They are aided by a wide variety of middle-class patriotic, antitax, and single-issue organizations

From *Who Rules America? Power and Politics, and Social Change* by G. William Domhoff (McGraw-Hill, 2006). Copyright © 2006 by McGraw-Hill Companies. Reprinted by permission.

that celebrate the status quo and warn against "big government." These opinion-shaping organizations are funded in good part by the corporate community, but they have some degree of independence due to direct-mail appeals and modest donations by a large number of middle-class conservatives. The corporate leaders play a large role in both of the major political parties at the presidential level and succeeded in electing a pro-corporate majority to Congress throughout the twentieth century. Historically, this majority in Congress consisted of Northern Republicans and Southern Democrats, but that arrangement changed gradually after the Voting Rights Act of 1965 made it possible for a coalition of African-Americans and white liberals to push the most conservative Southern Democrats into the Republican Party.

Since the last quarter of the twentieth century, the corporate-conservative coalition has been joined by the Christian Right, which consists of a wide range of middle-class religious groups concerned with a variety of social issues, including abortion, prayer in schools, teenage sexual behavior, homosexuality, gay marriage, and pornography. The alliance is sometimes an uneasy one because the corporate community and the Christian Right do not have quite the same priorities, yet they work together because of their common mistrust of government power.

The corporate community's ability to transform its economic power into policy influence and political access, along with its capacity to enter into a coalition with middle-class social and religious conservatives, makes it the most important influence in the federal government. Its key leaders are appointed to top positions in the executive branch and the policy recommendations of its experts are listened to carefully by its allies in Congress. This combination of economic power, policy expertise, and continuing political success makes the corporate owners and executives a *dominant class,* not in the sense of complete and absolute power, but in the sense that they have the power to shape the economic and political frameworks within which other groups and classes must operate. They therefore win far more often than they lose on the issues of concern to them.

Who Wins?

There are many issues over which the corporate-conservative and liberal-labor coalitions disagree, including taxation, unionization, business regulation, foreign trade, the outsourcing of jobs, and the funding of Social Security. Power can be inferred on the basis of these issue conflicts by determining who successfully initiates, modifies, or vetoes policy alternatives. This indicator, by focusing on relationships between the two rival coalitions, comes closest to approximating the process of power contained in the formal definition. It is the indicator preferred by most social scientists. For many reasons, however, it is also the most difficult to use in an accurate way. Aspects of a decision process may remain hidden, some informants may exaggerate or downplay their roles, and people's memories about who did what often become cloudy shortly after the event. Worse, the key concerns of the corporate community may never arise as issues for public discussion because it has the power to keep them off the agenda through a variety of means that are explained throughout later chapters.

Despite the difficulties in using the *Who wins?* indicator of power, it is possible to provide a theoretical framework for analyzing governmental decision-making that mitigates many of them. This framework encompasses the various means by which the corporate community attempts to influence both the government and the general population in a conscious and planned manner, thereby making it possible to assess its degree of success very directly. More specifically, there are four relatively distinct, but overlapping processes (discovered by means of membership network analysis) through which the corporate community controls the public agenda and then wins on most issues that appear on it. These four power networks, which are discussed in detail in later chapters, are as follows:

1. The *special-interest process* deals with the narrow and short-run policy concerns of wealthy families, specific corporations, and specific business sectors. It operates primarily through lobbyists, company lawyers, and trade associations, with a focus on congressional committees, departments of the executive branch, and regulatory agencies.
2. The *policy-planning process* formulates the general interests of the corporate community. It operates through a policy-planning network of foundations, think tanks, and policy-discussion groups, with a focus on the White House, relevant congressional committees, and the high-status newspapers and opinion magazines published in New York and Washington.
3. The *candidate-selection process* is concerned with the election of candidates who are sympathetic to the agenda put forth in the special-interest and policy-planning processes. It operates through large campaign donations and hired political consultants, with a focus on the presidential campaigns of both major political parties and the congressional campaigns of the Republican Party.
4. The *opinion-shaping process* attempts to influence public opinion and keep some issues off the public agenda. Often drawing on policy positions, rationales, and statements developed within the policy-planning process, it operates through the public relations departments of large corporations, general public relations firms, and many small opinion-shaping organizations, with a focus on middle-class voluntary organizations, educational institutions, and the mass media.

Taken together, the people and organizations that operate in these four networks constitute the political-action arm of the corporate community and upper class.

How the Power Elite Dominate Government

The power elite build on their structural economic power, their storehouse of policy expertise, and their success in the electoral arena to dominate the federal government on the issues about which they care. Lobbyists from corporations, law firms, and trade associations play a key role in shaping government on narrow issues of concern to specific corporations or business sectors, and the policy-planning network supplies new policy directions on major issues, along with top-level governmental appointees to implement those policies.

However, victories within government are far from automatic. As is the case in the competition for public opinion and electoral success, the power elite face opposition from a minority of elected officials and their supporters in labor unions and liberal advocacy groups. These liberal opponents are sometimes successful in blocking the social initiatives put forth by the Christian Right, but the corporate-conservative coalition itself seldom loses when it is united.

Appointees to Government

The first way to see how the power elite shapes the federal government is to look at the social and occupational backgrounds of the people who are appointed to manage the major departments of the executive branch, such as state, treasury, defense, and justice. If the power elite are as important as this book claims, they should come disproportionately from the upper class, the corporate community, and the policy-planning network.

There have been numerous studies of major governmental appointees under both Republican and Democratic administrations, usually focusing on the top appointees in the departments that are represented in the president's cabinet. These studies are unanimous in their conclusion that most top appointees in both Republican and Democratic administrations are corporate executives and corporate lawyers, and hence members of the power elite. Moreover, they are often part of the policy-planning network as well, supporting the claim that the network plays a central role in preparing members of the power elite for government service.

The Special-Interest Process

The special-interest process consists of the many and varied means by which specific corporations and business sectors gain the favors, tax breaks, regulatory rulings, and other governmental assistance they need to realize their narrow and short-run interests. The process is carried out by people with a wide range of experiences: former elected officials, experts who once served on congressional staffs or in regulatory agencies, employees of trade associations, corporate executives whose explicit function is government liaison, and an assortment of lawyers and public-relations specialists. The process is based on a great amount of personal contact, but its most important ingredients are the information and financial support that the lobbyists have to offer. Much of the time this information comes from grassroots pressure generated by the lobbyists to show that voting for a given measure will or will not hurt a particular politician.

Corporations spend far more money on lobbying than their officers give to PACs, by a margin of ten to one. In 2000, for example, the tobacco industry, facing lawsuits and regulatory threats, spent $44 million on lobbyists and $17 million on the Tobacco Institute, an industry public relations arm, but gave only $8.4 million to political campaigns through PACs. More generally, a study of the top 20 defense contractors showed that they spent $400 million on lobbying between 1997 and 2003, but only $46 million on campaign contributions.

The trend toward increasingly large tax breaks continued from 2001 to 2003, with the effective tax rate on corporations declining from 21.7 percent during the last years of the Clinton Administration to 17.2 percent in 2003. Forty-six of 275 major companies studied for 2003 paid no federal income taxes, a considerable increase from a similar study in the late 1990s. A new tax bill in October 2004 added another $137 billion in tax breaks for manufacturing and energy companies, with General Electric, which spent $17 million in lobbying fees in 2003, once again the biggest beneficiary. At the same time, other legal loopholes have allowed multinational corporations to increase the sheltering of profits in foreign tax havens by tens of billions of dollars.

Special interests also work through Congress to try to hamstring regulatory agencies or reverse military purchasing decisions they do not like. When the Federal Communications Commission tried to issue licenses for over 1,000 low-power FM stations for schools and community groups, Congress blocked the initiative at the behest of big broadcasting companies, setting standards that will restrict new licenses to a small number of stations in the least populated parts of the country. When the Food and Drug Administration tried to regulate tobacco, Congress refused authorization in 2000 in deference to the tobacco industry. The FDA is now so lax with pharmaceutical companies that one-third of its scientific employees have less than full confidence that it tests new drugs adequately, and two-thirds expressed a lack of complete confidence in its monitoring of the safety of drugs once they are on the market.

The special-interest process often is used to create loopholes in legislation that is accepted by the corporate community in principle. "I spent the last seven years fighting the Clean Air Act," said a corporate lobbyist in charge of PAC donations, who then went on to explain why he gave money to elected officials even though they voted for the strengthening of the Clean Air Act in 1990:

> How a person votes on the final piece of legislation is not representative of what they have done. Somebody will do a lot of things during the process. How many guys voted against the Clean Air Act? But during the process some of them were very sympathetic to some of our concerns.

Translated, this means there are forty pages of exceptions, extensions, and other loopholes in the 1990 version of the act after a thirteen-year standoff between the Business Roundtable's Clean Air Working Group and the liberal-labor coalition's National Clean Air Coalition. For example, the steel industry has thirty years to bring twenty-six large coke ovens into compliance with the new standards. Once the bill passed, lobbyists went to work on the Environmental Protection Agency to win the most lax regulations possible for implementing the legislation. As of 1998, after twenty-eight years of argument and delay, the agency had been able to issue standards for less than ten of the many hazardous chemicals emitted into the air.

The Big Picture

This book began with two seeming paradoxes. How can the owners and managers of highly competitive corporations develop the policy unity to shape government policies? How can large corporations have such great power in a democratic country? The step-by-step argument and evidence presented in previous chapters provide the foundation for a theory that can explain these paradoxes—a *class-domination theory of power* in the United States.

Domination means that the commands of a group or class are carried out with relatively little resistance, which is possible because that group or class has been able to establish the rules and customs through which everyday life is conducted. Domination, in other words, is the institutionalized outcome of great distributive power. The upper class of owners and high-level executives, based in the corporate community, is a dominant class in terms of this definition because the cumulative effect of its various distributive powers leads to a situation where its policies are generally accepted by most Americans. The routinized ways of acting in the United States follow from the rules and regulations needed by the corporate community to continue to grow and make profits.

The overall distributive power of the dominant class is first of all based in its structural economic power, which falls to it by virtue of its members being owners and high-level executives in corporations that sell goods and services for a profit in a market economy. The power to invest or not invest, and to hire and fire employees, leads to a political context where elected officials try to do as much as they can to create a favorable investment climate to avoid being voted out of office in the event of an economic downturn. This structural power is augmented by the ability to create new policies through a complex policy-planning network, which the upper class has been able to institutionalize because common economic interests and social cohesion have given the corporate community enough unity to sustain such an endeavor over many decades.

But even these powers might not have been enough to generate a system of extreme class domination if the bargains and compromises embodied in the Constitution had not led unexpectedly to a two-party system in which one party was controlled by the Northern rich and the other by the Southern rich. This in turn created a personality-oriented candidate-selection process that is heavily dependent on large campaign donations—now and in the past as well. The system of party primaries is the one adaptation to this constrictive two-party system that has provided some openings for insurgent liberals and trade unionists.

Structural economic power and control of the two parties, along with the elaboration of an opinion-shaping network, results in a polity where there is little or no organized public opinion independent of the limits set by debates within the power elite itself. There is no organizational base from which to construct an alternative public opinion, and there have been until recently no openings within the political system that could carry an alternative message to government.

Finally, the fragmented and constrained system of government carefully crafted by the Founding Fathers led to a relatively small federal government that is easily entered and influenced by wealthy and well-organized private citizens, whether through Congress, the separate departments of the executive branch, or a myriad of regulatory agencies. The net result is that the owners and managers of large income-producing properties score very high on all three power indicators: who benefits, who governs, and who wins. They have a greater proportion of wealth and income than their counterparts in any other capitalist democracy, and through the power elite they are vastly overrepresented in key government positions and decision-making groups. They win far more often than they lose on those issues that make it to the government for legislative consideration, although their lack of unity in the face of worker militancy in the 1930s made it possible for organized workers to have far more independence, income, and power than they ever had in the past.

Many Americans feel a sense of empowerment because they have religious freedom, free speech, and a belief that they can strike it rich or rise in the system if they try hard enough. Those with educational credentials and/or secure employment experience a degree of dignity and respect because there is no tradition of public degradation for those of average or low incomes. Liberals and leftists can retain hope because in recent decades they have had success in helping to expand individual rights and freedom—for women, for people of color, and most recently for gays and lesbians. But individual rights and freedoms do not necessarily add up to distributive power. In the same time period, when individual rights and freedoms expanded, corporate power also became greater because unions were decimated and the liberal-labor coalition splintered. This analysis suggests there is class domination in spite of a widening of individual freedoms and an expansion of the right to vote.

Sheldon Kamieniecki

Corporate America and Environmental Policy: How Often Does Business Get Its Way?

The findings reported in this study directly challenge prevailing assumptions both in- and outside the scholarly community about the regularity of business involvement in agenda building and policymaking as well as the ability of business to influence government decisions concerning pollution control and natural resource management. This outcome was unexpected. When I first began working on this book more than three years ago, I anticipated finding that American corporations are regularly involved in environmental agenda building and policymaking and that they exert a great deal of influence over government decision making. Like many, I accepted the conventional wisdom that business frequently opposes proposals that will improve environmental quality in order to protect its profits. After all, reports in the media nearly always place the blame for the defeat of environmental initiatives on the undue influence of business. As an environmentalist myself, I have been quite disappointed in the lack of progress the United States has made, especially recently, in the areas of pollution control and natural resource conservation. Most policy analysts attribute this lack of progress to the ability of corporate America to block or dilute critical federal legislation and to the inability of environmental groups to compete in the policymaking process. . . .

I was determined to . . . conduct a fair and balanced assessment of the role of business interests in environmental and natural resource policymaking.

As the data show, business interests do not participate in environmental policy debates at a high rate, and when they do, they have mixed success in influencing policy outcomes. These results generally hold when one examines agenda building in Congress, agency rulemaking, and, to some extent, the courts. Analyses of salient conflicts involving pollution control and natural resources also tend to bear this out. Business interests, instead, appear to select strategically the controversies in which they become involved and how much money they spend on lobbying activities of various kinds. A major conclusion of my work is that agenda building within the environmental policy domain is a highly complex process and cannot be explained by a single theory. This and other surprising related findings are the subject of this book. . . .

From *Corporate America and Environmental Policy,* by Sheldon Kamieniecki (Stanford Law and Politics, 2006), excerpts from Preface, Chapters 1, 2, and Conclusion. Copyright © 2006 by the Board of Trustees of Leland Stanford Jr. University. Reprinted by permission of Stanford University Press. www.sup.org

The central question of the book is, how often does business get its way on environmental issues? Do corporations, given the immense wealth and resources they command, exert an unequal and unfair influence over American government whereby they are able to compel elected representatives and agency officials to reject or compromise substantially appropriate and necessary environmental rules and regulations? A related concern, often ignored in the interest group literature, is the frequency with which firms are able to prevent environmental and natural resource policy proposals from even reaching the government agenda. Although recent research suggests that firms do not possess the amount of influence necessary to shape or block public policymaking on a consistent basis more generally, few studies have critically analyzed their ability to affect agenda setting specifically within the environmental policy sphere. This investigation addresses this issue by empirically assessing the ability of companies to affect legislative, administrative, and judicial decision making and mold the government's environmental and natural resource policy agenda since the beginning of the environmental movement. . . .

In particular, the size and wealth of business lobbying organizations have grown dramatically since World War Two, prompting some observers to argue that they are now too powerful and are undermining democracy and threatening the well-being of society. The weakening of the political parties, the rising costs of media advertising and election campaigns, and the increasing contributions by Political Action Committees (PACs) to candidates and parties have led to calls for reform in the way American elections are financed. Business interests, among others, are key targets of critics who demand the enactment of meaningful campaign finance reform at the federal level. The campaign finance reform legislation enacted in 2002 bans "soft money," among other things, and is a significant attempt to level the playing field. Loopholes in the act exist, however, and it will be necessary to adopt additional regulations in the future in order to correct inequities in the financing of campaigns. Thus, despite Madison's assurances, the question of how we allow business and other interest groups to form and participate but control their influence remains a dilemma in modern times. . . .

Corporate America and Environmental Policy: Opposing Views

The influence of business over environmental policy is often used as an example of the substantial and unfair leverage certain interest groups have over government actions, especially when compared to the level of influence of average citizens. Many believe that the power business wields in American politics threatens democracy and, among other things, undermines the nation's efforts to control pollution and conserve natural resources. Environmentalists assert that "big business" has continuously been an impediment to the formulation and implementation of clean air and water quality standards. Ranchers and land developers, they argue, have successfully fought endangered species protection;

oil, coal, and natural gas companies have opposed strict energy-conservation measures and have lobbied against the adoption of renewable sources of energy; mining companies have thwarted the revision of mining laws and regulations; and chemical companies have fought legislation intended to control pesticides, promote the safe disposal of hazardous waste, and abate old, abandoned toxic waste sites. . . .

Many critics maintain that interest groups subvert democracy, in part by pressing Congress to pass too much "special-interest" legislation that benefits the few at the expense of the majority and in part by blocking legislative initiatives they oppose even when those measures are favored by, or would benefit, the broad public. In addition, critics contend that campaign contributions by interest groups undermine democratic government and degrade the American electoral system. In contrast, Berry rejects these arguments, saying that interest groups help to link citizens to government: "They empower people by organizing those citizens with similar interests and expressing those interests to policymakers. In this regard, the growth of citizen groups reflects an expansion of organizing around interests that have too often received too little attention in Washington." Berry carefully avoids saying that business interests are no longer a force in American politics, but he does argue that their influence has significantly declined. . . .

Interestingly, Berry's findings and conclusions are a throwback to some of the positions of the early pluralists, namely that interest group politics is equitable and fair. For this reason, Berry and his contemporaries, such as Baumgartner and Leech who also share this view, are referred to as *neopluralists* in this volume. Specifically, neopluralists argue that the increasing number and size of citizen groups has furthered democracy and the public good by involving a broad range of interests in policymaking and by substantially countering the influence of business in the political system. The neopluralists, like the early pluralists, point to the positive aspects of group pressures on politics and government. Scholars who believe that public opinion also provides a check on the power of business are considered neopluralists as well. The degree to which environmental groups and public opinion mitigate business influence in environmental policymaking is examined in the present study. . . .

The Business Advantage?

Mark Smith's provocative investigation explores the widely held assumption that business dominates the policymaking process when it is unified on specific policy issues, thereby undermining democracy. Using the policy positions of the U.S. Chamber of Commerce as a guide, he identifies 2,364 unifying issues that were considered by Congress between 1953 and 1996. His list of unifying issues encompasses a wide range of policy areas including employment policy, labor-management relations, and clean air regulation. Agenda building in Congress over time is his dependent variable. Among the independent variables he analyzes are "public mood," public attitudes toward corporations, partisan composition of Congress, "presidential leadership opening" (that is, when partisan turnover in Congress runs in the president's favor), corporate PAC funding, and the state of the economy. Mark Smith finds that

> unity does not increase the direct influence of business and reduce democratic control by the citizenry. Instead, unity coincides with the opposite results. Issues marked by a common business position are precisely those for which government decisions are affected most strongly by election outcomes and the responsiveness of officeholders to their constituents. Policies match the collective desires of business only when citizens, through their policy preferences and voting choices, embrace ideas and candidates supportive of what business wants. To bolster its odds of winning in politics, business needs to seek backing from the broad public.

According to Mark Smith, therefore, only when the public supports the unified positions of business on policy issues does business achieve its legislative goals. When the public opposes the positions of business, however, Congress tends to follow the public will even though business is unified. Since all unifying policy issues are highly ideological, partisan, and salient. Congress nearly always follows the public on these issues. He concludes by stating, "The long-standing debates over unity among pluralists, elite theorists, and ruling class theorists have focused our attention in the wrong place. Widespread scholarly concerns about business unity are misplaced, for unifying issues are marked by the highest, rather than the lowest, degree of democratic control by the citizenry." Smith's interpretation of his findings places him in the neopluralist camp along with Baumgartner and Leech and Berry. . . .

Baumgartner and Jones report significant changes in the environmental interest group sphere and show dramatic growth in the numbers of environmental groups and the resources available to them. Based on their analysis, the number of environmental organizations nearly tripled from 1960 to 1990, and the combined staff reported by those groups increased nearly ten times. This surge in environmental group membership is one of the most important reasons for the enactment of so many major environmental laws during the 1970s and 1980s, often over the protests of powerful business lobbyists. . . .

This book provided a comprehensive investigation of how much corporate America has influenced agenda building and environmental policymaking since 1970. The study began by charting the development of business interests since the founding of the nation and by raising important issues about democratic theory and the role of business in American politics. A review of the literature on interest groups addressed collective-action issues and the emergence of citizen groups in the agenda-setting process. Research by the neopluralists suggests that public opinion and citizen groups have tempered the influence of business interests in social policymaking. Based on their findings, one would expect this to be the case in environmental and natural resource policy. Theories addressing certain political and economic variables, issue definition, framing processes, and agenda building were introduced and applied in the analysis of the role of business in Congress, at the EPA and natural resource agencies, in federal court, and in environmental and natural resource disputes. . . .

Major Findings

This book reports a number of major findings. In sharp contrast to the conventional wisdom that business interests actively oppose environmental and natural resource protection on a continuous basis, the data presented [clearly shows that] corporations do not take a position on proposed legislation in Congress about four-fifths of the time. The widely held belief that business frequently opposes environmental regulation and natural resource conservation is also not true. Regardless of how companies align (that is, unified or particularized), they tend to support environmental legislation more often than not. . . .

The study also reports several important findings concerning the influence of business over federal agencies and the courts. As the data indicate, the number of public comments on proposed environmental and natural resource rules and which segments of the population participate in the rulemaking process varies depending on the saliency and nature of the policy issue involved. As Golden discovers, a large percentage of those who submit comments are located outside Washington DC. The exceptionally large number of comments submitted by citizen groups on the natural resource rules examined in this research supports the position by the neopluralists that the dramatic rise in the number and size of such groups is effectively competing against the lobbying activities of business interests. Comments by corporations were generally hostile toward the EPA's efforts to promulgate new environmental regulations. Overall, public comments on proposed rules by EPA, the Forest Service, and the FWS have no or very little effect on the composition of final rules. Comments that contain new facts and information normally receive the closest attention by agency officials. Thus, as Golden finds, business does not exercise an undue influence over rulemaking involving environmental and natural resource issues. Instead, what kinds of rules are proposed to begin with is most important. This is determined by who occupies the White House and who the president appoints to senior positions in the environmental protection and natural resource agencies. . . .

The findings from the analyses of business influence in government institutions provide compelling reasons for investigating the influence of corporate interests within specific contexts involving disputes over environmental regulation and the use of natural resources. As this study indicated, in the end GE did not get its way in its fight to block the EPA's order that it clean up the PCBs it had dumped in the Hudson River. Likewise, the coal companies and utilities were unable to persuade Congress to exclude controls on sulfur dioxide emissions to reduce acid rain from the clean Air Act Amendments of 1990. In both cases, the scientific evidence concerning the negative impact of PCBs and SO_2 emissions on the environment and public health was overwhelming and undercut opposing political and economic forces in the debate over policy. Public concern was also high, prompting the FPA and Congress, respectively, to take action against the wishes of powerful economic interests.

The battle over controlling GHG emissions and climate change, however, presents a very different story. Extremely influential energy producers and consumers have teamed up to prevent the U.S. government from ratifying the Kyoto agreement and from taking a leadership role at the international level to address the climate change issue. The ratification of the Kyoto treaty by Russia represents a significant step forward to resolving the global climate change problem. Nonetheless, the global effort is considerably weakened without the participation of large CO_2 emitters such as the United States and Australia. It is unlikely that U.S. policy on climate change will reverse course during President Bush's second term.

In addition, the study explored the influence of business in three controversies concerning natural resource issues. Despite calls for reform, mining interests have successfully beaten back attempts to revise the General Mining Law of 1872. Sugarcane growers and development forces were able to thwart efforts to restore the Florida Everglades until scientists and environmentalists banded together and persuaded the federal government, particularly the U.S. Army Corps of Engineers and Congress, to take action. The state government, which has been continuously pressured from all sides, has waffled in its intentions to improve the wetlands ecosystem in South Florida. Environmentalists have been successful in attracting media attention, expanding the scope of conflict beyond the region and the state, and using the courts to protect the northern spotted owl and old-growth forests in the Pacific Northwest. The ESA continues to provide a strong pillar in the debate over logging old-growth trees on public lands. Revision of the ESA by the Republican-controlled White House and Congress in the coming years could place economic interests ahead of habitat protection and eventually spell the demise of the northern spotted owl and other endangered species across the country. . . .

Implications of the Study's Findings

This study's findings have a number of implications for the way analysts view the role of business in environmental and natural resource policymaking. At the aggregate level it is clear that business interests selectively choose which bills to oppose or support in Congress, and they do not, as environmentalists, media commentators, and some scholars assume, continuously and unrelentingly pressure legislators for favorable treatment. They are most likely to become active in critical and salient policy debates. Although their participation in the legislative process is far less than expected, the controversies in which they decide to become involved tend to be ones where there is much at stake for them *and* the environment. In this sense, the lobbying activities of business can have an enormous impact on the nation's effort to protect the environment and natural resources.

When business does choose to lobby Congress on environmental legislation, it more often supports rather than opposes such legislation. This result probably indicates that the views of business interests are often conveyed and considered during the initial writing of bills. The multiple indicators approach used by Mark Smith and employed in this research unfortunately does not include this somewhat hidden but critical facet of the agenda-building process in Congress. Of course, business interests will actively oppose legislation when their views are not reflected in legislative proposals and when there is much at stake. Such legislation is adopted when pressure from environmental groups and public opinion requires congressional representatives to take immediate action to address urgent pollution or natural resource problems. Congress is unable to always act according to the desires of the business community because of the existence of previous, and oftentimes landmark, law. In such cases corporations seldom get their way. . . .

Analysis of the six case studies, however, offers more support for the position of the neopluralists. Generally, when much is at stake, environmental groups tend to mobilize and provide an effective check on the influence of business interests. This is evident in the conflicts involving GE and the dumping of PCBs in the Hudson River, the promulgation of acid rain regulations, the restoration of the Everglades, and protection of the northern spotted owl and old-growth forests. Public opinion was a factor in all these controversies, though to varying degrees. Therefore, when conflicts are salient, environmental groups and public opinion tend to present an important, countervailing force to business interests. Mancur Olson would not have predicted this finding.

Finally, the overall results of the investigation have important implications for the influence of business in environmental and natural resource policymaking in particular, and democratic theory in general. Corporations strategically select which legislative debates to enter, and they take positions on environmental and natural resource legislation only a small percentage of the time. Furthermore, business interests do not exert an undue influence in the rulemaking process. Yet, they tend to win as many cases as they lose in the federal court of appeals. Overall, however, business does not get what it wants from government institutions a majority of the time, as some argue. This study's findings suggest that the influence of business in environmental and natural resource policymaking is modest at best.

The examination of the case studies presents a similar picture. Although business interests experienced early success in conflicts over the contamination of the Hudson River. SO_2 emissions, the pollution of the Everglades, and the logging of old-growth forests, they eventually were forced to bow to the demands of federal officials. This is not the situation, of course, in disputes over hardrock mining and climate change. In these instances, corporations have thus far been able to defeat efforts to reform the General Mining Act of 1872 and reduce GHG emissions. Based on the overall analysis of the environmental regulatory and the natural resource case studies, however, business interests do not often get their way. As this study shows, they tend to have a mixed rate of success in influencing the outcomes of salient policy controversies.

In addition to environmental groups and public opinion, other factors also mitigate the influence of business in agenda building and policymaking. Competing elites in the media and scientific community, for example, can point out differences between what corporations are claiming and the actual evidence. As this study revealed, the media played a central role in the controversy over the northern spotted owl and old-growth forests. What started out as a regional (Pacific Northwest) issue quickly expanded to the national level as a result of extensive media coverage of the plight of the owl and its habitat. The timber industry was thus forced to reduce logging on public land considerably. Likewise, scientists brought to light the negative impacts of PCB contamination of the Hudson River, SO_2 emissions on aquatic bodies and forests, and agricultural runoff in the Everglades. In each case business groups were forced to moderate significantly their stands. Federal district trial court judges, too, placed controls on pollution of the Everglades and logging in old-growth forests. This was only possible because of the existence of groundbreaking federal laws governing environmental and natural resource protection (for example, the Clean Water Act and the ESA). As James Madison suggested would generally happen in *Federalist Paper Number 10,* the environmental policy arena is characterized by a healthy balance between competing interests and stakeholders. The system of checks and balances between the three branches of government and the protection of individual rights allow business interests to pursue aggressively their aims but at the same time prevent them from completely destroying the environment and severely harming public health.

POSTSCRIPT

Is America Dominated by Big Business?

The key issue in this debate is the extent of the influence of corporate power over the making and administrating of government policies on issues that concern them. The dominant view is that neither the public nor mobilized noncorporate interests can effectively counterpose corporate interests. Two political scientists who have advocated this view in a lifetime of publications are G. William Domhoff and Thomas R. Dye. Domhoff's article in this debate contains selections from the fifth edition of his book *Who Rules America?* (McGraw-Hill, 2006). In an earlier book, *Changing the Powers That Be: How the Left Can Stop Losing and Win* (Rowman & Littlefield, 2003), he focused on how to fight this corporate power. Three of Dye's recent books are *Politics in America,* 7th ed. (Pearson Prentice Hall, 2007), *Who's Running America? The Bush Restoration* (Prentice Hall, 2003), and *Top Down Policymaking* (Chatham House, 2001). Other works supporting this view are Michael Parenti, *Democracy for the Few* (Thomson-Wadsworth, 2008); Melissa L. Rossi, *What Every American Should Know about Who's Really Running America* (Plume Book, 2007); Lou Dobbs, *War on the Middle Class: How Government, Big Business, and Special Interest Groups Are Waging War on the American Dream and How to Fight Back* (Viking, 2006); Charles Perrow, *Organizing America: Wealth, Power, and the Origins of Corporate America* (Princeton University Press, 2002); Peter Kobrak, *Cozy Politics: Political Parties, Campaign Finance, and Compromised Governance* (Lynne Rienner, 2002); Arianna Stassinopoulos Huffington, *Pigs at the Trough: How Corporate Greed and Political Corruption Are Undermining America* (Crown, 2003); Ted Nace, *Gangs of America: The Rise of Corporate Power and the Disabling of Democracy* (Berrett-Koehler, 2003); Dan Clawson et al., *Dollars and Votes: How Business Campaign Contributions Subvert Democracy* (Temple University Press, 1998); John B. Parrott, *Being Like God: How American Elites Abuse Politics and Power* (University Press of America, 2003); Russell Mokhiber and Robert Weissman, *On the Rampage: Corporate Predators and the Destruction of Democracy* (Common Courage Press, 2005); Paul Kivel, *You Call This Democracy? Who Benefits, Who Pays and Who Really Decides?* (Apex Press, 2004); and Charles Derber, *Hidden Power: What You Need to Know to Save Our Democracy* (Berret-Koehler, 2005).

Several authors advance the thesis that American corporations also seek to some degree to rule the world, including David C. Korten, *When Corporations Rule the World,* 2nd ed. (Kumarian Press, 2001); and Peter Alexis Gourevich and James J. Shinn, *Political Power and Corporate Control: The New Global Politics of Corporate Governance* (Princeton University Press, 2005).

For some pluralist arguments, see Stephen E. Frantzich, *Citizen Democracy: Political Activists in a Cynical Age,* 3rd ed. (Rowman & Littlefield, 2008); Feliz

Kolb, *Protest and Opportunities: The Political Outcomes of Social Movements* (Campus Verlag, 2007); Michael Rabinder James, *Deliberative Democracy and the Plural Polity* (University Press of Kansas, 2004); Kevin Danaher, *Insurrection: Citizen Challenges to Corporate Power* (Routledge, 2003); David S. Meyers et al., eds., *Routing the Opposition: Social Movements, Public Policy, and Democracy* (University of Minnesota Press, 2005); Jeffrey M. Berry, *The New Liberalism: The Rising Power of Citizen Groups* (Brookings Institution, 1999); and *Battling Big Business: Countering Greenwash, Infiltration, and Other Forms of Corporate Bullying* (Common Courage Press, 2002). Recently, the pluralist view is being reworked into political process theory; see Andrew S. McFarland, *Neopluralism: The Evolution of Political Process Theory* (University Press of Kansas, 2004).

ISSUE 11

Does Capitalism Undermine Democracy?

YES: Robert B. Reich, from "How Capitalism Is Killing Democracy," *Foreign Policy* (September/October 2007)

NO: Anthony B. Kim, from "Economic Freedom Underpins Human Rights and Democratic Governance," *Heritage Foundation Web Memo* (March 18, 2008)

ISSUE SUMMARY

YES: Robert B. Reich, Professor of Public Policy at the University of California, Berkeley, and former U.S. Secretary of Labor, accuses capitalism of undermining democratic governments' ability to serve the public good and advance the general welfare. The political power of the corporations exceeds that of the people so many nations with democratic elections do not function as democracies.

NO: Anthony B. Kim, a policy analyst at the Heritage Foundation's Center for International Trade and Economics, contends that economic progress through advancing economic freedom has allowed more people to discuss and adopt different views more candidly, ultimately leading societies to be more open, inclusive, and democratic.

One of the longstanding findings of the social sciences is the connection between economic development and democracy. Economic growth creates the need for skilled and professional workers and thus the expansion of education and the growth of the middle class. Over time the educated and the middle class pressure for rights and eventually the right to participate in the selection of leaders and to influence government policies. Economic growth over the long run also tends to create government support for freer markets and individual and organizations initiative, which can eventually increase opposition to despots. Indirectly, therefore, economic growth is a major cause of democracy.

But is this how economic growth impacts modern developed nations today? Economic growth also has produced powerful multinational corporations with concentrated economic power, and these powerful corporations are a threat to democracy. Corporations finance politicians' campaigns, lobby Congress, arrange to participate in the writing of legislation, and use their resources in many legal and even illegal ways to influence government to serve their interests or to oppose actions that would hurt their interests. The social sciences are united in this view of the alignment of power in America and many other nations. There is a debate, however, about whether this situation is a case of corporate control or only corporate influence. The latter allows other interests, including the public good, to also have influence over the government and thus make it more democratic, that is, rule of the people. The thesis of corporate control versus corporate influence is debated in Issue 10. Issue 11 examines whether capitalism, the driver of economic growth, is good or bad for democracy.

According to Reich, "Conventional wisdom holds that where either capitalism or democracy flourishes, the other must soon follow. Yet today, their fortunes are beginning to diverge." His thesis, as stated in his title, is that capitalism is killing democracy. It is undermining "the government's capacity to respond to citizens' concerns." He wrote before the current recession, which has revealed the chasm between the interests of the corporations and the people. Hundreds of billions of dollars have been spent by the federal government to bail out corporations. This helps to save some jobs, free up credit, minimize the losses suffered by pensions, and turn around the recession. Thus, individuals have been helped, but little has been spent directly for individuals except "cash for clunkers." The American public sees the American government as serving corporations first and individuals last. Anthony B. Kim is a salesman for capitalism. After all, he works for the American Enterprise Institute. But he backs up his argument that free enterprise spawns and strengthens democracy with solid data.

YES

Robert Reich

How Capitalism Is Killing Democracy?

It was supposed to be a match made in heaven. Capitalism and democracy, we've long been told, are the twin ideological pillars capable of bringing unprecedented prosperity and freedom to the world. In recent decades, the duo has shared a common ascent. By almost any measure, global capitalism is triumphant. Most nations around the world are today part of a single, integrated, and turbocharged global market. Democracy has enjoyed a similar renaissance. Three decades ago, a third of the world's nations held free elections; today, nearly two thirds do.

Conventional wisdom holds that where either capitalism or democracy flourishes, the other must soon follow. Yet today, their fortunes are beginning to diverge. Capitalism, long sold as the yin to democracy's yang, is thriving, while democracy is struggling to keep up. China, poised to become the world's third largest capitalist nation this year after the United States and Japan, has embraced market freedom, but not political freedom. Many economically successful nations—from Russia to Mexico—are democracies in name only. They are encumbered by the same problems that have hobbled American democracy in recent years, allowing corporations and elites buoyed by run-away economic success to undermine the government's capacity to respond to citizens' concerns.

Of course, democracy means much more than the process of free and fair elections. It is a system for accomplishing what can only be achieved by citizens joining together to further the common good. But though free markets have brought unprecedented prosperity to many, they have been accompanied by widening inequalities of income and wealth, heightened job insecurity, and environmental hazards such as global warming. Democracy is designed to allow citizens to address these very issues in constructive ways. And yet a sense of political powerlessness is on the rise among citizens in Europe, Japan, and the United States, even as consumers and investors feel more empowered. In short, no democratic nation is effectively coping with capitalism's negative side effects.

This fact is not, however, a failing of capitalism. As these two forces have spread around the world, we have blurred their responsibilities, to the detriment of our democratic duties. Capitalism's role is to increase the economic

Reprinted in entirety by McGraw-Hill with permission from *Foreign Policy* September/October 2007, pp. 38–42. www.foreignpolicy.com. © 2007 Washingtonpost.Newsweek Interactive, LLC.

pie, nothing more. And while capitalism has become remarkably responsive to what people want as individual consumers, democracies have struggled to perform their own basic functions: to articulate and act upon the common good, and to help societies achieve both growth and equity. Democracy, at its best, enables citizens to debate collectively how the slices of the pie should be divided and to determine which rules apply to private goods and which to public goods. Today, those tasks are increasingly being left to the market. What is desperately needed is a clear delineation of the boundary between global capitalism and democracy—between the economic game, on the one hand, and how its rules are set, on the other. If the purpose of capitalism is to allow corporations to play the market as aggressively as possible, the challenge for citizens is to stop these economic entities from being the authors of the rules by which we live.

The Cost of Doing Business

Most people are of two minds: As consumers and investors, we want the bargains and high returns that the global economy provides. As citizens, we don't like many of the social consequences that flow from these transactions. We like to blame corporations for the ills that follow, but in truth we've made this compact with ourselves. After all, we know the roots of the great economic deals we're getting. They come from workers forced to settle for lower wages and benefits. They come from companies that shed their loyalties to communities and morph into global supply chains. They come from CEOs who take home exorbitant paychecks. And they come from industries that often wreak havoc on the environment.

Unfortunately, in the United States, the debate about economic change tends to occur between two extremist camps: those who want the market to rule unimpeded, and those who want to protect jobs and preserve communities as they are. Instead of finding ways to soften the blows of globalization, compensate the losers, or slow the pace of change, we go to battle. Consumers and investors nearly always win the day, but citizens lash out occasionally in symbolic fashion, by attempting to block a new trade agreement or protesting the sale of U.S. companies to foreign firms. It is a sign of the inner conflict Americans feel—between the consumer in us and the citizen in us—that the reactions are often so schizophrenic.

Such conflicting sentiments are hardly limited to the United States. The recent wave of corporate restructurings in Europe has shaken the continent's typical commitment to job security and social welfare. It's leaving Europeans at odds as to whether they prefer the private benefits of global capitalism in the face of increasing social costs at home and abroad. Take, for instance, the auto industry. In 2001, DaimlerChrysler faced mounting financial losses as European car buyers abandoned the company in favor of cheaper competitors. So, CEO Dieter Zetsche cut 26,000 jobs from his global workforce and closed six factories. Even profitable companies are feeling the pressure to become ever more efficient. In 2005, Deutsche Bank simultaneously announced an

87 percent increase in net profits and a plan to cut 6,400 jobs, nearly half of them in Germany and Britain. Twelve-hundred of the jobs were then moved to low-wage nations. Today, European consumers and investors are doing better than ever, but job insecurity and inequality are rising, even in social democracies that were established to counter the injustices of the market. In the face of such change, Europe's democracies have shown themselves to be so paralyzed that the only way citizens routinely express opposition is through massive boycotts and strikes.

In Japan, many companies have abandoned lifetime employment, cut workforces, and closed down unprofitable lines. Just months after Howard Stringer was named Sony's first non-Japanese CEO, he announced the company would trim 10,000 employees, about 7 percent of its workforce. Surely some Japanese consumers and investors benefit from such corporate downsizing: By 2006, the Japanese stock market had reached a 14-year high. But many Japanese workers have been left behind. A nation that once prided itself on being an "all middle-class society" is beginning to show sharp disparities in income and wealth. Between 1999 and 2005, the share of Japanese households without savings doubled, from 12 percent to 24 percent. And citizens there routinely express a sense of powerlessness. Like many free countries around the world, Japan is embracing global capitalism with a democracy too enfeebled to face the free market's many social penalties.

On the other end of the political spectrum sits China, which is surging toward capitalism without democracy at all. That's good news for people who invest in China, but the social consequences for the country's citizens are mounting. Income inequality has widened enormously. China's new business elites live in McMansions inside gated suburban communities and send their children to study overseas. At the same time, China's cities are bursting with peasants from the countryside who have sunk into urban poverty and unemployment. And those who are affected most have little political recourse to change the situation, beyond riots that are routinely put down by force.

But citizens living in democratic nations aren't similarly constrained. They have the ability to alter the rules of the game so that the cost to society need not be so great. And yet, we've increasingly left those responsibilities to the private sector—to the companies themselves and their squadrons of lobbyists and public-relations experts—pretending as if some inherent morality or corporate good citizenship will compel them to look out for the greater good. But they have no responsibility to address inequality or protect the environment on their own. We forget that they are simply duty bound to protect the bottom line.

The Rules of the Game

Why has capitalism succeeded while democracy has steadily weakened? Democracy has become enfeebled largely because companies, in intensifying competition for global consumers and investors, have invested ever greater sums in lobbying, public relations, and even bribes and kickbacks, seeking laws that give them a competitive advantage over their rivals. The result is an arms race for political influence that is drowning out the voices of average citizens. In the United States, for example, the fights that preoccupy Congress, those that consume weeks or months of congressional staff time, are typically contests between competing companies or industries.

While corporations are increasingly writing their own rules, they are also being entrusted with a kind of social responsibility or morality. Politicians praise companies for acting "responsibly" or condemn them for not doing so. Yet the purpose of capitalism is to get great deals for consumers and investors. Corporate executives are not authorized by anyone—least of all by their investors—to balance profits against the public good. Nor do they have any expertise in making such moral calculations. Democracy is supposed to represent the public in drawing such lines. And the message that companies are moral beings with social responsibilities diverts public attention from the task of establishing such laws and rules in the first place.

It is much the same with what passes for corporate charity. Under today's intensely competitive form of global capitalism, companies donate money to good causes only to the extent the donation has public-relations value, thereby boosting the bottom line. But shareholders do not invest in firms expecting the money to be used for charitable purposes. They invest to earn high returns. Shareholders who wish to be charitable would, presumably, make donations to charities of their own choosing in amounts they decide for themselves. The larger danger is that these conspicuous displays of corporate beneficence hoodwink the public into believing corporations have charitable impulses that can be relied on in a pinch.

By pretending that the economic success corporations enjoy saddles them with particular social duties only serves to distract the public from democracy's responsibility to set the rules of the game and thereby protect the common good. The only way for the citizens in us to trump the consumers in us is through laws and rules that make our purchases and investments social choices as well as personal ones. A change in labor laws making it easier for employees to organize and negotiate better terms, for example, might increase the price of products and services. My inner consumer won't like that very much, but the citizen in me might think it a fair price to pay. A small transfer tax on sales of stock, to slow the movement of capital ever so slightly, might give communities a bit more time to adapt to changing circumstances. The return on my retirement fund might go down by a small fraction, but the citizen in me thinks it worth the price. Extended unemployment insurance combined with wage insurance and job training could ease the pain for workers caught in the downdrafts of globalization.

Let us be clear: The purpose of democracy is to accomplish ends we cannot achieve as individuals. But democracy cannot fulfill this role when companies use politics to advance or maintain their competitive standing, or when they appear to take on social responsibilities that they have no real capacity or authority to fulfill. That leaves societies unable to address the trade-offs between economic growth and social problems such as job insecurity, widening inequality, and climate change. As a result, consumer and investor interests almost invariably trump common concerns.

The vast majority of us are global consumers and, at least indirectly, global investors. In these roles we should strive for the best deals possible. That is how we participate in the global market economy. But those private benefits usually have social costs. And for those of us living in democracies, it is imperative to remember that we are also citizens who have it in our power to reduce these social costs, making the true price of the goods and services we purchase as low as possible. We can accomplish this larger feat only if we take our roles as citizens seriously. The first step, which is often the hardest, is to get our thinking straight.

Want to Know More?

Robert B. Reich argues that the effectiveness of democracy has waned in the face of the modern global market in *Supercapitalism: The Transformation of Business, Democracy, and Everyday Life* (New York: Alfred A. Knopf, 2007). He blogs regularly about global economics and politics at robertreich.blogspot.com.

Milton Friedman's classic *Capitalism and Freedom* (Chicago: University of Chicago Press, 1962) established economic freedom as a key precondition for political freedom. In *The Great Risk Shift: The Assault on American Jobs, Families, Health Care and Retirement—And How You Can Fight Back* (New York: Oxford University Press, 2006), Jacob S. Hacker examines a prosperous United States where citizens increasingly feel politically powerless. Martin Wolf refutes the allegation that the global economy undermines democracy in *The Morality of the Market* (Foreign Policy, September/October 2003).

For links to relevant Web sites, access to the *FP* Archive, and a comprehensive index of related *Foreign Policy* articles, go to www.ForeignPolicy.com.

Economic Freedom Underpins Human Rights and Democratic Governance

In her preface to the Department of State's recently published *Country Reports on Human Rights Practices for 2007*, Secretary of State Condoleezza Rice wrote: "These values [liberty, dignity, and rights] are the basic endowments of all human beings, and the surest way to protect and preserve them is through effective, lawful, democratic governance."[1] There is no distinct formula through which to guarantee this process, but an unequivocal linkage to ensuring this progression lies in economic freedom. As a fundamental element of enhancing human rights, economic freedom is an indispensable means toward promoting effective, lawful, and democratic governance.

A Valuable End in Itself

Economic freedom is a part of human liberty that is concerned with the material autonomy of the individual in relation to the government and other organized groups. As Friedrich Hayek once observed, "To be controlled in our economic pursuits means to be controlled in everything."[2] Hayek's observation on economic freedom is based on the truth that each person is a free and responsible being with an inalienable dignity and fundamental human rights that should come first in any political system.

It is not surprising to see that seven of the 10 countries identified as "the most systematic human rights violators"[3] (North Korea, Burma, Iran, Syria, Zimbabwe, Cuba, and Belarus) by the State Department's human rights report are "repressed" economies according to the *Index of Economic Freedom*, an annual publication by The Heritage Foundation and *The Wall Street Journal* that measures economic freedom around the world.[4] Government leaders in these countries put their own tyrannical political systems ahead of the people's economic freedoms. The concentration of power and wealth in the hands of unaccountable and autocratic political elites results in erosion and nullification of basic social and economic rights such as the rights to health, food, water, and education.

As the *Index* defines it, "the highest form of economic freedom provides an absolute absence of coercion or constraint of economic liberty beyond the

From *Heritage Foundation Web Memo*, #1861, March 18, 2008. Copyright © 2008 by Heritage Foundation. Reprinted by permission.

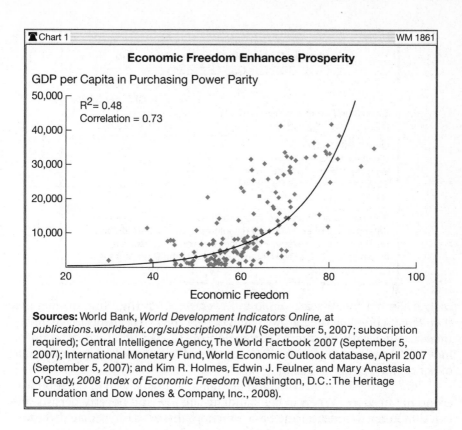

Chart 1   WM 1861

Economic Freedom Enhances Prosperity

GDP per Capita in Purchasing Power Parity

$R^2 = 0.48$
Correlation = 0.73

Economic Freedom

Sources: World Bank, *World Development Indicators Online,* at *publications.worldbank.org/subscriptions/WDI* (September 5, 2007; subscription required); Central Intelligence Agency, The World Factbook 2007 (September 5, 2007); International Monetary Fund, World Economic Outlook database, April 2007 (September 5, 2007); and Kim R. Holmes, Edwin J. Feulner, and Mary Anastasia O'Grady, *2008 Index of Economic Freedom* (Washington, D.C.: The Heritage Foundation and Dow Jones & Company, Inc., 2008).

extent necessary for citizens to protect and maintain liberty itself."[5] In other words, economic freedom is about individuals' basic economic rights to work, produce, save, and consume without the state's intimidation and infringement. It encompasses the freedom to engage in entrepreneurial activities, having choices in education and health care, fair taxation, and just treatment by the courts under the rule of law.

Greater economic freedom generates opportunities for people and creates sustainable wealth and respect for human rights. By reducing barriers to economic activities, economic freedom helps to create a framework in which people fulfill their dreams of success. This is well-documented in the *Index,* which identifies strong synergies among the 10 key ingredients of economic freedom, among which are openness to the world, transparency, and the rule of law.

Empirical findings confirm that greater economic freedom empowers people and improves their quality of life by unleashing opportunities and innovative ideas. As Chart 1 demonstrates, there is a strong positive relationship between economic freedom and prosperity. People in countries with greater economic freedom enjoy higher standards of living than people in countries with less economic freedom.

More important, there is another noticeable dimension to the relationship between economic freedom and prosperity; one that involves the evolution of economic freedom and standard of living over time. Table 1 shows

☎Table I   WM 1861

Change in Economic Freedom Score and GDP per Capita Growth

Change in Economic Freedom (%) *(1998 Index–2008 Index)*	Average GDP per Capita Growth (%) *(1996–2006)*
Over 2 (20 Countries)	5.50
Between 1 and 2 (25 Countries)	2.73
Between 0 and 1 (53 Countries)	2.55
Between −1 and 0 (36 Countries)	2.38
Below −1 (13 Countries)	1.68

Sources: International Monetary Fund, World Economic Outlook database, October 2007; Kim R. Holmes, Edwin J. Feulner, and Mary Anastasia O'Grady, *2008 Index of Economic Freedom* (Washington, D.C.: The Heritage Foundation and Dow Jones & Company, Inc., 2008).

that, measured by 10-year compound averages, countries' improvements in their *Index* scores and their growth rates of per capita GDP are positively related to each other with the simple correlation of 0.44. In other words, countries moving toward greater economic freedom tend to achieve higher growth rates of per capita GDP over time.[6]

Promoting and preserving human rights cannot be seen in isolation from economic freedom. When living standards are low and poverty persists, violence often replaces peace, and basic human rights are easily violated. Sustainable economic development backed by economic freedom thereby plays a vital role in supporting the expansion and protection of human rights.

A Vital Means to Democratic Governance

Greater economic freedom can also provide more fertile ground for effective and democratic governance. It empowers people to exercise greater control over their daily decision-making processes. In doing so, economic freedom ultimately nurtures political reform as well. Economic freedom makes it possible for independent sources of wealth to counterbalance political power and encourages the cultivation of a pluralistic society.

Debate over the direction of causality between economic freedom and democracy has been somewhat controversial due to the complex interplay between the two freedoms. However, the positive relationship is undeniable. Chart 2 shows the relationship between economic freedom and democratic governance measured by the Economist Intelligence Unit's democracy index.[7] They are clearly interrelated and together form a coherent whole.

It is undeniable that freedom has reached every area of the world over the past century. Economic freedom is a powerful building block for advancing effective and democratic governance. Yet the world needs to be mobilized behind that cause more effectively, and it needs to confront those who advocate ideologies of repression and extremism.

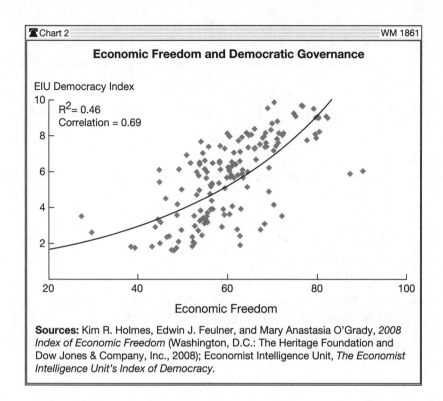

☎ Chart 2   WM 1861

Economic Freedom and Democratic Governance

EIU Democracy Index

$R^2 = 0.46$
Correlation = 0.69

Economic Freedom

Sources: Kim R. Holmes, Edwin J. Feulner, and Mary Anastasia O'Grady, *2008 Index of Economic Freedom* (Washington, D.C.: The Heritage Foundation and Dow Jones & Company, Inc., 2008); Economist Intelligence Unit, *The Economist Intelligence Unit's Index of Democracy.*

In his recent book, *Liberty's Best Hope: American Leadership for the 21st Century,* Heritage Foundation Vice President Kim Holmes highlights the need to build coalitions of freedom-loving countries around the world. He suggests inviting countries to join a common alliance of liberty through a "Global Economic Freedom Forum" and a "Liberty Forum for Human Rights" that would enshrine the powerful interplay of economic freedom, human rights, and political freedom.[8]

Conclusion

As President George W. Bush once noted, "Freedom can be resisted, and freedom can be delayed, but freedom cannot be denied."[9] This is why the United States should continue to stress freedom as a liberating moral force and the foundation of America's leadership for the future. It is the compelling force of economic freedom that empowers people, unleashes powerful forces of choice and opportunity, and nourishes other liberties. As the 21st century progresses, freedom's champions must join to advance their common cause of freedom, peace, and prosperity.

Notes

1. U.S. Department of State, *Country Reports on Human Rights Practices for 2007.*

2. Friedrich Hayek, *The Road to Serfdom* (Chicago, Ill.: The University of Chicago Press, 1944).

3. Jonathan Farrar, Acting Assistant Secretary, Bureau of Democracy, Human Rights, and Labor, "Remarks on the State Department's 2007 Country Reports on Human Rights Practices," March 11, 2008.

4. Kim R. Holmes, Edwin J. Feulner, and Mary Anastasia O'Grady, *2008 Index of Economic Freedom* (Washington, D.C.: The Heritage Foundation and Dow Jones & Company, Inc., 2008).

5. Ibid.

6. Countries are grouped by their *Index* score changes based on 10-year compound average growth rate. As shown in the number of countries in each group in the table, the countries are divided under a normal distribution curve.

7. Covering 192 countries, the EIU Democracy Index is based on five categories: electoral process and pluralism; civil liberties; the functioning of government; political participation; and political culture. The Index classifies: full democracy: scores of 8 to 10; flawed democracy: scores of 6 to 7.9; hybrid regimes: scores of 4 to 5.9; authoritarian regimes: scores below 4.

8. Kim R. Holmes, *Liberty's Best Hope: American Leadership for the 21st Century* (Washington, D.C.: The Heritage Foundation, 2008).

9. President George W. Bush, speech given in Prague, Czech Republic, June 2007.

POSTSCRIPT

Does Capitalism Undermine Democracy?

The foremost issue in understanding our society is the structure of power. Both Issues 10 and 11 address this phenomena. Issue 10 debates the power elite thesis, and Issue 11 debates the impact of capitalism on democracy. In 1962, Milton Friedman pretty much established that economic freedom is a key precondition for political freedom in his classic book *Capitalism and Freedom* (University of Chicago Press). His thesis became the common wisdom to which Reich referred and which he sought to refute. Other works that support Freeman's and Kim's view include Peter L. Berger, *The Capitalist Revolution: Fifty Propositions about Prosperity, Equality, and Liberty* (Basic Books, 1986); Andrew Bernstein, *The Capitalist Manifesto: The Historic, Economic and Philosophic Case for Laissez-Faire* (University Press of America, 2005); Dhanjoo N. Ghista, *Socio-Economic Democracy and the World Government: Collective Capitalism, Depovertization, Human Rights, Template for Sustainable Peace* (World Scientific, 2004); Michael G. Heller, *Capitalism, Institutions, and Economic Development* (Routledge, 2009); Dennis C. Mueller, *Capitalism and Democracy: Challenges and Responses in an Increasingly Interdependent World* (E. Elgar Pub., 2003); Arthur Seldon, ed., *The Virtues of Capitalism* (Liberty Fund, 2004); and Edward W. Younkins, *Champions of a Free Society: Ideas of Capitalism's Philosophers and Economists* (Lexington Books, 2008).

The works that are critical of capitalism's impact on democracy include Brian C. Anderson, *Democratic Capitalism and Its Discontents* (ISI Books, 2007); Noreena Hertz, *The Silent Takeover: Global Capitalism and the Death of Democracy* (Heinemann, 2001); Alex Callinicos, *An Anti-Capitalist Manifesto* (Polity Press, 2003); Mark A. Martinez, *The Myth of the Free Market: The Role of the State in a Capitalist Economy* (Kumarian Press, 2009); and Reich's Own *Supercapitalism: The Transformation of Business, Democracy, and Everyday Life* (Alfred A. Knopf, 2007). Jacob S. Hacker examines a prosperous United States where citizens increasingly feel politically powerless in *Great Risk Shift: The Assault on American Jobs, Families, Health Care and Retirement—And How You Can Fight Back* (Oxford University Press, 2006). A major response to the above critics of capitalism is Martin Wolf's "The Morality of the Market," *Foreign Policy* (September/October 2003), in which he tries to refute the allegation that the global economy undermines democracy. Two works which study the connection of capitalism and democracy more neutrally are Amiya Kumar Bagchi, *Perilous Passage: Mankind and the Global Ascendancy of Capital* (Rowman & Littlefield Publishers, 2005), and Peter Nolan, *Capitalism and Freedom: The Contradictory Character of Globalisation* (Anthem Press, 2007).

ISSUE 12

Should Government Intervene in a Capitalist Economy?

YES: **Joseph E. Stiglitz**, "Government Failure vs. Market Failure: Principles of Regulation," paper prepared for the conference "Government and Markets: Toward a New Theory of Regulation," February 1–3, 2008, Yulee, Florida

NO: **Walter Williams**, "Future Prospects for Economic Liberty," *Imprimis* (September 2009)

ISSUE SUMMARY

YES: Joseph E. Stiglitz, University Professor at Columbia University, argues that the government plays an essential role in enabling the market to work properly. Capitalism runs amok if it is not regulated to protect against abuse and ensure fairness.

NO: Walter Williams, Professor of Economics at George Mason University, argues that the founders defined a small role for government in the Constitution and protected the freedom of individuals. Now the role of government is increasing and individual freedoms are declining. The free market has achieved great prosperity for America and the intervention of government has had net negative impacts.

The expression "That government is best which governs least" sums up a deeply rooted attitude of many Americans. From early presidents Thomas Jefferson and Andrew Jackson, to America's most recent leaders, Ronald Reagan, George Bush, Bill Clinton, and George W. Bush, American politicians have often echoed the popular view that there are certain areas of life best left to the private actions of citizens.

One such area is the economic sphere, where people make their living by buying, selling, and producing goods and services. The tendency of most Americans is to regard direct government involvement in the economic sphere as both unnecessary and dangerous. The purest expression of this view is the economic theory of laissez-faire, a French term meaning "let be" or "let alone."

The seminal formulation of laissez-faire theory was the work of eighteenth-century Scottish philosopher Adam Smith, whose treatise *The Wealth of Nations* appeared in 1776. Smith's thesis was that each individual, pursuing his or her own selfish interests in a competitive market, will be "led by an invisible hand to promote an end which was no part of his intention." In other words, when people single-mindedly seek profit, they actually serve the community, because sellers must keep prices down and quality up if they are to meet the competition of other sellers.

Laissez-faire economics was much honored (in theory, if not always in practice) during the nineteenth and early twentieth centuries. But as the nineteenth century drew to a close, the Populist Party sprang up. The Populists denounced eastern bankers, Wall Street stock manipulators, and rich "moneyed interests," and they called for government ownership of railroads, a progressive income tax, and other forms of state intervention. The Populist Party died out early in the twentieth century, but the Populist message was not forgotten. In fact, it was given new life after 1929, when the stock market collapsed and the United States was plunged into the worst economic depression in its history.

By 1932, a quarter of the nation's workforce was unemployed, and most Americans were finding it hard to believe that the "invisible hand" would set things right. Some Americans totally repudiated the idea of a free market and embraced socialism, the belief that the state (or "the community") should run all major industries. Most stopped short of supporting socialism, but they were now prepared to welcome some forms of state intervention in the economy. President Franklin D. Roosevelt, elected in 1932, spoke to this mood when he pledged a "New Deal" to the American people. "New Deal" has come to stand for a variety of programs that were enacted during the first eight years of Roosevelt's presidency, including business and banking regulations, government pension programs, federal aid to the disabled, unemployment compensation, and government-sponsored work programs. Side by side with the "invisible hand" of the marketplace was now the very visible hand of an activist government.

Government intervention in the economic sphere increased during World War II as the government fixed prices, rationed goods, and put millions to work in government-subsidized war industries. Activist government continued during the 1950s, but the biggest leap forward occurred during the late 1960s and early 1970s, when the federal government launched a variety of new welfare and regulatory programs: the multibillion-dollar War on Poverty; new civil rights and affirmative action mandates; and new laws protecting consumers, workers, disabled people, and the environment. These, in turn, led to a proliferation of new government agencies and bureaus, as well as shelves and shelves of published regulations. Proponents of the new activism conceded that it was expensive, but they insisted that activist government was necessary to protect Americans against pollution, discrimination, dangerous products, and other effects of the modern marketplace. Critics of government involvement called attention not only to its direct costs but also to its effect on business activity and individual freedom.

YES

Joseph E. Stiglitz

Government Failure vs. Market Failure: Principles of Regulation

The subject of regulation has been one of the most contentious, with critics arguing that regulations interfere with the efficiency of the market, and advocates arguing that well-designed regulations not only make markets more efficient but also help ensure that market outcomes are more equitable. Interestingly, as the economy plunges into a slowdown, if not a recession, with more than 2 million Americans expected to lose their homes (unless the government intervenes), there is a growing consensus: there was a need for more government regulation. Responding to these calls—as if to close the barn door after all the horses have gotten out—the Federal Reserve has tightened some regulations. If it is the case that better regulations could have prevented, or even mitigated, the downturn, the country, and the world, will be paying a heavy price for the failure to regulate adequately. And the social costs are no less grave—as hundreds of thousands of Americans will not only have lost their homes but their lifetime savings. Home ownership has long been thought of as contributing to the strength of communities; with the share of home ownership falling, communities too will be weaker. The foreclosures will exacerbate the decline in housing prices, and property tax bases will erode—a further knock on effect of inadequate regulation.

When Upton Sinclair's novel *The Jungle* depicted the terrible sanitary conditions in America's stock yards, Americans turned away from meat; and the meat packing industry asked for government food safety regulation to restore confidence. When the Enron/WorldCom scandal eroded confidence in America's financial markets and accounting firms, there was again a demand for stronger regulation to restore confidence. Whether Sarbanes-Oxley went too far or not far enough may be debated; but what is not debatable is that such regulations were viewed, at least by many Americans, as essential for restoring confidence in America's markets, where scandal had touched every accounting firm, most of the major investment banks, and many of its leading corporations.

Today, America's air and water is cleaner—and Americans are living longer—because of environmental regulations. No one can imagine a world today without food, safety, and environmental regulations. The debate is only

From *Government and Markets: Toward a New Theory of Regulation*. Edited by Edward Balleisen and David Moss. Copyright © 2009 The Tobin Project. Reproduced with the permission of Cambridge University Press.

whether we have gone too far, and whether we could have gotten the desired results at lower costs.

The General Theory of Regulation

The general theory of regulation begins with a simple question: Why is regulation needed? [The answer is] . . . market failures. Adam Smith (it is widely believed) argued that markets by themselves are efficient. Arrow and Debreu established the sense in which that was true (Pareto efficiency, i.e., no one could be made better off without making someone else worse off), and the conditions under which it was true (perfect competition, no externalities, no public goods). Subsequently, Greenwald and Stiglitz showed that whenever information is imperfect or markets incomplete—that is, always—there is a presumption that markets are not (constrained) Pareto efficient. Thus, the notion that markets, by themselves, lead to efficient outcomes has, today, no theoretical justification: no one believes that the conditions under which that statement is true are satisfied.

Some advocates of free markets take it as a matter of faith that the magnitude of the inefficiencies are small (though no one has suggested how one might prove that); but more commonly advocates of free markets take it as a matter of faith that government attempts to correct market failures by and large make things worse. To be sure, there are examples of badly designed government regulations, but the disasters associated with unfettered markets at least provide a prima facie case for the desirability of *some* regulation.

Regulations can thus play an important role in addressing market failures. There are several particular categories of market failures to which I want to call attention. We have regulations designed to mitigate the extent of *externalities*. These include, for instance, zoning restrictions and environmental regulations. We have regulations designed to maintain competition (restrictions on anti-competitive practices), and to ensure that natural monopolies do not abuse their monopoly position (utilities regulations). We have a large set of regulations aimed at protecting consumers (ensuring that the banks where they deposit their money are sufficiently sound, that food and products are safe, or that they are not taken advantage of by unscrupulous merchants, advertising, or lenders). In several of these cases, as we shall note, disclosure is important; but the regulations go well beyond disclosure, for reasons which I explain below.

There are two further categories on which I want to comment, both related to *information problems*. The first concerns insurance. Private sector contractual arrangements often have what would appear to be "regulatory" structures. A fire insurance firm requires that the insured install sprinklers. Sometimes, insurance companies use the price system, i.e., they give a discount if sprinklers are installed. But sometimes they simply will not write the insurance policy if sprinklers are not installed. Many government regulations are similarly motivated: government absorbs risk, and to reduce its risk exposure, imposes constraints; it provides flood and earthquake insurance (explicitly in some cases and implicitly in others—if an earthquake occurs, it knows that it cannot deny assistance to anyone) and demands that houses be constructed so as to reduce the risk of loss. Because of moral hazard—or even because of a failure to perceive accurately the magnitude of the risk—individuals will take insufficient care.

The second category concerns what might be called certification. The meatpackers wanted certification that their products were produced in a safe and humane manner. They also knew that the only credible source of such certification was the government—if the meatpackers paid the certifiers directly, there would be a conflict of interest.

Recent troubles in accounting and rating agencies highlight the problems of private certification. The Enron scandal highlighted that the accounting firms' incentives were distorted; and while Sarbanes-Oxley improved matters, it did not fully resolve them. Similarly, with the rating agencies being paid by the financial firms to rate the complex products they were creating, it is perhaps no surprise that they gave AAA ratings to highly risky products.

Information is a public good. All individuals want to be assured that if they put money in a bank, the bank will be there when it comes time to withdraw the money. Government bank regulation is in part certification: it sets certain standards that a bank must satisfy—and inspects that it fulfills those standards. It could, of course, stop there, allowing individuals to deposit their money in "uncertified" banks (and in a sense, it does that—there are many non-certified financial institutions). But it goes beyond that: it does not allow banks to operate unless they satisfy certain conditions. And that, in part, is because it knows that if a bank fails, it may have to be bailed out. As one astute observer put it: there are two kinds of governments—those who provide deposit insurance and know it; and those who do so and don't know it. This in turn means that in order to mitigate the moral hazard problem, restrictions on banks have to be imposed.

Irrationality

The market failure approach growing out of an analysis of the standard assumptions required to establish the Pareto efficiency of the economy (the First Fundamental Theorem) is, however, only one of at least three strands of analysis underlying the demand for regulation. A second focuses on *market irrationality*. The standard competitive equilibrium model assumed that all individuals were rational; it explained why rational individuals (households) interacting with profit (or value) maximizing firms in a competitive marketplace might not result in Pareto efficient allocations. But individuals may not be rational and may deviate from rationality in systematic ways. Individuals (and even more so societies) have to be saved from themselves. Markets suffer from irrational exuberance and irrational pessimism. Individuals may not save adequately for their retirement.

Until the recent work on behavioral economics, economists typically looked askance at such paternalistic arguments for government intervention. Why, it was argued, should there be any presumption that governments are more rational or better informed than individuals? Who are we to impose our beliefs of what is rational on others? Part of the answer was provided by the classic theory of market failure: one might argue that so long as the individual only harms himself, there is no reason for government intervention. But individual actions may adversely affect others (there are, in effect, externalities). Regulation may reduce the likelihood of these adverse effects occurring and their impacts when they do. There is a special category of externalities that arises in democratic societies. Society cannot stand idly by when it sees someone starving—even if it is a result of the individual's own mistakes, say, not saving enough. Society will bail out the individual (or a bank which is too big to fail). Knowing that, individuals have an incentive to save too little (or banks to take too much risk). Knowing that, government should impose regulations to ensure that individuals do save enough (or banks do not undertake excessive risk).

But the new behavioral economics puts a new perspective on these issues: individuals may, in some sense, be better off if they are compelled to undertake some actions or are circumscribed from undertaking others. A potential alcoholic or drug addict may realize that he may be tempted to consume these toxic products and then become addicted. He knows *before he becomes addicted* that he will regret getting the addiction, but once he is addicted, will not be able to change his behavior. He therefore wants the government (or someone else) to make it impossible, or at least more difficult, to become addicted. (Matters are made worse by the fact that there are firms, such as those in the tobacco industry, who profit by taking advantage of addiction. By increasing the addictive properties of their products, they reduce the elasticity of demand and increase profitability.)

Similarly, individuals may know that they can easily be induced to save very little or a great deal, simply on the basis of the default set by the employer in choosing the fraction of income to put into a savings account. Accordingly, they might want the government to force the firm to undertake a kind of analysis that sets the default rate in ways which enable the individual to have a reasonably comfortable retirement, without sacrificing excessively current levels of consumption.

A formal welfare analysis of such regulations within the traditional welfare economics paradigm is, of course, difficult: Do we evaluate the impacts of the policy intervention using individuals' *ex ante* expected utility (their incorrect beliefs, for instance, about the consequences of their actions), or using *ex post* realized (average) utility?

Distributive Justice

There is a third category of rationale for government interventions: the best that can be said for the market economy is that it produces *efficient* outcomes; there is no presumption that it produces outcomes that are viewed as socially just. Regulations may be an important instrument for achieving distributive objectives, especially when governments face tight budgetary constraints (or other administrative constraints). CRA (Community Reinvestment Act) lending requirements or health insurance mandates may be an effective way of helping poor individuals when the government cannot afford other ways of helping them.

Some advocates of free markets appeal to Coase's conjecture (sometimes called Coase's theorem) that, even in the presence of externalities, individuals can bargain themselves to an efficient outcome, so long as there are clearly defined property rights. But such claims cannot be supported so long as there is imperfect information (e.g., concerning individuals' valuation of the external costs) or transactions costs, as there always are. Indeed, one of the standard arguments for regulation is that it economizes on transactions costs.

A variant of Coase's argument is that those injured should (be entitled to) sue those who are doing the injury. With a good tort legal system (including class action suits), individuals will have appropriate incentives. Interestingly, conservatives (like those in the Bush Administration) argue both for less regulation and reduced capacity to recover damages. They sometimes have a valid argument against the legal system: as currently constituted; in many areas it provides "excessive" recovery—providing excessive incentives for care—at the same time that in other areas it provides insufficient incentives (without class actions, the transactions costs are so large that recovery of damages is impossible).

More generally, sums required to compensate for damage done to individuals may not provide appropriate incentives; by linking the two together, incentives are not in general optimized. Moreover, in many cases, there is no adequate monetary incentive: someone whose child has died as a result of lead poisoning can never really be adequately compensated. *Ex post* compensation is not enough. We have to stop the bad behavior *ex ante,* if we can.

Other forms of market mechanisms, it is now realized, also are insufficient—reputation mechanisms help but do not ensure efficiency.

Regulations vs. Other Forms of Intervention

Critics of regulation argue the objectives of regulation can be achieved better at lower costs by using "market based" interventions, i.e., taxes and subsides. If smoking gives rise to an externality, tax smoking. If greenhouse gases give rise to global warming, tax greenhouse gas emissions. Price interventions have much to commend them: they are general, simple, and often have low transaction costs. But research over the last quarter century has clarified an important set of limitations. Indeed, the very conditions (such as imperfect and asymmetric information) that imply that markets by themselves do not in general lead to (constrained) Pareto efficient outcomes also imply that price interventions by themselves will not suffice.

i. Imperfect information and incomplete contracting

Most importantly, in the presence of imperfect information and incomplete contracting, optimal incentive schemes typically are highly non-linear (they do not take the form of a price intervention) and may even impose constraints (like rationing and terminations). In a sense, most regulations can be recast as (typically simple) forms of non-linear price schedules; but few price schedules, used in the private or public sector, are in fact anywhere near the complexities of those that emerge from optimal incentive schemes. Whether a particular regulatory structure is better or worse than a particular simplified non-linear price system may be hard to ascertain; and in any case, viewed through lens, the distinction between regulatory systems and (non-linear) price systems is more a matter of semantics than anything else.

There is, of course, a literature contrasting polar forms: a pure price system or a pure quantity (regulatory) system. But there is seldom reason to resort to such extremes, and in many cases, the standard formulation is simply not relevant.

Prices vs. Quantities

Nonetheless, much of the literature has been couched in exactly these extremes. It has been argued, for instance, that, depending on the nature of the shocks (to the demand and supply curves), quantity interventions (regulations) may lead to a higher level of expected utility than price interventions. Consider, for instance, the problem of greenhouse gases. Some have suggested that this is a classic case where quantity regulation is to be preferred. With price interventions, the level of greenhouse gas emissions is uncertain; a change in the demand or supply curve will mean that we will have less or more emissions than is desirable.

But the argument is hardly persuasive: global warming is related to the level of concentration of greenhouse gases in the atmosphere, and what matters for this is not the level of emissions in any particular year. There is, in fact, even some uncertainty about the relationship between emission levels and changes in concentration levels and about the relationship between the level of concentration of greenhouse gases and the (precise) change in climate. There will have to be, in any case, adjustments to the allowable levels of emissions over time. Using prices (emission taxes), there will have to be adjustments too, with one additional factor of uncertainty: the relationship between taxes and emissions. But provided that adjustments are made in a relatively timely way, there is little additional risk in the variables of concern, the level of concentration of greenhouse gases, and climate change.

But there are contexts in which regulations may be better than price interventions. If import supply functions are highly variable but domestic demand and supply conditions do not vary, then setting a tariff leads to high variability in price, domestic output, and production; setting a quota eliminates this costly source of "imported" risk. Tariffication (shifting from quotas to tariffs) may, accordingly, not be welfare enhancing. In general, with imperfect information (and incomplete contracting) it is optimal to use a complex set of "controls" which entail both (generalized) incentives and constraints.

Walter Williams    **NO**

Future Prospects for Economic Liberty

One of the justifications for the massive growth of government in the 20th and now the 21st centuries, far beyond the narrow limits envisioned by the founders of our nation, is the need to promote what the government defines as fair and just. But this begs the prior and more fundamental question: What is the legitimate role of government in a free society? To understand how America's Founders answered this question, we have only to look at the rule book they gave us—the Constitution. Most of what they understood as legitimate powers of the federal government are enumerated in Article 1, Section 8. Congress is authorized there to do 21 things, and as much as three-quarters of what Congress taxes us and spends our money for today is nowhere to be found on that list. To cite just a few examples, there is no constitutional authority for Congress to subsidize farms, bail out banks, or manage car companies. In this sense, I think we can safely say that America has departed from the constitutional principle of limited government that made us great and prosperous.

On the other side of the coin from limited government is individual liberty. The Founders understood private property as the bulwark of freedom for all Americans, rich and poor alike. But following a series of successful attacks on private property and free enterprise—beginning in the early 20th century and picking up steam during the New Deal, the Great Society, and then again recently—the government designed by our Founders and outlined in the Constitution has all but disappeared. Thomas Jefferson anticipated this when he said, "The natural progress of things is for liberty to yield and government to gain ground."

To see the extent to which liberty is yielding and government is gaining ground, one need simply look at what has happened to taxes and spending. A tax, of course, represents a government claim on private property. Every tax confiscates private property that could otherwise be freely spent or freely invested. At the same time, every additional dollar of government spending demands another tax dollar, whether now or in the future. With this in mind, consider that the average American now works from January 1 until May 5 to pay the federal, state, and local taxes required for current government spending levels. Thus the fruits of more than one-third of our labor are used in ways decided upon by others. The Founders favored the free market because

From *Imprimis*, September 2009. Copyright © 2009 by Hillsdale College. Reprinted by permission.

it maximizes the freedom of all citizens and teaches respect for the rights of others. Expansive government, by contrast, contracts individual freedom and teaches disrespect for the rights of others. Thus clearly we are on what Friedrich Hayek called the road to serfdom, or what I prefer to call the road to tyranny.

As I said, the Constitution restricts the federal government to certain functions. What are they? The most fundamental one is the protection of citizens' lives. Therefore, the first legitimate function of the government is to provide for national defense against foreign enemies and for protection against criminals here at home. These and other legitimate public goods (as we economists call them) obviously require that each citizen pay his share in taxes. But along with people's lives, it is a vital function of the government to protect people's liberty as well—including economic liberty or property rights. So while I am not saying that we should pay no taxes, I am saying that they should be much lower—as they would be, if the government abided by the Constitution and allowed the free market system to flourish.

And it is important to remember what makes the free market work. Is it a desire we all have to do good for others? Do people in New York enjoy fresh steak for dinner at their favorite restaurant because cattle ranchers in Texas love to make New Yorkers happy? Of course not. It is in the interest of Texas ranchers to provide the steak. They benefit themselves and their families by doing so. This is the kind of enlightened self-interest discussed by Adam Smith in his *Wealth of Nations*, in which he argues that the social good is best served by pursuing private interests. The same principle explains why I take better care of my property than the government would. It explains as well why a large transfer or estate tax weakens the incentive a property owner has to care for his property and pass it along to his children in the best possible condition. It explains, in general, why free enterprise leads to prosperity.

Ironically, the free market system is threatened today not because of its failure, but because of its success. Capitalism has done so well in eliminating the traditional problems of mankind—disease, pestilence, gross hunger, and poverty—that other human problems seem to us unacceptable. So in the name of equalizing income, achieving sex and race balance, guaranteeing housing and medical care, protecting consumers, and conserving energy—just to name a few prominent causes of liberal government these days—individual liberty has become of secondary or tertiary concern.

Imagine what would happen if I wrote a letter to Congress and informed its members that, because I am fully capable of taking care of my own retirement needs, I respectfully request that they stop taking money out of my paycheck for Social Security. Such a letter would be greeted with contempt. But is there any difference between being forced to save for retirement and being forced to save for housing or for my child's education or for any other perceived good? None whatsoever. Yet for government to force us to do such things is to treat us as children rather than as rational citizens in possession of equal and inalienable natural rights.

We do not yet live under a tyranny, of course. Nor is one imminent. But a series of steps, whether small or large, tending toward a certain destination will eventually take us there. The philosopher David Hume observed that liberty is seldom lost all at once, but rather bit by bit. Or as my late colleague Leonard Read used to put it, taking liberty from Americans is like cooking a frog: It can't be done quickly because the frog will feel the heat and escape. But put a frog in cold water and heat it slowly, and by the time the frog grasps the danger, it's too late.

Again, the primary justification for increasing the size and scale of government at the expense of liberty is that government can achieve what it perceives as good. But government has no resources of its own with which to do so. Congressmen and senators don't reach into their own pockets to pay for a government program. They reach into yours and mine. Absent Santa Claus or the tooth fairy, the only way government can give one American a dollar in the name of this or that good thing is by taking it from some other American by force. If a private person did the same thing, no matter how admirable the motive, he would be arrested and tried as a thief. That is why I like to call what Congress does, more often than not, "legal theft." The question we have to ask ourselves is whether there is a moral basis for forcibly taking the rightful property of one person and giving it to another to whom it does not belong. I cannot think of one. Charity is noble and good when it involves reaching into your own pocket. But reaching into someone else's pocket is wrong.

In a free society, we want the great majority, if not all, of our relationships to be voluntary. I like to explain a voluntary exchange as a kind of nonamorous seduction. Both parties to the exchange feel good in an economic sense. Economists call this a positive sum gain. For example, if I offer my local grocer three dollars for a gallon of milk, implicit in the offer is that we will both be winners. The grocer is better off because he values the three dollars more than the milk, and I am better off because I value the milk more than the three dollars. That is a positive sum gain. Involuntary exchange, by contrast, means that one party gains and the other loses. If I use a gun to steal a gallon of milk, I win and the grocer loses. Economists call this a zero sum gain. And we are like that grocer in most of what Congress does these days.

Some will respond that big government is what the majority of voters want, and that in a democracy the majority rules. But America's Founders didn't found a democracy, they founded a republic. The authors of *The Federalist Papers*, arguing for ratification of the Constitution, showed how pure democracy has led historically to tyranny. Instead, they set up a limited government, with checks and balances, to help ensure that the reason of the people, rather than the selfish passions of a majority, would hold sway. Unaware of the distinction between a democracy and a republic, many today believe that a majority consensus establishes morality. Nothing could be further from the truth.

Another common argument is that we need big government to protect the little guy from corporate giants. But a corporation can't pick a consumer's pocket. The consumer must voluntarily pay money for the corporation's product. It is big government, not corporations, that have the power to take our money by force. I should also point out that private business *can* force us to pay them by employing government. To see this happening, just look at the automobile industry or at most corporate farmers today. If General Motors or a corporate farm is having trouble, they can ask me for help, and I may or may not choose to help. But if they ask government to help and an IRS agent shows up at my door demanding money, I have no choice but to hand it over. It is big government that the little guy needs protection against, not big business. And the only protection available is in the Constitution and the ballot box.

Speaking of the ballot box, we can blame politicians to some extent for the trampling of our liberty. But the bulk of the blame lies with us voters, because politicians are often doing what we elect them to do. The sad truth is that we elect them for the specific purpose of taking the property of other Americans and giving it to us. Many manufacturers think that the government owes them a protective tariff to keep out foreign goods, resulting in artificially higher prices for consumers. Many farmers think the government owes them a crop subsidy, which raises the price of food. Organized labor thinks government should protect their jobs from non-union competition. And so on. We could even consider many college professors, who love to secure government grants to study poverty and then meet at hotels in Miami during the winter to talk about poor people. All of these—and hundreds of other similar demands on government that I could cite—represent involuntary exchanges and diminish our freedom.

This reminds me of a lunch I had a number of years ago with my friend Jesse Helms, the late Senator from North Carolina. He knew that I was critical of farm subsidies, and he said he agreed with me 100 percent. But he wondered how a Senator from North Carolina could possibly vote against them. If he did so, his fellow North Carolinians would dump him and elect somebody worse in his place. And I remember wondering at the time if it is reasonable to ask a politician to commit political suicide for the sake of principle. The fact is that it's unreasonable of us to expect even principled politicians to vote against things like crop subsidies and stand up for the Constitution. This presents us with a challenge. It's up to us to ensure that it's in our representatives' interest to stand up for constitutional government.

Americans have never done the wrong thing for a long time, but if we're not going to go down the tubes as a great nation, we must get about changing things while we still have the liberty to do so.

POSTSCRIPT

Should Government Intervene in a Capitalist Economy?

$\mathbf{A}$s with most good debates, the issue of the rightness of government intervention is difficult to decide. Part of the difficulty is that it involves the trade-off of values that are in conflict in real situations, and part of the difficulty is that it involves uncertain estimations of the future consequences of policy changes. Both experts and interested parties can differ greatly on value trade-offs and estimations of impacts. Government regulations and other interventions cost money for both administration and compliance. Nevertheless, Stiglitz argues that certain government actions will provide benefits that greatly exceed the costs, and Williams argues the contrary view, that the costs will be far greater than Stiglitz expects and probably will have net negative results. Part of the strength of Williams's argument is that regulations often fail to do what they are designed to do. Part of the strength of Stiglitz's argument is that there are many observable problems that need to be addressed, and for some of these government action seems to be the only viable option.

One aspect of the issue is the morality of businesses. Most commentators have a low opinion of business ethics and the way corporations use their power, and point to the recent corporate scandals as confirmation. Thus, it is easy to conclude that because they will not do what is right, they must be made to do what is right. For support of this view see Joel Bakan, *The Corporation: The Pathological Pursuit of Profit and Power* (Free Press, 2004); Justin O'Brien, *Wall Street on Trial: A Corrupted State?* (Wiley, 2003); Steve Tombs and Dave Whyte, *Unmasking the Crimes of the Powerful: Scrutinizing States and Corporations* (P. Lang, 2003); Jamie Court, *Corporateering: How Corporate Power Steals Your Personal Freedom—And What You Can Do about It* (Jeremy P. Tarcher/Putnam, 2003); Kenneth R. Gray et al., *Corporate Scandals: The Many Faces of Greed: The Great Heist, Financial Bubbles, and the Absence of Virtue* (Paragon House, 2005); Matthew Robinson and Daniel Murphy, *Greed is Good: Maximization and Elite Deviance in America* (Rowman & Littlefield Publishers, 2009); Frank Partnoy, *Infectious Greed: How Deceit and Risk Corrupted the Financial Markets* (Public Affairs, 2009); and Victor Perlo, *Superprofits and Crisis: Modern U.S. Capitalism* (International Publishers, 1988).

Some commentators, however, defend businesses in a competitive capitalistic market. Philosopher Michael Novak contends that the ethos of capitalism transcends mere moneymaking and is (or can be made) compatible with Judeo-Christian morality. See *The Spirit of Democratic Capitalism* (Madison Books, 1991) and *The Catholic Ethic and the Spirit of Capitalism* (Free Press, 1993). Another broad-based defense of capitalism is Peter L. Berger's The *Capitalist*

Revolution: Fifty Propositions about Prosperity, Equality and Liberty (Basic Books, 1988). For a feminist critique of capitalism, see J. K. Gibson-Graham, *The End of Capitalism (As We Know It): A Feminist Critique of Political Economy* (Blackwell, 1996). For a mixed view of capitalism, see Charles Wolf Jr., *Markets or Governments: Choosing Between Imperfect Alternatives* (MIT Press, 1993). A strong attack on government interventions in the market is Jonathan Rauch, *Demosclerosis: The Silent Killer of American Government* (Times Books, 1994).

For an in-depth understanding of the way that markets work and the role that institutions maintained by the state, including property rights, function to maintain markets, see Neil Fligstein, *The Architecture of Markets: An Economic Sociology of Twenty-First Century Capitalist Societies* (Princeton University Press, 2001). An interesting role of government is its bailing out failed corporations. See *Too Big to Fail: Policies and Practices in Government Bailouts* edited by Benton E. Gup (Praeger, 2004), and David G. Mayes et al., *Who Pays for Bank Insolvency?* (Palgrave Macmillan, 2004). Often self-regulation is better than government regulation. See Virgina Haufler, *A Public Role for the Private Sector: Industry Self-Regulation in a Global Economy* (Carnegie Endowment for International Peace, 2001).

ISSUE 13

Has Welfare Reform Benefited the Poor?

YES: David Coates, "Cutting 'Welfare' to Help the Poor," from *A Liberal Toolkit: Progressive Responses to Conservative Arguments* (Praeger, 2007)

NO: Stephanie Mencimer, "Brave New Welfare," *Mother Jones* (January/February, 2009)

ISSUE SUMMARY

YES: David Coates presents the argument for welfare reform, which is that most poverty is self-induced; the previous welfare program created poverty and many other problems; and the reform reduces poverty, improves the lives of the people who left welfare, and solves other problems.

NO: Stephanie Mencimer, staff reporter for *Mother Jones*, does not denigrate the current welfare law but documents the horrible way welfare is administered in many states. Many welfare workers deny many benefits to many people who qualify for welfare. Thus, many welfare benefits do not reach the poor.

In his 1984 book *Losing Ground: American Social Policy, 1950–1980* (Basic Books), policy analyst Charles Murray recommended abolishing Aid to Families with Dependent Children (AFDC), the program at the heart of the welfare debate. At the time of the book's publication, this suggestion struck many as simply a dramatic way for Murray to make some of his anti-welfare points. However, 14 years later this idea became the dominant idea in Congress. In 1996, President Bill Clinton signed into law the Work Opportunity Reconciliation Act and fulfilled his 1992 campaign pledge to "end welfare as we know it." Murray's thesis that welfare hurt the poor had become widely accepted. In "What to Do about Welfare," *Commentary* (December 1994), Murray argues that welfare contributes to dependency, illegitimacy, and the number of absent fathers, which in turn can have terrible effects on the children involved. He states that workfare, enforced child support, and the abolition of welfare would greatly reduce these problems. One reason why Congress ended AFDC was the emergence of a widespread backlash against welfare recipients. Much of the backlash, however, was misguided. It often rested on the assumptions that welfare is generous and that most people on welfare are professional loafers. In fact, over the previous two decades, payments to families with dependent children eroded considerably relative to the cost of living. Furthermore, most women with dependent children on welfare had intermittent periods of work, were elderly, or were disabled. Petty fraud may be common because welfare payments are insufficient to live on in many cities, but "welfare queens" who cheat the system for spectacular sums are so rare that they should not be part of any serious debate on welfare issues. The majority of people on welfare are those whose condition would become desperate if payments were cut off. Although many believe that women on welfare commonly bear children in order to increase their benefits, there is no conclusive evidence to support this idea.

Not all objections to AFDC can be easily dismissed, however. There does seem to be evidence that in some cases AFDC reduces work incentives and increases the likelihood of family breakups. But there is also a positive side to AFDC—it helped many needy people get back on their feet. When all things are considered together, therefore, it is not clear that welfare, meaning AFDC, was bad enough to be abolished. But it was abolished on July 1, 1997, when the Work Opportunity Reconciliation Act went into effect. Now the question is whether the new policy is better than the old policy.

It is too soon to obtain an accurate assessment of the long-term impacts of the Act. Nevertheless, AFDC rolls have declined since the Act was passed, so many conclude that it is a success rather than a failure. Of course, the early leavers are the ones with the best prospects of succeeding in the work world; the welfare-to-work transition gets harder as the program works with the more difficult cases. The crucial question is whether the reform will benefit those it affects. Already, many working former welfare recipients are better off. But what about the average or more vulnerable recipient?

In the readings that follow, David Coates presents a fair summary of the case for the benefits of welfare reform. Stephanie Mencimer tells the unseemly story of how many states seek to keep welfare payment to a minimum, and therefore cheat many people who need and deserve welfare.

YES

David Coates

Cutting "Welfare" to Help the Poor

Welfare states in the modern world aren't very old—60 or 70 years at most. Some parts are older—the German social insurance system started with Bismarck—but in general the provision of government help to the poor, the sick, the disabled, and the elderly is a recent phenomenon. Not all governments make that provision even now, but most do. Certainly in recent times, all governments in the advanced democracies have taken on a major welfare role, and that includes federal and state authorities here in the United States.

Yet in this, as in so much else, the United States has proved to be unique. Unique in coverage: No universal system of health care, free at the point of use, emerged here in the late 1940s as it did in much of Western Europe. Unique in delivery system: From the early 1950s, pensions and health care were tied directly to wage settlements here, in wage-and-benefit packages with few foreign parallels. Unique in timing: The United States set the pace in the 1930s with the New Deal, and again in the late 1960s with its own War on Poverty. Unique in vocabulary: The U.S. state pension system is known as *social security* and the term *welfare* is restricted to payments to the poor, giving it a stigma it lacks in much of Western Europe. And unique in fragility: The United States is the only major industrial democracy formally committed to the "ending of welfare as we know it," through the 1996 Personal Responsibility and Work Opportunity Reconciliation Act.

The result has been the consolidation in the United States of a publicly financed welfare system, which, in comparative terms, is now both residual and modest. It's residual in that it leaves the bulk of provision for the sick and the old to the private sector. It's modest in that the public provision made available (pensions apart) is less generous than that now commonplace in Western Europe and Japan. For many American liberals, there's something profoundly embarrassing about the richest country on earth getting by with the most limited welfare system in the advanced industrial world. But that's not how the Conservative Right sees it. On the contrary, having a residual and modest welfare state is, for them, one of the key reasons why the United States is the richest country on earth. Protecting that economic success then requires U.S. welfare provision to be made ever more residual and modest over time. In a manner and scale without precedence elsewhere, *cutting welfare*—either to the

From *A Liberal Toolkit: Progressive Responses to Conservative Arguments* by David Coates (Praeger, 2007). Copyright © 2007 by Greenwood Publishing Group. Reprinted by permission.

bone, or away completely—is regularly and seriously canvassed by conservative forces in the United States as the best way to help the poor. . . .

&@&

A Liberal Response

Oh, if it was only that simple. But, for the following reasons at least, it's not. . . .

There's More Poverty Out There Than You Might Think

12.7 percent of all Americans now live on incomes that fall at or below the official poverty lines. Even worse, of the 37 million people living in officially defined poverty in 2004, 13 million were children. That's equivalent to the entire populations of Sweden and Norway. The poverty rate for very young children in the United States in the first half-decade of the twenty-first century was slightly over 20 percent: That's one preschool child in every five. And around them are what the Economic Policy Institute (EPI) calls "the twice-poor," that is, Americans living on or below incomes that are only twice the officially defined level for their family size. Amazingly, more than 89 million Americans fell into that broader category in 2003—all close to poverty and all accordingly obliged to watch every penny. Collectively, the poor and the twice-poor now constitute 31 percent of the population—that's 3 in every 10 Americans. That's a lot of people in or near the poverty margin, no matter what Congress is or isn't being told by the people in suits.

What they experience is real poverty, in both the absolute and relative senses of the term. Currently, 39 million Americans are classified as "food insecure" and 40 percent of all those using food banks live in families in which at least one adult is working. . . . It doesn't help them—or indeed us—to be told that most of them have cars. Of course they do. Given the absence of adequate systems of public transport in vast swathes of the United States, how else are they meant to get to shops or to the food bank? A car in the United States isn't a luxury. It's a necessity; an extra financial burden that can't be avoided if doing the ordinary things of life is not to become nearly impossible. The Western European poor don't need cars to anything like the same degree, because the scale of public provision—the size of the social wage that everyone enjoys regardless of income—is so much larger in those countries.

That's one reason why it's simply untrue to claim that the American poor are better off than most ordinary Europeans and better off than the entirety of the Western European poor. Sadly, they're not. On the contrary, the child poverty rate in the United States is currently *four* times that of northern Europe.

There are *only three* Western European countries whose poor children have a lower living standard than do poor children in the United States. . . .

If All This Poverty Is Self-Inflicted, Then Masochism in the United States Is Amazingly Rife

This is why there's something particularly offensive about the speed and ease with which so many commentators on the American Right, instead of probing beneath the surface for the underlying causes of the "pathologies" of poverty they so dislike, move instead to demonize the poor, endlessly blaming them for making "bad choices" as though good ones were plentiful and immediately at hand. Telling young black women to marry the fathers of their children, for example, carries with it the premise that the men are there to be married. Yet "twelve percent of all black men between eighteen and thirty-four are [currently] in jail," a bigger proportion of "men away" than the United States as a whole experienced during the entirety of World War II. Unemployment rates among young black men are double those among their white contemporaries. "The problem is not that the nation's poorest women have systematically passed up good jobs and good marriage partners. The problem is that there are significant economic and cultural inadequacies in the choices available to them. They, like the rest of America, value children; but unlike the rest of America, they cannot easily support them." . . .

Given a Chance, Welfare Works Better Than Is Claimed

The payment of welfare stands accused by many on the American Right of creating poverty and damaging those to whom it is given. With one important caveat—welfare traps—to which we will come later, the claim is literally ludicrous. Welfare did not create poverty in America. Poverty was here long before the New Deal and long before Johnson's "war." Neither set of welfare initiatives created their clienteles. They simply responded to their prior existence. The poverty of the 1930s was of a mass kind, the product of a general economic collapse that was rectified not by welfare programs but by the United States' mobilization for war. Within it, however, were categories of the poor that had existed before 1929 and that continued to exist after 1941—the temporarily unemployed, the genetically infirm, widows, and the elderly. By the 1960s, those categories of the poor had been joined by another, one explicitly excluded from the coverage of the original New Deal. To get any sort of legislative package through a Congress whose committees were dominated by southern Democrats, Roosevelt had excluded black workers in the south. Servants and agricultural workers gained no benefits from the core programs of the New Deal. They survived instead in the invisible southern poverty, poverty which—as prosperity returned with the war—then drew them out of the south into the cities and industries of the northeast and the midwest. In the first half of the postwar period. African Americans increasingly exchanged *invisible* southern rural poverty for its *visible* urban northern equivalent. It was an exchange to which the welfare programs of the 1960s were a belated response.

So it was a case of poverty first, and welfare second, and not the other way around. It was also a case of a welfare response that, when properly funded, took the rate of poverty *down* not up: a response that over time definitely improved the lives of many categories of the American poor. The official poverty rate in 1959—the first year in the United States that it was taken—was 22.4 percent: By 1973, with the War on Poverty at its height, that rate had halved. Then, as programs were cut back in the 1970s and 1980s, the rate grew again. It was back to 14.5 percent by 1992, although it's slightly lower now, as we've seen. . . .

The Charity Illusion

Unless, of course, as the Cato people would have it, private charity would have stepped into the breach and done a better job. But there's just no evidence to sustain that claim. There's certainly no evidence that private charity could, or did, scratch more than the surface of the poverty experienced by the old, the infirm, and the widowed before the New Deal. And of the nature of things, no evidence can sustain the claim that if welfare were entirely removed (and tax levels cut accordingly), those benefiting from the tax cuts would then redirect all or most of their extra income into charitable endeavors. American altruism—although impressive by international standards—is not without limit, and because it isn't, the private sector can't be treated as a reliable and problem-free alternative to existing welfare programs. Charity-based welfare contains no mechanisms to guard against unevenness of provision, moralizing in the terms set for aid given, or the onset of "gift exhaustion" over time. The gathering of funds by private charities is in any case always time-consuming, intrusive, and administratively inefficient; and the distribution of funds as private handouts only serves to reinforce—for those who receive them—the very sense of dependency and impotence that conservatives are apparently so keen to avoid. . . .

The Fallacy of the Incompetent State

In any event, in making the pitch for the full privatization of welfare, the Charles Murrays and Michael Tanners of this world are not comparing like with like. They're also generalizing from an extraordinarily parochial base. They advocate the replacement of the American welfare system by an idealized and untested network of private charities, using as their evidence inadequacies in American public welfare policy since the 1970s. With few exceptions, they don't appear to have looked in any systematic way at Western Europe, where states have run welfare systems successfully for years. Nor have they engaged with—indeed have they even read—the fabulous and extensive scholarly literature on comparative welfare systems. If they had, they'd quickly have come to see that the great tragedy of Lyndon Johnson's War on Poverty was not that poverty won, but that the war itself was not pursued with sufficient consistency and zeal.

All governments—European and American alike—distribute income and dispense welfare. They're all, in James Galbraith's telling term, "transfer states," and inequality always shows what he called "the fingerprints of state policy." The War on Poverty required those fingerprints to distribute income downward, and initially it did. General poverty levels fell. But command of the war then shifted. Under Reagan and the two Bush administrations, the fingerprints were deployed differently. Income was consciously moved upward. Welfare systems can always be made to fail, if inadequately financed and led. An agency such as Federal Emergency Management Agency (FEMA) will always fail if it's led by cronies and managed by fools. But by the same token, welfare systems can always be made to work well if supplied with sufficient funds and commitment. Indeed, take a welfare system up to about 40 percent of gross domestic product (GDP)—when it's servicing the entire community and not just the poor—and popular support for it will rise, not fall. That's been the universal Western European experience. . . .

The Limits of Welfare-to-Work Programs in a World of Low Pay

The 1996 Act is the Republicans' ace card in their attempt to roll back the American welfare state, and they have one huge piece of evidence going in their favor: the dramatic fall in the number of people—especially young single mothers—in receipt of welfare since its passing. But the figures on caseload reduction, although real, are also deceptive, and we need to say so. They're deceptive in a *causal* sense: in that the full implementation of the Act coincided with a significant period of job growth in the American economy. When that growth stalled, so too did the rate of job take-up by single mothers. The figures on caseload reduction are deceptive, too, in a *social* sense. People came off welfare, but then ran into a whole series of new problems that the figures don't catch. Women fleeing domestic violence lost a vital source of autonomy from the men who had violated them. Young women with small children lost a significant percentage of their new wages on child care and transport costs; and the children themselves—whose enhanced well-being was, after all, a key aim of the new legislation—often found themselves in inadequate child care, looked after by undertrained and underpaid female staff. Women didn't stop providing child care. They simply stopped providing their own. And, overwhelmingly, the figures on caseload reduction are deceptive in an *economic* sense. Going off welfare, although it reduced the numbers, did not reduce the scale and rate of poverty among those who previously had been in receipt of aid. The Cato Institute's Michael Tanner has conceded as much, noting that "self-sufficiency appears to be eluding the grasp of many, if not most, former recipients." And of course it is, because (quite predictably) the vast majority of the jobs into which former welfare recipients were moved turned out to be *low-paid* jobs. Welfare-to-work moved people from government-sponsored poverty to private sector-based poverty, adding to their transport and child care costs as it did so. Workfare changed the source of poverty; but not the poverty itself. . . .

The "Welfare Poor" and the "Working Poor" Are on the Same Side

Republicans likes to present themselves as champions of the working poor against the welfare poor, implying that the interests of the two groups are in tension and painting the Democratic Party into a "tax-and-spend" corner as they do so. But the argument is false in both of its premises: The interests of the two are not in tension and the Republicans are not the defenders of the real interests of the working poor.

The existence of a large group of full-time workers—paid so little that they themselves are on the margin of poverty—actually traps the welfare poor a second time. If you're on welfare, you're poor. If you get out of welfare and into work, you'll still be poor, because the move will only take you into the bottom tier of the poorly paid. If the people in that low-pay group are then financially pressed—and they definitely are—it's not because of the weight of any welfare taxation that they carry. It's because their wages are low. It's not taxes that make them poor, but the lack of income growth. What really hurts the low paid is not the poverty of the people below them but the greed of the people above. As we read in Chapter 3, the truly unique feature of the recent American income story is the proportion of total income growth taken by the ultrarich. You remember, 24 percent of all income growth in the U.S. economy between 1997 and 2001 was taken by just 1 percent of the population, and it was taken at the end of a quarter-century in which wages remained flat for the majority of working Americans. What the working poor need is not welfare retrenchment but higher wages. They *and* the welfare poor need the creation of a high-wage, high-growth economy to ease the burden of poverty on them both. They both need full employment and rising wages in an economy in which there is a fair distribution of rewards. That's the kind of economy that the Republicans always promise in the run-up to elections, but it's also the kind of economy that after the elections, for 80 million Americans at least, the party regularly fails to deliver. . . .

Welfare Doesn't Trap the Poor in an Underclass—We Do

Welfare critics are right on at least this: There is a welfare trap, work disincentive issue in any welfare system. As people come off welfare and lose benefits, the effective tax rate on their own earnings can be extraordinarily high. Depending on the rules, in the move from welfare to work you might lose 60 cents of welfare provision for every dollar you earn, and effectively be only 40 cents better off—a rate of taxation against which the rich regularly howl when experiencing it themselves. So there is a problem of "disincentives to work" associated with welfare, one on which the Right regularly latch. But it's not the only, or indeed the main, problem currently facing young mothers in search of good jobs in America's inner cities. Good jobs are scarce because the middle-class workers have left those cities, taking the jobs with them. Available child care is poor because the programs have been cut. Young men are scarce because incarceration rates have been systematically ratcheted up. Suburban flight, welfare retrenchment, drugs, and the rise of a prison economy are the real villains here. As Barack Obama said, "the people of New Orleans weren't just abandoned during the hurricane. They were abandoned long ago—to murder and mayhem in the streets, to sub-standard schools, to dilapidated housing, to inadequate health care, to a pervasive sense of hopelessness." Underclasses don't create themselves. They're created. You can't be trapped unless somebody does the trapping.

The great thing about traps, however, is that they can be sprung. The solution to the disincentive effect of welfare payments is to phase in benefit reductions slowly—allowing people to earn and receive benefits in parallel until their incomes reach a tolerable level. . . .

Poverty Is a Matter of Choice—It's Just Not a Choice Made by the Poor

The ultimate irony here is that poverty, as the Republican Right regularly claims, is indeed a matter of choice. It's just not a choice that the poor themselves are called on to make. It's a choice made by the rest of us. In the main, for most of us, by how we vote, and for those who govern us, by how they legislate. They and us, not the poor, have the power to choose. We can choose, as an economy and a society, to meet the arrival of intensified global competition by outsourcing production, lowering American wages, and increasing income inequality. Or we can choose to reset the way we organize the economy and regulate trade to pull jobs back to the United States and to improve the quality of work and levels of remuneration attached to them. There is a choice to be made. If we take the first route, we'll create new sources of poverty for those low-skilled American workers currently in employment and extra barriers for those trying to move into work from welfare dependency. If we take the second, we'll have to dismantle much of the hidden welfare state now going to the rich, and perhaps not just to them. A proper system of rent subsidy for people on low incomes, for example, may have to be financed by phasing out the enormous tax subsidy currently provided to those of us fortunate enough to be buying rather than renting our houses. But at least the more affluent among us have a choice. The poor do not. Or perhaps more accurately, the affluent have the choice of making a big difference by making a small sacrifice. The poor, by contrast, have to labor mightily just to change their individual circumstances by merely an inch.

"Poor people and investment bankers have one thing in common. They both spend considerable energy thinking about money." Which is why, on this topic at least, the Republicans are both right and wrong. They're right: When discussing poverty, policy is ultimately a matter of making right choices. But they're also wrong. Over and over again, the choices they make are the wrong ones—and we need to say so.

Brave New Welfare

Georgia officials lied to Gabby's mom to keep her from getting a $100 monthly check. From red tape to dirty tricks and outright abuse, here's what awaits if your luck runs out.

In 2006, Letorrea Clark was 22 years old, unemployed, and living with her boyfriend in Homerville, a tiny town near the Okefenokee Swamp in southern Georgia, when she discovered she was pregnant. The timing wasn't ideal. Her boyfriend's job at the local can-manufacturing plant supported them both, but his largesse came at a price. The man was controlling, unfaithful, and jealous, a problem only enhanced by the wide array of drugs that filled his freezer. Clark had hit the stash, too, but the pregnancy pushed her to get clean and get out. She slept on a park bench until a friend helped her secure a place to stay.

Two-year-old Gabby and her mother are among thousands eligible for welfare who have been denied benefits as states push to trim the rolls.

Desperate, with her due date fast approaching, Clark decided to apply for Temporary Assistance for Needy Families (TANF), better known as welfare. But when she went to the local Division of Family and Children Services office, a caseworker told her—wrongly—that she couldn't apply until after the baby was born. "They basically said, 'Go get a job,'" says Clark. "I was eight months pregnant."

Gabby arrived by C-section a month later, and Clark brought the chubby newborn home to a sweltering trailer with a busted fridge, no air conditioning, and no running water. (Her ex had reneged on promises to get the water turned on.) Clark got by with help from her church and her landlord, who let her stay for free until she was able to move. Later, she found a job in a day care. But the center docked her paycheck for Gabby's care, an expense the state would have picked up had she been able to get on TANF. Sometimes she'd go home with just $20 at the end of the week.

Clark patched things together with food stamps and $256 a month in child support. But after nine months, Gabby's father stopped paying just long enough for Clark to get evicted. She went back to the welfare office, where caseworkers turned her away, saying—falsely again—that because she'd been getting child support she was ineligible for TANF.

What Clark didn't know was that Georgia, like many other states, was in the midst of an aggressive push to get thousands of eligible mothers like her off TANF, often by duplicitous means, to use the savings elsewhere in the

From *Mother Jones*, January/February 2009. Copyright © 2009 by Mother Jones. Reprinted by permission.

state budget. Fewer than 2,500 Georgia adults now receive benefits, down from 28,000 in 2004—a 90 percent decline. Louisiana, Texas, and Illinois have each dropped 80 percent of adult recipients since January 2001. Nationally, the number of TANF recipients fell more than 40 percent between then and June 2008, the most recent month for which data are available. In Georgia last year, only 18 percent of children living below 50 percent of the poverty line—that is, on less than $733 a month for a family of three—were receiving TANF.

Plunging welfare rolls were big news in the wake of Bill Clinton's 1996 welfare reform, which limited benefits and required recipients to engage in "work related" activities. Those declines coincided with record numbers of poor single mothers heading into the workplace and a significant drop in child poverty—proof, supporters said, that the new policy was a success. But the reform took effect at a time when unemployment was at a historic low—there were actually jobs for welfare moms to go to. In recent years, by contrast, TANF caseloads have been falling even as unemployment has soared and other poverty programs have experienced explosive growth. (Nearly 11 million more people received food stamps last year than did in 2000.) With the economy settling into a prolonged slump, this trend could be devastating.

Welfare is the only cash safety-net program for single moms and their kids, notes Rebecca Blank, an economist at the Brookings Institution and one of the nation's leading experts on poverty. "One has to worry, with a recession, about the number of women who, if they get unemployed, are not going to have anywhere to turn."

No longer the polarizing, racially tinged political issue it was when Ronald Reagan attacked "welfare queens," the welfare system today is dying a quiet death, neatly chronicled in the pages of academic and policy journals, largely unnoticed by the rest of us. Yet its demise carries significant implications. Among the most serious: the rise of what academics call the "disconnected," people who live well below the poverty line and are neither working nor receiving cash benefits like Social Security disability or TANF. Estimates put this group at roughly 2 million women caring for 4 million children, many dealing with a host of challenges from mental illness to domestic violence. "We don't really know how they survive," says Blank.

Women turned away from TANF lose more than a check. TANF is a gateway to education, drug rehab or mental health care, child care, even transportation and disability benefits—tools for upward mobility. Without those options, some women are driven to more desperate measures. In one of the towns in Georgia where I traveled to research this story, arrests of women for prostitution and petty crime went up as more and more families were pushed off welfare. And women are increasingly vulnerable to sexual assault and exploitation—sometimes, as I discovered, from the very officials or caseworkers who are supposed to help them. In the worst cases, they are losing custody of their children, precisely what TANF was designed to prevent. "I worry a lot about the kids in these families," Blank says. "We don't know where the kids are going."

One good thing did come from Letorrea Clark's final attempt to get on TANF. Federal law requires caseworkers to ask applicants about domestic violence, and when Clark mentioned that Gabby's father was stalking her, a concerned caseworker sent her to a shelter in another city. When the ex found Clark there, she was transferred to a shelter an hour away in Albany, a midsize town nestled among some of the nation's most impoverished rural counties.

The shelter staff did for Clark what the TANF office would not: extended her a lifeline. With their help, Clark and Gabby moved to a dingy one-room apartment in a low-slung brick complex filled with ex-cons and drug addicts, clients of the nonprofit group that runs the building. This is where I found them during several visits over the summer. Mother and daughter slept on a donated mattress; crates set inside an oversize, listing four-poster frame served as the box spring. Free rent made the roaches tolerable, but there were other liabilities. Upon Clark's arrival, the nonprofit group's caseworker asked her for sex. "He said, 'You ain't got nothing; you might as well,'" she said.

As we spoke in July, Clark sat in an overstuffed chair holding Gabby, a vivacious toddler whose head sprouted with braids. Clark was worried. She needed to get a job so she could keep food in the house; she was haunted by the possibility of losing Gabby if she didn't. But there were serious obstacles. She's been diagnosed with bipolar disorder and ADHD; "I don't like to be around a lot of people," she said. She can't drive and fears the bus because "I suffer from paranoia. I always think I'm going to fall off those seats."

Born in Hattiesburg, Mississippi, one of six children, Clark barely knows her father. She suspects both her mother and grandmother suffer from mental illness. One day when she was five, she told me, her mother whipped her back with an extension cord and then made her stand in a corner all night long. In kindergarten the next day, a concerned teacher lifted up her shirt and fell to her knees at the sight of so much blood. Social workers investigated but didn't take Clark away from her mother for another six years of crushing abuse.

In school, she languished in special education classes; her behavior turned violent. At 11, the state finally put her into foster care, and later, when foster families wouldn't have her, a mental hospital. Eventually she was returned to her mother, who coveted her monthly disability check. "When I turned 18, my mom wanted me to stay home to live off my tit," she says. Instead, "I saw an ad on TV for Job Corps and thought that was my ticket out." After she got her GED and became certified as a nursing assistant, Job Corps helped her find work in a nursing home, but the death of a woman she cared for left her rattled. She quit and was soon homeless. Somewhere along the way, she lost the disability benefits she'd received since she was a child. After she was raped in a crack house, Clark sought refuge in the only safe place she could think of: jail. "I hadn't ate in like two weeks," she says, so she went to Wal-Mart and started taking things off the shelves—a sandwich, soda, candy. "I knew I was going to get caught, but I just kept eating. I kept thinking that if I went to jail I could sleep."

After her sojourn in lockup, she met Gabby's father and moved in with him. While her pregnancy was unplanned, Clark believes that Gabby saved her life. "If I didn't have her, I'd have probably lost my mind," says Clark. "She's my pride and joy."

In his 1903 book *The Souls of Black Folk,* W.E.B. Du Bois described Albany as the capital of Georgia's "Black Belt." At the time, the area was home to 2,000 white people and 10,000 blacks; the cotton trade had collapsed, and Albany was a landscape of decaying one-room slave cabins occupied by tenant farmers eking out a meager existence from the depleted soil.

Things have improved since then, but only slightly. Despite the addition of an aquarium and civic center, the downtown looks much as it must have when Martin Luther King Jr. was jailed here after a civil rights protest in 1961. The main drags offer gas stations, dollar stores, and an outfit advertising $99 headstones. More than one-fifth of Albany families live below the poverty line—nearly twice the national average. About one in three adults is illiterate. Nearly 16 percent are unemployed. Eighty percent of children born here in 2007 had single mothers, many of them teenagers.

Despite those dismal demographics, in July 2006, only 143 adults in the 14 surrounding counties—some of whose demographics make Albany look downright prosperous—were receiving TANF benefits. The number had fallen 96 percent from 2002, according to the Georgia Budget and Policy Institute, though not because poverty was on the retreat: During the same period, unemployment in the area shot up 15 percent and food stamp use increased 24 percent.

After interviewing dozens of clients of Liberty House, the Albany domestic violence shelter where Clark sought refuge, I discovered that getting TANF in Albany is virtually impossible. While most of the women were eligible for benefits under state rules, many had been turned away for some reason or another. A caseworker incorrectly told one woman that she didn't qualify because her three kids—all under 15—were too old. Another, a 30-year-old with six kids between the ages of 2 and 12, had been in the shelter for a month after the district attorney from her hometown drove her there from the hospital. ("The guy that I was dating tried to kill me," she explained matter-of-factly.) She'd applied for TANF to get subsidized child care and go back to work. But a four-hour visit to the welfare office produced nothing but a promise that she'd receive a letter with an appointment date. A month later, she still hadn't gotten the letter. She says the county offered her three weeks of child care with the warning—false— that if she didn't find a job during that time, she wouldn't be eligible for TANF. "But if I find a job, I don't need TANF," she said with a laugh.

In 2006, the Georgia Coalition Against Domestic Violence conducted a survey to figure out why so many women were suddenly failing to get TANF benefits. They discovered that caseworkers were actively talking women out of applying, often using inaccurate information. (Lying to applicants to deny them benefits is a violation of federal law, but the 1996 welfare reform legislation largely stripped the Department of Health and Human Services of its power to punish states for doing it. Meanwhile, county officials have tried to head off lawyers who might take up the issue by pressing applicants to sign waivers saying they voluntarily turned down benefits.) Allison Smith, the economic justice coordinator at the coalition, says the group has gotten reports of caseworkers telling TANF applicants they have to be surgically sterilized before they can apply. Disabled women have been told they can't apply because they can't meet the work requirement. Others have been warned that the state could take their children if they get benefits. Makita Perry, a 23-year-old mother of four who did manage to get on TANF for a year, told me caseworkers "ask you all sorts of personal questions, like when the last time you had sex was and with who." Elsewhere, women are being told to get a letter proving they've visited a family-planning doctor.

Simply landing an appointment with a caseworker is an ordeal that can take 45 days, according to some of the women I interviewed—and applicants must clear numerous other hurdles, including conducting a job search, before being approved. Few complete the process. One study found that in April 2006, caseworkers in Georgia green-lighted only 20 percent of TANF applications, down from 40 percent in 2004. The lucky few who are accepted must often work full time in "volunteer" jobs in exchange for their benefits, which max out at $280 a month for a family of three.

Even as it blocks potential applicants, Georgia is also pushing current TANF recipients off the rolls at a rapid clip. Sandy Bamford runs a federally funded family literacy program in Albany where single mothers can get their GEDs. TANF allows recipients to attend school, but Bamford says officials routinely tell her clients otherwise: In a single month, one caseworker informed three of her students (incorrectly) that because they had turned 20, they could no longer receive benefits while completing their degrees. One was about to become the first in her family to graduate from high school. She quit and took a job as a dishwasher. Students as young as 16 have been told they must go to work full time or lose benefits. The employee who threatened to drop the students, says Bamford, became "caseworker of the month" for getting so many people off TANF.

As welfare officials go, B.J. Walker is something of a rock star. Appointed commissioner of Georgia's Department of Human Resources in 2004, Walker quickly became famous for her push to get virtually every adult off the state's public assistance rolls. By 2006, the state claimed Walker's agency had produced an astounding increase in the work participation rate of its TANF recipients, which in four years had jumped from 8 percent to nearly 70 percent.

Those numbers caught the attention of the Bush administration, which was in the midst of writing strict new regulations to require states to put 50 percent of their TANF caseloads into work activities, a target that only a handful of states had ever met. To unveil the new regs, administration officials brought Walker to Washington for a photo op and declared Georgia a model for other states.

To researchers, though, Georgia's rosy statistics looked too good to be true—especially given that Walker's own agency had found that the collapse of Georgia's textile industry and other manufacturing sectors left former TANF clients with far fewer job opportunities. In fact, even as the number of TANF recipients fell nearly 90 percent between January 2002 and November 2007, unemployment jumped 30 percent.

So how did Georgia put all those welfare moms to work? It didn't. As the Center on Budget and Policy Priorities' Liz Schott explained in a 2007 paper, "the increased work participation rate is primarily a factor of fewer families receiving assistance."

As for that "work participation," Stacy Haire, an outreach worker at Liberty House, says it's unlikely to help recipients find actual jobs. "They will put you at a police department. You'll be cleaning up behind toilets, picking up trash," she says. The TANF office once sent a client of hers to see a local government official about a job. The official told her he'd be glad to help out if she'd have sex with him. The woman filed a police report, but the man was never prosecuted. "That's what they can do in these towns," Haire says. "I see some sickening stuff."

Georgia isn't the only state that's found that dropping people from TANF is the easiest and cheapest way to meet federal work requirements. Texas reduced its caseloads by outsourcing applications to a call center, which wrongfully denied some families and lost others' applications altogether. In Florida, one innovative region started requiring TANF applicants to attend 40 hours of classes before they could even apply. Clients trying to restore lost benefits had once been able to straighten out paperwork with the help of caseworkers. In 2005, officials assigned all such work to a single employee, available two hours a week. The area's TANF caseload fell by half in a year.

Walker admits that Georgia has actively discouraged people from getting on TANF, primarily by emphasizing how meager the benefits are. "Two hundred eighty dollars a month does not make for a very good life," she told me. "This is really in the best interest of the children."

Walker acknowledges that some people struggle. "A lot of the people we see on TANF have made a mistake in choosing to have children," she offers. "We meet them at the front door and try to make sure that from day one they're engaged in some sort of productive activity." As for people like Clark who can't seem to get and keep a full-time job, Walker responds simply, "Can't? Won't."

Whatever their philosophical convictions, officials have another incentive for paring the TANF rolls: money. That's because the Clinton-era welfare reform turned what had been an entitlement program like Social Security—the more people needed help, the more money was spent—into a block grant, a fixed amount of money given to the states, regardless of need. The money, $16.5 billion a year, came mostly unencumbered by regulation. States could divert the funds to any program vaguely related to serving the needy.

Not only did the block grant doom the program to a slow death by inflation (by 2010, it will have lost 27 percent of its value), it also encouraged states to deny benefits to families, since they'd get the same amount of federal funds regardless of how many people received assistance. Georgia's share of the federal grant is nearly $370 million a year. "Even if caseloads go to zero, they get the same amount of money," notes Robert Welsh of the Georgia Budget and Policy Institute.

Some states have used surplus TANF money to expand child care, job training, and transportation to help recipients find jobs. But Georgia didn't use the bulk of its money for those programs—instead, it cut spending on child care and put the money into child protective services in the wake of a lawsuit against the state over the mistreatment of children in foster care. "The Feds are just fine with that," Walker insists. "We use our block grant to support other vulnerable families. That was the intent of the block grant."

Georgia is not alone in shifting its TANF money to other areas. The Government Accountability Office found in 2006 that many states were moving federal welfare funds away from cash assistance to the poor, or even "work supports" like child care, to plug holes in state budgets. Yet over the past 12 years, federal regulators have cited states only 11 times for misusing their TANF block grant, and only two suffered any financial penalty, according to Ken Wolfe, a spokesman for the Administration for Children and Families, which oversees the program. "As far as the federal government's concerned, it's not a big problem," he says.

On the run from an abusive boyfriend, Letorrea Clark struggles to keep food in the house for her daughter.

Terrell County, population 10,260, covers a rural corner of southwest Georgia not far from Jimmy Carter's boyhood peanut farm. Forty percent of the children here live below the poverty line; since the civil rights era the place has been known as "Terrible Terrell" because of the racial violence that erupted in the area. When I visited the Martin Luther King Jr. public housing project in the town of Dawson, a cluster of postwar-era brick buildings in the shadow of the Golden Peanut factory, three women sat in folding chairs, drinking Miller Lites under a big oak tree, bird-dogging the gaggle of children darting through the shirts flapping on laundry lines. One of them was a sturdy 30-year-old in a yellow T-shirt with three children, 13, 11, and 10, no husband, and no job.

The woman, who did not want her name used, had her first baby at 17, dropped out, and moved into the three-bedroom apartment where she's been ever since. For a decade, she had help from her children's father, who worked at the peanut factory. But three years ago they broke up, and he hasn't been heard from since. Not long ago, she got a letter from the state saying it had seized $900 from his tax refund for child support, but rather than sending it to his kids, the state would keep it as "back pay" for TANF checks she received years ago. She long ago exhausted her TANF benefits, which Georgia limits to 48 months over the course of a lifetime. She and the kids get $542 a month in food stamps; her electric bill alone runs $265 a month when the air conditioning's on.

So, as some women have always done in desperate times, she gets help from men. "Shit like that happens," she says. "If it was me, I probably wouldn't do stuff like that, but I got three babies to care for." She has held down jobs in the past, at Dawson Manufacturing, which made auto parts, and the Tyson chicken plant. But Dawson closed in 2007. Tyson won't rehire her because she had too many write-ups on the job. The only other major employer in town is Golden Peanut, right next door, but applying requires a trip to a temp agency in Sylvester, 45 miles away with no bus connection, which might as well be outer Mongolia for someone with no car and no money for gas. "I get on my knees and pray to that man above to make things change," she says.

In the meantime, she's getting by with help from her mom, and the man who slips in and out of her house when the kids aren't home. "I keep it on the down low from them," she explains. When she has bills due, her friend will give her $200 or $250, just about what she used to get in TANF benefits. "If he wants some and I need some money to keep the lights on, he hands out a pretty good penny," she says with a laugh.

Her experience isn't especially unusual. Toni Grebel, a relief worker at the Lord's Pantry, an Albany food bank, says she's heard many similar stories from her clients, who, at one time, were virtually all receiving TANF. Stacy Haire, the domestic violence outreach worker, says, "A lot of my clients, they're resorting to favors from men to get money." Albany police data show a sharp jump in arrests for prostitution and other crimes committed by women in 2005—shortly after the state began dumping its TANF caseloads.

Other women are turning to various illicit schemes: trading food stamps for cash to buy diapers; selling their kids' Social Security numbers to people with jobs, who use them to collect the Earned Income Tax Credit. One woman told me she got $800 each for her children's Social Security numbers, which she used to buy her kids summer clothes and new beds. "That money comes in handy. If you're not using it, why not help someone else?" she said.

One afternoon last fall, Letorrea Clark's caseworker from Liberty House, Ellen Folmar, stopped in to give her a ride to the post office. For a while, Clark had landed a job as a nanny, but that ended when school started. A Legal Aid lawyer helped her try to regain her lost disability benefits, but the appeal had recently been denied. Now, she'd lost her food stamp card. For the past few weeks, Gabby had subsisted on little but eggs and rice, and Clark was frantic.

Clark's life is a string of these sorts of crises. Mental illness wreaks havoc with her organizational skills. Medicaid doesn't pay for all her drugs, so when her child support money runs out, she doesn't always take the medication that keeps her stable. Finding no food stamp card at the post office, Clark fell apart. She was such a pathetic sight that a woman handed her $40. A weepy Clark got back in the van, consoled only after Folmar rounded up some emergency food from the shelter to tide the family over. "I got gravy!" Clark exclaimed with delight as she examined her bounty.

Back home later that week, Clark was happily entertaining a fellow Jehovah's Witness, who had a daughter Gabby's age. Gabby danced around the tiny space in her princess nightgown while Clark made the girls a brunch of eggs, bologna slices, tortilla chips, and apple juice cut with water to make it last longer. She put the paper plates on a plastic crate serving as a table. Clark was hoping her friend would get a job so that she could babysit her daughter. "Even in high school I worked with kids. That's my niche," she said. "That's the only thing that makes me happy. If it paid better, I'd be real happy."

As she talked, Clark stuck some donated chicken nuggets into the oven. She joked that her ADD was showing as she burned the first batch. As she started over, the two women swapped stories about ringing doorbells for the Lord. "I get a better response rate with Gabby," Clark said with a laugh. The Witnesses' generosity was on display in her apartment—a donated microwave, the TV, curtains, toys. Clark had piles of religious tracts in the apartment, some in Spanish, a language she was trying to learn from CDs, "so I can find me a Spanish husband," she joked.

The happy scene was but a temporary respite. Gabby's father had found Clark again. Two weeks later, her nonprofit landlord would tell her she had to move, citing budget woes. Shelter workers would search frantically to find her somewhere else to go. (They eventually found a place in yet another town.) Right now, though, Clark was focused on the chicken nuggets, and on Gabby, who climbed up, kissed her mother, and erupted into giggles. "I'm doing a good job with her," Clark said.

POSTSCRIPT

Has Welfare Reform Benefited the Poor?

There was considerable national agreement that the old welfare system had to be changed so that it would encourage people to find jobs and achieve self-sufficiency. Much success has been gained regarding this goal so far, but some analysts point out that numerous problems still remain. Coates focuses on the positive results of the new system and Mencimer focuses on shortcomings of the administration of the welfare.

Michael B. Katz, in *The Undeserving Poor: From the War on Poverty to the War on Welfare* (Pantheon Books, 1989), traces the evolution of welfare policies in the United States from the 1960s through the 1980s. Charles Noble traces the evolution of welfare policies into the late 1990s and argues that the structure of the political economy has greatly limited the welfare state, in *Welfare as We Knew It: A Political History of the American Welfare State* (Oxford University Press, 1997). Joel F. Handler carries the historical analysis of welfare in the United States to the present, in *Blame Welfare, Ignore Poverty and Inequality* (Cambridge University Press, 2007). Bruce S. Johnson criticizes welfare policies in the United States since the 1930s, in *The Sixteen-Trillion-Dollar Mistake: How the U.S. Bungled Its National Priorities from the New Deal to the Present* (Columbia University Press, 2001). For discussions of welfare reform, see Jeff Groggen and Lynn A. Karoly, *Welfare Reform: Effects of a Decade of Change* (Harvard University Press, 2005); Ron Haskins, *Work over Welfare: The Inside Story of the 1996 Welfare Reform Law* (Brookings Institution Press, 2006); Mary Reintsma, *The Political Economy of Welfare Reform in the United States* (Edward Elgar, 2007); Harrell R. Rodgers Jr., *American Poverty in a New Era of Reform* (M. E. Sharpe, 2006); Sharon Hayes, *Flat Broke with Children: Women in the Age of Welfare Reform* (Oxford University Press, 2003); Scott W. Allard, *Out of Reach: Place, Poverty, and the New American Welfare State* (Yale University Press, 2009); Frank Ridzi, *Selling Welfare Reform: Work-First and the New Common Sense of Employment* (New York University Press, 2009); and *Work, Welfare and Politics: Confronting Poverty in the Wake of Welfare*, edited by Frances Fox Piven et al. (University of Oregon Press, 2002). A great deal of information can be obtained from the reauthorization hearings in the House Committee on Education and the Workforce, *Welfare Reform: Reauthorization of Work and Child Care* (March 15, 2005). A new emphasis in current welfare policy involves faith-based programs, which are discussed in Mary Jo Bane and Lawrence M. Mead, *Lifting Up the Poor: A Dialogue on Religion, Poverty, and Welfare Reform* (Brookings Institution Press, 2003) and John P. Bartkowski, *Charitable Choices: Religion, Race, and Poverty in the Post-Welfare Era* (New York University, 2003). Most assessments of the 1996 welfare reform are positive. Two works that explore the negative consequences of this bill are Jane Henrici, ed., *Doing Without: Women and Work after Welfare Reform* (University of Arizona Press, 2006), and Kathleen M. Shaw et al., *Putting Poor People to Work: How the Work-First Idea Eroded College Access for the Poor* (Russell Sage Foundation, 2006). Many recognize that the key to reducing welfare rolls is to make work profitable. To understand welfare from this perspective, see *Making Work Pay: America after Welfare: A Reader,* edited by Robert Kuttner (New York Press, 2002), and Dave Hage, *Reforming Welfare by Rewarding Work: One State's Successful Experiment* (University of Minnesota Press, 2004). Two books that offer explanations as to why welfare provision is so minimal in the United States are Frank Stricker, *Why America Lost the War on Poverty—And How to Win It* (University of North Carolina Press, 2007), and Linda Gordon, *Pitied but Not Entitled: Single Mothers and the History of Welfare* (Free Press, 1994).

ISSUE 14

Is Competition the Reform That Will Fix Education?

YES: Clint Bolick, from "The Key to Closing the Minority Schooling Gap: School Choice," *The American Enterprise* (April/May 2003)

NO: Ron Wolk, from "Think the Unthinkable," *Educational Horizons* (Summer 2004)

ISSUE SUMMARY

YES: Clint Bolick, vice president of the Institute for Justice, presents the argument for school choice that competition leads to improvements and makes the case that minorities especially need school choice to improve their educational performance.

NO: Educator and businessman Ron Wolk argues that school choice and most other educational reforms can only be marginally effective because they do not get at the heart of the educational problem, which is the way students learn. Too much attention is directed to the way teachers teach when the attention should be placed on how to stimulate students to learn more. Wolk advocates giving students more responsibility for their education.

T he quality of American public schooling has been criticized for several decades. Secretary of Education Richard Riley said in 1994 that some American schools are so bad that they "should never be called schools at all." The average school year in the United States is 180 days, whereas Japanese children attend school 240 days of the year. American schoolchildren score lower than the children of many other Western countries on certain standardized achievement tests. In 1983, the National Commission on Excellence in Education published *A Nation at Risk,* which argued that American education was a failure. Critics of *A Nation at Risk* maintain that the report produced very little evidence to support its thesis, but the public accepted it anyway. Currently, much of the public still thinks that the American school system is failing and needs to be fixed. The solution most frequently proposed today is some form of competition from charter schools or a voucher system.

Today 99 percent of children ages 6 to 13 are in school. In 1900, only about 7 percent of the appropriate age group graduated from high school, but in 1990, 86 percent did. Another success is the extraordinary improvement in the graduation rates for blacks since 1964, when it was 45 percent, to 1987, when it was 83 percent. Now this rate is almost at parity with white graduation rates. And over two-thirds of the present American population have a high school degree. No other nation comes close to these accomplishments. Nevertheless, most voices are very critical of American education.

American education reforms of the past 40 years have focused on quality and on what is taught. In the late 1950s, the Soviet Union's launch of the first space satellite convinced the public of the need for more math and science in the curriculum. In the late 1960s and 1970s, schools were criticized for rigid authoritarian teaching styles, and schools were made less structured. They became more open, participatory, and individualized in order to stimulate student involvement, creativity, and emotional growth. In the 1980s, a crusade for the return to basics was triggered by the announcement that SAT scores had declined since the early 1960s. In the 1990s, the continued problems of public schools led many to call for their restructuring by means of school choice, that is, competition.

The debate today is whether competition will finally make American schools succeed. The answer depends on whether the current structure of schools is the main reason why schools seem to be failing. Many other trends have also affected school performance, so the structure of the school system may not be the key to the problem. For example, many argue that curriculum changes away from basics, new unstructured teaching techniques, and the decline of discipline in the classroom have contributed to perceived problems. Perhaps the quality of teachers needs to be raised. There is evidence that those who go into teaching score far lower on SATs than the average college student. In addition, societal trends outside the school may significantly impact school performance. Increasing breakdown of the family, more permissive childrearing, the substantial decline in the amount of time that parents spend with children, and the increased exposure of children to television are trends that many believe are adversely affecting school performance.

In the selections that follow, the costs and the benefits of school choice are debated. Clint Bolick argues that school choice applies to college education, and U.S. higher education is the envy of the world. The role of competition in producing excellence in business, sports, and elsewhere is well-known. And from the moral point of view, the parents should have the right to choose. Wolk argues that most educational reforms, including school choice, do not get at the heart of the educational problem, which is the way students are taught. Too much emphasis is placed on better teaching and not where it belongs, on students' learning. Wolk advocates shifting considerable responsibility from teachers to the students for their education.

YES

Clint Bolick

The Key to Closing the Minority Schooling Gap: School Choice

In a nation supposedly committed to free enterprise, consumer choice, and equal educational opportunities, school choice should be routine. That it is not demonstrates the clout of those dedicated to preserving the government's monopoly over public education. To listen to the education establishment, one would think that school choice is a radical, scary, alien concept. Indeed, the defenders of the status quo have convinced many voters that school choice is a threat to American society.

But school choice is not threatening, and it is not new. To the contrary, it is the norm in most modern nations. . . . Even in the U.S., non-government schools have long played a key educational role, often using public funds. America's college system—the world's envy—is built on school choice: Students can use the G.I. Bill, Pell Grants, and other forms of government aid to attend either public or private schools, including religious institutions. At the other end of the age spectrum, parents of preschoolers can use child care vouchers in private and religious settings. And under federal law, tens of thousands of disabled elementary and high school age children receive schooling in private schools at public expense. It is only mainstream K–12 schools in which the government commands a monopoly over public funds.

Thomas Paine, the most prescient of our founding fathers, is credited with first suggesting a voucher system in the United States. He wanted an educated, enlightened citizenry, but the idea that the government should operate schools was an alien concept to him and his generation. Instead, Paine proposed providing citizens with financial support that they could use to purchase education in private schools.

The great portion of early American "public" education took place in private schools. Even when states started creating government schools, the teachers often were ministers. The concept of "separation of church and state" is not in the U.S. Constitution, and was certainly never applied to education.

In 1869, Vermont adopted a school choice program for communities that did not build their own public schools, and Maine followed suit in 1873. To this day, both states will pay tuition for children to attend private schools, or public schools in neighboring communities. In Vermont, 6,500 children from 90 towns

From *The American Enterprise*, April/May 2003, pp. 30–33. Copyright © 2003 by American Enterprise Institute. Reprinted by permission. www.TAE.com

attend private schools at government expense; in Maine, 5,600 children from 55 towns do so. Those programs, in existence for more than a century and a quarter, have not destroyed the local public schools; to the contrary, both states boast a well-educated population.

But the goal of universal common schooling, fueled by the ideas of Horace Mann, helped make government schools the norm in the late nineteenth century. Thereafter, private schools typically served two groups: the elite, and those seeking a religious immersion different from the Protestant theology that dominated public schools. The latter, of course, were primarily Catholic immigrants.

The rise of Catholic schools bitterly annoyed Protestant public school advocates like Senator James Blaine (R-ME). Blaine struck back in 1876. His proposed amendment to the U.S. Constitution to prohibit any government aid to religious schools came just short of securing passage in Congress. His allies, however, lobbied state legislatures and succeeded in attaching "Blaine amendments" to approximately 37 state constitutions, which prohibited expenditure of public funds in "support" of sectarian (i.e., Catholic) schools. Anti-Catholic bigotry crested in an Oregon law, secured by the Ku Klux Klan, which *required* all children to attend government schools.

In the landmark 1925 decision *Pierce v. Society of Sisters,* the U.S. Supreme Court struck down that Oregon law, declaring that "The fundamental theory of liberty upon which all governments in this Union repose excludes any general power of the State to standardize its children by forcing them to accept instruction from public teachers only. The child is not the mere creature of the State; those who nurture him and direct his destiny have the right, coupled with the high duty, to recognize and prepare him for additional obligations." This principle of parental sovereignty remains a cornerstone of American law today. Though it remains constantly under attack, it continues to keep private educational options (among other rights) open to parents.

The modern case for school vouchers was first made by the Nobel laureate economist Milton Friedman in 1955. Instead of providing education as a monopoly supplier, Friedman suggested, government should just finance it. Every child would be given a voucher redeemable at a school of the parent's choice, public or private. Schools would compete to attract the vouchers. Friedman's proposal contained two insights that formed the intellectual foundations of the contemporary school choice movement: that parents, rather than government, should decide where children attend school, and that the economic rules which yield good services and products are not suspended at the schoolhouse door.

Support for school choice began to expand and diversify in the 1970s, when two liberal Berkeley law professors, Jack Coons and Steven Sugarman, began to consider school choice as a means of delivering educational equity. If forced busing plans had failed, Coons and Sugarman argued, why not give vouchers to poor and minority parents so they could choose the best education for their children? Coons and Sugarman adapted Friedman's proposal to their own ends: While Friedman advocated universal vouchers, Coons and Sugarman wanted to target them to disadvantaged populations. Friedman preferred a lightly regulated system, while Coons and Sugarman called for substantial government oversight. Still, there was the beginning of an alliance between freedom-seeking conservatives on the one hand and equality-seeking liberals on the other. That alliance eventually made the school choice programs of the 1990s a reality.

The main force generating support for vouchers, however, was the alarming decline in urban public schools. During the 1960s and 1970s, most urban public schools were ruined. Whites and middle-class blacks fled to the suburbs, leaving poor and mostly minority populations in rapidly worsening city public schools.

The problems of urban public schools were connected to a broader decline in public education. The 1983 study *A Nation at Risk* warned that large doses of mediocrity and failure had crept into American public schools. Meanwhile, starting in the 1980s, social scientists like James Coleman began showing that private and religious schools were succeeding in educating the very same poor, minority schoolchildren that government schools were failing. Many corroborating studies followed.

Also helping set the stage for a school choice movement was the 1990 Brookings Institution study by John Chubb and Terry Moe, *Politics, Markets & America's Schools*. Chubb and Moe set out to discover why suburban public schools and inner-city private schools generally produced good academic outcomes, while inner-city public schools were disasters. They found that whereas the first two types of schools were characterized by strong leaders with a clear mission and a high degree of responsiveness to parents, inner-city schools were not. Instead, urban public school districts were run by bloated bureaucracies whose principal constituencies were not parents, but politicians and unions.

A crucial factor distinguishing the successful and unsuccessful schools was the element of choice: Suburban parents could send their children to private schools, or move to different communities, if they were dissatisfied with their public schools. Private schools, obviously, were entirely dependent on satisfied parents. But inner-city public school parents were captives: They had no choice except to send their children to whatever the local government school offered. In school districts with tens or hundreds of thousands of students, they were powerless to do anything about the system.

Introducing choice in inner-city public schools, Chubb and Moe concluded—particularly giving parents the power to exit the public system altogether—would force the bureaucracy to respond to its customers rather than to politicians and special-interest groups. These findings created a scholarly foundation for school choice as a way not merely of helping children in failing government schools, but also as an essential prerequisite for reforming public school systems.

When the current school choice movement started to come together a decade or two ago, its leading protagonists could have met comfortably in a telephone booth. In an amazingly short period, it has grown into a sophisticated, passionate, and ecumenical movement. There are philanthropists, activists, public officials, clergy, lawyers, and parents, all willing to put aside ideological differences in pursuit of a common cause.

The movement's core argument is that parents, not government, should have the primary responsibility and power to determine where and how their children are educated. That this basic principle should require a vicious fight is testimony to the strength, determination, and ferocity of the reactionary forces defending today's educational status quo. Teacher unions, which form the cornerstone of our education establishment, are the most powerful special-interest group in America today. At the national level, they essentially own the Democratic Party. At the state level, they wield enormous influence over elected officials in both parties. At the local level, they frequently control school boards. They and their education allies dedicated all the resources at their disposal to defeat meaningful school choice anywhere it has presented itself.

For the education establishment, this battle is about preserving their monopolistic vise grip on American schooling. For parents—and our society— the stakes are much higher. Nearly 50 years after *Brown v. Board of Education,* vast numbers of black and Hispanic children do not graduate from high school. Many of those who do still lack the most basic skills needed for even entry-level jobs. As a result, many children in inner-city schools wind up on welfare or in jail. Children who most need the compensations of a quality edu- cation are instead regulated to dysfunctional schools. In climbing out of this morass we should not worry about whether a particular reform is too radical; we should worry about whether it is radical enough.

The school choice movement is not only a crusade to improve American education. It is also a true civil rights struggle. It is critical to the real lives of real people. The system has written off many of the people who most need choice—both the parents and their children. Minority citizens may be offered welfare payments, or racial preferences, but little is done to help them become productive, self-supporting citizens. Government schools and their liberal patrons implicitly assume that low-income children are incapable of learning. With little expected of these children, that becomes a self-fulfilling prophecy.

Meanwhile, conditions are different in most inner-city private schools. Not because they have greater resources than their public school counterparts (they typically have far fewer), or because they are selective (they usually accept all applicants), but rather because the operating philosophy is mark- edly different. At non-government schools, parents are not discouraged from involvement, they are *required* to play a role in the school and in their chil- dren's education. The children are expected to behave. They are expected to achieve. And research shows that they do.

Ultimately, we want school choice programs that are large and accessible enough to give government schools a serious run for their money. But initially, even a small program—publicly or privately funded—can begin to introduce inner-city parents to the previously unknown concept that there is an alterna- tive to failure. That creates a constituency for a larger program.

Any functioning program, no matter how small, will change the debate from one about hypotheticals to one about realities. When we can show that competition helps public schools, and that families are choosing good schools rather than, say, witch-craft schools, we can begin to debunk the myths of choice adversaries. In Milwaukee, where school choice has been pioneered, public opinion polls show that support for choice is stronger the closer one is to the program. Not only inner-city parents but also suburban parents now support school choice there.

Actual experience has shown that school choice programs do not "skim the cream" of students, as our detractors like to say, leaving only hard cases in the public schools. Instead (not surprisingly), school choice programs usually attract children who are experiencing academic or disciplinary problems in government schools. Many such children are on a downward trajectory. Just arresting that trajectory is an accomplishment, even if it doesn't show up immediately in improved test scores.

Academic research by Harvard's Paul Peterson and others shows that academic gains are modest in the first year or two of a school choice program, and begin to accelerate afterward. Longitudinal studies tracking choice students over many years seem likely to find higher high school graduation and college enrollment rates, plus other measures of success. If that happens, the debate over the desirability of school choice will be over. The pioneers of school choice will have shown how to rescue individuals from otherwise dark futures, as well as how to force our larger system of public education to improve itself for the good of all students.

Think the Unthinkable

For more than two decades, the United States has been struggling to improve public education. In April 1983 the federal report *A Nation at Risk* stunned the nation with its dire warning that "a rising tide of mediocrity" was swamping our schools. A spate of articles and editorials on the occasion of its twentieth anniversary last spring concluded that the schools today are not much better than they were then.

Five years after *A Nation at Risk,* in 1988, the first President Bush and the nation's governors, with much fanfare, set lofty education goals to be met by the year 2000, including the goals that every child would be ready for school and that the U.S. would be first in the world in math and science by the dawn of the new millennium. We didn't even come close to meeting any of the goals.

Now we have "No Child Left Behind," the sweeping and intrusive new federal law that more than doubles the amount of standardized testing. It promises, among other things, that a highly qualified teacher will be in every classroom by 2006 and that all children will be proficient in a dozen years. It, too, will inevitably fall well short of its noble objectives.

How could a country with such knowledge, wealth, and power and such stellar accomplishments in every other field of human endeavor try so hard and still be so far behind in education that it ranks among Third World nations?

The Wrong Questions Encourage the Wrong Answers

After pondering that conundrum for many years, I've come to believe it is because we are seeking answers to the wrong questions. In the current school-reform movement—and in every previous one—we have asked:

- How do we fix our broken public schools?
- How do we raise student achievement (meaning test scores)?

Not surprisingly, the answers to those questions nearly always focus on the school. We always accept the school as a given, which means we are essentially stuck with all the conventions and sacred cows of the traditional school. It almost guarantees that we will not be able, as they say, to "think outside the box."

From *Educational Horizons,* Summer 2004, pp. 268–279. Copyright © 2004 by Ron Wolk. Reprinted by permission.

The questions we should be asking are:

- How do we guide our kids through their very challenging formative years so that they emerge as responsible young adults with the skills and attitudes they need to function and thrive in a rapidly changing world?
- What do we want every child to achieve?

The answers to those questions must focus on a lot more than just school. Three short sketches from where I live—Providence, Rhode Island—make the point.

Jesse the Janitor.   Sixteen-year-old Jesse lived with his widowed mother and attended Coventry High School in Rhode Island. Bored to death and "fed up" with school, Jesse told the principal he intended to drop out. Although Jesse had been labeled "troubled," the principal knew Jesse liked to work and considered him to be a bright, mature young man. So he offered Jesse a deal: if Jesse would attend classes in the morning, he could work as a janitor in the afternoons for five dollars an hour.

Jesse accepted, and in the following months the school was never cleaner. Jesse got grass to grow where it hadn't grown before and even inspired his classmates to cease littering almost completely. Jesse now wants to go on to community college to study computer programming. Says his principal: "This kid is going to be a productive citizen someday, and I would not have been able to say that months ago."

Following Footsteps.   Michelle and Tiffany were sophomores at the Met school in Providence, perhaps the most unconventional high school in the nation. Students at the Met spend a couple of days a week out of school, working with mentors on term projects in the community. Each student has a personalized curriculum worked out in consultation with the parent, teacher (known as "adviser"), and mentor. Michelle and Tiffany decided that for their term project they would join a group of adults and retrace Martin Luther King Jr.'s Alabama Freedom March from Selma to Montgomery.

They read biographies of King, studied contemporary accounts of the march in newspapers and magazines, and plotted their day-by-day itinerary. Then, with their adviser's help, they arranged to stay with families along the route. The girls traveled for three weeks, interviewing civil rights leaders and participants in the march.

When the girls returned to school, they wrote a detailed account of their adventure. Michelle said she had never understood before all the fuss about voting, but she learned during that trip that people died so she could vote, and she vowed that her vote would never be wasted.

Learning Leadership.   To be admitted to Classical High School (arguably Providence's best), students must pass an examination. On her first day as a freshman, Maria, nervous and scared, sat in the auditorium as the principal told students to look to their left and right. One of those kids would not be there at graduation, he warned. As the months passed, Maria found school boring and irrelevant. She wondered if she might be one of the absent ones four years later.

Then Maria heard about a community organization called "Youth in Action" and joined. Suddenly she was immersed in meaningful and interesting work—designing an AIDS curriculum, gathering data for a local environmental-justice campaign, working with troubled children, speaking to groups, planning events, raising money. Maria became an officer and a member of the board of Youth in Action.

After graduating from high school and beginning college, Maria returned to Providence to speak at a meeting on educational opportunities for American adolescents. Poised, passionate, and articulate, she talked more about her work in the community than her high school experience. When she finished, she was complimented on her accomplishments and asked how much of her success she attributed to attending Classical and how much to participating in Youth in Action. Without hesitation, she said that the youth group was responsible for 95 percent of her growth.

Jesse was fortunate that his principal was perceptive enough and flexible enough to adapt to his needs and skills. Michelle and Tiffany learned about history and the meaning of citizenship by following their own interests. Maria blossomed through doing real work in the real world.

America Wasn't Listening

For those youngsters and millions like them, the conventional school with its rigid academic curriculum and inflexible procedures is neither the only way nor the best way to become educated—that is, if we accept Webster's definition of educate, which means "to rear, to develop mentally and morally." If our primary goal is to help children become competent and responsible adults, then the conventional school, at least after grade six, may be counterproductive.

That same message was delivered to the nation by a panel of researchers assembled by the White House Science Advisory Committee almost a decade before *A Nation at Risk*. Led by the noted sociologist James S. Coleman, the panel in 1974 published "Youth: Transition to Adulthood." The report began with this profound observation:

> As the labor of children has become unnecessary to society, school has been extended for them. With every decade, the length of schooling has increased, until a thoughtful person must ask whether society can conceive of no other way for youth to come into adulthood.
>
> If schooling were a complete environment, the answer would probably be that no amount of school is too much, and increased schooling for the young is the best way for the young to spend their increased leisure and society its increased wealth.

Coleman and his colleagues concluded, however, that schooling was far from a complete environment, and called for a "serious examination" of the institutional framework in which young people develop into adults.

They argued, "The school is not the world, and is not perceived by students as 'real.'" The panel recommended that high school play a lesser role in the lives of adolescents and that their learning be transferred to a variety of sites in the community where they can develop the skills and attitudes which society expects of responsible young adults.

If that 175-page report had galvanized the nation the way *A Nation at Risk* did, the past twenty-five years of education reform probably would have been much different and, arguably, much more productive.

Two years before Coleman's report appeared, a colleague of his, the sociologist Christopher Jencks, published his landmark study *Inequality: A Reassessment of the Effect of Family and Schooling in America*. Jencks found that not only is school not the complete environment, but he discovered no evidence that "school reform can be expected to bring about significant social changes outside of schools." The research showed that the outcomes of school depend largely on what goes in: i.e., the students. Middle- and upper-class kids tend to perform adequately; poor kids tend to do poorly. The schools that kids from affluent families attend do relatively well; the schools that poor kids attend do poorly.

That remains true today. The quality of a child's education in the United States depends mainly on where he lives, the color of her skin, and the socio-economic status of the family. . . .

The Good Old Days

There was a time when the responsibility for transforming kids into competent young adults was mainly the job of the family, shared by the church and, for six or eight years of children's lives, the public school. The responsibility was more easily fulfilled in the simpler era of the nineteenth century because the distractions were far fewer than they are in this cacophonous age of mass media. Today, neither the family nor the church wields the kind of influence on the young that it once did. That has left the school as the primary institution charged with shaping our young.

The school might have successfully filled the vacuum left by family and church had it changed as dramatically and continually as the rest of the world, but it didn't. The core of the school remains essentially as it was a century ago, even though the students and the world have changed radically. As a consequence, schools are declining in influence and effectiveness at the very time that kids are facing greater and more demanding challenges. Restoring the family and the church to their long-lost cultural dominance is unlikely. And because the school is in decline, we are leaving much of the social and intellectual development of our children to their peers, the media, and popular culture.

Needed: A New Education Strategy

It is not productive to criticize schools or to blame them for not changing over the decades or for not solving a problem they are not now equipped to solve. The rational course of action is to recognize where we are, what the main task is, and how to accomplish it. Our paramount goal should be to help kids progress successfully into adulthood. To accomplish that, our priorities should include, at least, the following:

- To help youngsters acquire the skills and knowledge they will need to function in a continually changing world. That means nourishing in them the motivation and ability to continue educating themselves.
- To guide them as they develop a system of positive values and ethics that will govern their day-to-day behavior and their relationships with others.
- To assist them in understanding their rights and responsibilities as members of a community and a democratic society.
- To give them the opportunity to explore the world of work and to recognize their obligation to support themselves and their families.

Schools have an important role to play in the development of the young, but it is not their only—or even the dominant—role. If we want children to become responsible adults, we need to forge an alternative or parallel system that offers a range of choices to young people and allows them to make decisions and change directions as they grow into adults.

The elements of such a new system already exist in some schools and communities across the country. Certainly, there are enough models available for states and municipalities to construct a system that addresses the varied needs of young people and offers them choices at critical times in their development. The challenge to policymakers in statehouses and school-district offices is to create some open space in the present system for new educational opportunities.

Here is a glimpse of what that system might look like and how it might come to be.

Proposed: A Parallel System to Educate the Young

On the premise that it is easier to make significant change by starting something new than by trying to reform something old, I would argue that each state should charter a nongeographic district that could include institutions located anywhere in the state. The charter district would be led by a superintendent with a relatively small administrative staff. The superintendent would be appointed by, and accountable to, a board, whose members would in turn be elected by the individual schools in the charter district. The state would exempt the charter district from all regulations governing public schools except those involving safety and civil rights.

The role of the district would be largely to coordinate and support innovation and experimentation in education and youth development. It would offer educational alternatives to the conventional schools. The charter district might be viewed as the research and development arm of the state's educational system. There would be two kinds of learning institutions in the charter district. Children from age five to age thirteen would attend "primary" schools, and children ages thirteen and over would enroll in secondary learning centers.

The primary schools could be new schools established by the state, schools chartered by nonprofit organizations (the way charter schools are today in most states), or existing innovative elementary schools that opt into the new charter district. Like many of the innovative elementary schools, the primary schools in the charter district could be organized around a theme or a particular pedagogy. All primary schools in the charter district would focus significantly on literacy, numeracy, and the arts. Students would be exposed to the disciplines—science, history, literature, biography, geography, and civics—through reading in those disciplines. The emphasis would be on reading and comprehension of concepts and ideas in those disciplines, not on coverage and memorization of enormous amounts of trivia. In addition, the primary school would nourish children's curiosity and inculcate good habits of mind and behavior.

To be admitted to a secondary learning center or school in the charter district, students would have to demonstrate mastery of reading comprehension and basic mathematics. The secondary learning centers would not be schools as such, but rather community-based organizations created by the state or operated under contract with the state by existing organizations. Their primary functions would be supervising young people and helping them manage their education. Secondary learning centers would be limited to about 200 "students."

In addition to the new secondary learning centers, the charter district could include innovative secondary schools that already exist in virtually every state. The Bill and Melinda Gates Foundation funds some of the more innovative schools, such as the New Country School in Minnesota, High Tech High in San Diego, the Met in Providence, and Best Practices High School in Chicago. Schools like those would add strength and diversity to the charter district. In addition, they would find the sanctuary and support that they often lack as outliers in the conventional system. (For additional examples of innovative schools, see Timothy J. Dyer, *Breaking Ranks: Changing an American Institution,* DIANE Publishing, November 1999, ISBN 0788183559, and Thomas Toch, *High Schools on a Human Scale: How Small Schools Can Transform American Education,* Beacon Press, April 2003, ISBN 080703245X.)

New Institutions and New Roles for Teachers and Students.   In the new secondary learning centers, the roles of teachers and students would change. Students would assume much more responsibility for their own education and would be assigned to an adult adviser: a teacher in most cases. Although advisers would teach, their primary function would be supervising fifteen to twenty students and helping them manage their learning and their time. The adviser and his or her students would remain together during the students' stay at the learning center. In schools practicing that model, students and advisers tend to become "families," forging close and productive relationships.

Personalized Curricula.   In consultation with advisers and parents, students would formulate personalized curricula. Each year they would choose from a menu of opportunities. Periodically, as they progressed, they would be able to change directions if they were so inclined. For example, they could participate in apprenticeships and internships with adult mentors in businesses, hospitals, government agencies, and other employers where they could experience the workplace and see the need for punctuality, attention to detail, and teamwork. They could volunteer to perform social and human services or work for worthy causes where they would observe democratic practices and politics in action.

Educational Travel. Youngsters would have opportunities for educational travel in the United States and abroad, both individually and in groups. Programs like Americorps could provide opportunities for high-school-age kids. Programs like Outward Bound could help young people test themselves and develop self-confidence. Previous efforts such as the Civilian Conservation Corps of the New Deal era could provide a useful model for such programs.

Extracurricular Activities.   As the role of high schools diminished, extracurricular activities would have to be provided largely through out-of-school clubs, teams, and youth organizations, perhaps coordinated by the secondary learning center. Many graduates attest that their most rewarding experiences in high school were activities such as chorus, band, debate, and athletics. To the extent that those activities met student needs, they would continue to command a significant amount of time and resources. However, because students would be spending much of their time in real-world situations, they might come to rely less on extracurricular activities to develop a sense of self-worth and to learn the values of teamwork, performance, effort, and proficiency.

Just-in-Time Instruction.   All the activities the students chose would be constructed to involve learning at several levels, including academic instruction. Students would have available "just-in-time" instruction: e.g., a student interning in a hospital might need to take a course in biology or anatomy; an intern in a bank might require instruction in math or accounting; a student apprenticing in a restaurant might need chemistry instruction. The secondary learning centers could make such instruction available both in person and online.

Technology.   A modest investment in research and development and a little imagination could produce software programs to provide "just-in-time" instruction. Simulations, computer games, chat rooms, CDs, Internet courses, and the like enable students to do almost everything that they could in a classroom: dissect a frog on the computer, conduct physics experiments, learn languages, study poetry read aloud by the poets themselves, conduct research, and carry on extensive discussions about issues. The infrastructure is already there: most schools in nearly every state already are wired to the Internet. Indeed, following the lead of the University of Phoenix, many of the nation's top universities and nearly seventy charter schools now offer online courses and degrees.

In-Person Instruction.   Technology by itself would not encompass the complete environment that students need to learn and grow. Secondary learning centers would offer live instruction either by contracting with a conventional school, arranging for courses in community or four-year colleges, or arranging for tutoring.

Flexible Scheduling.   Whether online or in person, instruction would not necessarily be delivered in semester courses of several classes a week. For example, an adviser and a small group of students might spend every day for two weeks in intense study of the Constitution, an area of mathematics, or the geography of the United States, but the decision to do so would arise from the needs and desires of the students—not from a pre-set curriculum.

The great philosopher and mathematician Alfred North Whitehead described the challenge this way: "The result of teaching small parts of a large number of subjects is the passive reception of disconnected ideas; not illumined with any spark of vitality. Let the main ideas which are introduced into a child's education be few and important and let them be thrown into every combination possible. The child should make them his own, and should understand their application here and now in the circumstances of his actual life."

Students at the Met School in Providence constantly demonstrate how effective and committed kids can be when they are working on something that interests them, which they have chosen. For example:

A Play of Her Own: A young woman in her junior year wrote a play for her term project. When she finished it, she decided to produce it. She selected the cast, designed the set, directed the play, rented the hall, printed and distributed announcements, sold the tickets, and played the lead. She symbolizes the independence and conscientiousness of students who engage in self-education, and she is not unusual.

His Father's War: A young man had long been intrigued by the fact that his father had served in Vietnam, but the father always declined to talk about his experience. The boy decided he had to visit Vietnam and he desperately wanted to take his father with him. He studied the history and geography of the country and read widely about the war; then he wrote a proposal that helped him raise enough money to cover travel expenses. He and his father spent several weeks visiting places in Vietnam where his father had been stationed. When they returned, the student wrote a detailed and thoughtful report about the experience and what he had learned about his father and himself.

"This is who I am":   Met students must write a seventy-five-page autobiography to graduate. Many students moan and resist. One student in particular insisted that he couldn't do it, that it was cruel and unusual punishment. When he walked across the stage to collect his diploma, that student's adviser noted that the young man had submitted a 100-page autobiography with the comment, "Until I wrote that paper, I didn't really know who I was."

In such projects, students learn a great deal and it becomes part of them, not just something to regurgitate on a test and forget. Doing real work in the real world—whether interning with a chef, a glassblower, or a hospital technician—requires some knowledge in a number of disciplines. Youngsters pursue that knowledge and assimilate it because they need it to do their work. Equally important, the work helps them to mature, gain confidence, and understand the power of learning. And their success in one endeavor tends to fuel their curiosity and lead to broader learning. . . .

It's the Students' Work, Stupid!   Students' work and accomplishments are at the heart of the new system. Common norm-referenced and criterion-referenced standardized testing would not be used. For diagnostic purposes and to assess value added, the charter district would use computer-adaptive online testing. In all the students' activities, teachers, mentors, and other adults would view the students' work and accomplishments to determine progress. Evaluating the work would be more complicated but far richer than assigning test scores. The evaluations of advisers and mentors would reveal infinitely more about a student's ability, attitude, and effort than simple letter grades.

At age sixteen, each student would have three options: continuing in the system for two more years; leaving to enroll in postsecondary education; or leaving to take a job, which could include the military, the Peace Corps, and other such occupations (which today is usually considered dropping out). If students left school at age sixteen for any reason, they would have the right to return to the system for two years before they turned twenty-one.

Instead of receiving a high school diploma, which tells an employer or a college admission officer virtually nothing about who a student is and what he or she has accomplished, students would receive a certificate of completion and a dossier. The dossier would list the courses they took, the internships they served, their volunteer work, and the organizations to which they belonged, along with the evaluations submitted by their adult supervisors. It would include selected samples of their work. Employers are much more likely to be satisfied with such an evaluation than colleges, suggesting that higher education needs to reassess admission requirements and find more substantive ways to evaluate student ability.

POSTSCRIPT

Is Competition the Reform That Will Fix Education?

Since school reformers have focused on school choice, the literature on it has mushroomed. The choice proposal first gained public attention in 1955, when Milton Friedman wrote about vouchers in "The Role of Government in Education," in Robert Solo, ed., *Economics and the Public Interest* (Rutgers University Press). More recent school choice advocates include Harry Brighouse, *School Choice and Social Justice* (Oxford University Press, 2000); Mark Schneider, *Choosing Schools: Consumer Choice and the Quality of American Schools* (Princeton University Press, 2000); Philip A. Woods, *School Choice and Competition: Markets in the Public Interest* (Routledge, 1998); Sol Stern, *Breaking Free: Public School Lessons and the Imperative of School Choice* (Encounter Books, 2003); Clint Bolick, *Voucher Wars: Waging the Legal Battle over School Choice* (Cato Institute, 2003); Clive R. Belfield and Henry M. Levin, *Privatizing Educational Choice* (Paradigm Publishers, 2005); James G. Dwyer, *Vouchers within Reason: A Child-Centered Approach to Education Reform* (Cornell University Press, 2002); and Emily Van Dunk, *School Choice and the Question of Accountability: The Milwaukee Experience* (Yale University Press, 2003). School choice is most strongly advocated for inner-city schools. See Frederick M. Hess, *Revolution at the Margins: The Impact of Competition on Urban School Systems* (Brookings Institution Press, 2002), and William G. Howell, *The Education Gap: Vouchers and Urban Schools* (Brookings Institution Press, 2002). For discussions between school choice systems, see *Public School Choice vs. Private School Vouchers*, edited by Richard D. Kahlenberg (Century Foundation, 2003). For a less partisan view, see Joseph P. Viteritti, *Choosing Equality: School Choice, the Constitution, and Civil Society* (Brookings Institute Press, 1999). For comparisons of school choice with other reforms, see Margaret C. Wang and Herbert J. Walberg, eds., *School Choice or Best Systems: What Improves Education?* (L. Erlbaum Associates, 2001). Some advocates of choice would limit the choices in major ways. Timothy W. Young and Evans Clinchy, in *Choice in Public Education* (Teachers College Press, 1992), contend that there is already considerable choice in public education, so they argue against a voucher system, which they feel will divert badly needed financial resources from the public schools to give further support to parents who can already afford private schools.

Important critiques of school choice include Albert Shanker and Bella Rosenberg, *Politics, Markets, and America's Schools: The Fallacies of Private School Choice* (American Federation of Teachers, 1991); Kevin B. Smith and Kenneth J. Meier, *The Case Against School Choice: Politics, Markets, and Fools* (M. E. Sharpe, 1995); Seymour Bernard Sarason, *Questions You Should Ask about Charter Schools and Vouchers* (Heinemann, 2002); Lois H. André Buchely, *Could It Be Otherwise? Parents and the Inequities of Public School Choice* (Routledge, 2005); Gary Miron and Christopher Nelson, *What's Public about Charter Schools? Lessons Learned about Choice and Accountability* (Corwin Press, 2002); R. Kenneth Godwin and Frand R. Kemerer, *School Choice Tradeoff: Liberty, Equity, and Diversity* (University of Texas Press, 2002); *School Choice: The Moral Debate,* edited by Alan Wolfe (Princeton University Press, 2003); Ronald G. Corwin and E. Joseph Schneider, *The School Choice Hoax: Fixing American's Schools* (Praeger, 2005).

ISSUE 15

Should Biotechnology Be Used to Alter and Enhance Humans?

YES: **President's Council on Bioethics,** from *Beyond Therapy* (Regan Books, 2009)

NO: **Michael J. Sandel,** from "The Case Against Perfection," *The Atlantic Monthly* (April 2004)

ISSUE SUMMARY

YES: The President's Council on Bioethics was commissioned by George Bush to report to him their findings about the ethical issues involved in the uses of biotechnology. Included in this selection are the expected positive benefits from the biotechnologies that are on the horizon.

NO: Political science professor Michael J. Sandel was on the President's Council on Bioethics but presents his private view in this selection, which is very cautionary on the use of biotechnology to alter and enhance humans. Many other uses of biotechnology he praises, but he condemns using biotechnology to alter and enhance humans. In these activities, humans play God and attempt inappropriate remaking of nature.

As a sociologist I feel that I am on relatively firm ground discussing the 19 other issues in this book. I am not on firm ground discussing the issue of how biotechnology should or should not be used. And I am not alone. The nation does not know what to think about this issue, at least not in a coherent way. But the discussion must begin because the issue is coming at us like a tornado. Already America is debating the use of drugs to enhance athletic performance. Athletes and body builders want to use them to build muscle, strength, and/or endurance, but much of the public do not approve. They have been outlawed for competitive sports, and users have been publicly discredited. Soon, however, parents will be able to pay for genetic engineering to make their children good athletes and perhaps even great athletes. Will that also be illegal? This is only the tip of the iceberg. Thousands of difficult questions will arise as the technology for designing babies will become more and more powerful. Stem cell research is currently a divisive issue. Are we blocking the development of technologies that can save thousands of lives by severely limiting stem cell research?

The classic expression of this issue is in the stories and legends of a very learned sixteenth-century German doctor named Faust. According to legend, he sold his soul to the devil in exchange for knowledge and magical power. The first printed version of the legend was by Johann Spiess, which was later used by Christopher Marlow as the basis for his famous play, *Dr. Faustus* (1593). Spiess and Marlow presented Faust as a scoundrel who deserved damnation. Some of the other representations of Faust made him a heroic figure who strived for knowledge and power for good. This theme was continued by the most famous Faust legend of all, written by Johann Wolfgang von Goethe in both a poem and a play. In the beginning, Faust's bargain with the Devil was for a moment of perfect happiness or contentment. The Devil, however, could not deliver this to Faust. More elements are added to the story, including women's love. In the end, Faust finds a moment of perfect contentment and happiness in helping others and dies because of the wager. But Goethe gives the story a Hollywood ending and Faust, the hero, goes to heaven.

Many of the issues in the biotechnology debate are found in the Faust legends. Both are focused on the search for knowledge and its use. Is the knowledge-seeking Faust a scoundrel or a saint? Will his knowledge be used for selfish or altruistic purposes? Is mankind better off with it or without it? If powerful new biotechnologies are able to make our babies safe from diseases and defects, certainly we should use them. By the same logic, we should also use them when they can enhance our children's physical and mental powers. Continuing this line of reasoning, we should also use them to enhance our physical and mental powers as adults. Sooner or later, however, we must face the Faustian myth, which suggests that at some point mankind's reach for knowledge may transcend man's proper role in the universe and be devilish. But this question takes us into realms where I get quickly lost. How do I discuss mankind's proper role in the universe? The wise thing for me to do is not to try, but to leave it to you and the readings.

The President's Council on Bioethics presents the reasons for using biotechnology to alter and enhance humans. They are simply the many benefits that biotechnology can produce. The Council also presented the case against using biotechnology for altering and enhancing humans. It is a very even-handed report. But I have not used that part of the report. Instead I have selected Michael J. Sandel to present the arguments against using biotechnology for altering and enhancing humans. Sandel is not even-handed. He is passionately against going down this road.

Beyond Therapy: Biotechnology and the Pursuit of Happiness

Chapter Five

Who has not wanted to escape the clutches of oppressive and punishing memories? Or to calm the burdensome feelings of anxiety, disappointment, and regret? Or to achieve a psychic state of pure and undivided pleasure and joy? The satisfaction of such desires seems inseparable from our happiness, which we pursue by right and with passion.

. . .

In these efforts at peace of mind, human beings have from time immemorial sought help from doctors and drugs. In a famous literary instance, Shakespeare's Macbeth entreats his doctor to free Lady Macbeth from the haunting memory of her own guilty acts:

> Macbeth. Canst thou not minister to a mind diseas'd,
> Pluck from the memory a rooted sorrow,
> Raze out the written troubles of the brain,
> And with some sweet oblivious antidote
> Cleanse the stuff'd bosom of that perilous stuff
> Which weighs upon the heart?
>
> Doctor. Therein the patient
> Must minister to himself.

Ministering to oneself, however, is easier said than done, and many people have found themselves unequal to the task without some outside assistance. For centuries, they have made use of external agents to drown their sorrows or lift their spirits.

. . .

The burgeoning field of neuroscience is providing new, more specific, and safer agents to help us combat all sorts of psychic distress. Soon, doctors may have just the "sweet oblivious antidote" that Macbeth so desired: drugs (such as beta-adrenergic blockers) that numb the emotional sting typically associated with our intensely bad memories.

. . .

From the President's Council on Bioethics, October 2003.

To be sure, these agents—and their better versions, yet to come—are, for now at least, being developed not as means for drug-induced happiness but rather as agents for combating major depression or preventing post-traumatic stress disorder (PTSD). Yet once available for those purposes, they could also be used to ease the soul and enhance the mood of nearly anyone.

. . .

By using drugs to satisfy more easily the enduring aspirations to forget what torments us and approach the world with greater peace of mind, what deeper human aspirations might we occlude or frustrate? What qualities of character may become less necessary and, with diminished use, atrophy or become extinct, as we increasingly depend on drugs to cope with misfortune? How will we experience our incompleteness or understand our mortality as our ability grows to medically dissolve all sorts of anxiety? Will the availability of drug-induced conditions of ecstatic pleasure estrange us from the forms of pleasure that depend upon discipline and devotion? And, going beyond the implications for individuals, what kind of a society are we likely to have when the powers to control memory, mood, and mental life through drugs reach their full maturity and are widely used?

. . .

I. What Are "Happy Souls"?

. . .

Because the happiness we seek we seek for *ourselves*—for *our* self, not for someone else's, and for our *self* or embodied soul, not for our bodies as material stuff—our happiness is bound up with our personhood and our identity. We would not want to attain happiness (or any other object of our desires) if the condition for attaining it required that we become someone else, that we lose our identity in the process.

The importance of identity for happiness implies necessarily the importance of memory. If experiencing our happiness depends upon experiencing a stable identity, then our happiness depends also on our memory, on knowing who we are in relation to who we have been.

. . .

But if enfeebled memory can cripple identity, selectively altered memory can distort it. Changing the content of our memories or altering their emotional tonalities, however desirable to alleviate guilty or painful consciousness, could subtly reshape who we are, at least to ourselves. With altered memories we might feel better about ourselves, but it is not clear that the better-feeling "we" remains the same as before. Lady Macbeth, cured of her guilty torment, would remain the murderess she was, but not the conscience-stricken being even she could not help but be.

. . .

[A]n unchecked power to erase memories, brighten moods, and alter our emotional dispositions could imperil our capacity to form a strong and coherent personal identity. To the extent that our inner life ceases to reflect the ups and downs of daily existence and instead operates independently of them, we dissipate our identity, which is formed through engagement with others and through immersion in the mix of routine and unpredictable events that constitute our lives.

. . .

II. Memory and Happiness

. . .

Our identity or sense of self emerges, grows, and changes. Yet, despite all the changes, thanks to the integrating powers of memory, our identity also, remarkably, persists *as ours*.

. . .

We especially want our memories to be not simply a sequence of disconnected experiences, but a narrative that seems to contain some unfolding purpose, some larger point from beginning to end, some aspiration discovered, pursued, and at least partially fulfilled.

Memory is central to human flourishing, in other words, precisely because we pursue happiness in time, as time-bound beings. We have a past and a future as well as a present, and being happy through time requires that these be connected in a meaningful way. If we are to flourish as ourselves, we must do so without abandoning or forgetting who we are or once were. Yet because our lives are time-bound, our happiness is always incomplete—always not-yet and on-the-way, always here but slipping away, but also always possible again and in the future. Our happiest experiences can be revivified. And, as we reminisce from greater distance and with more experience, even our painful experiences can often acquire for us a meaning not in evidence when they occurred.

The place of memory in the pursuit of happiness also suggests something essential about human identity, a theme raised in various places and in different ways throughout this report: namely, our identities are formed both by what we do and by what we undergo or suffer. We actively choose paths and do deeds fit to be remembered. But we also live through memorable experiences that we would never have chosen—experiences we often wish never happened at all. To some extent, these unchosen memories constrain us; though we may regret the shadows they cast over our pursuit of happiness, we cannot simply escape them while remaining who we really are. And yet, through the act of remembering— the act of discerning and giving meaning to the past as it really was—we can shape, to some degree, the meaning of our memories, both good and bad.

. . .

The capacity to alter or numb our remembrance of things past cuts to the heart of what it means to remember in a human way, and it is this biotechnical possibility that we focus on here. Deciding when or whether to use such biotechnical power will require that we think long and hard about what it means to remember truthfully, to live in time, and to seek happiness without losing or abandoning our identity. The rest of this discussion of "memory and happiness" is an invitation to such reflection.

A. Good Memories and Bad

. . .

[T]he significance of past events often becomes clear to us only after much rumination in light of later experience, and what seems trivial at one time may appear crucial at another. Neither can an excellent memory be one that remembers only what we *want* to remember: sometimes our most valuable memories are of events that were painful when they occurred, but that on reflection teach us vital lessons.

. . .

B. Biotechnology and Memory Alteration

It is a commonplace observation that, while some events fade quickly from the mind, emotionally intense experiences form memories that are peculiarly vivid and long-lasting. Not only do we recall such events long after they happened, but the recollection is often accompanied, in some measure, by a recurrence of the emotions aroused during the original experience.

. . .

When a person experiences especially shocking or violent events (such as a plane crash or bloody combat), the release of stress hormones may be so intense that the memory-encoding system is over-activated. The result is a consolidation of memories both far stronger and more persistent than normal and also more apt, upon recollection, to call forth the intense emotional response of the original experience. In such cases, each time the person relives the traumatic memory, a new flood of stress hormones is released, and the experience may be so emotionally intense as to be encoded as a new experience. With time, the memories grow more recurrent and intrusive, and the response— fear, helplessness, horror—more incapacitating. As we shall see, drugs that might prevent or alleviate the symptoms of PTSD are among the chief medical benefits that scientists expect from recent research in the neurochemistry of memory formation.

In fact, the discovery of hormonal regulation of memory formation was quickly followed up by clinical studies on human subjects demonstrating that memory of emotional experiences can be altered pharmacologically. In one particularly interesting series of experiments, Larry Cahill and his colleagues showed that injections of beta-blockers can, by inhibiting the action of stress hormones, suppress the memory-enhancing effects of strong emotional arousal.

. . .

[T]aking propranolol appears to have little or no effect on how we remember everyday or emotionally neutral information. But when taken at the time of highly emotional experiences, propranolol appears to suppress the normal memory-enhancing effects of emotional arousal—while leaving the immediate emotional response unaffected. These results suggested the possibility of using beta-blockers to help survivors of traumatic events to reduce their intrusive—and in some cases crippling—memories of those events.

. . .

"[A]lthough the pharmacology of memory alteration is a science still in its infancy, the significance of this potential new power—to separate the subjective experience of memory from the truth of the experience that is remembered—should not be underestimated. It surely returns us to the large ethical and anthropological questions with which we began—about memory's role in shaping personal identity and the character of human life, and about the meaning of remembering things that we would rather forget and of forgetting things that we perhaps ought to remember.

C. Memory-Blunting: Ethical Analysis

If we had the power, by promptly taking a memory-altering drug, to dull the emotional impact of what could become very painful memories, when might we be tempted to use it? And for what reasons should we yield to or resist the temptation?

At first glance, such a drug would seem ideally suited for the prevention of PTSD, the complex of debilitating symptoms that sometimes afflict those who have experienced severe trauma. These symptoms—which include persistent re-experiencing of the traumatic event and avoidance of every person, place, or thing that might stimulate the horrid memory's return[1]—can so burden mental life as to make normal everyday living extremely difficult, if not impossible.[2] For those suffering these disturbing symptoms, a drug that could separate a painful memory from its powerful emotional component would appear very welcome indeed.

Yet the prospect of preventing (even) PTSD with beta-blockers or other memory-blunting agents seems to be, for several reasons, problematic. First of all, the drugs in question appear to be effective only when administered during or shortly after a traumatic event—and thus well before any symptoms of PTSD would be manifested. How then could we make, and make on the spot, the *prospective* judgment that a particular event is sufficiently terrible to warrant preemptive memory-blunting? Second, how shall we judge *which* participants in the event merit such treatment? After all, not everyone who suffers through painful experiences is destined to have pathological memory effects. Should the drugs in question be given to everyone or only to those with an observed susceptibility to PTSD, and, if the latter, how will we know who these are? Finally, in some cases merely witnessing a disturbing event (for example, a murder, rape, or terrorist attack) is sufficient to cause PTSD-like symptoms long afterwards. Should we then, as soon as disaster strikes, consider giving memory-altering drugs to all the witnesses, in addition to those directly involved?

. . .

If the apparent powers of memory-blunting drugs are confirmed, some might be inclined to prescribe them liberally to all who are involved in a sufficiently terrible event. After all, even those not destined to come down with full-blown PTSD are likely to suffer painful recurrent memories of an airplane crash, an incident of terrorism, or a violent combat operation. In the aftermath of such shocking incidents, why not give everyone the chance to remember these events without the added burden of painful emotions? This line of reasoning might, in fact, tempt us to give beta-blockers liberally to soldiers on the eve of combat, to emergency workers en route to a disaster site, or even to individuals requesting prophylaxis against the shame or guilt they might incur from future misdeeds—in general, to anyone facing an experience that is likely to leave lasting intrusive memories.

Yet on further reflection it seems clear that not every intrusive memory is a suitable candidate for prospective pharmacological blunting. As Daniel Schacter has observed, "attempts to avoid traumatic memories often backfire."

Intrusive memories need to be acknowledged, confronted, and worked through, in order to set them to rest for the long term. Unwelcome memories of trauma are symptoms of a disrupted psyche that requires attention before it can resume healthy functioning. Beta-blockers might make it easier for trauma survivors to face and incorporate traumatic recollections, and in that sense could facilitate long-term adaptation. Yet it is also possible that beta-blockers would work against the normal process of recovery: traumatic memories would not spring to mind with the kind of psychological force that demands attention and perhaps intervention. Prescription of beta-blockers could bring about an effective trade-off between short-term reductions in the sting of traumatic memories and long-term increases in persistence of related symptoms of a trauma that has not been adequately confronted.[3]

The point can be generalized: in the immediate aftermath of a painful experience, we simply cannot know either the full meaning of the experience in question or the ultimate character and future prospects of the individual who experiences it. We cannot know how this experience will change this person at this time and over time. Will he be cursed forever by unbearable memories that, in retrospect, clearly should have been blunted medically? Or will he succeed, over time, in "redeeming" those painful memories by actively integrating them into the narrative of his life? By "rewriting" memories pharmacologically we might succeed in easing real suffering at the risk of falsifying our perception of the world and undermining our true identity.

Finally, the decision whether or not to use memory-blunting drugs must be made in the absence of clearly diagnosable disease. The drug must be taken right after a traumatic experience has occurred, and thus before the different ways that different individuals handle the same experience has become clear. In some cases, these interventions will turn out to have been preventive medicine, intervening to ward off the onset of PTSD before it arrives—though it is worth noting that we would lack even post hoc knowledge of whether any particular now-unaffected individual, in the absence of using the drug, would have become symptomatic.[4] In other cases, the interventions would not be medicine at all: altering the memory of individuals who could have lived well, even with severely painful memories, without pharmacologically dulling the pain. Worse, in still other cases, the use of such drugs would inoculate individuals in advance against the psychic pain that *should* accompany their commission of cruel, brutal, or shameful deeds. But in all cases, from the defensible to the dubious, the use of such powers changes the character of human memory, by intervening directly in the way individuals "encode," and thus the way they understand, the happenings of their own lives and the realities of the world around them.

. . .

1. Remembering Fitly and Truly.

Altering the formation of emotionally powerful memories risks severing what we remember from how we remember it and distorting the link between our perception of significant human events and the significance of the events themselves. It risks, in a word, falsifying our perception and understanding of the world. It risks making shameful acts seem less shameful, or terrible acts less terrible, than they really are.

Imagine the experience of a person who witnesses a shocking murder. Fearing that he will be haunted by images of this event, he immediately takes propranolol (or its more potent successor) to render his memory of the murder less painful and intrusive. Thanks to the drug, his memory of the murder gets encoded as a garden-variety, emotionally neutral experience. But in manipulating his memory in this way, he risks coming to think about the murder as more tolerable than it really is, as an event that should not sting those who witness it. For our opinions about the meaning of our experiences are shaped partly by the feelings evoked when we remember them. If, psychologically, the murder is transformed into an event our witness can recall without pain—or without *any* particular emotion—perhaps its moral significance will also fade from consciousness. If so, he would in a sense have ceased to be a genuine witness of the murder. When asked about it, he might say, "Yes, I was there. But it wasn't so terrible."

This points us to a deeper set of questions about bad memories: Would dulling our memory of terrible things make us too comfortable with the world, unmoved by suffering, wrongdoing, or cruelty? Does not the experience of hard truths—of the unchosen, the inexplicable, the tragic—remind us that we can never be fully at home in the world, especially if we are to take seriously the reality of human evil? Further, by blunting our experience and awareness of shameful, fearful, and hateful things, might we not also risk deadening our response to what is admirable, inspiring, and lovable? Can we become numb to life's sharpest sorrows without also becoming numb to its greatest joys?

. . .

There seems to be little doubt that some bitter memories are so painful and intrusive as to ruin the possibility for normal experience of much of life and the world. In such cases the impulse to relieve a crushing burden and restore lost innocence is fully understandable: If there are some things that it is better never to have experienced at all—things we would avoid if we possibly could—why not erase them from the memory of those unfortunate enough to have suffered them? If there are some things it is better never to have known or seen, why not use our power over memory to restore a witness's shattered peace of mind? There is great force in this argument, perhaps especially in cases where children lose prematurely that innocence that is rightfully theirs.

And yet, there may be a great cost to acting compassionately for those who suffer bad memories, if we do so by compromising the truthfulness of how they remember. We risk having them live falsely in order simply to cope, to survive by whatever means possible.

. . .

2. The Obligation to Remember.

Having truthful memories is not simply a personal matter. Strange to say, our own memory is not merely our own; it is part of the fabric of the society in which we live. Consider the case of a person who has suffered or witnessed atrocities that occasion unbearable memories: for example, those with firsthand experience of the Holocaust. The life of that individual might well be served by dulling such bitter memories,[5] but such a humanitarian intervention, if widely practiced, would seem deeply troubling: Would the community as a whole—would the human race—be served by such a mass numbing of this terrible but indispensable memory? Do those who suffer evil have a duty to remember and bear witness, lest we all forget the very horrors that haunt them?

. . .

Surely, we cannot and should not force those who live through great trauma to endure its painful memory *for the benefit of the rest of us.* But as a community, there are certain events that we have an obligation to remember—an obligation that falls disproportionately, one might even say unfairly, on those who experience such events most directly.[6] What kind of people would we be if we did not "want" to remember the Holocaust, if we sought to make the anguish it caused simply go away? And yet, what kind of people are we, especially those who face such horrors firsthand, that we can endure such awful memories?

The answer, in part, is that those who suffer terrible things cannot or should not have to endure their own bad memories alone. If, as a people, we have an obligation to remember certain terrible events truthfully, surely we ought to help those who suffered through those events to come to terms with their worst memories. Of course, one might see the new biotechnical powers, developed precisely to ease the psychic pain of bad memories, as the mark of such solidarity: perhaps it is our new way of meeting the obligation to aid those who remember the hardest things, those who bear witness to us and for us. But such solidarity may, in the end, prove false: for it exempts us from the duty to suffer-with (literally, to feel *com*-passion for) those who remember; it does not demand that we preserve the truth of their memories; it attempts instead to make the problem go away, and with it the truth of the experience in question.

4. The Soul of Memory, The Remembering Soul.

. . .

[W]e might often be tempted to sacrifice the accuracy of our memories for the sake of easing our pain or expanding our control over our own psychic lives. But doing so means, ultimately, severing ourselves from reality and leaving our own identity behind; it risks making us false, small, or capable of great illusions, and thus capable of great decadence or great evil, or perhaps simply willing to accept a phony contentment. We might be tempted to alter our memories to preserve an open future—to live the life we wanted to live before a particular experience happened to us. But in another sense, such interventions assume that our own future is not open—that we cannot and could never redeem the unwanted memory over time, that we cannot and could never integrate the remembered experience with our own truthful pursuit of happiness.

. . .

To have only happy memories would be a blessing—and a curse. Nothing would trouble us, but we would probably be shallow people, never falling to the depths of despair because we have little interest in the heights of human happiness or in the complicated lives of those around us. In the end, to have only happy memories is not to be happy in a truly human way. It is simply to be free of misery—an understandable desire given the many troubles of life, but a low aspiration for those who seek a truly human happiness.

Footnotes

1. There is no definitive diagnostic criterion for PTSD, but the core symptoms are thought to include persistent re-experiencing of the traumatic event, avoidance of associated stimuli, and hyperarousal. See *Diagnostic and Statistical Manual of Mental Disorders, Fourth Edition,* text revision, Washington, D.C.: American Psychiatric Association, 2000, pp. 463–486.

2. These symptoms are observed especially among combat veterans; indeed, PTSD is the modern name for what used to be called "shell shock" or "combat neurosis." Among veterans, PTSD is frequently associated with recurrent nightmares, substance abuse, and delusional outbursts of violence. There is controversy about the prevalence of PTSD, with some studies finding that up to 8 percent of adult Americans have suffered the disorder, as well as a third of all veterans of the Vietnam War. See Kessler, R. C., et al., "Post-Traumatic Stress Disorder in the National Comorbidity Survey," *Archives of General Psychiatry* 52(12): 1048–1060, 1995; Kulka, R. A., et al., *Trauma and the Vietnam War Generation: Report of Findings from the National Vietnam Veterans Readjustment Study,* New York: Brunner/Mazel, 1990.

3. Schacter, D., *The Seven Sins of Memory: How the Mind Forgets and Remembers,* New York: Houghton Mifflin, 2001, p. 183.

4. There is already ongoing controversy about excessive diagnosis of PTSD. Many psychotherapists believe that a patient's psychic troubles are generally based on some earlier (now repressed) traumatic experience which must be unearthed and dealt with if relief is to be found. True PTSD is, however, generally transient, and the search for treatment is directed against the symptoms of its initial (worst) phase—the sleeplessness, the nightmares, the excessive jitteriness.

5. Of course, many Holocaust survivors managed, without pharmacological assistance, to live fulfilling lives while never forgetting what they lived through. At the same time, many survivors would almost certainly have benefited from pharmacological treatment.

6. For a discussion of memory-altering drugs and the meaning of "bearing witness," see the essay by Cohen, E., "Our Psychotropic Memory," *SEED*, no. 8, Fall 2003, p. 42.

Michael J. Sandel  **NO**

The Case Against Perfection: Ethics in the Age of Genetic Engineering

The Ethics of Enhancement

A few years ago, a couple decided they wanted to have a child, preferably a deaf one. Both partners were deaf, and proudly so. Like others in the deaf-pride community, Sharon Duchesneau and Candy McCullough considered deafness a cultural identity, not a disability to be cured. "Being deaf is just a way of life," said Duchesneau. "We feel whole as deaf people and we want to share the wonderful aspects of our deaf community—a sense of belonging and connectedness—with children. We truly feel we live rich lives as deaf people."

In hopes of conceiving a deaf child, they sought out a sperm donor with five generations of deafness in his family. And they succeeded. Their son Gauvin was born deaf.

The new parents were surprised when their story, which was reported in the *Washington Post,* brought widespread condemnation. Most of the outrage focused on the charge that they had deliberately inflicted a disability on their child. Duchesneau and McCullough (who are lesbian partners) denied that deafness is a disability and argued that they had simply wanted a child like themselves. "We do not view what we did as very different from what many straight couples do when they have children," said Duchesneau.

Is it wrong to make a child deaf by design? If so, what makes it wrong—the deafness or the design? Suppose, for the sake of argument, that deafness is not a disability but a distinctive identity. Is there still something wrong with the idea of parents picking and choosing the kind of child they will have? Or do parents do that all the time, in their choice of mate and, these days, in their use of new reproductive technologies? . . .

Articulating Our Unease

Breakthroughs in genetics present us with a promise and a predicament. The promise is that we may soon be able to treat and prevent a host of debilitating diseases. The predicament is that our new-found genetic knowledge may also enable us to manipulate our own nature—to enhance our muscles, memories, and moods; to choose the sex, height, and other genetic traits of our children; to improve our physical and cognitive capacities; to make ourselves "better

From *The Atlantic Monthly,* April 2004. pp. 50–62. Copyright © 2004 by Michael J. Sandel, Ph.D. Reprinted by permission of the author.

than well." Most people find at least some forms of genetic engineering disquieting. But it is not easy to articulate the source of our unease. The familiar terms of moral and political discourse make it difficult to say what is wrong with reengineering our nature. . . .

When science moves faster than moral understanding, as it does today, men and women struggle to articulate their unease. In liberal societies, they reach first for the language of autonomy, fairness, and individual rights. But this part of our moral vocabulary does not equip us to address the hardest questions posed by cloning, designer children, and genetic engineering. That is why the genomic revolution has induced a kind of moral vertigo. To grapple with the ethics of enhancement, we need to confront questions largely lost from view in the modern world—questions about the moral status of nature, and about the proper stance of human beings toward the given world. Since these questions verge on theology, modern philosophers and political theorists tend to shrink from them. But our new powers of biotechnology make them unavoidable.

Genetic Engineering

To see how this is so, consider four examples of bioengineering already on the horizon: muscle enhancement, memory enhancement, height enhancement, and sex selection. In each case, what began as an attempt to treat a disease or prevent a genetic disorder now beckons as an instrument of improvement and consumer choice.

Muscles

Everyone would welcome a gene therapy to alleviate muscular dystrophy and to reverse the debilitating muscle loss that comes with old age. But what if the same therapy were used to produce genetically altered athletes? Researchers have developed a synthetic gene that, when injected into the muscle cells of mice, makes muscles grow and prevents them from deteriorating with age. The success bodes well for human applications. Dr. H. Lee Sweeney, who leads the research, hopes his discovery will cure the immobility that afflicts the elderly. But Dr. Sweeney's bulked-up mice have already attracted the attention of athletes seeking a competitive edge. The gene not only repairs injured muscles but also strengthens healthy ones. Although the therapy is not yet approved for human use, the prospect of genetically enhanced weight lifters, home-run sluggers, linebackers, and sprinters is easy to imagine. The widespread use of steroids and other performance-enhancing drugs in professional sports suggests that many athletes will be eager to avail themselves of genetic enhancement. The International Olympic Committee has already begun to worry about the fact that, unlike drugs, altered genes cannot be detected in urine or blood tests.

The prospect of genetically altered athletes offers a good illustration of the ethical quandaries surrounding enhancement. Should the IOC and professional sports leagues ban genetically enhanced athletes, and if so, on what grounds? The two most obvious reasons for banning drugs in sports are safety and fairness: Steroids have harmful side effects, and to allow some to boost their performance by incurring serious health risks would put their competitors at an unfair disadvantage. But suppose, for the sake of argument, that muscle-enhancing gene therapy turned out to be safe, or at least no riskier than a rigorous weight-training regime. Would there still be a reason to ban its use in sports? There is something unsettling about the specter of genetically altered athletes lifting SUVs or hitting 650-foot home runs or running a three-minute mile. But what exactly is troubling about these scenarios? Is it simply that we find such superhuman spectacles too bizarre to contemplate, or does our unease point to something of ethical significance? . . .

Designer Children, Designing Parents

The ethic of giftedness, under siege in sports, persists in the practice of parenting. But here, too, bioengineering and genetic enhancement threaten to dislodge it. To appreciate children as gifts is to accept them as they come, not as objects of our design, or products of our will, or instruments of our ambition. Parental love is not contingent on the talents and attributes the child happens to have. We choose our friends and spouses at least partly on the basis of qualities we find attractive. But we do not choose our children. Their qualities are unpredictable, and even the most conscientious parents cannot be held wholly responsible for the kind of child they have. That is why parenthood, more than other human relationships, teaches what the theologian William F. May calls an "openness to the unbidden."

Molding and Beholding

May's resonant phrase describes a quality of character and heart that restrains the impulse to mastery and control and prompts a sense of life as gift. It helps us see that the deepest moral objection to enhancement lies less in the perfection it seeks than in the human disposition it expresses and promotes. The problem is not that the parents usurp the autonomy of the child they design. (It is not as if the child could otherwise choose her genetic traits for herself.) The problem lies in the hubris of the designing parents, in their drive to master the mystery of birth. Even if this disposition does not make parents tyrants to their children, it disfigures the relation between parent and child, and deprives the parent of the humility and enlarged human sympathies that an openness to the unbidden can cultivate.

To appreciate children as gifts or blessings is not to be passive in the face of illness or disease. Healing a sick or injured child does not override her natural capacities but permits them to flourish. Although medical treatment intervenes in nature, it does so for the sake of health, and so does not represent a boundless bid for mastery and dominion. Even strenuous attempts to treat or cure disease do not constitute a Promethean assault on the given. The reason is that medicine is governed, or at least guided, by the norm of restoring and preserving the natural human functions that constitute health.

Medicine, like sports, is a practice with a purpose, a telos, that orients and constrains it. Of course what counts as good health or normal human functioning is open to argument; it is not only a biological question. People disagree, for example, about whether deafness is a disability to be cured or a form of community and identity to be cherished. But even the disagreement proceeds from the assumption that the point of medicine is to promote health and cure disease.

Some people argue that a parent's obligation to heal a sick child implies an obligation to enhance a healthy one, to maximize his or her potential for success in life. But this is true only if one accepts the utilitarian idea that health is not a distinctive human good, but simply a means of maximizing happiness or well-being. Bioethicist Julian Savulescu argues, for example, that "health is not intrinsically valuable," only "instrumentally valuable," a "resource" that allows us to do what we want. This way of thinking about health rejects the distinction between healing and enhancing. According to Savulescu, parents not only have a duty to promote their children's health; they are also "morally obliged to genetically modify their children." Parents should use technology to manipulate their children's "memory, temperament, patience, empathy, sense of humor, optimism," and other characteristics in order to give them "the best opportunity of the best life."

But it is a mistake to think of health in wholly instrumental terms, as a way of maximizing something else. Good health, like good character, is a constitutive element of human flourishing. Although more health is better than less, at least within a certain range, it is not the kind of good that can be maximized. No one aspires to be a virtuoso at health (except, perhaps, a hypochondriac). During the 1920s, eugenicists held health contests at state fairs and awarded prizes to the "fittest families." But this bizarre practice illustrates the folly of conceiving health in instrumental terms, or as a good to be maximized. Unlike the talents and traits that bring success in a competitive society, health is a bounded good; parents can seek it for their children without risk of being drawn into an ever-escalating arms race.

In caring for the health of their children, parents do not cast themselves as designers or convert their children into products of their will or instruments of their ambition. The same cannot be said of parents who pay large sums to select the sex of their child (for nonmedical reasons) or who aspire to bioengineer their child's intellectual endowments or athletic prowess. Like all distinctions, the line between therapy and enhancement blurs at the edges. (What about orthodontics, for example, or growth hormone for very short kids?) But this does not obscure the reason the distinction matters: parents bent on enhancing their children are more likely to overreach, to express and entrench attitudes at odds with the norm of unconditional love.

Of course, unconditional love does not require that parents refrain from shaping and directing the development of their child. To the contrary, parents have an obligation to cultivate their children, to help them discover and develop their talents and gifts. As May points out, parental love has two aspects: accepting love and transforming love. Accepting love affirms the being of the child, whereas transforming love seeks the well-being of the child. Each side of parental love corrects the excesses of the other: "Attachment becomes too quietistic if it slackens into mere acceptance of the child as he is." Parents have a duty to promote their child's excellence.

These days, however, overly ambitious parents are prone to get carried away with transforming love—promoting and demanding all manner of accomplishments from their children, seeking perfection. "Parents find it difficult to maintain an equilibrium between the two sides of love," May observes. "Accepting love, without transforming love, slides into indulgence and finally neglect. Transforming love, without accepting love, badgers and finally rejects." May finds in these competing impulses a parallel with modern science; it, too, engages us in beholding the given world, studying and savoring it, and also in molding the world, transforming and perfecting it.

The mandate to mold our children, to cultivate and improve them, complicates the case against enhancement. We admire parents who seek the best for their children, who spare no effort to help them achieve happiness and success. What, then, is the difference between providing such help through education and training and providing it by means of genetic enhancement? Some parents confer advantages on their children by enrolling them in expensive schools, hiring private tutors, sending them to tennis camp, providing them with piano lessons, ballet lessons, swimming lessons, SAT prep courses, and so on. If it is permissible, even admirable, for parents to help their children in these ways, why isn't it equally admirable for parents to use whatever genetic technologies may emerge (provided they are safe) to enhance their child's intelligence, musical ability, or athletic skill?

Defenders of enhancement argue that there is no difference, in principle, between improving children through education and improving them through bioengineering. Critics of enhancement insist there is all the difference in the world. They argue that trying to improve children by manipulating their genetic makeup is reminiscent of eugenics, the discredited movement of the past century to improve the human race through policies (including forced sterilization and other odious measures) aimed at improving the gene pool. These competing analogies help clarify the moral status of genetic enhancement. Is the attempt of parents to enhance their children through genetic engineering more like education and training (a presumably good thing) or more like eugenics (a presumably bad thing)?

The defenders of enhancement are right to this extent: Improving children through genetic engineering is similar in spirit to the heavily managed, high-pressure child-rearing practices that have become common these days. But this similarity does not vindicate genetic enhancement. On the contrary, it highlights a problem with the trend toward hyperparenting. . . .

The Pressure to Perform

Grubman's willingness to move heaven and earth, and even the market, to get his two-year-olds into a fancy nursery school is a sign of the times. It tells of mounting pressures in American life that are changing the expectations parents have for their children and increasing the demands placed on children to perform. When preschoolers apply to private kindergartens and elementary schools, their fate depends on favorable letters of recommendation and a standardized test intended to measure their intelligence and development. Some parents have their four-year-olds coached to prepare for the test. . . .

Some see a bright line between genetic enhancement and other ways that people seek improvement in their children and themselves. Genetic manipulation seems somehow worse—more intrusive, more sinister—than other ways of enhancing performance and seeking success. But morally speaking, the difference is less significant than it seems.

Those who argue that bioengineering is similar in spirit to other ways ambitious parents shape and mold their children have a point. But this similarity does not give us reason to embrace the genetic manipulation of children. Instead, it gives us reason to question the low-tech, high-pressure child-rearing practices we commonly accept. The hyperparenting familiar in our time represents an anxious excess of mastery and dominion that misses the sense of life as gift. This draws it disturbingly close to eugenics. . . .

Although liberal eugenics finds support among many Anglo-American moral and political philosophers, Jürgen Habermas, Germany's most prominent political philosopher, opposes it. Acutely aware of Germany's dark eugenic past, Habermas argues against the use of embryo screening and genetic manipulation for nonmedical enhancement. His case against liberal eugenics is especially intriguing because he believes it rests wholly on liberal premises and need not invoke spiritual or theological notions. His critique of genetic engineering "does not relinquish the premises of postmeta-physical thinking," by which he means it does not depend on any particular conception of the good life. Habermas agrees with John Rawls that, since people in modern pluralist societies disagree about morality and religion, a just society should not take sides in such disputes but should instead accord each person the freedom to choose and pursue his or her own conception of the good life.

Genetic intervention to select or improve children is objectionable, Habermas argues, because it violates the liberal principles of autonomy and equality. It violates autonomy because genetically programmed persons cannot regard themselves as "the sole authors of their own life history." And it undermines equality by destroying "the essentially symmetrical relations between free and equal human beings" across generations. One measure of this asymmetry is that, once parents become the designers of their children, they inevitably incur a responsibility for their children's lives that cannot possibly be reciprocal.

Habermas is right to oppose eugenic parenting, but wrong to think that the case against it can rest on liberal terms alone. The defenders of liberal eugenics have a point when they argue that designer children are no less autonomous with respect to their genetic traits that children born the natural way. It is not as if, absent eugenic manipulation, we can choose our genetic inheritance for ourselves. As for Habermas's worry about equality and reciprocity between the generations, defenders of liberal eugenics can reply that this worry, though legitimate, does not apply uniquely to genetic manipulation. The parent who forces her child to practice the piano incessantly from the age of three, or to hit tennis balls from dawn to dusk, also exerts a kind of control over the child's life that cannot possibly be reciprocal. The question, liberals insist, is whether the parental intervention, be it eugenic or environmental, undermines the child's freedom to choose her own life plan.

An ethic of autonomy and equality cannot explain what is wrong with eugenics. But Habermas has a further argument that cuts deeper, even as it points beyond the limits of liberal, or "postmeta-physical" considerations. This is the idea that "we experience our own freedom with reference to something which, by its very nature, is not at our disposal." To think of ourselves as free, we must be able to ascribe our origins "to a beginning which eludes human disposal," a beginning that arises from "something—like God or nature—that is not at the disposal of some *other* person." Habermas goes on to suggest that birth, "being a natural fact, meets the conceptual requirement of constituting a beginning we cannot control. Philosophy has but rarely addressed this matter." An exception, he observes, is found in the work of Hannah Arendt, who sees "natality," the fact that human beings are born not made, as a condition of their capacity to initiate action.

Habermas is onto something important, I think, when he asserts a "connection between the contingency of a life's beginning that is not at our disposal and the freedom to give one's life an ethical shape." For him, this connection matters because it explains why a genetically designed child is beholden and subordinate to another person (the designing parent) in a way that a child born of a contingent, impersonal beginning is not. But the notion that our freedom is bound up with "a beginning we cannot control" also carries a broader significance: Whatever its effect on the autonomy of the child, the drive to banish contingency and to master the mystery of birth diminishes the designing parent and corrupts parenting as a social practice governed by norms of unconditional love.

This takes us back to the notion of giftedness. Even if it does not harm the child or impair its autonomy, eugenic parenting is objectionable because it expresses and entrenches a certain stance toward the world—a stance of mastery and dominion that fails to appreciate the gifted character of human powers and achievements, and misses the part of freedom that consists in a persisting negotiation with the given.

Mastery and Gift

The problem with eugenics and genetic engineering is that they represent the one-sided triumph of willfulness over giftedness, of dominion over reverence, of molding over beholding. But why, we may wonder, should we worry about this triumph? Why not shake off our unease with enhancement as so much superstition? What would be lost if biotechnology dissolved our sense of giftedness?

Humility, Responsibility, and Solidarity

From the standpoint of religion, the answer is clear: To believe that our talents and powers are wholly our own doing is to misunderstand our place in creation, to confuse our role with God's. But religion is not the only source of reasons to care about giftedness. The moral stakes can also be described in secular terms. If the genetic revolution erodes our appreciation for the gifted character of human powers and achievements, it will transform three key features of our moral landscape—humility, responsibility, and solidarity.

In a social world that prizes mastery and control, parenthood is a school for humility. That we care deeply about our children, and yet cannot choose the kind we want, teaches parents to be open to the unbidden. Such openness is a disposition worth affirming, not only within families but in the wider world as well. It invites us to abide the unexpected, to live with dissonance, to reign in the impulse to control. A *Gattaca*-like world, in which parents became accustomed to specifying the sex and genetic traits of their children, would be a world inhospitable to the unbidden, a gated community writ large. . . .

It is sometimes thought that genetic enhancement erodes human responsibility by overriding effort and striving. But the real problem is the explosion, not the erosion, of responsibility. As humility gives way, responsibility expands to daunting proportions. We attribute less to chance and more to choice. Parents become responsible for choosing, or failing to choose, the right traits for their children. Athletes become responsible for acquiring, or failing to acquire, the talents that will help their team win.

One of the blessings of seeing ourselves as creatures of nature, God, or fortune is that we are not wholly responsible for the way we are. The more we become masters of our genetic endowments, the greater the burden we bear for the talents we have and the way we perform. Today when a basketball player misses a rebound, his coach can blame him for being out of position. Tomorrow the coach may blame him for being too short.

Even now, the growing use of performance-enhancing drugs in professional sports is subtly transforming the expectations players have for one another. In the past when a starting pitcher's team scored too few runs to win, he could only curse his bad luck and take it in stride. These days, the use of amphetamines and other stimulants is so wide-spread that players who take the field without them are criticized for "playing naked." A recently retired major league outfielder told *Sports Illustrated* that some pitchers blame teammates who play unenhanced: "If the starting pitcher knows that you're going out there naked, he's upset that you're not giving him [everything] you can. The big-time pitcher wants to make sure you're beaning up before the game." . . .

The Promethean impulse is contagious. In parenting as in sports, it unsettles and erodes the gifted dimension of human experience. When performance-enhancing drugs become commonplace, unenhanced ballplayers find themselves "playing naked." When genetic screening becomes a routine part of pregnancy, parents who eschew it are regarded as "flying blind" and are held responsible for whatever genetic defect befalls their child. . . .

If genetic engineering enabled us to override the results of the genetic lottery, to replace chance with choice, the gifted character of human powers and achievements would recede, and with it, perhaps, our capacity to see ourselves as sharing a common fate. The successful would become even more likely than they are now to view themselves as self-made and self-sufficient, and hence wholly responsible for their success. Those at the bottom of society would be viewed not as disadvantaged, and so worthy of a measure of compensation, but as simply unfit, and so worthy of eugenic repair. The meritocracy, less chastened by chance, would become harder, less forgiving. As perfect genetic knowledge would end the simulacrum of solidarity in insurance markets, perfect genetic control would erode the actual solidarity that arises when men and women reflect on the contingency of their talents and fortunes. . . .

There is something appealing, even intoxicating, about a vision of human freedom unfettered by the given. It may even be the case that the allure of that vision played a part in summoning the genomic age into being. It is often assumed that the powers of enhancement we now possess arose as an inadvertent by-product of biomedical progress—the genetic revolution came, so to speak, to cure disease, but stayed to tempt us with the prospect of enhancing our performance, designing our children, and perfecting our nature. But that may have the story backward. It is also possible to view genetic engineering as the ultimate expression of our resolve to see ourselves astride the world, the masters of our nature. But that vision of freedom is flawed. It threatens to banish our appreciation of life as a gift, and to leave us with nothing to affirm or behold outside our own will. . . .

POSTSCRIPT

Should Biotechnology Be Used to Alter and Enhance Humans?

The most often-cited arguments in favor of using biotechnologies for altering and enhancing humans are the benefits of protecting children from diseases, preventing handicaps and deficiencies, and enhancing physical and mental abilities. The main arguments against using biotechnology are the fear that something awful will happen and the moral arguments against playing God and too mightily interfering in nature. But what about the possibility of making people more moral in the sense of more caring, compassionate, cooperative, trusting, and helpful and less uncooperative, unsympathetic, and easily irritated? A number of scientists believe that these characteristics are fairly closely related to genes, so the moral improvement of the human race could be assisted by bioengineering. Furthermore, chemical treatments could help adults become less selfish and aggressive and become more altruistic and cooperative.

Thus, the moral argument can be used in favor of biotechnologies. In some sense, this is an old debate as the Faust legend indicates. Nevertheless, it is only recently that science has brought us to the doorstep of the bioengineering of humans. Two books from the mid-1980s serve as classics in this field. Jeremy Rivkin and Nicanor Perlas warn against bioengineering in *Algeny* (Penguin Books, 1984). They argue that biotechnology's destructive power far exceeds its potential benefits. Johnathan Glover reverses the weights for benefits and costs and champions bioengineering in *What Sort of People Should There Be?* (Penguin Books, 1984). More recent works that are opposed to bioengineering include Jeremy Rivkin, *The Biotech Century* (Tarcher/Putnam, 1998); Francis Fukuyama, *Our Posthuman Future* (Farrar, Strauss, and Giroux, 2002); and Bill McKibben, *Enough* (Henry Holt, 2003). More positive views of genetic engineering are found in the following: Eric S. Grace, *Biotechnology Unzipped: Promises and Realities* (Joseph Henry Press, 2006); Ramex Naam, *More Than Human: Embracing the Promise of Biological Enhancement* (Broadway Books, 2005); Gregory Stock, *Redesigning Humans: Our Inevitable Genetic Future* (Houghton Mifflin, 2002); Allan Buchanan et al., *From Chance to Choice: Genetics and Justice* (Cambridge University Press, 2000); and Emirates Center for Strategic Studies and Research, *Biotechnology and the Future of Society: Challenges and Opportunities* (Emirates Center for Strategic Studies and Research, 2004). For works that present multiple views, see Bernard E. Rollin, *Science and Ethics* (Cambridge University Press, 2006); Lori P. Knowles and Gregory E. Kaebnick, eds., *Reprogenetics: Law, Policy, and Ethical Issues* (Johns Hopkins University Press, 2007); Rose M. Morgan, *The Genetics Revolution: History, Fears, and Future of a Life-Altering Science* (Greenwood Press, 2006); Pete Shanks, *Human Genetic Engineering: A*

Guide for Activists, Skeptics, and the Very Perplexed (Nation Books, 2005); Gerald Magill, ed., *Genetics and Ethics: An Interdisciplinary Study* (Saint Louis University Press, 2004); Audrey R. Chapman and Mark S. Frankel, eds., *Designing Our Descendants: The Promises and Perils of Genetic Modifications* (Johns Hopkins University Press, 2003); Scott Gilbert et al., *Bioethics and the New Embryology: Springboards for Debate* (W.H. Freeman, 2005); Howard W. Baillie and Timothy K. Casey, eds., *Is Human Nature Obsolete? Genetics, Bioengineering, and the Future of the Human Condition* (MIT Press, 2005); and Rose M. Morgan, *The Genetic Revolution: History, Fears, and Future of a Life-Altering Science* (Greenwood Press, 2006). For discussions of human cloning, see Martha C. Nusbaum and Cass R. Sunstein, eds., *Clones and Clones: Facts and Fantasies about Human Cloning* (W. W. Norton, 1998), and President's Council on Bioethics, *Human Cloning and Human Dignity: An Ethical Inquiry* (Government Printing Office, 2002).

We leave to Colin Tudge ("The Future of Humanity," *New Statesman*, April 8, 2002), the final word on this subject. "On present knowledge, or even with what we are likely to know in the next two centuries, it would be as presumptuous to try to improve on the genes of a healthy human baby as it would be to edit sacred verse in medieval Chinese if all we had to go on was a bad dictionary. So all in all, human beings are likely to remain as they are, genetically speaking . . . and there doesn't seem to be much that meddling human beings can do about it. This, surely, is a mercy. We may have been shaped blindly by evolution. We may have been guided on our way by God. Whichever it was, or both, the job has been done a million times better than we are ever likely to do. Natural selection is far more subtle than human invention. 'What a piece of work is a man!' said Hamlet. 'How beauteous mankind is!' said Miranda. Both of them were absolutely right."

Internet References . . .

American Society of Criminology

The American Society of Criminology Web site is an excellent starting point for studying all aspects of criminology and criminal justice. This page provides links to sites on criminal justice in general, international criminal justice, juvenile justice, courts, the police, and the government.

http://www.asc41.com/

Crime Times

This *Crime Times* site lists research reviews and other information regarding the causes of criminal and violent behavior. It is provided by the nonprofit Wacker Foundation, publishers of *Crime Times*.

http://www.crimetimes.org/

Justice Information Center (JIC)

Provided by the National Criminal Justice Reference Service, the Justice Information Center (JIC) site connects to information about corrections, courts, crime prevention, criminal justice, statistics, drugs and crime, law enforcement, and victims, among other topics.

http://www.ncjrs.gov/

Crime and Social Control

*A*ll societies label certain hurtful actions as crimes and punish those who commit them. Other harmful actions, however, are not defined as crimes, and the perpetrators are not punished. Today the definition of crime and the appropriate treatment of criminals is widely debated. Some of the major questions are: Does street crime pose more of a threat to the public's well-being than white-collar crime? Billions of dollars have been spent on the "war on drugs," but who is winning? Would legalizing some drugs free up money that could be directed to other types of social welfare programs, such as the rehabilitation of addicts? Is the threat of nuclear terrorism legitimate or overstated?

- Is Street Crime More Harmful Than White-Collar Crime?
- Should Laws Against Drug Use Remain Restrictive?
- Are We Headed Toward a Nuclear 9/11?

ISSUE 16

Is Street Crime More Harmful Than White-Collar Crime?

YES: David A. Anderson, from "The Aggregate Burden of Crime," *Journal of Law and Economics* XLII (2) (October 1999)

NO: Jeffrey Reiman, from *The Rich Get Richer and the Poor Get Prison: Ideology, Class, and Criminal Justice*, 5th ed. (Allyn & Bacon, 1998)

ISSUE SUMMARY

YES: David A. Anderson estimates the total annual cost of crime including law enforcement and security services. The costs exceed $1 trillion, with fraud (mostly white-collar crime) causing about one-fifth of the total. His calculations of the full costs of the loss of life and injury comes to about half of the total costs. It is right, therefore, to view personal and violent crime as the big crime problem.

NO: Professor of philosophy Jeffrey Reiman argues that the dangers posed by negligent corporations and white-collar criminals are a greater menace to society than are the activities of typical street criminals.

T he word *crime* entered the English language (from the Old French) around A.D. 1250, when it was identified with "sinfulness." Later, the meaning of the word was modified: Crime became the kind of sinfulness that was rightly punishable by law. Even medieval writers, who did not distinguish very sharply between church and state, recognized that there were some sins for which punishment was best left to God; the laws should punish only those that cause harm to the community. Of course, their concept of harm was a very broad one, embracing such offenses as witchcraft and blasphemy. Modern jurists, even those who deplore such practices, would say that the state has no business punishing the perpetrators of these types of offenses.

What, then, should the laws punish? The answer depends in part on our notion of harm. We usually limit the term to the kind of harm that is tangible and obvious: taking a life, causing bodily injury or psychological trauma, and destroying property. For most Americans today, particularly those who live in cities, the word *crime* is practically synonymous with street crime. Anyone who has ever been robbed or beaten by street criminals will never forget the experience. The harm that these criminals cause is tangible, and the connection between the harm and the perpetrator is very direct.

But suppose the connection is not so direct. Suppose, for example, that A hires B to shoot C. Is that any less a crime? B is the actual shooter, but is A any less guilty? Of course not, we say; he may even be more guilty because he is the ultimate mover behind the crime. A would be guilty even if the chain of command were much longer, involving A's orders to B, and B's to C, then on to D, E, and F to kill G. Organized crime kingpins go to jail even when they are far removed from the people who carry out their orders. High officials of the Nixon administration, even though they were not directly involved in the burglary attempt at the Democratic National Committee headquarters at the Watergate Hotel complex in 1972, were imprisoned.

This brings us to the topic of white-collar crime. The burglars at the Watergate Hotel were acting on orders that trickled down from the highest reaches of political power in the United States. Other white-collar criminals are as varied as the occupations from which they come. They include stockbrokers who make millions through insider trading, as Ivan Boesky did; members of Congress who take payoffs; and people who cheat on their income taxes, like hotel owner and billionaire Leona Helmsley. Some, like Helmsley, get stiff prison sentences when convicted, though many others (like most of the officials in the Watergate scandal) do little or no time in prison. Do they deserve stiffer punishment, or are their crimes less harmful than the crimes of street criminals?

Although white-collar criminals do not directly cause physical harm or relieve people of their wallets, they can still end up doing considerable harm. The harm done by Nixon's aides threatened the integrity of the U.S. electoral system. Every embezzler, corrupt politician, and tax cheat exacts a toll on our society. Individuals can be hurt in more tangible ways by decisions made in corporate boardrooms: Auto executives, for example, have approved design features that have caused fatalities. Managers of chemical companies have allowed practices that have polluted the environment with cancer-causing agents. And heads of corporations have presided over industries wherein workers have been needlessly killed or maimed.

Whether these decisions should be considered crimes is debatable. A crime must always involve "malicious intent," or what the legal system calls *mens rea*. This certainly applies to street crime—the mugger obviously has sinister designs—but does it apply to every decision made in a boardroom that ends up causing harm? And does that harm match or exceed the harm caused by street criminals? In the following selections, David A. Anderson tries to calculate all the costs of all crimes. His message is that crime costs society far more than we realize. But for the debate on the relative costs of street vs. white-collar crime, his study shows that street crime costs society more than white-collar crime. According to Jeffrey Reiman, white-collar crime does more harm than is commonly recognized. By his count, white-collar crime causes far more deaths, injuries, illnesses, and financial loss than street crime. In light of this, he argues, we must redefine our ideas about what crime is and who the criminals are.

YES

David A. Anderson

The Aggregate Burden of Crime

Introduction

Distinct from previous studies that have focused on selected crimes, regions, or outcomes, this study attempts an exhaustively broad estimation of the crime burden. . . .

Overt annual expenditures on crime in the United States include $47 billion for police protection, $36 billion for corrections, and $19 billion for the legal and judicial costs of state and local criminal cases. (Unless otherwise noted, all figures are adjusted to reflect 1997 dollars using the Consumer Price Index.) Crime victims suffer $876 million worth of lost workdays, and guns cost society $25 billion in medical bills and lost productivity in a typical year. Beyond the costs of the legal system, victim losses, and crime prevention agencies, the crime burden includes the costs of deterrence (locks, safety lighting and fencing, alarm systems and munitions), the costs of compliance enforcement (non-gendarme inspectors and regulators), implicit psychic and health costs (fear, agony, and the inability to behave as desired), and the opportunity costs of time spent preventing, carrying out, and serving prison terms for criminal activity.

This study estimates the impact of crime, taking a comprehensive list of the repercussions of aberrant behavior into account. While the standard measures of criminal activity count crimes and direct costs, this study measures the impact of crimes and includes indirect costs as well. Further, the available data on which crime cost figures are typically based is imprecise. Problems with crime figures stem from the prevalence of unreported crimes, inconsistencies in recording procedures among law enforcement agencies, policies of recording only the most serious crime in events with multiple offenses, and a lack of distinction between attempted and completed crimes. This research does not eliminate these problems, but it includes critical crime-prevention and opportunity costs that are measured with relative precision, and thus places less emphasis on the imprecise figures used in most other measures of the impact of crime. . . .

Previous Studies

Several studies have estimated the impact of crime; however, none has been thorough in its assessment of the substantial indirect costs of crime and the crucial consideration of private crime prevention expenditures. The FBI Crime

From *Journal of Law and Economics,* vol. 42, October 1999, pp. 611–642. Copyright © 1999 by David A. Anderson. Reprinted by permission of the author.

Table 1

Previous Study	Focus	Not Included	$ (billions)
Colins (1994)	General	Opportunity Costs, Miscellaneous Indirect Components	728
Cohen, Miller, and Wiersema (1995)	Victim Costs of Violent and Property Crimes	Prevention, Opportunity, and Indirect Costs	472
U.S. News (1974)	General	Opportunity Costs, Miscellaneous Indirect Components	288
Cohen, Miller, Rossman (1994)	Cost of Rape, Robbery, and Assault	Prevention, Opportunity, and Indirect Costs	183
Zedlewski (1985)	Firearms, Guard Dogs, Victim Losses, Commercial Security	Residential Security, Opportunity Costs, Indirect Costs	160
Cohen (1990)	Cost of Personal and Household Crime to Victims	Prevention, Opportunity, and Indirect Costs	113
President's Commission on Law Enforcement (1967)	General	Opportunity Costs, Miscellaneous Indirect Components	107
Klaus (1994)	National Crime and Victimization Survey Crimes	Prevention, Opportunity, and Indirect Costs	19

Index provides a measure of the level of crime by counting the acts of murder, rape, robbery, aggravated assault, burglary, larceny, motor vehicle theft, and arson each year. The FBI Index is purely a count of crimes and does not attempt to place weights on various criminal acts based on their severity. If the number of acts of burglary, larceny, motor vehicle theft, or arson decreases, society might be better off, but with no measure of the severity of the crimes, such a conclusion is necessarily tentative. From a societal standpoint what matters is the extent of damage inflicted by these crimes, which the FBI Index does not measure.

Over the past three decades, studies of the cost of crime have reported increasing crime burdens, perhaps more as a result of improved understanding and accounting for the broad repercussions of crime than due to the increase in the burden itself. Table 1 summarizes the findings of eight previous studies. . . .

The Effects of Crime

The effects of crime fall into several categories depending on whether they constitute the allocation of resources due to crime that could otherwise be used more productively, the production of ill-favored commodities, transfers from victims to criminals, opportunity costs, or implicit costs associated with risks to life and health. This section examines the meaning and ramifications of each of these categories of crime costs.

Crime-Induced Production

Crime can result in the allocation of resources towards products and activities that do not contribute to society except in their association with crime. Examples include the production of personal protection devices, the trafficking of drugs, and the operation of correctional facilities. In the absence of crime, the time, money, and material resources absorbed by the provision of these goods and services could be used for the creation of benefits rather than the avoidance of harm. The foregone benefits from these alternatives represent a real cost of crime to society. (Twenty dollars spent on a door lock is twenty dollars that cannot be spent on groceries.) Thus, expenditures on crime-related products are treated as a loss to society.

Crimes against property also create unnecessary production due to the destruction and expenditure of resources, and crimes against persons necessitate the use of medical and psychological care resources. In each of these cases, crime-related purchases bid-up prices for the associated items, resulting in higher prices for all consumers of the goods. In the absence of crime, the dollars currently spent to remedy and recover from crime would largely be spent in pursuit of other goals, bidding-up the prices of alternative categories of goods. For this reason, the *net* impact of price effects is assumed to be zero in the present research.

Opportunity Costs

As the number of incarcerated individuals increases steadily, society faces the large and growing loss of these potential workers' productivity. . . . Criminals are risk takers and instigators—characteristics that could make them contributors to society if their entrepreneurial talents were not misguided. Crimes also take time to conceive and carry out, and thus involve the opportunity cost of the criminals' time regardless of detection and incarceration. For many, crime is a full-time occupation. Society is deprived of the goods and services a criminal would have produced in the time consumed by crime and the production of "bads" if he or she were on the level. Additional opportunity costs arise due to victims' lost workdays, and time spent securing assets, looking for keys, purchasing and installing crime prevention devices, and patrolling neighborhood-watch areas.

The Value of Risks to Life and Health

The implicit costs of violent crime include the fear of being injured or killed, the anger associated with the inability to behave as desired, and the agony of being a crime victim. Costs associated with life and health risks are perhaps the most difficult to ascertain, although a considerable literature is devoted to their estimation. The implicit values of lost life and injury are included in the list of crime costs below; those not wishing to consider them can simply subtract these estimates from the aggregate figure.

Transfers

One result of fraud and theft is a transfer of assets from victim to criminal. . . .

Numerical Findings

Crime-Induced Production

... Crime-induced production accounts for about $400 billion in expenditures annually. Table 2 presents the costs of goods and services that would not have to be produced in the absence of crime. Drug trafficking accounts for an estimated $161 billion in expenditure. With the $28 billion cost of prenatal drug exposure and almost $11 billion worth of federal, state, and local drug control efforts (including drug treatment, education, interdiction, research, and intelligence), the combined cost of drug-related activities is about $200 billion. Findings that over half of the arrestees in 24 cities tested positive for recent drug use and about one-third of offenders reported being under the influence of drugs at the time of their offense suggest that significant portions of the other crime-cost categories may result indirectly from drug use.

Table 2

Crime-Induced Production	$ (millions)
Drug Trafficking	160,584
Police Protection	47,129
Corrections	35,879
Prenatal Exposure to Cocaine and Heroin	28,156
Federal Agencies	23,381
Judicial and Legal Services—State & Local	18,901
Guards	17,917
Drug Control	10,951
DUI Costs to Driver	10,302
Medical Care for Victims	8,990
Computer Viruses and Security	8,000
Alarm Systems	6,478
Passes for Business Access	4,659
Locks, Sales, and Vaults	4,359
Vandalism (except arson)	2,317
Small Arms and Small Arms Ammunition	2,252
Replacements Due to Arson	1,902
Surveillance Cameras	1,471
Safety Lighting	1,466
Protective Fences and Gates	1,159
Airport Security	448
Nonlethal Weaponary, e.g., Mace	324
Elec. Retail Article Surveillance	149
Theft Insurance (less indemnity)	96
Guard Dogs	49
Mothers Against Drunk Driving	49
Library Theft Detection	28
Total	**397,395**

About 682,000 police and 17,000 federal, state, special (park, transit, or county) and local police agencies account for $47 billion in expenditures annually. Thirty-six billion dollars is dedicated each year to the 895 federal and state prisons, 3,019 jails, and 1,091 state, county, and local juvenile detention centers. Aside from guards in correctional institutions, private expenditure on guards amounts to more than $18 billion annually. Security guard agencies employ 55 percent of the 867,000 guards in the U.S.; the remainder are employed in-house. While guards are expected and identifiable at banks and military complexes, they have a less conspicuous presence at railroads, ports, golf courses, laboratories, factories, hospitals, retail stores, and other places of business. The figures in this paper do not include receptionists, who often play a duel role of monitoring unlawful entry into a building and providing information and assistance. . . .

Opportunity Costs

In their study of the costs of murder, rape, robbery, and aggravated assault, Cohen, Miller, and Rossman estimate that the average incarcerated offender costs society $5,700 in lost productivity per year. Their estimate was based on the observation that many prisoners did not work in the legal market prior to their offense, and the opportunity cost of those prisoners' time can be considered to be zero. The current study uses a higher estimate of the opportunity cost of incarceration because unlike previous studies, it examines the relative savings from a *crime-free* society. It is likely that in the absence of crime including drug use, some criminals who are not presently employed in the legal workforce would be willing and able to find gainful employment. This assumption is supported by the fact that many criminals are, in a way, motivated entrepreneurs whose energy has taken an unfortunate focus. In the absence of more enticing underground activities, some of the same individuals could apply these skills successfully in the legal sector. . . .

The Value of Risks to Life and Health

Table 3 presents estimates of the implicit costs of violent crime. The value of life and injury estimates used here reflect the amounts individuals are willing to accept to enter a work environment in which their health state might change. The labor market estimates do not include losses covered by workers' compensation, namely health care costs (usually provided without dollar or time limits) and lost earnings (within modest bounds, victims or their spouses typically receive about two-thirds of lost earnings for life or the duration of the injury). The values do capture perceived risks of pain, suffering, and mental

Table 3

The Value of Risks to Life and Health	$ (millions)
Value of Lost Life	439,880
Value of Injuries	134,515
Total	**574,395**

distress associated with the health losses. If the risk of involvement in violent crime evokes more mental distress than the risk of occupational injuries and fatalities, the labor market values represent conservative estimates of the corresponding costs of crime. Similar estimates have been used in previous studies of crime costs. . . .

The average of 27 previous estimates of the implicit value of human life as reported by W. Kip Viscusi is 7.1 million. Removing two outlying estimates of just under $20 million about which the authors express reservation, the average of the remaining studies is $6.1 million. Viscusi points out that the majority of the estimates fall between $3.7 and $8.6 million ($3 and $7 million in 1990 dollars), the average of which is again $6.1 million. The $6.1 million figure was multiplied by the 72,111 crime-related deaths to obtain the $440 billion estimate of the value of lives lost to crime. Similarly, the average of 15 studies of the implicit value of non-fatal injuries, $52,637, was multiplied by the 2,555,520 reported injuries resulting from drunk driving and boating, arson, rape, robbery, and assaults to find the $135 billion estimate for the implicit cost of crime-related injuries.

Transfers

More than $603 billion worth of transfers result from crime. After the $204 billion lost to occupational fraud and the $123 billion in unpaid taxes, the $109 billion lost to health insurance fraud represents the greatest transfer by more than a factor of two, and the associated costs amount to almost ten percent of the nations' health care expenditures. Robberies, perhaps the classic crime, ironically generate a smaller volume of transfers ($775 million) than any other category of crime. The transfers of goods and money resulting from fraud and theft do not necessarily impose a net burden on society, and may in fact increase social welfare to the extent that those on the receiving end value the goods more than those losing them. Nonetheless, as Table 4 illustrates, those on the losing side bear a $603 billion annual burden. . . .

There are additional cost categories that are not included here, largely because measures that are included absorb much of their impact. Nonetheless, several are worth noting. Thaler, Hellman and Naroff, and Rizzo estimate the erosion of property values per crime. An average of their figures, $2,024, can be multiplied by the total number of crimes reported in 1994, 13,992, to estimate an aggregate housing devaluation of $28 billion. Although this figure should reflect the inability to behave as desired in the presence of crime, it also includes psychic and monetary costs imposed by criminal behavior that are already included in this [article].

Julie Berry Cullen and Stephen D. Levitt discuss urban flight resulting from crime. They report a nearly one-to-one relationship between serious crimes and individuals parting from major cities. The cost component of this is difficult to assess because higher commuting costs must be measured against lower property costs in rural areas, and the conveniences of city living must be compared with the amenities of suburbia. Several other categories of crime costs receive incomplete representation due to insufficient data, and therefore

Table 4

Transfers	$ (millions)
Occupational Fraud	203,952
Unpaid Taxes	123,108
Health Insurance Fraud	108,610
Financial Institution Fraud	52,901
Mail Fraud	35,986
Property/Casualty Insurance Fraud	20,527
Telemarketing Fraud	16,609
Business Burglary	13,229
Motor Vehicle Theft	8,913
Shoplifting	7,185
Household Burglary	4,527
Personal Theft	3,909
Household Larceny	1,996
Coupon Fraud	912
Robbery	775
Total	**603,140**

make the estimates here conservative. These include the costs of unreported crimes (although the National Crime Victimization Survey provides information beyond that reported to the police), lost taxes due to the underground economy, and restrictions of behavior due to crime.

When criminals' costs are estimated implicitly as the value of the assets they receive through crime, the gross cost of crime (including transfers) is estimated to exceed $2,269 billion each year, and the net cost is an estimated $1,666 billion. When criminals' costs are assumed to equal the value of time spent planning and committing crimes and in prison, the estimated annual gross and net costs of crime are $1,705 and $1,102 billion respectively. Table 5 presents the aggregate costs of crime based on the more conservative, time-based estimation method. The disaggregation of this and the previous tables facilitates the creation of customized estimates based on the reader's preferred assumptions. Each of the general studies summarized in Table 1 included transfers, so the appropriate comparison is to the gross cost estimate in the current

Table 5

The Aggregate Burden of Crime	$ (billions)
Crime-Induced Production	397
Opportunity Costs	130
Risks to Life and Health	574
Transfers	603
Gross Burden	**$1,705**
Net of Transfers	**$1,102**
Per Capita (in dollars)	**$4,118**

study. As the result of a more comprehensive treatment of repercussions, the cost of crime is now seen to be more than twice as large as previously recognized.

Conclusion

Previous studies of the burden of crime have counted crimes or concentrated on direct crime costs. This paper calculates the aggregate burden of crime rather than absolute numbers, includes indirect costs, and recognizes that transfers resulting from theft should not be included in the net burden of crime to society. The accuracy of society's perspective on crime costs will improve with the understanding that these costs extend beyond victims' losses and the cost of law enforcement to include the opportunity costs of criminals' and prisoners' time, our inability to behave as desired, and the private costs of crime deterrence.

As criminals acquire an estimated $603 billion dollars worth of assets from their victims, they generate an additional $1,102 billion worth of lost productivity, crime-related expenses, and diminished quality of life. The net losses represent an annual per capita burden of $4,118. Including transfers, the aggregate burden of crime is $1,705 billion. In the United States, this is of the same order of magnitude as life insurance purchases ($1,680 billion), the outstanding mortgage debt to commercial banks and savings institutions ($1,853 billion), and annual expenditures on health ($1,038 billion).

As the enormity of this negative-sum game comes to light, so, too, will the need for countervailing efforts to redefine legal policy and forge new ethical standards. Periodic estimates of the full cost of crime could speak to the success of national strategies to encourage decorum, including increased expenditures on law enforcement, new community strategic approaches, technological innovations, legal reform, education, and the development of ethics curricula. Economic theory dictates that resources should be devoted to moral enhancement until the benefits from marginal efforts are surpassed by their costs. Programs that decrease the burden of crime by more than the cost of implementation should be continued, while those associated with negligible or positive net increments in the cost of crime should be altered to better serve societal goals.

A Crime by Any Other Name . . .

If one individual inflicts a bodily injury upon another which leads to the death of the person attacked we call it manslaughter; on the other hand, if the attacker knows beforehand that the blow will be fatal we call it murder. Murder has also been committed if society places hundreds of workers in such a position that they inevitably come to premature and unnatural ends. Their death is as violent as if they had been stabbed or shot. . . . Murder has been committed if society knows perfectly well that thousands of workers cannot avoid being sacrificed so long as these conditions are allowed to continue. Murder of this sort is just as culpable as the murder committed by an individual.

—Frederick Engels
The Condition of the Working Class in England

What's in a Name?

If it takes you an hour to read this chapter, by the time you reach the last page, three of your fellow citizens will have been murdered. *During that same time, at least four Americans will die as a result of unhealthy or unsafe conditions in the workplace!* Although these work-related deaths could have been prevented, they are not called murders. Why not? Doesn't crime by any other name still cause misery and suffering? What's in a name?

The fact is that the label "crime" is not used in America to name all or the worst of the actions that cause misery and suffering to Americans. It is primarily reserved for the dangerous actions of the poor.

In the February 21, 1993, edition of the *New York Times*, an article appears with the headline: "Company in Mine Deaths Set to Pay Big Fine." It describes an agreement by the owners of a Kentucky mine to pay a fine for safety misconduct that may have led to "the worst American mining accident in nearly a decade." Ten workers died in a methane explosion, and the company pleaded guilty to "a pattern of safety misconduct" that included falsifying reports of methane levels and requiring miners to work under unsupported roofs. The company was fined $3.75 million. The acting foreman at the mine was the only individual charged by the federal government, and for his cooperation

From Jeffrey Reiman, *The Rich Get Richer and the Poor Get Prison: Ideology, Class and Criminal Justice*, 5th ed. Published by Allyn and Bacon, Boston, MA. Copyright © 1998 by Pearson Education. Reprint by permission of the publisher.

with the investigation, prosecutors were recommending that he receive the minimum sentence: probation to six months in prison. The company's president expressed regret for the tragedy that occurred. And the U.S. attorney said he hoped the case "sent a clear message that violations of Federal safety and health regulations that endanger the lives of our citizens will not be tolerated."

Compare this with the story of Colin Ferguson, who prompted an editorial in the *New York Times* of December 10, 1993, with the headline: "Mass Murder on the 5:33." A few days earlier, Colin had boarded a commuter train in Garden City, Long Island, and methodically shot passengers with a 9-millimeter pistol, killing 5 and wounding 18. Colin Ferguson was surely a murderer, maybe a mass murderer. My question is, Why wasn't the death of the miners also murder? Why weren't those responsible for subjecting ten miners to deadly conditions also "mass murderers"?

Why do ten dead miners amount to an "accident," a "tragedy," and five dead commuters a "mass murder"? "Murder" suggests a murderer, whereas "accident" and "tragedy" suggest the work of impersonal forces. But the charge against the company that owned the mine said that they "repeatedly exposed the mine's work crews to danger and that such conditions were frequently concealed from Federal inspectors responsible for enforcing the mine safety act." And the acting foreman admitted to falsifying records of methane levels only two months before the fatal blast. Someone was responsible for the conditions that led to the death of ten miners. Is that person not a murderer, perhaps even a *mass murderer?*

These questions are at this point rhetorical. My aim is not to discuss this case but rather to point to the blinders we wear when we look at such an "accident." There was an investigation. One person, the acting foreman, was held responsible for falsifying records. He is to be sentenced to six months in prison (at most). The company was fined. But no one will be tried for *murder*. No one will be thought of as a murderer. *Why not?...*

Didn't those miners have a right to protection from the violence that took their lives? *And if not, why not?*

Once we are ready to ask this question seriously, we are in a position to see that the reality of crime—that is, the acts we label crime, the acts we think of as crime, the actors and actions we treat as criminal—is *created*: It is an image shaped by decisions as to *what* will be called crime and *who* will be treated as a criminal.

The Carnival Mirror

... The American criminal justice system is a mirror that shows a distorted image of the dangers that threaten us—an image created more by the shape of the mirror than by the reality reflected. What do we see when we look in the criminal justice mirror? ...

He is, first of all, a *he*. Out of 2,012,906 persons arrested for FBI Index crimes [which are criminal homicide, forcible rape, robbery, aggravated assault, burglary, larceny, and motor vehicle theft] in 1991, 1,572,591, or 78 percent, were males. Second, he is a *youth*. . . . Third, he is predominantly *urban*. . . . Fourth, he is disproportionately *black*—blacks are arrested for Index crimes at a rate three times that of their percentage in the national population. . . . Finally, he is *poor:* Among state prisoners in 1991, 33 percent were unemployed prior to being arrested—a rate nearly four times that of males in the general population. . . .

This is the Typical Criminal feared by most law-abiding Americans. Poor, young, urban, (disproportionately) black males make up the core of the enemy forces in the war against crime. They are the heart of a vicious, unorganized guerrilla army, threatening the lives, limbs, and possessions of the law-abiding members of society—necessitating recourse to the ultimate weapons of force and detention in our common defense.

. . . The acts of the Typical Criminal are not the only acts that endanger us, nor are they the acts that endanger us the most. As I shall show . . . , we have as great or sometimes even a greater chance of being killed or disabled by an occupational injury or disease, by unnecessary surgery, or by shoddy emergency medical services than by aggravated assault or even homicide! Yet even though these threats to our well-being are graver than those posed by our poor young criminals, they do not show up in the FBI's Index of serious crimes. The individuals responsible for them do not turn up in arrest records or prison statistics. *They never become part of the reality reflected in the criminal justice mirror, although the danger they pose is at least as great and often greater than the danger posed by those who do!*

Similarly, the general public loses more money . . . from price-fixing and monopolistic practices and from consumer deception and embezzlement than from all the property crimes in the FBI's Index combined. Yet these far more costly acts are either not criminal, or if technically criminal, not prosecuted, or if prosecuted, not punished, or if punished, only mildly. . . . *Their faces rarely appear in the criminal justice mirror, although the danger they pose is at least as great and often greater than that of those who do. . . .*

The criminal justice system is like a mirror in which society can see the face of the evil in its midst. Because the system deals with some evil and not with others, because it treats small evils as the gravest and treats some of the gravest evils as minor, the image it throws back is distorted like the image in a carnival mirror. Thus, the image cast back is false not because it is invented out of thin air but because the proportions of the real are distorted. . . .

If criminal justice really gives us a carnival-mirror of "crime," we are doubly deceived. First, we are led to believe that the criminal justice system is protecting us against the gravest threats to our well-being when, in fact, the system is protecting us against only some threats and not necessarily the gravest ones. We are deceived about how much protection we are receiving and thus left vulnerable. The second deception is just the other side of this one. If people believe that the carnival mirror is a true mirror—that is, if they believe the criminal justice system simply *reacts* to the gravest threats to their well-being—they come to believe that whatever is the target of the criminal justice system must be the greatest threat to their well-being. . . .

A Crime by Any Other Name . . .

Think of a crime, any crime. Picture the first "crime" that comes into your mind. What do you see? The odds are you are not imagining a mining company executive sitting at his desk, calculating the costs of proper safety precautions and deciding not to invest in them. Probably what you do see with your mind's eye is one person physically attacking another or robbing something from another via the threat of physical attack. Look more closely. What does the attacker look like? It's a safe bet he (and it is a *he*, of course) is not wearing a suit and tie. In fact, my hunch is that you—like me, like almost anyone else in America—picture a young, tough lower-class male when the thought of crime first pops into your head. You (we) picture someone like the Typical Criminal described above. The crime itself is one in which the Typical Criminal sets out to attack or rob some specific person.

It is important to identify this model of the Typical Crime because it functions like a set of blinders. It keeps us from calling a mine disaster a mass murder even if ten men are killed, even if someone is responsible for the unsafe conditions in which they worked and died. I contend that this particular piece of mental furniture so blocks our view that it keeps us from using the criminal justice system to protect ourselves from the greatest threats to our persons and possessions.

What keeps a mine disaster from being a mass murder in our eyes is that it is not a one-on-one harm. What is important in one-on-one harm is not the numbers but the *desire of someone (or ones) to harm someone (or ones) else*. An attack by a gang on one or more persons or an attack by one individual on several fits the model of one-on-one harm; that is, for each person harmed there is at least one individual who wanted to harm that person. Once he selects his victim, the rapist, the mugger, the murderer all want this person they have selected to suffer. A mine executive, on the other hand, does not want his employees to be harmed. He would truly prefer that there be no accident, no injured or dead miners. What he does want is something legitimate. It is what he has been hired to get: maximum profits at minimum costs. If he cuts corners to save a buck, he is just doing his job. If ten men die because he cut corners on safety, we may think him crude or callous but not a murderer. He is, at most, responsible for an *indirect harm*, not a one-on-one harm. For this, he may even be criminally indictable for violating safety regulations—but not for murder. The ten men are dead as an unwanted consequence of his (perhaps overzealous or undercautious) pursuit of a legitimate goal. So, unlike the Typical Criminal, he has not committed the Typical Crime—or so we generally believe. As a result, ten men are dead who might be alive now if cutting corners of the kind that leads to loss of life, whether suffering is specifically aimed at or not, were treated as murder.

This is my point. Because we accept the belief . . . that the model for crime is one person specifically trying to harm another, we accept a legal system that leaves us unprotected against much greater dangers to our lives and well-being than those threatened by the Typical Criminal. . . .

According to the FBI's *Uniform Crime Reports,* in 1991, there were 24,703 murders and nonnegligent manslaughters, and 1,092,739 aggravated assaults.

In 1992, there were 23,760 murders and nonnegligent manslaughters, and 1,126,970 aggravated assaults. . . . Thus, as a measure of the physical harm done by crime in the beginning of the 1990s, we can say that reported crimes lead to roughly 24,000 deaths and 1,000,000 instances of serious bodily injury short of death a year. As a measure of monetary loss due to property crime, we can use $15.1 billion—the total estimated dollar losses due to property crime in 1992 according to the UCR. Whatever the shortcomings of these reported crime statistics, they are the statistics upon which public policy has traditionally been based. Thus, I will consider any actions that lead to loss of life, physical harm, and property loss comparable to the figures in the UCR as actions that pose grave dangers to the community comparable to the threats posed by crimes. . . .

In testimony before the Senate Committee on Labor and Human Resources, Dr. Philip Landrigan, director of the Division of Environmental and Occupational Medicine at the Mount Sinai School of Medicine in New York City, stated that

> [I]t may be calculated that occupational disease is responsible each year in the United States for 50,000 to 70,000 deaths, and for approximately 350,000 new cases of illness.

. . . The BLS estimate of 330,000 job-related illnesses for 1990 roughly matches Dr. Landrigan's estimates. For 1991, BLS estimates 368,000 job-related illnesses. These illnesses are of varying severity. . . . Because I want to compare these occupational harms with those resulting from aggravated assault, I shall stay on the conservative side here too, as with deaths from occupational diseases, and say that there are annually in the United States approximately 150,000 job-related serious illnesses. Taken together with 25,000 deaths from occupational diseases, how does this compare with the threat posed by crime?

Before jumping to any conclusions, note that the risk of occupational disease and death falls only on members of the labor force, whereas the risk of crime falls on the whole population, from infants to the elderly. Because the labor force is about half the total population (124,810,000 in 1990, out of a total population of 249,900,000), to get a true picture of the *relative* threat posed by occupational diseases compared with that posed by crimes, we should *halve* the crime statistics when comparing them with the figures for industrial disease and death. Using the crime figures for the first years of the 1990s, . . . we note that the *comparable* figures would be

	Occupational Hazard	Crime (halved)
Death	25,000	12,000
Other physical harm	150,000	500,000

. . . Note . . . that the estimates in the last chart are *only* for occupational *diseases* and deaths from those diseases. They do not include death and disability from work-related injuries. Here, too, the statistics are gruesome. The National Safety Council reported that in 1991, work-related accidents caused

9,600 deaths and 1.7 million disabling work injuries, a total cost to the economy of $63.3 billion. This brings the number of occupation-related deaths to
34,600 a year and other physical harms to 1,850,000. If, on the basis of these
additional figures, we recalculated our chart comparing occupational harms
from both disease and accident with criminal harms, it would look like this:

	Occupational Hazard	Crime (halved)
Death	34,600	12,000
Other physical harm	1,850,000	500,000

Can there be any doubt that workers are more likely to stay alive and
healthy in the face of the danger from the underworld than in the work-
world? . . .

To say that some of these workers died from accidents due to their own
carelessness is about as helpful as saying that some of those who died at the
hands of murderers asked for it. It overlooks the fact that where workers are
careless, it is not because they love to live dangerously. They have production
quotas to meet, quotas that they themselves do not set. If quotas were set with
an eye to keeping work at a safe pace rather than to keeping the production-to-
wages ratio as high as possible, it might be more reasonable to expect workers
to take the time to be careful. Beyond this, we should bear in mind that the
vast majority of occupational deaths result from disease, not accident, and disease is generally a function of conditions outside a worker's control. Examples
of such conditions are the level of coal dust in the air ("260,000 miners receive
benefits for [black lung] disease, and perhaps as many as 4,000 retired miners
die from the illness or its complications each year"; about 10,000 currently
working miners "have X-ray evidence of the beginnings of the crippling and
often fatal disease") or textile dust . . . or asbestos fibers . . . or coal tars . . . ;
(coke oven workers develop cancer of the scrotum at a rate five times that of
the general population). Also, some 800,000 people suffer from occupationally
related skin disease each year. . . .

To blame the workers for occupational disease and deaths is to ignore the
history of governmental attempts to compel industrial firms to meet safety
standards that would keep dangers (such as chemicals or fibers or dust particles
in the air) that are outside the worker's control down to a safe level. This has
been a continual struggle, with firms using everything from their own "independent" research institutes to more direct and often questionable forms of
political pressure to influence government in the direction of loose standards
and lax enforcement. So far, industry has been winning because OSHA [Occu-
pational Safety and Health Administration] has been given neither the personnel nor the mandate to fulfill its purpose. It is so understaffed that, in 1973,
when 1,500 federal sky marshals guarded the nation's airplanes from hijackers,
only 500 OSHA inspectors toured the nation's workplaces. By 1980, OSHA
employed 1,581 compliance safety and health officers, but this still enabled
inspection of only roughly 2 percent of the 2.5 million establishments covered by OSHA. The *New York Times* reports that in 1987 the number of OSHA

inspectors was down to 1,044. As might be expected, the agency performs fewer inspections that it did a dozen years ago. . . .

According to a report issued by the AFL-CIO [American Federation of Labor and Congress of Industrial Organizations] in 1992, "The median penalty paid by an employer during the years 1972–1990 following an incident resulting in death or serious injury of a worker was just $480." The same report claims that the federal government spends $1.1 billion a year to protect fish and wildlife and only $300 million a year to protect workers from health and safety hazards on the job. . . .

Is a person who kills another in a bar brawl a greater threat to society than a business executive who refuses to cut into his profits to make his plant a safe place to work? By any measure of death and suffering the latter is by far a greater danger than the former. Because he wishes his workers no harm, because he is only indirectly responsible for death and disability while pursuing legitimate economic goals, his acts are not called "crimes." Once we free our imagination from the blinders of the one-on-one model of crime, can there be any doubt that the criminal justice system does *not* protect us from the gravest threats to life and limb? It seeks to protect us when danger comes from a young, lower-class male in the inner city. When a threat comes from an upper-class business executive in an office, the criminal justice system looks the other way. This is in the face of growing evidence that for every three American citizens murdered by thugs, at least four American workers are killed by the recklessness of their bosses and the indifference of their government.

Health Care May Be Dangerous to Your Health

. . . On July 15, 1975, Dr. Sidney Wolfe of Ralph Nader's Public Interest Health Research Group testified before the House Commerce Oversight and Investigations Subcommittee that there "were 3.2 million cases of unnecessary surgery performed each year in the United States." These unneeded operations, Wolfe added, "cost close to $5 billion a year and kill as many as 16,000 Americans.". . .

In an article on an experimental program by Blue Cross and Blue Shield aimed at curbing unnecessary surgery, *Newsweek* reports that

> a Congressional committee earlier this year [1976] estimated that more than 2 million of the elective operations performed in 1974 were not only unnecessary—but also killed about 12,000 patients and cost nearly $4 billion.

Because the number of surgical operations performed in the United States rose from 16.7 million in 1975 to 22.4 million in 1991, there is reason to believe that at least somewhere between . . . 12,000 and . . . 16,000 people a year still die from unnecessary surgery. In 1991, the FBI reported that 3,405 murders were committed by a "cutting or stabbing instrument." Obviously, the FBI does not include the scalpel as a cutting or stabbing instrument. If they did, they would have had to report that between 15,405 and 19,405 persons were killed by "cutting or stabbing" in 1991. . . . No matter how you slice it, the scalpel may be more dangerous than the switchblade. . . .

Waging Chemical Warfare Against America

One in 4 Americans can expect to contract cancer during their lifetimes. The American Cancer Society estimated that 420,000 Americans would die of cancer in 1981. The National Cancer Institute's estimate for 1993 is 526,000 deaths from cancer. "A 1978 report issued by the President's Council on Environmental Quality (CEQ) unequivocally states that 'most researchers agree that 70 to 90 percent of cancers are caused by environmental influences and are hence theoretically preventable.'" This means that a concerted national effort could result in saving 350,000 or more lives a year and reducing each individual's chances of getting cancer in his or her lifetime from 1 in 4 to 1 in 12 or fewer. If you think this would require a massive effort in terms of money and personnel, you are right. How much of an effort, though, would the nation make to stop a foreign invader who was killing a thousand people and bent on capturing one-quarter of the present population?

In face of this "invasion" that is already under way, the U.S. government has allocated $1.9 billion to the National Cancer Institute (NCI) for fiscal year 1992, and NCI has allocated $219 million to the study of the physical and chemical (i.e., environmental) causes of cancer. Compare this with the (at least) $45 billion spent to fight the Persian Gulf War. The simple truth is that the government that strove so mightily to protect the borders of a small, undemocratic nation 7,000 miles away is doing next to nothing to protect us against the chemical war in our midst. This war is being waged against us on three fronts:

- Pollution
- Cigarette smoking
- Food additives

. . . The evidence linking *air pollution* and cancer, as well as other serious and often fatal diseases, has been rapidly accumulating in recent years. In 1993, the *Journal of the American Medical Association* reported on research that found " 'robust' associations between premature mortality and air pollution levels." They estimate that pollutants cause about 2 percent of all cancer deaths (at least 10,000 a year). . . .

A . . . recent study . . . concluded that air pollution at 1988 levels was responsible for 60,000 deaths a year. The Natural Resources Defense Council sued the EPA [Environmental Protection Agency] for its foot-dragging in implementation of the Clean Air Act, charging that "One hundred million people live in areas of unhealthy air."

This chemical war is not limited to the air. The National Cancer Institute has identified as carcinogens or suspected carcinogens 23 of the chemicals commonly found in our drinking water. Moreover, according to one observer, we are now facing a "new plague—toxic exposure." . . .

The evidence linking *cigarette smoking* and cancer is overwhelming and need not be repeated here. The Centers for Disease Control estimates that cigarettes cause 87 percent of lung cancers—approximately 146,000 in 1992. Tobacco continues to kill an estimated 400,000 Americans a year. Cigarettes are widely estimated to cause 30 percent of all cancer deaths. . . .

This is enough to expose the hypocrisy of running a full-scale war against heroin (which produces no degenerative disease) while allowing cigarette sales and advertising to flourish. It also should be enough to underscore the point that once again there are threats to our lives much greater than criminal homicide. The legal order does not protect us against them. Indeed, not only does our government fail to protect us against this threat, it promotes it! . . .

Based on the knowledge we have, there can be no doubt that air pollution, tobacco, and food additives amount to a chemical war that makes the crime wave look like a football scrimmage. Even with the most conservative estimates, it is clear that *the death toll in this war is far higher than the number of people killed by criminal homicide!*

Summary

Once again, our investigations lead to the same result. The criminal justice system does not protect us against the gravest threats to life, limb, or possessions. Its definitions of crime are not simply a reflection of the objective dangers that threaten us. The workplace, the medical profession, the air we breathe, and the poverty we refuse to rectify lead to far more human suffering, far more death and disability, and take far more dollars from our pockets than the murders, aggravated assaults, and thefts reported annually by the FBI. What is more, this human suffering is preventable. A government really intent on protecting our well-being could enforce work safety regulations, police the medical profession, require that clean air standards be met, and funnel sufficient money to the poor to alleviate the major disabilities of poverty—but it does not. Instead we hear a lot of cant about law and order and a lot of rant about crime in the streets. It is as if our leaders were not only refusing to protect us from the major threats to our well-being but trying to cover up this refusal by diverting our attention to crime—as if this were the only real threat.

POSTSCRIPT

Is Street Crime More Harmful Than White-Collar Crime?

It is important to consider both the suffering and the wider ramifications caused by crimes. Anderson captures many of these dimensions and gives a full account of the harms of street crime. Today the public is very concerned about street crime, especially wanton violence. However, it seems relatively unconcerned about white-collar crime. Reiman tries to change that perception. By defining many harmful actions by managers and professionals as crimes, he argues that white-collar crime is worse than street crime. He says that more people are killed and injured by "occupational injury or disease, by unnecessary surgery, and by shoddy emergency medical services than by aggravated assault or even homicide!" But are shoddy medical services a crime? In the end, the questions remain: What is a crime? Who are the criminals?

A set of readings that support Reiman's viewpoint is *Corporate Violence: Injury and Death for Profit,* edited by Stuart L. Hills (Rowman & Littlefield, 1987); *Unmasking the Crimes of the Powerful: Scrutinizing States and Corporations,* edited by Steve Tombs and Dave Whyte (P. Lang, 2003); Joel Bakan, *The Corporation: The Pathological Pursuit of Profit and Power* (Free Press, 2004); Hazel Croall, *Understanding White Collar Crime* (Open University Press, 2001); Stephen M. Rosoff et al., *Looting, America: Greed, Corruption, Villians, and Victims* (Prentice Hall, 2003); *Readings in White-Collar Crime,* edited by David Shichor et al. (Waveland Press, 2002); and David Weisburd, *White-Collar Crime and Criminal Career* (Cambridge University Press, 2001). Most works on crime deal mainly with theft, drugs, and violence, and the injury and fear that they cause, including Leslie Williams Reid, *Crime in the City: A Political and Economic Analysis of Urban Crime* (LFB Scholarly Pub., 2003); Walter S. DeKeseredy, *Under Seige: Poverty and Crime in a Public Housing Community* (Lexington Books, 2003); Alex Alverez and Ronet Bachman, *Murder American Style* (Wadsworth, 2003); Claire Valier, *Crime and Punishment in Contemporary Culture* (Routledge, 2004); Matthew B. Robinson, *Why Crime? An Integrated Systems Theory of Antisocial Behavior* (Pearson, 2004); Ronald B. Flowers, *Male Crime and Deviance: Exploring Its Causes, Dynamics, and Nature* (C. C. Thomas, 2003); and Meda Chesney-Lind and Lisa Pasko, *The Female Offender: Girls, Women, and Crime,* 2nd ed. (Sage, 2004). Two works on gangs, which are often connected with violent street crime, are Martin Sanchez Jankowski, *Islands in the Street: Gangs and American Urban Society* (University of California Press, 1991), and Felix M. Padilla, *The Gang as an American Enterprise* (Rutgers University Press, 1992). William J. Bennett, John J. DiIulio, and John P. Walters, in *Body Count: Moral Poverty—and How to Win America's War Against Crime and Drugs* (Simon & Schuster, 1996), argue that moral poverty is the root cause of crime (meaning street crime). How applicable is this thesis to white-collar crime? One interesting aspect of many corporate, or white-collar, crimes is that they involve crimes of obedience, as discussed in Herman C. Kelman and V. Lee Hamilton, *Crimes of Obedience: Toward a Social Psychology of Authority and Responsibility* (Yale University Press, 1989).

For recent effort to calculate the costs of crime and law enforcement see Mark A. Cohen, *The Costs of Crime and Justice* (Routledge, 2005). Finally, there is a new type of crime that is increasingly troublesome: digital crime and terrorism. This is thoroughly examined by Robert W. Taylor et al., in *Digital Crime and Digital Terrorism* (Pearson/Prentice Hall, 2006).

ISSUE 17

Should Laws Against Drug Use Remain Restrictive?

YES: Herbert Kleber and Joseph A. Califano Jr., from "Legalization: Panacea or Pandora's Box?" *The World & I Online* (January 2006)

NO: **Peter Gorman**, from "Veteran Cops Against the Drug War," *The World & I Online* (January 2006)

ISSUE SUMMARY

YES: Herbert Kleber, the executive vice president of the Center on Addiction and Substance Abuse (CASA), and Joseph Califano, founder of CASA, maintain that drug laws should remain restrictive because legalization would result in increased use, especially by children. Kleber and Califano contend that drug legalization would not eliminate drug-related violence and harm caused by drugs.

NO: Author Peter Gorman states that restrictive drug laws have been ineffective. He notes that drug use and drug addiction have increased since drug laws became more stringent. Despite the crackdown on drug use, the availability of drugs has increased while the cost of drugs has decreased. In addition, restrictive drug laws, says Gorman, are racist and endanger civil liberties.

In 2008, the federal government allocated nearly $13 billion to control drug use and to enforce laws that are designed to protect society from the perils created by drug use. Some people believe that the government's war on drugs could be more effective but that governmental agencies and communities are not fighting hard enough to stop drug use. They also hold that laws to halt drug use are too few and too lenient. Others contend that the war against drugs is unnecessary; that, in fact, society has already lost the war on drugs. These individuals feel that the best way to remedy drug problems is to end the fight altogether by ending the current restrictive policies regarding drug use.

There are conflicting views among both liberals and conservatives on whether legislation has had the intended result of curtailing the problems of drug use. Many argue that legislation and the criminalization of drugs have been counterproductive in controlling drug problems. Some suggest that the criminalization of drugs has actually contributed to and worsened the social ills associated with drugs. Proponents of drug legalization maintain that the war on drugs, not drugs themselves, is damaging to American society. They do not advocate drug use; they argue only that laws against drugs exacerbate problems related to drugs.

Proponents of drug decriminalization argue that the strict enforcement of drug laws damages American society because it drives people to violence and crime and that the drug laws have a racist element associated with them. People arrested for drug offenses overburden the court system, thus rendering it ineffective. Moreover, proponents contend that the criminalization of drugs fuels organized crime, allows children to be pulled into the drug business, and makes illegal drugs more dangerous because they are manufactured without government standards or regulations. Hence, drugs may be adulterated or of unidentified potency. Decriminalization advocates also argue that decriminalization would take the profits out of drug sales, thereby decreasing the value of and demand for drugs. In addition, the costs resulting from law enforcement are far greater to society than the benefits of criminalization.

Some decriminalization advocates argue that the federal government's prohibition stance on drugs is an immoral and impossible objective. To achieve a "drug-free society" is self-defeating and a misnomer because drugs have always been a part of human culture. Furthermore, prohibition efforts indicate a disregard for the private freedom of individuals because they assume that individuals are incapable of making their own choices. Drug proponents assert that their personal sovereignty should be respected over any government agenda, including the war on drugs. Less restrictive laws, they argue, would take the emphasis off of law enforcement policies and allow more effort to be put toward education, prevention, and treatment. Also, it is felt that most of the negative implications of drug prohibition would disappear.

Opponents of this view maintain that less restrictive drug laws are not the solution to drug problems and that it is a very dangerous idea. Less restrictive laws, they assert, will drastically increase drug use. This upsurge in drug use will come at an incredibly high price: American society will be overrun with drug-related accidents, lost worker productivity, and hospital emergency rooms filled with drug-related emergencies. Drug treatment efforts would be futile because users would have no legal incentive to stop taking drugs. Also, users may prefer drugs rather than rehabilitation, and education programs may be ineffective in dissuading children from using drugs.

Advocates of less restrictive laws maintain that drug abuse is a "victimless crime" in which the only person being hurt is the drug user. Opponents argue that this notion is ludicrous and dangerous because drug use has dire repercussions for all of society. Drugs can destroy the minds and bodies of many people. Also, regulations to control drug use have a legitimate social aim to protect society and its citizens from the harm of drugs.

In the following selections, Henry Kleber and Joseph Califano explain why they feel drugs should remain illegal, whereas Peter Gorman describes the detrimental effects that he believes occur as a result of the restrictive laws associated with drugs.

YES

Herbert Kleber and Joseph A. Califano Jr.

Legalization: Panacea or Pandora's Box?

Introduction

Legalization of drugs has recently received some attention as a policy option for the United States. Proponents of such a radical change in policy argue that the "war on drugs" has been lost; drug prohibition, as opposed to illegal drugs themselves, spawns increasing violence and crime; drugs are available to anyone who wants them, even under present restrictions; drug abuse and addiction would not increase after legalization; individuals have a right to use whatever drugs they wish; and foreign experiments with legalization work and should be adopted in the United States.

In this, its first White Paper, the Center on Addiction and Substance Abuse at Columbia University (CASA) examines these propositions; recent trends in drug use; the probable consequences of legalization for children and drug-related violence; lessons to be learned from America's legal drugs, alcohol and tobacco; the question of civil liberties; and the experiences of foreign countries. On the basis of its review, CASA concludes that while legalization might temporarily take some burden off the criminal justice system, such a policy would impose heavy additional costs on the health care system, schools, and workplace, severely impair the ability of millions of young Americans to develop their talents, and in the long term overburden the criminal justice system.

Drugs like heroin and cocaine are not dangerous because they are illegal; they are illegal because they are dangerous. Such drugs are not a threat to American society because they are illegal; they are illegal because they are a threat to American society.

Any relaxation in standards of illegality poses a clear and present danger to the nation's children and their ability to learn and grow into productive citizens. Individuals who reach age 21 without using illegal drugs are virtually certain never to do so. Viewed from this perspective, substance abuse and addiction is a disease acquired during childhood and adolescence. Thus, legalization of drugs such as heroin, cocaine, and marijuana would threaten a pediatric pandemic in the United States.

While current prohibitions on the import, manufacture, distribution, and possession of marijuana, cocaine, heroin, and other drugs should remain,

As seen in *The World and I Online* journal, January 2006, from a report of The National Center on Addiction and Substance Abuse at Columbia University, September 1995. Copyright © 2006 by The National Center on Addiction and Substance Abuse (CASA) at Columbia University. Reprinted by permission.

America's drug policies do need a fix. More resources and energy should be devoted to prevention and treatment, and each citizen and institution should take responsibility to combat drug abuse and addiction in America. . . .

Legalization, Decriminalization, Medicalization, Harm Reduction: What's the Difference?

The term "legalization" encompasses a wide variety of policy options from the legal use of marijuana in private to free markets for all drugs. Four terms are commonly used: legalization, decriminalization, medicalization, and harm reduction—with much variation in each.

Legalization usually implies the most radical departure from current policy. Legalization proposals vary from making marijuana cigarettes as available as tobacco cigarettes to establishing an open and free market for drugs. Variations on legalization include: making drugs legal for the adult population, but illegal for minors; having only the government produce and sell drugs; and/or allowing a private market in drugs, but with restrictions on advertising, dosage, and place of consumption. Few proponents put forth detailed visions of a legalized market.

Decriminalization proposals retain most drug laws that forbid manufacture, importation, and sale of illegal drugs, but remove criminal sanctions for possession of small amounts of drugs for personal use. Such proposals suggest that possession of drugs for personal use be legal or subject only to civil penalties such as fines. Decriminalization is most commonly advocated for marijuana.

Medicalization refers to the prescription of currently illegal drugs by physicians to addicts already dependent on such drugs. The most frequently mentioned variation is heroin maintenance. Proponents argue that providing addicts with drugs prevents them from having to commit crimes to finance their habit and insures that drugs they ingest are pure.

Harm reduction generally implies that government policies should concentrate on lowering the harm associated with drugs both for users and society, rather than on eradicating drug use and imprisoning users. Beginning with the proposition that drug use is inevitable, harm reduction proposals can include the prescription of heroin and other drugs to addicts; removal of penalties for personal use of marijuana; needle-exchange programs for injection drug users to prevent the spread of AIDS and other diseases that result from needle sharing among addicts; and making drugs available at low or no cost to eliminate the harm caused by users who commit crimes to support a drug habit.

Variations on these options are infinite. Some do not require any change in the illegal status of drugs. The government could, for instance, allow needle exchanges while maintaining current laws banning heroin, the most commonly injected drug. Others, however, represent a major shift from the current role of government and the goal of its policies with regard to drug use and availability. Some advocates use the term "harm reduction" as a politically attractive cover for legalization.

Where We Are

Most arguments for legalization in all its different forms start with the contention that the "war on drugs" has been lost and that prevailing criminal justice and social policies with respect to drug use have been a failure. To support the claim that current drug policies have failed, legalization advocates point to the 80 million Americans who have tried drugs during their lifetime. Since so many individuals have broken drug laws, these advocates argue, the laws are futile and lead to widespread disrespect for the law. A liberal democracy, they contend, should not ban what so many people do.[1]

The 80 million Americans include everyone who has ever smoked even a single joint. The majority of these individuals have used only marijuana, and for many their use was brief experimentation. In fact, the size of this number reflects the large number of young people who tried marijuana and hallucinogenic drugs during the late 1960s and the 1970s when drug use was widely tolerated. During this time, drug use was so commonly accepted that the 1972 Shafer Commission, established during the Nixon Administration, and later, President Jimmy Carter called for decriminalization of marijuana.[2]

Since then, concerned public health and government leaders have mounted energetic efforts to de-normalize drug use, including First Lady Nancy Reagan's "Just Say No" campaign. As a result, current* users of any illicit drugs, as measured by the National Household Survey on Drug Abuse, decreased from 24.8 million in 1979 to 13 million in 1994, a nearly 50 percent drop. Over the same time period, current marijuana users dropped from 23 million to 10 million and cocaine users from 4.4 million to 1.4 million.[3] The drug-using segment of the population is also aging. In 1979, 10 percent of current drug users were older than 34; today almost 30 percent are.[4]

With these results and only 6 percent of the population over age 12 currently using drugs,[5] it is difficult to say that drug reduction efforts have failed. This sharp decline in drug use occurred during a period of strict drug laws, societal disapproval, and increasing knowledge and awareness of the dangers and costs of illegal drug use.

Several factors, however, lead many to conclude that we have not made progress against drugs. This feeling of despair stems from the uneven nature of the success. While casual drug use and experimentation have declined substantially, certain neighborhoods and areas of the country remain infested with drugs and drug-related crime, and these continuing trouble spots draw media attention. At the same time, the number of drug addicts has not dropped significantly and the spread of HIV among addicts has added a deadly new dimension to the problem. The number of hardcore** cocaine users (as estimated by the Office of National Drug Control Policy based on a number of surveys including the Household Survey, Drug Use Forecasting, and Drug

---

*Throughout this paper, "current" drug users refers to individuals who have used drugs within the past month, the definition used in most drug use surveys.

**Throughout this paper, "hardcore" users refers to individuals who use drugs at least weekly.

Abuse Warning Network) has remained steady at roughly 2 million.[6] The over-all number of illicit drug addicts has hovered around 6 million, a situation that many experts attribute both to a lack of treatment facilities[7] and the large numbers of drug-using individuals already in the pipeline to addiction, even though overall casual use has dropped.

Teenage drug use has been creeping up in the past three years. In the face of the enormous decline in the number of users, however, it is difficult to con-clude that current policies have so failed that a change as radical as legaliza-tion is warranted. While strict drug laws and criminal sanctions are not likely to deter hardcore addicts, increased resources can be dedicated to treatment without legalizing drugs. Indeed, the criminal justice system can be used to place addicted offenders into treatment. In short, though substantial problems remain, we have made significant progress in our struggle against drug abuse.

Will Legalization Increase Drug Use?

Proponents of drug legalization claim that making drugs legally available would not increase the number of addicts. They argue that drugs are already available to those who want them and that a policy of legalization could be combined with education and prevention programs to discourage drug use.[8] Some contend that legalization might even reduce the number of users, arguing that there would be no pushers to lure new users and drugs would lose the "forbidden fruit" allure of illegality, which can be seductive to children.[9] Proponents of legalization also play down the consequences of drug use, saying that most drug users can func-tion normally.[10] Some legalization advocates assert that a certain level of drug addiction is inevitable and will not vary, regardless of government policies; thus, they claim, even if legalization increased the number of users, it would have little effect on the numbers of users who become addicts.[11]

The effects of legalization on the numbers of users and addicts is an impor-tant question because the answer in large part determines whether legalization will reduce crime, improve public health, and lower economic, social, and health care costs. The presumed benefits of legalization evaporate if the number of users and addicts, particularly among children, increases significantly.

Availability

An examination of this question begins with the issue of availability, which has three components:

- **Physical**, how convenient is access to drugs.
- **Psychological**, the moral and social acceptability and perceived conse-quences of drug use.
- **Economic**, the affordability of drugs.

Physical
Despite assertions to the contrary, the evidence indicates that presently drugs are not accessible to all. Fewer than 50 percent of high school seniors and young adults under 22 believed they could obtain cocaine "fairly easily" or

"very easily."[12] Only 39 percent of the adult population reported they could get cocaine; and only 25 percent reported that they could obtain heroin, PCP, and LSD.[13] Thus, only one-quarter to one-half of people can easily get illegal drugs (other than marijuana). After legalization, drugs would be more widely and easily available. Currently, only 11 percent of individuals reported seeing drugs available in the area where they lived;[14] after legalization, there could be a place to purchase drugs in every neighborhood. Under such circumstances, it is logical to conclude that more individuals would use drugs.

Psychological

In arguing that legalization would not result in increased use, proponents of legalization often cite public opinion polls, which indicate that the vast majority of Americans would not try drugs even if they were legally available.[15] They fail to take into account, however, that this strong public antagonism towards drugs has been formed during a period of strict prohibition when government and institutions at every level have made clear the health and criminal justice consequences of drug use. Furthermore, even if only 15 percent of population would use drugs after legalization, this would be triple the current level of 5.6 percent.

Laws define what is acceptable conduct in a society, express the will of its citizens, and represent a commitment on the part of the Congress, the President, state legislatures, and governors. Drug laws not only create a criminal sanction, they also serve as educational and normative statements that shape public attitudes.[16] Criminal laws constitute a far stronger statement than civil laws, but even the latter can discourage individual consumption. Laws regulating smoking in public and workplaces, prohibiting certain types of tobacco advertising, and mandating warning labels are in part responsible for the decline in smoking prevalence among adults.

The challenge of reducing drug abuse and addiction would be decidedly more difficult if society passed laws indicating that these substances are not sufficiently harmful to prohibit their use. Any move toward legalization would decrease the perception of risks and costs of drug use, which would lead to wider use.[17] During the late 1960s and the 1970s, as society, laws, and law enforcement became more permissive about drug use, the number of individuals smoking marijuana and using heroin, hallucinogens, and other drugs rose sharply. During the 1980s, as society's attitude became more restrictive and anti-drug laws stricter and more vigorously enforced, the perceived harmfulness of marijuana and other illicit drugs increased and use decreased.

Some legalization advocates point to the campaign against smoking as proof that reducing use is possible while substances are legally available.[18] But it has taken smoking more than 30 years to decline as much as illegal drug use did in 10.[19] Moreover, reducing use of legal drugs among the young has proven especially difficult. While use of illegal drugs by high school seniors dropped 50 percent from 1979 to 1993, tobacco use remained virtually constant.[20]

Economic

By all of the laws of economics, reducing the price of drugs will increase consumption.[21] Though interdiction and law enforcement have had limited success in reducing supply (seizing only 25 percent to 30 percent of cocaine imports, for example)[22] the illegality of drugs has increased their price.[23] Prices of illegal drugs are roughly 10 times what they would cost to produce legally. Cocaine, for example, sells at $80 a gram today, but would cost only $10 a gram legally to produce and distribute. That would set the price of a dose at 50 cents, well within the reach of a school child's lunch money.[24]

Until the mid-1980s, cocaine was the drug of the middle and upper classes. Regular use was limited to those who had the money to purchase it or got the money through white collar crime or selling such assets as their car, house, or children's college funds. In the mid-1980s, the $5 crack cocaine vial made the drug inexpensive and available to all regardless of income. Use spread. Cocaine-exposed babies began to fill hospital neonatal wards, cocaine-related emergency room visits increased sharply, and cocaine-related crime and violence jumped.[25]

Efforts to increase the price of legal drugs by taxing them heavily in order to discourage consumption, if successful, would encourage the black market, crime, violence, and corruption associated with the illegal drug trade. Heroin addicts, who gradually build a tolerance to the drug, and cocaine addicts, who crave more of the drug as soon as its effects subside, would turn to a black market if an affordable and rising level of drugs were not made available to them legally.

Children

Drug use among children is of particular concern since almost all individuals who use drugs begin before they are 21. Furthermore, adolescents rate drugs as the number one problem they face.[26] Since we have been unable to keep legal drugs, like tobacco and alcohol, out of the hands of children, legalization of illegal drugs could cause a pediatric pandemic of drug abuse and addiction.

Most advocates of legalization support a regulated system in which access to presently illicit drugs would be illegal for minors.[27] Such regulations would retain for children the "forbidden fruit" allure that many argue legalization would eliminate. Furthermore any such distinction between adults and minors could make drugs, like beer and cigarettes today, an attractive badge of adulthood.

The American experience with laws restricting access by children and adolescents to tobacco and alcohol makes it clear that keeping legal drugs away from minors would be a formidable, probably impossible, task. Today, 62 percent of high school seniors have smoked, 30 percent in the past month.[28] Three million adolescents smoke cigarettes, an average of one-half a pack per day, a $1 billion a year market.[29] Twelve million underage Americans drink beer and other alcohol, a market approaching $10 billion a year. Although alcohol use is illegal for all those under the age of 21, 87 percent of high school seniors report using alcohol, more than half in the past month.[30] These rates of use persist despite school, community, and media activities that inform youths about the dangers of smoking and drinking and despite increasing public awareness of these risks. This record indicates that efforts to ban drug use among minors while allowing it for adults would face enormous difficulty.

Moreover, in contrast to these high rates of alcohol and tobacco use, only 18 percent of seniors use illicit drugs, which are illegal for the entire society.[31] It is no accident that those substances which are mostly easily obtainable—alcohol, tobacco, and inhalants such as those found in household cleaning fluids—are those most widely used by the youngest students.[32]

Supporters and opponents of legalization generally agree that education and prevention programs are an integral part of efforts to reduce drug use by children and adolescents. School programs, media campaigns such as those of the Partnership for a Drug-Free America (PDFA), and news reports on the dangers of illegal drugs have helped reduce use by changing attitudes towards drugs. In 1992, New York City school children were surveyed on their perceptions of illegal drugs before and after a PDFA campaign of anti-drug messages on television, in newspapers, and on billboards. The second survey showed that the percentage of children who said they might want to try drugs fell 29 points and those who said drugs would make them "cool" fell 17 points.[33] Another study found that 75 percent of students who saw anti-drug advertisements reported that the ads had a deterrent effect on their own actual or intended use.[34]

Along with such educational programs, however, the stigma of illegality is especially important in preventing use among adolescents. From 1978 to 1993, current marijuana use among high school seniors dropped twice as fast as alcohol use.[35] California started a $600 million anti-smoking campaign in 1989, and by 1995, the overall smoking rate had dropped 30 percent. But among teenagers, the smoking rate remained constant—even though almost one-quarter of the campaign targeted them.[36]

In separate studies, 60 to 70 percent of New Jersey and California students reported that fear of getting in trouble with the authorities was a major reason why they did not use drugs.[37] Another study found that the greater the perceived likelihood of apprehension and swift punishment for using marijuana, the less likely adolescents are to smoke it.[38] Because a legalized system would remove much, if not all of this deterrent, drug use among teenagers could be expected to rise. Since most, teens begin using drugs because their peers do[39]—not because of pressure from pushers[40]—and most drugs users initially exhibit few ill effects, more teenagers would be likely to try drugs.[41]

As a result, legalization of marijuana, cocaine, and heroin for adults would mean that increased numbers of teenagers would smoke, snort, and inject these substances at a time when habits are formed and the social, academic, and physical skills needed for a satisfying and independent life are acquired.

Hardcore Addiction

A review of addiction in the past shows that the number of alcohol, heroin, and cocaine addicts, even when adjusted for changes in population, fluctuates widely over time, in response to changes in access, price, societal attitudes, and legal consequences. The fact that alcohol and tobacco, the most accepted and available legal drugs, are the most widely abused, demonstrates that behavior is influenced by opportunity, stigma, and price. Many soldiers who were regular heroin users in Vietnam stopped once they returned to the United States where heroin was much more difficult and dangerous to get.[42] Studies have shown that even among chronic alcoholics, alcohol taxes lower consumption.[43]

Dr. Jack Homer of the University of Southern California and a founding member of the International System Dynamics Society estimates that without retail-level drug arrests and seizures—which reduce availability, increase the danger of arrest for the drug user, and stigmatize use—the number of compulsive cocaine users would rise to between 10 and 32 million, a level 5 to 16 times the present one.[44]

Not all new users become addicts. But few individuals foresee their addiction when they start using; most think they can control their consumption.[45] Among the new users created by legalization, many, including children, would find themselves unable to live without the drug, no longer able to work, go to school, or maintain personal relationships. In fact, as University of California at Los Angeles criminologist James Q. Wilson points out with regard to cocaine,[46] the percentage of drug triers who become abusers when the drugs are illegal, socially unacceptable, and generally hard to get, may be only a fraction of the users who become addicts when drugs are legal and easily available—physically, psychologically, and economically.

Harming Thy Neighbor and Thyself: Addiction and Casual Drug Use

To offset any increased use as a result of legalization, many proponents contend that money presently spent on criminal justice and law enforcement could be used for treatment of addicts and prevention.[47] In 1995, the federal government is spending $13.2 billion to fight drug abuse, nearly two-thirds of that amount on law enforcement; state and local governments are spending at least another $16 billion on drug control efforts, largely on law enforcement.[48] Legalization proponents argue that most of this money could be used to fund treatment on demand for all addicts who want it and extensive public health campaigns to discourage new use.

With legalization, the number of prisoners would initially decrease because many are currently there for drug law violations. But to the extent that legalization increases drug use, we can expect to see more of its familiar consequences. Costs would quickly rise in health care, schools, and businesses. In the long term, wider use and addiction would increase criminal activity related to the psychological and physical effects of drug use and criminal justice costs would rise again. The higher number of casual users and addicts would reduce worker productivity and students' ability and motivation to learn, cause more highway accidents and fatalities, and fill hospital beds with individuals suffering from ailments and injuries caused or aggravated by drug abuse.

Costs

It is doubtful whether legalization would produce any cost savings, over time even in the area of law enforcement. Indeed, the legal availability of alcohol has not eliminated law enforcement costs due to alcohol-related violence. A third of state prison inmates committed their crimes while under the influence of alcohol.[49] Despite intense educational campaigns, the highest number of arrests in 1993—1.5 million—was for driving while intoxicated.[50] Even if, as some legalization proponents propose, drug sales were taxed, revenues raised would be more than offset by erosion of the general tax base as abuse and addiction limited the ability of individuals to work.

Like advocates of legalization today, opponents of alcohol prohibition claimed that taxes on the legal sale of alcohol would dramatically increase revenues and even help erase the federal deficit.[51] The real-world result has been quite different. The approximately $20 billion in state and federal revenues from alcohol taxes in 1995[52] pay for only half the $40 billion that alcohol abuse imposes in direct health care costs,[53] much less the costs laid on federal entitlement programs and the legal and criminal justice systems, to say nothing of lost economic productivity. The nearly $13 billion in federal and state cigarette tax revenue[54] is one-sixth of the $75 billion in direct health care costs attributable to tobacco,[55] to say nothing of the other costs such as the $4.6 billion in social security disability payments to individuals disabled by cancer, heart disease, and respiratory ailments caused by smoking.[56]

Health care costs directly attributable to illegal drugs exceed $30 billion,[57] an amount that would increase significantly if use spread after legalization. Experience renders it unrealistic to expect that taxes could be imposed on newly legalized drugs sufficient to cover the costs of increased use and abuse.

Public Health

Legalization proponents contend that prohibition has negative public health consequences such as the spread of HIV from addicts who share dirty needles, accidental poisoning, and overdoses from impure drugs of variable potency. In 1994, more than one-third of new AIDS cases were among injection drug users who shared needles, cookers, cottons, rinse water, and other paraphernalia; many other individuals contracted AIDS by having sex, often while high, with infected injection drug users.[58]

Advocates of medicalization argue that while illicit drugs should not be freely available to all, doctors should be allowed to prescribe them (particularly heroin, but also cocaine) to addicts. They contend that giving addicts drugs assures purity and eliminates the need for addicts to steal in order to buy them.[59]

Giving addicts drugs like heroin, however, poses many problems. Providing them by prescription raises the danger of diversion for sale on the black market. The alternative—insisting that addicts take drugs on the prescriber's premises—entails at least two visits a day, thus interfering with the stated goal of many maintenance programs to enable addicts to hold jobs.

Heroin addicts require two to four shots each day in increasing doses as they build tolerance to its euphoric effect. On the other hand, methadone can be given at a constant dose since euphoria is not the objective. Addicts maintained on methadone need only a single dose each day and take it orally, eliminating the need for injection.[60] Because cocaine produces an intense, but short euphoria and an immediate desire for more,[61] addicts would have to be given the drug even more often than heroin in order to satisfy their craving sufficiently to prevent them from seeking additional cocaine on the street.

Other less radical harm reduction proposals also have serious flaws. Distributing free needles, for example, does not guarantee that addicts desperate for a high would refuse to share them. But to the extent that needle exchange programs are effective in reducing the spread of the AIDS virus and other diseases without increasing drug use, they can be adopted without legalizing drugs. Studies of whether needle exchange programs increase drug use have generally focused on periods of no longer than 12 months.[62] While use does not seem to increase in this period, data is lacking on the long-term effects of such programs and whether they prompt attitude shifts that in turn lead to increased drug use.

Some individuals do die as a result of drug impurities. But while drug purity could be assured in a government-regulated system (though not for those drugs sold on the black market), careful use could not. The increased numbers of users would probably produce a rising number of overdose deaths, similar to those caused by alcohol poisoning today.

The deaths and costs due to unregulated drug quality pale in comparison to the negative impact that legalization would have on drug users, their families, and society. Casual drug use is dangerous, not simply because it can lead to addiction or accidental overdoses, but because it is harmful per se, producing worker accidents, highway fatalities, and children born with physical and mental handicaps. Each year, roughly 500,000 newborns are exposed to illegal drugs in the womb; many others are never born because of drug-induced spontaneous abortions.[63] Newborns already exposed to drugs are far more likely to need intensive care and suffer the physical and mental consequences of low birth weight and premature birth, including early death.[64] The additional costs just to raise drug-exposed babies would outweigh any potential savings of legalization in criminal justice expenditures.[65]

Substance abuse aggravates medical conditions. Medicaid patients with a secondary diagnosis of substance abuse remain in hospitals twice as long as patients with the same primary diagnosis but with no substance abuse problems. Girls and boys under age 15 remain in the hospital three and four times as long, respectively, when they have a secondary diagnosis of substance abuse.[66] One-third to one-half of individuals with psychiatric problems are also substance abusers.[67] Young people who use drugs are at higher risk of mental health problems, including depression, suicide, and personality disorders.[68] Teenagers who use illegal drugs are more likely to have sex[69] and are less likely to use a condom than those who do not use drugs.[70] Such sexual behavior exposes these teens to increased risk of pregnancy as well as AIDS and other sexually transmitted diseases.

In schools and families, drug abuse is devastating. Students who use drugs not only limit their own ability to learn, they also disrupt classrooms, interfering with the education of other students. Drug users tear apart families by failing to provide economic support, spending money on drugs, neglecting the emotional support of the spouse and guidance of children, and putting their children at greater risk of becoming substance abusers themselves.[71] With the advent of crack cocaine in the mid-1980s, foster care cases soared over 50 percent nationwide in five years; more than 70 percent of these cases involved families in which at least one parent abused drugs.[72]

Decreased coordination and impaired motor skills that result from drug use are dangerous. A recent study in Tennessee found that 59 percent of reckless drivers who, having been stopped by the police, test negative for alcohol on the breathalyzer, test positive for marijuana and/or cocaine.[73] Twenty percent of New York City drivers who die in automobile accidents test positive for cocaine use.[74] The extent of driving while high on marijuana and other illegal drugs is still not well-known because usually the police do not have the same capability for roadside drug testing as they do for alcohol testing. . . .

Crime and Violence

Legalization advocates contend that *drug-related* violence is really *drug-trade-related* violence. They argue that what we have today is not a drug problem but a drug prohibition problem, that anti-drug laws spawn more violence and crime than the drugs themselves. Because illegality creates high prices for drugs and huge profits for dealers, advocates of legalization point out that users commit crimes to support their habit; drug pushers fight over turf; gangs and organized crime thrive; and users become criminals by coming into contact with the underworld.[75]

Legalization proponents argue that repeal of current laws, which criminalize drug use and sales, and wider availability of drugs at lower prices will end this black market and thus reduce the violence, crime, and incarceration associated with drugs.

Researchers divide drug-related violence into three types: systemic, economically compulsive, and psychopharmacological:[76]

- **Systemic violence** is that intrinsic to involvement with illegal drugs, including murders over drug turf, retribution for selling "bad" drugs, and fighting among users over drugs or drug paraphernalia.
- **Economically compulsive violence** results from addicts who engage in violent crime in order to support their addiction.
- **Psychopharmacological violence** is caused by the short or long-term use of certain drugs which lead to excitability, irrationality and violence, such as a brutal murder committed under the influence of cocaine.

Legalization of the drug trade and lower prices might decrease the first two types of violence, but higher use and abuse would increase the third. Dr. Mitchell Rosenthal, President of the Phoenix House treatment centers, warns, "What I and many other treatment professionals would expect to see in a drug-legalized America is a sharp rise in the amount of drug-related crime that is *not* committed for gain—homicide, assault, rape, and child abuse. Along with this, an increase in social disorder, due to rising levels of drug consumption and a growing number of drug abusers."[77]

In a study of 130 drug-related homicides, 60 percent resulted from the psychopharmacological effects of the drug; only 20 percent were found to be related to the drug trade; 3.1 percent were committed for economic reasons. (The remaining 17 percent either fell into more than one of these categories or were categorized as "other.")[78] U.S. Department of Justice statistics reveal that six times as many homicides, four times as many assaults, and almost one and a half times as many robberies are committed under the influence of drugs as are committed in order to get money to buy drugs.[79] Given these facts, any decreases in violent acts committed because of the current high cost of drugs would be more than offset by increases in psychopharmacological violence, such as that caused by cocaine psychosis.

The threat of rising violence is particularly serious in the case of cocaine, crack, methamphetamine, and PCP—drugs closely associated with violent behavior. Unlike marijuana or heroin, which depress activity, these drugs cause irritability and physical aggression. For instance, past increases in the New York City homicide rate have been tied to increases in cocaine use.[80]

Repeal of drug laws would not affect all addicts in the same way. Addicts engage in criminal behavior for different reasons. A small proportion of addicts is responsible for a disproportionately high number of drug-related crimes and arrests. Virtually all of these addicts committed crimes before abusing drugs and use crime to support themselves as well as their habits. Their criminal activity and drug use are symptomatic of chronic antisocial behavior and attitudes. Legally available drugs at lower prices would do little to discourage crime by this group. For a second group, criminal activity is associated with the high cost of illegal drugs. For these addicts, lower prices would decrease drug-related crimes. For a third group, legally available drugs would mean an opportunity to create illegal diversion markets, as some addicts currently do with methadone.[81]

Legalization advocates point to the exploding prison population and the failure of strict drug laws to lower crime rates.[82] Arrests for drug offenses doubled from 470,000 in 1980 to 1 million in 1993.[83] Some 60 percent of the 95,000 federal inmates are incarcerated for drug-law violations.[84]

Rising prison populations are generated in large part by stricter laws, tough enforcement, and mandatory minimum sentencing laws—policy choices of the public and Congress. But the growing number of prisoners is also a product of the high rate of recidivism—a phenomenon tied in good measure to the lack of treatment facilities, particularly in prison. Eighty percent of prisoners have prior convictions and 60 percent have served time before.[85] Despite the fact that more than 60 percent of all state inmates have used illegal drugs regularly and 30 percent were under the influence of drugs at the time they committed the crime for which they were incarcerated,[86] fewer than 20 percent of inmates with drug problems receive any treatment.[87] Many of these inmates also abuse alcohol, but there is little alcoholism treatment either for them or for those prisoners dependent only on alcohol.[88]

While strict laws and enforcement do not deter addicts from using drugs, the criminal justice system can be used to get them in treatment. Because of the nature of addiction, most drug abusers do not seek treatment voluntarily, but many respond to outside pressures including the threat of incarceration.[89]

Where the criminal justice system is used to encourage participation in treatment, addicts are more likely to complete treatment and stay off drugs. . . .[90]

Notes

1. Kurt Schmoke, "Decriminalizing Drugs: It Just Might Work—And Nothing Else Does," in *Drug Legalization: For and Against,* ed. Rod Evans and Irwin Berent (Lasalle: Open Court Press, 1992), p. 216; Merrill Smith, "The Drug Problem: Is There an Answer?" in Evans and Berent, eds., p. 84; Steven Wisotsky, "Statement Before the Select Committee on Narcotics Abuse and Control," in Evans and Berent, eds., p. 189.

2. National Commission on Marijuana and Drug Abuse, *Marijuana: Signal of Misunderstanding* (Washington, DC: GPO, 1972); Musto, p. 267.

3. U.S. Department of Health and Human Services, *Preliminary Estimates from the 1994 National Household Survey on Drug Abuse* (September 1995), pp. 2, 58.

4. Dept. of Health and Human Services (1995), p. 11.

5. Dept. of Health and Human Services (1995), p. 2.

6. Office of National Drug Control Policy (ONDCP), *National Drug Control Strategy: Strengthening Communities' Response to Drugs and Crime* (February 1995), p. 139.

7. ONDCP, *Breaking the Cycle of Drug Abuse* (September 1993), pp. 6–9.

8. Todd Austin Brenner, "The Legalization of Drugs: Why Prolong the Inevitable," in Evans and Berent, eds., p. 173; Schmoke, in Evans and Berent, eds., p. 218; Smith, in Evans and Berent, eds., p. 85.

9. Smith, in Evans and Berent, eds., pp. 83–86; Kevin Zeese, "Drug War Forever?" in *Searching for Alternatives: Drug-Control Policy in the United States,* eds. Melvyn Krauss and Edward Lazear (Stanford: Hoover Institute Press, 1992), p. 265.

10. Ethan Nadelmann, "The Case for Legalization," in *The Drug Legalization Debate,* ed. James Inciardi (Newbury Park: Sage Publications, 1991), pp. 39–40.

11. Michael Gazzaniga, "The Opium of the People: Crack in Perspective," in Evans and Berent, eds., p. 236.

12. Lloyd Johnston, Patrick O'Malley, and Jerald Bachman, *National Survey Results on Drug Use from the Monitoring the Future Study, 1975–1993* (Rockville: 1994), Vol. 1, p. 191 and Vol. 2, p. 144; Center on Addiction and Substance Abuse at Columbia University, *National Survey of American Attitudes on Substance Abuse* (July 1995).

13. Dept. of Health and Human Services *Preliminary Estimates from the 1993 National Household Survey: Press Release* (July 1994), p. 4.

14. Dept. of Health and Human Services (July 1994), p. 4.

15. See for example, Lester Grinspoon and James Bakalar, "The War on Drugs—A Peace Proposal," *The New England Journal of Medicine,* 330(5) 1994, pp. 357–60; Arnold Trebach, "For Legalization of Drugs" in *Legalize It? Debating American Drug Policy,* Arnold Trebach and James Inciardi, eds., (Washington: American University Press, 1993), p. 108.

16. Mark Moore, "Drugs: Getting a Fix on the Problem and the Solution," in Evans and Berent, eds., p. 152.

17. Johnston, O'Malley and Bachman, Vol. 1, p. 206.

18. Schmoke, in Evans and Berent, eds., p. 218; Brenner, in Evans and Berent, eds., p. 171; Wisotsky in Evans and Berent, eds., p. 210.

19. ONDCP (1995), p. 139; Centers for Disease Control, *Morbidity and Mortality Weekly Report,* 34(SS-3) 1994, p. 8.

20. Johnston, O'Malley and Bachman, Vol. 1, p. 79.

21. Moore in Evans and Berent, eds., p. 148; and Mark Moore, "Supply Reduction and Law Enforcement" in *Drugs and Crime,* Michael Tonry and James Wilson, eds., *Crime and Justice: A Review of Research,* Volume 13 (Chicago: University of Chicago Press, 1990), pp. 109–158; Michael Grossman, Gary Becker and Kevin Murphy, "Rational Addiction and the Effect of Price on Consumption," in Krauss and Lazear, eds., p. 83.

22. ONDCP (1995), p. 146.

23. Michael Farrell, John Strang and Peter Reuter, "The Non-Case for Legalization" in *Winning the War on Drugs: To Legalize or Not* (Institute of Economic Affairs: London, 1994).

24. Herbert Kleber, "Our Current Approach to Drug Abuse—Progress, Problems, Proposals," *The New England Journal of Medicine* 330(5), 1994, pp. 362–363; for higher estimates of the differences between illegal and legal costs see Moore, in Evans and Berent, eds., p. 148 and Wisotsky, in Evans and Berent, eds., p. 190.

25. Moore, in Evans and Berent, eds., pp. 129–130.

26. Center on Addiction and Substance Abuse at Columbia University, *National Survey of American Attitudes on Substance Abuse* (July 1995).

27. See for example, Wisotsky, in Evans and Berent, eds., p. 204.

28. Johnston, O'Malley and Bachman, Vol. 1, pp. 76–79.

29. K. Michael Cummings, Terry Pechacek and Donald Shopland, "The Illegal Sale of Cigarettes to US Minors: Estimates by State," *American Journal of Public Health,* 84(2) 1994, pp. 300–302.

30. Johnston, O'Malley and Bachman, Vol. 1, pp. 76–79.

31. Johnston, O'Malley and Bachman, Vol. 1, p. 79.

32. Lloyd Johnston, "A Synopsis of the Key Points in the 1994 Monitoring the Future Results" (December 1994), Table 1; Johnston, O'Malley and Bachman, Vol. 1, pp. 136–137.

33. Drug Strategies, *Keeping Score* (Washington, DC: 1995), p. 11.

34. Evelyn Cohen Reis et al., "The Impact of Anti-Drug Advertising: Perceptions of Middle and High School Students," *Archives of Pediatric and Adolescent Medicine,* 148, December 1994, pp. 1262–1268.

35. Johnston, O'Malley and Bachman, Vol. 1, p. 79.

36. "Hooked on Tobacco: The Teen Epidemic," *Consumer Reports,* March 1995, pp. 142–148.

37. Rodney Skager and Gregory Austin, *Fourth Biennial Statewide Survey of Drug and Alcohol Use Among California Students in Grades 7, 9, and 11,* Office

of the Attorney General, June 1993; Wayne Fisher, *Drug and Alcohol Use Among New Jersey High School Students,* New Jersey Department of Law and Public Safety, 1993.

38. David Peck, "Legal and Social Factors in the Deterrence of Adolescent Marijuana Use," *Journal of Alcohol and Drug Education,* 28(3) 1983, pp. 58–74.

39. Diedre Dupre, "Initiation and Progression of Alcohol, Marijuana and Cocaine Use Among Adolescent Abusers," *The American Journal on Addiction,* 4, 1995, pp. 43–48.

40. Ronald Simmons, Rand Conger and Leslie Whitbeck, "A Multistage Learning Model of the Influences of Family and Peers Upon Adolescent Substance Abuse," *Journal of Drug Issues* 18(3) 1988, pp. 293–315.

41. Simmons, Conger and Whitbeck, p. 304; Mark Moore, "Drugs: Getting a Fix on the Problem and the Solution," in Evans and Berent, eds., p. 143.

42. Musto, pp. 258–259.

43. Philip Cook, "The Effect of Liquor Taxes on Drinking, Cirrhosis, and Auto Accidents" in *Alcohol and Public Policy: Beyond the Shadow of Prohibition,* Mark Moore and Dean Gerstein, eds. (Washington, DC: National Academy Press, 1981), p. 256.

44. Jack Homer, "Projecting the Impact of Law Enforcement on Cocaine Prevalence: A System Dynamics Approach," *Journal of Drug Issues* 23(2) 1993, pp. 281–295.

45. Kleber, p. 361.

46. James Q. Wilson, "Against the Legalization of Drugs," *Commentary* (February 1990), pp. 21–28.

47. See for example, Schmoke in Evans and Berent, eds., p. 218.

48. ONDCP (1995), p. 138.

49. Bureau of Justice Statistics, *Survey of State Prison Inmates, 1991* (Washington, DC: 1993), p. 26.

50. Bureau of Justice Statistics, *Prisoners in 1994* (Washington, DC: 1995), p. 13.

51. Paul Aaron and David Musto, "Temperance and Prohibition in America: A Historical Overview," in Moore and Gerstein, eds., p. 172.

52. Drug Enforcement Administration (DEA), *How to Hold Your Own in a Drug Legalization Debate* (Washington, DC, 1994), p. 26, adjusted to 1995.

53. Center on Addiction and Substance Abuse at Columbia University (CASA), *The Cost of Substance Abuse to America's Health Care System, Final Report* (To be issued, 1995).

54. The Tobacco Institute (1994), adjusted to 1995.

55. CASA (To be issued, 1995).

56. Center on Addiction and Substance Abuse at Columbia University, *Substance Abuse and Federal Entitlement Programs* (February 1995).

57. CASA (To be issued, 1995).

58. Centers for Disease Control, National AIDS Clearinghouse (1994).

59. See for example, "Prescribing to Addicts Appears to Work in Britain: Interview with Dr. John Marks," *Psychiatric News,* December 17, 1993, pp. 8, 14.

60. Joyce Lowinson et al., "Methadone Maintenance," pp. 550–561; Jerome Jaffe, "Opiates: Clinical Aspects," pp. 186–194; and Eric Simon, "Opiates: Neurobiology," pp. 195–204 in *Substance Abuse: A Comprehensive Textbook,* 2nd ed., Joyce Lowinson, Pedro Ruiz and Robert Millman, eds. (Baltimore: Williams and Wilkins, 1992).

61. Mark Gold, "Cocaine (and Crack): Clinical Aspects," in Lowinson, Ruiz and Millman, eds., pp. 205–221.

62. Peter Lurie, Arthur Reingold et al., *The Public Health Impact of Needle Exchange Programs in the United States and Abroad,* 2 vols. (University of California, 1993).

63. Dept. of Justice (1992), p. 12; Paul Taubman, "Externalities and Decriminalization of Drugs," in Krauss and Lazear, eds., p. 99.

64. Dept. of Justice (1992), p. 12; Joel Hay, "The Harm They Do to Others," in Krauss and Lazear, eds., pp. 204–213.

65. Hay, in Krauss and Lazear, eds., p. 208.

66. Center on Addiction and Substance Abuse at Columbia University (CASA), *The Cost of Substance Abuse to America's Health Care System, Report 1: Medicaid Hospital Costs,* (July 1993), pp. 38–46.

67. Ronald Kessler et al., "Lifetime and 12-month prevalence of DSM-III-R psychiatric disorders in the United States: Results from the National Comorbidity Study," *Archives of General Psychiatry,* 51(1) 1994, pp. 8–19.

68. Dept. of Justice (1992), p. 11.

69. Centers for Disease Control, "Youth Risk Behavior Survey, 1991."

70. M. Lynne Cooper, Robert Pierce, and Rebecca Farmer Huselid, "Substance Abuse and Sexual Risk Taking Among Black Adolescents and White Adolescents," *Health Psychology* 13(3) 1994, pp. 251–262.

71. Dept. of Justice (1992), p. 9.

72. General Accounting Office, *Foster Care: Parental Drug Abuse Has Alarming Impact on Young Children* (Washington, DC: 1994).

73. Daniel Brookoff et al., "Testing Reckless Drivers for Cocaine and Marijuana," *The New England Journal of Medicine* 331(8) 1994, pp. 518–522.

74. Peter Marzuk, Kenneth Tardiff, et al., "Prevalence of Recent Cocaine Use among Motor Vehicle Fatalities in New York City," *Journal of the American Medical Association* 1990; 263, pp. 250–256.

75. See for example, Nadelmann, in Inciardi (1991), ed., pp. 31–32; Brenner, in Evans and Berent, eds., p. 174; Ira Glasser, "Drug Prohibition: An Engine for Crime," in Krauss and Lazear, eds., pp. 271–283; Milton Friedman, "The War We are Losing," in Krauss and Lazear, eds., pp. 53–57.

76. Paul J. Goldstein, "The Drugs/Violence Nexus: A Tripartite Conceptual Framework," *Journal of Drug Issues* (Fall 1985), pp. 493–516.

77. Mitchell Rosenthal, "Panacea or Chaos: The Legalization of Drugs in America," *Journal of Substance Abuse Treatment* 11(1) 1994, pp. 3–7.

78. Henry Brownstein and Paul J. Goldstein, "A Typology of Drug-Related Homicides" in *Drugs, Crime and the Criminal Justice System,* Ralph Weisheit, ed. (Cincinnati, OH: Anderson Publishing Co., 1990), pp. 171–191.

79. Bureau of Justice Statistics (1993), p. 22.

80. Kenneth Tardiff et al., "Homicide in New York City: Cocaine Use and Fire-arms," *Journal of the American Medical Association* 272(1) 1994, pp. 43–46.

81. Jon Chaiken and Marcia Chaiken, "Varieties of Criminal Behavior," (Santa Monica: Rand, 1982); HK Wexler and George De Leon, "Criminals as Drug Abusers and Drug Abusers Who Are Criminals," Paper presented to the Annual Convention of the American Psychological Association, Washington, DC, 1980; cited in George De Leon, "Some Problems with the Anti-Prohibitionist Position on Legalization of Drugs," *Journal of Addictive Diseases* 13(2) 1994, p. 38.

82. See for example, New York City Bar Association, "A Wiser Course: Ending Drug Prohibition," *The Record* 49(5) 1994, pp. 525–534.

83. Bureau of Justice Statistics (1995), p. 13.

84. Bureau of Justice Statistics (1995), pp. 1, 10.

85. Bureau of Justice Statistics (1993), p. 11.

86. Bureau of Justice Statistics (1993), p. 21.

87. General Accounting Office, *Drug Treatment: State Prisons Face Challenges in Providing Services* (Washington, DC: 1991).

88. Bureau of Justice Statistics (1993), p. 26.

89. De Leon, p. 38.

90. M. Douglas Anglin. "The Efficacy of Civil Commitment in Treating Narcotic Addiction" in *Compulsory Treatment of Drug Abuse: Research and Clinical Practice,* NIDA Research Monograph 86, 1988, pp. 8–34; Robert Hubbard et al., *Drug Abuse Treatment: A National Study of Effectiveness* (Chapel Hill: University of North Carolina Press, 1989).

Peter Gorman

Veteran Cops Against the Drug War

Howard Woolridge is outside of Utica, New York, heading east on horseback on a beautiful late summer day. He's wearing a T-shirt with the slogan "Cops Say Legalize Drugs. Ask Me Why." For the last 3,000 miles, he's been switching off between his two horses, Misty and Sam. But the T-shirt slogan has stayed the same.

The rangy, good-looking guy is also talking on the cell phone to a reporter back in North Texas. But he interrupts that conversation to speak to someone who pulls up next to him in a car. "That's right—cops say legalize," he tells the newcomer in a deep voice. "Why? Because if we do, we just might be able to keep drugs out of the hands of your 14-year-old."

"Right on!" the motorist shouts, and drives off.

Woolridge is not a lunatic and he's not been out in the sun too long, even if he did cross the United States on horseback in the summer heat. He's a retired law enforcement officer with 18 years on the job who finally decided that the war on drugs was more of a problem than the illicit drugs it was purporting to fight.

He's also a serious long-distance horseman, on the road this time since March 4, when he left Los Angeles for the 3,400-mile ride to New York Harbor. It's the second time Woolridge has crossed the United States to publicize the campaign to repeal most of the drug laws in this country. In 2003 he rode from Georgia to Oregon. When he finished this trip on October 5, looking out at the Statue of Liberty, he was honored by the Long Riders' Guild as only the second person known to have ridden horseback all the way across the country in both directions. And he'll still be wearing one of his "Ask Me Why" T-shirts, the same shirts he's been wearing for six years.

"When I first started wearing it," he says, "people in Texas thought I was crazy. They thought my idea would destroy Texas and America. They believed the government propaganda that millions of people would pick up heroin or methamphetamines and become junkies overnight if you legalized it." But in the last two to three years, he's seen a sea change in the attitude of the American public regarding the war on drugs.

Jailed over Medicinal Marijuana

"At any given Arby's, McDonald's, Rotary Club or veterans hall," he says, "people are overwhelmingly in favor of calling a halt to drug prohibition. Overwhelmingly."

From *The World & I Online*, January 2006. Copyright © 2006 by The World & I Online. Reprinted by permission. www.Worldandl.com

Many of the houses Woolridge is riding past carry plaques attesting to the Utica area's involvement in the Underground Railroad that once funneled runaway slaves from the south up to Canada. It makes him think about Bernie Ellis, a fellow soldier in the war against the drug war, who has lost his own freedom.

"For 10 years he provided free medical marijuana to three oncologists in the Nashville, Tennessee, area for their patients undergoing chemotherapy. He never once met the doctors, of course; it was all cloak-and-dagger. He'd bring the marijuana to an office worker who'd get it to the patient.

"Well, he finally got busted last year. Now he's looking at five years mandatory federal prison time, though that might go up to 10 because he had a shotgun on his farm when he got busted. And of course his million-dollar farm has been forfeited because he grew the medical marijuana there."

The phone goes quiet for a minute, and there's the sound of a strangled sob. "Sorry. Got a little choked up for a second," he says. He pauses to explain his T-shirt to a motorist, then he's back on the phone talking about Bernie. "This is a guy who broke the law to help people and is now facing the consequences of that. Poor son of a bitch. Next time I see him he'll be in prison."

Woolridge is not a lone ranger in the fight to legalize drugs. He's a founding member of an organization called Law Enforcement Against Prohibition or LEAP, an organization made up entirely of current or former members of law enforcement who feel the drug war's a failure and believe legalization and regulation are preferable to the incarceration of drug users and control of the drug market by organized crime.

Founded in March 2002 by five police officers, LEAP now counts about 3,000 members, from the ranks of policemen, prison guards, Drug Enforcement Administration (DEA) agents, judges and even prosecutors in 48 states and 45 foreign countries. The idea behind LEAP is that, as with the Vietnam Veterans Against the War, the call for an end to the drug war carries more weight when it comes from folks who were in the trenches.

"We're the ones who fought the war," said Jack Cole, LEAP's executive director, who retired from the New Jersey state police as a detective lieutenant after 26 years, including 14 in their Narcotics Bureau, mostly undercover. "And I bear witness to the abject failure of the U.S. war on drugs and to the horrors these prohibitionist policies have produced."

The LEAP Web site provides the statistical backup for that argument. "After nearly four decades of fueling the U.S. policy of a war on drugs with over half a trillion tax dollars and increasingly punitive policies, our confined population has quadrupled," it says. "More than 2.2 million of our citizens are currently incarcerated and every year we arrest an additional 1.6 million for nonviolent drug offenses—more per capita than any country in the world. . . . Meanwhile, people continue dying in our streets while drug barons and terrorists continue to grow richer."

To get that message out, LEAP members have given nearly 1,500 speeches since 2003. And they don't preach to the choir. "We don't do hemp rallies or Million Man Marijuana Marches," said Woolridge. "We do Kiwanis Clubs and PTA meetings and cop conventions. That's where the people we've got to reach go."

To parents and teachers and Rotarians and other cops, LEAP members tell their own stories, about their work and about how they came to feel the drug war was not the answer.

Woolridge, for instance, was a street cop in Michigan for 15 of his 18 years of service, before moving up to the rank of detective. "I didn't work directly with the drug war, in that I wasn't in narcotics," he said. "Still, as a detective I was constantly working with felonies that touched on the drug war. Eight of 10 burglary suspects I dealt with were on crack at the time. They were stealing for drug money."

The burglary victims "were all in real pain," he said. "And I got so fed up with it I began saying, 'Why not let these guys have all the crack they want until they die?' Now I'd say, 'Have all you want for a dollar.' That makes it their choice to live or die. Either way, you don't have people breaking into houses for drug money anymore."

"Dehumanizing" Drug Users

To Cole, who did work directly in narcotics, the whole concept of the war on drugs is wrong. "You declare war, you need soldiers. You have soldiers, they need an enemy. So we've effectively taken a peacekeeping force—the police— and turned them into soldiers whose enemies are the 110 million people who have tried illegal substances in the U.S."

To be an effective soldier, you've got to dehumanize your enemy. "When I started out in narcotics I believed everything they told me," said Cole, a no-BS kind of guy. "Drugs were bad. The people who did them were less than human. I was all for locking them up."

Worse, he said, he and others often applied what they called a little "street justice" to the people they were arresting. "In our training we were taught to believe that drug users were the worst people in the world and whatever we did to them to try to stop their drug use was justified."

What they did was kick in home or apartment doors and have every man woman and child inside lie on the floor. If people didn't cooperate immediately, they were thrown to the floor. Then the place was ransacked. "When we searched for drugs we pretty much did as much damage as possible. We'd break bureaus, turn over beds, smash mirrors, throw things on the floor. Didn't matter, because the people there weren't humans, right? And then, if we did find any drugs, we'd arrest everyone in the house: parents, sisters, brothers. And since we'd already kicked the door down when we came in, it would be left open and anyone who wanted to enter could steal what they wanted. We never cared about that."

Street justice didn't stop there, said Cole. In court, he said officers routinely changed testimony to insure convictions—times, locations, amounts of drug, "anything that couldn't be checked to catch the officer in a lie."

It didn't take long for Cole to reach the conclusion that the drug war and its street justice weren't for him. He was mostly going after small-timers, and his job, he came to feel, was to insert himself into voluntary, private business transactions. "To do that, I had to become someone's confidant, their best friend. And once I was, I would bust them."

But he, too, got hooked—on the adrenaline high of the game. "By the time I came to my senses, I was working on big-timers, and pitting your mind against theirs was a great rush," he said. "Also, it was hard to quit because we were considered by the public and our peers as heroes. And then, given that I'd worked with a lot of cops who applied bad street justice, I let myself believe that at least if I was the one catching [the dopers] they'd be legally caught, and I'd tell the truth and justice would prevail."

He laughed. "Know what was the worst? When I realized that I liked and respected a lot of the bad guys much more than I liked or respected the guys I was working with."

Prohibition: Has It Worked by Its Own Standards?

The stated goals of the war on drugs are to lower drug consumption, reduce addiction and dependence, and decrease the quality and quantity of illegal drugs available on American streets. Those have been the goals since President Richard Nixon first declared the war as part of his attempt to look tough on crime during the presidential election in 1968.

Since then, the strategy of prohibition has been ramped up by every succeeding administration. Few people in this country—or anywhere—have escaped the effects of the U.S. drug war, from the toll of burglaries and car thefts committed to pay for drugs, to the tax bills for prisons to hold the increasing percentages of citizens locked up for nonviolent drug-related crimes, to the millions of kids who've grown up without one or both parents as a result of drug convictions and drug addictions. Drug-related murders reach into the tens of thousands in this country, and the toll is much higher in drug-producing and-shipping nations, from Colombia to Afghanistan to Jamaica. Thousands of peace officers have died fighting the drug war. Whole countries have found themselves under the boot of the illegal drug industry, their governments controlled or intimidated by drug cartels, their politicians and police forces infiltrated, and honest public servants assassinated.

The assumption in American drug policy has always been that those are the impacts of illegal drugs themselves. But LEAP members have come to believe those are the wages not of drugs, but of the war on drugs. And they want the rest of the country to look closely at the costs of that strategy and what they see as its failures.

Despite the billions of dollars spent on the fight in nearly 40 years, LEAP members point out, the drug war has failed on every one of its own stated goals.

Drug consumption, for instance, shows little sign of dropping. Whereas in 1965, according to the Drug Enforcement Administration, fewer than 4 million Americans had ever tried an illegal drug, the figure is now more than 110 million. In 2000, the federal government estimated that there were about 33 million people in this country who had used cocaine at least once—a more than 700 percent increase over the total number of people 35 years before who had used any illegal drug.

Dependence and addiction? According to the Office of National Drug Control Policy (ONDCP), the federal agency that sets and administers U.S. drug policy, in 2002 more than 7 million Americans were either dependent on or abusing illegal substances—nearly double the number of people who had even tried such drugs when Nixon declared his war. Heroin addicts have jumped from a few hundred thousand in the 1960s to between 750,000 and one million today according to the ONDCP.

Attempts to decrease the quality of available drugs also have failed. In 1970, average street heroin in this country had a potency of 1 to 2 percent. In 2000, according to the DEA, that purity figure was 36.8 percent—although U.S. drug czar John Walters did praise anti-drug forces recently for reducing the strength of street heroin coming from South America to 32.1 percent. Similarly, street cocaine was roughly 2 to 4 percent pure in 1968—and a whopping 56 percent in 2001, according to the ONDCP. The average strength of the active ingredient (THC) in marijuana sold in this country more than doubled between the late 1970s and 2001.

Nor is there much good news on drug quantities and availability, at least not judging by the numbers of users and the prices on the street. The ONDCP estimates that Americans' use of cocaine and crack has dropped from 447 tons in 1990 to 259 tons in 2000. But the price of cocaine has dropped from $100 per gram in 1970 to $25 to $50 per gram in 2002—for cocaine that was many times stronger. At the wholesale level, a kilogram of cocaine (2.2 pounds at roughly 25 percent purity) cost $45,000 in New York City in 1970. Today, in any large city in the U.S., it costs less than $15,000 and it's about 65 percent pure.

Only marijuana showed a price increase. In 1970, a bag of Mexican ditchweed (roughly an ounce) cost $20. In 2005, that same bag costs nearly $50. But most Americans who can afford it don't smoke Mexican ditchweed. They smoke U.S.-grown sinsemilla, which runs up to $400 per ounce.

With availability, price, and quality making drugs as attractive as ever, the only other barometer of the success of the drug war might be if it's stopped anyone from trying drugs—an area where programs like DARE, a huge effort targeted at schoolkids—have had a noted lack of success. "It didn't stop George Bush, Bill Clinton, Al Gore or me from smoking pot," said Woolridge. "I don't think it probably ever stopped anyone."

Collateral Damage

The cops and prosecutors and judges who belong to LEAP think the bad results of the drug war go beyond its policy failures, even beyond the lives lost to drug violence and incarceration.

"Let's be honest," Cole said. "The war on drugs has taken an incredible toll in terms of the loss of our civil liberties, particularly in terms of the Fourth Amendment, from property forfeiture laws that fund law enforcement agencies to warrantless searches. It's promoted institutionalized racism, and it's created a systemic level of corruption among law enforcement unheard of prior to its initiation."

Law enforcement veterans like Cole and Woolridge believe the increase in institutional racism is one of the deepest wounds. They point out, for instance, that crack users (generally inner-city blacks) are subject to mandatory minimum sentences of five years for possession of five grams of crack, while powder cocaine users (generally middle-class whites) have to be caught with 500 grams to get the same mandatory sentence.

While ONDCP statistics show that whites use more than 70 percent of all illegal drugs, blacks are sentenced to prison for drug crimes seven times more often than whites.

"Imagine," said Cole, "one of the most racist places in the world: South Africa, 1993. At that time, the South African government was incarcerating black males at the rate of 859 per 100,000 population." And yet in 2004 in the United States—with more people and a higher percent of its population in prison than any country in the world—the incarceration rate for black males was 4,919 per 100,000 (compared to 726 overall).

He pointed to an FBI estimate that one in three black male babies born in the U.S. in 2004 have an expectation of going to prison during their lifetime. "That just blows my mind," he said.

LEAP members believe that a large percentage of the corruption found in U.S. police agencies is tied to drugs. In Texas, recent drug-related scandals included the Dallas fake-drugs operation, in which a snitch was paid more than $200,000 over a two-year period to provide local cops with drug dealers. The "dealers" turned out to be nearly all illegal immigrants; their "drugs" turned out to be crushed sheetrock and pool chalk.

And then there was Tulia, in the Texas Panhandle, in which a multi-county drug task force hired a corrupt deputy sheriff to rid the town of its drug problem; when it turned out there wasn't one, the deputy created one, and more than 40 people wound up arrested.

LEAP spokesmen see both of those high-profile Texas drug corruption cases as indicative of a much wider problem: officers cutting corners to get the arrest numbers that will keep the fuel line of federal and state anti-drug funding open. And those scandals don't begin to touch on the border patrol agents, police, and other law enforcement officials who have been corrupted because the drug money is so available.

More Law-Enforcement Corruption

Rusty White, another LEAP member, is a self-described redneck who grew up hard in east Texas and now, after many stops in other states and countries, lives just north of Fort Worth. At 13, he saw a friend shoot up black-tar heroin and decided he didn't like hard drugs. By 16, he'd been to juvenile detention five times and gotten kicked out of his high school "because I was traveling with an older crowd of bad-ass kids that I was trying to live up to."

In quick succession, he married, became a father, joined the Army and got divorced. After a second tour with the Army, he ended up in Florence, Arizona, where he went to work at the state penitentiary, which, he said, was "one of the most violent prisons in the United States at that time."

From 1973 to 1978, he worked as a guard on maximum security, death row, and administrative segregation cellblocks, dealing with horrors daily. "Life meant very little to those inside the walls," he said, noting that two prison guards were killed and mutilated by inmates in 1973. "And drugs were one of the biggest problems we had. They were the cause of most of the deaths and power struggles." And most of the drugs were brought in by family members of prison workers. "I got fed up with the corruption and left to go into the oil-drilling business in 1979," he said.

After working overseas for several years, White moved to Oklahoma. And there, he said, he got to see the war on drugs from a very different vantage point. "The county I lived in had a sheriff who controlled the drug market. And he did so with force. It was common knowledge that if you crossed him he could be—and had been—deadly."

But the same sheriff regularly flew around the county in National Guard helicopters, providing photo ops for news crews to show how tough he was on drugs. "The only thing he was getting rid of was the competition," said White disgustedly.

His only personal encounter with the sheriff and his machine occurred when White's brother-in-law, a small-time pot dealer, was busted. "He was poor, didn't have a car that ran, and was living off [government] commodities. Yet he was going to be played by the sheriff as a drug-dealing kingpin," the former prison guard said.

"Anyway, he's the father of three little ones, all younger than six, and when the police arrived, he offered to go with them willingly. But he asked that his kids be allowed to stay with an uncle who was there rather than dragging them down to the station. Well, you know how people feel about 'drug dealers.' The police said no, the kids were coming to the station to watch their father get busted, and then they'd be released to the uncle."

When the man's trial came up, White said, it turned out the district attorney didn't have any evidence against him as a big-time dealer. Nonetheless, he was offered a plea deal: Admit to being a big dealer and get a one- to three-year sentence. If he took it to trial, however, the prosecutor promised he'd ask for a full 10 years.

"He copped to the plea. But to see him struggle with having to lie in front of his kids and admit to something he hadn't done—well, I sort of snapped and screamed at the prosecutor and asked him if he'd thought he'd earned his money that day and why he was playing God, and he looked at me and answered, 'Because in this county, I am God.'"

A couple of years later, White said, the DA went back into private practice and shortly thereafter was arrested and convicted for dealing methamphetamines. "How the sheriff escaped that net, I don't know," White said. "But the thing to remember is that . . . this sort of thing is happening every day in the war on drugs, all over the country. And that abuse of trust and power is far more harmful to Americans than drugs could ever be."

No Place for "Anyone with a Conscience"

Shortly after his brother-in-law's conviction, White went back to work in the prison system, and became a drug-dog trainer and handler. It was the sort of work White said he was meant to do. "I tracked several escapees from the prison and even some cop killers using my track K-9s. We helped departments all over the state. I'd be sent to prisons to look for drugs—I had no problem with that. But the more we were used with other police organizations the more my conscience started to become a problem."

Two incidents stick in White's mind. Once while his partner was helping another officer, part of a joint was discovered in the ashtray of an old pickup belonging to an elderly man. The dogs were brought in, and in the camper shell on the back of the truck in which the old man lived the dogs sniffed out a briefcase with more than $9,000 in it. Because it was a drug dog that had alerted on it, the money was confiscated. "And they just stood around laughing as the old man begged them not to take his life savings. It just made me sick and ashamed. Heck, it's common knowledge that over 90 percent of the paper money in this country is tainted with a drug scent a dog can find. But using that to rob our people disgusts me. Heck, if you walk any K-9 into a bank vault the dog will mark on that money, too. How come that money isn't confiscated?"

The second incident occurred one night when White and his drug dog were called to help a local police department search a house for drugs. When he pulled up to the house, he asked to see the warrant. The officer told him it wasn't there yet but to go ahead and start the search, and it would be there shortly. "I told him that's just not how it works. I needed the warrant for the search to be legal. So I put my K-9 back into the truck and brought him back to the kennel. And then I got called on the carpet for refusing to assist."

White thought getting into trouble for following the law he'd sworn to uphold was just too much, so he quit. "Heck, there was so much corruption, even among K-9 handlers. If they didn't want someone with drugs caught they'd say the dog didn't mark. If they did, well, we heard of cases where guys went so far as to 'salt' the areas their dogs were searching to make sure someone got busted. It was so bad that, being honest, you couldn't do it. . . . I don't think anyone with a conscience can be part of law enforcement anymore."

Richard Watkins saw the same corruption inside prison that White did, but from a unique perspective. A decorated Vietnam veteran with a Ph.D. in education, Watkins worked at Texas' Huntsville prison for 20 years; the last several as warden of Holiday Unit, a 2,100-bed facility housing a range of criminals from nonviolent to violent/maximum security.

He was originally hired to revamp and professionalize the correctional officers training program—something the prison system was forced to do by federal mandate, and which Watkins said was badly needed. "It was just horrible. Corrupt, bad, just plain horrible," he said.

Watkins had always had reservations about the war on drugs. He figured the drug dealers wouldn't go away as long as there was a market. And looking at this country's experience with Prohibition, "and how that created mobsters and criminal gangs," he figured that legalizing drugs made more sense. When selling and drinking booze became legal in this country again, he said, "you had so much more control of it. You had supporting laws that managed the use of alcohol."

Watkins was first exposed to drugs in Vietnam. He didn't use them—he preferred alcohol—but he saw a lot of other guys getting high on marijuana and other drugs. Many of those men wound up in prison when they came home with addiction problems. "And in prison, you could always get whatever drugs you wanted. Heck, we arrested a mom one time who was putting a lip-lock on her son to pass him a balloon full of heroin. But most of the drugs came in through the guards. Drugs are packaged so small, it's almost impossible to keep them out. Think about that: If you can't keep drugs out of a maximum-security prison, you can't keep them out of schools or anywhere else."

Once drugs land someone in prison in Texas, he said, life's prospects get a lot dimmer. "We've got these minor players put in with professional criminals. If they weren't criminals going in they damn sure are when they get out. Imagine a system where we put people into a society that's really a training ground for criminals, then don't provide them with either schooling or treatment, then put them back on the streets where they came from. Do you really expect them to be reformed? Life doesn't work that way."

He wishes people wouldn't make the decision to use drugs. "But if they did use them, I wouldn't put them in prison. I'd rather see the money we spend on prisons going to give these kids the tools they need to make better choices."

Voices Opposing LEAP's Perspective

You might imagine that it would be easy to find law enforcement agencies and personnel who oppose LEAP's call for legalization and regulation as an alternative to the war on drugs. But neither the FBI nor the DEA would discuss the subject.

"Our job is to stop the flow of illegal drugs both at home and abroad, as well as to stop our citizens from wanting to use them, through education and prevention methods," said an ONDCP representative. "We will not discuss legalization or any organization which thinks that would be a solution."

Jack Cole wasn't surprised. "They're good soldiers," he said. "They're not allowed to question their commands. Our job is to simply have their commanders change their marching orders."

Mike Smithson, who runs LEAP's speakers bureau, said he's made more than 100 attempts to get law enforcement and drug policy officials to come out and debate LEAP, "and we've only been taken up on it five times. Policymakers generally say that debating us will lend us credence. We think they're just afraid. How can they defend a policy that is already being defended by every major drug dealer, cartel and drug-producing government worldwide?"

Woolridge says that on his entire ride from Los Angeles he's talked to only two officers who disagreed with LEAP's point of view. "One guy thought we'd destroy America if we legalized drugs. He was so angry when he couldn't find anything to write me a ticket for that he gave me the finger as he drove away. And there was a state trooper with 22 years on the job who told me to take off my shirt because it said 'Cops say legalize drugs,' and he didn't agree with that. I told him go make up his own shirt."

One person did agree to discuss his opposition to LEAP's stand was Sheriff John Cooke of Wells County in Colorado. Cooke is a member of a Rotary Club at which Howard Woolridge spoke. He was so taken aback by the idea of legalizing drugs that he demanded equal time and recently spoke to the Rotary Club himself.

"In my opinion, there are several reasons not to legalize drugs," Cooke told Fort Worth Weekly. First of all, when people say you're going to eliminate the black market, does that mean you're going to sell drugs to 12- and 15-year olds? Because if you don't, someone will. Law enforcement surely hasn't done a good job at keeping alcohol and cigarettes out of the hands of kids, so what makes them think they'll do any better with drugs? And if you don't sell drugs to them, there will be a black market created to sell to them. So I don't buy the end of the black market theory.

"Secondly, we already have social ills from the legal use of alcohol and tobacco. Why on earth would we want to turn other addictive substances loose on the public?

"Thirdly, these LEAP folks want to throw in the towel, say we've lost the drug war. But the thing is that I think we're winning the war on drugs. I think drug use is down. I think if we keep at it, we will win.

"Then there's the question of use. Right now, I believe that the threat of the hammer of law enforcement is keeping a great many people from doing drugs. The threat of prison time is a big hammer. I think if we legalized you'd see the number of people doing drugs in this country skyrocket. I believe we'd have a drug-dependent society . . . and I don't want to see America as a drug-dependent country."

Michael Gilbert, director of the Department of Criminal Justice at the University of Texas at San Antonio, said he doubted that there would be any sizeable black market aimed at teens if drugs were legalized. Gilbert is a LEAP member who worked in prisons—including Leavenworth—and with Justice Department agencies for more than 20 years.

"The reason there's so much money in the black market is not because of the small portion of destabilized street addicts we have, or even kids experimenting with drugs. It's because you have long-time productive millions [of people] who regularly purchase small quantities of the drugs of their choice but they don't use them in a way that becomes destructive to their lives," he said. "They're working, paying their taxes and so forth. The real money is from the enormous number of middle-class people who use drugs. So while you might still have a small market of teens purchasing drugs, it wouldn't be large enough to fund criminal enterprises as it does today."

While few policy makers will discuss the benefits of drug prohibition, several well-known former policy makers have come out against it. Among them are Nobel Prize-winning economist Milton Friedman, a former member of President Reagan's Economic Advisory Board; former Secretary of State (under Ronald Reagan) George P. Shultz; former governor of New Mexico Gary Johnson; former Baltimore Mayor Kurt Schmoke; and U.S. Rep. Dennis Kucinich of Ohio, a former presidential candidate.

Benefits of the LEAP Solution

None of the LEAP members interviewed for this article believes abusing drugs is a good choice. But that's different, they say, from the legal system further ruining people's lives because of that bad choice. They also figure that, like tattoos, hair color decisions, and bad marriages, drug use is a poor choice that society should only care about when it hurts other people. In town, running around in your yard naked and screaming at 4 a.m. breaks the social contract. On a ranch where no one else can see or hear, few people would care about it. Likewise, LEAP members figure, if you can do drugs and not break the social contract, go ahead. And in fact, the federal government figures that 72 percent of chronic drug users continue to function well in society, without harming others.

Even considering the harm that drugs can cause, however, LEAP members believe that the war on drugs is even more harmful. Legalizing drugs, on the other hand, would take profits out of the hands of criminals and hugely reduce the need for people to commit crime to pay for drugs, they say. Regulation would take drug manufacture out of the hands of bathtub chemists and put it into the hands of real chemists, eliminating many of the deaths from bad drugs—much like the end of Prohibition did for deaths from homemade booze. HIV and hepatitis C, rampant among needle-sharing junkies, could be significantly reduced with the availability of clean needles, reducing a major health-care burden for the country.

"Don't forget my favorite," Woolridge said. "If as Bush said, drug money funds terrorists, [then] legalizing drugs would take half a billion dollars a day out of Afghanistan alone, much of which is going to al Qaeda to buy weapons to be used to kill our boys. We could eliminate that overnight."

Legalization, in fact, would probably not increase drug use long-term, many believe—especially since nearly half the population has already tried it. "In all likelihood," Watkins said, "you would see a spike in use as we did with the end of alcohol prohibition. But that normalized pretty quickly, and would probably be the same with drugs. There would be a period of experimentation that would level out, and we'd be left with all the benefits and none of the negatives."

It was Sunday afternoon and Howard Woolridge and Misty were still in upstate New York, having made it from Utica to a ghetto in Schenectady. Woolridge was back on the phone again, when a woman approached him.

"What do you mean cops say legalize drugs?" she could be heard asking.

"Just that. Let's legalize drugs, take them off the street corner."

"What kind of drugs?"

"Heroin, crack, methamphetamine, anything you can think of."

"Are you crazy? I don't want my kids doing those drugs!"

"Neither do I," he told her. "They're no good. But that doesn't keep them from being sold on the corner in this very neighborhood, does it? I'd legalize them and get them into pharmacies. Keep your kids from being shot while walking down the street."

There was a pause and then she laughed. "I never thought of it that way before. You're making me think now."

POSTSCRIPT

Should Laws Against Drug Use Remain Restrictive?

Kleber and Califano assert that utilizing the criminal justice system to maintain the illegal nature of drugs is necessary to keep society free of the detrimental effects of drugs. Loosening drug laws is unwise and dangerous. They argue that international control efforts, interdiction, and domestic law enforcement are effective and that many problems associated with drug use are mitigated by drug regulation policies. They maintain that restrictive drug laws are a feasible and desirable means of dealing with the drug crisis.

Gorman charges that restrictive drug laws are highly destructive and discriminatory. He professes that if drug laws remain stringent, the result would be more drug users in prison and that drug abusers and addicts would engage in more criminal activity. Also, there is the possibility that more drug-related social problems would occur. Gorman concludes that society cannot afford to retain its intransigent position on drug legalization. The potential risks of the current federal policies on drug criminalization outweigh any potential benefits. Society suffers from harsh drug laws, says Gorman, by losing many of its civil liberties.

Proponents for less restrictive drug laws argue that such laws have not worked and that the drug battle has been lost. They believe that drug-related problems would diminish if more tolerant policies were implemented. Citing the legal drugs alcohol and tobacco as examples, legalization opponents argue that less restrictive drug laws would not decrease profits from the sale of drugs (the profits from cigarettes and alcohol are incredibly high). Moreover, opponents argue, relaxing drug laws does not make problems associated with drugs disappear (alcohol and tobacco have extremely high addiction rates as well as a myriad of other problems associated with their use).

Many European countries, such as the Netherlands and Switzerland, have a system of legalized drugs, and most have far lower addiction rates and lower incidences of drug-related violence and crime than the United States. These countries make a distinction between soft drugs (those identified as less harmful) and hard drugs (those with serious consequences). However, would the outcomes of less restrictive laws in the United States be the same as in Europe? Relaxed drug laws in the United States could still be a tremendous risk because its drug problems could escalate and reimposing strict drug laws would be difficult. This was the case with Prohibition in the 1920s, which, in changing the status of alcohol from legal to illegal, produced numerous crime- and alcohol-related problems.

Many good articles debate the pros and cons of this issue. These include "Who's Using and Who's Doing Time: Incarceration, the War on Drugs, and

Public Health," by Lisa Moore and Amy Elkavich (*American Journal of Public Health*, September 2008); "Too Dangerous Not to Regulate," by Peter Moskos (*U.S. News and World Report*, August 4, 2008); "Reorienting U.S. Drug Policy," by Jonathon Caulkins and Peter Reuter (*Issues in Science and Technology*, Fall 2006); "No Surrender: The Drug War Saves Lives," by John Walters (*National Review*, September 27, 2004), the current director of the Office of National Drug Control Policy; "Lighting Up in Amsterdam," by John Tierney (*New York Times*, August 26, 2006); "What Drug Policies Cost: Estimating Government Drug Policy Expenditures," by Peter Reuter (*Addiction*, March 2006); "An Effective Drug Policy to Protect America's Youth and Communities," by Asa Hutchinson (*Fordham Urban Law Journal*, January 2003); and "The War at Home: Our Jails Overflow with Nonviolent Drug Offenders. Have We Reached the Point Where the Drug War Causes More Harm Than the Drugs Themselves?" by Sanho Tree (*Sojourners*, May–June 2003).

ISSUE 18

Are We Headed Toward
a Nuclear 9/11?

YES: Brian Michael Jenkins, from "Terrorists Can Think Strategically: Lessons Learned from the Mumbai Attacks," Rand Corporation (January 2009)

NO: Graham Allison, from "Time to Bury a Dangerous Legacy—
Part I," *YaleGlobal Online* (March 14, 2008)

ISSUE SUMMARY

YES: Brian Michael Jenkins, senior advisor to the President of the
Rand Corporation, in testimony before the U.S. Senate Committee
on Homeland Security and Governmental Affairs, posited that a
team of terrorists could be inserted into the United States and carry
out a Mumbai-style attack, as terrorism has "increasingly become
an effective strategic weapon."

NO: Graham Allison, Harvard professor and director of the Belfer
Center for Science and International Affairs, affirms that we are
not likely to experience a nuclear 9/11 because "nuclear terrorism
is preventable by a feasible, affordable agenda of actions that . . .
would shrink the risk of nuclear terrorism to nearly zero."

$\mathbf{S}$ince the terrorist attacks of September 11, 2001, much has been written
about the specter of nuclear terrorism and the releasing of a dirty bomb (one
loaded with radioactive material) in an urban/civilian setting. The events of
September 11 have all but ensured the world's preoccupation with such an
event for the foreseeable future. Indeed, the arrest of a U.S. man that was
suspected of having dirty bomb materials indicates that such plans may indeed
be in the works between Al Qaeda and other terrorist cells. When this horror
is combined with the availability of elements of nuclear-related material in
places like the states of the former Soviet Union, Pakistan, India, Iraq, Iran,
North Korea, and many other states, one can envision a variety of sobering
scenarios.

Hollywood feeds these views with such films as *The Sum of All Fears* and
The Peacemaker, in which nuclear terrorism is portrayed as all too easy to carry

out and likely to occur. It is difficult in such environments to separate fact from fiction and to ascertain objectively the probabilities of such events. So many factors go into a successful initiative in this area. One must find a committed cadre of terrorists, sufficient financial backing, technological know-how, intense security and secrecy, the means of delivery, and many other variables, including luck. In truth, such acts may have already been advanced and thwarted by governments, security services, or terrorist mistakes and incompetence.

We do not know, and we may never know.

Regional and ethnic conflicts of a particularly savage nature in places like Chechnya, Kashmir, Colombia, and Afghanistan help to fuel fears that adequately financed zealots will see in nuclear weapons a swift and catastrophic answer to their demands and angers. Osama bin Laden's contribution to worldwide terrorism has been the success of money over security and the realization that particularly destructive acts with high levels of coordination can be "successful." This will undoubtedly encourage others with similar ambitions against real or perceived enemies.

Conversely, many argue that fear of the terrorist threat has left us imagining that which is not likely. They point to a myriad of roadblocks to terrorist groups' obtaining all of the elements necessary for a nuclear or dirty bomb. They cite technological impediments, monetary issues, lack of sophistication, and inability to deliver. They also cite governments' universal desire to prevent such actions. Even critics of former Iraqi leader Saddam Hussein have argued that were he to develop such weapons, he would not deliver them to terrorist groups nor would he use them except in the most dire of circumstances, such as his own regime's survival. They argue that the threat is overblown and, in some cases, merely used to justify increased security and the restriction of civil liberties.

The following selections reflect the debate about a nuclear 9/11. Jenkins focuses on the ability and resourcefulness of the terrorists and argues that recent events indicate a real ability to carry out such an attack. Allison focuses on the targets, the United States and the West, and insists that a coordinated strategy can stop such an event.

YES

Brian Michael Jenkins

Terrorists Can Think Strategically

Lessons Learned from the Mumbai Attacks

Mr. Chairman and Members of the Committee, it is an honor to appear before you today. The Mumbai attack was still ongoing when RAND initiated an analysis to determine what lessons might be learned from it. This analysis, part of RAND's continuing research on terrorism and homeland security, was documented in a report I co-authored along with other RAND analysts. Specifically, I contributed the sections on the terrorists' strategic motives and the execution of the attack.

We relied on both informed official sources and media reporting. My analysis benefited greatly from the detailed descriptions of the attack provided by officers from the New York Police Department, who were on the scene and whose reports were shared with law enforcement and others in the United States.

Copies of our report have been made available to members of the Committee. Additional copies are available here, and the report is also on RAND's website. For convenience, I have appended the key findings to my testimony. The following observations derive from this report and other relevant research.

Terrorism has increasingly become an effective strategic weapon. Earlier generations of terrorists seldom thought beyond the barrels of their guns. In contrast, the masterminds of the Mumbai terrorist attacks displayed sophisticated strategic thinking in their choice of targets and their efforts to achieve multiple objectives. They were able to capture and hold international attention. They sought to exacerbate communal tensions in India and provoke a crisis between India and Pakistan, thereby persuading Pakistan to redeploy troops to its frontier with India, which in turn would take pressure off of the Taliban, al Qaeda, and other groups operating along the Afghan frontier. All terrorist attacks are recruiting posters. The Mumbai attackers established their terrorist credentials and now rival al Qaeda in reputation.

Al Qaeda is not the only galaxy in the jihadist universe—new contenders have signed on to al Qaeda's ideology of global terror. Even as we have degraded al Qaeda's operational capabilities, the idea of a violent global jihad has spread from North Africa to South Asia. The Mumbai attack foreshadows

From *Testimony Series*, January 2009, pp. 1–4. Copyright © 2009 by Rand Corporation. Reprinted by permission via Copyright Clearance Center.

a continuing terrorist campaign in India. More broadly, it suggests that the global struggle against the jihadists is far from over.

Terrorists can innovate tactically to obviate existing security measures and confuse authorities.   Authorities are obliged to prevent the recurrence of the most recent attack, while knowing that other terrorists will analyze the security in place, devise new tactics, and do the unexpected. The Mumbai attackers did not plant bombs in crowded train coaches, as in the 2006 Mumbai terrorist attack. Instead, gunmen attacked the train station. They did not detonate car bombs as in the 1993 Mumbai attacks or the more recent terrorist attacks on hotels in Indonesia, Egypt, Jordan and Pakistan. They seized control of hotels where they started fires. Multiple attacks at different locations prevented authorities from developing an overall assessment of the situation.

Once again, terrorists have demonstrated that with simple tactics and low-tech weapons, they can produce vastly disproportionate results.   The Mumbai attack was sequential, highly mobile, and a departure from the now common suicide bombings, but the tactics were simple—armed assaults, carjackings, drive-by shootings, building takeovers, barricade and hostage situations. The attack was carried out by ten men armed with easily obtained assault weapons, semi-automatic pistols, hand grenades, and simple improvised explosive devices—little more than the arsenal of an infantryman in the 1940s—along with 21st century cell phones, BlackBerries, and GPS locators.

Terrorists will continue to focus on soft targets that offer high body counts and that have iconic value.   Nationally and internationally recognized venues that offer ease of access, certainty of tactical success, and the opportunity to kill in quantity will guide target selection. Public spaces are inherently difficult to protect. Major investments in target hardening make sense for government only when these provide a net security benefit, that is, when they do not merely displace the risk to another equally lucrative and accessible target.

Terrorists view public surface transportation as a killing field.   One of the two-man terrorist teams went to Mumbai's main train station and opened fire on commuters. While the attacks on the other targets were theoretically aimed at killing foreigners, the attack at the train station was aimed solely at slaughter. It accounted for more than a third of the total deaths.

This underscores a trend that should be a priority issue in the United States. Public surface transportation offers terrorists easily accessible, dense populations in confined environments—ideal killing zones for gunmen or improvised explosive devices, which remain the most common form of attack. According to analysis by the Mineta Transportation Institute's National Transportation Security Center, two-thirds of all terrorist attacks on surface transportation were intended to kill; 37 percent resulted in fatalities (compared with between 20 and 25 percent of terrorist attacks overall); 75 percent of the fatal attacks involved multiple fatalities; and 28 percent of those involved 10 or more fatalities.

Terrorist attacks on flagship hotels are increasing in number, in total casualties, and in casualties per incident.   This trend places increasing demands on hotel security. However, while terrorist attacks are spectacular, they are statistically rare in comparison to ordinary violent crime. In the past forty years, fewer than five hundred hotel guests in the entire world have been killed by terrorists, out of a total global hotel guest population at any time of nearly ten million.

Pakistan's principal defense against external pressure is not its nuclear arsenal, but its own political fragility—its government's less-than-full cooperation is preferable to the country's collapse and descent into chaos.   Pakistan continues to play a prominent and problematic role in the overlapping armed conflicts and terrorist campaigns in India, Afghanistan, and Pakistan itself. Al Qaeda, the Taliban, Lashkar-e-Taiba and other insurgent and terrorist groups find sanctuary in Pakistan's turbulent tribal areas. Historically, some of them have drawn on support from the Pakistan government itself. While the Government of Pakistan has been helpful in capturing some key terrorist operatives, Pakistan is accused of protecting others. And it has been understandably reluctant to use military force against its own citizens in the remote tribal areas where these groups reside. When it has used military force, government forces have not fared well. Public sentiment imposes further constraints. Many Pakistanis regard India and the United States, not al Qaeda or the Taliban, as greater threats to Pakistan's national security. This was perceived as an obstacle to U.S. counterterrorist efforts even before 9/11.

The success of the Mumbai attackers in paralyzing a large city and commanding the attention of the world's news media for nearly three days will encourage similar operations in the future.   Terrorists will continue to effectively embed themselves among civilians, taking hostages and using them as human shields to impede responders and maximize collateral casualties. We should expect to see more of this tactic.

Could a Mumbai-style attack happen in the United States?   It could. The difference lies in planning and scale. Assembling and training a ten-man team of suicidal attackers seems far beyond the capabilities of the conspirators identified in any of the local terrorist plots discovered in this country since 9/11. We have no evidence of that level of dedication or planning skills.

However, we have seen lone gunmen and pairs of shooters, motivated by mental illness or political cause, run amok, determined to kill in quantity. The Long Island Railroad, Empire State Building, LAX, Virginia Tech, and Columbine cases come to mind. In 1955, four Puerto Rican separatists opened fire in a then unguarded Capitol Building, wounding five members of Congress. Firearms are readily available in the United States. And some of the perpetrators of the attacks mentioned above planned for their attacks for months, while building their arsenals. Therefore, an attack on the ground, carried out by a small number of self-radicalized, homegrown terrorists armed with readily available weapons, perhaps causing scores of casualties, while still far beyond what we have seen in the terrorist plots uncovered thus far, is not inconceivable.

Could a team of terrorists, recruited and trained abroad as the Mumbai attackers were, be inserted into the United States, perhaps on a U.S.-registered fishing vessel or pleasure boat, to carry out a Mumbai-style attack? Although our intelligence has greatly improved, the answer again must be a qualified yes. It could conceivably happen here, although I would expect our police response to be much swifter and more effective than we saw in Mumbai.

Graham Allison  **NO**

Time to Bury a Dangerous Legacy–Part I

One month after the terrorist assault on the World Trade Center and the Pentagon, on October 11, 2001, President George W. Bush faced a more terrifying prospect. At that morning's presidential daily intelligence briefing, George Tenet, the director of central intelligence, informed the president that a CIA agent codenamed "Dragonfire" had reported that Al Qaeda terrorists possessed a 10-kiloton nuclear bomb, evidently stolen from the Russian arsenal. According to Dragonfire, this nuclear weapon was in New York City.

The government dispatched a top-secret nuclear emergency support team to the city. Under a cloak of secrecy that excluded even Mayor Rudolph Giuliani, these nuclear ninjas searched for the bomb. On a normal workday, half a million people crowd the area within a half-mile radius of Times Square. A noon detonation in Midtown Manhattan would kill them all instantly. Hundreds of thousands of others would die from collapsing buildings, fire and fallout in the hours thereafter. The electromagnetic pulse generated by the blast would fry cell phones and other electronic communication. The wounded would overwhelm hospitals and emergency services. Firemen would fight an uncontrolled ring of fires for days afterward.

In the hours that followed, Condoleezza Rice, then national security adviser, analyzed what strategists call the "problem from hell." Unlike the Cold War, when the US and the Soviet Union knew that an attack against the other would elicit a retaliatory strike or greater measure, Al Qaeda—with no return address—had no such fear of reprisal. Even if the president were prepared to negotiate, Al Qaeda has no phone number to call.

Concerned that Al Qaeda could have smuggled a nuclear weapon into Washington as well, the president ordered Vice President Dick Cheney to leave the capital for an "undisclosed location," where he would remain for weeks to follow—standard procedure to ensure "continuity of government" in case of a decapitation strike against US political leadership. Several hundred federal employees from more than a dozen government agencies joined the vice president at this secret site, the core of an alternative government that would seek to cope in the aftermath of a nuclear explosion that destroyed Washington.

Six months earlier the CIA's Counterterrorism Center had picked up chatter in Al Qaeda channels about an "American Hiroshima." The CIA knew that Osama bin Laden's fascination with nuclear weapons went back at least to

From *YaleGlobal Online*, March 14, 2008. Copyright © 2008 by Yale Center for the Study of Globalization. Reprinted by permission of YaleGlobal Online. www.yaleglobal.yale.edu

1992, when he attempted to buy highly enriched uranium from South Africa. Al Qaeda operatives were alleged to have negotiated with Chechen separatists in Russia to buy a nuclear warhead, which the Chechen warlord Shamil Basayev claimed to have acquired from Russian arsenals. The CIA's special task force on Al Qaeda had noted the terrorist group's emphasis on thorough planning, intensive training and repetition of successful tactics. The task force highlighted Al Qaeda's preference for symbolic targets and spectacular attacks.

As CIA analysts examined Dragonfire's report and compared it with other bits of information, they noted that the September attack on the World Trade Center had set the bar higher for future terrorist attacks. Psychologically, a nuclear attack would stagger the world's imagination. New York was, in the jargon of national-security experts, "target rich."

As it turned out, Dragonfire's report proved to be a false alarm. But the central takeaway from the case is this: The US government had no grounds in science or logic to dismiss this possibility, nor could it do so today.

There's no established methodology for assessing the probability of an unprecedented event that could have such catastrophic consequences. Nonetheless, in "Nuclear Terrorism" I state my considered judgment that if the US and other governments just keep doing what they are doing today, a nuclear terrorist attack in a major city is more likely than not by 2014.

Richard Garwin, a designer of the hydrogen bomb, whom Enrico Fermi once called, "the only true genius I had ever met," told Congress in March 2007 that he estimated a "20 percent per year probability of a nuclear explosion with American cities and European cities included." My Harvard colleague Matthew Bunn has created a model that estimates the probability of a nuclear terrorist attack over a 10-year period to be 29 percent—identical to the average estimate from a poll of security experts commissioned by Senator Richard Lugar in 2005.

Former Secretary of Defense William Perry has expressed his own view that my work may underestimate the risk. Warren Buffett, the world's most successful investor and legendary odds-maker in pricing insurance policies for unlikely but catastrophic events, concluded that nuclear terrorism is "inevitable." As he has stated: "I don't see any way that it won't happen."

The good news is that nuclear terrorism is preventable by a feasible, affordable agenda of actions that, if taken, would shrink the risk of nuclear terrorism to nearly zero. A global strategy to prevent this ultimate catastrophe can be organized under a Doctrine of Three No's: No loose nukes, no new nascent nukes, no new nuclear weapons. The first requires securing all nuclear weapons and weapons-usable material, on the fastest possible timetable, to a new "gold standard." The second does not allow for any new national capabilities to enrich uranium or reprocess plutonium. The third draws a line under the current eight and a half nuclear powers—the five members of the Security Council and India, Israel, Pakistan and North Korea—and says unambiguously: "Stop. No More."

The US cannot unilaterally sustain a successful strategy to prevent nuclear terrorism. Nor can the necessary actions simply be commanded, compelled or coerced. Instead, they require deep and steady international cooperation rooted in the recognition that nations share a common threat that requires a common strategy. A Global Alliance Against Nuclear Terrorism is therefore in order. The mission of this alliance should be to minimize the risk of nuclear terrorism by taking every action physically, technically and diplomatically possible to prevent nuclear weapons or materials from falling into the hands of terrorists.

Constructing such an alliance will require the US and other nuclear-weapons states to confront the question of a "fourth no": no nuclear weapons. While US or Russian possession of nuclear arsenals is not a major driver of Iran's nuclear ambitions, and while Osama bin Laden would not be less inter-ested in acquiring a nuclear weapon if the US eliminated its current arsenals, the proposition that nuclear weapons are necessary for the security of US and Russia but intolerably dangerous if acquired by Iran or South Africa is difficult to sell to nuclear have-nots.

The question of a categorical "fourth no" has come to the fore with the January 2007 opinion piece in the *Wall Street Journal* by George P. Shultz, William J. Perry, Henry A. Kissinger and Sam Nunn, calling upon the US and other states to act to realize their Non-Proliferation Treaty commitment and President Reagan's vision of "a world free of nuclear weapons." Towards that goal, the immediate agenda should be to devalue nuclear weapons and minimize their role in international affairs. This should begin with nuclear-weapons states pledging to the following principles: no new national enrichment, no nuclear tests, no first use of a nuclear bomb and no new nuclear weapons.

Faced with the possibility of an American Hiroshima, many are paralyzed by a combination of denial and fatalism. This is unwarranted. Through a combination of imagination, a clear agenda for action and fierce determination to pursue it, the countdown to a nuclear 9/11 can be stopped.

POSTSCRIPT

Are We Headed Toward a Nuclear 9/11?

There are many arguments to support the contention that nuclear and dirty bombs are hard to obtain, difficult to move and assemble, and even harder to deliver. There is also ample evidence to suggest that most, if not all, of the U.S. government's work is in one way or another designed to thwart such actions because of the enormous consequences were such acts to be carried out. These facts should make Americans rest easier and allay fears if only for reasons of probability.

However, Allison's contention that failure to assume the worst may prevent the thwarting of such terrorist designs is persuasive. Since September 11, it is clear that the world has entered a new phase of terrorist action and a new level of funding, sophistication, and motivation. It is dangerous for a nation to believe that because something is difficult it is unlikely to take place. The collapse of the USSR has unleashed a variety of forces, some positive and some more sinister and secretive. The enormous prices that radioactive material and nuclear devices can command on the black market make the likelihood of temptation strong and possibly irresistible.

If states are to err, perhaps they should err on the side of caution and preventive action rather than on reliance on the statistical probability that nuclear terrorism is unlikely. We may never see a nuclear terrorist act in this century, but it is statistically likely that the reason for this will not be lack of effort on the part of motivated terrorist groups.

Some important research and commentary on nuclear terrorism can be found in Elaine Landau, *Osama bin Laden: A War Against the West* (Twenty-First Century Books, 2002); Jan Lodal, *The Price of Dominance: The New Weapons of Mass Destruction and Their Challenge to American Leadership* (Council on Foreign Relations Press, 2001); Jessica Stern, *The Ultimate Terrorists* (Harvard University Press, 1999); Graham Allison, *Nuclear Terrorism: The Ultimate Preventable Catastrophe* (Times Books, 2004); Gavin Cameron, *Nuclear Terrorism: A Threat Assessment for the 21st Century* (St. Martin's Press, 1999); Charles D. Ferguson and William C. Potter, with Amy Sands . . . [et al.], *The Four Faces of Nuclear Terrorism* (Routledge, 2005); Robin M. Frost, *Nuclear Terrorism after 9/11* (Routledge for the International Institute for Strategic Studies, 2005); and Zbigniew Brzezinski, *The Choice: Global Domination or Global Leadership* (Basic Books, 2005).

Some recent general works on terrorism include Jonathan Barker, *The No-Nonsense Guide to Global Terrorism*, 2nd ed. (New Internationalist, 2008); Cornelia Beyer, *Violent Globalisms: Conflict in Response to Empire* (Ashgate, 2008); Michael Chandler and Rohan Gunaratna, *Countering Terrorism: Can We*

Meet the Threat of Global Violence? (Reaktion, 2007); Peter R. Neumann, *Old and New Terrorism: Late Modernity, Globalization and the Transformation of Political Violence* (Polity, 2009); John Robb, *Brave New War: The Next Stage of Terrorism and the End of Globalization* (John Wiley & Sons, 2007); Paul J. Smith, *The Terrorism Ahead: Confronting Transnational Violence in the Twenty-First Century* (M. E. Sharpe, 2008); and Ian Bellany, *Terrorism and Weapons of Mass Destruction: Responding to the Challenge* (Routledge, 2007).

United Nations Environment Program (UNEP)

The United Nations Environment Program (UNEP) Web site offers links to environmental topics of critical concern to sociologists. The site will direct you to useful databases and global resource information.

http://www.unep.ch

Worldwatch Institute Home Page

The Worldwatch Institute is dedicated to fostering the evolution of an environmentally sustainable society in which human needs are met without threatening the health of the natural environment. This site provides access to *World Watch* magazine and *State of the World 2000*.

http://www.worldwatch.org

William Davidson Institute

The William Davidson Institute at the University of Michigan Business School is dedicated to the understanding and promotion of economic transition. Consult this site for discussions of topics related to the changing global economy and the effects of globalization on society.

http://www.wdi.bus.umich.edu

World Future Society

The World Future Society is an educational and scientific organization for those interested in how social and technological developments are shaping the future.

http://www.wfs.org

Population Division: Department of Economic and Social Affairs

The Department of Economic and Social Affairs, Population Division, is responsible for monitoring and appraisal of the broad range of areas in the field of population.

http://www.un.org/esa/population/aboutpop.htm

The Future: Population/ Environment/Society

*T*he leading issues for the beginning of the twenty-first century include global warming, environmental decline, and globalization. The state of the environment and the effects of globalization produce strong arguments concerning what can be harmful or beneficial. Technology has increased enormously in the last 100 years, as have world-wide population growth, consumption, and new forms of pollution that threaten to undermine the world's fragile ecological support system. Although all nations have a stake in the health of the planet, many believe that none are doing enough to protect its health. Will technology itself be the key to controlling or accommodating the increase of population and consumption, along with the resulting increase in waste production? Perhaps so, but new policies will also be needed. Technology is driving the process of globalization, which can be seen as both good and bad. Those who support globalization theory state that globalization increases competition, production, wealth, and the peaceful integration of nations. However, not everyone agrees. This section explores what is occurring in our environment and in our current global economy.

- Are Declining Growth Rates Rather Than Rapid Population Growth Today's Major Global Population Problem?

- Is Humankind Dangerously Harming the Environment?

- Is Globalization Good for Humankind?

ISSUE 19

Are Declining Growth Rates Rather Than Rapid Population Growth Today's Major Global Population Problem?

YES: **Michael Meyer,** from "Birth Dearth," *Newsweek* (September 27, 2004)

NO: **Danielle Nierenberg and Mia MacDonald**, from "The Population Story . . . So Far," *World Watch* magazine (September/October 2004)

ISSUE SUMMARY

YES: Michael Meyer, a writer for *Newsweek International,* argues that the new global population threat is not world overpopulation but underpopulation in many countries. Declining birth rates will ultimately lead to declining population and increasing ratios of older people to younger people in many countries. This situation creates immense problems in supporting the elderly and maintaining a healthy economy.

NO: Danielle Nierenberg and Mia MacDonald counter those who fear negative consequences of stable or declining population. The worriers fail to notice the benefits of a stable population. Furthermore, the population decline thesis is overblown. The population of developed countries with healthy economies is likely to grow through immigration. Stable or declining population countries will only have to change some policies to avoid the anticipated serious problems.

Beginning in the late 1960s, demographers began to observe dramatic increases in population growth, particularly in the developing world. Some analysts feared terrible consequences. They warned of mass starvation of humans in the 1970s and 1980s due to overpopulation and advocated immediate action to limit population growth. By the mid-1970s, growth rates, particularly in the developing world, were such that the doubling of the world's population was predicted to occur in only a few decades. And indeed, as the last millennium was coming to an end, a billion people were added to the world's population in just 12 short years. Contrast this time frame with the fact that it had taken all of recorded history until 1830 for the planet to reach a population of 1 billion and 100 years for the second billion.

In the last decade of the millennium, however, something unforeseen happened. Population growth slowed, not only in the developed sector of the globe but also in the developing world. The UN Population Fund lowered its short-term and long-term projections. These recent trends have been surprising, as most observers had long believed that the built-in momentum of population growth in the last third of the twentieth century would have major impacts well into the new century. It turned out, however, that when people had the means to control their fertility, the birth rate dropped considerably. Now a new population debate is raging. One side says that further population growth is bad because of its impacts on the environment and the depleting of limited resources, and the other side worries about the economic crises that will be brought on by population declines. The anti-growth position fears that further population growth, though slower, will nevertheless increase starvation, deplete resources faster, accelerate global warming with possible catastrophic results, and badly damage the environment even to the point, possibly, of environmental collapse. The anti–population decline position fears that a high number of retirees per worker will reduce welfare, reduce innovation rates, increase deficits, cause crushing health care expenses, and other economic crises.

Michael Meyer describes how families in both the developed and developing worlds are choosing to have fewer children and chronicles what he believes to be an array of negative consequences associated with this population transition. Danielle Nierenberg and Mia MacDonald applaud the current demographic changes and argue that stable or declining population has many positive effects and manageable negative ones. They estimate that the optimal world population is about 2 billion. Much more than that is either unsustainable or must live constricted lives.

YES

Michael Meyer

Birth Dearth

Everyone knows there are too many people in the world. Whether we live in Lahore or Los Angeles, Shanghai or Sao Paulo, our lives are daily proof. We endure traffic gridlock, urban sprawl and environmental depredation. The evening news brings variations on Ramallah or Darfur—images of Third World famine, poverty, pestilence, war, global competition for jobs, and increasingly scarce natural resources.

Just last week the United Nations warned that many of the world's cities are becoming hopelessly overcrowded. Lagos alone will grow from 6.5 million people in 1995 to 16 million by 2015, a miasma of slums and decay where a fifth of all children will die before they are 5. At a conference in London, the UN Population Fund weighed in with a similarly bleak report: unless something dramatically changes, the world's 50 poorest countries will triple in size by 2050, to 1.7 billion people.

Yet this is not the full story. To the contrary, in fact. Across the globe, people are having fewer and fewer children. Fertility rates have dropped by half since 1972, from six children per woman to 2.9. And demographers say they're still falling, faster than ever. The world's population will continue to grow—from today's 6.4 billion to around 9 billion in 2050. But after that, it will go sharply into decline. Indeed, a phenomenon that we're destined to learn much more about—depopulation—has already begun in a number of countries. Welcome to the New Demography. It will change everything about our world, from the absolute size and power of nations to global economic growth to the quality of our lives.

This revolutionary transformation will be led not so much by developed nations as by the developing ones. Most of us are familiar with demographic trends in Europe, where birthrates have been declining for years. To reproduce itself, a society's women must each bear 2.1 children. Europe's fertility rates fall far short of that, according to the 2002 UN population report. France and Ireland, at 1.8, top Europe's childbearing charts. Italy and Spain, at 1.2, bring up the rear. In between are countries such as Germany, whose fertility rate of 1.4 is exactly Europe's average. What does that mean? If the UN figures are right, Germany could shed nearly a fifth of its 82.5 million people over the next 40 years—roughly the equivalent of all of east Germany, a loss of population not seen in Europe since the Thirty Years' War.

From *Newsweek*, vol. 144, issue 13, September 27, 2004, pp. 54–61. Copyright © 2004 by Newsweek, Inc. All rights reserved. Used by permission and protected by the Copyright Laws of the United States. The printing, copying, redistribution, or retransmission of the Material without express written permission via PARS International is prohibited.

And so it is across the Continent. Bulgaria will shrink by 38 percent, Romania by 27 percent, Estonia by 25 percent. "Parts of Eastern Europe, already sparsely populated, will just empty out," predicts Reiner Klingholz, director of the Berlin Institute for Population and Development. Russia is already losing close to 750,000 people yearly. (President Vladimir Putin calls it a "national crisis.") So is Western Europe, and that figure could grow to as much as 3 million a year by midcentury, if not more.

The surprise is how closely the less-developed world is following the same trajectory. In Asia it's well known that Japan will soon tip into population loss, if it hasn't already. With a fertility rate of 1.3 children per woman, the country stands to shed a quarter of its 127 million people over the next four decades, according to UN projections. But while the graying of Japan (average age: 42.3 years) has long been a staple of news headlines, what to make of China, whose fertility rate has declined from 5.8 in 1970 to 1.8 today, according to the UN? Chinese census data put the figure even lower, at 1.3. Coupled with increasing life spans, that means China's population will age as quickly in one generation as Europe's has over the past 100 years, reports the Center for Strategic and International Studies in Washington. With an expected median age of 44 in 2015, China will be older on average than the United States. By 2019 or soon after, its population will peak at 1.5 billion, then enter a steep decline. By midcentury, China could well lose 20 to 30 percent of its population every generation.

The picture is similar elsewhere in Asia, where birthrates are declining even in the absence of such stringent birth-control programs as China's. Indeed, it's happening despite often generous official incentives to procreate. The industrialized nations of Singapore, Hong Kong, Taiwan and South Korea all report subreplacement fertility, says Nicholas Eberstadt, a demographer at the American Enterprise Institute in Washington. To this list can be added Thailand, Burma, Australia and Sri Lanka, along with Cuba and many Caribbean nations, as well as Uruguay and Brazil. Mexico is aging so rapidly that within several decades it will not only stop growing but will have an older population than that of the United States. So much for the cliche of those Mexican youths swarming across the Rio Grande. "If these figures are accurate," says Eberstadt, "just about half of the world's population lives in subreplacement countries."

There are notable exceptions. In Europe, Albania and the outlier province of Kosovo are reproducing energetically. So are pockets of Asia: Mongolia, Pakistan and the Philippines. The United Nations projects that the Middle East will double in population over the next 20 years, growing from 326 million today to 649 million by 2050. Saudi Arabia has one of the highest fertility rates in the world, 5.7, after Palestinian territories at 5.9 and Yemen at 7.2. Yet there are surprises here, too. Tunisia has tipped below replacement. Lebanon and Iran are at the threshold. And though overall the region's population continues to grow, the increase is due mainly to lower infant mortality; fertility rates themselves are falling faster than in developed countries, indicating that over the coming decades the Middle East will age far more rapidly than other regions of the world. Birthrates in Africa remain high, and despite the AIDS epidemic its population is projected to keep growing. So is that of the United States.

We'll return to American exceptionalism, and what that might portend. But first, let's explore the causes of the birth dearth, as outlined in a pair of new books on the subject. "Never in the last 650 years, since the time of the Black Plague, have birth and fertility rates fallen so far, so fast, so low, for so long, in so many places," writes the sociologist Ben Wattenberg in "Fewer: How the New Demography of Depopulation Will Shape Our Future." Why? Wattenberg suggests that a variety of once independent trends have conjoined to produce a demographic tsunami. As the United Nations reported last week, people everywhere are leaving the countryside and moving to cities, which will be home to more than half the world's people by 2007. Once there, having a child becomes a cost rather than an asset. From 1970 to 2000, Nigeria's urban population climbed from 14 to 44 percent. South Korea went from 28 to 84 percent. So-called megacities, from Lagos to Mexico City, have exploded seemingly overnight. Birthrates have fallen in inverse correlation.

Other factors are at work. Increasing female literacy and enrollment in schools have tended to decrease fertility, as have divorce, abortion and the worldwide trend toward later marriage. Contraceptive use has risen dramatically over the past decade; according to UN data, 62 percent of married or "in union" women of reproductive age are now using some form of nonnatural birth control. In countries such as India, now the capital of global HIV, disease has become a factor. In Russia, the culprits include alcoholism, poor public health and industrial pollution that has whacked male sperm counts. Wealth discourages childbearing, as seen long ago in Europe and now in Asia. As Wattenberg puts it, "Capitalism is the best contraception."

The potential consequences of the population implosion are enormous. Consider the global economy, as Phillip Longman describes it in another recent book, "The Empty Cradle: How Falling Birthrates Threaten World Prosperity and What to Do About It." A population expert at the New America Foundation in Washington, he sees danger for global prosperity. Whether it's real estate or consumer spending, economic growth and population have always been closely linked. "There are people who cling to the hope that you can have a vibrant economy without a growing population, but mainstream economists are pessimistic," says Longman. You have only to look at Japan or Europe for a whiff of what the future might bring, he adds. In Italy, demographers forecast a 40 percent decline in the working-age population over the next four decades—accompanied by a commensurate drop in growth across the Continent, according to the European Commission. What happens when Europe's cohort of baby boomers begins to retire around 2020? Recent strikes and demonstrations in Germany, Italy, France and Austria over the most modest pension reforms are only the beginning of what promises to become a major sociological battle between Europe's older and younger generations.

That will be only a skirmish compared with the conflict brewing in China. There market reforms have removed the cradle-to-grave benefits of the planned economy, while the Communist Party hasn't constructed an adequate social safety net to take their place. Less than one-quarter of the population is covered by retirement pensions, according to CSIS. That puts the burden of elder care almost entirely on what is now a generation of only children. The one-child policy has led to the so-called 4-2-1 problem, in which each child will be potentially responsible for caring for two parents and four grandparents.

Incomes in China aren't rising fast enough to offset this burden. In some rural villages, so many young people have fled to the cities that there may be nobody left to look after the elders. And the aging population could soon start to dull China's competitive edge, which depends on a seemingly endless supply of cheap labor. After 2015, this labor pool will begin to dry up, says economist Hu Angang. China will have little choice but to adopt a very Western-sounding solution, he says: it will have to raise the education level of its work force and make it more productive. Whether it can is an open question. Either way, this much is certain: among Asia's emerging economic powers, China will be the first to grow old before it gets rich.

Equally deep dislocations are becoming apparent in Japan. Akihiko Matsutani, an economist and author of a recent best seller, "The Economy of a Shrinking Population," predicts that by 2009 Japan's economy will enter an era of "negative growth." By 2030, national income will have shrunk by 15 percent. Speculating about the future is always dicey, but economists pose troubling questions. Take the legendarily high savings that have long buoyed the Japanese economy and financed borrowing worldwide, especially by the United States. As an aging Japan draws down those assets in retirement, will U.S. and global interest rates rise? At home, will Japanese businesses find themselves competing for increasingly scarce investment capital? And just what will they be investing in, as the country's consumers grow older, and demand for the latest in hot new products cools off? What of the effect on national infrastructure? With less tax revenue in state coffers, Matsutani predicts, governments will increasingly be forced to skimp on or delay repairs to the nation's roads, bridges, rail lines and the like. "Life will become less convenient," he says. Spanking-clean Tokyo might come to look more like New York City in the 1970s, when many urban dwellers decamped for the suburbs (taking their taxes with them) and city fathers could no longer afford the municipal upkeep. Can Japanese cope? "They will have to," says Matsutani. "There's no alternative."

Demographic change magnifies all of a country's problems, social as well as economic. An overburdened welfare state? Aging makes it collapse. Tensions over immigration? Differing birthrates intensify anxieties, just as the need for imported labor rises—perhaps the critical issue for the Europe of tomorrow. A poor education system, with too many kids left behind? Better fix it, because a shrinking work force requires higher productivity and greater flexibility, reflected in a new need for continuing job training, career switches and the health care needed to keep workers working into old age.

In an ideal world, perhaps, the growing gulf between the world's wealthy but shrinking countries and its poor, growing ones would create an opportunity. Labor would flow from the overpopulated, resource-poor south to the depopulating north, where jobs would continue to be plentiful. Capital and remittance income from the rich nations would flow along the reverse path, benefiting all. Will it happen? Perhaps, but that presupposes considerable labor mobility. Considering the resistance Europeans display toward large-scale immigration from North Africa, or Japan's almost zero-immigration policy, it's hard to be optimistic. Yes, attitudes are changing. Only a decade ago, for instance, Europeans also spoke of zero immigration. Today they recognize the need and, in bits and pieces, are beginning to plan for it. But will it happen on the scale required?

A more probable scenario may be an intensification of existing tensions between peoples determined to preserve their beleaguered national identities on the one hand, and immigrant groups on the other seeking to escape overcrowding and lack of opportunity at home. For countries such as the Philippines—still growing, and whose educated work force looks likely to break out of low-status jobs as nannies and gardeners and move up the global professional ladder—this may be less of a problem. It will be vastly more serious for the tens of millions of Arab youths who make up a majority of the population in the Middle East and North Africa, at least half of whom are unemployed.

America is the wild card in this global equation. While Europe and much of Asia shrinks, the United States' indigenous population looks likely to stay relatively constant, with fertility rates hovering almost precisely at replacement levels. Add in heavy immigration, and you quickly see that America is the only modern nation that will continue to grow. Over the next 45 years the United States will gain 100 million people, Wattenberg estimates, while Europe loses roughly as many.

This does not mean that Americans will escape the coming demographic whammy. They, too, face the problems of an aging work force and its burdens. (The cost of Medicare and Social Security will rise from 4.3 percent of GDP in 2000 to 11.5 percent in 2030 and 21 percent in 2050, according to the Congressional Budget Office.) They, too, face the prospect of increasing ethnic tensions, as a flat white population and a dwindling black one become gradually smaller minorities in a growing multicultural sea. And in our interdependent era, the troubles of America's major trading partners—Europe and Japan—will quickly become its own. To cite one example, what becomes of the vaunted "China market," invested in so heavily by U.S. companies, if by 2050 China loses an estimated 35 percent of its workers and the aged consume an ever-greater share of income?

America's demographic "unipolarity" has profound security implications as well. Washington worries about terrorism and failing states. Yet the chaos of today's fragmented world is likely to prove small in comparison to what could come. For U.S. leaders, Longman in "The Empty Cradle" sketches an unsettling prospect. Though the United States may have few military competitors, the technologies by which it projects geopolitical power—from laser-guided missiles and stealth bombers to a huge military infrastructure—may gradually become too expensive for a country facing massively rising social entitlements in an era of slowing global economic growth. If the war on terrorism turns out to be the "generational struggle" that national security advisor Condoleezza Rice says it is, Longman concludes, then the United States might have difficulty paying for it.

None of this is writ, of course. Enlightened governments could help hold the line. France and the Netherlands have instituted family-friendly policies that help women combine work and motherhood, ranging from tax credits for kids to subsidized day care. Scandinavian countries have kept birthrates up with generous provisions for parental leave, health care and part-time employment. Still, similar programs offered by the shrinking city-state of Singapore—including a state-run dating service—have done little to reverse the birth dearth. Remember, too, that such prognoses have been wrong in the past. At the cusp of the postwar baby boom, demographers predicted a sharp fall in fertility and a global birth dearth. Yet even if this generation of seers turns out to be right, as seems likely, not all is bad. Environmentally, a smaller world is almost certainly a better world, whether in terms of cleaner air or, say, the return of wolves and rare flora to abandoned stretches of the East German countryside. And while people are living longer, they are also living healthier—at least in the developed world. That means they can (and probably should) work more years before retirement.

Yes, a younger generation will have to shoulder the burden of paying for their elders. But there will be compensations. As populations shrink, says economist Matsutani, national incomes may drop—but not necessarily per capita incomes. And in this realm of uncertainty, one mundane thing is probably sure: real-estate prices will fall. That will hurt seniors whose nest eggs are tied up in their homes, but it will be a boon to youngsters of the future. Who knows? Maybe the added space and cheap living will inspire them to, well, do whatever it takes to make more babies. Thus the cycle of life will restore its balance. . . .

**Danielle Nierenberg and
Mia MacDonald**

 **NO**

The Population Story . . . So Far

Forty years ago, the world's women bore an average of six children each. Today, that number is just below three. In 1960, 10–15 percent of married couples in developing countries used a modern method of contraception; now, 60 percent do.

To a considerable extent, these simple facts sum up the change in the Earth's human population prospects, then and now. In the mid-1960s, it was not uncommon to think about the human population as a time bomb. In 1971, population biologist Paul Ehrlich estimated that if human numbers kept increasing at the high rates of the time, by around 2900 the planet would be teeming with sixty million billion people (that's 60,000,000,000,000,000). But the rate of population rise actually peaked in the 1960s and demographers expect a leveling-off of human numbers this century.

Every couple of years the United Nations Population Division issues projections of human population growth to 2050. In 2002, UN demographers predicted a somewhat different picture of human population growth to mid-century than what the "population bombers" thought likely a generation ago. World population, growing by 76 million people every year (about 240,000 people per day), will pass 6.4 billion this year. The latest UN mid-range estimate says there will be about 8.9 billion people on Earth by 2050. And, according to this new scenario, total population will begin to shrink over the next hundred years.

These numbers are leading some people to say that the population bomb has been defused. A few nations, such as Italy and Japan, are even worried that birth rates are too low and that their graying populations will be a drain on the economy. (Some studies suggest that China, the world's most populous country, may also "need" more people to help support the hundreds of millions who will retire in coming decades.)

We're not out of the woods yet. While the annual rate of population growth has decreased since 1970—from about 2 percent to 1.3 percent today—*the rate is applied to a much larger population* than ever before, meaning that the added yearly increments to the population are also much larger. These numbers show that the largest generation in history has arrived: 1.2 billion people are between 10 and 19. In large measure, it will be their choices—those they have, and those they make—that determine where the global population meter rests by mid-century.

From *World Watch*, September/October 2004, pp. 14–17. Copyright © 2004 by Worldwatch Institute. Reprinted by permission. www.worldwatch.org

Population × Consumption

Potential for catastrophe persists. In many places, population growth is slowly smoldering but could turn into a fast burn. Countries as diverse as Ethiopia, the Democratic Republic of Congo, and Pakistan are poised to more than double their size by 2050 even as supplies of water, forests, and food crops are already showing signs of strain and other species are being squeezed into smaller and smaller ranges. Arid Yemen will likely see its population quadruple to 80 million by 2050. The UN estimates that populations in the world's 48 least-developed countries could triple by 2050. And if the world's women have, on average, a half a child more than the UN predicts, global population could grow to 10.6 billion by mid-century.

But it is a mistake to think that population growth is only a problem for developing countries. While consumption levels need to increase among the 2.8 billion people who now live on less than $2 a day, high rates of population growth combined with high levels of consumption in rich countries are taking a heavy toll on the Earth's natural resources:

- Carbon dioxide levels today are 18 percent higher than in 1960 and an estimated 31 percent higher than they were at the onset of the Industrial Revolution in 1750.
- Half the world's original forest cover is gone and another 30 percent is degraded or fragmented.
- Industrial fleets have fished out at least 90 percent of all large ocean predators—tuna, marlin, swordfish, cod, halibut, skate, and flounder—in just the past 50 years, according to a study in *Nature* in 2003.
- An estimated 10–20 percent of the world's cropland, and more than 70 percent of the world's rangelands, are degraded.

As global consumption of oil, meat, electricity, paper products, and a host of consumer goods rises, the impact of population numbers takes on a new relevance. Although each new person increases total demands on the Earth's resources, the size of each person's "ecological footprint"—the biologically productive area required to support that person—varies hugely from one to another. The largest ecofootprints belong to those in the industrialized world.

Further, new demographic trends can have significant impacts as well. Since 1970, the number of people living together in one household has declined worldwide, as incomes have risen, urbanization has accelerated and families have gotten smaller. With fewer people sharing energy, appliances, and furnishings, consumption actually rises. A one-person household in the United States uses about 17 percent *more* energy per person than a two-person home.

And while some nations are getting nervous about declining birth rates, for most of the world the end of population growth is anything but imminent. Although fertility rates are ratcheting down, this trajectory is not guaranteed. Projections of slower population growth assume that more couples will be able to choose to have smaller families, and that investment in reproductive health keeps pace with rising demand. But along the route to the eventual leveling-off of global population, plateaus are possible. And smaller families are not guaranteed in countries where government resources are strained or where health care, education, and women's rights are low on the list of priorities.

In the West African country of Niger, for example, the availability of family planning and reproductive health services has declined, while birth rates have increased. According to a recent report by the World Bank, the average woman in Niger will give birth to eight children in her lifetime, up from seven in 1998 and more than women in any other nation. Niger is already bulging with young people; 50 percent of the population is under age 15 and 70 percent is under 25.

Biology ≠ Destiny

A series of global conferences in the 1990s—spanning the Rio Earth Summit in 1992, the Cairo population conference (1994), the Beijing women's conference (1995), and the UN's Millennium Summit in 2000—put issues of environment, development, poverty, and women's rights on the global policy table. As a result, discussions of the relationship between growing human numbers and the Earth's ability to provide are increasingly framed by the realities of gender relations. It is now generally agreed that while enabling larger numbers of women and men to use modern methods of family planning is essential, it is not sufficient. Expanding the choices, capacities, and agency of women has become a central thread in the population story. Consumption—what we need and what we want—is, too.

Many studies have shown that women with more education have smaller, healthier families, and that their children have a better chance of making it out of poverty. Likewise, wealthier women and those with the right to make decisions about their lives and bodies also have fewer children. And women who have the choice to delay marriage and childbearing past their teens tend to have fewer children than those women—and there are millions of them still—who marry before they've completed the transition from adolescence. Equalizing relations between women and men is also a social good: not only is it just, but a recent World Bank report found that in developing countries where gender equality lags, efforts to combat poverty and increase economic growth lag, too.

Yet women's rights and voices remain suppressed or muted throughout the world. Over 100 million girls will be married before their 18th birthdays in the next decade, some as young as 8 or 9. Early childbearing is the leading cause of death and disability for women between the ages of 15 and 19 in developing countries. At least 350 million women still lack access to a full range of contraceptive methods, 10 years after the Cairo conference yielded a 20-year plan to balance the world's people with its resources. Demand for services will increase an estimated 40 percent by 2025.

The assault of HIV/AIDS is also increasingly hurting women: more than 18 million women are living with HIV/AIDS, and in 2003 women's rate of infection for the first time equaled men's. In the region hardest hit, sub-Saharan Africa, 60 percent of adults living with HIV are women. Two-thirds of the world's

876 million illiterates are women and a majority of the 115 million children not attending grade school are girls. In no country in the world are women judged to have political, economic, and social power equal to that of men.

Even in the United States, women's reproductive rights are increasingly constrained by the growing number of restrictions and conditions on choice imposed by state and federal laws. Like the U.S. lifestyle, the current Administration's blinkered view of sexuality has gone global. The United States has withheld $34 million from the UN Population Fund (UNFPA) every year of the Bush Administration due to a dispute over abortion. And the "global gag rule," a relic of the Reagan presidency reimposed by President Bush, binds U.S. population assistance by making taboo any discussion of abortion in reproductive health clinics, even in countries where it is legal.

The impacts reach more deeply than the rhetoric: due to the loss of U.S. population funds, reproductive health services have been scaled back or eliminated in some of the world's poorest countries, precisely where fertility rates are highest and women's access to family planning most tenuous. In Kenya, for instance, the two main providers of reproductive health services refused to sign a pledge to enforce the gag rule, with the result that they lost funds and closed five family planning clinics, eliminating women's access to maternal health care, contraception, and voluntary counseling and testing for HIV/AIDS. In Ethiopia, where only 6 percent of women use modern methods of contraception, the gag rule has cut a wide swath: clinics have reduced services, laid off staff and curtailed community health programs; many have suffered shortages of contraceptive supplies.

Need ↑ Funds ↓

A recent study by UNFPA and the Alan Guttmacher Institute estimated that meeting women's current unmet need for contraception would prevent each year:

- 23 million unplanned births;
- 22 million induced abortions;
- 1.4 million infant deaths;
- 142,000 pregnancy related-deaths (including 53,000 from unsafe abortions); and
- 505,000 children losing their mothers due to pregnancy-related causes.

The non-medical benefits are not quantified but are considerable: greater self-esteem and decision-making power for women; higher productivity and income; increased health, nutrition, and education expenditures on each child; higher savings and investment rates; and increased equality between women and men. We know this from experience: recent research in the United States, for example, ascribes the large numbers of women entering law, medical, and other professional training programs in the 1970s to the expanded choices afforded by the wide availability of the Pill.

Despite these benefits, vast needs go unmet as the Cairo action plan remains underfunded. The United States is not the only culprit. UNFPA reports that donor funds for a basic package of reproductive health services and population data and policy work totaled about $3.1 billion in 2003—$2.6 billion less than the level agreed to in the ICPD Program. Developing country domestic resources were estimated at $11.7 billion, a major portion of which is spent by just a handful of large countries. A number of countries, particularly the poorest, rely heavily on donor funds to provide services for family planning, reproductive health, and HIV/AIDS, and to build data sets and craft needed policies.

A year from now, donors will be expected to be contributing $6.1 billion annually, $3 billion more than what has already been spent. "A world that spends $800 billion to $1 trillion each year on the military can afford the equivalent of slightly more than one day's military spending to close Cairo's $3 billion external funding gap to save and improve the lives of millions of women and families in developing countries," says UNFPA's executive director, Thoraya Obaid. But as the world's priorities lie in other arenas, it is looking increasingly unlikely that the Cairo targets—despite their modest price tag in a world where the bill for a war can top $100 billion—will be met.

But it isn't only poor people in developing countries who will determine whether the more dire population scenarios pass from speculation to reality. Family size has declined in most wealthy nations, but the U.S. population grew by 32.7 million people (13.1 percent) during the 1990s, the largest number in any 10-year period in U.S. history. At about 280 million people, the United States is now the third most populous nation in the world and its population is expected to reach 400 million by 2050. A recent study suggests that if every person alive today consumed at the rate of an average person in the United States, three more planets would be required to fulfill these demands.

Whether or not birth rates continue to fall, consumption levels and patterns (affluence), coupled with technology, take on new importance. The global consumer class—around 1.7 billion people, or more than a quarter of humanity—is growing rapidly. These people are collectively responsible for the vast majority of meat-eating, paper use, car driving, and energy consumption on the planet, as well as the resulting impact of these activities on its natural resources. As populations surge in developing countries and the world becomes increasingly globalized, more and more people have access to, and the means to acquire, a greater diversity of products and services than ever before.

It is the combined effect of human numbers and human consumption that creates such potent flash-points. Decisions about sexuality and lifestyle are among the most deeply personal and political decisions societies and their citizens can make. The fate of the human presence on the Earth will be shaped in large part by those decisions and how their implications unfold in the coming years. This population story's ending still hasn't been written.

POSTSCRIPT

Are Declining Growth Rates Rather Than Rapid Population Growth Today's Major Global Population Problem?

William P. Butz labels the two sides of this debate implosionists versus explosionists in *The Double Divide: Implosionists and Explosionists Endanger Progress since Cairo* (Population Reference Bureau, September 2004). The implosionists argue that falling birth rates throughout the world cause major negative consequences. The explosionists counter that there will still be substantial world population growth, and countries with declining populations should be able to deal with the potential problems. They think that world leaders and organizations must still focus on the problems of population growth under conditions of increasing environmental constraints. Implosionists include Charles C. Mann, "The Coming Death Shortage," *The Atlantic Monthly* (May 2005); David R. Francis, "Now, Dangers of a Population Implosion," *Christian Science Monitor* (October 7, 2004); Denis Dutton "Now It's the Population Implosion," *New Zealand Herald* (July 23, 2003); Kerry Howley "Baby Bust!," *Reason* (July 2008); Phillip Longman, *The Empty Cradle: How Falling Birthrates Threaten World Prosperity and What to Do about It* (Basic Books, 2004); Wolfgang Lutz, Warren Sanderson, and Sergei Scherbov, eds., *The End of World Population Growth in the 21st Century: New Challenges for Human Capital Formation and Sustainable Development* (Earthscan Publishers, 2004); Richard Jackson and Neil Howe, *The Graying of the Great Powers: Demography and Geopolitics in the 21st Century* (Center for Strategic and International Studies, 2008); and Ronald Demos Lee, *Global Population Aging and Its Economic Consequences* (AEI Press, 2007). Explosionists include Werner Fornos, "A Global Concern: A Population Crisis Still Looms," *International Herald Tribune* (January 14, 2004); Michael Tobias, Bob Gillespie, and Elizabeth Hughes, eds., *No Vacancy: Global Responses to the Human Population Explosion* (Hope Publishing House, 2006); and K. Bruce Newbold, *Six Billion Plus: World Population in the Twenty-First Century* (Rowman & Littlefield Publishers, 2006).

The United Nations serves as an authoritative source on various population data, whether historical, current, or future oriented. One of the UN agencies, the United Nations Population Fund, or UNFPA, issues an annual State of the World Population, as well as other reports. See, for example, its *World Population Prospects: The 2008 Revision—Highlights* (2009). Two Washington private organizations, the Population Reference Bureau (PRB) and The Population Institute, publish a variety of booklets, newsletters, and reports yearly.

A particularly succinct discussion of the "demographic divide" is found in PRB's *The Demographic Divide: What It Is and Why it Matters,* (Mary Mederios and Carl Haub, 2008). Another source on population issues is the Population Council of New York.

ISSUE 20

Is Humankind Dangerously Harming the Environment?

YES: Lester R. Brown, from *Plan B 4.0, Mobilizing to Save Civilization* (Earth Policy Institute. 2009)

NO: Bjorn Lomborg, from "The Truth about the Environment," *The Economist* (August 4, 2001)

ISSUE SUMMARY

YES: Lester R. Brown, founder of the Worldwatch Institute and now president of the Earth Policy Institute, argues that population growth and economic development are placing increasingly harmful demands on the environment for resources and to grow food for improving diets.

NO: Bjorn Lomborg, a statistician at the University of Aarhus, Denmark, presents evidence that population growth is slowing down; natural resources are not running out; species are disappearing very slowly; the environment is improving in some ways; and assertions about environmental decline are exaggerated.

Much of the literature on socioeconomic development in the 1960s was premised on the assumption of inevitable material progress for all. It largely ignored the impacts of development on the environment and presumed that the availability of raw materials would not be a problem. The belief was that all societies would get richer because all societies were investing in new equipment and technologies that would increase productivity and wealth. Theorists recognized that some poor countries were having trouble developing, but they blamed those problems on the deficiencies of the values and attitudes of those countries and on inefficient organizations.

In the late 1960s and early 1970s, an intellectual revolution occurred. Environmentalists had criticized the growth paradigm throughout the 1960s, but they were not taken very seriously at first. By the end of the 1960s, however, marine scientist Rachel Carson's book *Silent Spring* (Alfred A. Knopf, 1962) had worked its way into the public's consciousness. Carson's book traces the noticeable loss of birds to the use of pesticides. Her book made the middle and upper classes in the United States realize that pollution affects complex ecological systems in ways that put even the wealthy at risk.

In 1968, Paul Ehrlich, a professor of population studies, published *The Population Bomb* (Ballantine Books), which states that overpopulation is the major problem facing mankind. This means that population has to be controlled or the human race might cause the collapse of the global ecosystems and the deaths of many humans. Ehrlich explained why he thought the devastation of the world was imminent:

> Because the human population of the planet is about five times too large, and we're managing to support all these people—at today's level of misery—only by spending our capital, burning our fossil fuels, dispersing our mineral resources and turning our fresh water into salt water. We have not only overpopulated but overstretched our environment. We are poisoning the ecological systems of the earth—systems upon which we are ultimately dependent for all of our food, for all of our oxygen and for all of our waste disposal.

In 1973, *The Limits to Growth* (Universe), by Donella H. Meadows et al., was published. It presents a dynamic systems computer model for world economic, demographic, and environmental trends. When the computer model projected trends into the future, it predicted that the world would experience ecological collapse and population die-off unless population growth and economic activity were greatly reduced. This study was both attacked and defended, and the debate about the health of the world has been heated ever since.

Let us examine the population growth rates for the past, present, and future. At about A.D. 1, the world had about one-quarter billion people. It took about 1,650 years to double this number to one-half billion and 200 years to double the world population again to 1 billion by 1850. The next doubling took only about 80 years, and the last doubling took about 45 years (from 2 billion in 1930 to about 4 billion in 1975). The world population may double again to 8 billion sometime between 2015 and 2025. At the same time that population is growing, people are trying to get richer, which means consuming more, polluting more, and using more resources. Are all these trends threatening the carrying capacity of the planet and jeopardizing the prospects for future generations?

In the following selections, Lester R. Brown warns that the population growth and the sevenfold expansion of the economy in the past half century is placing demands on the environment that exceed the earth's natural capacity. As a result we face many environmental problems. The one that Brown focuses on is the difficulty of increasing food production enough to feed growing populations with better diets and with declining natural resources. Bjorn Lomborg counters that the evidence supports optimism—not environmental pessimism. He maintains that resources are becoming more abundant, food per capita is increasing, the extinction of species is at a very slow rate, and environmental problems are transient and will get better.

YES

Lester R. Brown

Plan B 4.0: Mobilizing to Save Civilization

Selling Our Future

From time to time I go back and read about earlier civilizations that declined and collapsed, trying to understand the reasons for their demise. More often than not shrinking food supplies were responsible. For the Sumerians, rising salt levels in the soil—the result of a flaw in their irrigation system—brought down wheat and barley yields and eventually the civilization itself.

For the Mayans, soil erosion exacerbated by a series of intense droughts apparently undermined their food supply and their civilization. For other early civilizations that collapsed, it was often soil erosion and the resulting shrinkage in harvests that led to their decline.

Does our civilization face a similar fate? Until recently it did not seem possible. I resisted the idea that food shortages could also bring down our early twenty-first century global civilization. But our continuing failure to reverse the environmental trends that are undermining the world food economy forces me to conclude that if we continue with business as usual such a collapse is not only possible but likely.

The historic grain price climb in the last few years underlines the gravity of the situation. From mid-2006 to mid-2008, world prices of wheat, rice, corn, and soybeans roughly tripled, reaching historic highs. It was not until the global economic crisis beginning in 2008 that grain prices receded somewhat. But even then they were still well above the historical level.

The world has experienced several grain price surges over the last half-century, but none like this. These earlier trends were event-driven—a monsoon failure in India, a severe drought in the Soviet Union, or a crop-shrinking heat wave in the U.S. Midwest. The price surges were temporary, caused by weather-related events that were usually remedied by the next harvest. The record 2006–08 surge in grain prices is different. It is trend-driven. This means that working our way out of this tightening food situation depends on reversing the trends that are causing it, such as soil erosion, falling water tables, and rising carbon emissions.

As a result of persistently high food prices, hunger is spreading. One of the United Nations Millennium Development Goals is to reduce hunger and malnutrition. In the mid-1990s, the number of people in this category had

From *Plan B 4.0: Mobilizing to Save Civilization,* Earth Policy Institute, 2009. Copyright © 2009 by Earth Policy Institute. Reprinted by permission.

fallen to 825 million. But instead of continuing to decline, the number of hungry started to edge upward, reaching 915 million at the end of 2008. It then jumped to over 1 billion in 2009. With business as usual, I see a combination of the projected growth in population, the planned diversion of grain to produce fuel for cars, spreading shortages of irrigation water, and other trends combining to push the number of hungry people to 1.2 billion or more by 2015.

Rising food prices and the swelling ranks of the hungry are among the early signs of a tightening world food situation. At a time when progress is seen as almost inevitable, this recent reversal on the food front is a disturbing setback. More and more, food is looking like the weak link in our civilization, much as it was for the earlier ones whose archeological sites we now study.

Food: The Weak Link

As the world struggles to feed all its people, farmers are facing several trying trends. On the demand side of the food equation are three consumption-boosting trends: population growth, the growing consumption of grain-based animal protein, and, most recently, the massive use of grain to fuel cars.

On the supply side, several environmental and resource trends are making it more difficult to expand food production fast enough. Among the ongoing ones are soil erosion, aquifer depletion, crop-shrinking heat waves, melting ice sheets and rising sea level, and the melting of the mountain glaciers that feed major rivers and irrigation systems. In addition, three resource trends are affecting our food supply: the loss of cropland to non-farm uses, the diversion of irrigation water to cities, and the coming reduction in oil supplies.

The first trend of concern is population growth. Each year there are 79 million more people at the dinner table. Unfortunately, the overwhelming majority of these individuals are being added in countries where soils are eroding, water tables are falling, and irrigation wells are going dry. If we cannot get the brakes on population growth, we may not be able to eradicate hunger.

Even as our numbers are multiplying, some 3 billion people are trying to move up the food chain, consuming more grain-intensive livestock products. At the top of the food chain ranking are the United States and Canada, where people consume on average 800 kilograms of grain per year, most of it indirectly as beef, pork, poultry, milk, and eggs. Near the bottom of this ranking is India, where people have less than 200 kilograms of grain each, and thus must consume nearly all of it directly, leaving little for conversion into animal protein.

Beyond this, the owners of the world's 910 million automobiles want to maintain their mobility, and most are not particularly concerned about whether their fuel comes from an oil well or a corn field. The orgy of investment in ethanol fuel distilleries that followed the 2005 surge in U.S. gas prices to $3 a gallon after Hurricane Katrina raised the annual growth in world grain consumption from roughly 20 million tons per year to more than 40 million tons in both 2007 and 2008, creating an epic competition between cars and people for grain.

Turning to the supply-side constraints, soil erosion is currently lowering the inherent productivity of some 30 percent of the world's cropland. In some countries, such as Lesotho and Mongolia, it has reduced grain production by half or more over the last three decades. Kazakhstan, the site of the Soviet Virgin Lands project a half-century ago, has abandoned 40 percent of its grain-land since 1980. Vast dust storms coming out of sub-Saharan Africa, northern China, western Mongolia, and Central Asia remind us that the loss of topsoil is not only continuing but expanding.

In contrast to the loss of topsoil that began with the first wheat and bar-ley plantings, falling water tables are historically quite recent, simply because the pumping capacity to deplete aquifers has evolved only in recent decades. As a result, water tables are now falling in countries that together contain half the world's people. As overpumping spreads and as aquifer depletion contin-ues, the wells are starting to go dry. Saudi Arabia has announced that because its major aquifer, a fossil (non-replenishable) aquifer, is largely depleted, it will be phasing out wheat production entirely by 2016. A World Bank study shows that 175 million people in India are being fed by overpumping aquifers. In China, this problem affects 130 million people.

Climate change also threatens food security. After a certain point, rising tem-peratures reduce crop yields. For each 1 degree Celsius rise in temperature above the norm during the growing season, farmers can expect a 10 percent decline in wheat, rice, and corn yields. Since 1970, the earth's average surface temperature has increased by 0.6 degrees Celsius, or roughly 1 degree Fahrenheit. And the Intergovernmental Panel on Climate Change projects that the temperature will rise by up to 6 degrees Celsius (11 degrees Fahrenheit) during this century.

As the earth's temperature continues to rise, mountain glaciers are melt-ing throughout the world. Nowhere is this of more concern than in Asia. It is the ice melt from glaciers in the Himalayas and on the Tibetan Plateau that sustain the major rivers of India and China, and the irrigation systems that depend on them, during the dry season. In Asia, both wheat and rice fields depend on this water. China is the world's leading wheat producer. India is number two. (The United States is third.) These two countries also dominate the world rice harvest. Whatever happens to the wheat and rice harvests in these two population giants will affect food prices everywhere. Indeed, the projected melting of the glaciers on which these two countries depend presents the most massive threat to food security humanity has ever faced.

According to the latest information on the accelerating melting of the Greenland and West Antarctic ice sheets, ice melt combined with thermal expansion of the oceans could raise sea level by up to 6 feet during this century. Every rice-growing river delta in Asia is threatened by the melting of these ice sheets. Even a 3-foot rise would devastate the rice harvest in the Mekong Delta, which produces more than half the rice in Viet Nam, the world's number two rice exporter. A World Bank map shows that a 3-foot rise in sea level would inundate half the rice-land in Bangladesh, home to 160 million people. The fate of the hundreds of millions who depend on the harvests in the rice-growing river deltas and floodplains of Asia is inextricably linked to the fate of these major ice sheets.

As pressures on land-based food sources mounted after World War II, the world turned to the oceans for animal protein. From 1950 to 1996 the world fish catch climbed from 19 million to 94 million tons. But then growth came to a halt. We had reached the limits of the oceans before those of the land. Since 1996, growth in the world seafood supply has come almost entirely from fish farms. The spiraling demand for fish feed, most of it in the form of grain and soybean meal, is further intensifying pressure on the earth's land and water resources.

Advancing deserts—the result of overgrazing, overplowing, and deforestation—are encroaching on cropland in Saharan Africa, the Middle East, Central Asia, and China. Advancing deserts in northern and western China have forced the complete or partial abandonment of some 24,000 villages and the cropland surrounding them. In Africa, the Sahara is moving southward, engulfing cropland in Nigeria. It is also moving northward, invading wheat fields in Algeria and Morocco.

Farmers are losing cropland and irrigation water to nonfarm uses. The conversion of cropland to other uses looms large in China, India, and the United States. China, with its massive industrial and residential construction and its paving of roads, highways, and parking lots for a fast-growing automobile fleet, may be the world leader in cropland loss. In the United States, suburban sprawl is consuming large tracts of farmland.

With additional water no longer available in many countries, growing urban thirst can be satisfied only by taking irrigation water from farmers. Thousands of farmers in thirsty California find it more profitable to sell their irrigation water to Los Angeles and San Diego and leave their land idle. In India, villages are selling the water from their irrigation wells to nearby cities. China's farmers are also losing irrigation water to the country's fast-growing cities.

Lingering in the background is the prospect of declining oil use as a result of either declining production or efforts to cut carbon emissions—or, more likely, some combination of the two. The tripling of the world grain harvest over the last half-century is closely tied to oil. Today oil figures prominently in the farm economy, used in tillage, irrigation, and harvesting. Once oil production turns downward, countries will compete for a shrinking supply as they try to keep their agriculture producing at a high level. It was relatively easy to expand world food production when oil was cheap and abundant. It will be far more difficult when the price of oil is rising and the supply is declining.

Despite the growing need for new techniques to expand production, the backlog of unused agricultural technology is shrinking. In the more agriculturally advanced countries, farmers are using virtually all the available technology to raise land productivity. And agricultural scientists are not finding many new ways to raise yields. In Japan, the first country to launch a sustained rise in grain yield per hectare, rice yield increases have stalled, with little gain over the last 14 years. In China, the rapid rise in rice yields is now history. In both France and Egypt, wheat yields, which are among the world's highest, have been flat for roughly a decade. For the world as a whole, the rise in grainland productivity dropped from 2.1 percent a year from 1950 to 1990, to 1.3 percent from 1990 to 2008.

Some commentators point to genetically modified crops as a way out of this predicament. Unfortunately, no genetically modified grains have dramatically raised yields. Nor are they likely to do so. Scientists using conventional plant breeding techniques have already exploited most of the genetic potential for raising crop yields.

The bottom line is that harvest-expanding scientific advances are ever more difficult to come by as crop yields move closer to the inherent limits of photosynthetic efficiency. This limit in turn establishes the upper bounds of the earth's biological productivity, which ultimately will determine its human carrying capacity.

As the world's farmers attempt to expand the harvest, the trends that negatively affect production are partly offsetting advances in technology. The question now is, Could the environmental damage to world agriculture at some point entirely offset the gains from advancing technology, as it has already in Saudi Arabia and Yemen, where water shortages are shrinking grain harvests, or in Lesotho and Mongolia, where soil erosion is reducing harvests?

The question—at least for now—is not will the world grain harvest continue to expand, but will it expand fast enough to keep pace with steadily growing demand?

Business as usual is no longer a viable option. Food security will deteriorate further unless leading countries collectively mobilize to stabilize population, stabilize climate, stabilize aquifers, conserve soils, protect cropland, and restrict the use of grain to produce fuel for cars.

Our Global Ponzi Economy

Our mismanaged world economy today has many of the characteristics of a Ponzi scheme. A Ponzi scheme takes payments from a broad base of investors and uses these to pay off returns. It creates the illusion that it is providing a highly attractive rate of return on investment as a result of savvy investment decisions when in fact these irresistibly high earnings are in part the result of consuming the asset base itself. A Ponzi scheme investment fund can last only as long as the flow of new investments is sufficient to sustain the high rates of return paid out to previous investors. When this is no longer possible, the scheme collapses—just as Bernard Madoff's $65-billion investment fund did in December 2008.

Although the functioning of the global economy and a Ponzi investment scheme are not entirely analogous, there are some disturbing parallels. As recently as 1950 or so, the world economy was living more or less within its means, consuming only the sustainable yield, the interest of the natural systems that support it. But then as the economy doubled, and doubled again, and yet again, multiplying eightfold, it began to outrun sustainable yields and to consume the asset base itself. In a 2002 study published by the U.S. National Academy of Sciences, a team of scientists led by Mathis Wackernagel concluded that humanity's collective demands first surpassed the earth's regenerative capacity around 1980. As of 2009 global demands on natural systems exceed their sustainable yield capacity by nearly 30 percent. This means we are meeting current demands in part by consuming the earth's natural assets, setting the stage for an eventual Ponzi-type collapse when these assets are depleted.

As of mid-2009, nearly all the world's major aquifers were being over-pumped. We have more irrigation water than before the overpumping began, in true Ponzi fashion. We get the feeling that we're doing very well in agriculture—but the reality is that an estimated 400 million people are today being fed by overpumping, a process that is by definition short-term. With aquifers being depleted, this water-based food bubble is about to burst.

A similar situation exists with the melting of mountain glaciers. When glaciers first start to melt, flows in the rivers and the irrigation canals they feed are larger than before the melting started. But after a point, as smaller glaciers disappear and larger ones shrink, the amount of ice melt declines and the river flow diminishes. Thus we have two water-based Ponzi schemes running in parallel in agriculture.

And there are more such schemes. As human and livestock populations grow more or less apace, the rising demand for forage eventually exceeds the sustainable yield of grasslands. As a result, the grass deteriorates, leaving the land bare, allowing it to turn to desert. At some point the herds of ultimately emaciated cattle also collapse. In this Ponzi scheme, herders are forced to rely on food aid or they migrate to cities.

Three-fourths of oceanic fisheries are now being fished at or beyond capacity or are recovering from overexploitation. If we continue with business as usual, many of these fisheries will collapse. Overfishing, simply defined, means we are taking fish from the oceans faster than they can reproduce. The cod fishery off the coast of Newfoundland in Canada is a prime example of what can happen. Long one of the world's most productive fisheries, it collapsed in the early 1990s and may never recover.

Paul Hawken, author of *Blessed Unrest*, puts it well: "At present we are stealing the future, selling it in the present, and calling it gross domestic product. We can just as easily have an economy that is based on healing the future instead of stealing it. We can either create assets for the future or take the assets of the future. One is called restoration and the other exploitation."

The larger question is, If we continue with business as usual—with over-pumping, overgrazing, overplowing, overfishing, and overloading the atmosphere with carbon dioxide—how long will it be before the Ponzi economy unravels and collapses? No one knows. Our industrial civilization has not been here before.

Unlike Bernard Madoff's Ponzi scheme, which was set up with the knowledge that it would eventually fall apart, our global Ponzi economy was not intended to collapse. It is on a collision path because of market forces, perverse incentives, and poorly chosen measures of progress. We rely heavily on the market because it is in so many ways such an incredible institution. It allocates resources with an efficiency that no central planning body can match, and it easily balances supply and demand.

The market does, however, have some fundamental, potentially fatal, weaknesses. It does not respect the sustainable yield thresholds of natural systems. It also favors the near term over the long term, showing little concern for future generations. It does not incorporate into the prices of goods the indirect costs of producing them. As a result, it cannot provide the signals telling us that we are caught up in a Ponzi scheme.

In addition to consuming our asset base, we have also devised some clever techniques for leaving costs off the books—much like the disgraced and bankrupt Texas-based energy company Enron did some years ago. For example, when we use electricity from a coal-fired power plant we get a monthly bill from the local utility. It includes the cost of mining coal, transporting it to the power plant, burning it, generating the electricity, and delivering electricity to our homes. It does not, however, include any costs of the climate change caused by burning coal. That bill will come later—and it will likely be delivered to our children. Unfortunately for them, their bill for our coal use will be even larger than ours.

When Sir Nicholas Stern, former chief economist at the World Bank, released his groundbreaking 2006 study on the future costs of climate change, he talked about a massive market failure. He was referring to the failure of the market to incorporate the costs of climate change in the price of fossil fuels. According to Stern, the costs are measured in the trillions of dollars. The difference between the market prices for fossil fuels and an honest price that also incorporates their environmental costs to society is huge.

As economic decision makers—whether consumers, corporate planners, government policymakers, or investment bankers—we all depend on the market for information to guide us. In order for markets to work over the long term and for economic actors to make sound decisions, the markets must provide reliable information, including the full cost of products. But the market is giving us incomplete information, and as a result we are making bad decisions.

One of the best examples of this massive market failure can be seen in the United States, where the gasoline pump price was around $3 per gallon in mid-2009. This reflects only the cost of finding the oil, pumping it to the surface, refining it into gasoline, and delivering the gas to service stations. It overlooks the costs of climate change as well as the costs of tax subsidies to the oil industry (such as the U.S. oil depletion allowance), the burgeoning military costs of protecting access to oil in the politically unstable Middle East, and the health care costs of treating respiratory illnesses from breathing polluted air.

Based on a study by the International Center for Technology Assessment, these costs now total nearly $12 per gallon ($3.17 per liter) of gasoline burned in the United States. If these were added to the $3 direct cost of the gasoline, motorists would pay $15 a gallon for gas at the pump. In reality, burning gasoline is very costly, but the market tells us it is cheap, thus grossly distorting the structure of the economy.

A similar situation exists with food. If we paid the full cost of producing it—including the true cost of the oil used in producing it, the future costs of overpumping aquifers, the destruction of land through erosion, and the carbon dioxide emissions from land clearing—food would cost far more than we now pay for it in the supermarket.

In addition to ignoring indirect costs, the market does not value nature's services. This became abundantly clear in the summer of 1998 when China's

Yangtze River valley, home to nearly 400 million people, was wracked by some of the worst flooding in history. The resulting damages of $30 billion equaled the value of the country's annual rice harvest.

After several weeks of flooding, Beijing announced a ban on tree cutting in the Yangtze River basin. It justified this by noting that trees standing are worth three times as much as trees cut—the flood control services provided by forests were far more valuable than the lumber they contained. In effect, the market price had been off by a factor of three.

The market does not respect the carrying capacity of natural systems. For example, if a fishery is being continuously overfished, the catch eventually will begin to shrink and prices will rise, encouraging even more investment in fishing trawlers. The inevitable result is a precipitous decline in the catch and the collapse of the fishery.

Today we need a realistic view about the relationship between the economy and the environment. We also need, more than ever before, political leaders who can see the big picture. And since the principal advisors to government are economists, we need either economists who can think like ecologists—Sir Nicholas Stern and Herman Daly, a pioneer in ecological economics, are rare examples of this—or more ecological advisors. Market behavior—including its failure to include the indirect costs of goods and services, to value nature's services, and to respect sustainable-yield thresholds—is leading to the destruction of the economy's natural support systems, our own version of a Ponzi scheme. At some point the deteriorating relationship between the economy and its natural supports begins to take a political toll, contributing to state failure.

Bjorn Lomborg

 **NO**

The Truth about the Environment

Ecology and economics should push in the same direction. After all, the "eco" part of each word derives from the greek word for "home", and the protagonists of both claim to have humanity's welfare as their goal. Yet environmentalists and economists are often at loggerheads. For economists, the world seems to be getting better. For many environmentalists, it seems to be getting worse.

These environmentalists, led by such veterans as Paul Ehrlich of Stanford University, and Lester Brown of the Worldwatch Institute, have developed a sort of "litany" of four big environmental fears:

- Natural resources are running out.
- The population is ever growing, leaving less and less to eat.
- Species are becoming extinct in vast numbers: forests are disappearing and fish stocks are collapsing.
- The planet's air and water are becoming ever more polluted.

Human activity is thus defiling the earth, and humanity may end up killing itself in the process.

The trouble is, the evidence does not back up this litany. First, energy and other natural resources have become more abundant, not less so since the Club of Rome published *The Limits to Growth* in 1972. Second, more food is now produced per head of the world's population than at any time in history. Fewer people are starving. Third, although species are indeed becoming extinct, only about 0.7% of them are expected to disappear in the next 50 years, not 25–50%, as has so often been predicted. And finally, most forms of environmental pollution either appear to have been exaggerated, or are transient—associated with the early phrases of industrialisation and therefore best cured not by restricting economic growth, but by accelerating it. One form of pollution—the release of greenhouse gases that causes global warming—does appear to be a long-term phenomenon, but its total impact is unlikely to pose a devastating problem for the future of humanity. A bigger problem may well turn out to be an inappropriate response to it.

Can Things Only Get Better?

Take these four points one by one. First, the exhaustion of natural resources. The early environmental movement worried that the mineral resources on which modern industry depends would run out. Clearly, there must be some

From *The Economist*, August 4, 2001, pp. 63–65. Copyright © 2001 by The Economist Newspaper Ltd. Reprinted by permission via Copyright Clearance Center.

limit to the amount of fossil fuels and metal ores that can be extracted from the earth: the planet, after all, has a finite mass. But that limit is far greater than many environmentalists would have people believe.

Reserves of natural resources have to be located, a process that costs money. That, not natural scarcity, is the main limit on their availability. However, known reserves of all fossil fuels, and of most commercially important metals, are now larger than they were when The *Limits to Growth* was published. In the case of oil, for example, reserves that could be extracted at reasonably competitive prices would keep the world economy running for about 150 years at present consumption rates. Add to that the fact that the price of solar energy has fallen by half in every decade for the past 30 years, and appears likely to continue to do so into the future, and energy shortages do not look like a serious threat either to the economy or to the environment.

The development for non-fuel resources has been similar. Cement, aluminum, iron, copper, gold, nitrogen and zinc account for more than 75% of global expenditure on raw materials. Despite an increase in consumption of these materials of between two- and ten-fold over the past 50 years, the number of years of available reserves has actually grown. Moreover, the increasing abundance is reflected in an ever-decreasing price: *The Economist's* index of prices of industrial raw materials has dropped some 80% in inflation-adjusted terms since 1845.

Next, the population explosion is also turning out to be a bugaboo. In 1968, Dr. Ehrlich predicted in his best selling book, *The Population Bomb*, that "the battle to feed humanity is over. In the course of the 1970s the world will experience starvation of tragic proportions—hundreds of millions of people will starve to death."

That did not happen. Instead, according to the United Nations, agricultural production in the developing world has increased by 52% per person since 1961. The daily food intake in poor countries has increased from 1,932 calories, barely enough for survival, in 1961 to 2,650 calories in 1998, and is expected to rise to 3,020 by 2030. Likewise, the proportion of people in developing countries who are starving has dropped from 45% in 1949 to 18% today, and is expected to decline even further to 12% in 2010 and just 6% in 2030. Food, in other words, is becoming not scarcer but ever more abundant. This is reflected in its price. Since 1800, food prices have decreased by more than 90%, and in 2000, according to the World Bank, prices were lower than ever before.

Modern Malthus

Dr. Ehrlich's prediction echoes that made 170 years earlier by Thomas Malthus. Malthus claimed that, if unchecked, human population would expand exponentially, while food production could increase only linearly, by bringing new land into cultivation. He was wrong. Population growth has turned out to have an internal check: as people grow richer and healthier, they have smaller families. Indeed, the growth rate of the human population reached its peak, of more than 2% a year, in the early 1960s. The rate of increase has been

Figure 1

Slowing Up

World population 1750–2200*, bn

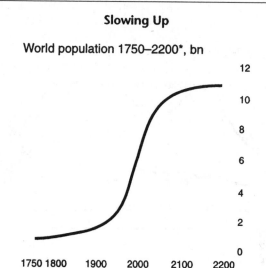

					12
					10
					8
					6
					4
					2
					0
1750 1800	1900	2000	2100	2200	

*UN medium-variant forecast from 2000
Source: UNPD

declining ever since. It is now 1.26%, and is expected to fall to 0.46% in 2050. The United Nations estimates that most of the world's population growth will be over by 2100, with the population stabilising at just below 11 billion (see Figure 1).

Malthus also failed to take account of developments in agricultural technology. These have squeezed more and more food out of each hectare of land. It is this application of human ingenuity that has boosted food production, not merely in line with, but ahead of, population growth. It has also, incidentally, reduced the need to take new land into cultivation, thus reducing the pressure on biodiversity.

Third, that threat of biodiversity loss is real, but exaggerated. Most early estimates used simple island models that linked a loss in habitat with a loss of biodiversity. A rule-of-thumb indicated that loss of 90% of forest meant a 50% loss of species. As rainforests seemed to be cut at alarming rates, estimates of annual species loss of 20,000–100,000 abounded. Many people expected the number of species to fall by half globally within a generation or two.

However, the data simply do not bear out these predictions. In the eastern United States, forests were reduced over two centuries to fragments totalling just 1–2% of their original area, yet this resulted in the extinction of only one forest bird. In Puerto Rico, the primary forest area has been reduced over the past 400 years by 99%, yet "only" seven of 60 species of bird have become extinct. All but 12% of the Brazilian Atlantic rainforest was cleared in the 19th century, leaving only scattered fragments. According to the rule-of-thumb,

Figure 2

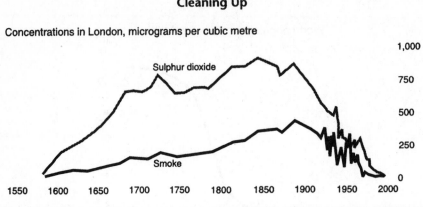

Cleaning Up

Concentrations in London, micrograms per cubic metre

Source: B. Lomborg

half of all its species should have become extinct. Yet, when the World Conservation Union and the Brazilian Society of Zoology analysed all 291 known Atlantic forest animals, none could be declared extinct. Species, therefore, seem more resilient than expected. And tropical forests are not lost at annual rates of 2.4%, as many environmentalists have claimed: the latest UN figures indicate a loss of less than 0.5%.

Fourth, pollution is also exaggerated. Many analyses show that air pollution diminishes when a society becomes rich enough to be able to afford to be concerned about the environment. For London, the city for which the best data are available, air pollution peaked around 1890 (see Figure 2). Today, the air is cleaner than it has been since 1585. There is good reason to believe that this general picture holds true for all developed countries. And, although air pollution is increasing in many developing countries, they are merely replicating the development of the industrialised countries. When they grow sufficiently rich they, too, will start to reduce their air pollution.

All this contradicts the litany. Yet opinion polls suggest that many people, in the rich world, at least, nurture the belief that environmental standards are declining. Four factors cause this disjunction between perception and reality.

Always Look on the Dark Side of Life

One is the lopsidedness built into scientific research. Scientific funding goes mainly to areas with many problems. That may be wise policy, but it will also create an impression that many more potential problems exist than is the case.

Secondly, environmental groups need to be noticed by the mass media. They also need to keep the money rolling in. Understandably, perhaps, they sometimes exaggerate. In 1997, for example, the Worldwide Fund for Nature issued a press release entitled, "Two-thirds of the world's forests lost forever." The truth turns out to be nearer 20%.

Table 1

The Price of a Life
Cost of saving one year of one person's life – 1993$

Passing laws to make seat-belt use mandatory	69
Sickle-cell anaemia screening for black new-borns	240
Mammography for women aged 50	810
Pneumonia vaccination for people aged over 65	2,000
Giving advice on stopping smoking to people who smoke more than one packet a day	9,800
Putting men aged 30 on a low-cholesterol diet	19,000
Regular leisure-time physical activity, such as jogging for men aged 35	38,000
Making pedestrians and cyclists more visible	73,000
Installing air-bags (rather than manual lap belts) in cars	120,000
Installing arsenic emission-control at glass-manufacturing plants	51,000,000
Setting radiation emission standards for nuclear-power plants	180,000,000
Installing benzene emission control at rubber-tyre manufacturing plants	20,000,000,000

Source: T. Tengs et al, *Risk Analysis,* June 1995

Though these groups are run overwhelmingly by selfless folk, they nevertheless share many of the characteristics of other lobby groups. That would matter less if people applied the same degree of scepticism to environmental lobbying as they do to lobby groups in other fields. A trade organisation arguing for, say, weaker pollution controls is instantly seen as self-interested. Yet a green organisation opposing such a weakening is seen as altruistic, even if a dispassionate view of the controls in question might suggest they are doing more harm than good.

A third source of confusion is the attitude of the media. People are clearly more curious about bad news than good. Newspapers and broadcasters are there to provide what the public wants. That, however, can lead to significant distortions of perception. An example was America's encounter with El Niño in 1997 and 1998. This climatic phenomenon was accused of wrecking tourism, causing allergies, melting the ski-slopes and causing 22 deaths by dumping snow in Ohio.

A more balanced view comes from a recent article in the *Bulletin of the American Meteorological Society.* This tries to count up both the problems and the benefits of the 1997–98 Niño. The damage it did was estimated at $4 billion. However, the benefits amounted to some $19 billion. These came from higher winter temperatures (which saved an estimated 850 lives, reduced heating costs and diminished spring floods caused by meltwaters) and from the well-documented connection between past Niños and fewer Atlantic hurricanes. In 1998, America experienced no big Atlantic hurricanes and thus avoided huge losses. These benefits were not reported as widely as the losses.

The fourth factor is poor individual perception. People worry that the endless rise in the amount of stuff everyone throws away will cause the world to run out of places to dispose of waste. Yet, even if America's trash output continues to rise as it has done in the past, and even if the American population doubles by 2100, all the rubbish America produces through the entire 21st century will still take up only the area of a square, each of whose sides measures 28 km (18 miles). That is just one-12,000th of the area of the entire United States.

Ignorance matters only when it leads to faulty judgments. But fear of largely imaginary environmental problems can divert political energy from dealing with real ones. The table, showing the cost in the United States of various measures to save a year of a person's life, illustrates the danger. Some environmental policies, such as reducing lead in petrol and sulphur-dioxide emissions from fuel oil, are very cost-effective. But many of these are already in place. Most environmental measures are less cost-effective than interventions aimed at improving safety (such as installing air-bags in cars) and those involving medical screening and vaccination. Some are absurdly expensive.

Yet a false perception of risk may be about to lead to errors more expensive even than controlling the emission of benzene at tyre plants. Carbon-dioxide emissions are causing the planet to warm. The best estimates are that the temperature will rise by some 2°–3°C in this century, causing considerable problems, almost exclusively in the developing world, at a total cost of $5,000 billion. Getting rid of global warming would thus seem to be a good idea. The question is whether the cure will actually be more costly than ailment.

Despite the intuition that something drastic needs to be done about such a costly problem, economic analyses clearly show that it will be far more expensive to cut carbon-dioxide emissions radically than to pay the costs of adaptation to the increased temperatures. The effect of the Kyoto Protocol on the climate would be minuscule, even if it were implemented in full. A model by Tom Wigley, one of the main authors of the reports of the UN Climate Change Panel, shows how an expected temperature increase of 2.1°C in 2100 would be diminished by the treaty to an increase of 1.9°C instead. Or, to put it another way, the temperature increase that the planet would have experienced in 2094 would be postponed to 2100.

So the Kyoto agreement does not prevent global warming, but merely buys the world six years. Yet, the cost of Kyoto, for the United States alone, will be higher than the cost of solving the world's single most pressing health problems: providing universal access to clean drinking water and sanitation. Such measures would avoid 2m deaths every year, and prevent half a billion people from becoming seriously ill.

And that is the best case. If the treaty were implemented inefficiently, the cost of Kyoto could approach $1 trillion, or more than five times the cost of worldwide water and sanitation coverage. For comparison, the total global-aid budget today is about $50 billion a year.

To replace the litany with facts is crucial if people want to make the best possible decisions for the future. Of course, rational environmental management and environmental investment are good ideas—but the costs and benefits of such investments should be compared to those of similar investments in all the other important areas of human endeavour. It may be costly to be overly optimistic—but more costly still to be too pessimistic.

POSTSCRIPT

Is Humankind Dangerously Harming the Environment?

Though a number of works (see below) support Lomborg's argument, his evidence has come under heavy attack (see Richard C. Bell, "How Did the Skeptical Environmentalist Pull the Wool over the Eyes of so Many Editors?" *WorldWatch* [March–April 2002] and *Scientific American* [January 2002]). The issue of the state of the environment and prospects for the future has been hotly debated for over 30 years, with little chance of ending soon. Two key issues are the potential impacts of global warming and the net effects of future agricultural technologies, which will be used to feed growing populations with richer diets. On the former, see Douglas Long, *Global Warming* (Facts on File, 2004); Robert Hunter, *Thermageddon: Countdown to 2030* (Arcade Pub., 2003); John Theodore Houghton, *Global Warming: The Complete Briefing,* 3rd ed. (Cambridge University, 2004); Andrew Simms et al., *Up in Smoke? Threats from, and Responses to, the Impact of Global Warming on Human Development* (New Economic Foundation, 2004); and the journal *The Ecologist* (March 2002). Ronald Bailey and others debunk the global warming "scare" in his edited book, *Global Warming and Other Eco-Myths: How the Environmental Movement Uses False Science to Scare Us to Death* (Prima, 2002). See also Patrick J. Michaels, *Meltdown: The Predicatable Distortion of Global Warming by Scientists, Politicians, and the Media* (Cato Institute, 2004). On food production issues and agriculture technologies, see Lester R. Brown, *Outgrowing the Earth: The Food Security Challenge in the Age of Falling Water Tables and Rising Temperatures* (Earth Policy Institute, 2004); *Bread for the World, Are We on Track to End Hunger? 14th Annual Report on the State of World Hunger* (Bread for the World Institution, 2004); and on agricultural technologies, see Vaclav Smil, *Feeding the World: A Challenge for the Twenty-First Century* (MIT Press, 2000).

Paul R. Ehrlich and Anne H. Ehrlich wrote *Betrayal of Science and Reason: How Anti-Environmental Rhetoric Threatens Our Future* (Island Press, 1996) to refute statements by those who do not agree with the messages of the concerned environmentalists. Julian Lincoln Simon counters with *Hoodwinking the Nation* (Transaction, 1999). For a debate on this issue, see Norman Myers and Julian L. Simon, *Scarcity or Abundance? A Debate on the Environment* (W. W. Norton, 1994).

Publications that are optimistic about the availability of resources and the health of the environment include Ronald Bailey, ed., *The True State of the Planet* (Free Press, 1995), and Gregg Easterbrook, *A Moment on the Earth: The Coming Age of Environmental Optimism* (Viking, 1995). Publications by some who believe that population growth and human interventions in the environment have dangerous consequences for the future of mankind include Joseph Wayne Smith, Graham Lyons, and Gary Sauer-Thompson, *Healing a Wounded World* (Praeger, 1997); Douglas E. Booth, *The Environmental Consequences of Growth* (Routledge, 1998); Kirill Kondratyev et al., *Stability of Life on Earth: Principal Subject of Scientific Research in the 21st Century* (Springer 2004); and James Gustive Speth, *Red Sky at Morning: America and the Crisis of the Global Environment* (Yale University Press, 2004).

Several works relate environmental problems to very severe political, social, and economic problems, including Michael Renner, *Fighting for Survival* (W. W. Norton, 1996); Michael N. Dobkowski and Isidor Wallimann, eds., *The Coming Age of Scarcity: Preventing Mass Death and Genocide in the Twenty-First Century* (Syracuse University Press, 1998); and one with a long timeframe, Sing C. Chew, *World Ecological Degradation: Accumulation, Urbanization, and Deforestation, 3000 B.C.–A.D. 2000* (Roman and Littlefield, 2001). An important series of publications on environmental problems is by the Worldwatch Institute, including two annuals: *State of the World* and *Vital Signs*.

ISSUE 21

Is Globalization Good for Humankind?

YES: Johan Norberg, from "Three Cheers for Global Capitalism," *The American Enterprise* (June 2004)

NO: Martin Hart-Landsberg, from "Neoliberalism: Myths and Reality," *Monthly Review* (April 2006)

ISSUE SUMMARY

YES: Author Johan Norberg argues that globalization is overwhelmingly good. Consumers throughout the world get better-quality goods at lower prices because the competition forces producers to be more creative, efficient, and responsive to consumers' demands. Even most poor people benefit greatly.

NO: Martin Hart-Landsberg, Professor of Economics at Lewis and Clark College, argues that globalization has "enhanced transnational capitalist power and profits at the cost of growing economic instability and deteriorating working and living conditions."

Globalization, which stands for worldwide processes, activities, and institutions, is a really big issue today. It involves world markets, world finance, world communications, world media, world religions, world popular culture, world rights movements, world drug trade, and so on. The focus of most commentators is on the world economy, which many believe promises strong growth in world wealth. Critics focus on the world economy's negative impacts on workers' wages, environmental protections and regulations, and national and local cultures. Many say that it is easy for Americans to feel positive toward globalization because America and its businesses, media, and culture are at the center of the globalized world, which ensures that America gains more than its proportional share of the benefits. But the real debate is whether globalization benefits all mankind. When the whole world is considered, there may be far more minuses to be weighed against the pluses. It is hard to settle this debate because so many different dimensions that are incomparable must be included in the calculation of the cost-benefit ratio.

The concept of globalization forces us to think about many complicated issues at the same time. There are technological, economic, political, cultural, and ethical aspects of globalization. Technological developments make possible the communication, transportation, coordination, and organization that make economic globalization possible. Political factors have made this a relatively free global economy. Restrictions on trade and production have been greatly reduced, and competition has greatly increased. The results have been increased production and wealth and celebration in financial circles. But competition creates losers as well as winners, so peoples throughout the world are protesting and resisting economic globalization. Many are also resisting cultural globalization because their own cultures are threatened. They feel that the global culture is materialistic, sexualized, secular, and egocentric—and they may be right. But many also consider the strengths of the global culture, such as championing human rights, democracy, and justice.

In the selections that follow, Johan Norberg reports on the benefits of the global economy and counters many of the arguments against globalization. His main argument is that the global economy stimulates faster economic growth, which improves the standard of living of all groups. Martin Hart-Landsberg opposes globalization because it adversely impacts workers, the environment, and the poor. To establish his argument, he attacks the theoretical underpinning of globalization—which is that free trade enhances economic growth that benefits everyone.

YES

Johan Norberg

Three Cheers for Global Capitalism

Under what is rather barrenly termed "globalization"—the process by which people, information, trade, investments, democracy, and the market economy tend more and more to cross national borders—our options and opportunities have multiplied. We don't have to shop at the big local company; we can turn to a foreign competitor. We don't have to work for the village's one and only employer; we can seek alternative opportunities. We don't have to make do with local cultural amenities; the world's culture is at our disposal. Companies, politicians, and associations have to exert themselves to elicit interest from people who have a whole world of options. Our ability to control our own lives is growing, and prosperity is growing with it.

Free markets and free trade and free choices transfer power to individuals at the expense of political institutions. Because there is no central control booth, it seems unchecked, chaotic. Political theorist Benjamin Barber speaks for many critics when he bemoans the absence of "viable powers of opposing, subduing, and civilizing the anarchic forces of the global economy." "Globalization" conjures up the image of an anonymous, enigmatic, elusive force, but it is actually just the sum of billions of people in thousands of places making decentralized decisions about their own lives. No one is in the driver's seat precisely because all of us are steering.

No company would import goods from abroad if we didn't buy them. If we did not send e-mails, order books, and download music every day, the Internet would wither and die. We eat bananas from Ecuador, order magazines from Britain, work for export companies selling to Germany and Russia, vacation in Thailand, and save money for retirement by investing in South America and Asia. These things are carried out by businesses only because we as individuals want them to. Globalization takes place from the bottom up.

A recent book about the nineteenth-century Swedish historian Erik Geijer notes that he was able to keep himself up to date just by sitting in Uppsala reading the *Edinburgh Review* and the *Quarterly Review*. That is how simple and intelligible the world can be when only a tiny elite in the capitals of Europe makes any difference to the course of world events. How much more complex and confusing everything is now, with ordinary people having a say over their own lives. Elites may mourn that they have lost power, but everyday life has vastly improved now that inexpensive goods and outside information and different employment opportunities are no longer blocked by political barriers.

From *American Enterprise*, June 2004, pp. 20–27. Copyright © 2004 by American Enterprise Institute. Reprinted by permission.

To those of us in rich countries, more economic liberty to pick and choose may sound like a trivial luxury, even an annoyance—but it isn't. Fresh options are invaluable for all of us. And the existence from which globalization delivers people in the Third World—poverty, filth, ignorance, and powerlessness—really is intolerable. When global capitalism knocks at the door of Bhagant, an elderly agricultural worker and "untouchable" in the Indian village of Saijani, it leads to his house being built of brick instead of mud, to shoes on his feet, and clean clothes—not rags—on his back. Outside Bhagant's house, the streets now have drains, and the fragrance of tilled earth has replaced the stench of refuse. Thirty years ago Bhagant didn't know he was living in India. Today he watches world news on television. The stand that we in the privileged world take on the burning issue of globalization can determine whether or not more people will experience the development that has taken place in Bhagant's village.

Critics of globalization often paint a picture of capitalist marauders secretly plotting for world mastery, but this notion is completely off the mark. It has mostly been pragmatic, previously socialist, politicians who fanned globalization in China, Latin America, and East Asia—after realizing that government control-freakery had ruined their societies. Any allegation of runaway capitalism has to be tempered by the observation that today we have the largest public sectors and highest taxes the world has ever known. The economic liberalization measures of the last quarter century may have abolished some of the recent past's centralist excesses, but they have hardly ushered in a system of laissez-faire.

What defenders of global capitalism believe in, first and foremost, is man's capacity for achieving great things by means of the combined force of market exchanges. It is not their intention to put a price tag on everything. The important things—love, family, friendship, one's own way of life—cannot be assigned a monetary value. Principled advocates of global economic liberty plead for a more open world because that setting unleashes individual creativity as none other can. At its core, the belief in capitalist freedom among nations is a belief in mankind. . . .

Today, we hear that life is increasingly unfair amidst the market economy: "The rich are getting richer, and the poor are getting poorer." But if we look beyond the catchy slogans, we find that while many of the rich have indeed grown richer, so have most of the poor. Absolute poverty has diminished, and where it was greatest 20 years ago—in Asia—hundreds of millions of people have achieved a secure existence, even affluence, previously undreamed of. Global misery has diminished, and great injustices have started to unravel. . . .

◄◎►

This progress is all very well, many critics of globalization will argue, but even if the majority are better off, gaps have widened and wealthy people and countries have improved their lot more rapidly than others. The critics point out that 40 years ago the combined per capita GDP of the 20 richest countries was 15 times greater than that of the 20 poorest, and is now 30 times greater.

There are two reasons why this objection to globalization does not hold up. First, if everyone is better off, what does it matter that the improvement comes faster for some than for others? Only those who consider wealth a greater problem than poverty can find irritation in middle-class citizens becoming millionaires while the previously poverty-stricken become middle class.

Second, the allegation of increased inequality is simply wrong.

The notion that global inequality has increased is largely based on figures from the U.N.'s 1999 *Human Development Report*. The problem with these figures is that they don't take into account what people can actually buy with their money. Without that "purchasing power" adjustment, the figures only show what a currency is worth on the international market, and nothing about local conditions. Poor people's actual living standards hinge on the cost of their food, their clothing, their housing—not what their money would get them while vacationing in Europe. That's why the U.N. uses purchasing-power-adjusted figures in other measures of living standards. It only resorts to the unadjusted figures, oddly, in order to present a theory of inequality.

A report from the Norwegian Institute for Foreign Affairs investigated global inequality by means of figures adjusted for purchasing power. Their data show that, contrary to conventional wisdom, inequality between countries has continuously *declined* ever since the end of the 1970s. This decline has been especially rapid since 1993, when globalization really gathered speed.

More recently, similar research by Columbia University development economist Xavier Sala-i-Martin has confirmed those findings. He found that when U.N. figures are adjusted for purchasing power, they point to a sharp decline in world inequality. Sala-i-Martin and co-author Surjit Bhalla also found independently that if we focus on inequality between *persons*, rather than inequality between *countries*, global inequality at the end of 2000 was at its lowest point since the end of World War II.

Estimates that compare countries rather than individuals, both authors note, grossly overestimate real inequality because they allow gains for huge numbers of people to be outweighed by losses for far fewer. For instance, country aggregates treat China and Grenada as data points of equal weight, even though China's population is 12,000 times Grenada's. Once we shift our focus to people rather than nations, the evidence is overwhelming that the past 30 years have witnessed a strong shift toward global equalization.

❦

One myth about trade is the notion that exports to other countries are a good thing, but that imports are somehow a bad thing. Many believe that a country grows powerful by selling much and buying little. The truth is that our standard of living will not rise until we use our money to buy more and cheaper things. One of the first trade theorists, James Mill, rightly noted in 1821 that "The benefit which derives from exchanging one commodity for another arises in all cases from the commodity received, not the commodity given." The only point of exports, in other words, is to enable us to get imports in return. . . .

Trade is not a zero-sum game in which one party loses what the other party gains. There would *be* no exchange if both parties did not feel that they benefited. The really interesting yardstick is not the "balance of trade" (where a "surplus" means that we are exporting more than we are importing) but the *quantity* of trade, since both exports and imports are gains. Imports are often feared as a potential cause of unemployment: If we import cheap toys and clothing from China, then toy and garment manufacturers here will have to scale down. But by obtaining cheaper goods from abroad, we save resources in the United States and can therefore invest in new industries and occupations.

⚬⚬⚬

Free trade brings freedom: freedom for people to buy and sell what they want. As an added benefit, this leads to the efficient use of resources. A company, or country, specializes where it can generate the greatest value.

Economic openness also leads to an enduring effort to improve production, because foreign competition forces firms to be as good and cheap as possible. As production in established industries becomes ever more efficient, resources are freed up for investment in new methods, inventions, and products. Foreign competition brings the same benefits that we recognize in economic competition generally; it simply extends competition to a broader field.

One of the most important but hard to measure benefits of free trade is that a country trading a great deal with the rest of the world imports new ideas and new techniques in the bargain. If the United States pursues free trade, our companies are exposed to the world's best ideas. They can then borrow those ideas, buy leading technology from elsewhere, and hire the best available manpower. This compels the companies to be more dynamic themselves.

The world's output today is six times what it was 50 years ago, and world trade is 16 times greater. There is reason to believe that the trade growth drove much of the production growth. One comprehensive study of the effects of trade was conducted by Harvard economists Jeffrey Sachs and Andrew Warner. They examined the trade policies between 1970 and 1989 of 117 countries. The study reveals a statistically significant connection between free trade and economic growth. Growth was between three and six times *higher* in free-trade countries than in protectionist ones. Factors like improved education turned out to be vastly less important than trade in increasing economic progress.

Over those two decades, developing countries that practiced free trade had an average annual growth rate of 4.5 percent, while developing countries that practiced protectionism grew by only 0.7 percent. Among industrial countries, the free traders experienced annual growth of 2.3 percent, versus only 0.7 percent among the protectionists. It must be emphasized that this is not a matter of countries earning more because *others* opened to *their* exports. Rather, these countries earned more by keeping their own markets open.

⚬⚬⚬

If free trade is constantly making production more efficient, won't that result in the disappearance of job opportunities? When Asians manufacture our cars and South Americans produce our meat, auto workers and farmers in the United States lose their jobs and unemployment rises. Foreigners and developing countries will increasingly produce the things we need, until we don't have any jobs left. If increasing automation means everything we consume today will be able to be made by half the U.S. labor force in 20 years, doesn't that mean that the other half will be out of work? Such are the horror scenarios depicted in many anti-globalization writings.

The notion that a colossal unemployment crisis is looming began to grow popular in the mid 1970s. Since then, production has been streamlined and internationalized more than ever. Yet far more jobs have been created than have disappeared. We have more efficient production than ever before, but also more people at work. Between 1975 and 1998, employment in countries like the United States, Canada, and Australia rose by 50 percent.

And it is in the most internationalized economies, making the most use of modern technology, that employment has grown fastest. Between 1983 and 1995 in the United States, 24 million more job opportunities were created than disappeared. And those were not low-paid, unskilled jobs, as is often alleged. On the contrary, 70 percent of the new jobs carried a wage above the American median level. Nearly half the new jobs belonged to the most highly skilled, a figure which has risen even more rapidly since 1995.

So allegations of progressively fewer people being needed in production have no empirical foundation. And no wonder, for they are wrong in theory too. Imagine a pre-industrial economy where most everyone is laboring to feed himself. Then food production is improved by new technologies, new machines, foreign competition, and imports. That results in a lot of people being forced to leave the agricultural sector. Does that mean there is nothing for them to do, that consumption is constant? Of course not; the manpower which used to be required to feed the population shifts to clothing it, and providing better housing. Then improved transport, and entertainment. Then newspapers, telephones, and computers.

The notion that the quantity of employment is constant, that a job gained by one person is always a job taken from someone else, has provoked a variety of foolish responses. Some advocate that jobs must be shared. Others smash machinery. Many advocate raising tariffs and excluding immigrants. But the whole notion is wrong. The very process of a task being done more efficiently, thus allowing jobs to be shed, enables new industries to grow, providing people with new and better jobs.

⋯⟨◉⟩⋯

Efficiency does, of course, have a flip side. Economist Joseph Schumpeter famously described a dynamic market as a process of "creative destruction," because it destroys old solutions and industries, with a creative end in view. As the word "destruction" suggests, not everyone benefits from every market transformation in the short term. The process is painful for those who have invested in or are employed by less-efficient industries. Drivers of horse-drawn cabs lost out with the spread of automobiles, as did producers of paraffin lamps when electric light was introduced. In more modern times, manufacturers of typewriters were put out of business by the computer, and LP records were superseded by CDs.

Painful changes of this kind happen all the time as a result of new inventions and methods of production. Unquestionably, such changes can cause trauma for those affected. But the most foolish way to counter such problems is to try to prevent them. It is generally fruitless; mere spitting into the wind. Besides, without "creative destruction," we would *all* be stuck with a lower standard of living. . . .

A review of more than 50 surveys of adjustments after trade liberalization in different countries shows clearly that adjustment problems are far milder than the conventional debate suggests. For every dollar of trade adjustment costs, roughly $30 is harvested in the form of welfare gains. A study of trade liberalization in 13 different countries showed that in all but one, industrial employment had already increased just one year after the liberalization. The process turns out to be far more creative than destructive.

If there are problems resulting from unshackled capitalism, they ought to be greatest in the United States, with its constant swirling economic transformations. But our job market is a bit like the Hydra in the legend of Hercules. Every time Hercules cuts off one of the beast's heads, two new ones appear. The danger of having to continue changing jobs all one's life is exaggerated: The average length of time an American stays in a particular job actually increased between 1983 and 1995, from 3.5 years to 3.8. Nor is it true, as many people believe, that more jobs are created in the United States only because real wages have stagnated or fallen since the 1970s. A growing proportion of wages is now paid in non-money forms, such as health insurance, stocks, 401(k) contributions, day care, and so forth, to avoid taxation. When these benefits are included, American wages have risen right along with productivity. Among poor Americans, the proportion of consumption devoted to food, clothing, and housing has fallen since the 1970s from 52 to 37 percent, which clearly shows that they have money to spare for much more than the bare necessities of life. . . .

Advocates of protectionism often complain of "sweatshops" allegedly run by multinational corporations in the Third World. Let's look at the evidence: Economists have compared the conditions of people employed in American-owned facilities in developing countries with those of people employed elsewhere in the same country. In the poorest developing countries, the average employee of an American-affiliated company makes *eight times* the average national wage! In middle income countries, American employers pay *three times* the national average. Even compared with corresponding modern jobs in the same country, the multinationals pay about 30 percent higher wages. Marxists maintain that multinationals exploit poor workers. Are much higher wages "exploitation"?

The same marked difference can be seen in working conditions. The International Labor Organization has shown that multinationals, especially in the footwear and garment industries, are leading the trend toward better working conditions in the Third World. When multinational corporations accustom workers to better-lit, safer, and cleaner factories, they raise the general standard. Native firms then also have to offer better conditions, otherwise no one will work for them. Zhou Litai, one of China's foremost labor attorneys, has pointed out that Western consumers are the principal driving force behind the improvements of working conditions in China, and worries that "if Nike and Reebok go, this pressure evaporates.". . .

~◎~

Corporations have not acquired more power through free trade. Indeed, they used to be far more powerful—and still are in dictatorships and controlled economies. Large corporations have chances to corrupt or manipulate when power is distributed by public officials who can be hobnobbed over luncheons to give protection through monopolies, tariffs, or subsides. Free trade, on the other hand, exposes corporations to competition. Above all, it lets consumers ruthlessly pick and choose across national borders, rejecting companies that don't measure up. . . .

Companies in free competition can grow large and increase their sales only by being better than others. Companies that fail to do so quickly go bust or get taken over by someone who can make better use of their capital, buildings, machinery, and employees. Capitalism is very tough—but mainly on firms offering outdated, poor-quality, or expensive goods and services. Fear of established companies growing so large as to become unaccountable has absolutely no foundation in reality. In the U.S., the most capitalist large country in the world, the market share of the 25 biggest corporations has steadily dwindled over recent decades.

Freer markets make it easier for small firms with fresh ideas to compete with big corporations. Between 1980 and 1993, the 500 biggest American corporations saw their share of the country's total employment diminish from 16 to 11 percent. During the same period, the average personnel strength of American firms fell from 17 to 15 people, and the proportion of the population working in companies with more than 250 employees fell from 37 to 29 percent.

Of the 500 biggest enterprises in the United States in 1980, one third had disappeared by 1990. Another 40 percent had evaporated five years later. Whether they failed to grow enough to stay on the list, died, merged, or broke up, the key lesson is that big corporations have much less power over consumers than we sometimes imagine. Even the most potent corporation must constantly re-earn its stripes, or tumble fast. . . .

Many people fear a "McDonaldization" or "Disneyfication" of the world, a creeping global homogeneity that leaves everyone wearing the same clothes, eating the same food, and seeing the same movies. But this portrayal does not accurately describe globalization. Anyone going out in the capitals of Europe today will have no trouble finding hamburgers and Coca-Cola, but he will just as easily find kebabs, sushi, Tex-Mex tacos, Peking duck, Thai lemongrass soup, and cappuccino. . . .

The world is indeed moving toward a common objective, but that objective is not the predominance of a particular culture, rather it is pluralism, the freedom to choose from a host of different paths and destinations. The market for experimental electronic music or film versions of novels by Dostoevsky may be small in any given place, so musicians and filmmakers producing such material could never produce anything without access to the much larger audience provided by globalization.

This internationalization is, ironically, what makes people believe that differences are vanishing. When you travel abroad, things look much the same as in your own country: The people there also have goods and chain stores from different parts of the globe. This phenomenon is not due to uniformity and the elimination of differences, but by the growth of pluralism everywhere. . . .

In the age of globalization, the ideas of freedom and individualism have attained tremendous force. There are few concepts as inspiring as that of self-determination. When people in other countries glimpse a chance to set their own course, it becomes almost irresistible. If there is any elimination of differences throughout the world, it has been the convergence of societies on the practice of allowing people to choose the sort of existence they please.

Global commerce does undermine old economic interests, challenge cultures, and erode some traditional power centers. Advocates of globalization have to show that greater gains and opportunities counterbalance such problems. . . .

Lasse Berg and Stig Karlsson record Chinese villagers' descriptions of the changes they experienced since the 1960s: "The last time you were here, people's thoughts and minds were closed, bound up," stated farmer Yang Zhengming. But as residents acquired power over their own livelihoods they began to think for themselves. Yang explains that "a farmer could then own himself. He did not need to submit. He decided himself what he was going to do, how and when. The proceeds of his work were his own. It was freedom that came to us. We were allowed to own things for ourselves."

Coercion and poverty still cover large areas of our globe. But thanks to globalizing economic freedom, people know that living in a state of oppression is not natural or necessary. People who have acquired a taste of economic liberty and expanded horizons will not consent to be shut in again by walls or fences. They will work to create a better existence for themselves. The aim of our politics should be to give them that freedom.

Neoliberalism: Myths and Reality

$\mathbf{A}$greements like the North American Free Trade Agreement (NAFTA) and the World Trade Organization (WTO) have enhanced transnational capitalist power and profits at the cost of growing economic instability and deteriorating working and living conditions. Despite this reality, neoliberal claims that liberalization, deregulation, and privatization produce unrivaled benefits have been repeated so often that many working people accept them as unchallengeable truths. Thus, business and political leaders in the United States and other developed capitalist countries routinely defend their efforts to expand the WTO and secure new agreements like the Free Trade Area of the Americas (FTAA) as necessary to ensure a brighter future for the world's people, especially those living in poverty. . . .

Therefore, if we are going to mount an effective challenge to the neoliberal globalization project, we must redouble our efforts to win the "battle of ideas." Winning this battle requires, among other things, demonstrating that neoliberalism functions as an ideological cover for the promotion of capitalist interests, not as a scientific framework for illuminating the economic and social consequences of capitalist dynamics. It also requires showing the processes by which capitalism, as an international system, undermines rather than promotes working class interests in both third world and developed capitalist countries.

The Myth of the Superiority of "Free Trade": Theoretical Arguments

According to supporters of the WTO and agreements such as the FTAA, these institutions/agreements seek to promote free trade in order to enhance efficiency and maximize economic well being. This focus on trade hides what is in fact a much broader political-economic agenda: the expansion and enhancement of corporate profit-making opportunities. In the case of the WTO, this agenda has been pursued through a variety of agreements that are explicitly designed to limit or actually block public regulation of economic activity in contexts that have little to do with trade as normally understood.

For example, the Agreement on Trade-Related Aspects of Intellectual Property Rights (TRIPS) limits the ability of states to deny patents on certain

From *Monthly Review*, April 2006, pp. 1–5, 8–12, 15–16. Copyright © 2006 by Monthly Review Foundation. Reprinted by permission of Monthly Review Foundation via the Copyright Clearance Center. References omitted.

products (including over living organisms) or control the use of products patented in their respective nations (including the use of compulsory licensing to ensure affordability of critical medicines). It also forces states to accept a significant increase in the length of time during which patents remain in force. The Agreement on Trade Related Investment Measures (TRIMS) restricts the ability of states to put performance requirements on foreign direct investment (FDI), encompassing those that would require the use of local inputs (including labor) or technology transfer. A proposed expansion of the General Agreement on Trade in Services (GATS) would force states to open their national service markets (which include everything from health care and education to public utilities and retail trade) to foreign providers as well as limit public regulation of their activity. Similarly, a proposed Government Procurement Agreement would deny states the ability to use non-economic criteria, such as labor and environmental practices, in awarding contracts.

These agreements are rarely discussed in the mainstream media precisely because they directly raise issues of private versus public power and are not easily defended. This is one of the most important reasons why those who support the capitalist globalization project prefer to describe the institutional arrangements that help underpin it as trade agreements and defend them on the basis of the alleged virtues of free trade. This is a defense that unfortunately and undeservedly holds enormous sway among working people, especially in the developed capitalist countries. And, using it as a theoretical foundation, capitalist globalization advocates find it relatively easy to encourage popular acceptance of the broader proposition that market determined outcomes are superior to socially determined ones in all spheres of activity. Therefore, it is critical that we develop an effective and accessible critique of this myth of the superiority of free trade. In fact, this is an easier task than generally assumed.

Arguments promoting free trade generally rest on the theory of comparative advantage. David Ricardo introduced this theory in 1821 in his *Principles of Political Economy and Taxation*. It is commonly misunderstood to assert the obvious, that countries have or can create different comparative advantages or that trade can be helpful. In fact, it supports a very specific policy conclusion: a country's best economic policy is to allow unregulated international market activity to determine its comparative advantage and national patterns of production. . . .

Like all theories, the theory of comparative advantage (and its conclusion) is based on a number of assumptions. Among the most important are:

- There is perfect competition between firms.
- There is full employment of all factors of production.
- Labor and capital are perfectly mobile within a country and do not move across national borders.
- A country's gains from trade are captured by those living in the country and spent locally.
- A country's external trade is always in balance.
- Market prices accurately reflect the real (or social) costs of the products produced.

Even a quick consideration of these assumptions reveals that they are extensive and unrealistic. Moreover, if they are not satisfied, there is no basis for accepting the theory's conclusion that free-market policies will promote international well being. For example, the assumption of full employment of all factors of production, including labor, is obviously false. Equally problematic is the theory's implied restructuring process, which assumes that (but never explains how) workers who lose their jobs as a result of free-trade generated imports will quickly find new employment in the expanding export sector of the economy. In reality, workers (and other factors of production) may not be equally productive in alternative uses. Even if we ignore this problem, if their reallocation is not sufficiently fast, the newly liberalized economy will likely suffer an increase in unemployment, leading to a reduction in aggregate demand and perhaps recession. Thus, even if all factors of production eventually become fully employed, it is quite possible that the cost of adjustment would outweigh the alleged efficiency gains from the trade induced restructuring.

The assumption that prices reflect social costs is also problematic. Many product markets are dominated by monopolies, many firms receive substantial government subsidies that influence their production and pricing decisions, and many production activities generate significant negative externalities (especially environmental ones). Therefore, trade specialization based on existing market prices could easily produce a structure of international economic activity with lower overall efficiency, leading to a reduction in social well being. . . .

Also worthy of challenge is the assumption that capital is not highly mobile across national borders. This assumption helps to underpin others, including the assumptions of full employment and balanced trade. If capital is highly mobile, then free-market/free-trade policies could produce capital flight leading to deindustrialization, unbalanced trade, unemployment, and economic crisis. In short, the free-trade supporting policy recommendations that flow from the theory of comparative advantage rest on a series of very dubious assumptions. . . .

Neoliberalism: The Reality

The post-1980 neoliberal era has been marked by slower growth, greater trade imbalances, and deteriorating social conditions. The United Nations Conference on Trade and Development (UNCTAD) reports that, "for developing countries as a whole (excluding China), the average trade deficit in the 1990s is higher than in the 1970s by almost 3 percentage points of GDP, while the average growth rate is lower by 2 percent per annum." Moreover,

> The pattern is broadly similar in all developing regions. In Latin America the average growth rate is lower by 3 percent per annum in the 1990s than in the 1970s, while trade deficits as a proportion of GDP are much the same. In sub-Saharan Africa growth fell, but deficits rose. The Asian countries managed to grow faster in the 1980s, while

reducing their payments deficits, but in the 1990s they have run greater deficits without achieving faster growth.

A study by Mark Weisbrot, Dean Baker, and David Rosnick on the consequences of neoliberal policies on third world development comes to similar conclusions. The authors note that "contrary to popular belief, the past 25 years (1980–2005) have seen a sharply slower rate of economic growth and reduced progress on social indicators for the vast majority of low- and middle-income countries [compared with the prior two decades].". . .

In an effort to keep growing trade and current account deficits manageable, third world states, often pressured by the IMF and World Bank, used austerity measures (especially draconian cuts in social programs) to slow economic growth (and imports). They also deregulated capital markets, privatized economic activity, and relaxed foreign investment regulatory regimes in an effort to attract the financing needed to offset the existing deficits. While devastating to working people and national development possibilities, these policies were, as intended, responsive to the interests of transnational capital in general and a small but influential sector of third world capital. This is the reality of neoliberalism.

The Dynamics of Contemporary Capitalism . . .

Mainstream theorists usually consider international trade, finance, and investment as separate processes. In fact, they are interrelated. And, as highlighted above, the capitalist drive for greater profitability has generally worked to pressure third world states into an overarching liberalization and deregulation. This dynamic has had important consequences, especially, but not exclusively, for the third world. In particular, it has encouraged transnational corporations to advance their aims through the establishment and extension of international production networks. This has led to new forms of dominance over third world industrial activity that involve its reshaping and integration across borders in ways that are ever more destructive of the social, economic, and political needs of working people.

During the 1960s and 1970s, most third world countries pursued state directed import-substitution industrialization strategies and financed their trade deficits with bank loans. This pattern ended suddenly in the early 1980s, when economic instabilities in the developed capitalist world, especially in the United States, led to rising interest rates and global recession. Third world borrowing costs soared and export earnings plummeted, triggering the third world "debt crisis." With debt repayment in question, banks greatly reduced their lending, leading to ever deepening third world economic and social problems.

To overcome these problems, third world states sought new ways to boost exports and new sources of international funds. Increasingly, they came to see export-oriented foreign direct investment as the answer. The competition for this investment was fierce. Country after country made changes in their investment regimes, with the great majority designed to create a more liberalized, deregulated, and "business friendly" environment. Transnational corporations responded eagerly to these changes, many of which they and their governments helped promote. And, over the years 1991–98, FDI became the single greatest source of net capital inflow into the third world, accounting for 34 percent of the total.

New technologies had made it possible for transnational corporations to cheapen production costs for many goods by segmenting and geographically dividing their production processes. They therefore used their investments to locate the labor intensive production segments of these goods—in particular the production or assembly of parts and components—in the third world. This was especially true for electronic and electrical goods, clothing and apparel, and certain technologically advanced goods such as optical instruments.

The result was the establishment or expansion of numerous vertically structured international production networks, many of which extended over several different countries. According to UNCTAD, "it has been estimated, on the basis of input-output tables from a number of OECD and emerging-market countries, that trade based on specialization within vertical production networks accounts for up to 30 percent of world exports, and that it has grown by as much as 40 percent in the last 25 years."

Despite the fierce third world competition to attract FDI, transnational corporations tended to concentrate their investments in only a few countries. In general, U.S. capital emphasized North America (NAFTA), while Japanese capital focused on East Asia, and European capital on Central Europe. The countries that "lost out" in the FDI competition were generally forced to manage their trade and finance problems with austerity. Those countries that "won" usually experienced a relatively fast industrial transformation. More specifically, they became major exporters of manufactures, especially of high-technology products such as transistors and semiconductors, computers, parts of computers and office machines, telecommunications equipment and parts, and electrical machinery.

As a consequence of this development, the share of third world exports that were manufactures soared from 20 percent in the 1970s and early 1980s, to 70 percent by the late 1990s. The third world share of world manufacturing exports also jumped from 4.4 percent in 1965 to 30.1 percent in 2003.

Mainstream economists claim that this rise in manufactured exports demonstrates the benefits of liberalization, and thus the importance of WTO-style liberalization agreements for development. However, this argument falsely identifies FDI and exports of manufactures with development, thereby seriously misrepresenting the dynamics of transnational capital accumulation. The reality is that participation in transnational corporate controlled production networks has done little to support rising standards of living, economic stability, or national development prospects.

There are many reasons for this failure. First, those countries that have succeeded in attracting FDI have usually done so in the context of liberalizing and deregulating their economies. This has generally resulted in the destruction of their domestic import-competing industries, causing unemployment, a rapid rise in imports, and industrial hollowing out. Second, the activities located in the third world rarely transfer skills or technology, or encourage domestic industrial linkages. This means that these activities are seldom able to promote a dynamic or nationally integrated process of development. Furthermore the exports produced are highly import dependent, thereby greatly reducing their foreign exchange earning benefits.

Finally, the transnational accumulation process makes third world growth increasingly dependent on external demand. In most cases, the primary final market for these networks is the United States, which means that third world growth comes to depend ever more on the ability of the United States to sustain ever larger trade deficits—an increasingly dubious proposition. . . .

Our Challenge

As we have seen, arguments purporting to demonstrate that free-trade/free-market policies will transform economic activities and relations in ways that universally benefit working people are based on theories and simulations that distort the actual workings of capitalism. The reality is that growing numbers of workers are being captured by an increasingly unified and transnational process of capital accumulation. Wealth is being generated but working people in all the countries involved are being pitted against each other and suffering similar consequences, including unemployment and worsening living and working conditions.

Working people and their communities are engaged in growing, although uneven, resistance to the situation. While increasingly effective, this resistance still remains largely defensive and politically unfocused. One reason is that neoliberal theory continues to provide a powerful ideological cover for capitalist globalization, despite the fact that it is both generated by and designed to advance capitalist class interests. Another is the dynamic nature of contemporary capitalism, which tends to mask its destructive nature. Therefore, as participants in the resistance, we must work to ensure that our many struggles are waged in ways that help working people better understand the nature of the accumulation processes that are reshaping our lives. In this way, we can illuminate the common capitalist roots of the problems we face and the importance of building movements committed to radical social transformation and (international) solidarity.

POSTSCRIPT

Is Globalization Good for Humankind?

Many believe that economic integration will spawn greater political integration and cultural integration to the benefit of mankind. Others believe that it will destroy some of the protections that people need. There is evidence on both sides, but little can be determined now. Both sides are predicting the future state of affairs, so until the future declares one view, the winner cannot be disproved.

There has been an explosion of books on globalization recently. A bestseller is Thomas Friedman's *The Lexus and the Olive Tree* (Farrar, Straus, Giroux, 2000), which tells the story of the new global economy and many of its ramifications. Friedman sees the United States as the nation that is best able to capitalize on that global economy, so it has the brightest future. Other works that explore the role of America in globalization include Jim Garrison, *America as Empire: Global Leader or Rogue Power?* (Berret-Koehler Publishers, 2004); Gary J. Hytrek and Kristine M. Zentgraf, *America Transformed: Globalization, Inequality, and Power* (Oxford University Press, 2008); Ulrich Beck et al., *Global America? The Cultural Consequences of Globalization* (Liverpool University Press, 2003); and Will Hutton, *World We're In: A Declaration of Interdependence: Why America Should Join the World* (W. W. Norton, 2003). Works that applaud globalization include Barry Asmas, *The Best Is Yet to Come* (AmeriPress, 2001); Diane Coyle, *Paradoxes of Prosperity: Why the New Capitalism Benefits All* (Texere, 2001); John Micklethwait and Adrian Wooldridge, *Future Perfect: The Challenge and Hidden Promise of Globalization* (Crown Business, 2000); and Jacques Bandot, ed., *Building a World Community: Globalization and the Common Good* (University of Washington Press, 2001).

Attacks on globalization are prolific and include Ronaldo Munck, *Globalization and Contestation: The New Great Counter-Movement* (Routledge, 2007); Robert Went, *Globalization: Neoliberal Challenge, Radical Responses* (Pluto Press, 2000); William K. Tabb, *The Amoral Elephant: Globalization and the Struggle for Social Justice in the Twenty-First Century* (Monthly Review Press, 2001); Walden Bello, *Future in Balance: Essays on Globalization and Resistance* (Food First Books, 2001); Vic George and Paul Wilding, *Globalization and Human Welfare* (Palgrave, 2002); Gary Teeple, *Globalization and the Decline of Social Reform* (Humanity Books, 2000); Noreena Hertz, *The Silent Takeover: Global Capitalism and the Death of Democracy* (Free Press, 2002); Alan Tomelson, *Race to the Bottom: Why a Worldwide Worker Surplus and Uncontrolled Free Trade Are Sinking American Living Standards* (Westview, 2000); Richard P. Appelbaum and William I. Robinson, eds., *Critical Globalization Studies* (Routledge, 2005); Joseph E.

Stiglitz, *Globalization and Its Discontents* (W. W. Norton 2003); Vincent Navarro, ed., *Neoliberalism, Globalization, and Inequalities* (Baywood, 2007); Peter Isard, *Globalization and the International Financial System: What's Wrong and What Can Be Done* (Cambridge, 2005); Thom Burnett and Alec Games, *Who Really Runs the World? The War Between Globalization and Democracy* (Disinformation, 2007); and Robert A. Isaak, *The Globalization Gap: How the Rich Get Richer and the Poor Get Left Further Behind* (Prentice-Hall, 2005).

For relatively balanced discussions of globalization, see Nick Bisley, *Rethinking Globalization* (Palgrave Macmillan, 2007); Arthur P. J. Mol, *Globalization and Environmental Reform: The Ecological Modernization of the Global Economy* (MIT Press, 2001), which points to the environmental degradation that results from globalization but also presents actions that retard degradation and improve environmental quality; Richard Langhome, *The Coming of Globalization: Its Evolution and Contemporary Consequences* (St. Martin's Press, 2001); Kamal Dervis, *Better Globalization: Legitimacy, Governance and Reform* (Brookings, 2005); Barbara Harris-White, ed., *Globalization and Insecurity: Political, Economic, and Physical Challenges* (Palgrave, 2002); *Global Transformations Reader: An Introduction to the Globalization Debate,* edited by David Held et al. (Policy Press, 2003); Tony Schirato and Jennifer Webb, *Understanding Globalization* (Sage, 2003); and *Globalization and Antiglobalization: Dynamics of Change in the New World,* edited by Henry Veltmeyer (Ashgate, 2004). For interesting discussions of the cultural aspects of globalization, see Paul Kennedy and Catherine J. Danks, eds., *Globalization and National Identities: Crisis or Opportunity* (Palgrave, 2001); Tyler Cowen, *Creative Destruction: How Globalization Is Changing the World's Cultures* (Princeton University Press, 2002); Alison Brysk, ed., *Globalization and Human Rights* (University of California Press, 2002); Elisabeth Madimbee-Boyi, ed., *Beyond Dichotomies: Histories, Identities, Cultures, and the Challenge of Globalization* (SUNY, 2002); and George Ritzer, *The Globalization of Nothing* (Pine Forge Press, 2007).

ISSUE 22

Is Big Government Bad?

YES: Jim DeMint, from *Saving Freedom* (Fidelis, 2009)

NO: Jeff Madrick, from *The Case for Big Government* (Princeton, 2008)

ISSUE SUMMARY

YES: Senator Jim DeMint argues that the federal government should be as limited as possible. It must protect the nation, guarantee freedom, provide justice and equal treatment, and provide a few other services that promote welfare, but it must avoid trying to solve all problems. Large government stifles the economy, wastes money and resources, reduces freedoms, and could expand to the point that it destroys the nation.

NO: Humanities professor Jeff Madrick argues that many government interventions in the economy since the end of World War II have been successful in furthering economic growth and addressing many problems that required government intervention. America is much better off because of many of the activities of the government.

This volume already contains a debate about whether the government should intervene in a capitalist economy, which overlaps with this debate about the appropriate size of government. The Tea Party, however, has made the size of the government the key political issue of the day, so it is necessary to examine the arguments for and against big government. According to the Tea Party, the stimulus, bailout, health care bill, regulations for Wall Street, and many other initiatives were bad because they increased the size and role of the federal government. Even if they accomplished some good things (which the Tea Party largely denies), they caused or will cause many bad things that make them very undesirable. According to them these policies gave the government too much power and control that endanger our freedoms and messes up our economy. The government lacks the competence to run any of the large corporations, so its interference will have mostly negative effects. Its regulations get in the way of efficient operations and are always poorly administered and thus accomplish little. Typically, they lead to the collusion of the regulatory agency with the businesses they regulate and possibly even extensive corruption.

There are many arguments against big government and DeMint covers many of them. His first and main argument is the incompetence of centralized government and his second argument is the perversion of government by special interests. Because elections are won by bundling together many special interests, the special interests rule to the detriment of the common good. The government is forced to serve these special interests, with disastrous results. DeMint mentions many wrongheaded actions that demonstrate how bad government actions can be even when the stated purposes have been honorable. Also the rights of individuals become subordinated to the demands of the special interests by the government's actions. Thus, the public must fight against the extension of the government to save our freedoms.

There are also many arguments for government actions to deal with problems that are not being addressed by other organizations and institutions. This, in turn, requires expanding government. The debate is actually not symmetrical. Although one side is adamantly against big government, the other side is not. Rather, the other side generally prefers small government to large government. They believe, however, that many problems must be addressed by the federal government because other institutions have not been able to adequately address them to date. They also disagree with the argument that the government almost always fails. Although some policies and agencies do fail, many succeed. The military not only has its failures and cost overruns (is that a business failure or a government failure?), but also has its successes. The same can be said for many other agencies and policies. Their argument is that the country needs many government-provided policies and services and this necessity results in big government.

At some point analysts should change the argument from whether big government is good or bad to figuring out what the government is good for and what it is not good for. In general, the public sector is good for public goods (which are provided for everyone) and the private sector is good for private goods (which individuals and organizations buy). For example, the police provide for public safety and law enforcement, while security guards provide security for a specific organization. Public schools educate all children in their districts, and private schools educate only those children whose parents pay for them. It seems to pro government side that modern complex life requires more and more public goods and a more active role for government. Next, the argument shifts to whether the public good should be provided at the federal, state, or local level. The anti-big-government view wants these issues addressed at the lowest level possible.

For this issue we have selected two authors who have written an entire book to argue their cases. Both strongly oppose the other side because they believe that their opponent's ideas, if implemented, could greatly harm America. Senator DeMint fights in the Senate against the big government ideas and policies of his colleagues, which he believes will lead to unlimited debt that will collapse the economy and bring on socialism and the loss of individual freedoms. Professor Jeff Madrick thinks that DeMint's views are nonsense. The many new activities of the government since the 1930s have greatly increased American prosperity and have improved life by addressing many societal problems.

YES

Jim DeMint

Freedom versus Big Government: Unlimited Government Leads to Unlimited Debt and Socialism

. . . **M**ost members of Congress act like the Constitution is no longer relevant and seem to believe we should continue to expand federal programs whenever and wherever we see fit. But no reasonably informed, thinking American could believe unrestrained government spending would be good for our country. I will discuss in later chapters the corruption, incompetence, mismanagement, and devastating societal impact of congressional meddling in all areas of American cultural and economic life. The focus of this chapter, however, is the financial condition of our country. The most compelling arguments to stop the growth of the federal government are our government's unsustainable levels of spending and debt, which could result in the financial collapse of our government and our private sector economic structure. . . .

Unlike politically manufactured crises, the catastrophic financial course of the federal government is an absolute fact. Without major reforms there is no plausible survivable scenario for our economy. This is not a problem that might occur in the distant future. The nation's debt, out-of-control spending, and loose monetary policy are creating worldwide economic insecurity. It seems inexplicable that Congress is completely ignoring this problem. . . .

Easy and cheap credit were allowing more people to buy homes and cars, accomplishing the dual goals of artificially raising the standard of living for lower-income Americans and keeping our economy running on steroids. The problem with steroids is they eventually destroy the people who use them. Loose monetary policy created a financial house of cards destined to crash. But unqualified borrowers and unscrupulous lenders were not the only ones who suffered. Much of the savings of responsible, hardworking Americans evaporated almost overnight. . . .

Mr. Walker's presentation, titled "Saving Our Future Requires Tough Choices Today," revealed that mandatory spending (required by law) for Social Security, Medicare, and Medicaid (entitlements) had grown from 16 percent of federal spending in 1966 to 40 percent of the entire federal budget in 2006. The large wave of baby boomers now reaching retirement age promises to make this problem much worse.

From *Saving Freedom: We Can Stop America's Slide into Socialism,* by Jim DeMint (Fidelis, 2009), pp. 85–88, 89–94, 103–104, 112–113, 127. Copyright © 2009 by Jim DeMint. Reprinted by permission of B&H Publishing, Nashville, TN.

Most of this spending has been taken from funds that should have been used for the primary constitutional responsibility of the federal government—defense. Military spending dropped from 43 percent in 1966 to 20 percent in 2006. While "smart bombs" and other new hightech weapons systems have lulled Americans into a false sense of security, our military is fighting with one hand tied behind its back. In the age of terrorism, our intelligence capabilities are woefully lacking. . . .

My point is this: there is a terrible cost to unrestrained government spending and debt. Part of that cost is the neglect of real national priorities such as defense. The other costs are the devaluation of our currency, the destruction of our private-sector economy, and the loss of wealth and quality of life for all Americans. . . .

Principles and Institutions

Government is an essential *institution* for the development and protection of freedom. We must have a framework of law, order, and justice for freedom to grow and thrive. Government makes the rules and enforces them much like the officials at a football game. Players and coaches have the freedom to do whatever they want as long as they follow the rules. When they don't, the officials throw a flag and impose a penalty. But the officials don't call the plays or decide who gets to play. Officials don't manage the game, and the federal government shouldn't try to manage America.

America's government has grown well beyond the constitutional framework provided by our founders. Our federal government is no longer the referee for our economy and culture; it is now the biggest player on the field. Our federal government is trying to manage many aspects of America's economy and social services. It is not an exaggeration to say the results have been catastrophic. Not only has the government inhibited the growth of our economy and undermined our culture, it has put our country on an unsustainable financial course that must be reversed immediately. . . .

The federal government is increasingly dysfunctional because congressmen and senators are focusing on their own priorities and the special interests of major political groups rather than the good of the nation. With so many competing interests, there is no agreement on what should be done. The only way to pass legislation is to ball up hundreds or even thousands of special interests favors into almost every bill. As long as a majority of congressmen have something they want in the bill, it passes.

Democracies become corrupt, incompetent, and dysfunctional when their focus turns from working for the good of the whole to serving the many interests of a wide range of subgroups. The reason for this dysfunction should be obvious; it is impossible for politicians and bureaucrats in Washington to manage a complex array of public and private functions at the national and international levels, while also trying to manage public and private functions within our fifty states and thousands of local communities.

That's why America was designed with a republican form of government, not a national government. We are a republic composed of fifty semi-independent states with separate legislatures and budgets. Each state has its own system of local governments to further disperse political power. The collective power of state and local governments was intended to counterbalance the power of the federal government. In addition, private enterprise with limited government interference was intended to disperse economic power to millions of independent decision-makers. . . .

The Tyranny of Special Interests

America's constitutionally limited, republican form of government is now alien to most members of Congress, federal judges, and federal agencies. These politicians, judges, and bureaucrats see themselves as rulers of all political, legal, economic, humanitarian, and cultural activities in America. They may delegate some responsibilities to other public and private entities; but make no mistake, the final say for all matters rests at the federal level.

As power has concentrated in Washington, every special interest in America has focused its attention on gleaning favor and money from the federal government. My office in Washington stays full with a parade of groups and lobbyists who want something from the federal government. Because the government now makes so many important decisions for so many interests and has control over so much money, lobbyists have grown like weeds in Washington. As Newt Gingrich has said:

> Lobbyists are a consequence of big government, not a cause of it. The more money centered in government the more value there will be in hiring a lobbyist. The more lobbyists are hired, the more politics will be dominated by the political contributions of the lobbyists and their employers. The more power the lobbyist and their employers amass over the politicians, the more politics will define the economy. It will become more profitable to influence a politician than to invent a product. If the market rejects you, or your ideas fail to compete, with your lobbyist's help you may be able to get government to protect you from your own failure.

The proliferation of special interests in Washington has created a threat to freedom quite different from the "tyranny of the majority." Majority interests in America are now secondary to the politics of special interests. The election of 2008 demonstrated how a political party could bundle the interests of numerous groups and create a new ruling majority—a new tyranny of special interests.

This new political dynamic is the antithesis of the intent of our Constitution and a serious blow to the cause of freedom. The rights of individuals, protected by equal justice and the rule of law, are now subjugated to the special rights of groups that are guaranteed by a strong, centralized government. The "common good" is now viewed as a conglomeration of disparate interests of multiple groups demanding special treatment.

There are a lot of good reasons for Americans to fight back against this centralization of special interest power in Washington, but the most important reason is it creates a dysfunctional government. It may be a cliché, but it's true; Washington is broken. Almost everything our federal government attempts to do becomes a disaster. We mandate that cars burn corn ethanol and cause a world food crisis. We combine social engineering with monetary policy and create a worldwide financial crisis. . . . We have left one catastrophe after another in our wake as we have attempted to save the world, dry every tear, and solve every problem. . . .

The federal farm program is [an] example of how parochial interests and earmarks can trump true national priorities. The farm program is a big government giveaway disguised as assistance to small farmers. It lavishes welfare-style subsidies on large corporate farmers, "hobby" farmers, and many agriculture-related businesses overflowing in profits. The most recent farm bill passed in May 2008 spent more than $600 billion. It was opposed by nearly every major editorial board and others from all political spectrums: the *New York Times, The Washington Post, USA Today, Los Angeles Times, National Review*, and more.

The bill contained outdated subsidy formulas giving welfare to millionaire farmers and continues to direct billions to food industries experiencing record profits. You are probably asking why, if just about all observers on the left and right condemned the bill, did it pass the House (318–106) and Senate (81–15). The answer is simple: special interest political power and earmarks.

- The Citizens against Government Waste found more than $2 billion in earmarks in the bill.
- *USA Today* found that more than $9 million in farm subsidies have gone directly to eight senators and four House members or their relatives.
- *The Washington Post* found at least $15 billion in wasteful farm subsidies.
- The Cato Institute uncovered an earmark to Plum Creek Timber for $500 million and noted that the company spent $2 million in lobbying and campaign contributions to secure the taxpayer handout.

Another problem with earmarks is they restrict the ability of our federal agencies to operate efficiently. For example, as congressmen and senators bemoan the nation's deteriorating roads and bridges, former Transportation Secretary Mary Peters explained that congressional earmarking was the major cause of our infrastructure problems:

> Wasteful spending over the last few decades has further degraded our ability to direct our limited transportation resources to the most productive investments. The clearest evidence of our failure to prioritize investments has been the disturbing growth of Congressional earmarks in surface transportation reauthorization bills, from a handful in the 1982 bill to more than 6,000 in the 2005 bill, SAFETEA-LU. The amount of the SAFETEA-LU earmarks was more than $23 billion. . . .

The High Cost of Socialism

Like Sancho in the Don Quixote story, Americans will bear the brunt of the good intentions of our knights in Congress. Despite political promises to reduce pain and to make things right for everyone, the top-down decision-making and bureaucratic management of government always deliver an inferior service at a higher price than competitive, free-market providers.

Once government begins to intervene into the free-enterprise system, the natural accountability of private sector risks and rewards is thrown out of balance. We have seen it in the financial crisis, in the auto and agriculture industries, in the deterioration and high cost of health-care services, and in America's government-run education system. The federal government's management of America's energy resources has also obscured the reliable economic balancing of supply and demand and left Americans heavily dependent on unreliable and high-cost energy suppliers.

Americans will not only pay for our slide toward socialism with inferior services; we will pay with high taxes and the devaluation of our dollar. Socialism creates a vicious cycle of political promises, government spending, and mounting debt. America's current debt, now at about $12 trillion, cannot be paid back under any plausible scenario. At our current rate of spending, we will not even be able to pay the interest on our debt without borrowing more money. In fact, we are already there. Our government has to borrow more money almost every day just to pay back the loans already coming due.

Absent major reforms and the downsizing of government, there are only two ways the government can deal with our current national debt: raise taxes dramatically and/or devalue our currency. The devaluation of our dollar will likely begin soon because other countries are already losing confidence in our ability to pay back our debt.

When the value of our dollar falls, everyone's quality of life declines because we can buy less with our current incomes. The value of our savings and investments also declines as the cost of everything we buy increases. If the government continues to spend and borrow more money—even to "bail" us out—we dig a deeper hole, and the value of the dollar will drop even more.

If politicians raise taxes to pay for more spending or to repay debt, everyone pays—even if the taxes are targeted at the "rich." Taxes take money out of the private economy and permanently increase the cost of government. Money left in the private economy is either spent or saved, both of which improve the overall economy.

When money stays in the private economy, there is an economic multiplier to every dollar spent. If you spend a dollar at the grocery store, the grocer uses it to pay an employee. That employee uses it to buy clothes at a local retailer who uses if to pay his employees . . . and on and on. Consumer spending strengthens our economy and creates jobs. Likewise, when money is saved or invested, it also creates jobs because savings and investments are used to finance the growth of companies with stocks or as loans to businesses or consumers.

Conversely, when money goes to the government in the form of taxes, it increases the size of government and creates a permanent cost to taxpayers. Every dollar the government spends this year becomes part of the baseline budget for next year. All new spending is added onto last year's spending. So when the government takes a dollar in taxes, it eliminates the economic multiplier in the private sector and creates a permanent cost compounded over time by bigger government.

Higher taxes don't solve problems; they weaken the private sector economy and grow the size of government. The question is not whether it is fair for someone to make millions while others struggle at minimum wage. The question is how do we help the guy making minimum wage make millions—or a least a decent income?

Principles and Institutions

Considering America's debt and current economic situation, the principle of limited government is not only a preferred conservative political philosophy; it is an urgent necessity for the survival of our republic. . . .

Another principle is that political power must be counterbalanced by private sector economic power. America's free enterprise capitalistic economic system with its millions of decision-makers is the foundational democratic institution in American. We cannot allow our government to become a major force in our private economy.

Freedom is protected by a wide range of public and private institutions guarding against the concentration of power. The concentration of power at the federal level destroys this balance, weakens other institutions of freedom, and destroys freedom itself. Americans must not continue to allow one institution of freedom, the federal government, to dominate and diminish the role of other institutions or to demean the individual values that made our country great and free.

Jeff Madrick  **NO**

The Case for Big Government

After World War II, almost all economists feared a reprise of the Depression. It was hard to imagine what could replace all the lost military demand. But the opposite occurred. After a pause in 1947, the economy grew as rapidly on average as it ever did before, and the incomes of most working Americans grew faster than ever before. The progressive turn of policy, despite a resurgence of antigovernment sensibility, did not deter growth. Nor did higher income tax rates, which were raised by Roosevelt during the Depression and were raised again to record levels during World War II, where they remained for more than a decade. The highest tax bracket reached approximately 90 percent, where it remained until 1964. To the contrary, bigger government seemed to go along with ever faster growth. Roosevelt had proposed a G.I. Bill of Rights in 1943, among other things, to provide aid for veterans to go to college and to buy a house. Congress raised objections, but in 1944 the G.I. Bill was passed. By the late 1950s, half of the returning sixteen million soldiers financed college or other training programs as a result. Millions of mortgages were guaranteed. The nation was thus directed in a particular way. The Marshall Plan under President Truman, and named after the secretary of state who strongly advocated it, provided billions of dollars of aid to rebuild Europe.

Dwight Eisenhower, as a former president, incurred the ire of the Republican right wing by proposing to expand Social Security coverage to another ten million workers—to include farm workers and professionals such as teachers, accountants, and dentists. He also increased benefits. Eisenhower said that it was simply clear that not all could save enough for retirement. Eisenhower also advocated the development and federal financing of a national highway system. He had strong support from the major auto companies, of course, and the bill passed in 1956. By the late 1950s, 90 percent of all homes in America were reachable by road, and often by highway. It was an explicit case of national government coordination and investment that deeply influenced the development of the nation into a new geography of suburbs, based on cheap gas, cheap property, and mostly free roads.

In these decades, the federal government financed and administered the antipolio vaccines. In the wake of the Soviet launch of the first space satellite, Sputnik, Congress passed the National Defense Education Act, providing billions of dollars of annual grants and loans to support higher education,

From *The Case for Big Government* by Jeff Madrick (Princeton University Press, 2008), pp. 56–61, 128, 138–140, 142–143. Copyright © 2008 by Princeton University Press. Reprinted by permission.

technical training, and other educational programs. Young people were further spurred to go to college. The National Institutes of Health, as an extension of late nineteenth-century government investment in health research, were expanded dramatically after World War II, and accounted for a high proportion of medical breakthroughs. Research and development (R&D) was undertaken in many federal agencies, not least the Defense Department, where the Internet had its origins. The federal government accounted for most of America's R&D, in fact, through the 1960s, topping out at 67 percent of all such research in 1963. Many economists contend that such intense research efforts account for greater American economic superiority in these years than any other single factor. The Supreme Court under Eisenhower, led by Johnson's appointee as chief justice, Earl Warren, ordered that public schools be integrated.

In the 1960s, President Johnson passed Medicare and implemented his War on Poverty, including health care for the poor under Medicaid. Regulatory changes were significant, and included landmark civil rights legislation, which protected voting rights for blacks, ended Jim Crow laws once and for all, and forbade gender and racial discrimination in labor markets. Other regulatory reforms involved cigarettes, packaging, motor vehicle safety, consumer credit, and the expansion of the authority of the Food and Drug Administration.

Between 1948 and 1970, the share of spending in GDP by the federal, state, and local governments rose from 16.5 percent to 27.5 percent, nearly eleven percentage points. Most of this increase was in social expenditures. Yet productivity, wages, and overall GDP grew very rapidly, as noted. What is the complaint then in light of all this success? It is hard to escape the conclusion as noted earlier in this section that government did not hurt but significantly helped economies to grow.

The Economic Benefits of Government

. . . Few economists disagree with the theory that some measure of public investment in infrastructure, education, and health care is necessary. Because public goods such as roads and schools benefit society overall more than any individual or business, such investment would not have been adequately undertaken by private firms. . . . Government support is required for primary education, roads, and the poor.

Far less frequently discussed is the fact that government can be the focus of needed and useful coordination. When railroads used different size track (gauge), government was needed to standardize them. By organizing communities to use a single public water system, government creates economies of scale for such a public good. The highway system was an immense act of coordination that probably couldn't have been attained through a private network; there is no example of one in the world, in any case. The system of international trade and currency valuation is a government-led example of coordination.

Similarly, regulations can and often do make economies work better. They can make information about products and services more open. They can reduce corruption, monopolistic pricing, and anticompetitive policies regarding research, innovation, and new products. They can temper financial speculation, which distorts the flow of capital toward inefficient uses and can often lead to costly corrections and serious recessions, as occurred yet again in 2008.

Some regulations can be poorly administered and reduce economic efficiency. Others will outlive their usefullness; they should be pruned and streamlined over time. But other regulations will be a short-term cost to business that the nation chooses to bear for quality of life and even a better economy. Maintaining the safety of products that consumers cannot judge for themselves is an example; but the safety and effectiveness of products also makes consumers more confident buyers of products. Environmental regulations adopted in the early 1970s have probably been costly to all of us, but they are a cost we bear for cleaner air and water and the diminution of global warming. It is no cause for alarm that regulations have multiplied as the economy supplies so many more goods and services to the people. As economies change and grow more complex, it is only natural that more oversight is needed.

At the still more liberal end of the political spectrum, some economists will argue—though not the American mainstream—that programs that help raise and make wages more equal, such as laws that facilitate union organizing, minimum wages, and equal rights, may well aid economic growth, not undermine productivity, by creating demand for goods and services, and also reinforcing faith in workers that they will be fairly rewarded for their effort. . . .

One of the key benefits of the larger post–World War II government, if in some quarters still a controversial one, is also that it makes the economy more stable. Well before Keynes's work during the Depression there were calls for government spending to create jobs and support incomes. Massive public works projects that reignited economic growth, such as Baron Hausmann's rebuilding of Paris, are common in history. But in the post–World War II era, such activities gained new theoretical justification from Keynes's theories. Both Keynesian liberals and some Friedmanite conservatives accepted, to one degree or another, that fiscal and monetary policy—deficit spending by the treasury or the adjustment of interest rates by the central bank—could help avoid or ameliorate recessions and thereby raise the rate of growth over time. A large government is itself, despite conservative arguments cited earlier, a bulwark against rapidly declining spending. Unemployment insurance, Social Security, and government employment itself are stabilizing factors.

If the size of government truly and directly caused the inflation of the 1970s and contributed demonstrably to slower economic growth, it would be reason for concern. But we have seen that it did not in the United States, and nations with far larger governments have produced neither more rapid inflation nor substandard levels of income for their citizens. The public goods and social programs of many countries—from Sweden and Norway to France and Germany—are significantly more generous than America's. . . .

In fact, enlightened regulation has been imperative for economic growth at least since Jefferson's policies for governing the distribution of land. When done well, regulation keeps competition honest and free, enables customers to know and understand the products they receive, and fosters new ideas. When neglected, abuse becomes easy, information in markets is suppressed, capital investment is channeled to wasteful and inefficient uses, and dangerous excesses occur. The open flow of products and services information is critical to a free-market economy. The conditions for healthy competition have simply not been maintained under a free-market ideology of minimal government that professes great faith in competition. Competition requires government oversight; the wool has been pulled over our eyes.

We now know the following. If federal, state, and local governments absorb roughly 35 percent of GDP in America, rather than the current roughly 30 percent, it will not inhibit growth and undermine entrepreneurial spirits, productivity, or prosperity if the spending is well-channeled. Government absorbs much more of national income in other nations whose prosperity is the equivalent of or perhaps superior to America's. In European nations, government spending absorbs approximately 40 percent of all spending, and standards of living are high. If government programs are managed well, they will on balance enhance productivity. A rise to 35 percent will raise approximately $700 billion a year to the federal, state, and local governments to provide protections to workers, finance social programs, maintain an adequate regulatory presence, and raise significantly the level of investment in transportation, energy, education, and health care. Part and perhaps all of this $700 billion can be paid for with higher taxes. . . .

. . . The most productive way to address rising global competition is not trade restrictions per se but for the government to invest in the nation. Consumer spending leaks to foreign imports and business investment leaks across borders. But potential returns to the economy from spending on transportation projects are at this point significant, partly due to years of neglect, and the jobs created to implement them largely stay at home. The proportion of the federal budget spent on investment in the nation—including transportation, science, technology, and energy—are well down from the levels of the 1970s. Federal spending on education as a proportion of GDP fell under Clinton but was raised under his successor, George Bush, and it remains slightly higher as a proportion of GDP than it was in the 1970s. Overall, public investment equaled nearly 3 percent of GDP in the 1970s, which would come to more than $400 billion today. Under Clinton it fell to halt of that proportion, and under Bush it rose but remains at less than 2 percent of GDP. Merely raising it to 1970s levels would produce $140 billion more a year to spend. To reemphasize, such spending usually creates domestic jobs and builds future productivity at the same time.

To take one estimate, a House Transportation Committee report cites a Federal Highway Administration model that claims that a $75 billion investment will create more than 3.5 million jobs and $464 billion in additional nationwide sales. Every $1 billion, in other words, yields 47,500 jobs and another $6 billion in sales. Spending has been so inadequate that such estimates can be accepted confidently. The Society of Civil Engineers suggest that much of America's infrastructure should get a grade of D. While these studies are hardly definitive, they are suggestive of the possibilities.

The most exciting potential returns are for high-quality pre-K education. A wide range of studies has been undertaken on several high-quality programs that have long been underway in the United States. The benefits of such programs include not only improving the ability of children to learn, but also long-term reduction in crime rates, reduced need for special education and repeating grades, and lower welfare enrollment rates. A conventional conservative economist such as James Heckman, a Nobel laureate who opposes college subsidies, nevertheless favors significant funding of preschool programs. Some estimate these programs create benefits that exceed costs by five to ten times. A highly sophisticated recent analysis by two economists estimates that if a high-quality program was instituted nationwide, the federal moneys spent would be fully paid for in increased tax revenues due to improved incomes and would reduce welfare, crime, and special education expenses. In other words, it would pay for itself. . . .

As a consequence of neglect and change, an adequate agenda for America is a lengthy one, but it is not an antigrowth agenda. It favors growth. Growing personal income is more necessary to a full life than is recognized, in part because the cost of some key needs rise very fast, in part because a wealthy society can finance innovation, and in part because a wealthy populace will find it easier and more congenial to pay for communal needs through taxes. But for too long, mainstream economists have accepted the notion that more savings and technology will alone lead to faster growth. The agenda for government is therefore inappropriately limited; government spending, for example, will allegedly erode savings. America has been able to test this economic philosophy for a full generation and it has failed. Years of below-par productivity growth, low and stagnating wages, inattention to basic needs, persistent poverty, and the undermining of assets necessary to future growth, including education, health care, energy alternatives, and transportation infrastructure are the consequences.

The gap between a growing economy and falling wages is the major contemporary mystery. Global competition and off-shoring may explain part of the gap, but the trend began decades ago. Research shows that a gap in worker compensation and productivity began to open up slowly in the late 1980s: typical workers got less than their historical share, while capital (profits) and high-income workers got more. This gap widened explosively in the 2000s.

Furthermore, there was little explanation as to why male incomes in particular fared especially poorly over this long period we have described. A major reason is the withdrawal of government from its traditional purposes.

POSTSCRIPT

Is Big Government Bad?

The debate between DeMint and Madrick cannot be resolved. DeMint does not like where America is today, but he is mainly worried about the future. Unless America changes in the way that he recommends our economy will collapse and the government will control our lives. Since this disaster is hypothetical, it cannot be proven and his arguments can be challenged. In contrast, Madrick assumes that the great progress that America achieved in the past through the expansion of social programs and policies for better conditions justifies new policies today. The experience of European countries lends support to his belief that similar policies will greatly benefit America, but he does not know this for sure. This impasse lets ideology dominate the debate. Nevertheless, considerable scholarship has argued each side for decades.

Quite a few recent books argue against big government and for limited government. American Enterprise Institute's president, Arthur C. Brooks, reveals in *The Battle: How the Fight Between Free Enterprise and Big Government Will Shape America's Future* (Basic Books, 2010) how recent political forces have greatly expanded the power of the state and adversely affected the free enterprise system, which is the main source of America's prosperity, welfare, and happiness. He recommends ways to reverse this threat to our way of life. Newt Gingrich (with Vince Haley and Rick Tyler) presents a similar analysis but focuses on many specific issues in *Real Change: From the World That Fails to the World That Works* (Regnery, 2008). He blames both Republicans and Democrats for America's failure. Serious change in the opposite direction is needed. Thomas E. Woods, Jr. argues in *Rollback: Repealing Big Government Before the Coming Fiscal Collapse* (Regnery, 2011) that big government will bring catastrophe. Peter Schweizer focuses on the recent economic crisis and blames it on big government in *Architects of Ruin: How Big Government Liberals Wrecked the Global Economy—and How They Will Do It Again If No One Stops Them* (HarperCollins, 2009). He tries to rebut the thesis that deregulation caused the financial collapse and argues that liberal soft-hearted and soft-headed policies are to blame. Timothy P. Carney blasts both big government and big business for exploiting the public in *The Big Ripoff: How Big Business and Big Government Steal Your Money* (Wiley, 2006). Lawrence D. Brown and Lawrence R. Jacobs largely agree with Carney's analysis in *The Private Abuse of the Public Interest: Market Myths and Policy Muddles* (University of Chicago Press, 2008) but argues that government is needed to create, maintain, support, and repair markets to ensure their proper functioning.

The defenders of an activist (and therefore big) government argue that it is necessary given the current circumstances and has produced great benefits in the past. Max Neiman makes a similar argument in *Defending Government:*

Why Big Government Works (Prentice Hall, 2009). William D. Eggers and John O'Leary also defend big government as capable of doing great things while admitting that it often fails to live up to its potential in *If We Can Put a Man on the Moon: Getting Big Things Done in Government* (Harvard Business Press, 2009). Ed Schultz explains in *Killer Politics: How Big Money and Bad Politics Are Destroying the Great American Middle Class* (Hyperion, 2010) why government often performs poorly. The main culprits are big money lobbyists. Most proponents of big government complain about the way our current government operates but believe that many of its problems can be corrected. See, for example, Kathleen M. Immordino, *Organizational Assessment and Improvement in the Public Sector* (CRC Press, 2010), Elaine C. Kamarck, *The End of Government—As We Know It: Making Public Policy Work* (Lynne Rienner, 2007), and Donald F. Kettl, *The Next Government of the United States: Why Our Institutions Fail Us and How to Fix Them* (W. W. Norton, 2009).

ISSUE 23

Do Women Make Better Leaders?

YES: Alice H. Eagly and Linda L. Carli, "The Female Leadership Advantage: An Evaluation of the Evidence," *The Leadership Quarterly* (2002)

NO: Herminia Ibarra and Otilia Obodaru, from "Women and the Vision Thing," *Harvard Business Review* (January 2009)

ISSUE SUMMARY

YES: Professor of social psychology at Northwestern University Alice Eagly and senior lecturer of psychology at Wellesley College Linda Carli review the literature on leadership and report that women have characteristics that make them better leaders for today's organizations.

NO: Professor of leadership and learning at the worldwide business school INSEAD Herminia Ibarra and her doctoral student Otilia Obodaru argue that men make better leaders because they have a genetic advantage of higher visionary skills than women. Women outperform men in some other skills useful to leadership but none as important as visioning that is critical for strategizing and understanding dynamic environments.

The Eagly and Carli team has authored another essay for this volume that argues that women face barriers to career success. Their advancement in work organizations is hindered in many ways at every step of their careers. The article for this issue, however, focuses on the comparison of the abilities of women and men relevant to leadership roles. It is based on a thorough review of the literature and includes seven pages of references that are not included here. This issue has not been decisively resolved because women have advantages over men on some traits that are useful for leadership but men have advantages on other characteristics. The debate therefore shifts to which characteristics are most important and what contexts require which leadership skills.

We need to stop for a minute and reflect on the massive change that this debate represents. Fifty years ago, this debate would have been unthinkable. Everyone thought that of course men were better leaders on average than women because they had the strength, confidence, and rationality to command and lead. Women on average could relate well but not command so well and more often than men their hearts would interfere with a cold rational appraisal of the issues. Here are some of the findings from studies published in the 1960s. Women were perceived as more sympathetic, humanitarian, compassionate, and dependent on others, while men had a behavioral orientation toward power, initiative, and prestige. Furthermore, it was generally assumed that the behaviors that were considered to be "female" generally conflicted with the role demands of supervisors. Over the past 50 years, the attitudes have changed and the research results have changed. Now there are even studies that show companies that have many female senior leaders are more profitable than companies that have few. Other studies focus on the competitive disadvantages of boys and men in various arenas. Past gender expectations seem to have been turned on their heads.

What are the personality characteristics of women that make them natural leaders? They are believed to be very intuitive, which would make them better able to discern subsurface business problems. Women are also better communicators, which helps them to work better in teams, which is increasingly demanded in modern organizations. Other traits useful for leadership that women tend to have more strongly than men are the ability to multitask, possess greater social sensitivity, better understand where people are coming from, demonstrate more empathy for employee and customer concerns, and be more tenacious. These findings support Eagly and Carli's conclusions. On the other hand, there are some gender differences that favor men, which support Ibarra and Obodaru's conclusions. The main difference is in strong visionary skills that Ibarra and Obodaru focus on. They argue that visionary skills help leaders identify opportunities and dangers and thus facilitate effective strategizing and make them better able to handle risks appropriately.

YES

Alice H. Eagly and
Linda L. Carli

The Female Leadership Advantage: An Evaluation of the Evidence

Introduction

After years of analyzing what makes leaders most effective and figuring out who's got the Right Stuff, management gurus now know how to boost the odds of getting a great executive: Hire a female.

The idea that women are effective leaders has jumped from the writers of feminist trade books on management to the mainstream press and is steadily making its way into the popular culture. Articles in newspapers and business magazines reveal a cultural realignment in the United States that proclaims a new era for female leaders. As *Business Week* announces that women have the "Right Stuff," *Fast Company* concurs that "The future of business depends on women." Even more startling is *Business Week*'s subsequent cover story on the "New Gender Gap," maintaining that "Men could become losers in a global economy that values mental power over might."

The sharp edge of these female advantage articles must be quite baffling to the many academic leadership researchers who have argued that gender has little relation to leadership style and effectiveness. They might be tempted to conclude that in our postmodernist world the voices of social scientists have not been accorded any special authority. However, to earn the trust of journalists and the public, leadership researchers must approach these issues with sophisticated enough theories and methods that they illuminate the implications of gender in organizational life. Toward this goal, we show that a careful sifting through social scientific evidence, separating wheat from chaff, suggests that contemporary journalists, while surely conveying too simple a message, are expressing some of the new realities associated with women's rise into elite leadership roles.[1]

To address these issues, researchers must confront the perennially important issue of what behaviors characterize effective leaders. Is it the firm execution of authority over subordinates or the capacity to support and inspire them? More likely, as situational theories of leadership contend, the effectiveness of leader behaviors depends on contextual variables, such as the nature of the task and the characteristics of the followers. Yet, historically, leadership has been construed as primarily a masculine enterprise, and many theories of

From *The Leadership Quarterly*, September 5, 2003, pp. 807–828. Copyright © 2003 by Elsevier Inc. Reprinted by permission via Rightslink.

leadership have focused on the desirability of stereotypically masculine qualities in leaders. Nevertheless, it is probable that stereotypically feminine qualities of cooperation, mentoring, and collaboration are important to leadership as well, certainly in some contexts and perhaps increasingly in contemporary organizations.

As we analyze these issues in this article, we contrast many of our views with those of Vecchio, who recently provided a review of some of the research relevant to the debate about female advantage. The basic questions that we address in this article and that demand attention in relation to these arguments are (a) whether men and women behave differently in leadership roles, (b) whether women receive prejudiced evaluations as leaders and potential leaders, and (c) whether leadership by women might be more effective or better meet the needs of organizations than leadership by men. Although Vecchio addressed the first and third of these questions, our conclusions differ from his, and he gave insufficient attention to the second question—the crucial issue of female disadvantage from discriminatory processes.

The Changing Concept of Female Leadership

Before delving into these issues of female advantage and disadvantage, we note that women's corporate and political leadership is on the rise. Whereas women held only 18% of managerial and administrative positions in the United States in 1972, by 2002 that percentage had increased to 46%. Moreover, in the Fortune 500, both the percentage of women among all corporate officers (15.7%) and CEOs (1.4%) are at all-time highs. Likewise, although women constitute only 14% of the Congress of the United States and 12% of state governors, 42% of the women who have ever served in the Senate are in office now, as are 26% of the women who have ever served as governors. Also, 43 of the 59 women who have ever served as presidents or prime ministers of nations came into office since 1990. Despite these changes, men, far more often than women, occupy positions conferring decision-making authority and the ability to influence others' pay or promotions.

The increase in female leaders has been accompanied by changes in theories and practices of leadership. Whereas in the past, leaders based their authority mainly on their access to political, economic, or military power, in postindustrial societies leaders share power far more and establish many collaborative relationships. Therefore, contemporary views of good leadership encourage teamwork and collaboration and emphasize the ability to empower, support, and engage workers. Trade books urge managers to put people first by using "resonance-building styles . . . that support commitment, involvement, active pursuit of the vision, and healthy, productive work relationships."

These contemporary approaches to leadership not only recommend a reduction in hierarchy but also place the leader more in the role of coach or teacher than previous models of leadership. Although the specifics of these views vary, most such discussions emphasize that leader roles are changing to meet the demands of greatly accelerated technological growth, increasing workforce diversity, intense competitive pressures on corporations and other organizations, and a weakening of geopolitical boundaries. As Kanter wrote:

> Managerial work is undergoing such enormous and rapid change that many managers are reinventing their profession as they go. With little precedent to guide them, they are watching hierarchy fade away and the clear distinctions of title, task, department, even corporation, blur. Faced with extraordinary levels of complexity and interdependency, they watch traditional sources of power erode and the old motivational tools lose their magic.

Is it possible that the changing nature of managerial work accords female leaders some advantages that they did not possess in the past? As we explain in this article, social scientists have often emphasized the prejudicial disadvantages that women face because of the construal of leadership in masculine terms. To the extent that modern characterizations of effective leadership have become more consonant with the female gender role, this female disadvantage may be eroding.

The gradual erosion of female disadvantage would be consonant with the emphasis of many popular mass-market management books on traditionally feminine communal behavior, involving creating a sense of community, empowering subordinates, and communicating and listening effectively. Indeed, writers of popular books on leadership have argued that effective leadership is congruent with the ways that women lead. For example, Rosener labeled women's leadership as interactive, involving collaboration and empowerment of employees, and men's leadership as command-and-control, involving the assertion of authority and the accumulation of power. Such authors construe men and women as quite different in the ways that they lead, with men relying on a somewhat antiquated leadership style that does not fit the needs of most contemporary organizations. These provocative descriptions of sex-typed leadership styles invite careful scrutiny from social scientists. . . .

Sex Differences and Similarities in Leadership Style

Task-Oriented, Interpersonally Oriented, and Autocratic–Democratic Styles

In the long-standing tradition of studying leadership style, most research conducted prior to 1990 distinguished between *task-oriented style* or *initiation of structure* and *interpersonally oriented* style or *consideration*. A somewhat less popular distinction was between leaders who (a) behave *democratically* and allow subordinates to participate in decision-making, or (b) behave *autocratically* and discourage subordinates from such participation. . . .

This synthesis found that leadership styles were somewhat gender-stereotypic in (a) laboratory studies generally conducted as experiments on group processes with student participants and (b) assessment studies using participants not selected for occupancy of leadership roles (e.g., samples of employees or students in university business programs). Specifically, in such research, women, more than men, manifested relatively interpersonally oriented and democratic styles, and men, more than women, manifested relatively task-oriented and autocratic styles. In contrast, sex differences were more limited in organizational studies, which examined managers' styles. Male and female managers did not differ in their tendencies to manifest interpersonally oriented and task-oriented styles. However, in these studies of managers, as in the laboratory and assessment studies, women manifested a somewhat more democratic (or participative) style and a less autocratic (or directive) style than men did.

This autocratic–democratic finding, which was based on 23 data sets and a heterogeneous set of measuring instruments, produced a relatively small mean effect size ($d = 0.22$). Nonetheless, 92% of the available comparisons went in the direction of a more democratic or participative style among women. The diversity of measures of autocratic and democratic tendencies, regarded as undesirable by Vecchio, can be regarded as a strength because the conclusion was not based solely on a particular measure and thus has potentially greater generalizability. Moreover, some confirmation of Eagly and Johnson's findings is contained in a later meta-analysis that surveyed studies published subsequent to their review. . . .

Based on analyses of their large database, Eagly and Johnson concluded that gender-stereotypic sex differences in leadership behavior were less common in organizational studies than in other types of studies because male and female managers were selected by similar criteria and subjected to similar organizational socialization—forces that tend to equalize the sexes. Among managers, a sex difference was detected only in a fairly narrow range of leadership behaviors assessed by measures of autocratic–democratic (or directive–participative) tendencies, which relate primarily to the exercise of power. These findings illustrate the value of comparing studies of different types: Without the context provided by the laboratory and assessment studies of persons not occupying managerial roles, any conclusion about the lessening of sex differences among managers would not have been convincing.

This meta-analysis included some possible interpretations of the autocratic–democratic sex difference—specifically, (a) the greater social skills of women (vs. men) may have facilitated collaborative, democratic leadership behavior and (b) such behavior may have been especially advantageous for women because it placated subordinates and peers who might otherwise have been resistant to female leadership. Although we do not concur with Vecchio's view that the demonstrated difference in autocratic–democratic tendencies is unimportant, we agree that this style's effectiveness depends on context as did Eagly and Johnson (1990, p. 249), who were "unwilling to argue that women's relatively democratic and participative style is either an advantage or disadvantage." Nonetheless, consistent with Fondas's analysis, democratic, participative leader behavior is more similar to the leadership styles advocated by contemporary managerial writers than is autocratic, directive behavior. . . .

Transformational, Transactional, and Laissez-Faire Styles

Debates about the leadership styles of women and men gained momentum in the 1990s because of new research attempting to identify the styles that are especially attuned to contemporary conditions. The new emphasis was on leadership that is *transformational* in the sense that it is future oriented rather than present oriented and that strengthens organizations by inspiring followers' commitment and creativity. As initially described by Burns and elaborated by Bass transformational leadership entails establishing oneself as a role model by gaining followers' trust and confidence. Transformational leaders state future goals, develop plans to achieve those goals, and innovate, even when their organization is generally successful. By mentoring and empowering followers, such leaders help followers to develop their potential and thus to contribute more effectively to their organization.

Leadership researchers contrasted transformational leaders to *transactional* leaders, who appeal to subordinates' self-interest by establishing exchange relationships with them. Transactional leadership involves managing in the conventional sense of clarifying subordinates' responsibilities, rewarding them for meeting objectives, and correcting them for failing to meet objectives. In addition, researchers distinguished a *laissez-faire* style that is marked by an overall failure to take responsibility for managing. These distinctions between aspects of leadership style are commonly assessed by the Multifactor Leadership Questionnaire, known as the MLQ.

Although Vecchio discounted the possibility that noteworthy gender effects might emerge in research on transformational and transactional leadership, researchers in this area have reasoned that transformational leadership might be particularly advantageous to women because of its androgynous qualities and, indeed, the substantial research literature comparing women and men on these styles has yielded interesting outcomes. . . .

In general, Eagly et al.'s meta-analysis revealed that, compared with male leaders, female leaders were (a) more transformational (significant in general and on all but one subscale) and (b) engaged in more of the contingent reward behaviors (i.e., exchanging rewards for followers' satisfactory performance) that are one component of transactional leadership. Also, male leaders were more likely than female leaders to manifest two other aspects of transactional leadership: active management by exception (attending to followers' mistakes and failures to meet standards) and passive management by exception (waiting for problems to become severe before intervening). Men were also higher on laissez-faire leadership (exhibiting widespread absence and lack of involvement). These sex differences were small, but prevailed in the meta-analysis as a whole as well as in auxiliary analyses of (a) the MLQ norming study, (b) the other studies that used the MLQ, and (c) the studies that used other measures of these styles. . . .

Sex differences in transformational and transactional leadership do have implications for female advantage arguments because researchers defined these styles in an effort to identify effective leadership. Substantiating these claims, a meta-analysis of 39 studies showed positive correlations between effectiveness and all components of transformational leadership as well as the contingent reward component of transactional leadership, the one aspect of transactional leadership on which women exceeded men. The norming study of the MLQ measure produced similar effectiveness findings, and in addition, showed negative relations between leaders' effectiveness and two of the remaining measures: (a) passive management by exception, which is one of the components of transactional leadership, and (b) laissez-faire leadership.

In view of these findings, the tendency of women to exceed men on the components of leadership style that relate positively to effectiveness (i.e., transformational leadership and the contingent reward aspect of transactional leadership) and the tendency of men to exceed women on the ineffective styles (i.e., passive management by exception and laissez-faire leadership) attest to women's abilities. Thus, research on transformational, transactional, and laissez-faire leadership styles does suggest female advantage, albeit a small advantage.

Prejudice and Discrimination Against Women as Leaders

Any female advantage in leadership style might be offset by disadvantage that flows from prejudice and discrimination directed against women as leaders. Prejudice consists of unfair evaluation of a group of people based on stereotypical judgments of the group rather than the behavior or qualifications of its individual members. When people hold stereotypes about a group, they expect members of that group to possess characteristics and exhibit behavior consistent with those stereotypes. Perceivers then tacitly assimilate information to their gender-stereotypic expectations and spontaneously fill in unknown details of others' behavior to conform to those expectations. These stereotypic inferences yield prejudice against individual group members when stereotypes about their group are incongruent with the attributes associated with success in certain classes of social roles. This incongruity tends to produce discrimination by lowering evaluation of such group members as potential or actual occupants of those roles.

According to Eagly and Karau, incongruity between expectations about women (i.e., the female gender role) and expectations about leaders (i.e., leader roles) underlie prejudice against female leaders. This explanation, based on Eagly's social role theory of sex differences and similarities in social behavior asserts that the activation of beliefs about women and men by gender-related cues influences people to perceive individual women as communal but not very agentic and individual men as agentic but not very communal. . . .

Male-dominated environments can be difficult for women. The Eagly et al. meta-analysis of Goldberg paradigm experiments thus demonstrated that female leaders received less favorable evaluations than their equivalent male counterparts in male-dominated leader roles, but were equally evaluated in roles that were not male-dominated. Congruent evidence in survey data emerged from an analysis of the Panel Study of Income Dynamics, which showed that, despite controls on numerous variables (e.g., human capital, family characteristics, skill requirements of occupations), working in male-dominated occupations increased men's chances of promotions (as assessed by substantial wage increases in successive years), but increased women's chances of leaving their jobs. Consistent with such findings, women appear to be disadvantaged in employment contexts in which advancement depends on sex homophilous male networks, which are especially prevalent in environments where men constitute a strong majority. . . .

In summary, research provides ample demonstration of bias against women as leaders, despite the failure of some reviewers to recognize important moderators of these effects. Our conclusions are strengthened by converging results from differing methods—specifically, organizational studies, survey research, and experiments that equate the objective characteristics of men and women. Women thus face discriminatory barriers mainly in male-dominated and masculine environments and with male evaluators. Because higher levels of authority and higher wages are concentrated in such environments and are controlled primarily by men, this prejudice is highly consequential for women's advancement. . . .

Conclusions

What Has Research Established Concerning Female Advantage and Disadvantage?

Research has shown that women possess both advantages and disadvantages as leaders, with the disadvantages arising primarily in roles that are male-dominated or otherwise defined in masculine ways. Many of the difficulties and challenges that women face arise from the incongruity of the traditional female role and many leader roles. This incongruity creates vulnerability whereby women encounter prejudicial reactions that restrict their access to leadership roles and negatively bias judgments of their performance as leaders.

Easing this dilemma of role incongruity requires that female leaders behave extremely competently while reassuring others that they conform to expectations concerning appropriate female behavior. The double-standard requirement to display extra competence makes it especially difficult for women to gain recognition for high ability and outstanding achievements. Therefore, successful female leaders generally work hard and seek leadership styles that do not unnecessarily elicit resistance to their authority by challenging norms dictating that women be egalitarian and supportive of others.

Given these constraints, transformational leadership may be especially advantageous for women because it encompasses some behaviors that are consistent with the female gender role's demand for supportive, considerate behaviors. The transformational repertoire, along with the contingent reward aspect of transactional leadership, may resolve some of the inconsistencies between the demands of leadership roles and the female gender role and therefore allow women to excel as leaders. Fortunately for women's progress as leaders, this positive, encouraging, inspiring style appears to have generalized advantages for contemporary organizations.

One feature of some of the findings that we have presented is that their magnitude is small. Critics such as Vecchio often suggest that such effects are therefore unimportant. Contrary to this view, methodologists have agreed that effects that can seem quite small in terms of most statistical metrics can have practical importance in natural settings. For example, the relation between taking aspirin and the prevention of heart attacks in a randomized double-blind experiment was only $r = .034$, yet this effect corresponded to 3.4% fewer people experiencing heart attacks, a drop meaningful enough to induce researchers to end the experiment prematurely because it was deemed unethical to deny the benefits of the treatment to the individuals in the control group. Similarly, small biases against women in performance evaluations, when repeated over individuals and occasions, can produce large consequences in terms of the distribution of women and men in senior management.

Why Are Women Rising?

The analyses that we have presented so far do not sufficiently explain the shift toward more women leaders. To address this, we suggest that several causes are at work, eroding female disadvantage and augmenting female advantage. Specifically, at the individual level, women's characteristics have changed. At the organizational level, leadership roles have changed and practices that constituted barriers to promoting women into positions of authority have eroded. At the cultural level, appointments of female leaders have come to symbolize progressive organizational change. We discuss each of these factors in turn and also acknowledge that the more distal causes of these changes are embedded in the weakening of the traditional family division of labor, the large increase in job roles that are managerial, and general political, bureaucratic, and economic pressures that favor gender equality.

Women Have Changed

As women shift more of their time from domestic to paid labor, they assume the personal characteristics required to succeed in these new roles. In addition to women's increased human capital investments, women's psychological attributes and related behaviors have changed in concert with their entry into formerly male-dominated roles. Especially relevant to leadership are findings showing that the career aspirations of female university students, women's self-reports of assertiveness, dominance, and masculinity, and the value that women place on job attributes such as freedom, challenge, leadership, prestige, and power have all become more similar to those of men. To the extent that risk-taking is relevant to leadership, it is notable the sex difference in the tendency to take risks has decreased. Given these changes, it is not surprising that social perceivers believe that women are becoming more masculine, particularly in agentic attributes, although not decreasing in feminine qualities.

Leadership Roles Have Changed

Some research indicates that the incongruity between leader roles and the female gender role have diminished. For example, Schein's "think manager, think male" studies have revealed that, in the United States, but not in several other nations, women, but not men, have adopted a more androgynous view of managerial roles. Although a definitive description of secular trends in stereotypes of leaders and managers awaits an appropriate meta-analysis, these changes may be modest. In general, consistent with the idea of *cultural lag,* the ideological aspects of culture, including stereotypes, are slower to change than shifts in social structure such as the actual content of roles. Therefore, gradual change in stereotypes of leaders is not inconsistent with change in leadership roles to emphasize qualities that are more consistent with the female gender role than traditional characterizations of leadership. As leadership roles change, a larger proportion of them provide environments that welcome women's managerial competence.

Organizational Practices Have Changed

Also important to women's rise is change in organizational practices, brought about in part by civil rights legislation, especially Title VII of the Civil Rights Act of 1967, which deemed sex discrimination in employment illegal in the United States. With the authority of such laws, discrimination has been challenged in the courts, and some organizations were then required to give women access to leadership roles. For example, several women in high executive positions in high-tech industry, including Carly Fiorina (CEO of HewlettPackard) and Patricia Russo (CEO of Lucent), spent critical periods of their careers at AT&T, which had been challenged for what the government deemed its "blatantly unlawful" discrimination against women. After signing a US$38 million consent decree containing provisions to remedy its discrimination, AT&T allowed quite a few women to rise as line managers, and some of these women have achieved distinction as executives.

These legal challenges have continued. Currently in the courts is a discrimination suit against Wal-Mart, which, if granted class-action status, would cover at least 500,000 female employees. This lawsuit may open up equitable managerial opportunities for women in the world's largest retail organization. Although obtaining legal remedies for sex discrimination is time-consuming, costly, and not always successful, they have proven to be a powerful force for increasing women's opportunities in managerial careers.

Organizational changes that are not necessarily driven by lawsuits have also increased the representation of women in leadership positions. To the extent that organizations have become less hierarchical and more driven by results than "old boy" networks, they reward talent over gender and present a more level playing field than do traditional organizations. In addition, the culture of many organizations now embraces the benefits of including women and minorities among their leaders. Such organizations may support women by encouraging mentoring and networking and establishing more family-friendly policies. Also critical is a clear message from executives at the top of the organization endorsing equitable opportunities. Special efforts of these types have increased women's access to leadership roles. For example, at Deloitte and Touche, a Big Five accounting firm that put forth such effort, the number of women in leadership positions tripled between 1992 and 1998. Also, because the U.S. federal government has strongly endorsed equal employment opportunity, it is noteworthy that, in the Senior Executive Service of a cabinet-level U.S. federal department that was particularly noted for its commitment to equal opportunity, female applicants fared somewhat better than equally qualified male applicants in recent years.

The Culture Has Changed

In view of changes in leader roles and organizational practices, female leaders have come to symbolize new types of leadership that connote greater effectiveness and synergy than leadership of the past. Appointments of women signal an organization's departure from past practices and help it to capture the symbols of innovation and progressive change. For example, the choice of Shirley Tilghman as President of Princeton University expressed this Ivy League university's transition to a progressive institution that fosters the talents of women as well as men. This new cultural symbolism may be fueled in part by exposure of the illegal and unethical business practices of Enron and other businesses led by men. Thus, after Smith Barney was exposed for fraudulent financial research, Sallie Krawcheck became CEO, symbolizing competence and honesty.

This symbolic shift in the meaning conveyed by appointments of women to high positions is one force underlying the surge of claims of female advantage in trade books and newspaper and magazine articles in the United States. However, concerning the specific issues of sex differences in leadership style and effectiveness, scientific evidence produces the narrower conclusions that we have set forth in this article. Nonetheless, consistent with this evidence, gender-fair organizations substantially enlarge the pool of talent from which they select their managers, and, for many managerial roles, the selection of women can increase organizations' chances of obtaining leaders who are especially effective under modern conditions.

Note

1. In this article, the terms *sex* and *sexes* denote the grouping of people into female and male categories. The terms *sex differences* and *similarities* are applied to describe the results of comparing these two groups. The term *gender* refers to the meanings that societies and individuals ascribe to these female and male categories. We do not intend to use these terms to give priority to any class of causes that may underlie sex and gender effects.

Herminia Ibarra and Otilia Obodaru

 **NO**

Women and the Vision Thing

Many believe that bias against women lingers in the business world, particularly when it comes to evaluating their leadership ability. Recently, we had a chance to see whether that assumption was true. In a study of thousands of 360-degree assessments collected by Insead's executive education program over the past five years, we looked at whether women actually received lower ratings than men. To our surprise, we found the opposite: As a group, women outshone men in most of the leadership dimensions measured. There was one exception, however, and it was a big one: Women scored lower on "envisioning"—the ability to recognize new opportunities and trends in the environment and develop a new strategic direction for an enterprise.

But was this weakness a perception or a reality? How much did it matter to women's ability to lead? And how could someone not perceived as visionary acquire the right capabilities? As we explored these issues with successful female executives, we arrived at another question: Was a reputation for vision even something many of them wanted to achieve?

A Brilliant Career

A leading services company CEO we'll call Anne Dumas typified in many ways the women we spoke with. The pillar of her leadership style was a principle taught to her 20 years ago by her first boss: Always stay close to the details. As she explained it: "I think strategy comes naturally from knowing your business and the forces that influence your market, clients, and suppliers—not at a high level but at a detailed level. Intermediaries kill your insight. You obviously can't monitor everything, but nothing should keep you from knowing in detail the processes on which your company runs—not supervising everything but understanding at a detailed level what is going on. Otherwise, you are hostage to people who will play politics. At best you don't have full information; at worst you're vulnerable to hidden agendas. My job is to go to the relevant detail level."

In her four years as CEO, Dumas had achieved some impressive results. She had doubled revenues and operating margins, given the company a new strategic direction, and undertaken a fundamental reorganization of the company's core processes and structures. More recently, she had turned her attention to developing her leadership team.

From *Harvard Business Review*, January 2009, pp. 62, 64–70. Copyright © 2009 by Harvard Business School Publishing. Reprinted by permission.

IDEA IN BRIEF

- Women outshine men in many areas measured by 360-degree assessments but score low on one key leadership capability: envisioning.
- Three theories could explain why. Women might use different processes than men for shaping the future. They might perceive that they have less license to go out on a limb. Or they might not buy into the value of being seen as visionary.
- Vision is a must-have for enterprise leadership, regardless of gender. Luckily, it's a capability that can be learned.

Yet Dumas knew she should somehow improve her communication effectiveness, particularly in her role as an executive member of her parent company's board. One challenge was her stylistic mismatch with her chairman, a broad-brush, big-picture thinker who often balked at what he perceived as excessive attention to detail. She found herself reluctant to favor "form over substance." She told us, "I always wonder what people mean when they say, 'He's not much of a manager but is a good leader.' Leader of what? You have to do things to be a leader." She went on to imply that so-called visionary behaviors might even be harmful. "We are in danger today of being mesmerized by people who play with our reptilian brain. For me, it is manipulation. I can do the storytelling too, but I refuse to play on people's emotions. If the string pulling is too obvious, I can't make myself do it."

Dumas's reluctance is not unusual. One of the biggest developmental hurdles that aspiring leaders, male and female alike, must clear is learning to sell their ideas—their vision of the future—to numerous stakeholders. Presenting an inspiring story about the future is very different from generating a brilliant strategic analysis or crafting a logical implementation plan, competencies on which managers like Dumas have built their careers.

Indeed, a whole generation of women now entering the C-suite owe their success to a strong command of the technical elements of their jobs and a nose-to-the-grindstone focus on accomplishing quantifiable objectives. But as they step into bigger leadership roles—or are assessed on their potential to do so—the rules of the game change, and a different set of skills comes to the fore.

Vision Impaired

Our research drew on 360-degree evaluations of 2,816 executives from 149 countries enrolled in executive education courses at Insead. As with most 360-degree exercises, these managers filled out self-assessments and invited subordinates, peers, supervisors, and other people they dealt with in a professional context, such as suppliers and customers, to evaluate them on a set of leadership dimensions. In total 22,244 observers participated. (See the sidebar "Critical Components of Leadership" for a description of the Global Executive Leadership Inventory, or GELI.)

As we looked for patterns within this data set, we focused on differences between the male and female leaders, both in terms of how they saw themselves and in terms of how the observers evaluated them. Certainly, there were plenty of data to work with, since 20% of the executives assessed and 27% of the evaluating observers were women. When analyzing the data, we controlled for the effects of the executives' age and level.

The first surprise for us, given prior published research, was that we found no evidence of a female "modesty effect." Quite the opposite: Women rated themselves significantly higher than men rated themselves on four of the 10 GELI dimensions we analyzed. And on the remaining dimensions, the women and men gave themselves ratings that were about the same.

Our analyses of how leaders were rated by their male and female associates—bosses, peers, and subordinates—also challenged the common wisdom. Again based on prior research, we'd expected gender stereotypes to lower the ratings of female leaders, particularly those given by men. That was not the case. If there was a gender bias, it favored female leaders: Male observers scored female leaders significantly higher than they scored male leaders on seven dimensions, and female observers scored them significantly higher on eight. (See the exhibit "Comparing the Ratings of Male and Female Leaders.")

Ratings on one dimension, however, defied this pattern. Female leaders were rated lower by their male observers (but not by women) on their capabilities in "envisioning." That deficit casts a large shadow over what would otherwise be an extremely favorable picture of female executives. The GELI instrument does not claim that the different dimensions of leadership are equal in importance, and as other research has shown, some do matter more than others to people's idea of what makes a leader. In particular, the envisioning dimension is, for most observers, a must-have capability.

Intrigued by this one apparent weakness, we looked more closely at the observers' ratings. Was a particular group responsible for bringing the envisioning scores down? Indeed one was. As shown in the exhibit "Who Says Women Aren't Visionary?" the male peers (who represented the majority of peers in our sample) rated women lower on envisioning. Interestingly, female peers did not downgrade women, contrary to the frequently heard claim that women compete rather than cooperate with one another. Our data suggest it's the men who might feel most competitive toward their female peers. Male superiors and subordinates rated male and female leaders about the same.

What It Means to Be Visionary

George H.W. Bush famously responded to the suggestion that he look up from the short-term goals of his campaign and start focusing on the longer term by saying, "Oh—the vision thing." His answer underlines vision's ambiguity. Just what do we mean when we say a person is visionary?

The distinction between management and leadership has long been recognized. Most agree that managing for continuous improvement to the status quo is different from being a force for change that compels a group to innovate and depart from routine. And if leadership is essentially about realizing

IDEA IN PRACTICE

When taking on more-strategic leadership roles, both men and women must come to grips with the vision thing. Here's a high-level plan for making that happen.

- **1. Get a vision test.** Undergo a 360-degree evaluation to explore the differences between how you see yourself and how others see you. Find out whether you have a vision gap to close and who perceives it. As Insead coaches say, if one person tells you that you have donkey ears, don't listen; if two people tell you, go buy yourself a saddle.

- **2. Gain a new respect.** Learn to appreciate vision as a matter of not just style but substance. It's not about meaningless mission statements but about strategic acumen and positioning know-how. Respect the size of the challenge you may face. If you pride yourself on your people skills, establishing the distance needed for a helicopter view may require reinventing your identity as a leader.

- **3. Leverage (or build) your network.** Strategic analysis demands a solid grasp of what is happening outside your group and firm. A good external network is the first line of defense against insular thinking. If you're like most executives we've studied, your network probably isn't strong enough to take you to the next level.

- **4. Learn the craft.** Much of envisioning can be learned the old-fashioned way: at the elbow of a master. Find role models and study how they develop and communicate strategic ideas. Then work with your leadership development organization or a good executive coach to identify training and tools to build your capabilities.

- **5. Beware of identity traps.** When you are very good at a needed task, the whole organization will conspire to keep you at it. Stop being so hands-on. Even if delivering on the details has always been your ticket to advancement, staying in the weeds is risky now.

- **6. Constantly communicate.** As your vision develops, find opportunities to articulate it. Don't wait until it's perfect. Try out draft versions along the way and even after the vision is mature. You'll never be seen as visionary if you don't get the word out.

- **7. Step up to the plate.** A vision doesn't come only from the outside; it comes from greater self-confidence. It is an internal presumption of competence: giving yourself latitude, believing in your ability, and assuming responsibility for creating a future for others.

change, then crafting and articulating a vision of a better future is a leadership prerequisite. No vision, no leadership.

But just as leadership is a question of what one does rather than what one is, so too is vision. It encompasses the abilities to frame the current practices as inadequate, to generate ideas for new strategies, and to communicate possibilities in inspiring ways to others. Being visionary, therefore, is not the same as being charismatic. It entails "naming" broad-stroke patterns and setting strategy based on those patterns. (See the sidebar "What Does It Mean to Have Vision?")

Visionary leaders don't answer the question "Where are we going?" simply for themselves; they make sure that those around them understand the direction as well. As they search for new paths, they conduct a vigorous exchange with an array of people inside and outside their organizations, knowing that great visions rarely emerge from solitary analysis. As "practical futurists," leaders also test new ideas pragmatically against current resources (money, people, organizational capabilities) and work with others to figure out how to realize the desired future. True strategists offer much more than the generic vision statements that companies hang on their walls; they articulate a clear point of view about what will transpire and position their organizations to respond to it. All of this adds up to a tall order for anyone in a leadership role. It's not obvious, however, why it should be a particular challenge for women.

Perception or Reality?

As we sought to understand why women fail to impress with their vision, research findings from prior studies were not much help. To begin with, most attempts to compare men's and women's styles have focused on how leaders are rated by subordinates. Yet, as we all know, leaders play a key role in managing stakeholders above, across, and outside their units. Moreover, the vast majority of studies ask participants either to rate hypothetical male and female leaders or to evaluate "the majority" of male or female leaders they know, rather than the actual, specific leaders they know well. Empirical studies of gender differences in leadership styles have often used populations of students, members of diverse associations, and nonmanagers, rather than the midlevel to senior business managers we are actually trying to understand.

We turned therefore to the experts who were living this reality every day: the women participating in our executive education programs. When we asked

---

CRITICAL COMPONENTS OF LEADERSHIP

T he Global Executive Leadership Inventory (GELI) is a 360-degree feedback instrument developed at Insead's Global Leadership Center by Manfred Kets de Vries, Pierre Vrignaud, and Elizabeth Florent-Treacy. To identify significant dimensions of exemplary leadership, they interviewed more than 300 senior executives over the course of three years. The emerging questionnaire was then validated on an international sample of more than 300 senior executives and MBA students. The result, GELI, measures degrees of competency in these dimensions of global leadership, which it defines as follows[1]:

Envisioning
Articulating a compelling vision, mission, and strategy that incorporate a multicultural and diverse perspective and connect employees, shareholders, suppliers, and customers on a global scale.

Empowering
Empowering followers at all levels of the organization by delegating and sharing information.

Energizing
Energizing and motivating employees to achieve the organization's goals.

Designing and aligning
Creating world-class organizational design and control systems and using them to align the behavior of employees with the organization's values and goals.

Rewarding and feedback
Setting up the appropriate reward structures and giving constructive feedback.

Team building
Creating team players and focusing on team effectiveness by instilling a cooperative atmosphere,

promoting collaboration, and encouraging constructive conflict.

Outside orientation
Making employees aware of outside constituencies, such as customers, suppliers, shareholders, and other interest groups, including local communities affected by the organization.

Global mind-set
Inculcating a global mentality, instilling values that act as a glue between the regional or national

cultures represented in the organization.

Tenacity
Encouraging tenacity and courage in employees by setting a personal example in taking reasonable risks.

Emotional intelligence
Fostering trust in the organization by creating—primarily by setting an example—an emotionally intelligent workforce whose members are self-aware and treat others with respect and understanding.

1. GELI contains two additional dimensions, life balance and resilience to stress, which we did not analyze in our study, since many observers were unable to provide evaluations on them.

how they would interpret our data, we heard three explanations. First, several women noted that they tended to set strategy via processes that differed from those used by their male counterparts. This suggests that what may in fact be visionary leadership is not perceived that way because it takes a different path. Second, we heard that women often find it risky to stray away from concrete facts, analyses, and details. And third, many women betrayed negative attitudes toward visionary leadership. Because they thought of themselves as grounded, concrete, and no-nonsense, and had seen many so-called visionary ideas founder in execution, they tended to eye envisioning behaviors with some suspicion. Each of these interpretations invited serious consideration.

THEORY 1: Women are equally visionary but in a different way. Several of the women who had taken the GELI survey argued that it is not that women

COMPARING THE RATINGS OF MALE AND FEMALE LEADERS

In the 360-degree assessments of participants in Insead's executive education program, female leaders received higher ratings than male leaders in most dimensions of leadership. But in one dimension—envisioning—women were rated lower than men.

	Which leaders rated themselves higher?	Which leaders did male observers rate higher?	Which leaders did female observers rate higher?
Envisioning	Neither	Men	Women
Empowering	Neither	Neither	Neither
Energizing	Women	Women	Women
Designing and aligning	Women	Women	Women
Rewarding and feedback	Neither	Women	Women
Team building	Neither	Women	Women
Outside orientation	Women	Women	Women
Global mind-set	Neither	Neither	Neither
Tenacity	Neither	Women	Women
Emotional intelligence	Women	Women	Women

lack vision but that they come to their visions in a less directive way than men do. One executive put it like this: "Many women tend to be quite collaborative in forming their vision. They take into account the input of many and then describe the result as the group's vision rather than their own." Another said, "I don't see myself as particularly visionary in the creative sense. I see myself as pulling and putting together abstract pieces of information or observations that lead to possible strategies and future opportunities."

Vivienne Cox, CEO of BP Alternative Energy, is known for having an "organic" leadership style. She led a team that crafted a strategy for moving BP into alternative energy in a more unified and substantial way, by combining a set of peripheral businesses such as solar, wind, and hydrogen-fired power plants into one new low-carbon-powered unit that BP would invest billions in. Ask those involved how the new strategy came about, and the answer always involves multiple players working collaboratively. One of her key lieutenants described Cox's approach like this: "She thinks about how to create incentives or objectives so that the organization will naturally find its own solutions and structures. It encourages people to be thoughtful, innovative, and self-regulating." Cox herself claims that her role is to be a "catalyst." She consistently articulates a management philosophy in which the leader does not drive change but, rather, allows potential to emerge.

Interestingly, the processes these women describe do not hinge just on a collaborative style. They also rely on diverse and external inputs and alliances. At BP Alternative Energy, Cox spent much of her time talking to key people outside her business group and the company in order to develop a strategic perspective on opportunities and sell the idea of low-carbon power to her CEO and peers. Her ideas were informed by a wide network that included thought leaders in a range of sectors. She brought in outsiders who could transcend a parochial view to fill key roles and invited potential adversaries into the process early on to make sure her team was also informed by those who had a different view of the world. Our results hint at an interesting hypothesis: By involving their male peers in the process of creating a vision, female leaders may get less credit for the result.

THEORY 2: Women hesitate to go out on a limb.   Some women responded to our findings by noting that they need to base their marching orders on concrete facts and irrefutable analysis, not unprovable assertions about how the future will take shape. Here, two Democratic candidates for the 2008 U.S. presidential race offer an interesting parallel. Barack Obama was viewed as a visionary, a charismatic communicator offering a more hopeful if undetailed future. Hillary Clinton was viewed as a competent executor with an impressive if uninspiring grasp of policy detail. According to a recent *New Yorker* article by George Packer, Clinton as much as admitted that she does not inspire through rhetoric and emotion. She said: "A President, no matter how rhetorically inspiring, still has to show strength and effectiveness in the day-to-day handling of the job, because people are counting on that. So, yes, words are critically important, but they're not enough. You have to act. In my own experience, sometimes it's putting one foot in front of the other day after day."

Might women feel they have to choose between being seen as competent and in control or being visionary? Recall Anne Dumas, our services executive, and her pride in having a vast, detailed knowledge of what is happening in her firm. Often, she told us, she'd called on that reservoir of data to defend her position against challenges. The same attitude comes through in the observation of a management consultant who told us, "Men speak more confidently and boldly on an issue, with very little data to back it up. Women want to have a lot of data and feel confident that they can back up what they are saying."

A common obstacle for female leaders is that they often lack the presumption of competence accorded to their male peers. As a result, women are less likely to go out on a limb, extrapolating from facts and figures to interpretations that are more easily challenged. When a situation is rife with threat—when people, male or female, expect that they are "guilty until proven innocent"—they adopt a defensive, often rigid, posture, relying less on their imagination and creativity and sticking to safe choices.

The presumption-of-competence effect is compounded by gender stereotypes that lead us to expect emotional, collaborative women and rational, directive men. When men communicate from the heart or manage participatively, it's taken as evidence of range, an added plus. Women's emotional communication or inclusive process, by contrast, is implicitly viewed as proof of an incapacity or unwillingness to do otherwise, even if the situation calls for it.

THEORY 3: Women don't put much stock in vision.   Do men and women really have different leadership styles? Certainly a lot of ink has been spilled on the question, but the answer provided by hundreds of studies, subjected to meta-analysis, is no. When other factors (such as title, role, and salary) are held constant, similarities in style vastly outweigh the differences. The occasional finding that women are slightly more people oriented and participative tends not to hold up in settings where there are few women—that is, in line positions and upper management. But put aside the science and ask individuals for their opinion on whether men and women have different leadership styles, and most women (and men) answer yes.

This can only complicate the solution to the vision deficit. It's one thing for a woman who suspects she is wrongly perceived to resolve to change certain behaviors in order to convey the competence and substance she has to offer. It's quite another thing when her own self-conception has become colored by the same biases.

Our interviews with female executives highlighted one potential difference in attitude between the genders that could explain women's lower ratings on envisioning. We suspect women may not value envisioning as a critical leadership competency to the same extent that men do or may have a more skeptical view of envisioning's part in achieving results. Over and over again in our discussions with women, we heard them take pride in their concrete, no-nonsense attitude and practical orientation toward everyday work problems. We were reminded of a comment made by Margaret Thatcher: "If you want anything said, ask a man; if you want anything done, ask a woman." Many of the women we interviewed similarly expressed the opinion that women were more thorough, had a better command of detail, and were less prone to self-promotion than men. Like Anne Dumas, they valued substance over form as a means of gaining credibility with key stakeholders. A pharmaceutical executive elaborated further: "I see women as more practical. Although the women in my organization are very strategic, they are also often the ones who ground the organization in what is possible, what can or cannot be done from the human dimension."

Making the Leadership Transition

Women may dismiss the importance of vision—and they may be reassured by the many claims made over the years about their superior emotional intelligence—but the fact remains that women are a minority in the top ranks of business organizations. Our findings suggest to us that the shortfall is in no small part due to women's perceived lack of vision.

The findings of a 2008 study by Catalyst researchers Jeanine Prime and Nancy Carter and IMD professors Karsten Jonsen and Martha Maznevski

WHAT DOES IT MEAN TO HAVE VISION?

Across studies and research traditions, vision has been found to be the central component in charismatic leadership and the essence of the oft-noted distinction between management and leadership. But what does it look like in action? As detailed by the Global Executive Leadership Inventory, behaving in a visionary way is a matter of doing three things well:

Sensing opportunities and threats in the environment
- simplifying complex situations
- foreseeing events that will affect the organization

Setting strategic direction
- encouraging new business
- defining new strategies
- making decisions with an eye toward the big picture

Inspiring constituents
- challenging the status quo
- being open to new ways of doing things
- inspiring others to look beyond limitations

concur. In it, more than 1,000 executives from nine countries (all alumni of executive education programs) were asked for their impressions of men and women in general as leaders. Both men and women tended to believe that the two genders have distinct leadership strengths, with women outscoring men on some behaviors, and men outscoring women on others. But here's the catch: When people were asked to rate the behaviors' relative importance to overall leadership effectiveness, the "male" behaviors had the edge. Across countries, "inspiring others"—a component of our envisioning dimension—landed at the top of the rankings as most important to overall leadership effectiveness. And what of the areas of leadership where men agreed that women were stronger? Let's take women's standout advantage: their much greater skill at "supporting others." That one ranked at the bottom of the list. As a component of overall leadership effectiveness, it was clearly not critical but merely nice to have.

We've seen how these priorities play out at close hand, in the personal stories of women we study. Particularly at midcareer, when senior management sizes up the leadership potential of competent managers, they take their toll. A manager we'll call Susan offers a cautionary tale. A strong performer, Susan rose through the functional ranks in logistics and distribution, thanks to her superior technical and people skills and belief in running a tight ship.

As a manager she prided herself on her efficient planning and organizing and her success in building a loyal, high-performing team. But her boss saw her capabilities differently. By this point in her career, he expected her to sense emerging trends or unexploited opportunities in the business environment, to craft strategy based on a view of the business as opposed to a view of her function, and to actively work to identify and bring on board stakeholders. Eventually a proposal came from outside her division calling for a radical reorganization of it. Still focused on making continuous improvement to the existing operation, Susan lacked the networks that would have helped her spot shifting priorities in the wider market and was blindsided by the idea.

It's often observed that the very talents that bring managers success in midlevel roles can be obstacles to their taking on bigger leadership roles. That was Susan's situation, and it's possible that it is a common trap for women. Having had the message drummed into their heads that they must be rational, nonemotional, and hyperefficient, they might actually place a higher value than men on knowing the details cold and getting the job done. That, in turn, makes their leadership transition more difficult, because they stick with what they know longer. Another woman we interviewed, this one an investment banker, captured the scale of the challenge. "It's like my whole basis for existence is taken away from me," she told us, "if I can't rely on the facts." Her words reminded us that an executive's accustomed approach and style define who she is as a leader. To walk away from them is to be left without a clear sense of identity.

The challenge facing women, then, is to stop dismissing the vision thing and make vision one of the things they are known for. In a senior leadership role, it's the best use of their time and attention. It's a set of competencies that can be developed. And of all the leadership dimensions we measured, it's the only thing holding women back.

POSTSCRIPT

Do Women Make Better Leaders?

Eagly and Carli provide considerable evidence that women are superior to men on average on a number of traits that are useful for leadership responsibilities. Ibarra and Obodaru present good evidence that men are superior to women on the vision trait and then argue that vision is key to some of the most important activities of top leadership. Could the resolution of these two arguments be that women leaders are better for some organizations and men leaders are better for other organizations? Women leaders may elicit more productivity from their staffs and men leaders may be better at breaking new ground. In the final analysis, however, it must be remembered that the differences are small though noticeable, and the comparison of averages must not be used to judge individuals.

The issue of women and leadership has received considerable attention. A lot of change has already occurred over the past several decades, but more change is necessary to improve the performance of American organizations. Half of all managerial positions are occupied by women, but women are scarce at the highest levels of large corporations. This is explained in part by the fact that some highly competent women want to balance career and family life in such a way that they do not attain the highest level that they are capable of. It is also partly explained by prejudice.

For further explorations of the issue of women and leadership we suggest the following studies. Alice H. Eagly and Linda L. Carli's more recent book, *Through the Labyrinth: The Truth about How Women Become Leaders* (Harvard Business School Press, 2007), examines many issues besides the relative competence of women versus men for leadership. They also examine whether family responsibilities hold women back, whether discrimination is still a serious problem, what is the psychological basis for the prejudice toward female leaders, whether people resist women's leadership, whether women lead differently than men, and how do women try to overcome the many obstacles to their advancement to high leadership positions. Douglas M. Branson focuses on employment discrimination and the glass ceiling in *The Last Male Bastion: Gender and the CEO Suite in America's Public Companies* (Routledge, 2010). He examines the restraints on advancement for women and advises how to get to the top based on the research. His earlier book that deals with the barriers to women's advancement is *No Seat at the Table: How Corporate Governance and Law Keep Women out of the Boardroom* (New York University Press, 2007). Patricia Werhane et al. cover many aspects of women leadership in *Women in Business: The Changing Face of Leadership* (Praeger Publishers, 2007).

Several books that give advice on how women can advance are Anna Marie Valerio, *Developing Women Leaders: A Guide for Men and Women in Organizations*

(Wiley-Blackwell, 2009); Ella L. J. Edmondson Bell with Linda Villarosa, *Career GPS: Strategies for Women Navigating the New Corporate Landscape* (Amistad, 2010); Molly D. Shepard, Jane K. Stimmler, and Peter J. Dean, *Breaking into the Boys' Club: 8 Ways for Women to Get Ahead in Business* (M. Evans, 2009); Manuela Barreto, Michelle K. Ryan, and Michael T. Schmitt, eds., *The Glass Ceiling in the 21st Century: Understanding Barriers to Gender Equality* (American Psychological Association, 2009); Peninah Thomson and Jacey Graham, with Tom Lloyd, *A Woman's Place Is in the Boardroom: The Roadmap* (Palgrave Macmillan, 2008); Judith Baxter, *The Language of Female Leadership* (Palgrave Macmillan, 2010).

For an older examination of the female advantage for leadership, see Sally Helgesen, *The Female Advantage: Women's Ways of Leadership* (Doubleday Currency, 1990), and Ann M. Morrison, Randall P. White, Ellen Van Velsor, and the Center for Creative Leadership, *Breaking the Glass Ceiling: Can Women Reach the Top of America's Largest Corporations?* (Addison-Wesley, 1992). For a historical coverage of women in business, see Carol H. Krismann, *Encyclopedia of American Women in Business: From Colonial Times to the Present* (Greenwood Press, 2005).

Contributors to This Volume

EDITOR

KURT FINSTERBUSCH is a professor of sociology at the University of Maryland at College Park. He received a B.A. in history from Princeton University in 1957, a B.D. from Grace Theological Seminary in 1960, and a Ph.D. in sociology from Columbia University in 1969. He is the author of *Understanding Social Impacts* (Sage Publications, 1980), and he is the co-author, with Annabelle Bender Motz, of *Social Research for Policy Decisions* (Wadsworth, 1980) and, with Jerald Hage, of *Organizational Change as a Development Strategy* (Lynne Rienner, 1987). He is the editor of *Annual Editions: Sociology* (McGraw-Hill/Contemporary Learning Series); *Annual Editions: Social Problems* (McGraw-Hill/Contemporary Learning Series); and *Sources: Notable Selections in Sociology,* 3rd ed. (McGraw-Hill/Dushkin, 1999).

AUTHORS

CONSTANCE AHRONS is co-chair of the Council on Contemporary Families. She is a therapist and author of three books: *The Good Divorce, Divorced Families,* and *We're Still Family.* She is Professor Emerita from the Department of Sociology and former Director of the Marriage and Family Therapy Doctoral Training Program at the University of Southern California in Los Angeles.

GRAHAM ALLISON is an American political scientist and professsor at the John F. Kennedy School of Government at Harvard. He is renowned for his book *Remaking Foreign Policy: The Organizational Connection,* co-written with Peter Szanton, which was published in 1976 and had some influence on the foreign policy of the administration of President Jimmy Carter. Since the 1970s, Allison has also been a leading analyst of U.S. national security and defense policy.

DAVID A. ANDERSON is a Blazer Associate Professor of Economics. He teaches many courses including law and economics, as well as the economics of crime. He is the author of *Environmental Economics* (Southwestern, 2004).

FRED BARNES was the executive editor of *The Weekly Standard* from 1985 to 1995. He has a news TV talk show.

GARY S. BECKER is a university professor in the Department of Economics and Sociology and professor in the Graduate School of Business at the University of Chicago. He is a senior fellow at the Hoover Institute and past president of the American Economic Association.

LAWRENCE D. BOBO is the Martin Luther King Jr. Centennial Professor at Stanford University, where he is also director of the Center for Comparative Study in Race and Ethnicity and director of the Program in African and African American Studies. He is a founding co-editor of the *Du Bois Review: Social Science Research on Race,* published by Cambridge University Press. He is co-author of the award-winning book *Racial Attitudes in America: Trends and Interpretations* (Harvard University Press, 1997). His next book, *Prejudice in Politics: Public Opinion, Group Position, and the Wisconsin Treaty Rights Dispute,* Harvard University Press, 2006.

CLINT BOLICK is vice president of the Institute for Justice and has litigated many crucial school choice decisions. His book *Voucher Wars: Waging the Legal Battle over School Choice* has just been published by the Cato Institute.

LESTER R. BROWN was the founder and president of the Worldwatch Institute, a nonprofit organization dedicated to the analysis of the global environment. He served as advisor to Secretary of Agriculture Orville Freeman and served as administrator of the International Agricultural Service in that department. In 1969, he helped James Grant establish the Overseas Development Council. He is the author and co-author of numerous books.

LINDA L. CARLI is a senior lecturer in the Department of Psychology at Wellesley College. Her research has focused on women's leadership and the obstacles women face when in leadership roles.

DAVID COATES is the Worrel Professor of Anglo-American Studies in the Political Science Department at Wake Forest University. He just published *The Liberal Toolkit: Progressive Answers to Conservative Arguments,* from which the reprinted articles were taken.

CURTIS CRAWFORD is the editor and co-author of the Web site www .DebatingRacialPreference.org.

JIM DEMINT, United States senator from South Carolina since 2005, serves on four different senatorial committees, including the Joint Economic Committee and the Committee on Banking, Housing, and Urban Affairs.

ALICE H. EAGLY is professor of social psychology at the Weinberg College of Art and Sciences, Northwestern University. Her research has focused on attitude theory and social role theory as a theory of sex differences, as well as sociopolitical attitudes. She was recently named Distinguished Scientist Lecturer by the APA for 2009.

BARBARA EPSTEIN was a writer and founding co-editor of *The New York Review of Books.*

PETER GORMAN is an investigative journalist and former editor-in-chief of *High Times* magazine.

MARTIN HART-LANDSBERG is professor of economics and director of the Political Economy Program at Lewis and Clark College.

E. JEFFREY HILL is associate professor of family life at Brigham Young University. He teaches in the Home and Family Living undergraduate program; the Marriage, Family, and Human Development graduate program; and in the MBA program at the Marriott School of Management.

HUMAN RIGHTS CAMPAIGN is the largest national gay, lesbian, bisexual, and transgender political organization, with members throughout the country.

HERMINIA IBARRA is an expert on professional and leadership development. She has written numerous articles on innovation, networking, career development, women's careers and professional identity. Her book *Working Identity: Unconventional Strategies for Reinventing Your Career* (Harvard Business School Press, 2003) documents how people reinvent themselves at work.

ROBERT F. KENNEDY Jr. is an environmental and political activist. He is an environmental lawyer and co-host of *Ring of Fire* on the Air America Radio Network and also serves as a senior attorney for the Natural Resources Defense Council.

ANTHONY B. KIM researches international economic issues, with a focus on economic freedom and free trade, at the Heritage Foundation.

HERBERT KLEBER has been a pioneer in research and treatment of substance abuse for over 35 years. From 1968 to 1989, he founded and headed the Drug Dependence Unit at Yale University. Dr. Kleber is the author of more than 200 papers, and the co-editor of the *American Psychiatric Press Textbook of Substance Abuse Treatment*. He has received numerous prestigious awards, two honorary degrees, is listed as one of the "Best Doctors in America" and "Best Doctors in New York," and was elected in 1996 to be a member of the Institute of Medicine of the National Academy of Science.

MARK KRIKORIAN has headed the Center for Immigration Studies since 1995. He holds a master's degree from the Fletcher School of Law and Diplomacy, a bachelor's degree from Georgetown University, and spent two years at Yerevan State University in then-Soviet Armenia. Before joining the Center he held a variety of editorial and writing positions.

JAMES KURTH is a Claude Smith Professor of Political Science at Swarthmore College, where he teaches defense policy, foreign policy, and international politics. He is also editor of *Orbis*.

BJORN LOMBORG is a statistician at the University of Aarhus and the author of the controversial book *The Skeptical Environmentalist: Measuring the Real State of the World* (Cambridge University Press, 2001).

JEFF MADRICK is the editor of *Challenge* magazine, the author of *The End of Affluence* (1995) and other books, a frequent contributor to *The New York Review of Books,* and a visiting professor of humanities at The Cooper Union in New York.

ELIZABETH MARQUARDT is the director of the Center for Marriage and Families and authored *Between Two Worlds: The Inner Lives of Children of Divorce* (Crown, 2005).

STEPHANIE MENCIMER is a contributing editor of *The Washington Monthly*. She was previously an investigative reporter for *The Washington Post* and a staff writer for *Legal Times*. A native of Ogden, Utah, and a graduate of the University of Oregon, Mencimer won the 2000 Harry Chapin Media Award for reporting on hunger and poverty.

MARY C. NOONAN is an assistant professor at the University of Iowa in the Department of Sociology. She received her Ph.D. in sociology and her master's in public policy from the University of Michigan. Her research interests include gender, work, and family issues.

JOHAN NORBERG has been in charge since 1999 of ideas policy at the Swedish think tank Timbro, where he is editor of smedian.com, a Swedish-language journal of cultural afffairs and ideas. His recent book is *In Defense of Global Capitalism* (Cato Institute, 2003).

KATE O'BEIRNE is the editor of *National Review* and a frequent panelist on TV news shows.

OTILIA OBODARU worked for 4 years as a Human Resources Consultant for AIMS Romania. Her research interest is focused on career management.

ROBERT B. REICH is professor of public policy at the Goldman School of Public Policy at the University of California at Berkeley. He has served in three national administrations, most recently as secretary of labor under President Bill Clinton. He has written 11 books, including *The Work of Nations,* which has been translated into 22 languages; the best-sellers *The Future of Success* and *Locked in the Cabinet;* and his most recent book, Aftershock: The Next Economy and America's Future.

JEFFREY REIMAN is the William Fraser McDowell Professor of Philosophy at American University in Washington, D.C. He is the author of *Justice and Modern Moral Philosophy* (Yale University Press, 1992) and *The Rich Get Richer and the Poor Get Prison: Ideology, Class, and Criminal Justice,* 6th ed. (Allyn and Bacon, 2001). He is also editor, with Paul Leighton, of *Criminal Justice Ethics* (Prentice Hall, 2001).

MICHAEL J. SANDEL is the Anne T. and Robert M. Bass Professor in the Political Science Department at Harvard. His most recent book is *Public Philosophy: Essay on Morality in Politics* (Harvard University Press, 2005).

PETER SPRIGG serves as vice president for policy at the Family Research Council and oversees FRC research, publications, and policy formulation. He is also the author of the book *Outrage: How Gay Activists and Liberal Judges Are Trashing Democracy to Redefine Marriage* (Regnery, 2004) and the co-editor of the book *Getting It Straight: What the Research Shows about Homosexuality.*

WALTER WILLIAMS is the John M. Olin Distinguished Professor of Economics at George Mason University. He holds a B.A. from California State University at Los Angeles and an M.A. and a Ph.D. in economics from UCLA. He has received numerous fellowships and awards, including a Hoover Institution National Fellowship and the Valley Forge Freedoms Foundation George Washington Medal of Honor. A nationally syndicated columnist, his articles and essays have appeared in publications such as *Economic Inquiry, American Economic Review, National Review, Reader's Digest, Policy Review,* and *Newsweek.* Dr. Williams has authored six books, including *The State Against Blacks* (later made into a PBS documentary entitlted *Good Intentions*) and *Liberty versus the Tyranny of Socialism.*

RON WOLK is a former vice president of Brown University and is chairman of the board of Editorial Projects in Education. He founded *Education Week* and *Teacher Magazine.* He edited, with Blake Hume Rodman, *Classroom Crusaders: Twelve Teachers Who Are Trying to Change the System* (Jossey-Bass Publishers, 1994).